Racial and Ethnic Relations in America

FIFTH EDITION

S. Dale McLemore
The University of Texas at Austin

Harriett D. Romo
The University of Texas at Austin

Allyn and Bacon
Boston   London   Toronto   Sydney   Tokyo   Singapore

Editor-in-Chief, Social Sciences: Karen Hanson
Series Editor: Sarah Dunbar
Editorial Assistant: Jennifer Muroff
Marketing Manager: Karon Bowers
Sr. Editorial Production Administrator: Susan McIntyre
Editorial Production Service: Ruttle, Shaw & Wetherill, Inc.
Text Design and Electronic Composition: Denise Hoffman
Photo Researcher: Susan Duane
Composition Buyer: Linda Cox
Manufacturing Buyer: Megan Cochran
Cover Administrator: Linda Knowles

Library of Congress Cataloging-in-Publication Data

McLemore, S. Dale.
    Racial and ethnic relations in America / S. Dale McLemore,
Harriett D. Romo. —5th ed.
        p.   cm.
    Includes bibliographical references and index.
    ISBN 0-205-19956-9
        1. Minorities—United States. 2. United States—Ethnic relations.
    3. United States—Race relations. I. Romo, Harriett. II. Title.
    E184.A1M35 1997
    305.8'00973—dc21   96-37717
                                                            CIP

Printed in the United States of America
10 9 8 7 6 5 4 3 2 1   03 02 01 00 99 98 97

Photo Credits: Page 1, Library of Congress; Page 19, Adriana Rovers; Page 45, Library of Congress; Page
69, Library of Congress; Page 101, The Bettman Archive; Page 129, Steve Latham, AP Photo/Gadsdan
Times; Page 155, AP/Wide World Photos; Page 193, © Robert Harbison; Page 225, © Will Hart; Page 256,
Library of Congress; Page 285, Doug Mills, AP/Photo; Page 319, Library of Congress; Page 353, © Robert
Harbison; Page 377, Wide World Photos; Page 409, © Will Faller; Page 437, © Will Faller.

Dedicamos este libro
a nuestras familias.

This book is dedicated
to our families.

Contents

3   The Rise of Anglo American Society   45

4   The Golden Door   69

5 Nativism, Scientific Racism, and Immigration Restriction 101

6 Prejudice and Discrimination 129

7 Japanese Americans 155

8   Mexican Americans: From Colonized Minority to Political Activists   193

13 Native Americans: A Struggle to Maintain Political and Cultural Pluralism   353

14 The New Immigration   377

15 Reducing Prejudice and Discrimination   409

16 The Future of Ethnicity in America   437

Preface

At a time when many people assumed that racial and ethnic tensions throughout the world would gradually diminish, they seemed, instead, to increase. Serious disagreements and open warfare among Serbs, Croats, and Bosnians in the former Yugoslavia, between Russians and Chechens and Armenians and Azerbaijanis in the former Soviet Union, between Tamils and Sinhalese in Sri Linka, between Tutsis and Hutus in Rwanda and Burundi, between English speakers and French speakers in Canada, and between Arabs and Jews in the Middle East all remind us that racial and ethnic divisions are prominent in the lives of people in many parts of the modern world. These conflicts remind us too that, although the United States contains numerous racial and ethnic groups whose encounters with one another are unique, some aspects of the fascinating and important problems that we will study are common to humankind.

This volume continues the basic strategy of discussion and analysis that was used in the previous editions. It focuses on interracial and interethnic relations in the United States and rests on ideas derived from (1) the sociological analysis of intergroup processes and (2) the history of the interactions of American racial and ethnic groups. We take this approach because the study of social processes—such as competition, conflict, segregation, stratification, accommodation, fusion, and separation—is inherently temporal. We believe that an understanding of the interactions of different racial and ethnic groups is most effectively grasped through an examination of the history of their relations with one another.

Our processual-historical approach moves, broadly speaking, from the beginnings of contact among different groups in North America to the pressing racial and ethnic problems of the contemporary United States; but as we discuss various groups and issues, we must move flexibly back-and-forth over the pertinent spans of American history. Along the way we consider a wide range of sociological issues such as racial and ethnic differences, various processes through which one group may be included within another, the reactions of natives to foreigners, various aspects of racism, racial and ethnic prejudice and discrimination, class and ethnic stratification, vertical mobility, stereotyping, social distance, authoritarianism, the effect of social pressures on behavior, segregation, desegregation, variations in economic adaptations to discrimination, and the processes through which ethnic groups form, organize, and disappear. Each topic introduced advances the central ideas of the book.

Although our overall approach has not changed, this volume differs in many ways from the fourth edition. Every chapter has been updated and rewritten, in most cases extensively. The basic goal in each case, as before, has been to reveal a set of Key Ideas concerning racial and ethnic relations and to show how these ideas apply to the racial and ethnic problems that now confront our nation. Three important substantive changes are that (1) greater attention has been given to the crucial family and occupational roles of women within several of the groups discussed; (2) greater attention has been given to the current immigration to America; and (3) four especially divisive current issues—the debate over the book *The Bell Curve,* the debates over bilingual education, immigration restriction, and affirmative action—are discussed in special "Flashpoint" sections located in Chapters 5, 9, 14, and 15. The Flashpoints may be read in any order, but we believe the complex issues addressed in each case will best be understood if they are read within the context in which they appear. In addition to the Key Ideas in each chapter that are intended to help you identify and grasp the main points in the analysis, the Key Terms in each chapter have been boldfaced in the text and listed, along with their definitions, at the end of each chapter.

In the course of the presentation we touch, all too briefly, on some aspects of the experiences of many different groups in America. Short, but important discussions focus on several groups who were prominent during the colonial period, including the Native Americans, Anglo Americans, African Americans, Irish Americans, and German Americans. Short discussions also focus on several groups who were prominent during the nineteenth century, including the Irish Americans, German Americans, Chinese Americans, Italian Americans, and Jewish Americans. The main analyses of specific groups occur, however, in Chapters 7 through 13. These chapters focus on the Japanese Americans, Mexican Americans, African Americans, and Native Americans. Each of these chapters is organized to help us apply and amplify the ideas presented in the earlier chapters. Chapter 14 enlarges our treatment of the current immigrant stream but also includes a more detailed look at the largest refugee group to reach America—the Vietnamese. Chapter 15 addresses the problems of reducing racial and ethnic prejudice and discrimination, and Chapter 16 closes the presentation with some conjectures suggested by our analysis concerning the future of racial and ethnic relations in America.

The choice of groups to be discussed is not intended to slight the members of the many other groups that might have been studied and have contributed in so many different ways to the development of the United States. We have not intended, in any case, to present a complete profile of any given group. The choices were dictated chiefly by our desire to illuminate the main racial and ethnic dilemmas faced by the United States as seen through the lenses of a set of Key Ideas. For this reason, you may find it is helpful to read the Key Ideas and Key Terms pertaining to a given chapter both before and after reading the chapter itself. This procedure may help you to distinguish between the central points of the discussions and the many details that are useful in understanding those points.

We are indebted to many people, the first of whom are the many scholars whose efforts have produced the rich literature on which this volume is based and whose continued research is rapidly increasing our knowledge of racial and ethnic relations in the United States and throughout the world. More specifically, we thank Karen Hanson and Sarah Dunbar, our editors, and the staff at Allyn & Bacon for their support throughout the writing and preparation of this book. We wish to give special thanks to Ana Romo, who helped us through the maze of computer problems that arose as we worked to complete the final manuscript; to Jean Flores, who helped prepare some of the figures that appear in the book; and for the continuous support and valuable suggestions we have received from Ricardo Romo. We are grateful, too, for the help we have received at various stages of the work from John Sibley Butler, Jack Gibbs, Greta Gilbertson, Joel Heikes, Lionel Lewis, and Arthur Sakamoto.

Natives and Newcomers

The popular image of Americanization is that new immigrants arrive by ship at the port of New York and within three generations become fully included in American society. The reality is that newcomers enter American society in many different ways and may or may not "fit" into all parts of it.

Send these, the homeless, tempest-tost, to me:
I lift my lamp beside the golden door.

—Emma Lazarus

e pluribus unum

—Motto on the Great Seal of the
United States of America

The United States of America is frequently described as a nation of nations. Most Americans cannot trace their stay in this land to more than five or six generations, and only the American Indians can claim to have been here for more than five centuries.[1] As a result, many Americans still think of themselves as having a "nationality" in addition to their identity as Americans.[2] Despite the romantic claim that Americans are the product of an international melting pot, that they are the first "self-created People in the history of the world" (MacLeish 1943:115), newspapers, magazines, and television bring us daily reminders—often through accounts of intergroup disagreements and conflict— that the fabric of modern American society is comprised largely of people who are immigrants from, or are the descendants of immigrants from, Africa, China, Cuba, El Salvador, England, Germany, India, Ireland, Italy, Korea, Mexico, Poland, Puerto Rico, Russia, Syria, Turkey, Vietnam, and many other places around the globe. Our cultural, racial, and religious diversity has been a source both of pride and of problems.

Here are a few of the many questions that have frequently been raised concerning the meaning of this diversity. Who wishes to be considered, and will be accepted as, full participants in American society? If Americans trace their national origins to other countries, do they think of themselves *first* as Americans and *then* as members of a **racial group** (a term that emphasizes physical appearance) or an **ethnic group** (a term that emphasizes cultural heritage)? Behind questions such as these lie some others of critical importance. If many people in the United States have divided group loyalties, how is the underlying unity of the nation affected? Should divided loyalties be encouraged as sources of variety and strength or discouraged as sources of disunity and distrust? Whether they are discouraged or not, will these types of groups naturally disappear with the passage of time? Some of these perplexing questions call for factual answers. Others are concerned mainly with the goals, values, and purposes of American society as a whole and of the various groups within it.

We will explore various aspects of these and other questions as we analyze the experiences of different groups that are a part of the fabric of American society. We are especially interested in the question, "Is there a preordained, general social process through which groups of newcomers and their descendants travel to become established in the economic and social mainstream of American life?" This question has aroused debate throughout American history; and for most of that time, people have generally believed that there is a single, basic, route to Americanization. As the twentieth century unfolded, however, the matter became more clouded, and an increasing number of people maintained that there is more than one general process that operates to change groups of newcomers and their descendants into Americans. Portes and Rumbaut (1990:7–8), for example, argued that the ethnic diversity of our newcomers is greater now than ever before; and they find the idea that there is a uniform process leading to Americanization to be "increasingly implausible." They state that "there are today first-generation millionaires who speak broken English, foreign-born mayors of large cities, and top-flight immigrant engineers and scientists in the nation's research centers: there are also those, at the other extreme, who cannot even take the first step toward [Americanization] because of the insecurity linked to an uncertain legal status."

We begin our exploration of these ideas by sketching very briefly a popular image of the general social process most Americans have assumed is the basic route to Americanization for individuals and groups. As will become clear, however, our brief description draws heavily on the experiences of certain groups of newcomers who arrived during a particular period of our history. For that reason, we may suspect even now that the popular image is not entirely accurate. Later, we will introduce a number of important competing ideas to help us understand fully how a person's identity may be transformed from that of a "foreigner" to that of an "American."

A Popular Image of Americanization

The principal stages through which a newcomer to our shores is generally presumed to travel have been portrayed in many biographies, novels, plays, movies, and scholarly books and articles. Both in fact and in legend, millions of people have crossed the oceans in search of economic, religious, and other opportunities in the United States. The central image is familiar: A ship enters New York harbor within view of the Statue of Liberty; the weary and awe-stricken immigrants are cleared through Ellis Island ("The Gateway to the New World") for entry into the United States; after clearance, they come ashore and seek a place to live in an area where some or many others from their home country have settled. Those who arrived earlier may already have established "national churches, immigrant-aid societies, foreign-language newspapers, and other institutions" (Petersen 1980:239) to form an immigrant community within the city.

The life of the "greenhorn," though exciting, is filled with problems to solve and obstacles to overcome. He or she must find a place to live, find a job, and cope with the countless difficulties that arise daily when a person is trying to learn a new language and adopt a new way of living. The old-country ways and ideas are no longer appropriate. The newcomer must rapidly learn the "American way" to speak, dress, think, and act.

Gradually, the greenhorn begins to "learn the ropes," to speak and act less like someone F.O.B. ("fresh off the boat") and more like an "American." But even an immigrant who wishes to do so probably will not be able to make a complete transition to the new way of life. His or her name, speech, dress, manners, religious observances, food preferences, place of residence, or type of occupation may continue to mark him or her as "foreign." In most cases, in fact, newcomers do not want to be divorced entirely from the old-country ways. They may wish to be accepted as Americans in all ways that are essential to their livelihood and immediate welfare; they may wish for the members of their families to be able to participate as fully as they like in the mainstream of American life; but they may find life's greatest pleasures and satisfactions in the sights, smells, sounds, and companionship that exist only in the ethnic community—Chinatown, Little Dublin, or Little Italy—that the members of their national group have developed. Nevertheless, these **first-generation** Americans who are unable or unwilling to give up certain elements of their foreign culture and society may hope that their children will move further in the direction of losing their identities as foreigners and will become completely "American."

The immigrants' children, the **second generation,** may learn many of the old-country ways from their parents and may also be unable or unwilling to drop all vestiges of their parents' culture and behavior.[3] They will attend the public schools and become much more fluent in English than their parents; and they may fail to learn, or may actively reject, certain features of the old-country ways. When these second-generation Americans are grown, they will move up the ladder of economic success and out of the old neighborhood. They may even marry someone of a different **ethnicity**[4] or change their name to something that sounds more "American." Still, many elements of the old culture may persist either by preference or by necessity, and the individuals may be regarded by themselves or by others as still remaining in some significant ways "ethnics." Such people have one foot in the new or "host" society and one in the immigrant society; there are both advantages and disadvantages to being in this position. On the positive side, a person who is bicultural may enjoy "the best of both" cultural worlds; on the negative side, the individual may not feel completely "at home" in either culture.

Finally, according to the familiar image being sketched, the grandchildren of the immigrants, the **third generation,** will move completely into the mainstream of American life. Their parents will not have transmitted to them a noticeable portion of the old culture. This failure of transmission may occur partly because the parents do not wish to have the children maintain an ethnic identity (other than American) and partly because the parents themselves do not know enough of the old culture to transmit it. The children of the third generation may learn to speak a few words of the old-country language, especially if the grandparents are still alive, and they may learn certain old-country recipes, folk songs, and proverbs; they may feel a strong sense of attachment to the country of their grandparents and to other Americans who share a similar ethnic heritage; but they will speak standard English, and questions concerning their nationality will seldom arise. The third-generation Americans will have completed, for all practical purposes, the process of Americanization set into motion by their grandparents. The individual has now become a full member of the host society, sharing equally with the other established members in the distribution of social rewards. He or she may "rise" to any position the society has to offer.

Although the familiar image we are tracing assumes that the end result of Americanization is the replacement of the heritage of one's grandparents by the "American" heritage, the process in fact may have other outcomes. We discuss these alternatives extensively throughout this book; but, to suggest one important possibility now, let us note that in contrast to becoming a "full-fledged American" through the **three-generations process,** members of the third generation sometimes choose to reemphasize one or more aspects of their ancestry (Waters 1990).[5] Instead of shedding the last vestiges of the heritage of their grandparents (or great-grandparents), they may feel that something valuable has been lost and, therefore, may work to recover their cultural roots and reconstruct the ethnic community.

Our description of the Americanization process so far has been very general; and although no time period was specified, the examples refer mainly to the experiences of groups that came to the United States from Europe during a period of high immigration between 1880 and 1924. We may now state tentatively that, as applied to European groups, the "specifically *national* aspect of most ethnic groups rarely survives the third generation in any significant terms" (Glazer and Moynihan 1964:313). This is *one* description—and as we will see, a highly controversial one—of the sequence of stages through which members of successive generations may pass to become "completely American."

Even if this account is accepted as a general description of the way some immigrant groups have changed within American society, certain aspects of it must still be altered to fit many other cases. To illustrate, for many *individuals* the process has been completed by the end of the second generation; in some individual cases it has continued beyond the third. And in contemporary America, many particulars of the account must be altered. Many people are now likely to arrive in an airplane, rather than a ship; they often already have jobs; and their views of America depend now not so much on the letters and personal accounts of relatives (though these are still important) as on the images they have received through movies, television, contacts with Americans in their homelands, or in previous trips to America. And, because of the global reach of American culture, they may already have taken on many aspects of it before their arrival.

A number of different terms used in both popular and scholarly discourse refer to the transformation of a person's or group's identity from foreign to American. The idea is frequently suggested that the foreigner becomes an American through a process of "melting" or "merging." We will have much to say about this; for the moment, let us refer to the process of Americanization simply as one of **inclusion.** When a person or group first enters a society, they may be included only in a physical sense. They may be "in" the society but, socially speaking, not "of" it. *Our primary interest is in how a person or group does or does not become more nearly "fitted into" the various parts of a society.*

◈ Some Non-European Instances

If we were to attempt to explain what has happened to American Indians during the past four centuries in terms of the popular image of Americanization, it would instantly be clear that the three-generations description simply does not fit this case at all. Indians did not enter American society as immigrants; they preceded it. For the most part, they were brought involuntarily into what became American society. They entered, not through immigration, but through conquest and the occupation of their territories.

The African ancestors of most Black Americans came to the United States as bonded servants or slaves. They, too, obviously did not emigrate to the United States in the sense we have discussed. Although much human migration involves, to some degree, both voluntary and involuntary elements, it is clear that the involuntary element was enormously greater in the migration of the ancestors of most Black Americans than was true of any other group that has come to the United States.[6] It also is clear that after many more than three generations, Black Americans, on average, have not entered fully into the mainstream of American life and become simply "Americans."

Mexican Americans present a somewhat more complicated case. Like the American Indians, the ancestors of some Mexican Americans were brought into the United States involuntarily through conquest. The ancestors of some others, however—and this is by far the largest category—have migrated more or less voluntarily to the United States from Mexico. Many of those in the latter group, however, did not consider the border between the two countries to be very important psychologically and did not think of themselves as immigrants to a foreign country (Alvarez 1985). Like Black Americans and American Indians, most Mexican Americans have not completed the process of inclusion within three generations.

Why have some groups in the past not merged uniformly into American society? Is it likely, given still longer periods of time, that even the groups that have not gone through the three-generations process will gradually be included fully? And will the newcomers who now are reaching America follow the three-generations pattern? Stated more generally, the primary question we consider here and throughout the book is this: *What factors affect whether, to what extent, and at what rate the members of a given group are included within American society?*

◈ Some Factors Affecting Inclusion

Differences in Social Power

White Americans have been not only the largest group throughout most of the history of the United States, but they have also been the most *powerful* group. Their members have been more highly represented in positions of authority within the government, military services, and economic and educational organizations of the society than those of any other group. In these positions, they have played the greatest role in making decisions that affected the course of the relations among different groups. The many other racial and ethnic groups that have been represented in our society have been both smaller in size and less powerful. In all human societies, some group or groups will have greater social power and, therefore, a greater capacity to *control* than others; and the kinds of relations these more or less powerful groups have with one another represent a vital element in the operation of the society.[7] Racial and ethnic relations, not only in the United States but throughout the world, may be viewed as revealing some of the social consequences that may arise when one group is more powerful and dominates another.

Often the power of a **dominant** (most powerful) **group** is accepted as legitimate by those below them, and the commands of its members are willingly obeyed; however, sometimes the **subordinate** (less powerful) **groups** do not wish to obey, and then the dominant group may rely on coercion, leading to overt or covert conflicts between the groups. *The relative power or degree of dominance of various racial and ethnic groups, rather than their sheer size, is of paramount sociological significance.* We note in passing that all segments of a dominant group do not necessarily share the group's power equally. In our society, for instance, men and members of the upper classes have generally wielded greater power than women and members of the lower classes.

Throughout American history, the most powerful group also has been the largest group; but in many societies that is not the case, and it is the differences in social power that are of greatest significance in our analysis. We therefore use the terms **majority** and **minority** to indicate differences in group power rather than differences in size. Our concern is *the extent to which the minority group's behavior and life circumstances are related to the superior control exercised by the majority.*

But a majority group's power is always limited in some respects. Minority-group members, even those who are extremely oppressed, do exert some influence, however small, over the development of intergroup relations; hence, however strongly the rate of a group's inclusion within American society may be affected by the extent to which the White Americans desire or resist their inclusion, the rate is also always affected by the extent to which a minority group's members desire or resist inclusion. In the case of any given minority, the extent to which the relations between the interacting groups reflect the desires of the majority and those of the minority is a question that can be settled only by specific research. For example, the existence of neighborhoods that are settled primarily by one ethnic group or another does not by itself demonstrate either that the concentrations have arisen primarily because the majority has enforced separation (**segregation**) or that the minorities have chosen separation (**congregation**). *It is absolutely essential in any case that we study the historical sequences that have created the dominant–subordinate group relations.*[8]

Voluntary or Involuntary Entrance

Our discussion has indicated that the members of groups that choose to become a part of American society are more likely to follow the three-generations process than those who enter the society involuntarily. Those who enter voluntarily may seek full inclusion, make great efforts to learn English, and be willing to alter many ways of acting that were customary in their homeland. People who are enslaved or conquered, on the other hand, may be reluctant to become members of the society that is responsible for those acts. Their goal may be to escape from the new society that has been imposed on them or to drive the invaders out and return to their former way of life.[9] Note, however, that even though a voluntary entrance into American society may initially lead people to be more favorable toward the adoption of its culture, and an involuntary entrance may favor the rejection of Americanization, the possibility exists that the two types of entrance may not necessarily lead to different results.

Americanization may be viewed, even by those who migrate voluntarily, as having both desirable and undesirable aspects. For example, the members of a racial or ethnic group may view full inclusion within American life mainly as a process whereby a cherished way of life is gradually eroded or destroyed rather than as progress. Although they may have chosen to enter the society, they still may struggle valiantly to maintain a separate ethnic identity. From this standpoint, a major problem for newcomers is the difficulty of *resisting* inclusion. At the same time, an effort by newcomers to maintain a distinctive identity may stir resentment among other Americans, who may say (or think), "If you don't like it here, why don't you go back where you came from?" Frequently, too, the members of an immigrant group may be uncertain regarding whether or in what ways inclusion should be sought. Nearly all Jews, for instance, may agree that the members of their group should learn English and be permitted to attend the public schools, but they may disagree sharply concerning the extent to which their religious ceremonies should be conducted in English.

Group Size, Concentration, and Time of Entry

It is well known that majority-group members are much more concerned about the presence of minority-group members and give much more evidence of rejecting them in those locations in which the minority is relatively large and in which the minority group has grown rapidly in size.[10] If the minority group actually becomes larger than the dominant group, the concern of the dominant-group members may be greater still. This situation has been common in the experience of Black Americans in many towns in the southern United States and of Mexican Americans and American Indians in many towns of the southwestern and western portions of the United States. When the minority is the larger group, the majority may erect many types of social barriers between itself and the minority. In these circumstances, the majority may be particularly sensitive, and may react violently to even the slightest sign that these barriers are eroding.

The economic conditions of the receiving country at the time a group arrives are critical factors affecting the group's reception. When the country has been in periods of economic expansion and more "hands" have been needed to do the work, immigrants have been encouraged to move to the United States; during such times they have been accepted more willingly than during depressions. When many Americans have been out of work, the fear that "they" are taking "our" jobs away provides a powerful motive to resist the inclusion of newcomers. In addition to the timing of a group's entry, the length of time that has elapsed since the members of a group first arrived is also an important factor affecting inclusion. Lieberson and Waters (1988:43) found that among those who described their ancestry as "American" in the decennial census of 1980, 98 percent "have at least three generations' residence" in the United States.

Ethnic and Racial Similarity

Another factor affecting the rate of inclusion of a minority group within the United States is the similarity between the culture (ethnicity) of the minority and the culture of the majority. People whose native languages are Chinese, Korean, or Japanese, for instance, may experience more difficulty in mastering the speech patterns and inflections of the English language than those whose native languages are Dutch, German, or Spanish. And since Judeo-Christian beliefs are dominant within the United States, those who have been raised in a different religious tradition may find many "American" ways difficult to accept. The same is true of American approaches to politics, education, courtship, marriage, and many other aspects of life.

A final factor affecting inclusion to be mentioned here—though many others will be uncovered in the course of our analysis—is the racial (physical) identification of the individual or group. Although White Americans have generally shown some hostility toward all foreigners, they have been more willing to accept the members of some groups than others. The history of the United States shows, in particular, that White resistance to inclusion is greater against those who are defined as "non-White" than against those who are considered to be "White." For reasons we will discuss later, White Americans generally have considered those labeled as non-White to be inferior and unacceptable as social equals.[11]

The discussion so far has suggested some of the factors that may be important in helping us to understand why some groups apparently have been fully included in American life within three generations and others have not; and we have stressed along the way the special importance of visible physical and sociocultural differences. These differences are key elements in our discussion.

Race and Ethnicity:
A Conceptual Note

The terms *race* and *ethnicity* have been assigned a variety of meanings and are the subjects of continuing debate. Each term refers in part to the fact that people may believe they and certain other people are the descendants of common or related ancestors and, further, that those of common ancestry comprise natural social groups or categories.[12]

Among those who perceive that they share with others some trait that is taken to denote common ancestry, there may develop a sense of "interconnectedness," "peoplehood," or group identification.

Race.   As we have noted, in current use racial group or category designations refer mainly to aspects of a person's physical heritage, whereas ethnic group or category designations refer mainly to aspects of a person's sociocultural heritage. People tend to *assume* that groups based on physical and social inheritance are of special importance and are *immutable* (Allport 1958:106; Petersen 1980:239). The plausibility of this viewpoint rests primarily on the centuries-old observation that family members usually resemble one another more in both appearance and behavior than do unrelated individuals.[13]

The practice of distinguishing between people's heritages primarily in physical terms or primarily in sociocultural terms is widely accepted. Its common acceptance, and the social groupings that are generally recognized thereby, provide the underpinnings for the analyses of this book; but let us note that *the boundaries between and within racial and ethnic groups are not nearly as sharp and fixed as many people assume.* In fact, they overlap, are blurred, and may change.

To illustrate, let us briefly consider some issues that arise in the process of attempting to determine a person's racial group membership. In everyday situations, most people are defined by themselves and others as belonging to a particular racial group even when they are aware that some racial "mixing" has occurred. They are thought to *be* (and are treated as being) members of this race *or* that race *or* some other race. Under these circumstances it is easy to assume that the boundaries of this system are "real" and have been imposed on us by nature. In fact, however, the conclusion that a person is a member of a single race involves a much larger element of choice and social agreement than may be apparent. The most frequently chosen defining trait, skin color, obviously varies by degrees. Some "White" people have skins that are as dark as or darker than the skins of some "non-White" people; hence, a common defining racial trait (skin color) cannot be used to establish sharp boundaries. Since all of the other visible traits (e.g., eye shape, nose shape) that are commonly employed suffer this same defect, any effort to establish sharp boundaries among the races on the basis of any one of these commonly used physical traits is bound to be imperfect and, to a considerable extent, arbitrary. Blumenbach, an early anthropologist, appreciated this point far better than many later observers. In his words, the "innumerable varieties of mankind run into one another by insensible degrees" (quoted by King 1971:113).

The problem of overlapping boundaries cannot be surmounted by combining the various traits, either. It is true that in the United States people who trace their origins to Europe are more likely to be called "White" than are people who trace their origins to Asia and Africa (i.e., geographical origin and skin color are **correlated**), but some people who trace their origins to Europe may have darker skins than some people who trace their ancestry to Asia and Africa (i.e., the correlation of geographical origin and skin color is not perfect). As a third trait is added, and then a fourth and a fifth, the probability that all of the traits will lead to the same racial assignments declines.[14] The low levels of correlation among clusters of these different socially accepted criteria of racial grouping explains why scholars who have employed the criteria of skin color, head shape, nose shape, geographical location, and so on, either singly or in combination, have frequently disagreed concerning how many human races there are. Linnaeus distinguished 4 races, Buffon distinguished 6, Deniker concluded there are 29, Coon and colleagues constructed 30, and Quatrefages listed 150 (Dunn and Dobzhansky 1964:110; Loehlin, Lindzey, and Spuhler 1975:33). These illustrations run directly counter to the prevalent idea that the "races" people usually distinguish on the basis of visible physical traits are quite distinctive, specific, unvarying entities. People may be grouped into the same or different races depending on the criteria that are used as defining traits.[15]

These considerations support the conclusion that, *although people commonly think of races, and sometimes ethnic groups, as sharply distinguishable biological entities, their boundaries, in fact, are set by social agreement.* Whatever sharpness racial and ethnic boundaries may have springs from the fact that people react to the members of these socially recognized groups in quite different, socially important ways.

The logic of this conclusion has led some students of racial and ethnic groups to argue that the concept of race is a sociopolitical rather than a scientific concept and to recommend that it be abandoned completely as a scientific term (Littlefield, Lieberman, and Reynolds 1982:644). It has also led to a demand by a growing group of Americans who consider themselves to be "multiracial" that the U.S. Bureau of the Census expand its question on racial identification to include a "multiracial" or "mixed" category. The impetus for this demand was that by 1990 there were 1.5 million interracial couples in the United States who were the parents of 4 million children (Smith 1996:A16). This demand that the reality of cross-race offspring be acknowledged, however, was opposed by some Black and Hispanic groups who said the proposal "reeks of racism and perpetuates the false notion that racial purity exists"; or as Judy Scales-Trent, a professor of law and author of a book on racial identification, stated, the proposal "smacks of Nazi ideology" (Smith 1996:A16).[16] Another author objected that "this proposal simply creates another category which multiracial people must force themselves into"; she stated that she views herself as being "black and white" and wished to "be able to check any boxes that apply" (Funderburg 1996:A15). The existence of this controversy highlights an important point: *The "races" that we recognize derive their significance from the fact that important social consequences follow from their use.*

Ethnicity.   Although the concept of ethnicity usually emphasizes a person's sociocultural heritage, "a biological connotation sometimes adheres still to 'ethnic'" (Petersen 1980:235);[17] but even when a person's appearance or behavior is generally acknowledged to derive exclusively from culture, there is a common tendency to treat the characteristic as a fixed, all-or-none matter and to miss entirely the flexibility of the group boundaries thus created.

In addition, there is a strong tendency to create derogatory images of various groups' members. Both majority-group and minority-group members may well believe that "we" who share certain sociocultural characteristics are more honest, or skillful, or loyal, or humane than "they" who share other sociocultural traits. Such judgments about **in-groups** and **out-groups** are made routinely and with little reflection in our daily lives, and they may seem to rest on hard experience and firm foundations. Even when such views are poorly founded, they nevertheless exist as social realities and guide social behavior. They also create formidable barriers to intergroup understanding and the full inclusion of minority groups within a society.

As we analyze racial and ethnic relations in America, we must recognize the social reality of the racial and ethnic categories that exist in our society and, simultaneously, maintain an awareness that these categories have not been imposed on us by nature. They are created by the members of social groups (even when physical traits are used as building materials); and they are, in principle, subject to reconstruction. Since there is no firm line of division between the concepts of *race* and *ethnicity,* people often use *ethnicity* as a general term that includes race.

Some scholars have argued that the alteration of our existing racial and ethnic categories will occur naturally with the passage of time. The argument is that racial and ethnic distinctions are inherently at odds with the requirements of a modern urban-industrial, scientific-rational society and that, consequently, "the forces of history" are against the maintenance of such distinctions. To understand this argument, let us turn briefly to some ideas pertaining to a related sociological problem.

From Traditional to Modern Racial and Ethnic Relations

A central concern of sociologists is to describe and understand what happens when a society undergoes the enormous shift from **traditional** to **modern.** In western Europe, for example, the transformation was from the traditional patterns of social life in a feudal system to the radically different patterns of life that characterize modern industrial societies. Traditional societies are regulated mainly by custom and are organized primarily in terms of kinship. The members of families work together and form the basic economic unit of the society. Since neighboring families live in essentially the same way, mutual understanding and cooperative activity are promoted, and a strong sense of community attachment, **cohesion** (or **solidarity**), develops. In such a setting, religion is a powerful force that tends to permeate all segments of individual and community life. The pervasiveness of religion combines with the force of custom and tradition to maintain a slowly changing, comparatively static social order. The ordinary person in a society of this type lives a hard life in many respects but finds compensation in the continuous social support of family, friends, and religious leaders. These supports create within the individual a strong sense of belonging to a valuable community; and they foster the impression that the social order in which the individual lives is timeless and unchanging.

The defining properties of modern societies are frequently portrayed as the exact opposites of those contained or implied in the description of traditional societies. If the central tendency of traditional societies is to maintain strong families and communities in which people live with a sense of belonging and purpose, the central tendency of modern societies is to weaken the bonds of families and communities and to atomize the individual. Within modern societies, economic activities shift away from the family to the city and the corporation. Work tasks are more likely to be divided and organized according to rational plans than according to custom. Instead of engaging in the same kinds of work, family members and neighbors usually engage in different kinds of work. In this way, the intimate knowledge and mutual understanding of one another that are cultivated when people work together at the same activities are hindered. Individuals who work together are less likely to develop strong personal ties within a modern setting. For one thing, people move around so frequently in modern societies that it is difficult to develop enduring personal bonds. Life in general becomes more hurried and more bureaucratic. The individual's sense of commitment to his or her family and community declines.

This comparison of the traditional and modern forms of social life suggests mainly the losses that individuals suffer in the shift from the former to the latter. But the picture may also be painted primarily in terms of the ways in which individuals gain. The term *modern* usually connotes progress for both the individual and the society. For the individual, modern life represents a release from the bonds of traditional life—a life in which the individual's place is determined largely by **ascribed characteristics** such as family status, sex, and age. Under modern conditions, the individual's place presumably depends more heavily on **achieved characteristics** such as educational level and occupational skill.

At the societal level, modernization is frequently advocated as a way to decrease poverty, disease, and death rates and to increase material abundance and the enjoyment of life. Modern life is seen by many as more enlightened and more efficiently organized than traditional life. Moreover, those who emphasize the advantages of modern life frequently assume either that the individual's attachment and loyalty to kinship and community groups will be transferred to other groups within modern societies or that, in fact, traditional loyalty to family and community may be maintained because they are compatible with the efficient operation of a modern nation. In any event, the ability to transfer allegiance if one wishes liberates the individual from the accidental restraints of birth and tradition, and enables him or her to pick and choose personal attachments more freely. From this standpoint, a traditional form of social organization that demands loyalty to the family, clan, tribe, or village and prevents a person from changing group memberships is "inefficient." In modern life, rewards are *supposed* to be distributed on the basis of the **principle of achievement** rather than on the basis of the **principle of ascription.** Giving individuals rewards for their achievements is regarded as "fair," whereas giving rewards to individuals because they have been born into privileged groups is considered "unfair."

With these ideas in mind, it is easy to understand why many sociologists believed that racial and ethnic distinctions would become decreasingly important in the modern world. It was assumed that the historical trend of American society would be away from tradition and toward modernity. From this perspective, social distinctions based on racial and ethnic differences are obsolete remnants of the traditional form of social organization. From this perspective, the ties that bind individuals to racial and ethnic groups in American society are expected to continue to become progressively weaker. Racial and ethnic loyalties and consciousness should decline. If they do not, this fact is likely to be seen as a problem that needs to be solved.

Several issues are raised by the ideas just presented. For instance, even though there is much evidence to support our general description of the positive and negative changes that accompany modernization, there is still cause to wonder whether such changes *must* occur.[18] If racial and ethnic consciousness has been declining throughout the twentieth century, why have civil rights activities become more prominent in the United States since the 1950s? And why is it true that "Everywhere one looks, ethnic division persists" (Spickard 1989:11)? Perhaps certain levels of traditional loyalty to family and tribe increase, rather than decrease, the efficiency of a modern nation by providing people with necessary social attachments and ways to "recharge their batteries" as they face the "future shock" of rapid social and cultural change.

These considerations suggest that we may not take for granted the idea that racial and ethnic differences automatically will decline as a society becomes more modern. Numerous conflicts almost certainly will arise between dominant and subordinate groups as a society reorganizes along new lines. Nevertheless, even if the process is not automatic, should not the passage of time generally lead interacting racial and ethnic groups gradually to adjust to one another and become more alike? The implications of various answers to these questions must be examined in detail. We begin this examination in Chapter 2.

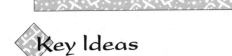

Key Ideas

1. Many people assume that the usual and normal course of Americanization requires three generations. In this view, the adult grandchild of the immigrant generally is, and should be, fully Americanized.

2. A basic sociological task is to try to understand the factors affecting whether, to what extent, and at what rate the members of a particular group have been included within a given society.

3. Many factors may affect the rate at which different groups move toward full inclusion within a society. Some of the most important of these factors, among many others, are: (a) the wishes and relative power of the majority and the minority; (b) whether the group's entry into the society was largely voluntary or involuntary;

(c) the relative size, rate of increase, and degree of concentration of the minority; (d) the time at which the minority entered the society; (e) the cultural similarity of the majority and minority; and (f) the racial similarity of the majority and minority.

4. Numerous problems exist in the effort to classify people as members of specific racial and ethnic groups. A basic problem is that the boundaries between and within racial and ethnic groups overlap and, in many ways, are blurred. Even though people commonly think of races, and sometimes ethnic groups, as sharply distinguishable biological entities, their boundaries are not set by nature but, rather, are set by social agreement; hence, these boundaries are flexible rather than fixed. Additionally, people in different socially recognized racial and ethnic groups may share some visible, supposedly defining, characteristics.

5. Judgments about in-groups and out-groups are made routinely and may rest on poor foundations. Such judgments nevertheless exist as social realities and guide social behavior. They serve as significant barriers to intergroup understanding and the inclusion of minority groups within a society.

6. Many scholars have assumed that as societies move away from traditional forms of social organization, loyalties based on kinship and cultural similarity tend to recede in importance or disappear. These forms of loyalty (based on the principle of ascription) are thought to be incompatible with the requirements of modern social organization (based on the principle of achievement). From this point of view, the kinship and cultural loyalties that remain or periodically revive within a modern nation are problems to be solved. An opposing point of view stresses the importance of family and community loyalties as psychological supports for people who live in an urban, industrial, and bureaucratic society.

Key Terms

achieved characteristics   Those characteristics of a person, such as educational level and occupation, that may be acquired through his or her efforts and performance.

ascribed characteristics   Those characteristics of a person that are assigned to him or her by birth, such as family status, sex, and age.

cohesion (solidarity)   A strong sense of attachment and allegiance among the members of a group leading to tightly knit families and communities.

congregation   The concentration of a group of people within a particular area primarily because they wish to be together.

correlation   The strength of the tendency of two or more variables to occur together.

dominant group   The most powerful group within a society.

ethnic group   A group or category of people whose inclusion in the group or category is based primarily on similarities of nationality, religion, language, or other aspects of a person's sociocultural heritage. The term also may be used more broadly to include racial groups.

ethnicity   The "sense of peoplehood" shared by those who believe they are members of a given ethnic group; a person's ethnic identification.

first generation   People of foreign birth who have immigrated to the United States.

inclusion   A general term used to designate all social processes that lead to the merger of a minority group with a majority group.

in-group   A group of people who share certain traits and characterize themselves as "we."

majority   *See* dominant group.

minority   *See* subordinate group.

modern   The defining characteristics of a contemporary industrial, urban, bureaucratic society.

out-group   The members of any group that lies beyond the circle of those who characterize themselves as "we" and are referred to as "they."

principle of achievement   The belief that individuals should be rewarded on the basis of their individual efforts and performances rather than on the basis of inheritance.

principle of ascription   The belief that certain inherited characteristics should determine their holder's share of society's rewards.

racial group   A group or category of people whose inclusion in the group or category is based primarily on inherited physical characteristics such as skin color, hair texture, and facial form.

second generation   People who are born in the United States whose parents were immigrants.

segregation   The concentration of a group of people within a particular area primarily because the majority group has left them little choice.

subordinate group   A group that is less powerful than the most powerful group in a society.

third generation   People who are born in the United States whose parents are second-generation Americans.

three-generations process   An intergenerational sequence through which an ethnic group loses its distinctiveness within three generations.

traditional society   A society based on the members' allegiance to its shared communal practices and the authority of the family.

Notes

1. We assume here that a generation is approximately twenty-five years.

2. There is no completely satisfactory way to identify different racial and ethnic groups. The practice followed in this book is intended to be both neutral and as close as possible to the contemporary preferences of the groups involved. We usually use a term of group reference followed by the word *American.*

3. Immigrants to a new country may bring with them infants and young children who also, technically, are members of the first generation; but the children's experiences while growing up in the new country usually resemble those of their siblings who are born in the new country. From a sociopsychological standpoint, therefore, these individuals are best viewed as members of the second generation.

4. "A convenient term for [a] sense of 'peoplehood' is 'ethnicity'" (Gordon 1964:24).

5. This phenomenon, in which "what the son wishes to forget the grandson wishes to remember," is often referred to as Hansen's thesis or "law" (Hansen 1938:9).

6. Schermerhorn (1970:98) presented a classification of migrations according to the amount of coercion involved. Slave transfers are the most coercive type.

7. For a comprehensive treatment of the concept of control and of its importance in sociological analysis, see Gibbs (1989).

8. Heraclitus, a scholar of ancient Greece, put it this way: "He who watches a thing grow has the best view of it."

9. An influential analysis of minority groups in terms of their goals was presented by Wirth (1945:347–372).

10. As (1) the ratio of the incoming minority to the resident population increases and (2) the influx becomes more rapid, the probability of conflict increases (Williams 1947:6–7). This viewpoint has been referred to as the visibility-discrimination hypothesis, the competition

hypothesis, and the minority size hypothesis (Burr, Galle, and Fossett 1991:833).

11. Distinctions are also made within the White group. Dark-skinned Whites are generally less acceptable to the dominant group than are Whites of lighter skin. For an excellent discussion of this point, see Warner and Srole (1946:285–286).

12. *Social groups* are small aggregates of people who know one another and interact on a personal level. *Social categories* are large aggregates of people who share one, or several, social characteristics.

13. The idea that clans, tribes, nations, and races owe their resemblances to shared blood was discredited by the discoveries of Mendel and others. A person's characteristics result not from "blood" but from the operation of separate particles ("genes") of the germ plasm of the parents (Dobzhansky 1962:27). The genetic elements are either present or absent; they do not "mix." An element may be present within the gene structure of an individual (the genotype) but find no expression whatever in the visible characteristics of the individual (the phenotype). The unexpressed characteristic is nonetheless still there.

14. Swedes typically are thought to be tall, long-headed, blond, and blue-eyed; but a study of Swedish people found only 10.1 percent of those studied to have *all four* of these traits (Loehlin, Lindzey, and Spuhler 1975:22).

15. Genetic approaches to defining races are based on counting the *frequencies* with which genes appear within different "breeding populations." Loehlin, Lindzey, and Spuhler (1975: 33) concluded there may be as many as 1 million "local breeding populations" (i.e., races) within the human species!

16. Some opposition also stems from a fear that if people could select a multiracial category, the size of the groups that are presently recognized would be decreased in the census counts and the smaller numbers would weaken

their influence in political matters (Smith 1996:A16).

17. Petersen (1980:234) states that "ethnic" comes from the Greek *ethnikos,* meaning a nation or race, and that "nation" comes from the Latin *nasci,* meaning "to be born"; hence, both ethnicity and nationality are derived from terms that originally referred to a group's biological heritage.

18. Blumer (1965), for example, argued that modern societies are more likely to adapt to the preexisting patterns of interethnic relations than the other way around.

Together or Apart?

Some Competing Views

The process of assimilation is complex. Some people favor a complete merger of the majority and the minority. Others advocate lower levels of merger. Defining a group's goals allows for a better understanding of what assimilation means to them.

*They must cast off the European skin, never to resume it. They must look
forward to their posterity rather than backward to their ancestors.*

—John Quincy Adams

*America is God's crucible. The great melting pot where all the races
of Europe are melting and reforming!*

—Israel Zangwill

*Thus "American civilization" may come to mean the perfection of the
cooperative harmonies of "European civilization" . . . a multiplicity in a
unity, an orchestration of mankind.*

—Horace Kallen

*The Indians are not willing to come to live near to the English. . . . A place
must be found somewhere remote from the English, where they must have
the word constantly taught, and government constantly exercised.*

—John Eliot

Chapter 1 introduced the view that we cannot merely assume racial and ethnic differences will decline automatically as a society becomes more modern. Numerous conflicts
will almost certainly arise between dominant and subordinate groups as a society reorganizes along new lines. These conflicts may strengthen rather than weaken group divisions, and the level of disagreement between the groups may increase. Even so, shouldn't
we expect interacting groups within a given society *usually* to adjust to one another and
become more alike with the passage of time? An important answer to this question was
provided by the theorist Robert E. Park.

Two Assimilation Theories

The Cycle of Race Relations

Park was deeply interested in the experiences of racial and cultural groups throughout
the world. His professional work on this subject covered a span of more than thirty
years. The framework of his thought was presented in a now-famous theory called
the **cycle of race relations.** Park expressed his view as follows: "In the relations of races
there is a cycle of events which tends everywhere to repeat itself. . . . The race relations
cycle . . . *contacts, competition, accommodation* and *eventual assimilation,* is apparently
progressive and irreversible. Customs regulations, immigration restrictions and racial

barriers may slacken the tempo of the movement; may perhaps halt it altogether for a time; but cannot change its direction; cannot at any rate, reverse it" (emphasis added; Park [1926]1964:150*).

The stages of this cycle are "the processes by which the integration of peoples and cultures have always and everywhere taken place" (Park 1964:104). Groups of people first come into contact through exploration or migration. Once they are in contact, a competition between the groups is set into motion for land, natural resources, and various goods and services, a competition in which violent conflict frequently erupts. After a period of time, Park said, overt conflict becomes less frequent as one of the two groups establishes dominance over the other. The groups develop some fairly regular or customary ways of living together; at this point, they are said to have accommodated to one another.[1]

Beginning with the first contacts, various individuals within the two groups learn some of the language, customs, sentiments, and attitudes of those in the other group. This process, initiated in the contact phase of the groups' relations with one another, gains momentum as the groups compete for such advantages as land and social dominance; and it accelerates during the more or less stable period of accommodation. As the groups continue to live together, there occurs, according to Park (1964:205), a "progressive merging" of the smaller group into the larger. The members of the smaller group increasingly adopt the language, manners, and public customs of the larger group. Except in the case of physical differences, this process has "erased the external signs which formerly distinguished the members of one [group] from those of another." When the external signs have been "erased" and the members of the smaller group can no longer be distinguished from those of the larger group, **assimilation** has occurred. Although Park lists *eventual* assimilation as the final stage in the cycle, the **assimilation process** *commences with contact and occurs throughout the cycle,* reaching its completion when all distinguishing external signs of group membership in the smaller group have disappeared.

Now, compare the cycle described by Park with the popular view of Americanization presented in Chapter 1. Park, of course, was attempting to understand the results of racial and ethnic contacts "always and everywhere," whereas our interest is centered on the United States. Even though the popular account and Park's account differ in some ways, they nevertheless appear to be entirely compatible in their main features. For this reason, the popular view of Americanization may be regarded as a "special case" of Park's general theory.

Another outstanding and controversial contribution to the development of ideas and concepts dealing with the subject of assimilation is the work of Milton M. Gordon (1964). Gordon effectively made the point that it is useful to think in terms of several specific **subprocesses of assimilation** rather than of a single broad process; and he identified several important subprocesses. He also distinguished three main **ideologies of**

---

*When an author originally published his/her ideas at an earlier date we have included that date for historical reference. The later publication date is a more recent edition of the work and is cited in the references. These dual dates appear throughout the text.

assimilation that have been significant in the development of the United States as a nation. And he organized these ideas and concepts into a theory of assimilation that has stimulated a great deal of debate.

We have noted two opposing views concerning the effects of modernization on differences among ethnic groups. The first argued that ethnic groups in a modernizing society gradually become more similar to one another; the second argued that differences among ethnic groups are increased and sharpened by the forces of modernization (Olzak and Nagel 1986:1–2). The theories of Park and Gordon, and assimilation theories in general, are consistent with the first view, that ethnic differences decline with modernization. They are consistent, additionally, with the idea that as ethnic differences decline the society's underlying order and unity rest increasingly on a consensus among the different groups concerning basic values and norms. For this reason, assimilation theories are generally referred to as **consensus** or **order theories.**

Those who favor the view that modernization increases the differences among ethnic groups emphasize that ethnic conflict has risen throughout the world during recent decades. Assimilation theories have been attacked particularly (1) for seeming to confuse the idea of assimilation as an historical reality or matter of fact with the idea of assimilation as a desirable condition that groups should work to achieve, (2) for seeming to give insufficient attention to the power differences and social conflicts that exist among racial and ethnic groups, and (3) for being inapplicable to the experiences in America of non-Whites and those who have entered the society involuntarily. Also, the basic term *assimilation* is itself a matter of dispute. Even though the word has a precise ring to it and is used in technical discussions, people with quite different or incompatible ideas may use it to describe their particular points of view on racial and ethnic problems. As Park ([1913]1964:204) said in his earliest paper on this topic, "It is not always clear . . . what assimilation means."[2]

These and other criticisms have stimulated the development of a number of alternative theories that we will discuss at pertinent places throughout the book. The most important of these alternatives for our purpose is the **theory of internal colonialism,** which is explained in Chapter 8 and plays an important role in our discussions of the experiences of Mexican Americans, African Americans, and Native Americans.[3] At the core of this theory is the distinction we made in Chapter 1 between the experiences and goals of those who are included in our society voluntarily and those who are included involuntarily. In contrast to assimilation theories, internal colonial theory forecasts the *eventual separation* of the interacting groups. It emphasizes that power and value conflicts exist between dominant and subordinate groups and that social conflicts center on these differences; hence, it is an example of **conflict theory.**

The implications of the major ideas introduced so far must be examined in much greater detail. We begin with a brief discussion of three of the subprocesses of assimilation described by Gordon (1964). To illustrate the ideas being presented, we refer to certain events drawn from the early colonial period of American history; and, in so doing, we make certain statements concerning colonial American society that will be discussed further in Chapter 3. We also present a brief summary of the main features of Gordon's **theory of assimilation subprocesses.**

Subprocesses of Assimilation

The European "discovery" of the Western Hemisphere near the end of the fifteenth century was followed by a long period of competition among several European nations for control of the land and resources of the new territories. By the time the English established their first successful colonies in Jamestown, Virginia (1607), and Plymouth, Massachusetts (1620), the Spanish and Portuguese had been colonizing the New World for more than a century; and the Spanish had already established permanent settlements in what are now Florida, New Mexico, and California. All of the territories claimed and occupied by these and other European powers had been held previously by various indigenous, so-called "Indian," peoples. As the Jamestown and Plymouth colonies expanded—by armed conquest and other techniques—the English became the dominant or occupying group in an increasingly large territory. The Native Americans were gradually forced either to retreat to lands that the English did not occupy or, if they wished to be included in English colonial society, to remain where they were on terms set by the English.

This process of expansion and domination by the English led, in time, to the seizure of New Netherland, which had been established earlier by the Dutch. New Amsterdam (1626) became New York (1664), giving the English tentative control of a strip of coastal territory stretching from Massachusetts to Virginia. During the next three decades, the mainly English population of this still-expanding territory became much larger in size, gained a stronger grip on the land, and came increasingly to think of itself as comprised of "Americans." As this sense of "Americanness" developed, the Anglo Americans distinguished more sharply between themselves and more recent newcomers, who were likely to be regarded as "foreigners."

These considerations support a very important point: *By the last quarter of the seventeenth century, the Anglo Americans had become established as the "native" group along the Atlantic seaboard from Massachusetts to Virginia.* Obviously, this does not mean the Anglo Americans were natives in the same sense that the Indians were natives. It does mean they had displaced the Indians as the principal occupants of the land and had established their own ways of living as dominant. In this way, the Anglo Americans established their culture and institutions as the basic elements of American life, at least tentatively. From their perspective, then, the extent to which someone was an "American" could now be determined in a rough way by a comparison with the accepted Anglo American pattern. The more nearly a person approximated this pattern, the more nearly "American" he or she was judged to be.[4]

Let us examine "the Anglo American pattern" more closely and attempt to describe some of its component parts. Consider, for instance, some of the main features of Anglo American culture. English was the accepted language, and foreigners were expected to learn and use it; Protestant religious ideas were dominant, and non-Protestant practices were discouraged; the system of law and government that was being established throughout the territory clearly was imported from England, as was the system of business practices that was established. It is true, of course, that various non-English elements were being added to the culture of the Anglo Americans. Many foods, planting practices, hunting methods, and other knowledge that were crucial to survival in North America were being borrowed from the Native Americans; and many other cultural items were being contributed by other groups. Dutch place names, for example, had already supplanted Native American names in some parts of New York and continue to be used there even now. Moreover, many aspects of English culture had been affected by the "long intimate and cranky relationship" (Tuchman 1988:57) that had existed between the English and the Dutch prior to 1664; and, in addition to the Dutch, New Amsterdam contained people of Swedish, French, Portuguese, Jewish, Spanish, Norwegian, Polish, Danish, African, and German descent, as well as several other ethnicities when the English arrived there.[5] Given this diversity, the culture of the *Anglo Americans* was no longer identical to that of the English. Nevertheless, in its major contours and social structure, it was distinctively English. It was a transplanted "sprig" of English life growing on foreign soil.

Within this context, we may say that as the Native Americans or the Dutch or the members of the many other groups that were already present in the English colonies abandoned their previous cultural practices and took up those of the colonists, they were undergoing one form of what Gordon called **cultural assimilation.** In this case the term refers to the subprocess of assimilation through which the members of a subordinate group gradually relinquish their own culture and, *at the same time,* acquire that of the dominant group. Since this subprocess of inclusion involves the *substitution* of one heritage and behavior pattern for another, we will refer to it as **cultural assimilation by substitution.** We also will examine cases of cultural assimilation in which the subordinate group keeps most or at least a significant portion of its own heritage (McFee 1972). In those cases we will use the term **cultural assimilation by addition.** Obviously, when this type of cultural assimilation occurs, the subordinate group remains distinguishable.

The complete "merging" of one group into another requires more, however, than cultural assimilation by substitution. It also requires that additional types of assimilation take place; and among these we focus on structural assimilation and marital assimilation. In Gordon's terms, structural assimilation focuses on the type of human relationships sociologists call **primary relationships.** These relationships are predominant within families, friendship groups, and "social" clubs, but are not typical of relationships at work, in schools, in commerical transactions, at political meetings, and in places of public recreation. The latter are called **secondary relationships.**

Our analysis will be greatly aided by dividing Gordon's structural assimilation subprocess into two subprocesses, one for social settings where secondary relationships are paramount and one for settings in which primary relationships are paramount. **Secondary structural assimilation** refers to equal-status relationships between subordinate- and dominant-group members in the "public" sphere. **Primary structural assimilation** refers to close, personal interactions between subordinate- and dominant-group members in the "private" sphere.[6]

The final step of ethnic "disappearance" to be included in our analysis (though not the final step distinguished by Gordon) is **marital assimilation.** This subprocess refers to the gradual merging of subordinate and dominant groups through intermarriage. In many cases, merging takes place directly as members of the dominant group marry partners from various subordinate groups; often, however, it takes place less directly as out-group marriages occur between the members of more-or-less assimilated groups.[7] To continue our previous illustration, the Native Americans, Africans, Dutch, and others, could be considered *fully* assimilated at the most personal levels of association only when friendships and marriages among these groups and the dominant group were taking place without regard to racial or ethnic distinctions.

The four subprocesses of assimilation that are directly pertinent to the kind of assimilation that may lead to a situation in which subordinate and dominant groups become indistinguishable from one another (excluding for the moment cultural assimilation by addition) are: (1) cultural assimilation by substitution, (2) secondary structural assimilation, (3) primary structural assimilation, and (4) marital assimilation.[8] We will generally refer to the third and fourth subprocesses simply as secondary and primary assimilation. Please note that *secondary assimilation appears in the list ahead of primary assimilation.* The reasoning here is simply that since people in modern societies typically meet and interact with one another in impersonal settings before they become close friends, assimilation into jobs, schools, political parties and positions, and neighborhoods might be expected to precede primary assimilation. The meaning and value of these distinctions will become progressively clearer as we move through our analysis.

A Theory of Assimilation Subprocesses

In a theory embodying these ideas and concepts, Gordon (1964:71) states that all of the subprocesses we have identified may be under way simultaneously and "may take place in varying degrees"; however, the rate of change expected at each level depends on its place in the preceding list; hence, cultural assimilation should proceed more rapidly than secondary assimilation, and so on. In sharp contrast to Park's view, however, the various subprocesses do not identify distinct and inevitable stages of assimilation. According to this theory, *a group may assimilate culturally without necessarily proceeding through the remaining levels of assimilation.* The condition of "cultural assimilation only" may "continue indefinitely" (Gordon 1964:77). Past a certain point, however (and in this way Gordon's theory bears an important resemblance to Park's), assimilation in all respects becomes inevitable. *The crucial point in the process for Gordon is the formation of primary group relations.* Once the minority group enters "into the social cliques, clubs, and institutions of the core society at the primary group level" marital assimilation will follow (Gordon 1964:80).

These ideas permit us to delineate more sharply the degrees and types of assimilation that have occurred or have not occurred between a given dominant group and any given subordinate group. If we compare the Native Americans and Dutch, for example, we may now say that although most of the Anglo Americans expected these ethnically distinctive peoples who lived among them to undertake cultural assimilation by substitution, this task posed greater problems for the Native Americans than for the Dutch. For one thing, the "distance" between the ideas, beliefs, manners, and physical appearance of the Native Americans and those of the Anglo Americans was far greater than that between the latter and the Dutch; so a greater change on the Native Americans' part was involved in their cultural assimilation (if they chose to undertake it). For another thing, and partly as a consequence of cultural differences and similarities, the dominant group was more willing to accept the members of some groups than of others; so the Dutch as a group were more acceptable from the beginning than the Native Americans.

These same considerations apply to the ease or difficulty with which secondary assimilation occurred among Native Americans. Any efforts they might have made to participate in the schools, jobs, or civic life of American communities may well have been met by rejection and hostility; and, in many cases, they were expected to remain on reservations or beyond the frontier of settlement. Even more emphatically, primary and marital assimilation were generally actively opposed. The White, Protestant, European, Dutch, on the other hand, faced no insuperable barriers to a steady movement through the remaining levels of assimilation. Even so, we must conclude—*in direct opposition to the three-generations idea*—that many of the Dutch did *not* move through all of the subprocesses within three generations and that many did not wish to do so. Even though the Anglo Americans and the Dutch were able to understand one another fairly easily and to establish many forms of cooperation, the Dutch language was maintained in some families far beyond three generations, as were preferences for Dutch friends and marriage partners.

We mentioned earlier that, in addition to various concepts and a theory of assimilation, Gordon also presented a description of three systems of belief (ideologies) concerning assimilation. *An understanding of these ideologies is crucial to our analysis of the processes through which groups come together, partially or completely, or remain apart.* Before considering these ideologies, it is important to note a problem that lies at the center of many debates but raises issues going far beyond the scope of this book. Our discussion necessarily involves considerations of both (1) the beliefs different people hold concerning how the ethnic groups of our society *ought* to relate to one another and (2) the beliefs that are presented in competing theories that are meant *to explain the actual relationships* that now exist, have existed, or may exist between the various groups. The problem is that, although it is easy to state the distinction between these two matters, it is by no means easy (some would say it is impossible) to maintain it in our thinking.

The assimilationist ideologies and **anti-assimilationist ideologies** we will discuss are intended to be statements of the first type, that is, sets of beliefs concerning what various people think *ought* to be; but these sets of beliefs also afford valuable frameworks for organizing the evidence that people use to help them decide whether interethnic relations are getting "better," "worse," or remaining the same and, beyond that, to reach decisions concerning the kinds of actions or social policies that might be of value in the effort to change the way ethnic groups relate to one another. Additionally, many of the concepts comprising these statements also appear as elements of the theories that are constructed to help us understand the realities of social life.

With these points in mind, we now turn to a consideration of the ideologies of assimilation outlined by Gordon.

Three Ideologies of Assimilation

The Anglo Conformity Ideology

We have said that, from the standpoint of the Anglo American ethnic group in colonial America, an "American" was someone who fitted exactly (or closely resembled) the pattern of life, standards of behavior, and racial type the Anglo Americans preferred. He or she spoke English, was Protestant, was of the so-called White physical type, had an English surname, and practiced the customs, behavior, and manners of the Anglo Americans. This definition of the term *American* fostered the idea that, to assimilate into Anglo American society, alien individuals and groups should accept the society and "merge" with it. This belief has been labeled the **Anglo conformity ideology** of assimilation.[9]

From this perspective also, the overwhelming majority of the members of colonial groups that were considered to be racially non-White, such as the Native Americans and Africans, *could never satisfy all of the requirements of complete assimilation even if they were disposed to try.* Although the dominant group exerted pressure on all subordinate groups to adopt Anglo conformity, only the members of White ethnic groups were considered eligible candidates for full inclusion into the society. The members of non-White groups who conformed to the expectations of the dominant group by adopting the Anglo American culture still were not permitted, as a rule, to move freely into the economic and political life of the Anglo Americans, let alone into their private social gatherings and families. Anglo conformity assimilation, therefore, always has been more difficult to complete for non-Whites than for Whites.

To summarize these points, we may say that complete Anglo conformity assimilation exists when:

1. A minority group's members exhibit a very high degree of cultural assimilation and, simultaneously, lose all or nearly all of their native culture. Cultural assimilation has occurred by the *substitution* of the majority group's culture for the native culture rather than by the *addition* of the former to the latter. Some vestiges of the native culture may be acceptable to the majority group and may even be regarded as "colorful" and "quaint." These cultural remnants include such things as special holiday celebrations; ethnic foods and recipes; and folk costumes, dances, and songs.
2. The minority's members exhibit a very high degree of secondary assimilation in education, occupations, places of residence, civic participation, and mass recreation (i.e., in the *public sphere* of secondary relations); and they participate little or not at all in such activities organized specifically for members of their own ethnic group (i.e., the *private sphere* of secondary relations). They have equal civil standing with the majority. Equality of opportunity is guaranteed. The law is "colorblind." It prohibits both discrimination against them and preferential treatment in their favor.

3. They exhibit a very high degree of primary assimilation. Friendship choices are made without reference to race or ethnicity.
4. They exhibit a very high degree of marital assimilation. Choices of mates are made without reference to race or ethnicity.

This **model of assimilation** is depicted in Figure 2.1. It represents a mental image of the ideal solutions the members of any group may prefer to the problems of inter-group relations. The **Anglo conformity model** depicts a set of ideal goals or *standards* toward which an out-group's members may elect or be expected to move. Those who accept this model measure any given group's "progress" in American society by compar-ing the group's actual location in regard to each subprocess of assimilation to the ideals set forth in the model.

The argument presented so far is that the English colonial efforts during the sev-enteenth century created an Anglicized version of *the very meaning of the word "Ameri-can"* and that Anglo conformity was established tentatively as the accepted way to

Subprocesses of Assimilation	Level of Minority's Participation in Majority Group High ———— Low		Level of Minority's Participation within Own Group High ———— Low
1. Cultural assimilation:	X ———————— (very high acceptance of the majority's culture)	AND	———————— X (very low acceptance of own group's culture)
2. Secondary assimilation:	X ———————— (very high "integration" in education, occupations, residence, civic matters, and mass recreation with majority)	AND	———————— X (very low "integration" in religious, health and welfare, and "social" recreational activities within own group)
3. Primary assimilation:	X ———————— (very high acceptance of majority-group friends)	AND	———————— X (very low acceptance of own-group friends)
4. Marital assimilation:	X ———————— (very high acceptance of majority-group mates)	AND	———————— X (very low acceptance of own-group mates)

FIGURE 2.1   A Model of Assimilation: Anglo Conformity
(X indicates a person's preferences, or goals, concerning the assimilation of minority groups)

achieve full inclusion. Those who championed this view looked down on the members of any group that departed very much from the Anglo American ideal or who appeared not to wish to become Americans. If a person believed that Anglo American norms or standards of behavior were normal and desirable, then he or she would probably also believe that the norms of others were abnormal and undesirable; thus, using Anglo conformity as the ideal, groups could be graded as more or less desirable according to how closely they resembled the Anglo American pattern at the outset, how rapidly they departed from their own cultural and social patterns, and how "successfully" they came to resemble the Anglo Americans. From this viewpoint, American nationality did not arise as "a blending of all the people" in the colonies; an "'American' was a modified Englishman" (Schwarz 1995:62).

This view of Americanization was not accepted by all members of the dominant group, of course; but by the end of the first century of English colonization, it had become paramount. Its continued force into the second century of colonization depended on the continuing dominance of the Anglo American group itself. And that dominance was threatened in some ways we will discuss in Chapter 3. We turn first to two major assimilationist alternatives to the ideology of Anglo conformity. The first of these to develop in American society was the ideology of the melting pot.

The Melting Pot Ideology

In 1783, J. Hector St. John Crevecoeur ([1782]1976:25–26) asked, "What, then, is the American, this new man?" and then proposed the following answer: "He is neither a European nor the descendant of a European. . . . Here individuals of all nations are melted into a new race of men." The basic belief lying behind the **melting pot ideology** is that the culture and society of each ethnic group should be blended with the culture and society of the host group to produce a new and different culture and society. While racial and ethnic groups should move toward the culture and society of the host, giving up their distinctive characteristics along the way, the host culture and society themselves also should change.

As is true of Anglo conformity, the melting pot view embraces the idea that minority groups in America should become indistinguishable from the majority. It adds to Anglo conformity, however, the further idea that the host culture and society will also "melt" so that the new society will reflect the proportionate influences of the groups that have gone into its making. The melting pot ideology is thoroughly assimilationist but rejects the idea that the Anglo American core should remain as it was before assimilation occurred. This **melting pot model** of assimilation, depicted in Figure 2.2 on page 30, outlines the vision of complete assimilation proposed by advocates of the ideology of the melting pot. Although a complete merger of groups would occur here, as in the Anglo conformity ideology, the Anglo American core would also be substantially changed. Advocates of this ideology believe the new host society resulting from the blend of the previously separate groups would be most consistent with the fundamental ideals of the United States.

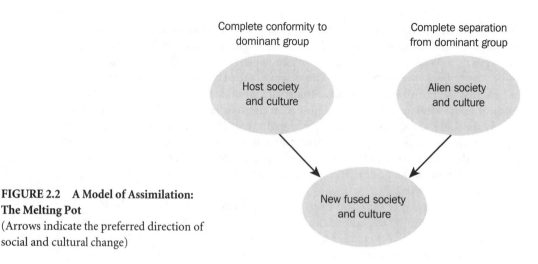

Complete conformity to dominant group

Complete separation from dominant group

Host society and culture

Alien society and culture

New fused society and culture

FIGURE 2.2   A Model of Assimilation: The Melting Pot
(Arrows indicate the preferred direction of social and cultural change)

The Ideology of Cultural Pluralism

Although the idea of cultural pluralism is quite old in American thought, its formulation as an explicit ideology is usually traced to the writings of Jewish philosopher Horace Kallen (Gordon 1964:141; Meister 1974:53–61). Beginning in 1915, Kallen attacked the idea that it was necessary for ethnic groups to give up their distinctive cultures or lose their distinctiveness in order to be *completely American.* Kallen argued in favor of an **ideology of cultural pluralism** based on the belief that the members of every American ethnic group should be free to participate in all of the society's major institutions (e.g., schools, jobs, politics), while simultaneously retaining or elaborating their own ethnic heritage.

In Kallen's view, neither the Anglo conformity nor the melting pot ideologies outlined acceptable goals for America. True Americanism, he thought, required us to protect and nurture the various distinctive cultures that exist within the United States. Unlike the other two assimilationist ideologies we have discussed, which assume (or hope) that intergroup relations will end in a merger in which the distinctive groups will become indistinguishable, cultural pluralism is based on the idea that the members of minority groups should be accepted as *completely Americanized and assimilated without being required to disappear as distinctive groups.* For our purposes, pluralism of this type exists when:

1. A minority group's members exhibit a very high degree of cultural assimilation but retain a large or an elaborated portion of their native heritage for use within the group. They are bilingual and bicultural. Cultural assimilation has occurred through the *addition* of the majority's culture to the minority's culture rather than by the *substitution* of the former for the latter. The differences of the majority and the minority are mutually accepted and respected.

2. The minority's members exhibit a very high degree of structural assimilation in education, occupations, places of residence, political participation, and mass recreation (i.e., desegregation in the *public sphere*); but they also remain very highly segregated in the religious, health care, welfare, and "social" recreational activities of their ethnic group (i.e., the "ethnic group" or *private sphere* of secondary relations). They have equal civil standing with the majority. Equality of opportunity is guaranteed. The law is "colorblind." It prohibits both discrimination against them and preferential treatment in their favor.

3. They exhibit a low level of primary assimilation. Friendship choices depend substantially on racial and ethnic identities.

4. They exhibit very low marital assimilation. Out-marriage is strongly discouraged. Mates are chosen almost exclusively from within the racial or ethnic group.

This version of pluralism, depicted in Figure 2.3, outlines the vision of complete assimilation proposed by advocates of the ideology of cultural pluralism.[10]

Subprocesses of Assimilation	Level of Minority's Participation in Majority Group High ———— Low		Level of Minority's Participation within Own Group High ———— Low
1. Cultural assimilation:	X ———————— (very high acceptance of the majority's culture)	AND	X ———————— (very high acceptance of own group's culture)
2. Secondary assimilation:	X ———————— (very high "integration" in education, occupations, residence, civic matters, and mass recreation with majority)	AND	X ———————— (very high "integration" in religious, health and welfare, and "social" recreational activities within own group)
3. Primary assimilation:	———————— X —— (low acceptance of majority-group friends)	AND	X ———————— (very high acceptance of own-group friends)
4. Marital assimilation:	———————————— X (very low acceptance of majority-group mates)	AND	X ———————— (very high acceptance of own-group mates)

FIGURE 2.3   A Model of Assimilation: Cultural Pluralism
(X indicates a person's preferences, or goals, concerning the assimilation of minority groups)

The goals of this version of pluralism (like those of Anglo conformity) include the acceptance of the Anglo American culture as the "standard" pattern of the country but present a *different* model of intergroup merger—one that rejects Anglo conformity and the melting pot but emphatically accepts the desirability of complete Americanization. It is vital to grasp the idea that, from this perspective, if a group were to achieve the goals outlined here, then it would have completed the requirements of assimilation. Its members would be viewed *as being as completely American as if they had lost their distinctiveness in accordance with the goals of Anglo conformity or the melting pot.* Advocates of this view wish to be an integral part of the society's cultural, educational, occupational, and political mainstream. We will refer to this model of assimilation as cultural pluralism or simply as pluralism.[11]

Those who favor pluralism, Anglo conformity, or the melting pot specify different degrees and methods of intergroup merger while envisioning high levels of similarity and cooperation in regard to the mainstream of the culture and society. Both pluralists and Anglo conformists expect high levels of assimilation along the cultural dimension (though differing on whether it is desirable for this to occur by addition or by substitution) and in the public sphere of secondary assimilation. The aim of the pluralist model is to show that individuals and groups may become "100 percent Americans" without following the paths of Anglo conformity or the melting pot. Pluralists believe that high levels of societal unity and harmony are consistent with the maintenance of ethnic diversity in the cultural, personal, and marital arenas.

The possible degrees of merger with, and separation from, the majority that a person prefers may actually range between a complete merger with the majority and a complete separation from it; and these possibilities exist at each of the four levels of assimilation. Pluralism, therefore, offers a broader range of possible models than either Anglo conformity or the melting pot. It also raises a major question: How much diversity is compatible with national unity? Many people who wish to live in a culturally diverse society may reject the model of cultural pluralism we have described as containing a dangerous degree of separation; hence, they may prefer a model in which the groups may be distinguishable but nevertheless be closer together in some respects than is shown in Figure 2.3. Please note that such a model of pluralism could be depicted using the framework of Figure 2.3 but, in this case, some of the X's shown in the figure would be placed at different points along the four assimilation dimensions.

Two Anti-Assimilationist Ideologies: Separatism and Secessionism

The pluralism shown in Figure 2.3 is also rejected by some pluralists who desire a still higher degree of separation. They may suggest that separate school systems, separate economies, and even separate states or autonomous regions within the United States should be established. They may also believe that whenever such separate institutions cannot be organized, the rights of the minority should be legally protected through the establishment of proportionate quotas in schools, jobs, and political offices. Pluralists of this type may object to the idea that only members of minority groups should be bilingual. Perhaps English should not be the general language in all parts of the country or within every institutional setting; and perhaps the members of the majority should also be expected to be bilingual. Equality of results, not of opportunity, is the goal.[12]

We will simplify the problem of discussing innumerable possible pluralisms by distinguishing only one other model of pluralism as a contrast to the one portrayed in Figure 2.3. Our second pluralist model—**the separatist model**—is generally anti-assimilationist in "tone" and intent. For our purposes, complete pluralism *of this second type* exists when:

1. A minority group's members exhibit a low degree of cultural assimilation and retain or construct a distinctive heritage for use in most of life's everyday activities. Only some members of the group will master the dominant culture and become bilingual and bicultural. Among these, cultural assimilation takes place by *addition* rather than by *substitution*. The differences of the majority and the minority are mutually accepted and respected.
2. The minority's members exhibit a low degree of secondary assimilation in both the *public* and *private* social spheres. Their education, occupations, places of residence, political participation, recreation, religious observances, and health and welfare activities are separated from those of the broader society insofar as that is possible within the framework of a single society. The minority's members are legally protected against coercive efforts to force them to assimilate in any respect. The law is not "colorblind." *Each group's share of public offices and benefits depends on the group's relative size.*
3. They exhibit very low primary assimilation. Out-group friendships are strongly discouraged.
4. They exhibit very low marital assimilation. Out-marriage is strongly discouraged. Mates are chosen almost exclusively from within the racial or ethnic group.

This second version of pluralism is depicted in Figure 2.4 on page 34.

This **pluralist model** advocates a high degree of separation in the cultural, public, and social lives of the dominant and subordinate groups; so we will refer to it as the **ideology of separatism** or simply as *separatism*. Please note, however, that separatism in this sense is still not based on a desire to bring about a complete separation. A separatist view that advocates a group's complete separation or withdrawal from the society is called an **ideology of secession**. Secession is well illustrated by the withdrawal of the southern states from the United States in 1861 and by the breakup of the Soviet Union in 1991.

We have attempted to show that the ideology of pluralism embraces varying degrees of merger and separation. The view shown in Figure 2.3 proposes one form of plu-

Subprocesses of Assimilation	Level of Minority's Participation in Majority Group		Level of Minority's Participation within Own Group
	High ———— Low		High ———— Low
1. Cultural assimilation:	————X—— (low acceptance of the majority's culture)	AND	X———————— (very high acceptance of own group's culture)
2. Secondary assimilation:	————X—— (low "integration" in education, occupations, residence, civic matters, and mass recreation with majority)	AND	X———————— (very high "integration" in religious, health and welfare, and "social" recreational activities within own group)
3. Primary assimilation:	——————X (very low acceptance of majority-group friends)	AND	X———————— (very high acceptance of own-group friends)
4. Marital assimilation:	——————X (very low acceptance of majority-group mates)	AND	X———————— (very high acceptance of own-group mates)

FIGURE 2.4   A Model of Separatism
(X indicates a person's preferences, or goals, concerning the assimilation of minority groups)

ralism that is decidedly assimilationist in "tone" and intent. Even though this cultural form of pluralism contains certain separatist elements, these are activated mainly in the sphere of private relations. Advocates of this kind of separateness emphasize that it does not detract from the unity of the nation but instead, by permitting different racial and ethnic groups to retain their distinctiveness without discrimination, creates especially loyal citizens. The form of pluralism depicted in Figure 2.4, however, is anti-assimilationist. Here the separatist elements are much more significant than in the cultural form and are definitely a challenge to the unity of the nation and the loyalty of its citizens. Indeed, this form of separatism may precede or lead to the secession of disaffected groups.

The three ideologies of assimilation and two ideologies of separation presented offer alternative sets of goals that individuals and groups may choose to pursue and to prescribe for others. Although they are not commonly referred to by the names we have given them, or in such detail, aspects of these models are often brought to public notice and enter public debate. For example, in speeches on national holidays or at patriotic celebrations speakers often say that "America is a melting pot"; or they may celebrate the fact that millions of immigrants have reached our society over the years and found the opportunities needed to enter the mainstream and live "the American dream." In his famous "I Have a Dream" speech, Dr. Martin Luther King, Jr., outlined his vision (or assimilation model) for future relations among the races.

Although assimilationist images are by far the most widely accepted in our society, separatist or secessionist views have always been present; and some of the advocates of these views are prominent in American history. Various representatives of the Native American peoples, Tecumseh for example, presented eloquent defenses of the desires of these groups to leave American society and to regain their former independence. As we shall see later, Marcus Garvey played a similar role among African Americans; and as a young man Malcolm X also argued for a type of separatism, although he later changed his position to a more moderate form of pluralism.

The Models of Assimilation as Descriptions

Recall that, in addition to affording statements of what one may believe *ought* to occur, the models we have presented may also be used as frameworks for *describing* the relations that have existed in the past or that currently exist between groups. When they are used in this way, the models suggest the following interesting and debatable question: To what extent do these competing views afford accurate descriptions of what *has actually occurred* in American society during the past two or three centuries? Since we will be reviewing various kinds of evidence bearing on this question throughout the remainder of this book, our comments at this point are only preliminary.

We have asserted that by the end of the colonial period, Anglo conformity was the most widely accepted ideology within the dominant Anglo American group; and our previous examples of the way English culture became Anglo American culture through innovation and the adoption of Native American, African, Dutch, and other cultural elements during the colonial period illustrated the operation of social processes that led to the fusing or "melting" of many cultural elements. Other examples showed that the fusing process has continued in American society since that time. But since a fusing of cultural elements is expected to occur in both the Anglo conformity model and in the melting pot model, these examples may be cited as evidence that we have been moving toward either of these two sets of goals.

Persuasive arguments have been presented on both sides. For example, Park's theory states that "eventually" subordinate groups take on the characteristics of the dominant group; and, although we did not label it as such at the time, this is the expected result based on Anglo conformity. But the melting pot has also had strong advocates. One of the most influential arguments supporting this interpretation of the American experience was the **frontier thesis** of historian Frederick Jackson Turner (1920). According to Turner, the western American frontier functioned as a great leveler of persons and a blender of cultures. On the frontier, people had to adapt to the harsh conditions confronting them by devising and sharing solutions to the problems presented. People borrowed freely from the various cultures there and, in the process, developed a new American culture that contained significant contributions from the various participating cultures and societies but was distinctly different from any of them.

The process of cultural accumulation that started on the Atlantic seacoast during the seventeenth century has continued as American society has grown and changed. For example, many types of previously "foreign" foods, beliefs, words, and phrases and various styles of dress, music, and dance have gradually become accepted as "American." In addition, when U.S. citizens are asked today to name their "nationality," an increasingly large proportion of them say "American." Consider also that the "English" culture on which the early Anglo American culture rested was itself the product of an extremely long period of cultural merging; hence, the Anglo American culture that developed during the colonial period consisted not only of English, Dutch, Native American, African, and many other elements then present in North America but also of the fused elements of thousands of other cultures that existed on the earth during a period of several millenia before Europeans were even aware of the Western Hemisphere's existence. The English language of today, for instance, reflects the fact that tens of thousands of words taken from the Celts, Romans, Danes, and Norman French, among others, were organized around an Anglo-Saxon core which, in turn, consisted of elements borrowed from many additional languages (Bryson 1990:46–47). In the long view of history, *all* modern cultures and societies are constructed from a vast accumulation of sociocultural elements from the past. As illustrated in a comment by Linton (1936:326–327), the "solid American citizen" may thank "a Hebrew deity in an Indo-European language that he is 100 percent American."

These examples introduce a point that we will stress in Chapter 16. It is vital that analyses of intergroup relations include clear statements concerning the *lengths of the periods of time* that are assumed to be needed for given sociocultural changes to take place. One may accept, for example, both that the English culture of 1600 consisted of fused elements from a large number of other cultures and that the processes of "melting" continued in America during the colonial period without necessarily accepting the idea that the melting pot model affords the best description of the actual effects of assimilation in America during the period since the country gained its independence.

Consider some points that have been raised in favor of the claim that contemporary American society is not mainly a product of a melting pot fusion of various societies and cultures during the past two or three centuries. Although we have noted that vast sociocultural changes have certainly taken place in American society since colonial times, this society has continued to consist of a variety of different racial and ethnic groups. Many minority groups either did not wish to "melt" into the "mainstream" of the society or were prevented from doing so. Many groups have remained distinctive even after they have adopted high levels of cultural assimilation; consequently, several scholars have argued that despite the profound changes that have occurred in and enriched American culture and society, the Anglo American foundation that initially defined the society's basic characteristics and structure (e.g., its language, laws, commercial organization, and basic values) has not thus far been altered markedly by the melting process.

From this perspective, changes in the defining features of Anglo American society have been comparatively small. The argument here is that although a high level of "melting" has taken place, the melting has been mainly in the direction of Anglo conformity. This view proposes that those who adopt the melting pot metaphor are, in fact, usually referring to the processes that lead to Anglo conformity. As expressed by Herberg (1960:21), "Our cultural assimilation has taken place not in a 'melting pot,' but rather in a **'transmuting pot'** in which all ingredients have been transformed and assimilated to an idealized 'Anglo-Saxon' model" (emphasis added). In a similar vein, Glazer and Moynihan (1964:v) observed in relation to New York that "The point about the melting pot . . . is that it did not happen"; and, in Hirschman's (1983:398) opinion, the melting pot metaphor has been significant mainly as "a political symbol used to strengthen and legitimize the ideology of America as a land of opportunity where race, religion, and national origin should not be barriers to social mobility."

At least three reservations are crucial in relation to these judgments. First, the Anglo American framework underlying American society has certainly not been static; second, if the processes of change continue for an indefinite period into the future, they "eventually" may well transform even the basic structure of the society; and third, the melting process may have produced a higher degree of mutual blending in some areas of the country than in others (Adams 1934). These valid considerations do not, however, afford a sufficient basis for stating conclusively that the fusion of the cultures of the natives, the later newcomers, and the indigenous population has significantly altered the foundations of the dominant culture thus far.

Whether a person favors either an Anglo conformity or a melting pot interpretation of the past, the coming chapters will make clear that sociocultural diversity has existed in America from the first; and, as is true for nearly all modern societies, it is still a multicultural society. Given these facts, the advocates of pluralism maintain that, despite the dominant group's continuous pressures on them, most subordinate-group Americans have given only lip service to the two ideologies favoring sociocultural fusion and that, in fact, pluralism has had many more adherents than is generally acknowledged. They argue that now the time has come for the American people to synchronize their ideology with social reality. Let us now, they say, recognize and promote our diversity instead of continuing to place pressure on the members of subordinate groups to move toward a single social pattern.

Critics of pluralism, of course, do not agree that pluralist ideology (as distinct from the fact of sociocultural diversity) has played a significant role in our history; but even if that were true, they would question the wisdom of endorsing pluralism as an accepted way to become an American; and they would raise questions that point to some important theoretical objections. For instance, will the acceptance of pluralism lead to a hardening of the group divisions that exist among us, promote intergroup hostility and conflict, and threaten the unity and stability of American society? Can the members of a subordinate group maintain their balance between the social forces pressuring them toward fusion on the one hand, and separation on the other? Won't they, perhaps over a period of several generations, be drawn inevitably toward one or the other of these competing poles?

These questions pose serious problems for pluralist theory. The existence of constantly opposing pressures favoring either total conformity to the dominant group at one extreme, or secession at the other, suggests that cultural pluralism is inherently unstable. No group, critics say, can stop just at the point of assimilation defined by cultural-pluralist philosophy. The group must continue beyond the exact degree of merger it prefers toward one or the other of the two opposing poles. Either the submersion of the minority within the dominant group or the separation (possibly accompanied by open warfare) of the groups is the inevitable result. Contemporary examples of the latter outcome include the ethnic conflicts between Azerbaijan and Armenia accompanying the dissolution of the Soviet Union and between Serbia, Croatia, and Bosnia-Herzegovina accompanying the dissolution of Yugoslavia.

The main reasons for supposing that pluralism will not necessarily collapse in one direction under the centripetal pressures to conform or in the opposite direction under the centrifugal forces of separation are derived from America's political experience as the world's oldest continuing democracy. The framers of the U.S. Constitution recognized that many different groups would struggle to gain control of the society; so they sought to write a legal document that would achieve a balance of social forces by providing ample checks against dangerous accumulations of power. To help reach this goal, they divided power among the three main branches of government, between the central government and the states, and between the large states and the small. The extent of the framers' success is a complex subject with a long history of debate behind it, and some skeptics doubt that American democracy could continue under an explicit policy of pluralism.

We have already seen that the Anglo Americans became the most powerful group in American society during the colonial period; but, as revealed in Chapters 3, 4, and 5, the fluctuating levels of immigration during the eighteenth, nineteenth, and twentieth centuries periodically raised the fears of natives that newcomers would gain control of the system and replace them as the dominant group. The struggle for political power in America has therefore taken place to some extent along ethnic lines; and, as a part of this struggle, the dominant group has frequently used ethnic discrimination to prevent "domination by ethnic strangers" (Horowitz 1985:188). An important issue for a pluralist society therefore is that, since ethnic groups would continue to be distinctive and visible, the dominant group's fears of losing control would not subside and the society's equilibrium could not be maintained.

The pluralist position in political theory, however, is that the competing interests of groups embedded within an explicitly plural ethnic system may be stable indefinitely. This position is based on the idea that since many types of interest groups, including ethnic groups, seek out government officials and attempt to influence the officials' actions, the resulting decisions reflect the balancing of many points of view (e.g., Riesman, Denney, and Glazer 1950).[13] Ethnic diversity, not uniformity, is seen as the key to the maintenance of a vigorous democracy. As stated by Wirth (1945:355), pluralism's advocates believe it is "one of the necessary preconditions of a rich and dynamic civilization under conditions of freedom."

To summarize, each of the models presented in this chapter helps us to state clearly and to compare both the *goals* different individuals and groups in American society believe they and others *ought* to pursue (i.e., they may serve as models of particular ideologies) and the *actual location* of any given individual or group (on average) in regard to the five subprocesses of assimilation we have selected for our analysis (i.e., they may serve as descriptions). Stated differently, the models help us to specify both (1) what the members of any group, individually or collectively, *want* and (2) *how near to or far from those goals* any individual or group actually is. The three theories of assimilation we have presented—Park's race cycle theory, Gordon's theory of subprocesses, and Turner's frontier thesis—represent efforts to explain how assimilation occurs and to forecast the probable future of intergroup relations in America. The value of these theories depends on how closely their explanations correspond to social reality.

Two of the ideologies of assimilation—the melting pot ideology and the ideology of cultural pluralism—emerged in reaction to the dominant group's demand that ethnic groups rapidly fuse with the existing society. Both of these alternatives to Anglo conformity have emphasized the advantages of accepting diverse elements into the mainstream of American life. In its cultural form, pluralism holds that minority groups may retain or construct distinctive heritages and, at the same time, live in harmony and equality with the dominant society. In its separatist form, pluralism is less confident about the goodwill of the majority and focuses on what it believes to be basic flaws in the society. It sees majority and minority groups more as adversaries than as cooperating partners in a joint venture. Separatists do not accept the basic values of the dominant group, and they consider the levels of distinctiveness permitted under cultural pluralism to be unsatisfactory. True democracy, from the separatist perspective, cannot occur when the majority has the power to control the destiny of a minority's members. A minority's ability to protect its rights depends, according to this line of reasoning, on a high degree of independence in the economic, political, and educational areas, and in more personal matters. Separatism shades into the more extreme position of secessionism, which represents the ultimate challenge to the goals of all three assimilationist ideologies.

The implications of the major ideas introduced so far must be examined in much greater detail in relation to the actual experiences of different groups within American society. We begin this effort in Chapter 3 by expanding our discussion of the way the Anglo Americans consolidated their power on the Atlantic Coast of North America.

Key Ideas

1. Several scholars have maintained that when racial or ethnic groups come into contact, a specific sequence of events is set into motion. Robert E. Park's theory, the cycle of race relations, for example, held that racial and ethnic contact led to competition, accommodation, and eventual assimilation. Park's theory assumed that these processes always occurred in that order.

2. The subject of assimilation is complex. It is important to think separately about *the facts* of assimilation and *the goals* that may be pursued. In regard to facts, it is helpful to focus on a set of specfic subprocesses of assimilation rather than on a single general process. In regard to goals, it is helpful to identify competing ideologies.

3. Milton M. Gordon has identified seven subprocesses of assimilation. Our analysis relies on three of these subprocesses: cultural assimilation, structural assimilation, and marital assimilation. We divide cultural assimilation into two subprocesses: cultural assimilation by substitution and cultural assimilation by addition. We also divide structural assimilation into two subprocesses: secondary structural assimilation and primary structural assimilation. Altogether, we distinguish five subprocesses of assimilation: (1) cultural assimilation by substitution, (2) cultural assimilation by addition, (3) secondary structural assimilation, (4) primary structural assimilation, and (5) marital assimilation.

4. According to Gordon's theory, each of the assimilation subprocesses may occur simultaneously and in varying degrees, and the rate of change in each one will correspond to its position in the list in Key Idea 3. In contrast to Robert E. Park's view, *a group may assimilate culturally without necessarily proceeding through the remaining stages.* As primary assimilation advances, however, Gordon's theory agrees with Park's that *assimilation in all respects becomes inevitable.*

5. Gordon also specified three main ideologies of assimilation that favor particular goals of assimilation. The models of assimilation based on these ideologies do not represent the actual levels of assimilation of any particular group or groups; *they represent, rather, the goals* toward which a group may elect or be expected to move. The models may also be used to help specify how near to or far from the goals an individual or group actually is.

6. Anglo Americans had become established as the dominant group along the Atlantic seaboard from Massachusetts to Virginia by the end of the seventeenth century. They had displaced the Native Americans and established their own ways of living as dominant. The more nearly a person approximated the Anglo American ethnic model, the more nearly "American" he or she was judged to be. This perspective on assimilation is called the Anglo conformity ideology.

7. The melting pot ideology and the ideology of cultural pluralism are prominent assimilationist views opposing the idea that Anglo conformity is the *only* way to become a "100 percent" American and also the idea that people of White Anglo-Saxon ancestry necessarily make the most desirable citizens.

8. The melting pot ideology, like the ideology of Anglo conformity, favors a complete merger of the majority and the minority. Unlike in Anglo conformity, in the melting pot model both the majority and the minority are expected to change, creating a new society and cultural identity.

9. The ideology of cultural pluralism opposes the complete merger of minorities with the majority. It seeks instead various degrees of merger and separation depending on the type of assimilation under consideration. Many pluralist models may be constructed. One example, which we refer to as cultural pluralism, stresses equality of opportunity for minority-group citizens plus the right to retain their cultural and social distinctiveness. In this form, the minority seeks to master the culture of the dominant group without losing its own culture. It also seeks secondary assimilation *in the public sphere.* This approach, therefore, is decidedly assimilationist with respect to the nation's central institutions even though separation in the private spheres of life is preserved.

10. Anti-assimilationist ideologies of pluralism advocate higher levels of separation among groups than does cultural pluralism. An example of this form of pluralism, which we refer to as separatism, seeks not only the preservation of a minority's culture but also a high degree of separation in many other ways as well. Advocates of this view may urge separate schools, economies, and governments. The resulting social arrangements would be pluralist but would involve a great deal more actual and legal separation than would cultural pluralism. Although the emphasis here is on separation rather than on merger, the minority would still be a part of the larger society. It would not attempt to secede or to overthrow the government by force.

11. The most extreme anti-assimilationist view is secessionism. Secessionists advocate a total separation of ethnic groups.

Key Terms

Anglo conformity   An ideology based on the belief that non-Anglo individuals and groups should accept Anglo American society and conform to its patterns of culture, social institutions, and social and private life.

Anglo conformity model   Outlines a vision of complete assimilation in which subordinate groups accept and conform to the Anglo American patterns of culture, social institutions, and social and private life.

anti-assimilationist ideology   A system of beliefs that opposes assimilation.

assimilation   The general process of inclusion through which newcomers are transformed from outsiders into full members of a group or society.

assimilation process   The specific, continuous changes that occur as newcomers are brought into the group.

conflict theories   Theories emphasizing that power and value differences exist between dominant and subordinate groups and that social conflicts are normal consequences of these differences.

consensus (order) theories   Theories emphasizing that the underlying order and unity of society rest on a consensus concerning basic values and norms of behavior among the different groups within it.

cultural assimilation by addition   The subprocess of inclusion through which the members of a subordinate group acquire the culture of the dominant group but retain or elaborate a significant portion of their own culture.

cultural assimilation by substitution   The subprocess of inclusion through which the members of a subordinate group gradually relinquish their own culture and acquire that of the dominant group.

cycle of race relations   Robert E. Park's theory stating that when groups come into contact with each other they set into motion an inevitable and irreversible chain of events leading to intergroup competition, accommodation, and the eventual assimilation of the smaller group into the larger.

frontier thesis   Frederick Jackson Turner's theory stating that the western American frontier functioned as a great leveler of persons and a blender of cultures to create a social melting pot.

ideology of assimilation   A system of beliefs concerning how society should bring minority groups within it into full participation in society.

ideology of cultural pluralism   An ideology based on the belief that the members of every American ethnic group should be free to participate in all of the society's major institutions (e.g., schools, jobs, politics) while simultaneously retaining or elaborating their own ethnic heritage and social institutions.

ideology of secession   A separatist view that advocates a group's complete separation or withdrawal from the society.

ideology of separatism   A system of beliefs based on the assumption that there should be a high degree of separation in the cultural, public, and social lives of dominant and subordinate groups.

marital assimilation   The subprocess of inclusion through which the dominant and subordinate groups gradually merge through intermarriage.

melting pot ideology   An ideology based on the belief that the culture and society of each subordinate group should be blended with the culture and society of the host group to produce a new and different culture and society.

melting pot model   Outlines the vision of complete assimilation shared by those who accept the ideology of the melting pot.

model of assimilation   A hypothetical conception of the way in which a smaller group that is outside a larger group becomes an integral part of, or is included within, the larger group.

pluralist model   Outlines the vision of complete assimilation proposed by advocates of the ideology of pluralism.

primary structural assimilation   The subprocess of inclusion through which dominant- and subordinate-group members engage in close, personal interactions with members of the other group.

primary relationships   Warm, close human relationships that are regulated mainly by sentiments of liking and affection and are characteristic of small, tightly knit groups such as the family.

secondary relationships   Human relationships that take place outside of small, tightly knit groups such as the family and are regulated mainly by conventional social roles and norms, administrative rules, and laws.

secondary structural assimilation   The subprocess of inclusion through which dominant-group and subordinate-group members engage in nondiscriminatory interactions within occupational, educational, civic, neighborhood, and public recreational settings.

separatist model   Outlines a pluralist vision of intergroup relations in which the cultures, institutions, and social lives of subordinate groups are highly separated from those of the dominant group.

subprocesses of assimilation   Specific types, levels (or components) of the general process of assimilation. The subprocesses identified by Milton M. Gordon are cultural assimilation, structural assimilation, marital assimilation, identificational assimilation, attitude-receptional assimilation, behavior-receptional assimilation, and civic assimilation.

theory of assimilation subprocesses   Gordon's theory of assimilation, which identifies seven subprocesses of assimilation, operating simultaneously and at varying rates of speed to bring about various types of intergroup mergers. The theory states that cultural assimilation may occur without necessarily leading to the remaining forms of assimilation; however, once primary assimilation occurs, the other forms inevitably follow.

theory of internal colonialism   Maintains that if a group enters a society involuntarily, power and value conflicts will characterize the relations between the dominating and dominated groups until social conflicts between the groups result in their eventual separation.

transmuting pot   The idea that the melting pot metaphor is often used to describe the social processes that lead, in fact, to Anglo conformity.

 # Notes

1. An accommodation exists when the "antagonism of the hostile elements is, for the time being, regulated, and conflict disappears as overt action, although it remains latent as a potential force" (Park and Burgess 1921:665). It may last for many generations or for only a short period.

2. For appraisals of Park's theory see Hirschman (1983:399–402) and McKee (1993:

134–137). See also criticisms advanced by Stanfield (1988).

3. Some additional theories discussed center on concepts such as ethnogenesis, ethnic enclaves, middleman minorities, social class conflict, dual labor markets, split labor markets, and intergroup competition.

4. Although it is useful for comparison to think of Anglo Americans as sharing a single

set of standards, there is a substantial diversity within this "host," "charter," or "core" group. Gordon (1974:74) employed one term, the *core subsociety,* to refer to middle-class Anglo American standards and another term, the *core group,* to refer to the standards of the entire Anglo American group.

5. Eighteen languages were spoken in New Amsterdam at the time it was annexed by the English (Hansen 1945:39).

6. Gordon's (1964:31–38) analysis clearly recognized the importance of the distinction between secondary and primary relationships, but he did not carry both terms over into the naming of the subprocesses of assimilation.

7. We consider in later chapters some problems in assessing various aspects of marital assimilation.

8. Gordon (1964:71) also distinguished four other subprocesses of assimilation that will not appear directly in our analysis. These are identificational assimilation (a sense of peoplehood based exclusively on the host society), attitude-receptional assimilation (the absence of prejudice), behavior-receptional assimilation (the absence of discrimination), and civic assimilation (the absence of value and power conflicts).

9. This term is generally accepted and will be used in this book. Gordon (1964:85) attributed it to Cole and Cole (1954).

10. For a related effort to describe an ideal or perfect cultural pluralism, see Murguía (1989:109-111).

11. Horton (1966:708) called this view *consensual pluralism.* Gordon (1964:88) suggested the term *liberal pluralism.*

12. Scholars who focus on interethnic relations in developing countries generally refer to this form of pluralism as cultural pluralism (Horowitz 1985:135–139).

13. Mills (1956) maintained that a relatively small number of people actually make the decisions that appear to be made through democratic procedures.

The Rise of Anglo American Society

The Anglo American group became dominant in the seventeenth century and established its standards as paramount. This group's legacy in the United States has been the dominance of the English language and customs and English ideas of commerce, law, government, and religion.

You will do well to inoculate the Indians by means of blankets,
as well as to try every other method that can serve to
extirpate this execrable race.

—Sir Jeffrey Amherst

. . . all children born of any negro or other slave, shall be slaves as
their fathers were for the term of their lives.

—Maryland Law of 1664

The process through which many immigrants and their descendants appear to have passed to become full members of American society was described briefly in Chapter 1. For those considered to be members of the "White race" this process appears frequently to have required a period of about three generations. In Chapter 2 we sketched some of the events that, by 1700, enabled the English to gain control over a strip of land along the Atlantic seacoast of North America and to generate and adopt the Anglo conformity ideology of assimilation. We also reviewed two additional ideologies of assimilation—the melting pot and cultural pluralism—and an anti-assimilationist ideology—separatism.

This chapter has two main purposes. First, we discuss further how the Anglo American group came into existence in the seventeenth century and established its standards as paramount. Second, we describe certain crucial variations in the operation of the processes of intergroup adjustment during the colonial period. Some groups (for example, the Dutch, the Scotch-Irish, and the Germans) were propelled more or less strongly toward a merger with the Anglo American group; but two other prominent groups, the Native Americans[1] and Africans as noted in Chapter 2, generally were held at or desired to remain at a distance. The varying degrees and qualities of assimilation and separation experienced by different groups during these formative years left a lasting imprint on the social order of the Anglo Americans. This imprint continues even now to affect intergroup relations in the United States.

 The English Legacy

Hardly more than a century after their successful beginnings at Jamestown, Virginia (1607), and Plymouth, Massachusetts (1620), the thirteen American colonies of the English were well established. By that time, the English language, English customs, and

English ideas of commerce, law, government, and religion were predominant through-out the region. The conditions in the New World promoted, and sometimes required, new ways of doing things; so the various elements of English culture and society had been modified in myriad and complex ways to produce the complicated mixture of peoples and cultures of the new "American" society and culture. A consideration of some early developments within this new society—English in broad outline but with many non-English elements—is crucial to an understanding of racial and ethnic relations in America today. To illustrate, we first review how certain legal and political traditions were transplanted from Europe to America.

Both Jamestown and Plymouth were founded by commercial companies that hoped to establish profitable businesses in America. These companies, operating under a charter granted by King James I, worked with varying degrees of success to colonize the territories granted to them. The London Company landed 104 men and boys in 1607 to construct a trading post that was named Jamestown. When the second boatload of settlers arrived early in the next year, the original group had been reduced by disease and conflicts with Indians to less than half their original number. The next several years were filled with misery and discouragement for these early settlers, and their suffering was made worse by the seeming pointlessness of their efforts (Burner, Fox-Genovese, and Bernhard 1991:34; Morison 1972:87–90). As employees of the company, most of these unfortunates had little stake in the enterprise. As would be true later for hundreds of thousands of others, they were expected to work as bonded servants for a specified number of years (usually seven) in order to pay for their passage and keep. Moreover, little was produced in the colony during the early years that could be sent to England for sale; consequently, the investors in the London Company were not making the profits they had hoped for; and, unless changes were made, the entire enterprise was in danger of failing.

Three important changes were made in the organization of the Jamestown colony. First, the king for a time discontinued his direct control of the colony. Second, the company (now the Virginia Company) began to grant settlers land and stock in the company so that they, too, would have a stake in its success. Third, in 1619, the company permitted a representative assembly to be established. This assembly, which has been widely hailed as the beginning of representative democracy in America, could enact any law that was not contrary to the laws of England. The king retained veto power, but the Virginia settlers had a great deal of control over their own affairs.

Like most other Europeans, the investors in Jamestown thought it possible that gold and silver would be discovered by the expeditions they financed. They also hoped to establish a profitable trade in furs and other goods with the Indians and to use products from the forests to supply England's navy. No riches in precious metals were to be found in the Chesapeake Bay area, however, and factionalism threatened the very existence of the colony; but the discovery that Virginia was an excellent place to grow tobacco provided the economic foundation that was needed for the colony to survive. In Morison's (1972:90) words, "Virginia went tobacco-mad" and by 1618 "exported 50,000 pounds' weight of tobacco to England."

Many investors in the London and Virginia companies suffered financial losses; so, understandably, they may have considered their efforts in America to be a failure. Yet from the vantage point of the present, the events at Jamestown were of the greatest significance in establishing the social and cultural framework of the English colonies and of their descendant, the United States.

The second early success in the colonization of English America also occurred under the sponsorship of the Virginia Company: the founding of Plymouth by the Pilgrims. In this case though, as is well known, the 102 Pilgrims who agreed to cross the Atlantic on the *Mayflower* sought to separate themselves from the Church of England in order to practice their own version of the Protestant faith, as well as to find improved economic conditions. And so it is not surprising to learn that the variation of English life they founded emphasized not only English ideas and ways but also those of their particular Protestant religious group. This fact played an extremely important role in the subsequent English immigration to America and in shaping the value system that became predominant in colonial American society.

Another group of dissenters from the Church of England also gained a charter to establish a colony in New England; and in 1630 some 800 members of this group, who wished to practice a "purified" version of Protestantism, emigrated to Massachusetts Bay. There they established several colonies (including Boston) that were more religious than commercial in nature, which attracted many people to them for religious reasons. During the first ten years, between 15,000 and 20,000 more Puritans reached the Massachusetts Bay Colony (Burner, Fox-Genovese, and Bernhard 1991:37; Jordan and Litwack 1987:25). Possibly twice that number had arrived in other portions of the lands claimed by England, making this the first period of heavy immigration to America.

The comparatively large size of the English immigration at this time is significant. Consider, by contrast, what happened in New Netherland. The Dutch companies that founded New Netherland were attempting to colonize at roughly the same time as the English, but their efforts to increase the population were not as successful. At one point, the Dutch West India Company offered large grants of land along the Hudson River to members of the company who would finance the passage of fifty families. This inducement did not, however, lead to the volume of immigration that was taking place in the English colonies. When the English occupied this territory (1664), the population of the English colonies may have been six or seven times as large as that of New Netherland. The task of conquest, therefore, was greatly simplified, and New Netherland was captured without a struggle. English control of the coast now stretched without interruption from Massachusetts through Virginia. These considerations remind us again that as Anglo American society expanded, the *standards* of the new society were being established. The very meaning of the terms *American* and *foreigner* was coming into being, as was the idea that the metamorphosis of the latter into the former required conformity to the Anglo American pattern of living.

These newly established standards involved more than ethnicity, however. Europeans had been taught throughout the Christian era that all people are brothers, but they nevertheless considered some peoples to be inferior to others (Gossett 1963:8–11). To illustrate, each European national group exhibited **ethnocentrism**—the practically universal tendency to consider one's own society to be superior to all others (Sumner [1906]1960:27). Consequently, this attitude resulted in more favorable treatment for members of the in-group than members of the out-group. Despite their ethnocentrism, however, the European nationalities shared many **folkways,** customary practices that regulate every aspect of life, ranging from what kind of clothing is acceptable to how many spouses a person may have, and **mores,** which are folkways that concern society's welfare (Sumner [1906]1960:18). On the basis of their shared folkways and mores (centered on Christianity), the European groups distinguished themselves as "civilized" and the Indians as inferior "savages." Although some individual Europeans considered the Indians' ways of life to be pure and noble, the belief grew and spread during the seventeenth century that the cultural differences between Europeans and non-Europeans were so great that neither the Indians nor the Africans were suitable materials for complete assimilation into the developing society of the Whites.

The ethnocentrism of the English at the beginning of the colonization period may have included some hostility based on differences in skin color; however, as we shall soon see, Indian–White relations and Black–White relations in the English colonies appear not to have been shaped markedly by the **doctrine of White supremacy,** which was based on the belief that Whites were becoming dominant because they were biologically superior to other racial groups (Fredrickson 1971:242–252). This doctrine (to which we return in Chapter 5) has been elaborated mainly in the last two centuries and, thus, is a product of the modern era.

Indian–English Relations

To understand the past and present experience of the American Indians, we must begin with two central facts. First, the Indians discovered America. Archaeological evidence indicates that there were people in Alaska by 25,000 B.C.; they had reached South America by 15,000 B.C. (Spencer, Jennings, et al. 1977:6–12). Thus, when the ancestors of some Anglo Americans disembarked from the *Mayflower,* the ancestors of some American Indians were already there to meet them. From the time of the early contacts to the present, the Indians' lands gradually have been occupied by invaders.

The second fact to be noted concerns the diversity of societies and cultures among the Indian tribes. At the outset, at least two hundred different tribes or bands stretched across the continent (Spicer 1980a:58). These societies possessed cultures that varied in many significant ways. Consider, for example, the diversity of languages. At least two hundred separate languages (not counting dialects) were spoken among the Indians at the time of first contact.[2] Although the members of these societies could communicate with one another through interpreters and sign language, their languages sometimes differed from one another as much as English and Chinese. Even closely related languages might differ as much as French and Spanish (Spencer 1977a:37–39).

The Indian societies differed also in the way they made their living and the manner in which they were organized. Many of the tribes were hunting and gathering societies; others lived primarily from small-scale gardening; still others had developed more advanced agricultural methods. These societies ranged from very small, simply organized groups to comparatively large, highly organized groups. The diversity of Indian cultures and societies was so great, as we shall see, that they were seldom able to lay aside their differences in order to face the invaders in a unified way; hence, the interactions among the different groups resulted in a bewildering array of changing relationships.

The Iroquois Confederacy, for example, consisted of an alliance of five tribes: Cayugas, Mohawks, Oneidas, Onondagas, and Senecas. This organization probably was formed before the arrival of the Europeans as a defensive measure in a longstanding conflict between the Iroquois and the Algonkians. By the time the Europeans arrived, the Iroquois were among the most politically and militarily active people in the Northeast. They had achieved dominance over a large region and had established an active trading network throughout it (Nash 1974:13–25).

A different confederation of Indian tribes was present in the Chesapeake Bay area when the English founded Jamestown. This confederation, named "Powhatans" after their leading chief, already had had some unpleasant contacts with Europeans and was therefore somewhat suspicious of these newcomers. The Powhatans did not, however, attempt immediately to expel the English settlers, although they greatly outnumbered them. Since the Powhatans were engaged in warfare with other Indian tribes, they hoped to form an alliance with the English. Besides, the Indians had no way of knowing about the dangers of European diseases or the size of the immigration to come.[3] Had the Indians wished to end Jamestown, they could have done so easily. In fact, the colony would not have survived its first winter without the Powhatans' help.

During the early years, the Jamestown settlers did not have a fixed policy toward the Indians. The king had given the land to the Virginia Company, but he had left the problem of dealing with the Indians to the colonists. The colonists knew that the Indians might reject their efforts to make use of the land or take possession of it; consequently, it was not at all clear how this delicate matter was to be handled. The ethnocentrism of the English, of course, led them to hope that the Indians would recognize the "superiority" of English culture, welcome its "benefits," cede their lands, become converted to Christianity, and serve willingly as a labor force for the colonists. The Indians, however, soon made it plain that they saw their own culture as superior and were not going to volunteer to perform the hard labor that would be required to make Jamestown a self-sustaining enterprise. When the colonists attempted to force the Indians to work, conflict between the two groups erupted.

Despite a slow start, the population of Jamestown grew rapidly after tobacco production commenced. Beginning with the struggling survivors of the first three years (about 60 people), the population reached 1,200 in 1624 (Jordan and Litwack 1987:21). This rapid increase in population created a great demand for additional land for tobacco plantations, which in turn led to increased friction with the Indians. By 1622, the Powhatans realized they had made a serious mistake; so they launched a full-scale effort to drive the colonists out. They killed almost one-third of the invaders but did not succeed in ending the colony. They did succeed, however, in convincing this particular group of English people that there could be no lasting accommodation between the groups. The hope of Christianizing and "civilizing" the "savages" was abandoned as an official policy.[4] Beyond this point, the English generally sought to seize the Indians' lands and to subjugate or eliminate the Indians themselves.

The Indians responded in kind. In 1644, they tried again—though by now they were much weaker—to drive the English into the sea. Again, they inflicted heavy casualties on the Whites but could not end English colonization. At the conclusion of this conflict, the English signed a treaty with the Powhatans that, in effect, initiated the reservation system. The treaty, in Nash's (1974:65) words, "recognized that assimilation of the two peoples was unlikely and guaranteed to the indigenous people a sanctuary from white land hunger and aggression." In this way, the Whites set into motion a method of conquest that was used repeatedly for more than two centuries. As a rule, major conflicts were ended through the signing of treaties that assured the Indians certain "reserved" lands, which, after a while, would be infiltrated, seized, and occupied. Each time, new reservations would be created over which the Indians would be guaranteed permanent control. Soon, however, a new round of encroachments would begin.

The relationships between the Puritans and the Indians of several tribes in the Massachusetts Bay region were similar to those that developed in Virginia. The initial contacts, made with the Wampanoags, generally were friendly; and, as in Virginia, the assistance of the Indians proved to be essential to the survival of the colonists.[5] The Indians of Massachusetts also were eager to establish trade relations and military alliances with the colonists; and, in fact, an alliance between the Puritans and Massasoit, Chief of the Wampanoags, was kept in force for over forty years.

The alliance with Massasoit did not prevent the colonists from occupying Indian lands, however. At first this practice caused little difficulty because the Indian population in eastern Massachusetts already had been greatly reduced by epidemics introduced by European fishermen and explorers (Snipp 1989:20–21). But as the main Puritan immigration commenced in the 1630s, the desire for land mounted and so did friction between the groups.

To an even greater extent than in Virginia, the policy of the English toward the Indians in New England was ambivalent. The English definitely wished to occupy the Indians' land, which might have the effect of driving the Indians away, but they also were eager to force the Indians to discontinue their "heathenish" beliefs and rituals and adopt the "civilized" religion and culture of the English, which required that they remain close at hand.

The Puritans' ambivalence may be seen in the arguments that arose among them concerning their right to occupy the land. Roger Williams, for example, maintained that the king had no right to give away the Indians' land and that the colonists were occupying it illegally. Although the leaders of the Plymouth colony considered Williams to be a radical, his belief that the Indians' land should be purchased from them already had become the basis for the official American Indian policies of Spain and Holland. Most of the English, though, did not accept the idea that the Indians were the true owners of the land. Various legal doctrines were advanced to justify taking the land, the most important of which was the doctrine of *vacuum domicilium*.[6] According to this view, the land claimed by the American Indians was in reality "unoccupied." This curious contention rested on the conviction that, to be occupied, land had to be put to "civilized" uses. Civilized uses, in turn, were the very ones to which the Puritans wished to put the land. One passenger of the *Mayflower*, argued as follows: "Their land is spacious and void, and they are few, and do but run over the grass, as do also the foxes and wild beasts. They are not industrious . . . to use either the land or the commodities of it, but all spoils . . . for want of manuring, gathering, ordering, etc. . . . So it is lawful now to take a land which none useth" (Quint, Cantor, and Albertson 1978:11).[7]

In short, the "failure" of the indigenous population to use the land in ways that the settlers deemed appropriate was interpreted by many Puritans to mean that the land was "unoccupied" and could be used as they saw fit. As the settlers acquired additional land, either by seizure or through some form of purchase, they encountered the Indians of various tribes and attempted to bring them under English rule. As the frontier moved south and west, various small groups of Indians were left behind in "reserved" areas and "praying" villages. The English expected these Indians to adopt English culture in every particular way as rapidly as possible and, simultaneously, to discontinue all of their Indian ways of thinking and acting. This did not mean that the English were prepared to permit the Indians who succeeded in mastering English culture to occupy positions of leadership and wealth within Puritan society, to enter into their homes as equals, or to marry into their families. It meant that the Indians were to be tolerated within the physical limits of New England, provided they appeared to the eye to be "civilized."

The Indians, for their part, had shown strong resistance to becoming a part of Anglo American society. They wished to retain their own tribal identities, traditions, and institutions. From their viewpoint, they were the civilized hosts whereas the Whites were the barbaric invaders. Consequently, some Indian leaders, such as the Wampanoag Chief Metacom (whom the English called King Philip), mounted several unsuccessful attempts to unite the tribes in the region and to drive the English out.

By the last quarter of the seventeenth century, the Anglo American colonists of Virginia and New England had devised a two-pronged policy toward the Indians. The Indians were expected either to give up whatever lands the colonists wanted and to move peacefully beyond the frontier, or they were to remain within the confines of Anglo American settlement under watchful eyes. A refusal by the Indians to accept one of these alternatives could lead to their annihilation or forcible removal from the area. In this way, the Indians either were excluded physically from participation in Anglo American society or were permitted to cling to the lower rungs of the social ladder. Despite the numerous differences that existed among the various tribes, including such things as the extent to which they had allied themselves with the colonists, all of those in America at the time of the "discovery" soon were considered by the majority of the English to be essentially alike. The label "Indian" was applied to all of the indigenous people. Eventually, they came to be regarded as unassimilable and ineligible for full membership in the new host society being created. This view was not shared by all of the Anglo Americans, however. Even though the ideology of separatism was paramount for more than two centuries, some members of the dominant group continued to hope to "civilize" and assimilate the Indians; and during the latter third of the nineteenth century, the ideology of Anglo conformity regained supremacy in Indian affairs (see Chapter 12).

The situation of Indian–English contact, first in the Northeast and then later in other parts of North America, illustrates clearly the way interracial and interethnic contacts may lead to repeated and persistent conflicts as the participants struggle to gain control of land and other resources and to establish themselves as the dominant group. Indian–English contacts also represent our first illustration of a vital point to be developed in Chapters 8 through 13: *Minority groups that have a strong sense of group identity and are socially self-sufficient at the time they become subordinate are likely to resist assimilation strongly for long periods of time.* Minorities of this type are highly unlikely to pass, in only a few generations, through the process of assimilation described by Park's race-cycle theory or Gordon's assimilation theory. After three generations, most Indians exhibited low levels of cultural assimilation into Anglo American society; and they exhibited very low levels of secondary, primary, and marital assimilation.

Servants and Slaves

African or Black people were represented among the first groups to arrive among the Spanish explorers in the New World, but the initial instance of Black "immigration" to what is now the United States occurred in Virginia in 1619.[8] It is recorded that the Virginia settlers bought "twenty Negers," who arrived on a Dutch warship (Frazier 1957:3). Although not much is known about the treatment of these twenty people, one thing appears to be established: They "were not slaves in a legal sense" (Franklin and Moss 1988:53). They were purchased as indentured or bonded servants rather than as absolute slaves. As we have noted, many of the White people who were a part of the English colony in Virginia also had come there under a similar arrangement.

Englishmen who were impoverished or had been convicted of a crime sometimes were sold into bondage for a specified number of years. Even free men sometimes were willing to accept a period of servitude in return for their passage to the New World. This system was recognized in England as legal and profitable to all parties, and the servants under this arrangement were sometimes referred to as slaves (Handlin 1957:7–9). Through such contracts, England profited by reducing the number of people who were public charges; the purchaser of the servants profited by having cheap, "slave" labor available for a fixed period; and the servants profited by having the opportunity to escape their unpleasant circumstances at home and, perhaps, to get a new start in life. Even during the period of indenture, a slave had certain rights and was, therefore, legally protected from excessive harshness by the master. Initially, these protections apparently applied to the Black bonded servants as well as to the Whites. English law during this period provided that "a slave who had been baptized became infranchised" (Frazier 1957:23). Those who were so treated might then become free. Although it is probable that Black servants were not treated in exactly the same way as White servants, even in the early years, much evidence favors the view that the laws regulating the rights and obligations of servitude applied to the members of both races and all nations.[9]

The main issues that provoked racial distinctions in legislation were the question of the length of the term of service, the problem of the standing of Christianized slaves, and the legal position of the children of slaves. For at least twenty years after Black servants were introduced into Virginia, many employers had a definite preference for White laborers and were also unwilling to commit themselves for long periods to the support of servants. As time passed, however, the profitability of Black labor increased and so, understandably, did the masters' desire for it; hence, by the 1660s, both Maryland and Virginia had taken legal steps to make the attainment of freedom more difficult for Black slaves. For example, in 1664, Maryland's legislature passed an act that required all non-Christian slaves, especially "Negroes," to serve for life (Degler 1972:71). This particular law was later repealed to prevent unscrupulous masters from marrying their White female servants to Black male servants in order to force the women into longer periods of servitude and to gain possession of their children. In the meantime, however, the noose around the freedom of Black people was permanently tightened. Since the law of 1664 had left open the possibility that Christianized Blacks might someday become free, a new law was passed stating that baptism did not amount to manumission (i.e., being freed).

A similar process of legalizing lifetime slavery for Blacks, even those who were Christians, occurred in Virginia. In 1661, a law imposing penalties on runaway slaves distinguished clearly between Black and White runaways and implied that the period of indenture for at least some Blacks was forever (Franklin and Moss 1988:54). Another law passed in the same year made this racial distinction hereditary. The ability of any Black person to gain freedom in Virginia seems to have ended by 1682. In that year, a law was passed establishing Black slavery for life, whether an individual had been baptized or not. In hardly more than sixty years, then, the Africans who had entered the colonies of Maryland and Virginia descended from a legal position similar to that of the indentured servants from other nations to a status of lifelong bondage. But the gap in status was not yet absolute. The terms *servant* and *slave* were still sometimes used interchangeably.

The possibility remained that at least some White people also might be reduced to the type of slavery that had been forced on Blacks, which in return influenced the choices of Whites who might otherwise have chosen to come to Maryland and Virginia. White servants frequently wrote letters to their relatives and friends back home warning them not to come to these colonies and, in some cases, begging for help. One Richard Frethorne ([1623]1988:36), for example, wrote his parents that "there is nothing to be gotten here but sickness and death." He pleaded with them to redeem his debt. Travelers also told of the harshness of White servitude.[10] Such places as Pennsylvania and New York, therefore, frequently were more attractive to free-born immigrants who feared they might be bound over as servants if they went to Maryland or Virginia. In the latter colonies, the masters' desire to encourage the immigration of White settlers and an increasing preference for Black labor on the plantations led to a gradual strengthening of the position of the White slaves (Handlin 1957:15). The Blacks, who had come to the colonies involuntarily and who did not write horror stories to those back home, were unable to benefit from this small source of protection. Neither were they able, at this point, to become enfranchised through baptism and thus claim the protection of the laws of England. In this way, the condition of the White servants gradually improved whereas the condition of the Black slaves slowly became worse.

The spread of the plantation system of agriculture increased the width of the status gap between Black and White servants. Black laborers could not desert the plantation and disappear among the citizenry nearly so easily as could White laborers. Therefore, the masters' investment in Black laborers was protected. Furthermore, Black women and children could be used in the fields along with the men, thus decreasing the number of unproductive hands at the masters' disposal (Frazier 1957:29–30).

As the plantation economy developed throughout the South, it was obvious to the members of the planter class that the fewer rights laborers had and the harder they were required to work, the lower would be the cost of their labor and the larger would be the planters' profits. Thus, the planters encouraged measures that moved the Blacks further from the status of human beings and closer to the status of mere property. Under these conditions, the Blacks had descended, by the beginning of the eighteenth century, into a state of complete, legally defenseless bondage. The term *slave* became unambiguous. The conclusion now had been reached that to be a slave *meant* that a person was of African descent. An African heritage, and particularly black skin, had become its symbols. The equation of "Black" with "slave" became fixed, making it impossible even for "free" Blacks to enjoy their legal rights.

The relegation of the African slaves to the status of property also increased the masters' desire to own more of them; and the increasing size of the slave population brought with it some new problems for the Whites. The importation of slaves increased so rapidly that in some places the planters became alarmed by the possibility that the slaves would become too numerous to control. Georgia, for example, attempted at first to prevent the importation of Black slaves entirely so that rebellions would be less likely to occur and the colony would be easier to defend. In South Carolina, the number of Black slaves had become so large by 1700 that the planters were permitted to have no more than six adult Black males for each White servant (Frazier 1957:32). Nevertheless, the White–Black ratio throughout the southern colonies declined sharply. In 1670 it was higher than 14 to 1; but by 1730, it had declined to less than 3 to 1; and by 1750, it had reached 1.5 to 1.[11]

The concern of the dominant group was well placed. Despite the fact that the masters took extraordinary precautions to keep the slaves under their dominion, slave resistance was a problem from the first. This fact frequently has been obscured by the claim that as long as they were well fed and were not treated harshly, the Black slaves were usually happy, contented people—what Jacobs and Landau (1971:100) called the *Gone With the Wind* version of slavery. This view of Black people was used to justify slave-holding; but a closer inspection of the historical record contradicts the thesis that Black slaves were happy and did not resist their enslavement. At the time of their acquisition—usually by purchase from African slave traders who captured their victims in the valleys of the Gambia, Niger, and Congo rivers—many slaves resisted vigorously. Frequently, as they were being transported through the infamous "Middle Passage" to the New World, many incidents occurred aboard ship. There were instances in which the slaves overcame the crews and captured the ships on which they were imprisoned. These revolts were so common that "they were considered one of the principal hazards of the slave trade" (Frazier 1957:85). Moreover, when escape or attack seemed impossible, many slaves jumped overboard to their deaths.[12]

The resistance to slavery by no means ended after the slaves arrived in America. Throughout the nearly two-and-one-half centuries of American slavery, most of the main forms of overt and covert resistance known to mankind were employed. From the beginning, individual slaves revolted against the system by running away. Considering the difficulties of all other forms of resistance, this may have been the most effective way to strike back. But even running away presented great difficulties of survival for one person alone. Some slaves were convinced that such an effort was hopeless (Rawick 1996:61). In many cases, fugitive slaves banded together and established independent "maroon communities" in various inaccessible places. They also sometimes were able to find protection and long-term sanctuary within Indian societies. Probably the most famous instance of maroon communities being established in conjunction with Indian societies is that of the Black Seminoles.[13] Black slaves in South Carolina and Georgia learned that they could escape across the border into Florida and enjoy either full freedom under the Spanish or an extremely favorable form of vassalage with the Seminoles. Among the Seminoles, the fugitive slaves typically established separate communities, adopted many aspects of Indian culture and, in some cases, intermarried with the Indians (Mulroy 1993:6–21).

The likelihood of escape by running away was dramatically improved near the beginning of the nineteenth century. At this time, the existing arrangements for assisting fugitive slaves, primarily those in the northern states, were enlarged and made more efficient as the complicated network of people and facilities known as the **Underground Railroad** gradually took form. Several "tracks" to the North developed; however, during the decades immediately preceding the Civil War, the center of the Railroad's activities was Ohio. Hundreds of "stations" and "conductors" assisted the fugitives in their long journey to havens in the North and in Canada.

Also during the nineteenth century, individual forms of resistance to slavery were supplemented by organized resistance. As a preventive measure, the Whites often separated slaves of the same tribe. Most slaves were not permitted to speak their native tongues or to retain their African names; and they were permitted to travel only for short distances and under careful surveillance. White slave patrols were used extensively to police the activities of Blacks and to interfere with any disapproved organizational efforts. In most places, it was illegal for a slave to learn to read or write or for anyone to teach a slave these skills. News of slave unrest was suppressed to diminish the possibility that such news might generate or strengthen resistance in other places. In brief, the masters were at great pains to keep the slaves in a state of ignorance and to disrupt communications among them. Under such circumstances, planning and executing a revolt was no easy matter.

We return to the issue of slave resistance in Chapter 10. For the moment though, we emphasize that the relations of Blacks and Whites during the period discussed illustrates the process through which the White American majority came into being and placed non-White people into a subordinate position. By the beginning of the eighteenth century, the Blacks as a group were physically within the developing Anglo American society and played an absolutely vital economic role there; but they were not candidates for full membership in the society. They were not encouraged, in many cases not permitted, to undergo cultural assimilation; and after three generations they certainly exhibited low levels of secondary, primary, and marital assimilation. As was true for the Indians, the human interactions and acceptance that are necessary for the "eventual" assimilation of Park's race-cycle theory to take place did not exist. The statuses of Indian and Black groups had been degraded during the seventeenth century. Therefore no one knew where or when the descent would end. To the questions, "What is an American?" and "How does a person become an American?" a majority of the members of the dominant group had adopted one answer—Anglo conformity. They also had established policies that raised barriers in the paths of any Indians and Africans who might also wish to adopt that same answer.

The eighteenth century created some challenges to Anglo American dominance. The first test came from a very heavy immigration to America of the Irish, particularly the so-called Scotch-Irish of Ulster.[14] A second test came from a heavy immigration of Germans; and the revolutionary war of 1776 represented a third. Let us turn first to the immigration from Ireland.

The Colonial Irish

The Irish began to arrive in the English colonies almost at once. By 1610, according to Adamic (1944:315), hundreds of the Irish had reached Jamestown. Throughout the seventeenth century, many more fled from the troubled Emerald Isle to the Atlantic colonies.

The largest and most discussed prerevolutionary immigration from Ireland to colonial America, however, consisted mainly of people from Northern Ireland (Ulster). Many people living in Ulster at this time were descendants of immigrant Scots who had been brought to Northern Ireland by the English early in the seventeenth century to work the Plantation of Ulster.[15] In contrast to the other citizens of Ireland, who were predominantly Catholic, the Irish of Scots descent were mainly Presbyterians. Although the Presbyterianism of these people was involved in their departure from Ireland, economic reasons were probably much more important. Presbyterians, as well as Catholics, were the targets of new laws passed by the Protestant English rulers of Ireland. One law permitted absentee English landowners, who owned the lands on which most Irish lived and worked, to raise rents as high as they wished. As the landowners raised the rents, the Irish were reduced to a state of poverty. Greeley (1971:28) quoted Jonathan Swift as stating that "The rise of our rents is squeezed out of the very blood, and vitals, and clothes,

and dwellings of the tenants, who live worse than English beggars." Under these conditions, a large number of the Irish, particularly those of Scots descent, decided to go to
America, beginning markedly around 1717.

More pertinent to our present discussion than their reasons for leaving, however,
is the reception that awaited them in the colonies. At first, the Scotch-Irish headed
mainly for New England where, in general, they were met with reserve. Although these
people were from the British Isles, were mainly Protestants, and were needed to help settle the frontier, they definitely were not accepted wholeheartedly by the now-native
Americans. They clearly were regarded as "foreigners" who deviated in certain undesirable ways from the Anglo American ideal pattern of behavior. They were said to drink
too much, to fight too much, and to be generally ill-tempered, troublesome, and coarse
of speech. Ulstermen generally were regarded "as illiterate, slovenly, and filthy" (Burner,
Fox-Genovese, and Bernhard 1991:72). These presumed differences created friction between the Americans and the Scotch-Irish. In one case, for example, a Scotch-Irish Presbyterian meeting house was destroyed (Hansen 1945:49). In another instance, "a mob
arose to prevent the landing of the Irish" (Jones 1960:45). In 1718, the Scotch-Irish were
blamed for a shortage of food in Boston (Seller 1984:141); and a Boston newspaper
stated in 1725 that the difficulty created by the newcomers "gives us an ill opinion of
foreigners, especially those coming from Ireland" (Jones 1960:46).

Pennsylvania soon became the most frequent destination of the Scotch-Irish immigrants. Not only did the way they were treated in New England have something to do
with this, but also William Penn was actively advertising in Europe for settlers, especially
for the frontier areas. So the Ulster Irish were greeted in a much friendlier way in Pennsylvania. Even here though, as the number of Irish immigrants mounted, certain interethnic problems arose. For example, it was said that unless something was done, the
Scotch-Irish would "soon make themselves Proprietors of the Province" (Jones 1960:
46).

The newcomers apparently were not great respectors of property; they frequently
"squatted" on land without paying for it. There was also a strong mutual antagonism
between the German and Scotch-Irish settlers of Pennsylvania that led to numerous disturbances. Before long, the Pennsylvania authorities began to discourage the continuation of the Scotch-Irish immigration, so this particular immigrant stream began to
move heavily into the frontier regions of Virginia and the Carolinas (Jones 1980:
899–900) where they were in constant conflict with the Indians (Burner, Fox-Genovese,
and Bernhard 1991:72).

The case of the Scotch-Irish affords an early example of the mixed reactions exhibited by Americans toward most later arrivals. On the one hand, immigrants frequently have been actively recruited to meet labor shortages and populate frontier areas;
but, on the other hand, Americans have been afraid the newcomers would compete for
land and jobs and would not conform to Anglo American folkways and mores. Perhaps
they would, instead, establish an alternative pattern of life or, worse yet, establish themselves as a new dominant group. This ambivalence usually has been displayed in various
acts of violence and other forms of hostility against members of the minority ethnic

groups. Some of the difficulties encountered by the colonial Scotch-Irish require us to consider them the first large American immigrant minority group.[16]

The feelings of rejection and the acts of hostility were not one-sided, however. The Scotch-Irish came to America mainly in groups and tended to stick together after they arrived. They were quite conscious of themselves as a distinctive nationality group and did not mingle easily with the host Anglo Americans. Indeed, they "nurtured a profound hatred for the English" (Burner, Fox-Genovese, and Bernhard 1991:94); and, as mentioned previously, they surely did not get along well with the other noticeable immigrant minority group of the day—the Germans. They were "avid politicians" who "demanded a voice in the lawmaking process" but who "totally disregarded the law if it did not suit them" (Burner, Fox-Genovese, and Bernhard 1991:72).

Given this outline of the entry of the Scotch-Irish into American society, what may be said concerning the course of their inclusion into American life? As Park's formulation of the cycle of race relations would lead us to expect, the contacts between the Scotch-Irish and the other main groups in American society at that time—majority and minorities alike—produced a certain amount of competition and conflict. A gradual accommodation was achieved, however, aided by the migration of the Scotch-Irish to the frontier areas in large numbers. So far, so good. But how rapidly did the Scotch-Irish move toward the fourth stage of Park's race cycle, *eventual* assimilation? To expand our understanding here, we refer to the five subprocesses of assimilation derived from Gordon's theory that were presented in Chapter 2.

By the standards of Anglo conformity, the Scotch-Irish were good candidates for complete assimilation in three generations. They were White Protestants from the British Isles; and, although the research evidence on these matters is far from complete, most writers agree that those elements of culture (e.g., speech, dress, manners) that served readily to distinguish them from the Anglo Americans were fairly rapidly laid aside. This cultural transformation, however, does not mean that the second-generation Scotch-Irish (or even the third) became socially indistinguishable from the dominant group. Many, if not most, were likely to select working partners and friends who were Scotch-Irish, and they were likely to marry someone who was Scotch-Irish; hence, secondary, primary, and marital assimilation were still incomplete when cultural assimilation (primarily by substitution) was well advanced. Even though by the time of the Revolutionary War the descendants of the early Scotch-Irish immigrants were for most practical purposes a functioning part of the Anglo American host group, it still is not correct to state, as many writers have, that the Scotch-Irish were at this point assimilated into American society in the Anglo conformity style.[17]

We conclude, then, that the Scotch-Irish were not completely assimilated into the Anglo-American majority, even culturally, by the end of the eighteenth century; nevertheless, the various types of assimilation leading toward Anglo conformity were all underway.[18] The main results of these different processes was to help solidify the American majority as a White, Protestant group of British origin. Even though the Scotch-Irish had created certain difficulties for the dominant Anglo Americans, there was never any widespread doubt that the Scotch-Irish could and, given time, would conform to the

Anglo American pattern. Moreover, in the opinion of some scholars, even the increased immigration of Catholic Irish before the Revolution did not seriously slow the movement of the Irish into American life (Diner 1996:163). The case of the colonial Germans, however, presented a more serious problem to the majority.

The Colonial Germans

At approximately the same time that the Scotch-Irish settlers were coming to New England and Pennsylvania, a large number of Germans and German-Swiss were moving to America.[19] As was true for the Scotch-Irish, Pennsylvania proved to be the most popular destination, although some members of the German group went originally to New York, Virginia, the Carolinas, and Georgia. These people, generally referred to as the "Dutch" (from *Deutsch*) or the "Palatines," were quite noticeable to the Anglo Americans. Many of them were members of various Protestant religious sects (e.g., the Mennonites), who dressed distinctively, settled together in rural areas, and did their best to maintain the language and customs of the old country. Although the majority of those who came later were less militantly Protestant, they still usually clustered in farming regions and held themselves apart from all other groups.

The primary area of settlement lay to the west of Philadelphia. Here the Germans, or "Pennsylvania Dutch" as they still are called, established prosperous and well-managed farms. They quickly earned a reputation for thrift, diligence, and farming skill that has continued to the present. And their numbers grew rapidly. By 1766, Benjamin Franklin estimated that one-third of the colony's people were German (Wittke 1964: 71).[20]

This large immigration of people who spoke German, who differed clearly from the Anglo Americans in culture, and who tended to settle cohesively in isolated areas aroused a strong antipathy among many of the "old" Americans. Some of the complaints against the Germans were identical to some lodged against the Scotch-Irish. They were said to "squat" illegally on other people's land, and their manners and morals were frequently thought to be rude and unseemly. To a much greater extent than the Scotch-Irish, however, the Germans posed an apparent threat of disloyalty. It was feared that they might set up a separate German state or even, as Benjamin Franklin put it, "Germanize us instead of our Anglifying them, and will never adopt our Language or Customs" (Kamphoefner 1996:152). At one point, a law was passed requiring immigrant Germans to take an oath of allegiance and, during the French and Indian War, many among the Anglo American and Scotch-Irish groups suspected the Germans of sympathizing with the French.

An important result of these differences and suspicions was to intensify the Germans' determination to survive as a group and, thereby, to slow the rate at which they and their descendants adopted the traditions of the Anglo Americans. The German language, only slightly modified by contact with English, was transmitted quite faithfully from the first to the second generation and even from the second to the third. The Germans did not wish to attend English-speaking schools or to participate in the political affairs of the dominant group. The sect Germans, such as the Mennonites, refused to bear arms, to hold public office, and sometimes even to pay taxes.

Since German farmers tended to build stone and heavy wood houses and barns, to buy adjacent lands, and to establish orchards and raise large families, they did not move readily; hence, they were likely to remain in close contact with others of their nationality. They organized publishing houses, German-language newspapers, and fairs and other celebrations to bring their people together on a regular basis. Although the sect Germans were more cohesive than the church Germans (such as the Lutherans), by the end of the eighteenth century, a German's friends still were likely to be Germans; and intermarriage, though increasing, was still low. Consequently, the Germans, especially in Pennsylvania, maintained their sense of ethnic distinctiveness beyond the third generation.

It seems fair to say that in terms of each of the subprocesses we have identified, the assimilation of the Germans into the majority group was slower than that of the Scotch-Irish and was accompanied by greater friction and hostility. This resistance to assimilation meant that the Germans were viewed with greater suspicion by the Anglo Americans. Nevertheless—and this is an important qualification—the German presence in large numbers in American society *did* strengthen further the dominant position of the White Protestants. Suppose, for example, that the Germans had succeeded in "Germanizing" the Anglo Americans and the Scotch-Irish. The dominant group in American society still would have been White and Protestant. It also still would have been European in culture, even if not of British origin. This is another way of noting that there were important similarities as well as differences between the Anglo American and German groups, similarities that, through time, enabled the Anglo American majority to maintain its basic pattern of life as the "standard" pattern.

The Revolutionary Period

Some interesting evidence bearing on the group cohesiveness of the colonial Germans and the Anglo Americans as well as on the group cohesiveness of the Anglo American group itself is provided by the alignments that took place during the Revolutionary War. Although many claims have been made that particular ethnic groups were solidly behind Washington and the Congress, it appears that the lines of cleavage varied from colony to colony.

The Scotch-Irish of Pennsylvania, for instance, evidently were strongly behind the patriot cause, but in New England the Scotch-Irish served on both sides; and in the backcountry of the southern colonies, some were on the loyalist side and some fought at one time or another for both sides (Jones 1980:901–902). The Germans also present a mixed picture. In Pennsylvania, many of the Germans subordinated their dislike of the Scotch-Irish and joined with them against the local loyalists. In Georgia, on the other hand, most of the Germans supported the British. In all probability, the majority of the ordinary German settlers were largely indifferent to the Revolution.

The cleavages within the Anglo American group were regional to some extent, but there also were important social and economic lines of demarcation. The decisive point for the present discussion, however, is this: The majority of those who actively participated in the Revolution, who led the Revolution, and who held the reins of government when the Revolution ended were members of the Anglo American group. This group had become dominant during the seventeenth century and had successfully met the challenges posed by the Scotch-Irish and the Germans during the colonial period. Now a sizable portion of this group had gained full control of the political institutions of the country, thus strengthening still further their claim to represent the ideal pattern for all Americans to follow. More than ever before, to be accepted as fully American one had to conform to the Anglo American model of behavior and appearance.

The events of the first three decades of the existence of the United States worked generally in the direction of consolidating the acceptance of Anglo American ethnicity as the "standard" or "semi-official" ethnicity of America. One important factor in this trend was a greatly decreased flow of immigrants to the United States between 1793 and 1815. The Napoleonic Wars in Europe interfered markedly with the free flow of international traffic and were the primary cause of the decline in immigration. Since the existing ethnic groups were not being reinforced by sizable infusions from their homelands, the pressures on them to conform to the dominant Anglo American pattern were more effective than might otherwise have been the case.

Another important factor that reinforced the dominance of the Anglo Americans was that by 1790 four out of five Americans were immigrants from the British Isles or their descendants (Easterlin 1980:479). Moreover, and despite the fact that more immigrants had arrived during the eighteenth than in the seventeenth century, most of the American population by this time was native born (Easterlin 1980:477); hence, people who were "native Americans" were becoming an increasingly large proportion of the population.

A third significant factor aiding the consolidation was the success of the Anglo American leaders in strengthening the powers of the postrevolutionary central government. The colonial immigrants from the British Isles were accustomed to the existence of social class differences in wealth and prestige, and these differences were present from the earliest days of the colonization; but these immigrants also believed in democracy and became accustomed to having a share of the power that was vested mainly in a comparatively few wealthy people. Those in the "lower orders" respected wealth but they also respected education and favored as leaders men like Washington, Adams, Jefferson, Franklin, and Madison who were both wealthy and educated (Sydnor 1965:60); consequently, many of those who led the Revolution and the formation of the American government were men of property. These men also felt a strong central government was needed to protect their interests. In *The Federalist Papers,* Hamilton ([1787]1961:66) argued that unless the national government was strengthened, the states would soon become separate nations. Concerns of this sort led Congress to convene a meeting of leaders in 1787 to amend the Articles of Confederation. Early in the convention, however, the delegates decided to draft a new document—the Constitution.

Practically all of the delegates who came to the convention represented the dominant White Protestant Americans, in general, and were members of the wealthier portion of that group, in particular. They were an aristocracy of wealth, education, and social position. The Constitution that was finally approved by the states benefited many groups that were not specifically represented in the convention. Still, there were economic tensions between Americans who were property owners or merchants, on the one hand, and those who were poor and in debt, on the other; and these economic differences led to some lengthy, occasionally violent, conflicts (Rubenstein 1970).

But this is not the place to engage in the debate over the motives of the framers of the Constitution.[21] The point, rather, is that during the first five years of the postwar period, many internal divisions threatened the very existence of the United States and, simultaneously, the shaky dominance of the White Protestant Americans over a vast territory. The ratification of a new Constitution, written and supported by wealthy representatives of the White Protestant group, was an important step in the direction of consolidating in law the dominant position of this group.

Let us review the argument that has been presented. The effects of the events commencing with the original settlement of Jamestown and Plymouth by people of English ethnicity combined to establish an American nation that was primarily a "fragment" of English culture and society. Outstanding among these events were the conquest of New Netherland; the exclusion of the Indians and Africans from full participation in the developing society; the assimilation of various types and degrees of a large number of Scotch-Irish and German immigrants; the successful Revolutionary War against Britain; the successful beginning of Constitutional government; and the decreased flow of immigrants following the Revolution.

We emphasize again that although the social order that had been established by the end of the eighteenth century was decisively patterned after English society and culture, the pattern itself was not inflexible. The developing *American* society and culture not only affected the immigrants, Indians, and Africans who were in contact with it but was, in return, to some degree affected by them. The crucial argument being presented is that the transformations taking place within this dynamic setting were predominantly toward the fixed Anglo American sociocultural pattern. The upshot was that, by the end of the Napoleonic Wars in 1815, the Anglo conformity ideology was more firmly established as the normal and accepted view of assimilation than ever before. At this point, the White Protestant Anglo Americans were the unquestioned majority in American society. On the surface at least, it may have seemed only a matter of time until practically all of the Europeans and their descendants would be culturally assimilated by substitution and, perhaps, in every other way.[22]

The Indians and Blacks, of course, were still very visible, and there was no prospect that they would soon disappear. These groups simply lay beyond the practical scope and intentions of the Anglo Americans; they were not genuine candidates for Anglo conformity. The assumption of the dominant group was that America was to be "a White man's country." Fully assimilated Americans and potential Americans were *by definition* White and Protestant.

Much more difficult for the dominant group to accept was the continuing visibility of certain European groups, such as the sect Germans. As stated earlier, a number of the Mennonite groups lived largely apart from all others and clung jealously to their own traditions, language, and religious observances. One who believed in the goals of the Anglo conformity ideology could argue, of course, that it was wrong for these groups to resist assimilation. The resistors could argue, in turn, that it would be wrong not to maintain their own group life and culture. Here we see an example of the way some groups worked to find an alternative to Anglo conformity as the solution to the problem of intergroup adjustment in America. These groups were dissatisfied with the idea that they should "melt" into the Anglo American majority, but they were unable to present a different view that would be accepted by the dominant group. Their inability to *state* such a view, however, did not prevent them from attempting to *live* along different lines. *Pluralism and separatism, thus, were realities in America long before they were expressed systematically as ideologies.*

We have seen that the Anglo conformity ideology encountered, survived, and ultimately was strengthened by the challenges of eighteenth-century immigration and the American Revolution; however, the seeds of three rival ideologies—the melting pot, cultural pluralism, and separatism—already were present in American thought. The first two ideologies reached maturity during the first and second halves of the twentieth century, respectively; whereas the third has appealed more or less strongly to different groups at different times. In Chapter 4 we develop these thoughts further against the background of the additional challenges to Anglo conformity that were presented by the heavy immigrations of the nineteenth and twentieth centuries.

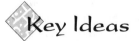

Key Ideas

1. The dominant group in American society was created as people of English ethnicity settled along the Atlantic seacoast and gradually extended their political, economic, and religious control over the territory. This group's structure, folkways, and mores may be traced to (a) the English system of law, (b) the organization of commerce during the sixteenth century, and (c) English Protestant religious ideas and practices, especially Puritanism.

2. By 1700, the Anglo Americans had replaced the American Indians as the "native" American group along the Atlantic seacoast. Those who came from the outside were likely to be regarded as "foreigners." The more nearly aliens resembled the Anglo Americans in appearance and in patterns of behavior, the more nearly "American" they were thought to be. The Indians and Blacks had been defined as

ineligible to participate fully in the developing society. Although Indians often could choose to remain physically within the boundaries of English colonial society, they usually chose not to. Blacks, on the other hand, were required to remain within those boundaries. In both cases, however, their physical inclusion was combined with social exclusion.

3. The Indian tribes were present for thousands of years before the arrival of the European explorers and colonists. This land belonged to them.

4. There were at least two hundred tribes in what is now the United States. The tribes spoke at least two hundred mutually unintelligible languages and exhibited varying levels of social, economic, and political organization. The tribe was the social unit to which the Indians gave their primary allegiance. Larger confederations of tribes were rare and only loosely organized.

5. Indian–English relations illustrate the point that minority groups that are cohesive and self-sufficient at the time they are brought into a society are likely to resist assimilation for a long time.

6. Africans in the English colonies did not at first occupy the status of chattel slaves. Their status was similar to that of the White bonded servants. In little more than half a century, however, their social position was that of mere property and slaves for life. African ancestry had become synonymous with the status of slave.

7. The argument that the slaves were generally happy and contented ignores many facts. They used every conceivable form of resistance to oppression. Given the oppressiveness of the slave system, however, most of the resistance was unorganized.

8. The position of the Anglo American majority and, consequently, the preeminence of its pattern of living were challenged during the eighteenth century by heavy immigrations from Northern Ireland (Ulster) and from the German states of central Europe. Even though these groups exhibited many of the cultural and social characteristics of the Anglo American majority, to some extent they both became the objects of hostility and discrimination. They were the first large immigrant minorities in American history.

9. The complete assimilation of the Scotch-Irish and German groups did not occur within three generations. Each subprocess of assimilation—cultural (by substitution or addition), secondary, primary, and marital—probably occurred more rapidly among the Scotch-Irish than among the Germans; however, the Scotch-Irish were still a fairly distinct group late into the nineteenth century, and some would argue that they have not completely lost their distinctiveness even today.

10. The experience of the Scotch-Irish and Germans illustrates the point that groups may reach a high level of cultural assimilation but remain incompletely assimilated in some other respects.

11. Although the Scotch-Irish and German groups posed challenges to the Anglo Americans and their version of the "semi-official" pattern of American life, the outcome served to strengthen the main features of the ideology of Anglo conformity. The experience seemed to prove that White Protestant Europeans could and would conform to the Anglo American pattern.

12. The results of the Revolutionary War and, later, the Constitutional Convention left the Anglo American majority in firm control of American society. This position was strengthened further by a decrease in European migration during the period between 1793 and 1815.

13. By 1815, the Anglo conformity ideology was practically unchallenged. To become "fully American," one had to be White and had to be, or become, Protestant. By this definition, non-White peoples such as Blacks and Indians were not, and could not become, full-fledged Americans.

Key Terms

doctrine of White supremacy   The belief that the growing dominance of the Whites throughout the world was a result of biologically inherited differences in ability among racial groups.

ethnocentrism   The tendency to consider one's own society to be superior to all others.

folkways   The customs or practices the members of a society have adopted as answers to life's problems.

mores   Those folkways that concern society's welfare.

Underground Railroad   An elaborate network of people who used their resources and homes to help Southern slaves flee to the North and freedom. Both White abolitionists and free Blacks helped in these efforts.

Notes

1. Some descendants of the indigenous population of the United States prefer to be identified by specific tribal names or the term *Native American.* Snipp (1989:5) stated that this term appears to be declining in popularity among Indians and that the term *American Indian* is preferable. We use *Indians, American Indians, Native Americans,* and various tribal names as identifiers.

2. Some writers say there was an even greater diversity of cultures and languages. Cook (1981:118) stated that there were approximately 400 different cultures and 500 languages. Jordan and Litwack (1987:2) stated there were "some twelve hundred different dialects and languages."

3. There is disagreement concerning the size of the American Indian population at this

time in various parts of the New World. Scholars have presented estimates of the total number of Indians north of Mexico ranging between 900,000 and 18 million (Snipp 1989:6). Snipp concluded that the Indian population of North America probably was no smaller than 2 million and no larger than 5 million (Snipp 1989:10, 63). Estimates for Mexico and the rest of the Western Hemisphere also vary widely. Embree (1970:18) estimated there were around 10 million in all; Wagley and Harris (1958:15) stated there may have been as many as 20 million; and Thornton (1996:44) estimated the total at around 75 million.

4. The Spanish, in contrast, maintained a major missionary effort for over three centuries.

5. Governor William Bradford claimed that Squanto (Tisquantum) had been sent by God to help the settlers (Jordan and Litwack 1987:25). Squanto had been kidnapped and taken to England by Captain George Waymouth in 1605 and had learned to speak English (Dennis 1977:4).

6. Two other popular legal theories were "the right of just war" and "the right of discovery" (Fredrickson 1971:35).

7. We thank W. Allen Martin for suggesting this quotation.

8. The term *African American* seems currently to be preferred by more Americans of African descent than any other. Many people, however, prefer the term *Black;* and we use the terms interchangeably.

9. Jordan (1972:86) stated "that there is simply not enough evidence" to settle the question.

10. Migration is strongly influenced by information that is distributed through social networks of relatives and friends (Bodnar 1985:57–84).

11. Calculated from Burner, Fox-Genovese, and Bernhard (1991:74).

12. Bennett (1964:41) reported that "So many dead people were thrown overboard on slavers that it was said that sharks would pick up a ship off the coast of Africa and follow it to America." Burner, Fox-Genovese, and Bernhard (1991:78) estimated that about 10 million slaves embarked on the Middle Passage and that about 2 million of these "died in transit."

13. This group is also known as Seminole Blacks, Indian Blacks, Seminole freedmen, and Afro-Seminoles (Mulroy 1993:1).

14. There is general agreement that around 250,000 Ulstermen of Scots descent and between 100,000 and 200,000 Germans came to America before the Revolution (Conzen 1980: 407; Dinnerstein and Reimers 1975:2; Greeley 1971:31; and Jones 1960:22, 29).

15. This group traditionally has been referred to as Scotch-Irish (or Scots-Irish). Although we treat them as Irish, many of its members may have been more Scot than Irish. Present-day demographers estimate that by 1790 more than 8 percent of the U.S. population was Scottish, while about 6 percent was from Ulster (Lieberson and Waters 1988:39). At the same time, nearly 4 percent of the Irish population of the United States was not from Ulster. This sizable population was predominantly Catholic, and some scholars say that by the time of the American Revolution, there were more Catholic Irish than Protestant Irish in America (Diner 1996:163). Some also argue that the emphasis on the Ulster Irish creates the impression that the Catholic Irish contributed little to the development of colonial America. No such implication is intended here.

16. In Leyburn's (1970:65–76) opinion, the Scotch-Irish were "full Americans almost from the moment they took up their farms in the backcountry."

17. Dinnerstein and Jaher (1970:4–5) stated that "Within three generations . . . (the) Scotch-Irish dropped their 'foreign' characteristics, assimilated to the dominant culture, and disappeared."

18. As recently as 1972, a number of seemingly assimilated groups (including the Irish Protestants) still differed from one another in regard to certain basic values (Taylor 1981).

19. The *Mayflower* of German immigration, the *Concord,* arrived in Philadelphia in 1683. The small group of immigrant families aboard was led by Franz Daniel Pastorius, an able and well-educated man who was the first to issue a public protest against slavery in America (Adamic 1944:168–169).

20. Franklin's estimate appears to have been accurate. Present-day demographers estimate that in 1790 the English comprised around 35 percent of Pennsylvania's population and that the Germans comprised around 33 percent. (Lieberson and Waters 1988:39).

21. For discussions see Lutz (1987) and Middlekauff (1987).

22. While we assume from this perspective that the majority pattern remained essentially unchanged, we also assume that, as the minority groups adopted the host culture, they made enormous contributions to the development of the society (Gordon 1964:73; Lipset 1979: 103).

The Golden Door

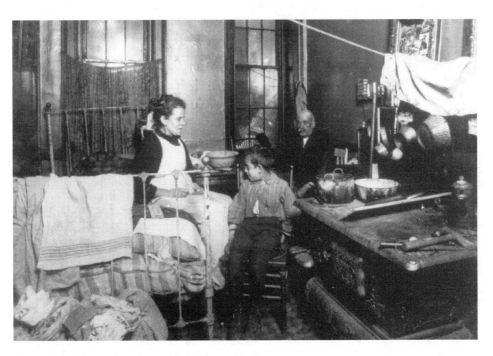

*As greater numbers of immigrants from diverse ethnic
and racial groups came to the United States, they
encountered increasingly difficult economic conditions
and heightened discrimination.*

. . . the Great Migration was not only one of people but of talents, skills, and cultural traditions.

—Max Lerner

A nation in a state of peace and safety, ought not to deny a hospitable reception to the fugitive from oppression or misfortune at home.

—William Rawle

People do not cross continents and oceans without considerable thought, nor do they uproot themselves from family, friends, and familiar terrain without significant strain.

—Leonard Dinnerstein and David M. Reimers

The greatest human migration in the history of the world has occurred since 1815. Uncounted millions of people have left their ancestral farms and villages to live in cities and cross the oceans. Although the specific reasons for migration varied substantially according to the time and place, the main factors contributing to this great movement of people were rapid changes in agriculture, population size, and industrial production. A significant effect of the workings of these three great factors was to reduce large numbers of farmers to a condition of poverty and thus, simultaneously, to "push" them off the land and "pull" them toward jobs in other places.[1]

Two results of the improvement of agricultural methods were especially important. First, the surplus of food made possible a rapid growth in population. In fact, during the seventeenth and eighteenth centuries, the population of Europe more than doubled. Second, the new methods made possible and profitable the farming of larger areas of land with fewer workers. These facts increased the efforts of the more powerful landowners to enlarge their lands. Consequently, many small private farms and much land held in common were gradually "enclosed" by the large landowners. With their farms gone, many people faced the choice of remaining as paupers where they were or moving in the hope of finding work and better living conditions elsewhere.

The choice was by no means easy. In many cases, people did not have the money required to make the journey and stay alive until work was found. Even if there were enough money to send one person ahead (usually a young male), the family members left behind frequently remained in desperate condition. To be sure, the increasing numbers of factories and the growth of cities created jobs for large numbers of the rural poor. But the growth of the population was so rapid that there were seldom enough jobs for those who wished to work. In addition, just as is true today, the number of jobs available fluctuated with the ups and downs of business activity.

The millions of people who were uprooted by these great changes from a preindustrial to an industrial form of social organization comprised the migrant "streams" or

TABLE 4.1   Immigration to the United States,
1820–2000*

Years	Number	Rate**
1820–1830	151,824	1.2
1831–1840	599,125	3.9
1841–1850	1,713,251	8.4
1851–1860	2,598,214	9.3
1861–1870	2,314,824	6.4
1871–1880	2,812,191	6.2
1881–1890	5,246,613	9.2
1891–1900	3,687,564	5.3
1901–1910	8,795,386	10.4
1911–1920	5,735,811	5.7
1921–1930	4,107,209	3.5
1931–1940	528,431	.4
1941–1950	1,035,039	.7
1951–1960	2,515,479	1.5
1961–1970	3,321,677	1.7
1971–1980	4,493,314	2.1
1981–1990	7,338,062	3.1
1991–2000*	9,789,853	3.5
Total	66,783,867	3.4

Sources: U.S. Immigration and Naturalization Service, *1994 Statistical Yearbook*, 1996:26–28; U.S. Bureau of the Census, *Statistical Abstract of the United States*, 1995:9.

*Projected.
**Per 1,000 U.S. population.

"waves" that flowed out of their native lands and into other countries. The United States has been, overall, the most popular destination. Between 1820 (when the U.S. government began keeping official records on immigration) and 1994, more than 61 million newcomers to this country were counted; and by the year 2000 the number was projected to exceed 66 million (Table 4.1). Many other countries—Russia, Canada, Argentina, Brazil, and Australia, to name only a few—also have received millions of immigrants. Whether people chose to go to one country or another depended to a large extent on such things as the likelihood that work would be found, the availability of transportation, and the presence of friends and relatives in the country of destination.

The waves of immigrants arriving at America's shores have tended to peak when economic conditions within the United States were good and to recede when there were economic downturns (Olzak 1986:25).[2] But, as has been suggested already, much more than the "pull" of the American economy was involved in the uprooting and movement of so many people. The convergence of many different forces has led to three fairly distinct and astonishingly large immigrant streams to the United States. During the period of the **first great immigrant stream** (1820–1889), people from countries located in western and northern Europe were predominant; during the period of the **second great immigrant stream** (1890–1924), people from southern and eastern Europe were predominant; and during the period of the **third great immigrant stream** or the **new immigration** (1946–present), people from Latin America and Asia have thus far been predominant. The decade from 1880 to 1889 combined high immigration from both of the first two great streams and was a period of transition from the first to the second. For reasons to be discussed later, immigration dropped dramatically after 1924, resumed after 1946, and assumed some new and distinctive traits after 1965.

The First Great Immigrant Stream

America was not really a very popular destination for emigrants during the decade of the 1820s. An economic panic destroyed many of the opportunities the emigrants were seeking, so immigration into the United States was comparatively low; however, the number of immigrants almost quadrupled within the next ten years. As the number of immigrants increased, the number of letters that were exchanged between Europe and America also increased. The newcomer's letters described their travels and new lives in America, leading to increases in the number of people who wished to come here and to increases in the number of agencies to help people arrange their travel and find employment. These changes helped make America more attractive to the millions of people who left Europe in the next two decades. During that period, more than 4 million people swelled the ranks of the first great stream. Although even larger numbers of people arrived in some later periods, the number arriving in the 1850s was the largest ever in comparison to the existing total population of the United States.

As was true of the colonial immigration, more people in the first stream came from Ireland, Germany, and the United Kingdom than from any other countries. With only one exception,[3] these three countries were among the top three until the last decade of the nineteenth century. The largest absolute number of first-stream immigrants arrived during the 1880s (see Figure 4.1).

The Nineteenth-Century Irish

As had been true earlier, the large immigration of the Irish preceded that of the Germans. For thirty years the Irish continued to arrive in larger numbers than the Germans, though the totals for both groups rose sharply. As this movement of people reached a

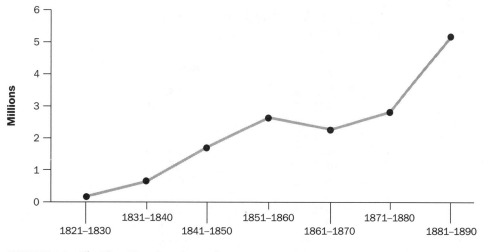

FIGURE 4.1   The First Great Immigrant Stream
Number of Immigrants by Decade, 1821–1890

Source: U.S. Immigration and Naturalization Service, *1994 Statistical Yearbook,* 1996:26.

peak during the 1850s, however, the German immigration became heavier than the Irish; and it remained so throughout the following decades of the nineteenth century. Table 4.2, on page 74, shows Irish immigration figures from 1820 to 1994.

To understand these large migrations, it is necessary to consider what was happening to many small farmers in Europe during this time. The basic problem consisted of a combination of a high population density, an unsound system of land tenure, and a high reliance on the potato.

The Potato Famine.   In 1815, Ireland was the most densely populated country in Europe (Jones 1976:69). The end of the Napoleonic Wars brought about a deflation of land values, a decline of foreign markets for wheat, and a decrease in the number of jobs available. The saving feature in the situation for the Irish was the potato. It was fairly easy to cultivate, and it took only an acre or so of land to support a family. As future events proved, however, this heavy reliance on the potato was ill-advised. The potato could not be preserved, it was hard to transport, and it was hard on the soil.

A foreshadowing of later events occurred in the early 1820s when the potato crop failed and famine followed. Although this famine was not nearly so severe as the one that led to the heaviest Irish immigration, many people left the country at this time. Despite this famine (and a relaxation by England of restrictions on immigration from Ireland), the vast majority of the Irish preferred to remain in Ireland. For the moment, there was enough food to go around. But a series of disagreements between landowners and tenants made it more difficult for people to lease land on which to support their

TABLE 4.2   Irish Immigration to the
United States, 1820–1994

Years	Number
1820–1830	54,338
1831–1840	207,381
1841–1850	780,719
1851–1860	914,119
1861–1870	435,778
1871–1880	436,871
1881–1890	655,482
1891–1900	388,416
1901–1910	339,065
1911–1920	146,181
1921–1930	211,234
1931–1940	10,973
1941–1950	19,789
1951–1960	48,362
1961–1970	32,966
1971–1980	11,490
1981–1990	31,969
1991–1994	46,564
Total	4,771,697

Source: U.S. Immigration and Naturalization
Service, *1994 Statistical Yearbook,* 1996:
26–28.

families, leading to an increase in the tempo of out-migration. During this period, a substantial proportion of the Irish immigrants to America still, as in colonial times, were Protestants; however, during the 1830s, an important change occurred in the character of the movement. By the latter part of that decade, most of the immigrants were Roman Catholics from the south and west of Ireland.

Two decisive blows came in the mid-1840s. A particularly virulent form of potato rot struck the Irish crop, destroying not only the potatoes in the ground but also many of those already stored. Between one-third and one-half of the Irish potato crop was destroyed by the disease. Then the potato gardens all over Ireland withered and died in the space of a few days. At this point, people finally realized that Ireland simply could not support so large a population. Therefore many people left in what soon became a general "flight from hunger."

As the famine spread, some people simply waited patiently in their cottages to die. Others took to the road, wandering from place to place begging for food. Those who could arrange passage to England or America did so. Within a year, at least a half million people had starved to death, while perhaps a million more had died of fever. Those who survived were in desperate condition (Jones 1960:109; 1976:67). During the next several years, the total number of Irish emigrants—the so-called famine Irish—reached unprecedented figures. By the mid-1850s, approximately 2 million people representing all social classes had left Ireland (Jones 1976:69). "The famine," wrote Diner (1996:164), "swept up Irish people, regardless of age, gender, or skill level." For a vast segment of the population, forced emigration became "the only alternative to death" (Greeley 1975:31).

Natives' Reactions.   Most of the Irish who arrived in America were poverty stricken. They had no money to proceed westward on their own, and they usually got out of the coastal cities only when they were needed in inland factories and mines and to help construct canals and railroads. Consequently, the conditions in the "little Dublins" and Irish "shanty towns" that sprang up along the East Coast were very poor (Wittke 1964:134). People were crowded together in tenements, and sometimes twenty or more families lived in a single house or apartment. The houses tended to be poorly lighted and ventilated; diseases such as cholera were rampant. Amidst all this, the "drink menace" increased in severity, the Irish reputation as ruffians and brawlers grew, and family ties were weakened. Although there was little serious crime among the Irish, they nevertheless were arrested frequently for minor offenses. These characteristics contributed to many native Americans' view of the Irish as an ignorant, practically barbaric, people. Cartoons often depicted them as apes "with a shillelagh in one hand and a pint of booze in the other" (Greeley 1975:6). All of these things contributed to the Americans' hostility toward the Irish and made their task of getting established in America still more difficult. Employers often preferred workers from other groups, resulting in many posted notices saying "No Irish Need Apply" (Jones 1976:78–79).

Aside from their high concentration in the eastern cities and towns and the behavior that the dominant group found to be offensive, two features of the social organization of the Irish worried the native Americans. The first of these was their conspicuous Roman Catholicism. During the eighteenth century, the Irish founded the first Catholic churches in the United States (Diner 1996:163); and the spread of Catholicism in the United States between 1825 and 1855 was due primarily to them. Subsequently, the Irish dominated the Catholic hierarchy in America. Wittke (1964:152) reported that "in 1836 the diocese of New York and half of New Jersey contained about 200,000 Catholics and of the 38 priests 35 were Irish and 3 were German." As Irish laborers were drawn from the East Coast to work on canals and railroads, new Roman Catholic parishes were created to serve them.

The Irish attracted the unfavorable notice of the native Americans in still another way. They were very active in politics. The Irish peasants had a history of conflict with their English overlords and were well acquainted with many of the techniques of organizing and carrying through political campaigns. The Irish, said Adamic (1944:344), "took to politics like ducks to water." In most cities, they were solidly behind the Democratic Party and tended to vote as a bloc on critical issues. In cities like New York and Boston, the "Irish vote" became increasingly important. As their numbers grew, the Irish became especially visible in various public service jobs and political offices. Angry natives frequently claimed that the Irish sold their votes to the Democratic city political machines in return for jobs and other favors. As we shall see, the fears of the natives led to various organized efforts to regulate and curb immigration.

The Irish reacted to the hostility of the Protestant Americans and to the problems of adapting to their new environment in much the same way as most immigrants before and after them. The ethnic communities they established arose in part because of, and were strengthened by, the rejection they faced in their interactions with members of the host society. Immigrants need, first of all, to solve the problem of making a living; to do that, they frequently rely on others of their nationality group for help. Moreover, the strange and hostile world of the natives typically stimulates the immigrants' desire to associate in a reassuring and friendly way with others of the same nationality—to eat together and engage in familiar recreational or religious activities. These forces encourage the members of a given nationality group to congregate to form benevolent societies, churches, patriotic organizations, newspapers, and social clubs. The ethnic group that is formed through this process, in the words of Francis (1976:169), is "exclusively the result of processes originating in the host society itself." The group is dependent on the host society for the satisfaction of almost all its basic needs and is under strong pressure to move toward a mastery of the host group's culture. Although the ethnic society that has been constructed within the host society is intrinsically valuable to its members, and although they make vigorous efforts to retain it, its major purpose is to establish a place for its members *within* the host society.

Women Immigrants.   The Irish who immigrated in the nineteenth century shared many experiences with their compatriots of the eighteenth century. For example, both groups responded in large numbers to economic pushes in their homeland and sought a better life in America; both groups joined with others of their nationality to construct ethnic communities; and both groups were subjected to hostility and rejection by Americans. They did differ, though, in the strength of the incentive for single men or women to leave the country. During the early decades, most immigrants were single, able-bodied males; but with the onset of the great famine, the number of women fleeing Ireland became roughly equal to the number of men. As the century advanced, the proportion of women became steadily larger (Diner 1996:163–167). By the first decade of the twentieth century, approximately 109 Irish women arrived for every 100 Irish men (Steinberg 1989:162).

This shift in the relative proportions of women immigrants was related to shifts in English colonial policy in Ireland. By the nineteenth century, control of most of the land had been placed into the hands of the English government and a few Protestant and absentee landowners. This policy greatly reduced the amount of farming land available to the Irish, especially the Catholics, and strengthened their tradition of permitting only eldest sons to inherit lands and leases. Subdividing land among all heirs was resisted because smaller plots simply could not support families. As a result, younger sons were left with few economic options. The main alternatives were to find work on someone else's farm or to migrate. Frequently men were forced to delay marriage or to remain unmarried. But the effect of these changes on women were even more profound. Faced with few opportunities to marry and even fewer employment opportunities than the men, "young women, even more often than men, decided to emigrate" (Steinberg 1989: 164).

Under these conditions, domestic service in America—an occupation shunned by the women of most ethnic groups—became an attractive option for Irish women. Employers of domestic servants preferred single women and women who could speak English. Large numbers of Irish women met both of these qualifications. For their part, the single Irish women wanted jobs that assured them of food, shelter, and protection in an alien environment. These factors combined to stimulate an active commerce on both sides of the Atlantic to bring employers of domestics and "Bridgets" together in America; consequently, Irish women were much more likely than the women of the other main groups to go into domestic "service" when they reached the United States. According to Steinberg (1989:163), among "immigrants arriving between 1899 and 1910, 40 percent of the Irish were classified as servants."

The nineteenth-century immigration of the Irish illustrates how the industrialization of western Europe led to a rapid growth of population, the consolidation of land holdings, widespread food shortages, and a massive flight from hunger. It shows, too, how the capitalist economies increasingly operated across national borders. To a larger extent than previously, the destinations and patterns of settlement of the Irish immigrants were affected by the efforts of growing American industries to meet their needs for labor. Most of the Irish men were manual laborers who were forced to take whatever work was available; large numbers of Irish women had little choice but to accept domestic service. The revolutionary effects of industrialization, only barely noticeable before the 1840s, became increasingly visible later in the century.

The Nineteenth-Century Germans

As was true for the Irish, the majority of German immigrants were small farmers who had been driven from their lands by widespread crop failures and financial difficulties. By the 1840s, the situation of many small farmers in Germany had become desperate. Weather conditions had been poor; the price of food was rising. Many small farmers were deeply in debt. According to Hansen (1945:225), "overpopulation, hunger and employment were the topics that dominated all discussions of social conditions."

The potato crop failed in Germany in the 1840s, just as it did in Ireland. Although the crop failure created a social crisis in Germany, the situation was not as bad as in Ireland because the Germans had not relied so heavily on a single crop. Nevertheless, many people were eager to leave before things became still worse. The fear that waiting longer might be a mistake was heightened by a widely circulated rumor that the United States was on the verge of prohibiting immigration. This rumor encouraged many people to leave immediately. Hence, even though hunger was involved, the "America fever" that developed in Germany at this time was not so directly a flight from famine as was the case in Ireland. During this period, the number of Germans emigrating to America jumped very sharply. Table 4.3 shows German immigration figures from 1820 to 1994.

TABLE 4.3 German Immigration
to the United States, 1820–1994

Years	Number
1820–1830	7,729
1831–1840	152,454
1841–1850	434,626
1851–1860	951,667
1861–1870	787,468
1871–1880	718,182
1881–1890	1,452,970
1891–1900	505,152
1901–1910	341,498
1911–1920	143,945
1921–1930	412,202
1931–1940	114,058
1941–1950	226,578
1951–1960	477,765
1961–1970	190,796
1971–1980	74,414
1981–1990	91,961
1991–1994	42,667
Total	7,126,132

Source: U.S. Immigration and Naturalization
Service, *1994 Statistical Yearbook,* 1996:
26–28.

As large numbers of people in Germany became interested in emigrating to the United States, several colonization societies were formed on both sides of the Atlantic. One of the most famous of these organizations made an effort to settle German immigrants near St. Louis in the 1830s (Jones 1976:125). In the 1840s, another organization sent thousands of German settlers to Texas with the "avowed object of peopling Texas with Germans" (Hansen 1945:231). And, in the 1850s, an effort was made to settle Germans in Wisconsin. Altogether, Germany contributed more immigrants to America during the nineteenth century than any other country. By the end of the century, Germans were "the single largest ethnic minority in 27 states" (Dinnerstein and Reimers 1975:25).

During this time, travel literature concerning America had become especially popular in Germany. In addition to guidebooks, periodicals, and pamphlets published and disseminated by travel agents, there were books written by those who had traveled in America or had already migrated. Most important of all were personal letters. When letters arrived, they frequently were read aloud in the midst of audiences. Their impact on the listeners ordinarily was great. The widespread interest in America within Germany and the increasing availability of travel literature led to the formation of village reading clubs. In this way, many people received information concerning the United States and became interested in moving there.

As in the eighteenth century, the Germans were comparatively unfamiliar with the language and institutions of the Anglo Americans; and their efforts to preserve their ethnic distinctiveness in America were very noticeable. Although the Germans were widely distributed throughout the United States, they built up large concentrations in cities like Chicago, Milwaukee, St. Louis, Cincinnati, and New York. For example, by the middle of the nineteenth century most of the large German population of New York lived in an area lying just north of the Irish district. Within this area, nearly all of the businesses were owned and operated by Germans, and German was the principal spoken language. There were in this district German schools, churches, restaurants, saloons, newspapers, and a lending library; and the Germans, no less than the Irish, formed numerous mutual-aid societies and benevolent associations to assist the immigrants to deal with the complexities of the strange new environment.

The German language became so prominent in many communities that the public schools either offered bilingual instruction in English and German or German was offered as an optional course of study, sometimes from the earliest grades. In some instances where the German population predominated, German was the language of instruction and English-speaking students—as a report from Missouri stated—either were "deprived of school privileges or else (were) taught in the German language" (Kloss 1977:89). During the 1840s, Cincinnati placed German and English on an equal footing as languages of instruction (Wittke 1964:229). The growth of German as a spoken language and as a language of instruction led to conflicts between German and English speakers. For instance, in 1875 the Germans of New York City staged "a great protest demonstration" following an announcement that German instruction in the schools was to be abolished (Kloss 1977:91). In subsequent years, some Germans fought for the continuance of German instruction in the schools and against the teaching of many other foreign languages. They maintained that German should have a favored status because it was an especially important language of science, literature, and international communication. At the same time, German theories of education also were playing a central role in the development of American public school systems.

Political Participation.   Another important feature of German immigration during the nineteenth century concerned politics. Germany at this time was still not a unified nation. The governments of the separate states were controlled by numerous princes. As the economic conditions of Germany worsened, there was an increasing desire, especially among intellectuals and young people, for large-scale reforms. The demands for solutions to the problems of hunger and unemployment and for a more democratic form of government led to revolutions in 1848 and 1849. These uprisings were crushed but clearly "highlighted the severity of social problems" (Weggert 1992: 228). The revolutionary leaders, many of whom were distinguished people of property, education, and high social standing, fled from the country and eventually made their way to the United States. These so-called **Forty-eighters** numbered only a few thousand and represented only a small proportion of the German immigration to the United States during this period, but they played an important role in determining the reaction of native Americans to the entire German immigration.

Many of the Forty-eighters were radical reformers who were disappointed to find that the United States was not a democratic utopia. They were shocked by slavery, corrupt political machines, the lack of civil rights for women, American Puritanism, and many other aspects of American life. In general, American life seemed to them to be "half-barbarian" (Wittke 1964:193). They openly criticized the shortcomings of American democracy, advocated the abolition of slavery and the U.S. Senate, as well as the office of President; and they hoped to transform the United States into a land of complete freedom of thought, rationality, and high culture (Jones 1960:155; Wittke 1967:8). They also founded athletic organizations (called **Turnvereine**) that became known as centers of radical reform and sponsored numerous newspapers to circulate their views.[4]

The Republican Party (formed in 1854) attracted many of the Forty-eighters. The Republicans' stand against slavery and in favor of foreign-born citizens were especially appealing to many German idealists. Germans, such as Carl Schurz, were so conspicuous during Lincoln's campaign for the presidency in 1860 that many observers have claimed his victory in the midwestern states was due to a bloc-vote by the Germans. Although this claim underestimates the deep divisions between and within the German American and German immigrant communities, it highlights the extent to which the Forty-eighters contributed to a sharp increase in German political participation in the United States and, perhaps, in the other main spheres of secondary assimilation as well (Conzen 1980:421; Jones 1960:162).

The radicals within the German immigrant group were sharply opposed by the large majority of German Americans who reached the United States before the 1840s. Many of the German Lutheran immigrants of the preceding century had moved very noticeably in the direction of Anglo conformity in their church services. The American Lutheran church had substituted English for German as the language of worship, and the traditional Lutheran beliefs and practices had been modified accordingly. The Missouri Synod, formed by the more recent Lutherans, emphasized the preservation of the German language and traditional beliefs and practices. These modifications led to acrimonious feuds between colonial and nineteenth-century German Lutherans.

Changing Patterns of Immigration

The Civil War created a comparative lull in immigration but certainly did not stop it. Over 2.3 million immigrants arrived during the 1860s, and still more arrived during the succeeding ten years (refer back to Table 4.1 and Figure 4.1). More significant than the sheer numbers, however, is that during the 1871–1880 period, a noticeable change began to occur in the national origins of the newcomers. Before the war, the largest numbers of immigrants were from Germany, Ireland, and the United Kingdom. During and after the war, these groups continued to grow rapidly and, in time, were augmented by large numbers of northwestern Europeans from Scandinavia. Immigration from Scandinavia during the decade preceding the war was about 21,000; but during the 1861–1870 decade, the number of newcomers from Norway and Sweden increased more than fivefold. In the years between 1871 and 1880, the number almost doubled again. However, the comparative increases among those arriving from southern and eastern Europe—particularly from Italy, Austria-Hungary, and Russia—were still more dramatic. By the 1890s, these countries were the leading countries of origin for immigrants to America.

As time passed, it became obvious that the federal government ultimately would be required to assume a major role in the control of immigration. The shift to federal control was launched in 1875 when the U.S. Supreme Court ruled that only the U.S. Congress was empowered by the Constitution to regulate immigration (Bernard 1980: 489). In contrast to an earlier ruling, the Court now said that all of the regulations that had been enacted over the years by the states and cities were unconstitutional. As if to stress the point, Congress passed the 1875 Immigration Act that sought to bar various types of "undesirable immigrants," such as those who engaged in "lewd" or "immoral" conduct (Abrams 1984:108; Cafferty, Chiswick, Greeley, and Sullivan 1984:43).

The 1880s were very significant both for the absolute number of immigrants arriving then and because that decade was the high point of the first immigrant stream. More immigrants came from Germany, the United Kingdom, and Scandinavia than ever before or since, and more came from Ireland than at any time since the peak in the 1850s. At the same time, however, the immigrant stream from southern and eastern Europe continued to increase rapidly.

As time passed, the receiving facilities in New York—located at the southern end of Manhattan Island in a former place of amusement called Castle Garden—became increasingly crowded. New York was by far the most popular landing site for European immigrants. During the years Castle Garden served as the city's port of entry (1855–1891), more than 7.5 million aliens were received there (Bolino 1985:3). At the end, however, the overcrowded conditions at Castle Garden and the misuse of the depot for political purposes led the federal government to take control of immigration and to open a new receiving station just offshore on Ellis Island. The new facility "was officially dedicated on New Year's Day, 1892" (Bolino 1985:4).

For more than thirty years, Ellis Island served as the "golden door" for approximately 16 million immigrants and became, along with the nearby Statue of Liberty, a symbol of hope, freedom, and opportunity. The island also developed a somewhat sinister reputation. Many people who attempted to enter the country there were detained and were subsequently deported. For the many who were denied entrance and were sent back to their homelands, Ellis Island became "The Isle of Tears" (Bolino 1985:44).[5] Kraut (1982:55) states that even those who were admitted after only a few hours on Ellis Island frequently considered the experience "the most traumatic part of their voyage to America." The immigrants feared being detained or separated from their families, and they feared the physical examination to discover contagious diseases. They also had difficulty communicating with the inspectors and, when the immigrants could not spell their names, they often entered the United States with new, "Ellis Island" names (Kraut 1982:54–57). It is estimated that more than one hundred million Americans today are descended from those whose first taste of their adopted land took place at Ellis Island (Horn 1988:63).

During this period, the number of immigrants arriving from each of the main countries of the first stream declined from their high levels during the 1880s; and, for the first time, more newcomers arrived from Italy, Austria-Hungary, and Russia than from Germany, Ireland, and the United Kingdom (see Figure 4.2). This second immigrant stream continued and increased during the first two decades of the twentieth century. So the first decade of the twentieth century proved to be the high point of immigration not only of the second stream but also of any decade thus far. Immigrants from Italy, Russia, and Austria-Hungary were the most numerous in all but the three years preceding 1924. By that year, three laws aimed at restricting immigration from southern and eastern Europe (discussed in Chapter 5) had taken effect; and as immigration from Europe ebbed, Canada and Mexico became the leading countries of origin for immigrants.

The Second Great Immigrant Stream

Soon after Ellis Island opened, officials began to comment on the change in the "types" of newcomers who were arriving. In addition to the Austrians, Hungarians, Italians, and Russian Jews, the second immigrant stream contained significant numbers of Bohemians, Bulgarians, Croatians, Greeks, Lithuanians, Moravians, Poles, Serbs, Slovaks, Slovenes, and others from southern and eastern Europe. These newcomers seemed even more foreign to Americans than the earlier foreigners from northern and western Europe. Many of the "old" first-stream foreigners, now in their second or third generation as Americans, had assimilated culturally by substitution, were well represented in the economic and political mainstream, and appeared to be moving toward complete Anglo conformity assimilation; consequently, there was no longer any real question of their "assimilability." But these "new" second-stream immigrants appeared to pose a more difficult problem.[6]

What was so unusual about the second-stream immigrants? Their languages, of course, were further removed from English than was true of most of the first-stream immigrants. Some of their religious practices, too, were quite different from the prevailing Protestant and Anglicized Catholic services. Their dress, manners, and foods also seemed especially alien. But, in addition to these cultural differences, many Americans soon came to believe that there was something "artificial" about the second immigrant stream. American employers were eager to tap the large pools of cheap European labor,

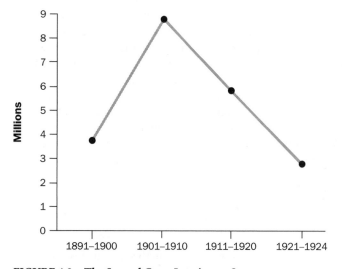

FIGURE 4.2   The Second Great Immigrant Stream
Number of Immigrants by Decade, 1891–1924

Source: U.S. Immigration and Naturalization Service, *1994 Statistical Yearbook,* 1996:27; U.S. Bureau of the Census, *Historical Statistics of the United States, Colonial Times to 1957,* 1960.

so they sent recruiting agents to whip up interest in American jobs. At the same time, rapid improvements in ocean travel greatly increased competition for passengers among steamship lines. Specialized agents also encouraged people throughout the southern and eastern European areas to emigrate.[7] The changes in the organization of the global economic system that we first noted in our discussion of the nineteenth-century Irish were now well underway. The second-stream immigrants were, like most of their predecessors, poverty-stricken peasants who were being forced off the land by industrialization; but these people, accustomed to life in small villages and farms, arrived in an America that was now well along the road of change from an agrarian to an industrial and urban nation.

The frontier had been declared officially "closed" after the census of 1890. There was no more free land for immigrants to clear and settle. As the demand for land increased, so did its price; and the immigrants increasingly could not escape the port cities in which they had landed. Given the location of Ellis Island, the city of New York, in particular, was flooded with immigrants. Even when they were able to leave port cities like New York, Boston, Baltimore, Philadelphia, or New Orleans, the immigrants usually wound up in inland cities like Cleveland, Chicago, Pittsburgh, or St. Louis (Novotny 1974:133).[8] The main jobs available were as unskilled laborers on the railroads or in factories; and by 1900, second-stream immigrant groups were the main source of workers for nearly all segments of industrial production (Kraut 1982:86). Since in nearly all cases the immigrants could afford only the least expensive housing, ethnic slums developed in all of America's major cities. Disease was rampant. Novotny (1974:138) reported that "nearly 40 percent of the slum dwellers suffered from tuberculosis." The promise of a new life in America thus became a shattered dream for large numbers of immigrants. Not surprisingly, many of these disappointed people returned to their homelands at the first opportunity.

We should note though that despite the hardships and disappointments, many of those who went back home—especially young, single, men—later returned to the United States. The emergence of a pattern of two-way or cyclical migration represents another important distinction between the first and second immigrant streams (Portes and Bach 1985:31).

The Italians

Probably the most prominent group of newcomers and urban dwellers at this time were the Italians. Several factors made this group particularly conspicuous. First, of course, were their sheer numbers and the rate at which they arrived (see Table 4.4). Well over 3 million Italians reached the United States during the thirty-year period beginning in 1890.[9] Second, a large majority of the Italians arriving at this time were from the southern regions. The people from these regions were overwhelmingly illiterate, landless peasants who were escaping from a harsh physical climate, overpopulation, economic dislocations, and an oppressive social class structure (Alba 1985:23–27, 38–40; Lopreato 1970:25–33).

Third, and somewhat surprising, these agricultural people did not move in large numbers directly into farming occupations when they reached America. To be sure, the changing American economy offered fewer encouragements than previously for those wishing to leave the cities; however, despite their lack of urban and industrial skills, the southern Italians generally preferred to remain in the cities (Alba 1985:47). But they were "too many and too late" (Schermerhorn 1949:232); so the men of this group frequently had to accept the pick-and-shovel jobs at the bottom of the occupational hierarchy that few others wanted. They also were drawn to occupations that required little in the way of initial capital. For instance, Italian men were nearly eight times as likely as other White workers to be "hucksters and peddlers" (Lieberson and Waters 1988:126). Nevertheless, despite these problems, possibly 40 percent of the men found work in skilled blue-collar and lower white-collar jobs (Alba 1996:173).

Comparatively few Italian women made the journey to America during this period. Among Italians arriving between 1899 and 1910, there were "only 27 women for every 100 men" (Steinberg 1989:162). In most cases, fathers, husbands, or other male family members left their families behind as they traveled to the new country; so most of the women who made the crossing were going to join other family members who already were established abroad. Under these circumstances, separated families were reunited, new families were formed readily, and Italian women were not pressured to enter the paid labor force; hence, unlike Irish women, only a small proportion of them

TABLE 4.4 Italian Immigration
to the United States, 1820–1994

Years	Number
1820–1830	439
1831–1840	2,253
1841–1850	1,870
1851–1860	9,231
1861–1870	11,725
1871–1880	55,759
1881–1890	307,309
1891–1900	651,893
1901–1910	2,045,877
1911–1920	1,109,524
1921–1930	455,315
1931–1940	68,028
1941–1950	57,661
1951–1960	185,491
1961–1970	214,111
1971–1980	129,368
1981–1990	67,254
1991–1994	48,841
Total	5,421,949

Source: U.S. Immigration and Naturalization
Service, *1994 Statistical Yearbook,* 1996:
26–28.

accepted paid employment. Those who did went mainly into the "needle trades."[10] Few were forced to accept domestic service (Steinberg 1989:165).

A fourth way in which the southern Italian immigrants stood out was that, to an unusual degree, this group contained a large proportion of males who did not intend to remain in America—so-called **sojourners** (or **birds of passage**). These immigrants, rather, wished to make their fortunes and return with honor to the homeland (Lopreato 1970:14–15; Piore 1979). Jones (1976:196) quoted a successful Italian American, Stefano Miele, as follows: "If I am to be frank, then I shall say that I left Italy and came to America for the sole purpose of making money." Lopreato (1970:110) observed that the Italians' "zeal for assimilation in American life left something to be desired." And Caroli (cited by Alba 1996:173) reported that approximately 1.5 million Italians returned to Italy between 1900 and 1914.

A final, though hardly unique, characteristic of the Italian immigration is that a large proportion of the group's members were obliged to occupy housing that was in many instances unfit for human habitation. The conditions in the Italian slums were frequently so terrible that they were widely publicized. Since many Americans did not understand the circumstances giving rise to the squalid conditions in the slums, the residents themselves, or their culture, often were blamed. As had been true of the Irish in an earlier period, it was assumed that the Italians were "just naturally" depraved.

Natives' Reactions.   Among the Americans' mental images of the Italians, one received special notoriety. The Italians acquired a reputation for criminality. Newspapers throughout the country described in lurid detail extortions and murders attributed to the "Mafia" (or "Cosa Nostra"). Many Americans feared that a notorious criminal organization had been imported by the southern Italians and now posed a serious foreign threat to democratic methods of assuring law and order. Although there is little doubt that Mafia-like organizations did develop among the Italians at this time, there is substantial disagreement concerning the reasons for it and the extent to which there was anything peculiarly Italian about it. Among the first-generation Italians, for example, crime rates were no higher than among other immigrant groups; and they were actually lower than those of native Americans (Schermerhorn 1949:250). A study in Massachusetts in 1912 showed that the Italian-born were greatly underrepresented in the prison population of the state (Jones 1976:213). In Alba's (1985:36) opinion, most accounts of organized crime among Italian Americans mistakenly dwell on events in Sicily and on southern Italian culture; and they falsely portray "organized crime as an alien and almost accidental growth in American soil . . . rather than as a native product that demanded the energies of numerous ethnic groups." He argued further that the criminal gangs that operated within Italian American communities probably were not organized at a higher level and "had essentially died out by 1920" (Alba 1985:62–63). The higher levels of organization did not occur until the 1930s, with Prohibition, and were not confined to people of Italian ancestry.

Peculiarly Italian or not, the idea that America's Little Italys were "seething hotbeds of crime" (Schermerhorn 1949:250) was commonly believed.[11] This belief helped to fuel a rising level of native hostility during this period. It also had another effect of considerable interest to us. It helped to awaken among the Italians a sense of ethnic identity.

Ethnic Identity.   As in the cases of the Indians and Blacks (and later the Asians), Americans tended to lump all people from Italy into the same category. But the immigrants themselves had a very different view of the matter, at least at first. The immigrants who left Italy came not as Italians but as representatives of particular villages, cities, or regions. The cleavages among the "Italians" themselves were very deep. Since Italy had only recently become united, the cultural and economic differences between the northerners and southerners were wide. The people in the north felt and acted superior to the people in the south. And even among the southerners, the social differences among the peoples from different villages and regions were pronounced. Consequently, as Lopreato (1970:104) stated, "When the Italians came to the United States they imported a pitiful tendency to mistrust and avoid all those who did not share their particular dialect and customs." This identification of the individual with groups smaller than the Italian nation was evident in the residential patterns in New York (Alba 1996:174).

Various Little Italys developed along separate streets or city blocks, each one exhibiting village, provincial, or regional loyalties (Wittke 1964:441). Neapolitans, for instance, gathered around Mulberry Bend; Sicilians clustered on Elizabeth and Prince Streets; and Calabrians lived on a portion of Mott Street (Alba 1985:48–49; Riis [1890]1957:41–52). As had been true for immigrant groups to America from the earliest days, this method of organizing enabled the immigrants to give and receive help from people like themselves and to bask in the warmth and security of their friendship. Here people could speak their native language, eat food prepared in the "proper" way, and escape the insults and inconveniences encountered in the "outside" world. The ethnic slum, for all its terrible faults, served in certain ways to shield and protect the immigrant. But, to repeat, the Americans did not usually recognize the distinctions that existed among the immigrants from Italy. Consequently, hostility and rejection were directed at the "Italians." They were called "wops," "dagos," "guineas," and "the Chinese of Europe" (Dinnerstein and Reimers 1975:40); hence, in Schermerhorn's (1949:250) words, "The Sicilians, the Neapolitans, and Calabrians thus became conscious of their common destiny as Italians in America." The hostility of the dominant group "Italianized them" (Lopreato 1970:171).

The process, illustrated by the Italians, by which people from the same geographic regions join together to form a new ethnic group within a different society is a form of **ethnogenesis** (Greeley 1971; Singer 1962).[12] This process may occur initially because the members of a group share certain historical and cultural characteristics. From this perspective, the importance of these shared characteristics derives from the common experiences of the group's members in the new society, especially the experience of rejection by the dominant group (Portes and Bach 1985:25). This common experience in turn provides a basis for a *transformed* ethnicity, one that is not a simple derivative of the society from which the immigrants came (Alba 1985:9; Geschwender, Carroll-Seguin, and Brill 1988:516). As Lurie (1982:143) expressed it, "Immigrant communities usually were not communities when they came; their ethnic identities were, to a surprising extent, constructed in America."

Sephardic and Ashkenazaic Jews

If the Italians were the most conspicuous portion of the second immigrant stream, the Jews were only slightly less so. Although Jews had been present in the United States since the colonial period, the largest wave arrived from Russia during the period of the second immigrant stream. The earliest Jews, the **Sephardim**, were from Spain, Portugal, and Holland. The Sephardim were few in number, but they played an important role in establishing Jewry in America. A second and much larger wave of Jewish immigrants originated in Germany and areas dominated by German culture (Sklare 1975:263). The same forces that led the other large groups of nineteenth-century Germans to come to the United States stimulated the immigration of German Jews as well. Many of the Forty-eighters were representatives of this group. The German Jews, the first of several Jewish groups from countries in central and eastern Europe (the **Ashkenazim**), so outnumbered the Sephardim that they soon became the primary force within Jewish American life.

German Jews.   The rise of the German Jews was not due entirely to their numbers, however. Of great importance also is that the German Jews had undergone a comparatively high level of cultural assimilation by substitution in Germany. The identification of the German Jews as Germans continued in the United States. According to Wittke (1964:329), the Jews participated in the activities of the *Turnvereine* and generally supported German cultural activities. Hence, the political and social characteristics of the German Jews were more prominent than their religion; and their religious practices were themselves much less distinctive than those of the Orthodox Jews who arrived both before and after them.

Most of the German Jews were participants in the Reform movement. The Reform synagogue differed from the Orthodox in such things as using little Hebrew in religious services, seating men and women together, celebrating Sunday as the Sabbath, approving intermarriage, and omitting prayers for the restoration of the Jewish state (Schermerhorn 1949:391). When combined, these factors stimulated a comparatively rapid cultural assimilation by substitution and a very rapid secondary structural assimilation of the German Jews in the United States. As the members of this group spread out across the country, many of them rose rapidly into the middle and upper classes. One of the most celebrated occupations of both first- and second-stream Jews was that of itinerant peddler. This line of work appealed to Jews, as it did Italians, because the cost of going into business was so low (Gold and Phillips 1996:189). Lieberson and Waters (1988:126) reported that in 1900 Russian men (most of whom presumably were Jewish) were over twenty-three times as likely to be "hucksters and peddlers" as were other White men in the labor force. "The new immigrant who was fired with ambition to succeed but hamstrung by limited capital," Kraut (1982:95) observed, ". . . took up the peddler's . . . pushcart." Some of America's great department stores—including Macy's, Gimbel's, Bloomingdale's, Filene's, Goldwater's, and Sears Roebuck—grew from such beginnings (Jones 1976:164–165). By the time the Russian Jews began to arrive in significant numbers, the German Jews already were established as the elite of American Jewry (Sklare 1975:263)—a status reflected by a strict pattern of within-group and intercity marriage alliances (Baltzell 1964:57). The rapid movement of the German Jews toward the mainstream of American cultural and secondary structural life suggested that in time—perhaps the fabled three generations—they would proceed through the remaining phases of assimilation and would disappear as a distinctive group.

Russian Jews.   That the full Anglo conformity assimilation of the German Jews did not occur may be due to the arrival of the extremely numerous and culturally distinctive Jews of the second immigrant stream. Between 1.5 and 2 million Russian Jews arrived in the United States as a part of the second immigrant stream.[13] Like the German Jews, the Russian Jews had at one time lived in Germany; and their main language was Yiddish, a mixture of Hebrew and German. Because of this historical unity, these two groups are both considered to be Ashkenazaic Jews; but after centuries of separation, the German and Russian groups were markedly different. Unlike German Jews, Russian Jews had been forced to live apart from the dominant group in certain parts of the country known as the Pale of Settlement. They had been oppressed by various restrictive laws (such as the military draft) and by organized violence (pogroms). Under these conditions, they had remained strongly united and had maintained their native culture and language to a high degree. Moreover, in contrast to the German Jews, the Russian Jews had every intention of keeping their culture intact in the New World. Most of the men wore beards, they organized Jewish schools to teach the ancient religious ways, they held strictly to the Sabbath and the dietary laws, and they dressed in distinctive ways. Even the German Jews considered these newcomers to be social inferiors and did not wish to associate with them (Schermerhorn 1949:393). It was, Glazer wrote, "as if a man who has built himself a pleasant house and is leading a comfortable existence suddenly finds a horde of impecunious relatives descending upon him" (quoted by Baltzell 1964:58). But the German Jews were concerned about the welfare of their co-religionists and also feared that their unusual manner of dress and other folkways might stimulate anti-Semitism among native Americans. For these reasons, the German Jews extended a broad range of assistance to the Russian Jews (Gold and Phillips 1996:188–189).

Italians and Russian Jews

Like the Italians, the Russian Jews were largely trapped in the port cities of the East, especially the Lower East Side of New York. Despite the efforts of Jewish Americans to assist the newcomers in relocating to other parts of the country, most of them remained in the newly formed urban ghettos. The Russian Jews also resembled the Italians in having had little previous experience in urban living. Most of them had come from small villages. Finally, the members of these two second-stream immigrant groups did not come to America with the desire to assimilate.

These similarities between the Italians and the Russian Jews do not mean that their reactions to the new environment were identical. For example, although neither group wished at first to assimilate in America, their reasons were quite different. The Italians, as we noted previously, typically did not bring their families, planning instead to make a fortune and return with it to the homeland. Although the Russian Jews brought their families and planned to remain permanently in America, they did not wish to give up the ancient culture they had so zealously defended in eastern Europe.

Two other differences between the Italians and the Russian Jews are noteworthy. The first of these has to do with the psychological impact of American urban living on the members of the two groups. It is an understatement to say that thousands of people in all of the second-stream groups were bitterly disappointed by the conditions they found in the New World. They were exploited at every turn, not only by the Americans but also by many of their own countrymen who "knew the ropes."[14] They were forced to work at unfamiliar jobs, at low wages, and with no job security. Usually, they had no choice but to move into the tenement slums with their crowding, noise, filth, lack of sanitation, and crime.[15] Understandably, many people felt beaten, homesick, and lonely. Both the Italians and the Jews were subject to these tremendous pressures. The Jews, however, were somewhat more insulated than the Italians. As bad as the conditions were, the Jews found in America a degree of freedom from persecution unimagined under the rulers of eastern Europe. Moreover, since the Jews had come over in families, including an unusually high proportion of children under the age of fourteen, they had quickly erected a cultural tent, so to speak, which gave them added protection against the insults and deprivations that were common in the lives of immigrants. They were extremely eager to make use of their new freedom and, consequently, embraced the opportunities that existed in public education and politics much more rapidly than did the Italians.

The second notable difference between the two largest groups of the second immigrant stream concerns the types of skills they possessed and the economic possibilities that were available to them. Although neither group was really familiar with the requirements of urban-industrial living, more Jews than Italians happened to possess occupational skills that could be put to quick use in such a setting. Ironically, some of the varied restrictions that had been placed on the Jews in eastern Europe had forced them into activities that now were of some value. An example of the way some of their previous skills helped the Jews to develop a distinctive wedge into the economy was their heavy concentration in the needle trades (Novotny 1974:138). By 1900, Russian (probably mostly Jewish) men were over thirty times more likely to be tailors than were other White men in the labor force (Lieberson and Waters 1988:126). They began making all types of clothing. Soon the garment industry in New York was run disproportionately on Jewish labor (Kraut 1982:82). Their concentration in this industry became so great that they effectively monopolized it in a short time (Gold and Phillips 1996:189). In addition, though, many of the Jews were experienced merchants and were especially resistant "to serving as a mere source of labor power" (Portes and Bach 1985:38). The Russian Jews, as had the German Jews, sought to establish themselves as entrepreneurs and owners of property. For instance, to return to the "huckster-and-peddler" example, although both the Italians and the Russian Jews were attracted disproportionately to these occupations, the latter were much more likely to be found there than the former.

Although it was advantageous to the Jews, relative to the other immigrant groups, to have some readily saleable skills, they nonetheless worked under poor and oppressive conditions. The garment industry was so competitive that it was very difficult for its workers, large numbers of whom were women and children, to eke out a living. They worked extremely long hours, for very low wages, under unsanitary conditions; and they encountered vigorous, sometimes physical, resistance when they organized labor unions to represent their interests. Moreover, the garment shops frequently were extremely dangerous places to work. In one notorious instance, 146 workers were killed when the Triangle Shirtwaist Company's factory in New York was gutted by fire (Burner, Fox-Genovese, and Bernhard 1991:647–650).[16]

There was another deplorable side to all of this that affected the members of many immigrant groups at that time and, in fact, continues to affect immigrants even in the present period.[17] Several industries, including the garment industry, subcontracted or "farmed out" sizable shares of their work to people who labored in their homes; so large numbers of Jewish homes became "sweatshops." Jacob Riis ([1890]1957:80) observed in 1890 that "the homes of the Hebrew quarter are its workshops also." Not only were the working conditions in these home sweatshops frequently worse than those in the facto- ries, but also the contractors often exploited an especially vicious aspect of the piece- work payment arrangement. They gradually reduced the prices paid for each piece of work, thereby forcing the workers to increase their productivity in order to keep their earnings at the same level. A frequent result of this method was to force women and children to work as many as eighteen hours a day (Novotny 1974:141–142). As Riis ([1890]1957:80) noted, all of the members of the family, young or old, helped with the work "from earliest dawn until mind and muscle give out together."

Our comparison of some of the differences between the way the Italians and Jews responded to the American setting illustrates a very important point: Although the members of these groups came to America as immigrant laborers and constructed eth- nic communities in response to native hostility, their communities nevertheless may have represented significantly different modes of adaptation. The neighborhoods of both groups served residential and economic functions; but the economic function ap- pears to have played a more decisive role in shaping the character of the ethnic neigh- borhoods established by the Jews. Although these neighborhoods resembled one an- other in appearance and served to shield their residents from the indignities heaped upon them by the dominant group, the Jewish neighborhoods are frequently cited as ex- amples of an entrepreneurial approach by immigrants to the problems of adapting to a new setting. A number of other American ethnic groups—including the Asian Indians, Chinese, Cubans, Greeks, Koreans, and Japanese—also are named frequently as exam- ples of this mode of adaptation.

Whether the immigrants of the second stream worked mainly as common laborers for members of the dominant group or for others of their own ethnicity, the human suffering engendered among all of them by the conditions of slum life in America at that time is truly incalculable. Despite great odds, the various second-stream immigrant groups endured and gradually made niches for themselves in American society, though not necessarily through the three-generations process. But, they were neither "a cluster of creative, ambitious, and optimistic individuals on the path from rags to riches" nor "a faceless mass of unskilled labor, sadistically exploited by robber barons" (Kraut 1982: 75). In time, as the story of their courage, determination, and success became widely known, they became models of what one may accomplish in America through hard work and perseverance; but when their struggle was most intense, native Americans generally did not see the second-stream immigrants as a confirmation of the American dream. They saw instead a massive renewal of the assault by aliens on the folkways and mores of American life. Once again, as in the earlier peak periods of immigration, the Americans increasingly feared that their social dominance and well-being were threatened; and, as a remedy, they increasingly demanded various forms of restrictions on immigration.

Immigration Restriction: A Preview

Various arguments and studies alleging that the immigrants of the second stream were inherently inferior to those of the first stream led Congress to pass a series of laws that, by 1924, effectively closed the golden door. The 1924 law introduced the use of the **national-origins principle** in the calculation of immigration quotas. This principle was based on the idea that the members of some racial or ethnic groups are inherently superior and preferable as immigrants to those of other groups. Its application had the effect of granting preferences to immigrants from countries of the colonial and first immigrant streams. The national-origins principle became the subject of angry political debate and, in time, the cornerstone of American immigration policy. The effects of the important law of 1924 were reinforced by the Great Depression during the 1930s and again by World War II in the 1940s, producing during those two decades the lowest rate of immigration in American history.

The United States has faced a dilemma throughout the twentieth century in its efforts to regulate the flow of immigration while, at the same time, attempting to honor its historic commitment to accept the "huddled masses" of the world. This dilemma has been intensified as rapid increases in the size of the world's population and dizzying changes in the methods of transportation and communication have, in effect, decreased the size of the world. In the short period between 1924 and the end of World War II, the world "shrank" dramatically. The forces of industrialization and urbanization that were just becoming apparent during the first great immigrant stream now encircled the globe, and their influences strongly shaped the character of international migration.

As the world changed, so did the United States. In contrast to the "open door" of the nineteenth century, a proliferation of laws, regulations, and legal agencies were created to deal with the increasing complexities of immigration. This contrast will be apparent as we move now from the issues of the second stream to those of the third. We return in Chapter 5 to a deeper consideration of the intergroup conflicts that led to immigration restriction.

The Third Great Immigrant Stream

By the end of World War II, a large number of people had been displaced from their homes and had become **refugees.**[18] Another important development following World War II was a worldwide increase in labor migrations from the poor to the rich nations (Massey 1981:58). These developments were joined by important changes in the immigration policies of the United States that favored the admission of refugees, the members of new immigrants' families, and skilled and technical workers. Taken together, these events helped produce a third great immigrant stream to the United States or the new immigration.

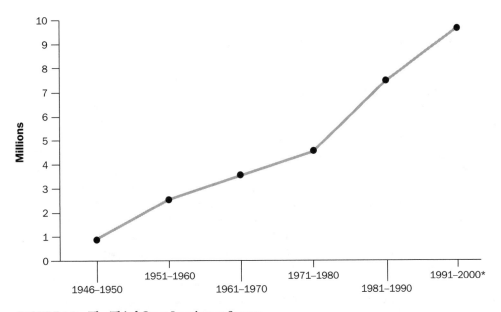

FIGURE 4.3   The Third Great Immigrant Stream
Number of Immigrants by Decade, 1946–1994.

Source: U.S. Immigration and Naturalization Service, *1994 Statistical Yearbook,* 1996:26; U.S. Bureau of the Census, *Statistical Abstract of the United States 1995,* 1995:9.

*1995–2000 (Projected)

The third immigrant stream started slowly at the end of World War II but gathered steam in each subsequent decade (see Figure 4.3). By the 1980s, the number of immigrants in the third stream had reached a level not seen since the earliest decade of the twentieth century; and if the current level of immigration continues, 1991–2000 will witness the largest number of newcomers of any decade in our history. Please notice though that, in relation to the total population of the United States, these massive increases in the foreign-born population still are well below those produced by the second immigrant stream (refer back to Table 4.1).[19]

Figure 4.3 and Table 4.1 show in different ways that the third immigrant stream increased in volume more sharply after the 1960s than it had up to that time. The main reason for this large shift is that in 1965 the United States government made some far-reaching changes in the country's basic immigration law, the Immigration and Nationality Act of 1952 (INA). The new law, the Immigration and Nationality Act Amendments (INAA), was passed in 1965 and went into effect in 1968. Its purpose was to make America's immigration law more democratic, more humane, and fairer to all of the world's countries. To make entry into the United States more democratic, the INAA discarded the system of quotas that gave preference to immigrants from the countries of the colonial and first immigrant streams.

Rejection of the
National-Origins Principle

The legal changes that laid the groundwork for these basic shifts in the character of American immigration began during World War II. In 1943, a program to admit temporary agricultural workers from Mexico was initiated;[20] and in 1948 Congress passed the Displaced Persons Act. It was clear by then that the patchwork of immigration laws adopted during the preceding decades needed to be put into better order.

Legislation designed to systematize, and to some extent liberalize, the existing laws was introduced into Congress. The result of this effort, the INA of 1952 (McCarran-Walter Act), continued the established quota approach for the nations of the Eastern Hemisphere and, consequently, was severely criticized by those who wished to do away with the national-origins principle. The INA, however, provided that members of all races could become citizens, eliminated sexual discrimination in admissions, introduced "special preference" designations for people who had talents or skills that were needed in the United States, and increased the number of relatives of citizens and permanent residents who could be brought into the country above the quota limits (U.S. Immigration and Naturalization Service 1996:A.1–12). And it granted the government the power to admit additional people as "parolees" (Reimers 1985:26). In 1953, Congress passed the Refugee Relief Act; and in 1957 it passed the Refugee Escape Act (U.S. Immigration and Naturalization Service 1996:A.1–12, A.1–13).

Despite the loosening of restrictions permitted under the INA, the various refugee and displaced persons acts, and the government's parole power, criticisms of the national-origins principle of admission continued to mount. Consequently, in 1965, the INA was amended (the Hart-Celler Act). This act broke sharply with the idea that the members of some racial or ethnic groups were inherently superior to those of other groups and were, therefore, to be preferred as immigrants. The national-origins quota system was abolished "eliminating national origin, race, or ancestry as a basis for immigration to the United States" (U.S. Immigration and Naturalization Service 1996:A.1–14). The new quota system raised the total who might be admitted annually from 150,000 to 290,000 people, beginning in 1968. A ceiling of 170,000 was set for all countries outside of the Western Hemisphere; no single country was assigned more than 20,000 visas per year. In addition, for the first time, an upper limit of 120,000 people annually was set on the entire Western Hemisphere, though no limits were set on any given country within it. As the volume of immigration from Mexico, Central America, the Caribbean, and South America rose, however, the pressure to assign limits to specific countries of the Western Hemisphere also rose. So, in 1976, the Western Hemisphere Act established a 20,000-visa-per-year limit for each country in this hemisphere (U.S. Immigration and Naturalization Service 1996:A.1-15).

The 1965 INAA also established a new preference system aiming first to reunite family members; second, to permit certain professional and skilled workers to enter the country; and third, to provide a place of asylum for refugees (Seller 1984:156). For example, among the seven preference categories listed, preferences one, two, four, and five

(74 percent of the total) were allocated to family members. Preferences three and six were allocated to professional and skilled workers (20 percent of the total), and preference seven was reserved for refugees (6 percent of the total) (Keely 1980:17; Maldonado and Moore 1985:14). Of special importance was that the immediate relatives of U.S. citizens (i.e., spouses, children, and parents) were eligible to enter above the existing numerical limits. A summary of these laws is presented in Chapter 5, Table 5.2.

Three Sociocultural Effects of the New Laws

An important post–World War II responsibility of the United States was to assist in the rebuilding of Europe and the relocation of the hundreds of thousands of people who had been displaced by the war. The United States at that time also was entering a new period of high international tension in which the country engaged in a global effort to "contain communism." Large numbers of World War II refugees and refugees from countries with communist governments sought asylum in the United States. The laws concerning refugees and displaced persons, and also the government's parole authority, were responses to these new global realities; and, as we have seen, refugees have been an important part of the third stream.

Since most of the refugees entering the United States in the decades immediately following World War II came mainly from countries represented in the first and second immigrant streams, the third immigrant stream seemed at the outset—with one major exception, Mexicans—to be mainly a resumption of the first and second streams. As had been true in the earlier periods, Germany, Canada, the United Kingdom, and Italy were among the countries that were most prominently represented (see Figure 4.3).

Racial and Ethnic Composition.   A second consequence of the new laws—especially of the INAA—was to help alter the racial and ethnic composition of the third immigrant stream and also increase its volume. The rejection of the national-origins principle as the basis for setting the size of each country's quota meant that the European countries, which had provided the overwhelming majority of America's immigrants in the past, no longer enjoyed a special preference. Each country outside of the Western Hemisphere (i.e., all of Europe, Asia, Africa, and Australia) was now eligible to send up to 20,000 emigrants per year, but the total of all Eastern Hemisphere countries could not exceed 170,000. Since this total permitted fewer than nine of the dozens of eligible countries to reach their individual quotas, the INAA, in effect, set into motion a competition among the emigrants from different countries to fill their country's quota as quickly as possible in order to reach their maximum share of the total. And since no country in the Western Hemisphere was limited to only 20,000 entries, the emigrants from any given country were eligible to occupy all of the 120,000 spaces allotted to the entire Western Hemisphere, which also encouraged early applications.

As matters developed, the majority of those who entered the United States in the years immediately following the passage of the INAA originated in the poorer countries of Central and South America, Asia, and the Caribbean Islands. This pattern of immigration was then enlarged and accelerated as the new residents became citizens and exercised their right to bring in members of their immediate families above the quota limits.[21] The overall result was that European immigrants, who comprised the overwhelming majorities of the colonial, first, and second immigrant streams declined sharply as a proportion of the total number of immigrants, whereas the proportion of those from Latin America and Asia rose to become, by 1980, the largest share. In addition, by far the largest numbers of refugees, who—like immediate family members—were eligible to enter above the quota limits, came from these same regions of the world. The societies and cultures primarily represented in the new immigration, then, differed markedly from all of the previous great immigrations. This consequence of the INAA—called by many commentators "the browning of America"—has aroused once again many of the same fears expressed by natives during the previous periods of high immigration.

Undocumented Workers.

The many pressures faced by poor people throughout the world generate a strong "push" that encourages them to migrate from their home countries, while the economic opportunities that exist in the world's richer countries provide an enticing "pull" for them to migrate to those countries. Although the changes in America's immigration policies initiated by the INAA were viewed as liberalizing the law—particularly the rejection of the national-origins principle and the emphasis on family reunification—there still existed quota limits. Additionally, the labor certification procedures established by Congress made the entrance of many types of workers more difficult. Many of the people who wished to enter the United States in pursuit of work therefore were excluded by the visa limits or were unable to find a job in advance (as required by law); consequently, many of these workers found ways to enter without acquiring the proper papers. The combined force of the economic gap that exists between the rich and poor nations of the world and the changes that were made in America's immigration laws resulted in a large increase in the number of "undocumented" or "illegal" immigrants. The exact size and impact of the undocumented immigrants has been the subject of furious debate.

Each of the three topics we have reviewed—the increase in the number of refugees immigrating to the United States, the changes in the racial and ethnic composition of the new immigration as compared to the earlier immigrant streams, and the rise in undocumented immigration—has contributed to the contemporary debate over immigration. We will examine these issues further in Chapter 14.

In summary, Chapters 3 and 4 examined the inclusion process of the first and second streams of immigrants and noted various objections and arguments that have been advanced against newcomers to America's shores. These arguments frequently have been presented in support of efforts to curb immigration. We also have introduced some preliminary information concerning the third immigrant stream. We turn in Chapter 5 to a further consideration of some of the arguments that regularly arise during periods of high immigration, especially those arising from Americans' ethnocentrism, and the role these arguments may play as shapers of America's immigration policies.

Key Ideas

1. The greatest human migration in history has occurred since 1815. Millions of people have come to the United States as parts of three great immigrant streams. The first two great streams, which overlapped in the nineteeth and early twentieth centuries, were completed by 1924. The largest groups of immigrants in the first stream originated in Ireland, Germany, the United Kingdom, Canada, and Scandinavia. The largest groups in the second stream originated in Italy, Austria-Hungary, and Russia.

2. The immigrants from every country have tended to cluster together with others from their land of origin. In the process, they have formed ethnic communities for mutual aid and the reconstruction of their ethnic institutions and heritages.

3. The waves of immigrants arriving at America's shores tended to peak when economic conditions within the United States were good and to recede when there were economic downturns. The patterns of emigration from the countries of origin were similar. During times of famine or economic or political disruption, large numbers of people were "pushed" from their homes and "pulled" toward opportunities in new lands.

4. Before the Civil War, the Irish and Germans arrived in the largest numbers. These migrations were precipitated largely by rapidly growing populations and crop failures. Both groups were politically active and appeared to the Anglo Americans to threaten their dominance; consequently, both groups aroused the hostility of the native Americans and heightened their fear of uncontrolled immigration.

5. After the Civil War, the effects of industrialization on both sides of the Atlantic brought great increases in the number of immigrants from southern and eastern Europe. The second-stream immigrants, like the first stream before them, seemed to threaten the integrity of the Anglo American society and culture. As their numbers rose, the demand for immigration restriction also rose.

6. Each of the three great immigrant streams aroused the fears of native Americans concerning such issues as competition for jobs, possible disloyalty, and the effects of foreign radicalism.

7. The experiences of the largest group to reach America during the second immigrant stream, the Italians, illustrated the process of ethnic-group formation called ethnogenesis. The members of this ethnic group became "Italian" in response to the conditions and pressures that existed within the American society.

8. The experiences of the second largest group of the second immigrant stream, the Jews, illustrated some of the important factors that affect the adjustment of an immigrant group to a new society. Important among these factors are whether individuals or family groups are most prevalent, whether men or women are more numerous, the extent to which the group already shares a common identity, and the kinds of occupational skills they possess.

9. More liberal policies toward political and military refugees, the search for jobs among the peoples of the poor countries of the world, and changes in America's immigration laws have helped stimulate a third great immigrant stream to the United States.

10. The immigrants of the third stream differ from those of the first and second streams not only in their countries of origin but also in the diversity of their social and economic backgrounds and in their destinations. They have come mainly from Asia and Latin America and represent a broad range of educational and occupational levels.

11. The third immigrant stream has revived many of the questions concerning the effects of immigrants on American society that were of interest during the earlier periods of massive immigration. Many people again wonder whether the newcomers will fit into the existing structure of American life or will alter it fundamentally.

 **Key Terms**

Ashkenazim   Jews from countries in central and eastern Europe.

ethnogenesis   The social processes through which people (1) from the same geographic regions join together to form a new ethnic group within a different society; (2) revive the functions of an ethnic group that has lost all or most of a previous role; or (3) bring together in a new, broader ethnic group several groups that are thought to be related.

first great immigrant stream   The large emigration to America between 1820 and 1889 of people who originated primarily in the countries of western and northern Europe.

Forty-eighters   German refugees who came to America after the failed revolutions of 1848 and 1849.

national-origins principle   Previously applied to the calculation of immigration quotas; based on the idea that the members of some racial or ethnic groups are inherently superior and, therefore, preferable as immigrants to those of other groups.

refugees   People who are outside of their country of nationality and are unable or unwilling to return to that country because of persecution or a well-founded fear of persecution.

second great immigrant stream   The large emigration to America between 1890 and 1924 of people who originated primarily in the countries of southern and eastern Europe.

Sephardim   Jews from Spain, Portugal, and Holland.

sojourners (birds of passage)   People who are, or intend to be, in a country temporarily.

third great immigrant stream (the **new immigration**)   The large emigration to America between 1945 and the present comprised of people who originated primarily in the countries of Latin America and Asia.

Turnvereine   Organizations formed by Germans in America that focused on athletic activities and became known as centers of radical reform.

Notes

1. We rely on the "push–pull" image to help identify some important factors that encourage migration but do not imply that human beings are robots "drawn from their homes against their wills, as if by a 'distant magnet'" (Kraut 1982:9). The decision to emigrate is based on many factors (see also Portes and Rumbaut 1990:8–14, 223–224).

2. Some evidence indicates that this historic relationship has reversed since the end of World War II (Portes and Bach 1985:57).

3. More immigrants arrived from France than Germany during the 1820s.

4. By 1852, Forty-eighters controlled half of the 133 German-language newspapers in the United States (Wittke 1964:193).

5. After 1924, Ellis Island was no longer used to receive immigrants. It became a detention center and point of deportation. In 1965, President Lyndon B. Johnson declared Ellis Island to be a part of the Statue of Liberty National Monument (Bolino 1985:42, 52); and in 1989 the Ellis Island Immigration Museum was opened to the public.

6. A congressional commission (the Dillingham Commission) portrayed the immigrants of the second stream as something "new" in American history who could not be expected to become good Americans, as had the "old" immigrants.

7. Portes and Bach (1985:5) note that deliberate labor recruitment may reveal a shortcoming of orthodox economic ("push–pull") theories of immigration.

8. Approximately 75 percent of the residents of Boston, Chicago, Cleveland, Detroit, and New York in 1910 were immigrants or the children of immigrants (Kraut 1982:77).

9. The United States was not the only destination of Italian immigrants. Many sought work in other European countries and millions went to Argentina and Brazil (Alba 1985:39).

10. These trades include "dressmakers, milliners, seamstresses, and tailoresses, and could be stretched to include workers in textile mills" (Steinberg 1989:153).

11. Baltzell (1964:30) reported that when New York's Mayor Fiorello La Guardia criticized his fellow Republican President Herbert Hoover, Hoover wrote to him saying "You should go back where you belong. . . . The Italians are preponderantly our murderers and boot-leggers."

12. This process also has been called "emergent ethnicity" (Yancey, Ericksen, and Juliani 1976).

13. The official statistics concerning the Jews are less reliable than for many other groups because some Jews are listed only as nationals of the particular countries from which they came (Schermerhorn 1949:398).

14. Many immigrants relied on others of their group who could speak English to get jobs for them and to handle all relations with the employer—including receiving their pay.

15. Notorious Jewish gangsters included "Bugsy" Siegel, Meyer Lansky, and Arnold Rothstein; but, according to Gold and Phillips (1996:183), "Jewish criminality was generally of the nonviolent type."

16. The "shirtwaist" was a fashionable blouse that had a high collar, full bosom, and narrow, pleated waist. Most of the 500 employees of the factory were young Jewish and Italian women (Burner, Fox-Genovese, and Bernhard 1991:647–648).

17. See, for example, Jane H. Lii, "Week in Sweatshop Reveals Grim Conspiracy of the Poor," *New York Times* (March 12, 1995:1); "7 Thais Plead Guilty in Sweatshop Slavery Case," *New York Times* (February 11, 1996:12).

18. Refugees apply for admission while they are outside of the United States; asylees apply from within the United States (Immigration and Naturalization Service 1996:76).

19. These numerical increases have resulted in a rise in the percent of the U.S. population that is foreign born. Even so, the relative size of the foreign-born portion of the population in 1990 was less than 60 percent that of 1920 (7.9 versus 13.2 percent) (U.S. Bureau of the Census 1995:52).

20. This "temporary" program continued until 1964 (see Chapter 9).

21. Immigration specialists refer to this type of pattern as a "chain migration."

Nativism, Scientific Racism, and Immigration Restriction

Rapid increases in immigration sharpened competition between immigrants and natives for jobs and political power. Pseudoscientific views about the inferiority of foreigners flourished. Anti-foreign sentiments resulted in immigration restrictions.

*As a nation we began by declaring that "all men are created equal."
When the Know-Nothings get control, it will read "all men are created
equal except Negroes and foreigners and Catholics."*
—Abraham Lincoln

*. . . it is on the moral qualities of the English-speaking race that
our history, our victories, and all our future rest.*
—Henry Cabot Lodge, Sr.

*In thim days America was th' refuge iv th' oppressed in the wurruld. . . .
But as I tell ye, 'tis diff'rent now. 'Tis time we put our back again' th' open
dure an' keep out the savage horde.*
—"Mr. Dooley"

ativism

From the earliest days of colonization, the dominant group encouraged voluntary immigration with alternating enthusiasm and resentment. Although the effort to subdue the continent, physically as well as politically, helped create systems of bonded servitude and slavery, these sources of labor alone were never sufficient. Clearing the land, tilling the soil, and producing raw materials for the mother country all required large numbers of newcomers.

The host group's reaction to the immigrants, as discussed previously, depended on such things as the size of the incoming group, the rate at which they arrived, their concentration, and the similarity between their culture and the Anglo American culture. If a group arrived in large numbers and behaved in ways that the members of the host society regarded as "too" different, the Anglo Americans became alarmed and reacted in "protective" ways. Under such conditions, the usual levels of anti-foreign activity increased greatly. Despite these fluctuating views, Americans generally came to prefer policies that encouraged a heavy flow of immigrants from Europe. After the United States gained independence, an "open door" immigration policy was adopted. The basic assumption behind this policy was that immigrants helped the country economically.

The door to America was never entirely open, however. The fear that foreigners would not understand or respect democratic institutions, or would in some way work to undermine them, was voiced during the debates over the Constitution. In the first flush of their new-found freedom, the Americans suspected that Catholics might be monarchist subversives and that immigrants from France might attempt to foment the kind of unrest that had led to the French Revolution. These fears concerning the safety of the fragile new republic created a widespread **xenophobia.**

A contest over the requirements for naturalization during the 1790s is an early illustration of the hostility that natives often feel toward foreigners, called **nativism.** The first federal laws concerning naturalization, passed in 1790, provided that "any free white person" who had lived in the United States for two years could apply for citizenship (Ueda 1980:737). By implication, of course, Black slaves, Native Americans, and indentured Whites were excluded as potential citizens. These laws also ruled out applicants who were not of "good moral character" (Cafferty, Chiswick, Greeley, and Sullivan 1984:40). For the most part during this time, immigration and naturalization was left to state and local governments.

Nativism increased sharply with the onset of the first great immigrant stream. Many Americans believed this new influx of foreigners represented a serious threat to their way of life. Their reaction included vitriolic attacks on Catholicism and the Pope, on the pauperism and illiteracy of the immigrants, and on the political rights of naturalized citizens. It also included an increasing number of proposals that laws be passed to restrict immigration, limit the rights of immigrants, and increase the length of time needed to become a naturalized citizen.

As the Irish population in America grew, and many of its members moved into various political and municipal jobs, there was an outburst of anti-Catholic propaganda. Many Americans believed the authoritarian organization of the Catholic church was incompatible with the democratic institutions and ideals of American society. Many newspaper accounts, books, pamphlets, and speeches claimed that the Irish Catholics were emissaries of the Pope who were working to undermine American traditions and overthrow the government of the United States. In 1834, for instance, the famous inventor Samuel F. B. Morse wrote several widely publicized statements claiming that the papal conquest was underway (Morse [1835]1976:61).[1] In 1836, an infamous tract, *The Awful Disclosures of Maria Monk,* portrayed monasteries and convents as dens of immorality (Monk [1836]1976:77). Anti-Catholic sentiments also were expressed in conflicts over the Catholics' opposition to the use of the King James version of the Bible in public schools and to their demands that state funds be used to support parochial schools.

The opposition to Catholicism was fused with a frequent, and not completely untrue, complaint that Europe was using America as a "dumping ground" for its paupers and criminals. There was widespread fear that the immigrants did not understand the American political system and could easily be manipulated by corrupt leaders. The Irish were accused of using rough, "un-American" methods to rig the outcomes of elections. Instances of bloc voting, electoral fraud, and voter intimidation were cited to show that the very foundation of American democracy was being undermined. Apparently, in some of the large cities, it was common practice for immigrants to be illegally naturalized the day before an election (Jones 1960:154). Moreover, the continued interest of the Irish in the political affairs of Ireland increased the fear that they were not loyal to the United States.

The Germans also were targets of the growing xenophobia of the native Americans. The Germans were feared because they were presumed to be revolutionaries. Even Americans who did not accept the exaggerated charges against immigrants and naturalized citizens nonetheless did not like the German revolutionaries who fled to America in 1848. As noted earlier, the members of this group were thought to be atheists and radicals who were contemptuous of American traditions.

The idea that immigrants were destroying the basic fabric of American society seemed even more plausible because of the rising controversy between the North and the South over slavery, westward expansion, and economics. As the possibility increased that the Union would collapse, various political parties were formed to protect the rights and privileges of natives and to combat immigration and immigrants. For example, in 1845, the Native American Party was formed. This new party's purpose was to devise "a plan of concerted political action in defense of American institutions against the encroachments of foreign influence" (Feldstein and Costello 1974:147). The Native American Party's Declaration of Principles argued that the natives were rapidly becoming "a minority in their own land." And it recited some of the charges mentioned previously: The newcomers were working for foreign governments; they were mainly Europe's unwanted criminals, paupers, and imbeciles; they sought unfair political advantage by organizing along ethnic lines; and they "offered their votes and influence to the highest bidder" (Feldstein and Costello 1974:153).

The Native American Party did not succeed on a national scale; but, it was soon followed by one that did—the American or "Know-Nothing" Party. The name of the party came from the fact that its members answered "I know nothing" whenever people sought information concerning its principles (Faulkner 1948:345). The party's slogan was "America for the Americans" (Jones 1960:157). Its platform urged that only native Americans be permitted to hold public office. The Know-Nothings opposed the admission of paupers into the country and believed that the period required for naturalization should be extended to twenty-one years. By 1854, the Know-Nothings had gained enough strength to elect a number of state governors and U.S. congressmen and to dominate several state legislatures. But, by the election of 1856, conflicts between the North and the South overshadowed immigration as a threat to national life. Thus the party's presidential candidate, former President Millard Fillmore, was soundly defeated.

The Civil War gave numerous foreigners a chance to demonstrate their loyalty either to the Union or the Confederacy. "In both sections of the country," according to Jones (1960:170), "immigrants responded to the call to arms as readily as did the natives." But the immigrants' loyalty had not removed all anti-alien sentiments. For example, in 1863, the Irish in New York staged three days of violence directed against both the White Republican establishment and against Blacks. These so-called Draft Riots were a protest against the practice of permitting rich draftees to avoid military service, which the largely poor Irish were unable to do; however, most of the rioters' attacks were on Blacks. A wave of anti-Irish reaction followed the Draft Riots, suggesting again that the war had not submerged all nativism.

The conflicts between the native Americans and the peoples of the first great immigrant stream subsided markedly immediately following the Civil War. Most Americans still believed that immigrants should discard their foreign ways and adopt the basic pattern of American life as soon as possible; however, even when the first stream resumed following the Civil War, the hostility of the natives toward the newcomers did not revive proportionately. The people from northern and western Europe had proven they could and would fit into the dominant Anglo American mold; in other words, they were assimilable. Indeed, many of those whose fathers and mothers had arrived during the 1840s and 1850s now exhibited high levels of cultural and secondary structural assimilation and had, for many practical purposes, joined the ranks of the natives; whereas many of those whose grandparents had arrived during the 1820s and 1830s were undergoing primary structural and marital assimilation. The continuation of the first immigrant stream, therefore, no longer was met with intense nativism.

The beginning of the second immigrant stream, however, aroused new doubts. As its volume overtook, and then surpassed, that of immigration from northern and western Europe, many people became alarmed again. As noted previously, the peoples of the second immigrant stream seemed to many Americans to be even more foreign than those of the first stream. Their manners and customs appeared to many to threaten the very basis of Americanism, since their arrival in large numbers as a part of America's shift from an agrarian to an industrial economy made it seem that the newcomers were directly responsible for the many problems associated with industrialization. For example, during this period, workers began to organize labor unions in an attempt to ensure employment and decent working conditions. These organizational efforts were, to put it mildly, not well received by the owners and managers of industry. Working men's strikes and picket lines were met by private armies and strikebreakers. Sabotage, assassinations, and open warfare were increasingly common in coal mines, steel mills, and railroads (Rubenstein 1970:29). Since many of these conflicts involved immigrant workers, xenophobia increased. These events in the East added strength to a movement initiated by conflicts between native workers and Chinese immigrants on the West Coast to end America's historic open door policy and to establish legal restrictions on immigration into the United States.

The charges against the Chinese emphasized the usual economic and political claims relating to the disadvantages of accepting immigrants; but now certain pseudo-scientific beliefs about the nature of racial differences were prominently added to these usual arguments. Immigrants were to be hated and excluded, according to this new theory, not only because they were a threat to the American working class and were the carriers of radical political ideas, but also because they were presumed to represent the "defeated" and, therefore, biologically "unfit" portions of their respective races. This new line of thought—called **scientific racism**—developed rapidly during the last quarter of the nineteenth and the first quarter of the twentieth centuries.

Scientific Racism

Racial Differences

We noted in Chapter 1 that many people believe racial categories are specific, unvarying entities. In fact, however, the boundaries of races (and, more obviously, ethnic groups) are set by social agreement. The traits ordinarily selected to form the basis of the social definitions of race are, of course, visible and biological. Such visible traits as skin color, head shape, eye form, hair texture, and so on are biologically inherited. As we emphasized, however, none of the traits that most people view as "racial" can be used to establish clear-cut lines of division among the races. The apparent sharpness of racial boundaries in the United States springs from the fact that Americans believe race to be important. So when they see another person, they generally (and without reflection) identify that person as a member of some racial group. After people have been classified, ethnocentrism leads the members of each group to treat in-group members more favorably than out-group members.

Europeans were keenly aware of the physical differences between themselves and others and wondered whether their social dominance over the Native Americans and Africans might be related to the physical differences. The main line of division on this issue lay between the competing ideas of **hereditarianism** and **environmentalism.** This important, though imprecise, division has appeared repeatedly in human thought as people tried to explain the differences in human behavior and patterns of living. From colonial times to the present, many Americans have accepted as a fact the idea that the social dominance of White people is a reflection of innate or inborn differences in ability. Many other Americans, on the other hand, have rejected this idea. The opposing views of hereditarians and environmentalists also have figured prominently in the effort to explain and justify the unequal distribution of goods, services, and privileges in society.

Throughout the first half of the nineteenth century, the debate over the relative qualities and standing of the races intensified. Slavery in America, and the various justifications of it, moved increasingly toward the center of political, moral, and scientific controversy. Scientists and nonscientists, proslavery advocates and abolitionists, Christians and non-Christians all argued over whether Blacks were members of a separate and inferior species. The political and moral battles were decided, in principle at least, in favor of the unity of humanity by the emancipation of the slaves, the victory of the Northern armies in the Civil War, and the extension of full citizenship rights to Black Americans. The scientific and scholarly controversy, however, was only beginning.

The fusion of several intellectual trends during the latter half of the nineteenth century fueled the dispute concerning racial differences. Charles Darwin's theory of organic evolution profoundly affected thought in nearly every field. Among social thinkers, Darwin's ideas were used to argue that individuals, nations, and races were engaged in a struggle to select the "fittest" and that, therefore, social dominance was a sign of natural superiority. The advocates of **social Darwinism** believed that socially dominant groups are those who have demonstrated their biological "fitness" in the struggle for survival.

Darwin's ideas also were highly compatible with an influential, though later discredited, interpretation of European and American history that flourished during the period of the second immigrant stream. On the basis of studies of the origin of European languages, many scholars were persuaded that the tall, blond, blue-eyed peoples of northern and western Europe were the modern remnants of an extremely talented race called the "Nordics" (or "Teutons") who, in turn, were descended from the ancient Aryans of India (Gossett 1963:84–122). Although the theory contained numerous— sometimes contradictory—strands of thought, it fostered the impression that ethnic groups, as well as races, exhibited different inherited traits. The theory held, for instance, that of all the Nordic peoples, the Anglo-Saxons were the most freedom-loving, democratic, self-reliant, ethical, and disciplined; they were believed to have made the most important contributions to English and American life. The Nordic group, as a whole, were said to have a special talent for political organization that enabled its members to form representative governments and create just laws even when they were a numerical minority (Higham 1963:137). From this perspective, members of the Nordic portion of the White race were destined to rule over all races, including the shorter "Alpine" and the darker-skinned "Mediterranean" portions of the White race. These arguments led many people to believe that the theories of social Darwinism and Nordic supremacy had been "scientifically proven."

Social Darwinism also held that White people were more intelligent than other people, which strengthened a line of argument that has always been at the core of the race-differences controversy. More than two centuries ago, Buffon, a pre-Darwinian evolutionist, concluded that although Blacks were "endowed with excellent hearts, and possess the seeds of every human virtue," they possessed "little genius" (Gossett 1963:36). Thomas Jefferson, who was strongly influenced by the environmentalist thought of European philosophers and believed that Black people were brave, adventuresome, musical, and had good memories, nevertheless thought they were inferior in the ability to reason (Gossett 1963:42). Despite a later friendship and correspondence with the gifted mathematician Benjamin Banneker, a Black man, Jefferson apparently entertained doubts about the mental ability of Blacks until his death (Bardolph 1961: 31–32). At the time Buffon and Jefferson presented their opinions, however, many others believed that the races were inherently equal and that it was the harshness of slavery that prevented Blacks in America from advancing intellectually (Gossett 1963:41).

The dispute over racial differences in intelligence gained momentum throughout the nineteenth century and, as we soon discuss, is still with us today. But the argument today revolves around a type of evidence that did not exist in Jefferson's time—evidence based on standardized tests of mental ability. Let us examine briefly the origin of these tests, their role in the continuing debate on racial differences in mental ability, and their effects on American immigration policies.

Mental Testing and Immigration

The idea that there are racial differences in mental ability was vigorously supported by Francis Galton, Darwin's cousin, in his studies of British men of distinction. Galton (1869) initiated the field of mental testing. He argued that nature (heredity), not nurture (environment), was responsible for the rise of people to eminence. From Galton's perspective, no social barriers could suppress the naturally talented person, and no social enrichment could cause an untalented person to become successful. He accepted the doctrine of White supremacy but feared that the "Anglo-Saxon race" was degenerating genetically. Galton advocated various measures that were intended to promote genetic improvement, which he called **eugenics**. The eugenics movement in England sought to lower the reproductive rates of the Irish, who were thought to be of low intelligence (Miller 1995:163–164).

Galton and his followers assumed that each person was endowed at birth with a certain intellectual capacity that could be measured with appropriate types of mental tests. In 1905, the inventors of the most influential type of mental testing procedure, Alfred Binet and Thomas Simon, combined various ideas to produce the first "scale" of intelligence (Klineberg 1937:323);[2] however, *they did not believe their scale was a measure of innate intelligence.*[3] It was intended originally to be used only as a tool to assist in identifying children with learning problems. In 1912, William Stern compared children's performances by dividing each child's mental age (MA) by his or her chronological age (CA) to obtain the child's "intelligence quotient" (IQ; Klineberg 1937:323).[4]

The Binet-Simon scale was developed at about the time the peak of the second immigrant stream to the United States was reached. As we have seen, at about this time the pressure was mounting to adopt policies of restricting admissions on the basis of racial or ethnic identity. The restrictionist's efforts were aided greatly by the evidence from a massive mental testing program conducted by the Army during World War I. This program tested more than 1.7 million men and was the first large mental-testing effort. It also stimulated a period of intense scholarly and public interest in the question of racial differences in intelligence.

The data gathered during the Army's testing program have served ever since as an important reference point concerning many crucial questions. What, exactly, is "intelligence"? How independent of prior training and experience are the questions and tasks used in intelligence testing? Is human intelligence a unitary thing, or is it composed of different elements? The Army reported the results of the intelligence program based on the findings of an *alpha* test (designed for those who were literate in English) and a *beta* test (designed for those who were illiterate or did not understand English).[5]

The results of the Army's studies had a tremendous impact on scholars, policy makers, and the lay public. In general, Black people and immigrants did not score as well on the tests as native Whites even when efforts were made to take into consideration group differences in schooling and experience. In terms of the average (median) alpha scores, White recruits of native birth ranked first, foreign-born White recruits ranked second, northern Black recruits ranked third, and southern Black recruits ranked fourth. The beta score median differences were generally smaller and more favorable for the Black recruits, but the rank order of the four groups was unchanged.

In an important contribution to the developing controversy concerning racial and ethnic differences in intelligence, C. C. Brigham (1923) analyzed the Army data further and presented them in *A Study of American Intelligence*, "a companion volume" to *America, A Family Matter* by C. W. Gould (1922). Gould's book argued for restrictions on immigration to the United States and against "racial mixing." Brigham's analysis strengthened the case for special restrictions on immigrants from the countries of southern and eastern Europe. His analysis showed that on the combined alpha and beta scores, the foreign-born recruits from countries representing the first immigrant stream exceeded the average (mean) for foreign-born recruits from countries representing the second immigrant stream.

Brigham asserted that these differences among the racial and ethnic groups could not be explained by differences in social and economic backgrounds but were due to group differences in heredity. He concluded that "the results which we obtain by interpreting the data by means of the race hypothesis support . . . the thesis of the superiority of the Nordic type" (Brigham 1923:182). This interpretation seemed to confirm that the immigrants from northern and western Europe were intellectually superior to (and, therefore, more assimilable than) those from southern and eastern Europe.

The Army's test program results seemed overwhelmingly to support the hereditarian perspective on group differences in intelligence. Most psychologists at this time were "of the opinion that the inherent mental inferiority of [immigrants and non-Whites] had been scientifically demonstrated" (Thompson 1934:494). At this point, most ordinary citizens were convinced the matter had been settled once and for all. Indeed, the hereditarian view seemed so compelling to so many that the nation's immigration policies were radically altered to reflect what was taken to be established fact.

The Rise of Environmentalism

As the number of studies comparing the IQ scores of different racial and ethnic groups continued to mount, many scholars had second thoughts. They wondered if, after all, such things as a person's social status, language, educational level, and test experience might make a *big* difference in test scores. Even Brigham reconsidered his earlier position and stated that "it is absurd" to combine different test scores as he had done previously (Brigham 1930:160). In a retraction that has delighted environmentalists ever since, Brigham (1930:165) offered this conclusion: "The more recent test findings . . . show that comparative studies of various national and racial groups may not be made with existing tests, and . . . that one of the most pretentious of these comparative racial studies—the writer's own—was without foundation."

Brigham was not alone in his change of mind. Earlier criticisms that the intelligence tests were influenced by factors other than native ability were elaborated. Certain questions of method were explored more fully; and the Army data themselves were subjected to further, and in some cases, different types of analyses. In addition, many scientists in the United States (and elsewhere) were shocked by the grossly exaggerated "master race" philosophy that was being espoused in Germany by Adolph Hitler during this time. Hitler justified the Nazis' persecution of "racial inferiors," particularly Jews and Gypsies, as necessary to establish the "New Order" of the "Aryans." In a study at this time of the opinions of people who were specialists in the field of racial differences, Thompson (1934) found that *96 percent of the scientists did not accept* racial superiority or inferiority as an established fact, and only 46 percent of those surveyed believed the hypothesis of race inferiority was even "reasonable."

In the period just preceding World War II, scholarly opinion (though not that of the general public) had reached a position far removed from the early 1920s. Although there were still some scientists who accepted the hereditarian thesis, most agreed that both heredity and environment affected an *individual's* mental test scores in some complicated, poorly understood way. For most researchers the question was no longer, "Is intelligence determined by heredity *or* environment?" but "How do heredity and environment combine to produce the scores obtained on intelligence tests?" Environmentalists had established that the earlier hereditarian interpretations were incorrect and oversimplified. They had shown clearly that factors, such as the test taker's previous experience, socioeconomic status, self-esteem, and motivation, could influence the test results.[6]

In the ensuing debates among scholars surrounding the proper interpretation of these points, the weight of informed opinion continued to shift toward an emphasis on the role of environmental factors in producing group differences in intelligence test scores. For instance, it was demonstrated that some Blacks scored as high on intelligence tests as any Whites and that a large number of Blacks even exceeded the average intelligence test score for Whites. Even a leading hereditarian, H. E. Garrett (1945:495), admitted that some test differences, though not all, may "be explained in socio-economic terms."[7]

A further consequence of the years of study and debate was that the key issues became more technical. For this reason, the remainder of our brief summary necessarily focuses on only a few important points and, especially, on some statistical arguments that lie at the heart of the contemporary controversy. This emphasis is influenced by our belief that an understanding of the competing views must include an examination of those arguments.

Comparing Races.   Consider again the view presented in Chapter 1 and earlier in this chapter, that although people commonly think of races, and sometimes ethnic groups, as sharply distinguishable biological entities, their boundaries, in fact, are set by social agreement. Most of the evidence concerning group differences is based on studies in which people either have identified themselves as members of particular groups or have been assigned to groups by others on the basis of commonly accepted visible traits. "It is hard to believe," Ryan (1995:27) said, "that [cognitive ability] would follow the haphazard lines of self-reported ethnicity." From this perspective, categories such as "Black" and "White" *are not valid biological categories.* There is massive evidence showing that the visible (phenotypic) races are not isolated breeding populations (genotypic races) but rather are highly intermixed; therefore, no strong claim can be made that a given difference between these groups (such as an average IQ difference) reflects biological differences.[8]

From this perspective, until a valid *biological* method of setting racial boundaries is discovered, *no statistical argument,* however sophisticated, can demonstrate that an average difference between races has a genetic basis. Nevertheless, statistical arguments are still widely used and often are accepted as demonstrating that average group differences in IQs have a genetic basis. For this reason, it is essential for anyone who wishes to understand the IQ controversy to be conversant with the main statistical arguments.

Spearman's Theory.   The statistical arguments begin with the common finding that people's performances on different mental tests are positively correlated. Those who do well on one test are likely also to do well on another.[9] The degree of positive correlation between different tests, however, may vary. Charles Spearman (1904) posited that the observed pattern of the test results occurred because each test measured some aspect of peoples' inherited general intellectual ability.[10]

Spearman's theory of mental testing has been a pillar of hereditarian thinking throughout the twentieth century and also has been very controversial. Two basic issues concern (1) his method of calculating the value of general intelligence (called factor analysis)[11] and (2) his belief that general intelligence is inherited biologically and cannot be changed by education or effort. He did accept the idea that specific types of skill or knowledge are subject to change.

A penetrating critique of Spearman's methods and interpretation was presented by L. L. Thurstone (1935). In contrast to Spearman's theory of general intelligence, Thurstone argued that there were various clusters of mental abilities (Gould 1981:296). Suppose, for instance, that we had the test scores from four highly correlated tests, two of which tested people's verbal skills and two of which tested their mathematical skills. Spearman's method of analyzing the scores would yield a measure of general intelligence based on all four tests. Thurstone's method would provide a measure of verbal intelligence and also a measure of mathematical intelligence. Thurstone concluded that there was not a single factor that measured intelligence but rather that there were several "primary mental abilities," or different types of intelligence, that were measured differently by different tests.[12]

What can we learn from this disagreement about measures of intelligence? Two main points are of great importance. First, Spearman and Thurstone agreed that their different techniques for analyzing test results were *mathematically equivalent*. Both were "correct" from a computational viewpoint. However, the second point is, when Thurstone's method was used, "general intelligence" vanished! The big question raised by Thurstone's studies is this: How can one claim that general intelligence is biologically fixed if an alternative, but equally accurate, method of computing factors shows that there are several different types of intelligence rather than a single general type (Gould 1981:253, 302)?[13] Researchers who follow Thurstone's lead search for patterns of differences among intellectual functions rather than seeking a way to rank racial and ethnic groups on a single scale of general intelligence (Loehlin, Lindzey, and Spuhler 1975: 177–188).

By the late 1960s, public discussions of intelligence had shifted away from the question of the relative importance of heredity and environment toward devising ways to improve intellectual achievement through deliberate changes in people's environments. Many studies and demonstration projects provided evidence that better nutrition, living conditions, and educational methods could bring about dramatic improvements in academic achievement and in IQ scores. As we will discuss later, large government programs, such as the Head Start preschool program for low-income children, were launched to achieve these purposes. Public policy at this point seemed no longer to rest on the belief that mental ability is fixed by nature but rather on the belief that it can be molded substantially by improving our knowledge and our environment.

Hereditarianism Revisited

Those who were confident that the nation's educational and other social problems could be solved primarily through environmental changes were shocked by an article published by Arthur Jensen late in 1969. This article revived the dispute over the relative influence on mental ability of heredity and environment and initiated another period of acrimonious scholarly and public debate. Jensen conducted a review of 141 studies of intelligence testing and was convinced that heredity's influence on intelligence was far greater than that of the environment. He acknowledged that "no one . . . questions the role of environmental factors" on intelligence test scores, but he believed that the environment's role was comparatively small (Jensen 1969:79). From his viewpoint, efforts to improve schooling and social programs could do little to increase mental achievement or raise IQs.

Jensen's main approach to an understanding of the relative contributions of heredity and environment to the development of mental ability relied on **estimates of heritability.** These estimates were based on comparisons of the IQ test scores of people who were either related or unrelated and were raised either in similar or in dissimilar environments, for example, identical twins (reared together or apart), siblings, cousins, and unrelated people. Jensen (1976:103) concluded that about 80 percent of the differences in intelligence existing among *individuals* were due to differences in their genetic endowments. His interpretation went well beyond this point, however, to state that the average *group* differences between Black and White Americans in IQ scores were best explained mainly in genetic terms.[14]

An avalanche of disagreement followed the publication of Jensen's review. Some authors responded by showing that the estimates Jensen relied on were much too high.[15] An especially important attack, however, was aimed at his interpretation of heritability estimates. Such estimates are based on evidence gathered from *specific* populations (e.g., the members of one racial or ethnic group) at a particular time and, if they are accurate, may be used properly to study differences only *within that population.*[16] This means that, even if the high estimates of heritability used by Jensen were accurate for one group, they still could not be used correctly to study differences *between* that group and any other.

The problem here lies in the fact that a *biologically inherited characteristic may develop differently in different environments.* Consider this example: Under favorable nutritional and living conditions the members of a particular population will attain an average adult height (which is a highly heritable trait) that is above the average adult height that *this same group of people* would have attained under less favorable conditions (e.g., scarce food supplies). In *each* case—under the favorable conditions or under the unfavorable conditions—the variations in adult height *within* the population would be due to genetic causes (assuming that everyone in the population shared equally the favorable or unfavorable conditions); however, the difference *between* the average height of the population when conditions were favorable and the average height of this *same* population when conditions were unfavorable would be due *entirely* to the differences in the favorable and unfavorable environments.

We see in this hypothetical example that a trait may be highly heritable yet play *absolutely no role* in producing an average difference *between* populations that *live under different environmental conditions.*[17] When we apply this reasoning to the case of the average IQ differences *between* Blacks and Whites, we see that *all* of the average differences between them in this respect may be due to the different conditions under which these populations have lived for several centuries even if intelligence is highly heritable. As Layzer (1995:659) stated, "The reported differences in average IQ tell us *nothing whatever* about any average genetic differences that may exist" (emphasis added).

One other especially interesting point was raised during this period. In a comparison of fourteen countries, Flynn (1987) found that since 1950 there had been an average increase in IQ scores of around fifteen points. Did this "massive increase" mean that the average person in 1987 was more intelligent than the average person in 1950? Flynn argued that "the real-world problem-solving ability called intelligence" was no more evident in the 1980s than in the 1950s. In his opinion, IQ tests measure "abstract problem solving ability" and, therefore, "psychologists should stop saying that IQ tests measure intelligence" (Flynn 1987:185–188).[18]

Flynn's recommendation came shortly before yet another round of vitriolic exchanges in the IQ debate—one that equaled, or perhaps exceeded, the scholarly and public attention and anger following Jensen's article in 1969.

Flashpoint 1: *The Bell Curve*

Two years after the publication of Jensen's explosive article, Richard Herrnstein (1971), a professor of psychology at Harvard, added fuel to the fire in an exploration of some possible implications of the hereditarian thesis for the future of American society. His argument was set forth as a logical syllogism and was based on the assumption that differences in intelligence are largely hereditary. If differences in intelligence are mainly inherited, Herrnstein said, and if educational and occupational success require intelligence, then a person's general social standing will be determined to some extent by his or her inherited intelligence.

Given this chain of reasoning, Herrnstein argued that one of American democracy's most cherished principles—the principle of achievement—is leading toward a strange result. In a society in which **vertical social class mobility** is affected substantially by individual ability, the more intelligent members of the lower classes will rise in the social hierarchy, leaving the less talented behind. Ironically, therefore, the ultimate effect of weakening the barriers to social mobility—of increasing what most Americans consider to be "fairness"—may be the creation of an "hereditary meritocracy." Since such a **stratification system** would be based increasingly on genetically inherited intelligence, children born into rich and powerful families of high standing generally would become rich and powerful adult members of the upper class, whereas children born into poor and downtrodden families of low standing generally would remain members of a lower class throughout their lives.

In the book *The Bell Curve*,[19] Herrnstein and Murray (1994) undertook to demonstrate that this dismal hypothetical scenario is in fact in the process of becoming a reality in America. They argued that several trends during the twentieth century had created a "cognitive elite" comprised of people of high intelligence. As occupational specialties proliferated and became more technical and as colleges increasingly based admissions on an individual's ability to do well on standardized tests, those who succeeded in college increasingly were channeled into specialized "high IQ professions" characterized by high pay and high prestige. This cognitive stratification in education and occupations has led, and will continue to lead, they said, to the increasing isolation of the brightest Americans from the rest of society (Herrnstein and Murray 1994:25, 91).

Had the authors limited their analysis to this highly debatable thesis,[20] perhaps *The Bell Curve* would not have generated such a storm of protest; but they did not. The first twelve chapters of their analysis used data concerning only White Americans, but in Chapter 13 the authors introduced the incendiary subject of ethnic differences in IQ. They acknowledged that many readers would turn first to Chapter 13 and that "race is often on people's minds when they think about IQ" (Herrnstein and Murray 1994:272). We should therefore not be surprised that the racial aspect of the work provided much of the force that propelled the book into the center of a heated public controversy. In the year following its publication, hundreds of thousands of copies of the book were sold, hundreds of magazine and newspaper articles and editorials about it were published, and numerous television and radio programs gave it attention.

One surprising thing about the book was that it contained so little that was new. It did contain a number of new analyses based on an important longitudinal data set, and the statistical methods employed were up-to-date.[21] The main ideas of the book, though, were not very different from those advanced by the early IQ testers. Herrnstein and Murray followed Galton in assuming that differences in intelligence are genetically inherited; they followed Spearman in assuming that IQ tests measure general intelligence and that this measure is a true reflection of innate intelligence;[22] and they followed Jensen in relying on estimates of heritability, though the estimate they used was lower than Jensen's. Herrnstein and Murray (1994:105) stated "that the genetic component of IQ is unlikely to be smaller than 40 percent or higher than 80 percent" and adopted "a middling estimate of 60 percent heritability."

The Bell Curve contained eight chapters exploring the relationship of IQ to a number of social problems among *White* Americans. The authors presented the findings in a series of graphs showing the relationship of IQ and socioeconomic status (SES) to various social problems. For instance, they found that being in poverty was directly related both to a person's SES and IQ; but the relationship to IQ was stronger. More specifically, adults who grew up in poverty were themselves more likely to be in poverty than those who grew up in a more favorable SES; and, also, adults who were in a low "cognitive class" (had low IQs) were more likely to be in poverty than those who were in a high cognitive class; but, overall, IQ was a more important factor than SES in predicting which *White* group would be suffering most from various social problems.

Herrnstein and Murray's discussion of ethnic differences in IQ in their disputed Chapter 13 reviewed past findings on this subject and argued that the inequalities in IQ among ethnic groups were not due to bias in the tests or to differences in SES. Continuing the logic of the analyses of the earlier chapters, Chapter 14 presented the authors' findings on inequalities *among* Latinos, Whites, and Blacks in education, occupations, poverty, unemployment, single motherhood, welfare dependency, crime, and adherence to middle class values. The authors concluded that the higher prevalence of problem behaviors among some minorities may be traced in part to their lower average IQs and also to the conclusion that the lower-average IQs were due in part to genetic differences. We will highlight only four of the many issues raised in this phase of the controversy.

First, several of the book's critics focused on Herrnstein and Murray's misuse of statistics (see, e.g., Cole 1995; Kamin 1995; Suzuki 1995). Herrnstein and Murray showed in graph after graph that low IQ was more strongly correlated with undesirable social outcomes and behaviors than was SES. The authors made the "strong causal claim" (Gould 1994:146) that their findings showed "that intelligence itself, not just its correlation with socioeconomic status, is responsible for these group differences" (Herrnstein and Murray 1994:117);[23] yet, on the same page on which Herrnstein and Murray made this claim, they conceded that "cognitive ability accounts for only small to middling proportions of the variation among people." They acknowledged that the amount of variation explained by IQ is "usually less than 10 percent and often less than 5 percent." How can such weak connections be held to support their strong claim?

A *second* problem in the authors' handling of statistics was reported by Hauser (1995; see also Institute for Research on Poverty 1995). From the standpoint of social policy, as well as social theory, an extremely important question is "Can intelligence be raised?" Herrnstein and Murray (1994:389–416) recognized the importance of this question and devoted a separate chapter to it. They reviewed many of the efforts that have been made along this line, including nutritional approaches, formal schooling (including special school programs), preschool programs (such as Head Start), and adoption at birth from an unfavorable to a favorable family environment. Their summary conclusion was that "Taken together, the story of attempts to raise intelligence is one of high hopes, flamboyant claims, and disappointing results" (Herrnstein and Murray 1994:389). They went on to state that we should not expect any known environmental intervention, except perhaps adoption at birth, to affect intellectual ability.

In an earlier discussion, however, Herrnstein and Murray (1995:290–292) had reported that during the twenty years before 1990, the gap between the scores of Blacks and Whites on the National Assessment of Educational Progress had been reduced by an amount equal to two to three IQ points. Hauser (1995) went back to the original source from which Herrnstein and Murray had taken their data and found that Herrnstein and Murray had neglected to adjust the scores for differences in age (as they had done earlier in a similar calculation). When Hauser recalculated the scores with the proper adjustment for age, he concluded that Herrnstein and Murray's highest estimate of the amount of IQ change during the period was definitely too low and that their lowest estimate may have been less than half of the actual amount of change. Hauser (1995:152) noted wryly about his findings, that a change in the IQ gap of this size in a twenty-year period is "not bad" for a supposedly "immutable" quantity. He concludes that "we are quite capable of changing the academic achievement of American students on a large scale" and that *The Bell Curve* is a "flawed and destructive" work (Hauser 1995:153).

The *third* criticism of the book that we consider here is less clear cut and more debatable than the previous two; but it may be more important. Many outraged commentators argued that *The Bell Curve* was a cleverly written political brief presented in the guise of objective, dispassionate science. The authors used many sophisticated statistics, but their analysis was flawed. The entire work seemed to be aimed mainly at supporting the authors' attack on the federal government's immigration, education, welfare, and affirmative-action policies and programs.

Consider the way Herrnstein and Murray handled the frequent error, which we discussed earlier, of assuming that if IQ is substantially heritable *within* a population, then the average IQ difference *between* two populations also must be at least partially inherited. Herrnstein and Murray (1994:298) agreed emphatically that *all* of the differences between two populations may be due to environmental causes; nevertheless, they then argued strongly for an hereditarian interpretation. In the process, they highlighted the evidence favoring the genetic hypothesis while skipping very lightly over the evidence opposing it (Gould 1994:142). Although such a procedure may be acceptable in an openly political debate, it is a highly questionable tactic in a book whose authors claim they wish to shed the light of objective scholarship on topics that are "so sensitive that hardly anyone writes or talks about them in public" (Herrnstein and Murray 1994:xxi).[24]

Consider also the authors' discussion of Flynn's finding that IQ scores have risen by about fifteen points throughout the world during the last generation. They agreed that "the instability of test scores across generations should caution against taking the current ethnic differences as etched in stone" (Herrnstein and Murray 1994:309); yet the primary message of the book was that these differences *are* "etched in stone." They might well have given greater attention to the studies of geneticists and neurologists that cast doubt on the possibility of understanding group differences in intelligence without a much more advanced knowledge of the structure and development of the human brain and nervous system. For instance, there is evidence that the number of neural connections that are formed during a child's fetal and postnatal development are affected by various environmental factors (Holt 1995).[25] But, on the basis of nothing more than the evidence reported in their book, Herrnstein and Murray easily could have argued that we should *increase* our efforts to improve people's environments instead of insisting that "the available repertoire of social interventions" has failed to do the job. Considerations such as these strongly suggest that effective interventions to improve peoples' abilities, such as a good education for all preschool and school-age children, should be pursued aggressively.

Consider now a *fourth* issue raised by Herrnstein and Murray. We pointed out that the main assumptions and arguments underlying *The Bell Curve* are a contemporary version of the social Darwinism of the nineteenth century. At the time *The Bell Curve* was published, people from Latin America and Asia comprised the bulk of the third immigrant stream. So the book echoed the fears of the nativists of the nineteenth and early twentieth centuries that the rising tide of non-Nordic immigrants was intellectually inferior to the native population and would lower America's mental level. In a short section on immigration that was reminiscent of the work of the early advocates of intelligence testing and immigration restriction, Herrnstein and Murray (1994:359) raised anew the specter of racial deterioration. They estimated the IQ averages for different groups, as follows: 105 for East Asians; 100 for Whites; 91 for Pacific Islanders and Latinos; and 84 for Blacks. Their estimate of the overall average for third-stream immigrants was about 95. Based on these calculations, Herrnstein and Murray (1994:364) argued that the average IQ of Americans may be dropping. They recognized that in the past America has been very successful in attracting immigrants "who were brave, hard-working, imaginative, self-starting—and probably smart" (Herrnstein and Murray 1994:361); but then they advanced reasons for thinking that, overall, the contemporary period of immigration may be less successful than were the previous periods.

This line of reasoning was very prominent during the second immigrant stream. Recall that this period was rife with nativist, social Darwinist, and racist ideas. These elements combined with the findings of the mental-testing movement to prepare the way for large-scale immigration restriction in America. In the period immediately following World War I, all of the needed ideological and political forces coalesced in support of the Immigration Act of 1924. The passage of this law took place after decades of agitation in favor of immigration restriction. The first major step in this process occurred in 1882 with a law intended to reduce to near zero the immigration of Chinese people into America. We now examine briefly the major events that culminated in the 1924 act, beginning with the campaign to exclude the Chinese.

Immigration Restriction

The Chinese

Before the California gold rush, only a handful of Chinese had come to America. During the three decades following 1848, however, more than 228,000 Chinese arrived (see Table 5.1).[26] The majority of these immigrants came to California to assist with mining, building railroads, and other jobs requiring hard manual labor. As was true of most European immigrants, the Chinese who came to the United States were peasants driven

TABLE 5.1   Chinese Immigration to the United States, 1820–1994

Years	Number
1820–1850	46
1851–1860	41,397
1861–1870	64,301
1871–1880	123,201
1881–1890	61,711
1891–1900	14,799
1901–1910	20,605
1911–1920	21,278
1921–1930	29,907
1931–1940	4,928
1941–1950	16,709
1951–1960	9,657
1961–1970	34,764
1971–1980	124,326
1981–1990	346,747
1991–1994	170,191
Total	1,084,567

Source: U.S. Immigration and Naturalization Service, *1994 Statistical Yearbook,* 1996: 26–28.

out by changing patterns of landownership that increasingly concentrated wealth in the hands of a comparatively small ruling group. The peasants' situation was made even worse by the pressure western governments placed on the rulers of China to open their country to foreign trade (Lai 1980:218). As a consequence of these changes, approximately 2.5 million people left China for other parts of the world (Jiobu 1988:32). The Chinese who immigrated to the United States, therefore, were only a small part of this much more extensive emigration.

Most of the Chinese came to California, where their presence soon became the subject of political debate and public protest. White miners in many of the mining camps passed resolutions excluding the Chinese from the camps and, in some cases, launched physical attacks against them (Boswell 1986:356). In 1852, the governor of California recommended that some action be taken to stem the "tide of Asiatic immigration" (Daniels 1969:16). The action taken by many Whites during the next three decades was to harrass, expel, and sometimes slaughter hundreds of Chinese people—all of which went largely unpunished (tenBroek, Barnhart, and Matson 1954:15). For example, Chinese people were attacked or expelled in thirty-four communities in California, nine in Washington, and in many locations in Alaska, Colorado, Nevada, Oregon, and Wyoming (Tsai 1986:67). Very serious assaults occurred in Los Angeles, where nineteen Chinese were killed; Rock Springs, Wyoming, where twenty-eight Chinese were killed; and along the Snake River, where ten Chinese were killed (Crane and Larson [1940]1978:47; Locklear [1960]1978:244; Tsai 1986: 70–71). General expulsions of Chinese people occurred in Seattle and Tacoma, Washington, and Humboldt County, California; and millions of dollars in property were confiscated or destroyed (Karlin [1940] 1978 and [1954]1978; Lynwood [1961]1978).

In 1854, a former U.S. Commissioner to China expressed the fear that America faced an "inundation of oriental barbarism" in the form of Chinese "coolie" labor (Curran 1975:79).[27] Anti-coolie clubs were organized beginning in 1862—the same year in which Governor Leland Stanford argued that the Chinese immigrants represented "an inferior race" and would "exercise a deleterious influence upon the superior natives" (Curran 1975:81). Another important action in 1862 was that Congress authorized the construction of a transcontinental railroad. The building of the railroad required a large number of laborers to do hard and dangerous work for low wages. So the Central Pacific Company began to hire large numbers of Chinese immigrant workers. Uncounted numbers of these workers lost their lives in the process of building the railroad. Jiobu (1988:35) quoted the historian Alexander Saxton as saying in this regard that "No man who had any choice would have chosen to be a common laborer on the Central Pacific during the crossing of the High Sierra." When the transcontinental railroad was completed in 1869, thousands of men (most of whom were Chinese) were thrown out of work and into direct competition with native workers for other jobs.

Native workers and small businessmen considered the Chinese workers to be the "slave laborers" of big business and deeply resented what they considered to be unfair competition (Boswell 1986:357–358; Hirschman and Wong 1986:5). This resentment led to the formation of a Workingman's Party that campaigned with the slogan "The Chinese Must Go!" (McWilliams 1949:174). A statement by this party in 1877 claimed that "white men, and women, and boys, and girls . . . cannot compete with the single Chinese coolie in the labor market" and, further, that "none but a degraded coward and slave would make the effort" (Kitano and Daniels 1988:22–23). The clamor for action, especially in California, became so strong that by 1880 both major political parties came out against permitting the Chinese to come to America to work, adding impetus to a trend toward immigration restriction.

Eighteen eighty-two was a watershed year in American immigration history. The number of immigrants reaching the United States in that year exceeded all previous years. Also in 1882, Congress enacted a comprehensive immigration law that prohibited the admission of convicts, lunatics, idiots, and people who were deemed likely to become public charges (Abrams 1984:108). Of special relevance to us here is that Congress voted in the Chinese Exclusion Act of 1882 to suspend for ten years the entrance of workers from this specific nation and also to declare them to be ineligible to become citizens of the United States. The previous exclusions of immigrants had been based on the personal characteristics of different individuals, but now a new element had gained official recognition. For the first time, American policy endorsed the idea that an entire group of people might be undesirable as immigrants and unfit for citizenship because of their race or nationality! As Reimers (1985:4) expressed it, "With the passage of this act the Chinese became the first and only nationality to be barred by name."

The Chinese Exclusion Act sharply reduced the number of Chinese coming into the United States.[28] It did not, however, stop discrimination and violence against those who already were here. Throughout the 1880s, the Chinese continued to be the objects of physical assaults, evictions, and other forms of harrassment. The political pressure to impose even greater restrictions on them was maintained. Within the next two decades, the rights of the Chinese in this country were curtailed, and the laws preventing the entrance of Chinese laborers into the United States and its possessions were extended in 1892 and were made "permanent" in 1902 (Lai 1980:221). Although the Chinese were able to gain some protection in the following years through court cases, they still were subject to various forms of discrimination. In many communities they were segregated in schools, refused service in public places, and barred from residence in certain towns. In some states, they were prohibited from marrying Whites (Lai 1980:223). Not until 1943, when China and the United States were allies in World War II, was the Chinese Exclusion Act repealed.

When exclusion went into effect, Chinese men outnumbered Chinese women in the United States by more than 200 to 1 (Chow 1996:113). This numerical imbalance between the sexes declined very slowly throughout the years of exclusion and still was higher than 2 to 1 when exclusion ended more than six decades later. These adverse sex ratios slowed family formation among the Chinese in America (Hing 1993:54); nevertheless, those who were able to find spouses married, had children, and commenced the work of establishing Chinese American institutions. They also started numerous small enterprises, such as garment factories, laundries, and restaurants that required little capital and could be maintained by hard work, long hours, low wages, and low profit margins (Lai 1980:224). Many Chinese women combined working at home and raising a family with outside employment—often as domestic servants (Chow 1996:116).

After the Chinese Exclusion Act was repealed in 1943, China was given a token immigration quota of 105 admissions per year (Lai 1980:226). Chinese immigrants and legal residents now were permitted to become American citizens. By that time, however, large numbers of Chinese people were American-born descendants of the nineteenth-century Chinese and already were citizens who had settled in all parts of the country. The period of the most rapid growth of the Chinese population in the United States was yet to come, however, as we will discuss in relation to the third immigrant stream in Chapter 14.

The Immigration Act of 1924

The second great immigrant stream reached its peak in the decade before World War I, though it continued at a high level during the 1911–1920 period (see Table 4.1). Resentment of immigrants by Americans (many of whom were themselves recent arrivals)[29] led to an almost continuous agitation to push Congress into passing laws that would restrict, or halt entirely, the immigration of the members of various national groups.

By 1917, pressures from those who feared racial deterioration and the inundation of American institutions by "hordes" of European and Asian immigrants had reached a high level. In that year the federal government passed an immigration act that barred alcoholics, stowaways, vagrants, and people who had had an attack of insanity (Cafferty, Chiswick, Greeley, and Sullivan 1984:44). This law also defined an "Asiatic barred zone" that expanded the list of Asian peoples to include not only Chinese and Japanese but also people from all other Asian countries except the Philippines (Hing 1993:32–33).[30] The most controversial portion of the Immigration Act of 1917, however, was the requirement that all immigrants must pass a literacy test before entering the country. President Woodrow Wilson vetoed the bill stating that it embodied "a radical departure from the tradition . . . of this country," but his veto was overturned by Congress (Jones 1975:228).

The Immigration Act of 1917 did little to reduce the flow of immigration. In 1921, the Emergency Quota Act (the Johnson Act) for the first time introduced a quantitative formula placing a general limitation on the number of immigrants who could be admitted in a single year (approximately 350,000); consequently, this act represented an historic departure from the open-door policy (Abrams 1980:27). The basic strategy of the law was to increase the *proportion* of all admittees who would be from the European countries that contributed most heavily to the colonial and first immigrant streams, while simultaneously decreasing the total number of legal immigrants. This dual result was obtained, moreover, without legislating specifically against particular nationalities. To produce this diplomatically tricky outcome, the act restricted immigration from Europe, Africa, the Near East, Australia, and New Zealand to 3 percent of the number of foreign-born members of each nationality counted in the United States census of 1910. Since a larger number of foreign-born immigrants in 1910 were from the countries of northern and western Europe than from any of the other places of origin, this legislation favored the countries of the colonial and first immigrant streams. By this time the nineteenth-century immigrants from Ireland, Germany, the United Kingdom, Canada,

Scandinavia, France, and the other European countries were sufficiently assimilated into the dominant group (at least culturally) that additional people of those ethnicities were not considered a threat to the dominant group.

At this point, immigration from other countries of the Western Hemisphere was not of great concern; so no quotas were set for these nations. Paradoxically, despite its general focus on groups, the new law established a preference system that permitted certain people to enter the United States on a nonquota basis (e.g., artists, lecturers, singers, nurses, ministers, and professors; U.S. Immigration and Naturalization Service 1996: A.1–6). The application of the quantitative formula of the 1921 law to the calculation of quotas had a dramatic effect on the size and sources of American immigration. Previously, the annual immigration from all nations averaged more than 850,000 people, around 79 percent of whom came from countries of the second immigrant stream; after the 1921 act, annual immigration was reduced to around 355,000, about 44 percent of whom came from countries of the second stream. Still, these changes did not satisfy the strongest advocates of immigration restriction; consequently, the restrictionists continued to press for a stricter law. The Immigration Act of 1924 (the Johnson-Reid Act) was the result.

This law continued the quota strategy of the act of 1921 but altered it in four main ways. First, it changed the "base" year initially from 1910 to 1890; second, the annual quota for all countries was set at 165,000 for the period 1924–1929; third, beginning in 1929, the annual quota for all countries was lowered to 150,000; and fourth, beginning in 1929 (using 1920 as the base year), the national-origins principle was to be used in the calculation of the annual quota of each country. For instance, if 30 percent of the Americans in 1920 were of English origin, then the annual quota for English immigrants would have been 45,000 (i.e., 30 percent of 150,000). Since in both 1890 and 1920 most Americans either were from Ireland, Germany, the United Kingdom, Canada, France, and Scandinavia, or were descended from people from those countries, the 1924 law led to a still higher proportion of admissions for the people of the countries of the colonial and first streams than had the 1921 law (Cafferty, Chiswick, Greeley, and Sullivan 1984:53). In short, with the quota formulas that were adopted, the limits of overall immigration were lowered while the proportions set for the more "desirable" immigrants were increased, as was intended. The Immigration Act of 1924 resulted in a dramatic change in America's historic "open door" policy by implementing restrictions that permitted close control over immigration.

There was one other especially significant aspect of the Immigration Act of 1924 that we return to in Chapter 7. The act completely cut off immigration from Japan. Everything considered, the golden door was left only slightly ajar. Table 5.2 presents a summary of some of the most important immigration legislation passed from the time of the first federal law until 1990.

To recapitulate, nativist, and social Darwinist thought flourished during the last third of the nineteenth century and the first quarter of the twentieth. These currents of thought were greatly strengthened by the findings and interpretations of IQ researchers, leading in the 1920s to laws that sharply reduced the acceptance of immigrants into America. The xenophobia of nativists was strengthened and apparently justified by the

TABLE 5.2   A Chronology of Selected Federal Immigration Laws, 1875–1990

Year	Law	Major Provisions
1875	Immigration Act	Barred "undesirables."
1882	Chinese Exclusion Act	Suspended immigration of Chinese workers; declared the Chinese ineligible for citizenship. (The suspension of immigration became "permanent" in 1902.)
1917	Immigration Act	Required immigrants to take a literacy test. Created an Asian barred zone.
1921	Immigration Act (Johnson Act)	Set a quota of 3% of the number of foreign-born of each nationality counted in the census of 1910.
1924	Immigration Act (Johnson-Reid Act)	Reduced quota to 2% of the number of foreign-born of each nationality counted in 1890 census; set total at 165,000; created "national origins" approach; excluded the Japanese.
1929	Implementation of "national-origins" provisions of 1924	Replaced 2% quota with the percent of people of each nationality in 1920; set total at 150,000
1943	Repeal of the Chinese Exclusion Act	Gave the Chinese a quota under the "national origins" provision.
	Braceros Act	Permitted Mexican laborers to enter the U.S. on a temporary basis.
1948	Displaced Persons Act	Permitted "nonquota" entrance of refugees from Europe.
1952	Immigration and Nationality Act (INA) (McCarran-Walter Act)	Continued quota principle; gave Japan a quota; introduced special preference categories; created parole power for the president.
1953	Refugee Relief Act	Permitted 189,000 nonquota refugee admissions.
1965	Amendments to the INA (Hart-Cellar Act)	National-origins quota principle abolished; annual ceiling raised to 290,000; limit of 120,000 set on the Western Hemisphere; set limit of 20,000 for each country of the Eastern Hemisphere; created seven–tiered preference system.
1976	Western Hemisphere Act	Set limit of 20,000 for each country of the Western Hemisphere.
1980	Refugee Act	Regulated refugee policy; established for first time grants of asylum under U.N. criteria.
1986	Immigration Reform and Control Act (IRCA) (Simpson-Rodino Act)	Provided legalization procedures, employer sanctions, and rules for foreign agricultural workers.
1990	Immigration Act	Raised annual ceiling to 700,000; revised naturalization requirements and enforcement procedures.

doctrines of scientific racism. The rise of IQ testing and the early analyses of the Army's test data by scholars such as C. C. Brigham joined with the charges of nativists to create the appearance that the immigrants of the colonial and first immigrant streams were naturally superior in intellectual capacities to the immigrants of the second immigrant stream and to African Americans. The IQ test results fanned the natives' fears concerning racial deterioration and helped to prepare the way for the restrictive immigration laws of 1921 and 1924. These laws shifted America's policy away from excluding only individuals who were considered undesirable to a policy of restricting admissions on the basis of racial or ethnic group identity. Although the Chinese had been excluded earlier, until after World War I the idea of excluding immigrants on the basis of their *group membership* rather than their *individual qualifications* had not been extended to any other groups (Ware 1937:592).

The restrictive legislation of the 1920s was followed by the Great Depression of the 1930s and World War II in the 1940s. The combined effects of these events produced the lowest rates of emigration to America on record. Numerous changes in American immigration law since then have been based on assumptions that are more nearly consistent with the ideals and traditions of eighteenth- and early nineteenth-century America and run counter to those embodied in the 1921 and 1924 acts. For example, the various acts passed since World War II to assist refugees reaffirmed America's commitment to aid the human beings who are displaced through war and oppression; and the 1965 amendments to the Immigration and Nationality Act of 1952 abandoned the nativist and racist principles embraced by the 1921 and 1924 acts. Individual rather than group characteristics once again became paramount.

Nevertheless, the continued rapid rise of the world's population coupled with increasing refugee and labor migrations have made a return to the open door policy unattractive; so numerous laws have been enacted since World War II to continue to regulate and limit immigration and naturalization (see Table 5.2). Although the influence of nativist and racist ideas on immigration laws waned after 1924, these influences still exist in America and appear to have increased during the 1980s and 1990s. The decisive role played by the results of IQ tests in the framing of immigration policies after World War I so far has not been resumed; but the IQ controversy again erupted with the appearance of *The Bell Curve*, which was published during the contemporary period of increasing nativism and xenophobia. We return to some of these issues in Flashpoint 3 in Chapter 14.

Chapters 2 through 5 have shown that the members of the dominant Anglo American group in the United States have exhibited strong views concerning the desirability of various groups of "outsiders" and that these views have been defended in economic, political, cultural, and racial terms. We have seen, too, that these views have been accompanied by different types and degrees of physical, social, and legal reactions. In all of the circumstances we have considered, greater or lesser degrees of conflict have been present. In some cases the conflicts were relatively mild and of short duration, whereas in other cases they were severe and prolonged.

What underlying factors have guided these patterns of likes and dislikes, acceptances and rejections? This question has intrigued students of racial and ethnic relations since the early years of the twentieth century and indeed was the central focus of inquiry among students of racial and ethnic relations in America until the 1960s. Two main assumptions guided research during this earlier period. The first assumption was that the discriminatory behavior of the dominant group should be the principal object of analysis; and the second assumption was that the key to understanding the levels of discrimination among both dominant-group and subordinate-group members was an understanding of their levels of prejudice. Work along these lines became, in Metzger's (1971:637) words, "a kind of official orthodoxy" in the field of racial and ethnic relations. The main theoretical arguments and research are summarized and discussed in Chapter 6.

Key Ideas

1. Each of the three great immigrant streams has aroused the fears of Americans concerning such issues as competition for jobs, possible disloyalty, and the effects of foreign "radicalism." Increasing fear has been accompanied by increases in hostile actions directed toward immigrants, including demands that immigration be restricted.

2. The shift from the first to the second great immigrant stream brought with it a new concern for physical differences between natives and foreigners. This concern was heightened during the latter decades of the nineteenth century by developments in several fields of scholarly research that resulted in scientific racism.

3. In addition to the rise of scientific racism, the conviction grew that the characteristic called "intelligence" basically determines the superiority of one race to another.

4. The studies of Francis Galton initiated a movement to develop tests to measure innate intellectual ability. The most successful tests created for this purpose were paper-and-pencil tests. They enabled testers to calculate a single score called the intelligence quotient (IQ) on each individual and to compare the scores of different individuals and the average scores of groups.

5. The U.S. Army conducted a massive study of intelligence test scores among its recruits during World War I. When the average IQ scores of the members of different ethnic groups were calculated, White Americans of colonial and first-stream immigrant ancestry ranked higher on average than the groups comprising the second immigrant stream; and the average of Whites was higher than for non-Whites. These findings seemed to confirm the ideas of scientific racism.

6. The efforts to define and measure human intelligence have raised many questions. Many scholars vigorously deny that a single mental quality that may be called general intelligence exists or that intelligence can be arrayed hierarchically in terms of single scores. Even when IQ scores are accepted as having some well-defined meaning, there are many objections to the idea that the scores represent an inborn quality. Environmental as well as biological factors are known to affect people's performances on tests, and there has been no conclusive demonstration of the role played by biological factors. Moreover, even if accurate estimates of the heritability of intelligence *within* populations were available, they would afford no evidence concerning the roles of hereditary or environmental factors in creating average intellectual differences *between* populations.

7. The work of Jensen in 1969 and of Herrnstein and Murray in 1994 seemed to be based on new genetic and statistical knowledge. The underlying ideas put forward by hereditarians during these two phases of the IQ debate, however, were still those introduced by Galton in the nineteenth century and Spearman in the first decade of the twentieth. The debate produced no compelling evidence that human beings possess something that may be called general intelligence, that such a factor is determined primarily by biological inheritance, or that intelligence is immutable.

8. The United States began to move away from the open door policy in 1882. Certain individuals were ruled to be undesirable; and, through the passage of the Chinese Exclusion Act, American policy endorsed for the first time the principle that an entire group of people might be unfit for admission or citizenship because of their race or ethnicity .

9. The IQ studies conducted during the period from 1904 to 1924, including the U.S. Army's massive IQ testing program during World War I, provided an important underpinning for the quota laws to restrict immigration that were enacted in 1921 and 1924. These immigration acts were designed to restrict admissions in a way that favored the countries that were most heavily represented in the colonial and first immigrant streams. The application of quotas, based first on the number of foreign-born residents of the United States and then on the national-origins principle, achieved the desired results.

Key Terms

environmentalism   The belief that social differences arise mainly because of different environmental circumstances.

estimates of heritability   Estimates of the extent to which various individual traits are biologically inherited.

eugenics   The study and use of techniques that are intended to strengthen populations genetically.

hereditarianism   The belief that the social differences among groups arise mainly because of genetically inherited differences.

nativism   Actions and policies based on the hostility of natives toward foreigners.

scientific racism   A set of beliefs that includes (1) the belief that racial and ethnic groups form a natural hierarchy of superiors and inferiors; (2) the belief that the White race is superior to the non-White races; and (3) the belief that the "Nordic" segment of the White race is superior even to its other segments.

social Darwinism   The view that groups become socially dominant because they have been more successful than their competitors in the struggle to survive and, therefore, are biologically the "fittest."

stratification system   A hierarchy of social strata reflecting the distribution of society's rewards (e.g., power, wealth, property) to various people.

vertical social class mobility   The upward or downward movement of individuals from one social class to another.

xenophobia   Fear of foreigners.

Notes

1. Alarm was expressed over the "Irish Papists" in 1728 (Adamic 1944:36).

2. The idea behind the Binet-Simon scale is that a child has normal intelligence or an appropriate mental age if he or she can answer questions that most children of the same chronological age also can answer.

3. Among Binet's principles for interpreting the tests was that the scores do not define anything innate or permanent.

4. A child with a "mental age" of 62 months and a chronological age of 62 months has a quotient of 1.00 (62/62). Multiplying by 100 yields an IQ score of 100.

5. The alpha test was intended to measure such things as the *ability* to take oral directions and solve arithmetical problems, but also included questions that depended on a person's knowledge (e.g., "The author of *The Raven* is: Stevenson, Kipling, Hawthorne, Poe?"). The beta test included tasks such as visualizing ac-

curately the number of cubes in a picture (Yerkes 1921:163, 227).

6. This list has continued to be refined and extended. Blau (1981), for example, traced the combined effects on children's IQ scores of more than a dozen additional factors and found that factors reflecting social differences account for between 40 and 70 percent of the difference between the IQ averages of Black and White children.

7. In studies of the IQ scores of Black children who had lived in New York and Philadelphia for different lengths of time, Klineberg (1935) and Lee (1951) showed that the longer the children had lived in the North, the better their average scores became.

8. This interpretation was strengthened by the results of a worldwide study of population genetics (Cavalli-Sforza, Menozzi, and Piazza 1994). The study confirmed the environmentalist assumption that at the genetic level, and

despite the many visible differences in physical traits, all socially recognized human races are remarkably alike and that there is no scientific basis for saying that one race is genetically superior to another.

9. A correlation's coefficient may range between a perfect positive (or direct) relationship of +1.00 and zero or between a perfect negative (or inverse) relationship of −1.00 and zero. The larger the coefficient is in either direction, the stronger is the relationship.

10. Spearman called the calculated value of general intelligence "g" (Gould 1981:256–272).

11. Spearman developed the "principal components" method of factor analysis to analyze the correlations among mental test scores. Our simplified account rests, here and elsewhere, on S. J. Gould's (1981; 1994) excellent discussions of these issues.

12. Thurstone's method is called "rotation to simple structure." This example is presented by S. J. Gould (1981:254–255, 300). Thurstone generally identified seven primary mental abilities involving verbal comprehension, word fluency, computational skill, spatial visualization, associative memory, perceptual speed, and reasoning (Gould 1981:302).

13. Although Thurstone was not an environmentalist, he demonstrated nevertheless that factor analysis does not prove the existence of general intelligence (Gould 1981:306–307).

14. Jensen (1969:78) acknowledged that "the full range of human talents is represented in all the major races of man" and that "it is unjust to allow . . . an individual's racial or social background to affect the treatment accorded him."

15. See, for example, Eckberg (1979:101), Ehrlich and Feldman (1977:138), and Taylor (1980:10–74).

16. Nearly all of the estimates were based on White samples.

17. The famous sociologist Charles Horton Cooley offered a fine early example to illustrate this point: If a person sowed mixed grain while walking straight across a field comprised of different kinds of soil, then all the seeds would flourish in some soils, a few would flourish in some soils, and in some places nothing would grow (Cooley [1897]1995:419).

18. Many people concluded that psychologists should stop trying to measure mental abilities at all on the grounds that the tests are biased and are used in ways that have deleterious consequences for minority children, such as "tracking" them into special classes and schools (Thernstrom 1992:134).

19. The book's title refers to the bell-shaped curve that is produced when a mathematical equation, called a "normal distribution," is displayed graphically. IQ tests are designed to produce test score results that approximate a normal distribution.

20. It is a rehash of "the tenets of social Darwinism" (Gould 1994:139).

21. The data set was the National Longitudinal Survey of Youth (NLSY). They used the technique of regression analysis, which is a standard way of examining the relationship of one variable to another while "holding other variables constant."

22. They acknowledged that there are several theories of intelligence, but they also made the highly dubious claim that the evidence favoring "a general factor of cognitive ability" is "beyond significant technical dispute" (Herrnstein and Murray 1994:13–19, 22).

23. Kamin (1995:90) observed that "The confusion between correlation and causation permeates the largest section" of the book.

24. Easterbrook (1995:39) states that "The most disquieting aspect of *The Bell Curve* is its insistence on phrasing as detached data analysis what is in truth an ideological argument about social policy."

25. Several critics noted that "The people who say intelligence is genetic are the ones with no training in genetics" (Evan Balaban, quoted by Easterbrook 1995:37). Howard Gardner (1995:61), a proponent of multiple intelligence, said that "the science in the book . . . has

now been supplanted by the development of the cognitive sciences and neurosciences."

26. By 1990, the U.S. population of Chinese ancestry had crossed the 1.5 million mark (U.S. Bureau of the Census 1995:53).

27. "Coolies" were workers who were paid only a subsistence wage and who frequently were involuntary or indentured immigrants.

28. Merchants and students still were permitted to enter.

29. Restrictionists "are often children of immigrants who wear their second-generation patriotism outwardly and aggressively" (Portes and Rumbaut 1990:26).

30. Filipinos were exempted because the Philippine Islands were an American colony, and Filipinos were legally American nationals.

Prejudice and Discrimination

Prejudice may arise from many sources, including the views of family or peers, or it may come from strong identification with a particular group.

*. . . we must sound the inside and see what springs
set us in motion.*
—M. E. de Montaigne

Men begin with acts, not with thoughts.
—William Graham Sumner

Since the formation of the dominant Anglo American group, its members have to some extent resented, downgraded, and harassed the members of all foreign groups. We have seen, however, that people from countries of the first immigrant stream generally have been more acceptable to the Anglo Americans than those from countries of the second immigrant stream. And regardless of their place of origin, Whites have been more acceptable than non-Whites. Our analysis has shown, therefore, that the historical sequence of intergroup contacts in America created a particular pattern of social "layers" among America's ethnic groups, an **ethnic stratification system,** in which the groups differed in power and prestige. Although the members of the dominant group have rated all other groups as "beneath" them socially and have tried to keep each group "in its place," they have displayed greater hostility toward some groups than others. Why?

Suppose a White employer has the choice of hiring a White person or a Black person of equal qualifications and that the White person is chosen. Suppose further that the employer is overheard to say, "Most Black employees are unreliable, and I don't like that." In addition to knowing about the employer's action in choosing the White candidate for the job, we now know something about what he or she believes and feels. Is the employer prejudiced? Has he or she discriminated? Is the person a racist?

To answer such questions, we need more information. For instance, although there is widespread agreement that the term **prejudice** refers to an attitude, some observers argue that an attitude concerning a person or group should be considered a prejudice only if it is a judgment that is not based on fact or experience. This presumably is what Ambrose Bierce had in mind when he defined prejudice as "a vagrant opinion without visible means of support." Similarly, most people agree that the term **discrimination** refers to an overt action, but it is used by some to refer only to actions that spring from prejudice. And, although these terms generally connote an unfavorable attitude or action, they may be used to refer to attitudes and actions that are favorable to a particular person or group. In short, there are no precise or universally accepted definitions of prejudice and discrimination. For our purposes, prejudice is an *unfavorable attitude* toward people because they are members of a particular racial or ethnic group, whereas discrimination is an *unfavorable action* toward people because they are members of a particular racial or ethnic group. Both prejudice and discrimination may vary by degrees and, therefore, may range from extremely high to extremely low levels.

With these definitions in mind, let us now consider the meaning of the term **racism.** The term *racism* today, in contrast to scientific racism, usually refers to an unfavorable attitude, and perhaps an unfavorable action, toward people who are members of particular racial or ethnic groups; it may or may not specify the type of relationship that exists between unfavorable attitudes and actions; and the idea of group ranking may be more or less salient. Clearly, this meaning of racism is more complicated and flexible than are the meanings we have given to prejudice and discrimination[1] and, as Hacker (1992:19) stated, "goes beyond prejudice and discrimination." In many contemporary discussions of racism one must infer from the context how the concept is being used. In this form, the concept has the advantage of drawing attention to the complex web of interconnections between the beliefs, attitudes, and actions of individuals, on the one hand, and the social and historical contexts within which these elements emerged, on the other. It reminds us that the reality of ethnic stratification is located in social systems, as well as in the attitudes and actions of individuals. Nevertheless, for many analytical purposes it is useful to focus specifically on prejudice and discrimination, on their relationship to one another, and on their many sources. That is the chief goal of the present discussion.

Consider again the hypothetical situation of the White and Black job applicants. The possibility was raised in this example that the White employer rejected the Black applicant because the employer was prejudiced. This idea may be diagrammed as shown in Figure 6.1.

This way of viewing the relationship of prejudice to discrimination is very common. And it is easy to see why. Much of our everyday experience seems to confirm the idea that peoples' actions are an indication of the way they think and feel about things. From this point of view, a person *first* has an attitude about something, and *then* he or she acts as a result of that attitude; so if a person harbors a prejudice we may assume (perhaps mistakenly) that the person may engage in discrimination. Conversely, if we are aware that a person has performed an act of discrimination, we may assume (again, perhaps mistakenly) that the person is prejudiced. We may describe either of these situations as examples of racism if, for some reason, the relationship of prejudice to discrimination is not at issue.

Where does the reasoning represented in Figure 6.1 lead? Let us begin with the basic principles that generally are considered to define the ideals that *ought* to guide the thought and actions of Americans. Our leaders frequently assert that Americans believe in freedom, equality, and justice for *all*. They remind us that these cherished ideals are set forth in precious documents such as the Declaration of Independence, the Preamble to the Constitution, the Bill of Rights, and the Gettysburg Address. We are expected to

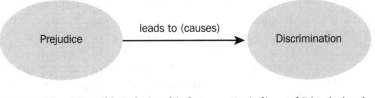

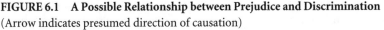

FIGURE 6.1   A Possible Relationship between Prejudice and Discrimination
(Arrow indicates presumed direction of causation)

learn and accept that, as expressed by President Franklin D. Roosevelt, "A good American is one who is loyal to this country and to our creed of liberty and democracy" (Schlesinger 1992:37). Roosevelt used the word "creed"—with its somewhat religious overtones—to signify that *believing* in certain "high" principles, such as liberty, democracy, and justice, is required of true Americans.

Myrdal ([1944]1964:3–4, 209) placed this set of beliefs, which he called the **American Creed,** at the center of *An American Dilemma*—his famous and influential analysis of American racial problems. Myrdal stated that this creed includes the belief that each individual should have equal access to justice and opportunity; that the principle of achievement (introduced in Chapter 1) should be the basis for judging individuals; and, consequently, that discrimination on the basis of ascribed characteristics (such as race, ethnicity, sex, and color) is unfair. The American Creed holds that in a democratic society, discrimination has no place and should be eradicated. But how is this to be done? The logic of Figure 6.1 indicates that to eradicate discrimination, we must first attempt to eliminate prejudice.

Now we consider two difficult questions. First, "How are people's prejudices to be altered?" Presumably, the answer depends primarily on our ability to discover and affect the sources of prejudice. Many different sources of prejudice have been proposed; but prominent among these are the process of learning one's culture (at home, at school, and among peers), the human tendency to identify strongly with particular human groups, and the process of psychological development (involving frustration, anxiety, personality "needs," and so on). This situation may be diagrammed as shown in Figure 6.2.

The relative importance of the different sources of prejudice shown in Figure 6.2 has been the subject of a great deal of research. Some studies emphasize only one of the sources, whereas others stress the importance of viewing them together. And here we arrive at the second of the two difficult questions: "Is discrimination caused entirely, or even mainly, by prejudice?"

We will attempt to examine only a few of the many issues raised by these two questions. We begin at the beginning with the proposed answers to the first question.

Theories of Prejudice

Cultural Transmission Theories of Prejudice

One important type of theory holds that children learn prejudice in much the same way they learn to speak a particular language, dress in a given manner, or use certain eating utensils. From this viewpoint, the building blocks of prejudice are contained within the society's culture and are transmitted to children in a natural way as they are exposed to the culture in the home and community. Two aspects of a culture are particularly closely related to the extent and kind of prejudice found in a given society. The first aspect has to do with the shared beliefs that the members of one group have about the members of the other groups in the society; the second has to do with a culture's prescriptions

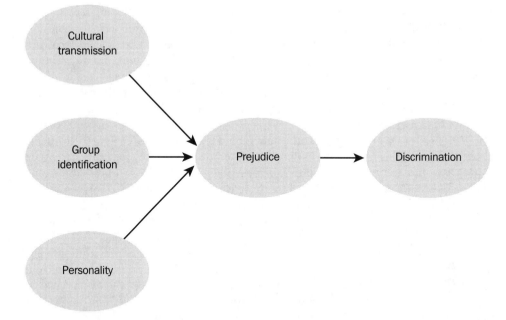

FIGURE 6.2   Major Direct Causes of Prejudice and Indirect Causes of Discrimination
(Arrows indicate presumed direction of causation)

concerning the degrees of intimacy or "nearness" that one group's members should permit or desire from any other group's members.

To illustrate the first point, consider the kind of "information" children are likely to receive regarding various other ethnic groups in America. They are likely to learn—by instruction and by accident—that the members of different groups possess a cluster of distinctive traits including, for instance, such things as that the Germans are hardworking, the Mexicans are lazy, the Italians are artistic, the Irish are quick-tempered, the Jews are mercenary, and the French are amorous. Even the children of quite "liberal" parents are likely to acquire such ideas as they come into contact with a wider circle of people in the neighborhood and school. The extent to which these shared beliefs exist within a society's culture and are transmitted more or less intact from one generation to the next has stimulated a large number of studies of **stereotypes.**

Stereotypes.   As is true of the term *prejudice,* stereotypes have been defined in a number of ways. For example, stereotypes have been defined as "pictures in our heads" (Lippmann 1922:16); "an exaggerated belief associated with a category" (Allport 1958: 187); "character profiles attributed to in-groups and out-groups" (Brown 1986:534); and "cognitive categories people use when thinking about groups" (Jussim, Nelson, Manis, and Soffin 1995:228).

Each of these definitions may be applied beyond the study of racial and ethnic relations. Also, even though none of the definitions specifies the direction of stereotypes, in practice people use the term primarily to call attention to beliefs that present an out-group in an uncomplimentary way. Furthermore, most people use the term to signify, in agreement with Allport, an exaggerated or false belief. Indeed, the statement "that is a stereotype" usually means "that is a false generalization."[2] For our purposes a stereotype is a shared, but not scientifically validated, belief concerning the characteristics of the members of different racial or ethnic groups as compared to some reference group. This definition recognizes as stereotypes the favorable images that in-groups ordinarily cherish about themselves; however, our main interest centers on the derogatory images that the members of in-groups frequently share about out-groups as compared to themselves or some other group. We assume that the presence of a derogatory stereotype within a culture indicates that those who subscribe to it harbor prejudices concerning the members of a given group. And since those who accept negative stereotypes appear to have a tendency to attribute any nonstereotypical behavior of out-groups to luck or favorable circumstances (and thus to "explain away" disconfirming evidence), we assume further that stereotypes assist to sustain prejudices (Hewstone 1989:37).

The major research tradition concerning the content of racial and ethnic stereotypes was started by Katz and Braly (1933) at Princeton. These researchers compiled a list of adjectives that may be used to describe the traits of members of a given racial or ethnic group and asked the students in the study to select five words from the list that they thought to be the most typical of each group. To illustrate their method, if each participant in a study were to describe Germans as hardworking, intelligent, progressive, practical, and brave, then these five traits would comprise the stereotype of Germans.[3] Katz and Braly found that more than a third of the students believed that Germans were stolid, Italians were passionate, English were intelligent, Jews were mercenary, Americans were industrious, Blacks were lazy, Irish were pugnacious, Chinese were superstitious, Japanese were intelligent, and Turks were cruel. The researchers contended that these high levels of agreement cannot be understood as a reflection of the actual experiences of the study participants and must, therefore, represent the influence of beliefs that exist within the culture and are widely shared.

Other studies of stereotypes conducted since 1933 have revealed that stereotypes are affected to some extent by contemporary events.[4] For example, public opinion polls in 1942 and 1966 showing that the proportion of the respondents who described the Germans as warlike and the Japanese as sly fell from 67 percent and 63 percent in 1942, respectively, to 16 percent and 19 percent in 1966 (Ehrlich 1973:30). Subsequent studies also have shown significant changes in the stereotype of Blacks held by White university students. For example, Katz and Braly (1933) found that 84 percent of the White students listed "superstitious" as the leading trait of Blacks. This proportion had declined to 41 percent by 1950 (Gilbert 1951) and by 1967 this trait was no longer a part of the stereotype of Black Americans (Karlins, Coffman, and Walters 1969). In 1993, Wood and Chesser (1994:20) found that the main trait attributed to Blacks by the White university students in their study was "loud." They also found that of the traits listed for Blacks by Katz and Braly in 1933 (superstitious, lazy, happy-go-lucky, ignorant, and musical), only "lazy" remained in 1993; and the proportion of students listing that trait had declined sharply from 75 percent to 25 percent (Wood and Chesser 1994:20). Despite these gains, however, Blacks still were stereotyped negatively more frequently than

Whites, Hispanics, and Asians. In a survey of Los Angeles County, for instance, Bobo (1996:895) found that on presumed traits, such as intelligence, willingness to receive welfare, and congeniality, Whites received the most favorable ratings, Blacks received the most unfavorable ratings, and Hispanics and Asians were intermediate.

Contemporary events may affect not only the traits that are included in a stereotype but also the candor of a study's participants. Both Gilbert (1951) and Karlins, Coffman, and Walters (1969) found that students were more resistant than previously to carrying out the instructions of the study. By then, criticisms of stereotyping were widely known and the students "sensed that *characterizing* ethnic groups at all would be interpreted as an ignorant and immoral thing to do" (Brown 1986:591). In short, the students' decreasing willingness to stereotype suggests that they may have wished to present themselves in a favorable light to the researchers, as well as to themselves (Dovidio and Gaertner 1993:188). This kind of distortion, known as **social desirability bias,** occurs when people give answers they believe they are expected to give rather than their true opinions (Lobel 1988:30).[5]

The media of communication, as well as the home and neighborhood, also may transmit stereotypes (Ehrlich 1973:32). An early study of popular fiction by Berelson and Salter (1946) found that Blacks and Jews were greatly underrepresented among the fictional characters and were usually presented in stereotyped ways. Studies of the materials presented in movies, in magazines, on television, and in school textbooks led to similar findings. For example, the ideal American was presented in some elementary school textbooks as a White, Protestant, of northern European background (Elson 1964). On the basis of the many studies that have been conducted, it seems safe to conclude that stereotypes are indeed an integral part of American culture and that people learn them as an ordinary consequence of associating with other members of the society.

Social Distance.   A related, but distinct, research tradition also offers compelling evidence that the very process of learning American culture teaches an individual specific prejudices. As people grow up in America, they learn more than that various racial and ethnic groups are thought to be intelligent, ambitious, dull, slovenly, and so on. They also learn that some of these traits are preferable to others and that, therefore, it is more desirable to associate with the members of some groups than others. People learn to desire social closeness to the members of some groups and **social distance** from the members of others.

The concept of social distance was presented by Simmel ([1908] 1950) and developed further by Park (1924), but the main research technique for the study of social distance was introduced by Bogardus (1933). Bogardus's method consisted of asking people to consider a list of different kinds of social contacts they would be willing to permit with the members of various racial and ethnic groups. The types of social contacts shown in the list represent various points running from a high willingness to permit social contact (e.g., "Would admit to close kinship by marriage") to, at the other extreme, a low willingness to permit social contact (e.g., "Would exclude from my country").[6] Social distance studies have shown that people who differed widely in such things as occupation, education, and geographical location were nonetheless similar in regard to the pattern of social distance they wished to seek between themselves and the members of various racial and ethnic groups.

The pattern discovered by Bogardus should not surprise the student of American immigration history. In general, people from the British Isles and from northern and western Europe (who were highly represented in the colonial and first immigrant streams) were ranked near the top of the list. People from southern and eastern Europe were next in order, and people of the racial minorities were ranked near the bottom. In short, the general pattern of social distance that is transmitted from generation to generation in the United States resembles the pattern that was created through the historical sequences of intergroup contact that we already have observed.

As in the case of stereotypes, the conclusion seems warranted that the normal development of people within American society predisposes them to regard some racial and ethnic groups more favorably than others. We cannot know, of course, whether a person's behavior will correspond to the answers given on a paper-and-pencil social distance form; but we may assume that the person at least has learned the answers he or she is expected to give under these circumstances.

Group Identification Theories of Prejudice

We turn now to the second of the three main types of causes of prejudice shown in Figure 6.2, group identification. The importance of a person's group memberships as a molding force has been stated powerfully by Sumner ([1906]1960) in his famous book *Folkways*. In Sumner's ([1906]1960:27) view, as discussed in Chapters 1 and 3, a fundamental fact concerning human groups is that as their members are drawn together by a common interest and come to see themselves as an in-group, outsiders are likely to be described in terms that are scornful and derogatory, reflecting negative stereotypes. In the United States, for example, such terms as "dago," "nigger," "kike," "honkey," "spick," "mick," "limey," "chink," "gringo," and so on have been applied frequently to out-groups as terms of extreme disrespect.

The tendency to rate all out-groups as lower than the in-group—ethnocentrism— is a pervasive sentiment. Children normally learn very early to distinguish the groups to which they belong from all others; and they usually have a strong attachment to, and preference for, their own group and its ways. The group's preferences become their preferences; its standards, their standards; its beliefs, their beliefs; and its enemies, their enemies. To grow up as a member of a given group is automatically to place that group at the center of things and to adopt its evaluations as the best. Prejudice and hostility toward members of out-groups and favoritism toward members of the in-group are seen as predictable consequences of this natural ethnocentrism.[7]

The idea that this universal phenomenon is a potent cause of prejudice is quite plausible, and it easily fits many of the facts of everyday experience; but it has some shortcomings. For example, loyalty to one's ethnic in-group is sometimes accompanied by an admiration for some specific accomplishments of the members of out-groups (Williams 1964:22). Even in the midst of war a hated enemy may be granted a grudging respect for his or her skill or daring. Such departures from perfect ethnocentrism, however, do not necessarily mean that an enemy out-group that is respected in some particular way is generally rated above the in-group. Additionally, many cases exist in which in-group members have rejected their own group and joined another. As Williams (1964:23) remarked, "history is replete with voluntary exiles, expatriates, out-group emulators, social climbers, renegades, and traitors."

Social Self and Identity.   Why is ethnocentrism so prevalent? An interesting answer to this question grows out of **social self theory** (Mead 1934) and **social identity theory** (Tajfel and Turner 1979). According to social self theory, human infants initially view the world only from their own perspective; they are unable to see it from the perspectives of others. Indeed, at the outset children have no conception of themselves as distinct individuals; however, as children mature and learn to communicate symbolically with family members (primarily through language), they become aware of themselves as distinct individuals who are members of particular groups. Social identity theorists argue that an individual's developing self-concept consists of his or her personal identity and also of various social identities that correspond to the groups of which the person is a member;[8] consequently, according to social identity theory, as people strive to maintain their self-esteem, they may draw strength and pride both from their own accomplishments and through being affiliated with groups having relatively high prestige. In this way, a person's sense of self-worth may be raised either by accepting an exaggerated view of the value and importance of his or her groups or by downgrading the value and importance of the groups of others. Pride in one's group may become excessive and give rise to prejudice.

But what happens to the self-esteem of children who grow up as members of an ethnic group that occupies a position of low prestige in the social hierarchy? In-groups usually react to out-group hostility by becoming prouder and more determined to maintain their social identities; but domination by an out-group may set into motion an often vicious cycle, called a **self-fulfilling prophecy** (Merton 1957:423). For example, if subordinate group children learn that others do not expect them to do well in school, then they may become anxious; their anxiety may impair their efforts and lead to below-par results; and these results may be taken as "proof" that the initial low expectations were justified. But the process may not end there. The subordinate-group children themselves may now have doubts about their academic ability, lowering their self-esteem and their expectations of themselves; their lowered expectations may lead to still higher anxiety, a further decrease in efforts, a further decline in performance, and so on in a vicious descending spiral.

The possibility that the self-esteem and group pride of subordinate-group children may be damaged through the action of self-fulfilling prophecies has led to a large number of research studies. For example, some interesting discoveries were based on the use of a technique called the "dolls test," pioneered by Clark and Clark (1939; 1958). In this test, children were asked questions about two dolls that were identical except for their skin and hair color. The Clarks' most startling findings were that the majority of Black children preferred a white doll to a brown doll, preferred to play with the white doll, thought that the white doll was "nice," and said that the brown doll "looks bad." These results seemed to show that the children had accepted the racist views of the dominant group and that their self-esteem had been damaged.

By 1970, so much research had confirmed the idea that the self-esteem of Black children was comparatively low that it had come to seem "almost unassailable" (Heiss and Owens 1972:360). Taken together, the main thrust of much research on the self-esteem of Black children supported the Clarks' judgment that children who learn they are members of a subordinate group and accept that opinion may experience incalculable, possibly irreversible, damage to their personalities. The U.S. Supreme Court accepted this view in the famous school desegregation case *Brown v. Topeka Board of Education* (1954). The Court held that to segregate children "from others of similar age and qualifications solely because of their race generates a feeling of inferiority as to their status in the community that may affect their hearts and minds in a way unlikely ever to be undone" (Osofsky 1968:477).[9]

Nevertheless, a growing body of research raised questions about this view. McCarthy and Yancey (1971) suggested that the case for low Black self-esteem was very weak. A number of other studies found no evidence that Blacks generally had low self-evaluations (Heiss and Owens 1972; Lerner and Buehrig 1975; Rosenberg and Simmons 1972). Some researchers believed, in fact, that one might make a stronger case for the idea that Blacks had higher average self-esteem than Whites (Drury 1980; Simmons 1978). After a thorough review of the literature, Stephan (1988:13) concluded that, "four decades of research on self-esteem indicate that blacks do not have lower self-esteem than whites."

A number of other questions have been raised concerning the earlier studies including possible changes that have occurred since the 1960s, problems of research method (Bachman and O'Malley 1984), and problems of ambiguous concepts and theory (Broman, Neighbors, and Jackson 1988). Porter and Washington (1979) argued that the concept of self-esteem has not been subjected to sufficient analysis. In a similar vein, Hughes and Demo (1989:154) argued that feelings of high personal worth may coexist with feelings of low personal control and concluded that racial inequality has a much greater effect on the latter element than on the former; and Rosenberg and colleagues (1995) found that children's performance in school was more closely tied to their specific (academic) self-esteem than to their overall self-esteem.

We close our consideration of the role of group identification in generating ethnocentrism, prejudice, and discrimination by noting briefly a highly controversial perspective. As we have seen, sociologists generally seek the roots of these phenomena in the way individuals develop within particular human groups; but some theorists believe there also is something in the genetic structure of human beings that predisposes them, but does not force them, in the direction of in-group preference (van den Berghe 1978). Lopreato (1984) argued that through both cultural and biological evolution, human beings have developed a predisposition to prefer to marry and live with people who are culturally and phenotypically like themselves. If so, the existence of a predisposition that influences people in the choice of reproductive partners may also help "explain such phenomena as ethnic conflict and ethnocentrism" (Lopreato 1984:310).[10]

Personality Theories of Prejudice

The various cultural transmission and group identification theories of prejudice have received a substantial amount of support, but they afford an incomplete view of what a person learns during the process of growing up. It is possible that the ways different individuals learn to react to problems and the kinds of personalities they develop also are important in understanding prejudice. Why, for example, do some people accept the racial and ethnic prejudices that are common in their home community whereas others reject them?

Many everyday comments concerning prejudice reflect the idea that some kind of conscious or unconscious personality "need" or problem lies behind racial and ethnic prejudice. We may hear prejudice explained, for example, in terms of "insecurity," "an inferiority complex," or "a closed mind." Such remarks suggest that prejudice may perform some important functions for the personality of the prejudiced person—to help the person in some way to cope with his or her inner conflicts and tensions.

Frustration. One popular personality theory of prejudice is related to the widespread observation that a person who is frustrated is likely to direct his or her anger toward some external object, sometimes in an aggressive way. The scholarly version of this idea, called the **frustration–aggression hypothesis,** stated that (1) frustration always leads to aggression, and (2) aggression is always the result of frustration (Dollard et al. 1939). This formulation of the hypothesis was too simple and sweeping (Baron 1977:22; Berkowitz 1969:2) and was revised later to recognize that aggression could be caused by things other than frustration (Miller 1941:30).[11]

People may not behave aggressively immediately after being frustrated. For instance, a person who causes frustration may be too powerful to attack directly or openly (e.g., one's boss). In such cases, the frustration experienced by the individual may have no feasible outlet but may instead await a safe or convenient substitute target. This situation leads to the frequent admonition to an angry person that he or she should not "take it out on me" (or the dog). Such a safe substitute target is called a **scapegoat** (Allport 1958:236). Since the anger that lies behind scapegoating may be released against a wide variety of targets, it is called **free-floating hostility** (Allport 1958:337).

Proponents of the frustration–aggression hypothesis believe that ethnic prejudices develop in response to people's need to cope with the frustrations in their daily lives. Ethnic groups in America, especially the newest arrivals and those in racial minorities, frequently provide scapegoats for the free-floating hostility of the majority.[12] Scapegoating, however, may set into motion a self-fulfilling prophecy. A person who scapegoats senses, if only vaguely, that he or she has committed an injustice; the sense of injustice may generate guilt; and guilt may be accompanied by a fear that the injured person will retaliate. The combination of guilt and fear now may become a new source of frustration, which arouses additional aggressive feelings. Scapegoating appears to feed on itself and increase, rather than diminish, free-floating hostility.

This intriguing theory seems consistent with many observations from daily experience, but it leaves many questions unanswered. Why, for instance, do some frustrated people use the members of minority groups as scapegoats whereas other, perhaps even more frustrated, people do not (Allport 1958:210, 332)? And how does the idea of scape-goating—which makes sense in the case of majority-group prejudices—apply to the frustrations experienced by members of ethnic minorities? When minority-group members strike out in apparent frustration against members of the majority, they can hardly be said to have selected a safe substitute target (Simpson and Yinger 1972:218–219).

We turn now, very briefly, to another theory that relies on personality dynamics to help explain ethnic prejudice—the theory that some people possess an **authoritarian personality**.

Authoritarian Personality.   Following World War II, a group of scholars set out to try to understand the causes of the extreme ethnic prejudices that became prominent with the rise of fascism in Europe during the 1930s and the Holocaust during the 1940s (Adorno, Frenkel-Brunswick, Levinson, and Sanford 1950). On the basis of intensive case studies, the researchers concluded that people who scored high on a questionnaire called the F-Scale (for Fascism) possessed a distinctive cluster of personality traits that predisposed them to be ethnocentric and prejudiced toward out-groups. They were found to be rigidly conventional, submissive, uncritical of in-group authority, preoccupied with power and "toughness," sexually inhibited, and intolerant of people who are members of out-groups. The authors argued that people with this type of personality, called authoritarians, had been raised by domineering adults who relied on harsh discipline to enforce rigid obedience. Children who are raised in this way, the theory holds, grow up to have a highly antidemocratic and ethnocentric view of the world that leads to a high level of intolerance toward all out-groups.

Hundreds of studies have been conducted to test various aspects of the authoritarian personality theory, wherein the F-Scale has been devoted to different purposes. High levels of authoritarianism appear to be especially prominent among people who show a generalized hatred of one or more out-groups and are attracted to organizations founded on out-group hatred. Overall, the findings of the many studies of authoritarianism support the view that an authoritarian personality structure, like frustration, is one among the many sources of ethnic prejudice.

Which Theory Is Best?

What conclusion may be reached from this brief review regarding the causes of prejudice? Evidently, many factors are at work. The culture of a society contains within it many ideas and beliefs concerning various racial and ethnic groups. Therefore, children learn these traditions as a normal part of growing up. Moreover, since these traditions are the source of children's basic sense of group membership or identity, they are inextricably woven into the children's conception of their own sense of self. Still further, many individuals regularly use the members of particular out-groups as scapegoats for their frustrations; and some individuals organize their lives around out-group hatred. We follow Allport (1958:212) in stating our most important conclusion regarding the diverse theories of prejudice: "Each has something to teach us. None possesses a monopoly of insight."[13]

So far we have focused on prejudice and assumed that (1) the reduction or elimination of discrimination requires an understanding of its causes; (2) prejudice is the cause of discrimination; and, therefore, (3) to reduce or eliminate discrimination, one must first attack the causes of prejudice. We did question, however, whether prejudice is in fact the only cause of discrimination; and now we state that the pattern of causation depicted in Figures 6.1 and 6.2 is seriously deficient. Instead of placing all of our emphasis on the effect prejudice has on discrimination, we should place at least equal emphasis on the reverse pattern.

Figure 6.3 suggests two conclusions that run counter to the idea that prejudice is the sole cause of discrimination. First, three entirely new types of factors are now shown on the right side of the figure as causes of discrimination. This indicates that certain causal factors generate discrimination directly rather than indirectly through a prior effect on prejudice. Second, the arrow pointing from discrimination to prejudice in Figure 6.3 indicates, in contrast to our usual reasoning, that discrimination is a cause of prejudice.

Theories of Discrimination

We have seen several ways in which prejudice may lead to discrimination. But how can the direction of this process be reversed? Our discussion of cultural transmission emphasized that children just seem to absorb the society's stereotypes and social distance

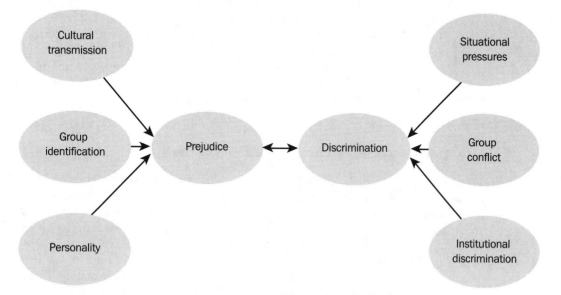

FIGURE 6.3   **Major Direct and Indirect Causes of Prejudice and Discrimination**
(Arrows indicate presumed direction of causation)

norms. Children also learn an enormous amount through imitation. They see their parents, older siblings, and neighbors performing certain acts, and they mimic those acts. In many of these cases, children literally do not know what they are doing and, in many cases, their actions are not accompanied by the same emotions that are present in the person they are imitating. As children "go through the motions," they do not necessarily understand why an action is being performed and may not have inner experiences during the act resembling those of the "model."

In this way, children frequently learn to hurl an epithet (or a rock) at members of an out-group *before* they know whom they are attacking or why. The discriminatory act, in this instance, precedes the expected internal condition. Only gradually, through direct and indirect instruction, does the child come to experience the prejudice he or she is "supposed" to feel. Once the prejudice is learned, the child may then experience it as coming before a given act of discrimination. The individual thus may say to others (and believe) that he or she has discriminated *because* he or she thinks or feels in a particular way; however, from a broader perspective, the feeling of prejudice that precedes a given act of discrimination may itself have been preceded by other acts of discrimination.

This is not the only way that discrimination may lead to prejudice. Discrimination by those who are wealthy and powerful may *create group differences* which then foster prejudice. Myrdal ([1944]1964:1066) illustrated this point by describing a particular self-fulfilling prophecy. Suppose that the initial relationship of the White and Black groups in America was determined *in part* by some degree of race prejudice on the side of the Whites, that the prejudice led to discrimination, and that the discrimination caused Blacks to have a lower standard of living than Whites. Under these conditions, Myrdal said, the lower standard of living among Blacks would stimulate and increase White prejudice, increase discrimination, and lower the Blacks' standard of living still further. In this example, each side of the prejudice–discrimination equation "fed back" on the other side. Each side, then, "caused" the other in a circular and—from the standpoint of democratic values—vicious way. With these ideas as a background, we move now to a consideration of the three types of theories of discrimination (which also are indirectly types of theories of prejudice) shown in Figure 6.3.

Situational-Pressures Theories of Discrimination

Theories of this type are based on the well-known fact that what people "preach" (their creeds) may not always correspond to what they "practice" (their deeds). In other words, there frequently is a gap between a "creed" and a "deed." A familiar example of a **creed–deed discrepancy** involves dominant-group members who feel it is necessary for social reasons to avoid frequent, open association with members of minority groups. Such a person may confide, "I am not prejudiced, you understand; some of my best friends are _____; but what would my neighbors or business associates think?" This example illustrates a simple but fundamental sociological idea: *The social pressures exerted on individuals in different social situations may cause them to vary their behavior in* *ways that do not correspond to their inner beliefs and preferences.* Once again we see that it may be a mistake either to infer prejudice from a given act of discrimination or to infer tolerance from a failure to discriminate.

A seminal exploration of the creed–deed discrepancy was conducted by LaPiere (1934). He and a Chinese couple traveled some ten thousand miles together in the United States, stopping at 251 hotels, motels, and restaurants. Despite the high levels of prejudice and discrimination against the Chinese in the United States at that time, they were refused service only once. After the trip was over, LaPiere mailed questionnaires to all of the proprietors involved asking whether they would accept "members of the Chinese race" as customers. Among those who answered the questionnaire (51 percent), about 92 percent stated they *would not* accept Chinese as guests. In other words, a large proportion of the proprietors (or their employees) who already had demonstrated they would sometimes accept Chinese guests claimed they would discriminate if faced with the choice.

In a society in which the standards of fairness hold that people should be judged on merit, one would expect frequent occurrences of creed–deed discrepancies in which people claim to be less prejudiced than they are; and, for that reason, many claims of tolerance in America are "taken with a grain of salt" (i.e., are considered to be hypocritical). But why would the Americans in LaPiere's study have wished to be thought less tolerant than they actually were? Perhaps the answer goes something like this: In the actual situations, many social elements came into play. The Chinese couple did not fit the prevailing negative stereotype, and they were accompanied by a distinguished-looking White man. Under these conditions, the travelers met almost no discrimination; but in the hypothetical situation described in the questionnaire, the proprietors' stereotypes, prejudices, and fears of dominant-group disapproval were not restrained by concrete circumstances. The discrepancies between the proprietors' (or their employees') fair treatment of the Chinese guests and their statements that they would discriminate probably were due much more to differences between the characteristics of the actual and hypothetical situations than to the individuals' levels of prejudice.

A number of other investigators pursued the question raised by LaPiere's study: Why do people's attitudes and actions frequently fail to correspond? Lohman and Reitzes (1952:242) argued that in modern industrial society "attitudes toward minority groups may be of little consequence in explaining an individual's behavior." To test this idea, they compared the attitudes and behavior of White workers who were members of a union that admitted Blacks without reservation but who lived in a neighborhood where Black residents were unwelcome. As members of the union, all workers were expected by other union members to ignore racial differences and to stand together on common interests such as wages and working conditions. As residents of the neighborhood, the White workers were expected by their neighbors to act on the assumption that admitting Blacks to the neighborhood as residents would lower property values. The study showed that behavior depended more on group membership than on individual attitudes. In the job situation, the White workers united with Black workers for their common advantage; at home, however, the White workers accepted the view of the neighborhood improvement association, rejecting Blacks as neighbors.

These and other studies demonstrated that prejudice and discrimination do not necessarily go together, raising a serious objection to the presumption that prejudice is "the" cause of discrimination. Several investigators have studied this problem under more controlled conditions. In one study, DeFleur and Westie (1958) asked forty-six White students to participate in a nationwide campaign for racial integration. Twenty-three of the students had very unfavorable attitudes toward Blacks; the remaining twenty-three had very favorable attitudes. To test the extent of a person's willingness to act in a manner consistent with his or her prejudice level, the researchers asked the students to be photographed with a Black person of the opposite sex and to sign release agreements to permit the pictures to be used in various phases of the campaign. The study showed that prejudice was positively related to discrimination (i.e., unwillingness to sign the releases); however, it also revealed that nine of the presumably unprejudiced students were less willing than the average to have their photographs used, and that five of the presumably prejudiced students were more willing than the average to release their photographs. DeFleur and Westie interpreted these discrepancies in terms of differing peer-group pressures.

A similar study by Linn (1965) also found a large number of cases in which a person's verbal attitude did not match his or her willingness to sign a release to permit a photograph to be used under different circumstances. Green (1972) used the photograph-release approach and found that, regardless of their expressed racial attitude, White people's willingness to pose with a Black person of the opposite sex diminished as the pose became more intimate. He agreed with DeFleur and Westie that peer pressures in different social situations lead to inconsistencies between expressed attitudes and actual behavior. Warner and DeFleur (1969) proposed that although attitudes do play a role in causing behavior, social norms, group memberships, and other situational factors also affect the relationship.[14]

These studies show that people who appear to be unprejudiced may, under some conditions, discriminate and that people who appear to be prejudiced may not discriminate. The specific social pressures arising in particular situations seem, in many instances, to outweigh personal prejudice as a cause of discrimination. This observation reveals a very important point about the way human beings reason about the causes of their own behavior and that of other people. Most of us have *a strong tendency to overestimate the importance of attitudes as causes of behavior and to underestimate the importance of situational factors*. This tendency, called the **fundamental attribution error**, has been demonstrated in many studies (Brown 1986:169, 176).

Situational-pressures theories evidently differ from the three types of theories of prejudice discussed previously. Not only do they focus primarily on behavior, but they also emphasize the current determinants of behavior rather than those growing out of the socialization process. As valuable as these theories are, they divert attention from the fact that people also are members of broad groups that may be competing with one another for the possession of many socially desired ends—such things as property, prestige, and power. Intergroup conflicts may arise from the fact that different groups occupy more or less favorable positions in the social order (or structure) and wish either to maintain or to improve those positions. Our two remaining types of theories focus on the consequences of group factors as determinants of discrimination and, indirectly, of prejudice.

Group Conflict Theories of Discrimination

In Chapters 2 and 3 we noted briefly how the American Indians and Europeans struggled for possession of the land; and in Chapters 4 and 5 we saw how the fear that immigrants would take jobs away from Americans led to nativist movements and campaigns to restrict immigration. These conflicts between groups for the control of land and jobs, to name only two important resources, led to relatively fixed social arrangements in which the members of the more powerful groups enjoyed greater privileges and higher social standing than those in the less powerful groups. A system of ethnic domination and subordination (or stratification) had been born.

Noel (1968) argued that the combination of differences in group power, competition for scarce resources, and ethnocentrism invariably leads to this result. Moreover, not only does such a system of stratification presumably come into existence but it also endures because the dominant groups gain by it. To illustrate, if minority-group workers are forced into the hardest, dirtiest, lowest-paying jobs, then majority-group workers may occupy the "better" jobs and thereby realize an economic gain (Glenn 1966:161). Quite aside from any feelings of antipathy that the majority-group workers may harbor or develop, they may discriminate because they, and perhaps all of the other members of their group, profit by such actions. Any feelings of antipathy that exist may themselves be understood as "secondary to the conflict for society's goodies" (Lieberson 1980:382).

Two issues are of special interest in regard to gaining economic advantages. First, the historical record we have reviewed leaves little room for doubt that in the past the members of given minority groups (e.g., Blacks and Native Americans) have received lower economic rewards than they would have in the absence of discrimination. One still may wonder, nonetheless, about the answer to the following question: Do some Americans still "pay a price" today for being members of minorities?

If taken at face value, the answer to this question seems obvious: "Yes, minority-group workers pay a price in the job market." For instance, the median[15] income of Black families in the United States in 1994 was $21,548, whereas the median for White families was $39,308 (U.S. Bureau of the Census 1995:48). The ratio of these two medians ($21,548/$39,308) is about .55, which shows that, overall, Black familes received 55 cents for every dollar received by White families. A moment's reflection will reveal, however, that this income difference by itself does not demonstrate the presence of discrimination by Whites. There may be other pertinent differences between dominant- and subordinate-group members, such as in education or experience, that must be taken into account if we are to understand what is producing the overall difference in family incomes. Several studies along this line have been conducted; in Chapters 7, 9, and 11 we will consider some of their results. For the present though, and in anticipation of the finding that there is still discrimination against minorities in the job market, let us focus attention here on another question: If, on average, the members of the majority gain economically through discrimination, who benefits most—the employers or the dominant-group workers?

Many writers have followed Karl Marx in asserting that the main beneficiaries of dominant-group discrimination are the employers (the ruling or capitalist class). In a system of ethnic discrimination the majority workers will receive higher pay than the minority workers; but, the Marxian view maintains, the majority workers' belief that they are profiting from the system is an illusion based on short-term calculations. For instance, if White employers encourage the hostility of the majority workers toward minority workers because it helps maintain a large low-wage labor pool, which enables the employers to cut costs and increase profits, then the net result for the majority workers is that their share of the pie is actually smaller in the long run than it would have been had they united with the minority workers against the employers. From this point of view, the behavior of the dominant-group workers is mistaken and "irrational." Beck (1980:148) summarized this position as follows: "Racism in a capitalist society is an ideology fostered and maintained by employers to insure the fractionalization of the working class."

Many writers reject the Marxian analysis and argue instead that high discrimination levels among White workers actually do serve to increase their economic rewards, just as they suppose (Myrdal [1944]1964:68). This theme was pursued by Bonacich (1972; 1973; 1975; 1976). She agreed with the Marxian writers that economic competition is at the root of ethnic antagonisms but disagreed that the conflict between White and Black workers is economically "irrational." She attacked the Marxian notion that capitalists deliberately create a division between different groups of workers in order to subordinate them both. After all, if the employers of labor actually adopt such a strategy, then they must pay one group of workers (e.g., Whites) more than is necessary, thus increasing their operating costs and reducing their profits.

Her alternative, **split labor market theory,** stated that the antagonism of White workers toward minority workers stems from the fact that the White workers received higher pay for performing the same jobs from the beginning. From this perspective, the capitalist class does not *create* but is *faced with* a split labor market (Bonacich 1972: 549). A split labor market is characterized by conflict among three key groups: business people (capitalists), higher-paid labor (e.g., Whites), and cheaper labor (e.g., Chinese, Latinos; Bonacich, 1972:553). In these terms, the main economic interests of the two laboring groups are not essentially alike (as in the Marxian analysis); they are fundamentally different. Higher-paid labor is genuinely threatened by the presence of cheaper labor. Since it is in the interest of the capitalist class to cut costs by hiring the least expensive workers, the capitalists may attempt to substitute the cheaper workers for the higher-paid ones.

How can the higher-paid laborers control the quite real threat against them that is posed by the cheaper laborers? Two main methods are available. The first is simply to exclude the cheaper laborers from the territory in which the higher-paid laborers work. This method frequently has been employed by workers all over the world. We have seen already in Chapter 5 that the United States excluded Chinese laborers beginning in 1882; and, as we shall see in Chapter 7, the same strategy was used later against the Japanese. In both cases, the hostility of the White workers, rather than of the employers, provided the force behind the exclusionist efforts.

The second main method used by higher-paid labor to combat cheaper labor is to organize unions that are committed to preserving the wage distinctions among ethnic groups. If the higher-paid group is sufficiently well organized and powerful, it may be able to force the employers either to continue paying different wages for the same work or to "reserve" the higher-paying jobs for dominant group workers. In either case, the employers may attempt to use the cheaper laborers as strikebreakers. If they succeed, the position of the higher-paid workers may be undermined and wages may decline (Bonacich 1972:554; 1976:40; Olzak 1986:23).

Several other studies have sought to discover whether the employers or the dominant-group workers gain most by a system of discrimination. Although the evidence is not conclusive, it seems likely that the antagonism between majority-group and minority-group workers in the United States arises in part because there is a *genuine conflict* between them over economic and other rewards (Bobo 1988; Glenn 1966). Consequently, as shown by Burr, Galle, and Fossett (1991:844), as the relative size of the minority population increases (and becomes more visible) in a given location, dominant-group discrimination and the levels of inequality between the groups also increase; and these changes increase the probability of collective violence between the competing groups.

One **collective violence theory** based on the competition perspective was presented by Olzak and Shanahan (1996). These authors maintain that the likelihood of racial and ethnic conflict is low when ethnic and racial groups occupy segregated areas and there is little competition for jobs and resources. When two or more groups compete for the same jobs, however, and the dominant group attempts to exclude or subordinate competitors, then the subordinate groups resist and group conflict and violence may occur. Since intergroup competition increases during economic recessions and depressions and when there is an increasing supply of workers from migration, these conditions favor higher levels of collective violence. Riots might be instigated either by minorities who feel that they are not getting good jobs or by the dominant group who wish to maintain their position.

Our discussion has centered on economic conflict between groups; but the debate is not limited to this issue. Dollard (1957) argued that Whites gained through discrimination in other ways as well. For instance, throughout most of the history of the United States, especially in the South, White men realized a "sexual gain" because they had sexual access to Black women, while sexual relations between Black men and White women were taboo. Citing still another advantage Whites enjoyed over Blacks, the "prestige gain," Dollard (1957:173–187) emphasized that the traditions of the South required Black people to be completely submissive in the presence of Whites. Indeed, the southern "etiquette of race relations" required that Blacks smother the Whites in adulation, defer to their wishes, and praise their goodness, wit, and skill (Doyle 1937). These requirements guaranteed that Whites regularly received the satisfactions that come to human beings who believe themselves to be superior and are so treated.

Dollard's analysis seems compelling; but even here, as in the case of economic gains, it is not certain that the sexual, social, and psychological gains for Whites of the White supremacy system outweighed their costs, especially in the long run. There were many noneconomic costs involved in maintaining a rigid system of subordination. For instance, it is possible that the costs to the dominant group in feelings of guilt, fear, and anxiety counterbalanced whatever satisfactions they may have received. This theme has been pursued in many works of literature, as well as in social science. In a moving passage Smith (1963:28) stated: "I began to understand . . . as the years passed, that the warped, distorted frame we have put around every Negro child from birth is around every White child also. . . . And I know that what cruelly shapes and cripples the personality of one is as cruelly shaping and crippling the personality of the other."

Taken together, the results of the many studies and literary insights concerning the total effects of the system of White supremacy in the United States afford a basis for the claim that the members of the dominant group have discriminated systematically against the members of subordinate racial and ethnic groups because they believed they gained by it, however misguided such a belief may have been. The prejudice generated by this intergroup conflict was then used to help explain and justify the existing social arrangements.

Whether these conclusions are correct is a matter of considerable practical importance. If White workers or White employers do not truly gain by possessing ethnic prejudices and by discriminating, then they have, in fact, a strong incentive to discontinue such beliefs and practices. From this vantage point, one may argue that when people are informed and evaluate their true interests correctly, they may then cooperate to bring about needed social changes. On the other hand, if any substantial segment of the dominant group is actually profiting from the system of subordination, then they may be expected to resist changes tooth and nail.

Although the emphasis in group conflict theories is on the relative gains and losses among groups that occupy different locations within the social structure, rather than on the attitudes and behavior of individuals, they nevertheless contain the assumption that prejudice plays an important role as an accompaniment to and justification for discrimination. Also, from this perspective, the forms of intergroup discrimination are comparatively overt. One may locate specific individuals within the dominant group who refuse to hire or promote minority workers, who pay minority workers less than dominant workers for performing the same job, who demand sexual favors in return for employment, and so on. However, some scholars have argued that even if, miraculously, individual prejudice and overt discrimination were to be eliminated completely, the normal operation of American society would still guarantee a high level of discrimination against subordinate racial and ethnic groups. Even if no one tried to discriminate, this argument runs, our traditional social arrangements—our institutions—would ensure discriminatory results.

Institutional Discrimination Theories

American racial and ethnic relations entered a critical period during the 1960s and, as the rioting in Los Angeles and other cities in the spring of 1992 reminded us, were still unsettled over a quarter of a century later. The events of both periods may have been generated to a considerable extent by a paradox. By the mid-1960s, the civil rights movement had scored numerous successes, especially on the legal front, symbolized by the 1954 Supreme Court school desegregation order in *Brown v. Topeka Board of Education*. During the same period, national opinion polls showed that White Americans were becoming less prejudiced. A study conducted by scholars at the National Opinion Research Center (NORC), for example, found that public approval of school desegregation had risen from 30 percent in 1942 to 63 percent in 1963; and by 1982, 90 percent of all

Americans accepted the principle of school desegregation (Schuman, Steeh, and Bobo 1985:75, 77). The NORC study also found that Whites' approval of neighborhood desegregation had risen from 35 percent in 1942 to 64 percent in 1963 (Hyman and Sheatsley 1964:18–19). By 1976, 88 percent of the Whites who were questioned in a study conducted by the Institute for Social Research (ISR) agreed that Black people have a right to live wherever they can afford. In 1984, the overall level of anti-Black prejudice had declined to the lowest level on record (Firebaugh and Davis 1988:261).[16] The paradox was that despite these many evidences of declines in prejudice, White Americans still seemed generally unwilling to support "policies promoting racial economic equality" (Kluegel 1990:513).

These shifts in attitudes may have been part of a general shift among Americans in the direction of a greater tolerance of diversity.[17] Alternatively, the decline in prejudice revealed by public opinion polls may be another illustration of social desirability bias. Several writers have emphasized that "old-style bigotry" or "old-fashioned racism" may have been replaced by a much more guarded "modern racism" (McConahay 1986). To illustrate, although the majority-group members who were polled generally rejected global stereotypes and blatant forms of discrimination, they still opposed fundamental changes in race relations (Bobo 1988:88–91). The targets of their opposition had not changed, but these targets now were attacked indirectly rather than directly (Pettigrew and Martin 1989:171–172). Opponents of school desegregation, for instance, might agree to the abstract principle that school desegregation was desirable but, at the same time, insist that this objective should be reached through neighborhood desegregation rather than through busing. In the meantime, most actual efforts to expand either busing or neighborhood desegregation might be opposed. In addition, many dominant-group members now reject the idea that Whites are genetically superior to other groups but still may argue that the problems faced by minority-group Americans is evidence of insufficient effort on their part (Kluegel 1990:513).[18] Hence, the apparently nonracist acceptance of the goal of desegregating schools and the rejection of White superiority may be "fronts" for continuing, more carefully veiled racism (Pettigrew and Martin 1987:46).

During this entire period of apparently decreasing prejudice and increasing opportunity, some members of minority groups (and in particular many Black Americans, Mexican Americans, and American Indians) noticed that significant improvements were not taking place in their own lives. At best, the rate of improvement seemed painfully slow;[19] and in many ways, after a period of improvement, there followed a period of decline. For example, a *Newsweek* poll published in April 1992 (Morganthau et al. 1992:21) found that 51 percent of Black Americans felt that the quality of life for Blacks had gotten worse during the preceding ten years. The article also repeated some generally known but still sobering figures concerning the very high rates among Blacks of infant mortality, homicide, and imprisonment. An important question that loomed in the minds of many people was, "How can so many changes occur in the laws and in the attitudes of the majority but not be reflected in the actual living conditions of some of the members of minority groups?"

An intriguing answer to this question was presented by Carmichael and Hamilton (1967) in their influential book *Black Power*. The answer these authors suggested was that the *ordinary operations* of American institutions discriminate against subordinate groups. Schools, hospitals, factories, banks, and so on do not need to be staffed by prejudiced people in order to achieve discriminatory results. For example, most employers have certain formal educational requirements for hiring, such as a high school or college diploma. When these requirements are applied uniformly (and many would add "fairly") to all those who apply, the *automatic* result is to exclude those who have been deprived of an equal opportunity to gain the necessary credentials. If people have been subject to discrimination in the schools, then they are less likely to have graduated; therefore, they cannot qualify for a job that requires a diploma. Even if the people who conduct the hiring procedure are completely tolerant as individuals, the rules of the organization they represent require them to accept only those who have proper diplomas, test scores, certificates, and licenses. In this case, we see that the discrimination that occurs in one institutional setting may carry over into a related institutional setting (Feagin 1977). To illustrate further, a father's difficulties in finding employment may lead his son to drop out of school to go to work. The son, too, may then later encounter the same employment problems as the father. Here we see how unintentional discrimination may place a self-fulfilling prophecy into operation both within and between generations.

Another type of institutional discrimination in employment arises because the members of a minority "lack some ability or qualification intentionally denied to them in the past" (Feagin 1977:189). If an employer requires that a person must have worked in one job for ten years in order to be qualified for another job, anyone who was deliberately excluded from the first job cannot be qualified for the second. For instance, during periods of economic expansion, employers frequently have not hired Black workers until no other workers were available. Then, during slack periods, the Black workers frequently were the first to lose their jobs. Under those circumstances, it was very difficult for Black workers to accumulate the years of seniority needed to qualify for many jobs. Therefore, wherever seniority rules were used in hiring and firing, and were applied uniformly, the Black workers were at a disadvantage. The employers in this situation may have been able to say truthfully that they were not prejudiced and were not discriminating even though the application of the seniority rules may have worked to the disadvantage of the Black workers.

Note that the main claim of institutional discrimination theories is that prejudice *presently* is not required to keep the system of discrimination intact. They acknowledge that prejudice initially may have played a role in producing the existing system and do not deny that prejudice still produces some discrimination.[20] The central idea was expressed by Baron (1969:144) as follows: "There is a carefully articulated interrelation of the barriers created by each institution. Whereas the single institutional strand standing alone might not be so strong, the many strands together form a powerful web."

Both group conflict theories and institutional discrimination theories emphasize that discrimination has important sources other than individual prejudice. This idea is exceptionally important in the present period. Many White Americans now recognize that their forebears profited from discrimination against minority groups; some also acknowledge that the effects of past discrimination have not been entirely erased. It is not always easy to see, however, that as prejudice levels decline, intergroup competition and traditional institutional arrangements may continue as before and may benefit disproportionately all or most members of the dominant group. Consequently, the complaint frequently is heard, "I haven't discriminated against anyone, so why should I pay for the mistakes of the past?" The answer supported by group conflict and institutional discrimination theories is that White Americans still receive a direct "bonus" for being White even if they do nothing to "earn" it or are unaware they have received it.

We have noted Myrdal's ([1944]1964:3–4) contention that, despite glaring discrepancies between many Americans' actions and the ideals of the American Creed, most Americans recognize that each individual is entitled to respect and the "inalienable rights to freedom, justice, and a fair opportunity." This position implies that prejudice and discrimination are morally wrong and, ideally, should be eliminated. In Chapter 15, we consider some of the methods of reducing racial and ethnic prejudice and discrimination that have been tried and studied.

We reviewed in Chapters 1 through 5 how American society developed a system of dominant–subordinate group relations. In Chapter 6, we have explored various sociological and psychological theories that help us understand why human beings create systems of dominance and subordination. We turn in the following chapters to a more detailed examination of how and why America's ethnic stratification system developed and has operated in relation to groups that have faced very high levels of discrimination, beginning with an analysis of the experiences of one non-White immigrant minority—the Japanese and Japanese Americans.

Key Ideas

1. Although prejudice (a negative attitude) is usually thought to precede and be the cause of discrimination (a negative action), discrimination also may precede prejudice and be a cause of it. Moreover, a person may be prejudiced but not discriminate and discriminate without being prejudiced.

2. Prejudice arises from several sources. Among the most important of these are:
   a. The transmission of specific attitudes and beliefs from one generation to the next: Children learn their group's stereotypes of different out-groups. They also learn which groups are to be admired and which should be held at a great social distance.
   b. The sense of group identity, belongingness, and loyalty that people ordinarily develop toward their own group's members and culture: Pride in one's own group may easily shade into or stimulate prejudice toward the groups of others.
   c. The effort to manage the personal frustrations and personal problems: People frequently exhibit an exaggerated, seemingly "irrational" hostility toward the members of out-groups. Such prejudices appear to have more to do with people's inner tensions and conflicts than with the characteristics of the members of the hated group(s).

3. Discrimination arises from several important sources, some of which do not directly involve prejudice:

   a. The social pressures that are exerted to ensure people's conformity to the norms of their group: Even when people do not personally desire to ostracize or harm the members of an out-group, they may be expected to do so by the other members of their own group. Those who violate the in-group norms may themselves be ostracized by the in-group members.

   b. The conflicts that occur between groups as they struggle over power, wealth, and prestige: Whether or not it is caused by prejudice, discrimination is a tool used in the struggle to gain advantages over other groups. Partly for this reason, dominant-group members generally enjoy higher incomes, more desirable jobs, less unemployment, and more social deference than the members of other groups.

   c. The normal operations of the society's institutions: Equal opportunity and fair play within a given institutional sector (e.g., the economy) may not lead to equal results. The lingering effects of past discrimination or the existence of discrimination within a related institution (e.g., education) may lead to the disproportionate disqualification of the members of minority groups. The rules of organizations may automatically discriminate.

Key Terms

American Creed   A value system based on the idea that individuals should have equal access to justice and opportunity.

authoritarian personality   A personality syndrome in which the individual is rigidly conventional, submissive, uncritical of in-group authority, preoccupied with power and "toughness," sexually inhibited, and intolerant of people who are members of out-groups.

collective violence theory   Maintains that there is little likelihood of racial and ethnic conflict when ethnic and racial groups occupy segregated areas and there is little competition for jobs and resources. This theory proposes that riots occur when racial or ethnic groups must compete for scarce jobs. Collective violence is even more likely when migration increases the numbers of workers competing for those scarce jobs.

creed–deed discrepancy   A gap between what people say they believe and their actions.

discrimination   Unfavorable actions toward people because they are members of a particular racial or ethnic group.

ethnic stratification system   A particular pattern of social "layers" among ethnic groups in which the groups differ in power and prestige.

free-floating hostility   Hostility that may be released aggressively against a wide variety of targets.

frustration–aggression hypothesis   States that frustration always leads to aggression and aggression is always the result of frustration.

fundamental attribution error A strong tendency to overestimate the importance of attitudes and to underestimate the importance of situational factors as causes of behavior.

prejudice An unfavorable attitude toward people because they are members of a particular racial or ethnic group.

racism Usually refers to an unfavorable attitude, and perhaps an unfavorable action, toward people who are members of particular racial or ethnic groups; it may or may not specify the type of relationship that exists between unfavorable attitudes and actions; and the idea of group ranking may be more or less salient.

scapegoat A safe, convenient substitute target of aggression.

self-fulfilling prophecy A cycle, often vicious, that begins with a false definition of the situation that evokes a new behavior which makes the originally false conception come true.

social desirability bias The distortion that occurs when people give answers they believe they are expected to give rather than their true opinions.

social distance Refers to the grades and degrees of understanding and intimacy which characterize personal and social relations generally.

social identity theory States that as people strive to maintain their self-esteem, they may draw strength and pride both from their own accomplishments and through being affiliated with groups having high prestige.

social self theory States that as children mature and learn to communicate symbolically, primarily through language, they develop an awareness of themselves as distinct individuals who are members of particular groups.

split labor market theory States that the antagonism of dominant-group workers toward subordinate-group workers arises because the price of the workers' labor in the two groups differs initially.

stereotype A shared, but not scientifically validated, belief concerning the characteristics of the members of different racial or ethnic groups as compared to some reference group.

 # Notes

1. Van Oudenhoven and Willemsen (1989:15) stated that "Racism always implies prejudice and may encompass discrimination as well. The relations between these different concepts . . . are generally not straightforward and simple."

2. It usually is unclear just how exaggerated a belief must be before it is to be regarded as a stereotype.

3. Some standard is required to determine when a trait is to be considered "typical."

Brown (1986:592) suggested that "*typical* means true of a higher percentage of the group in question than of people in general." This is known as the "diagnostic ratio" approach to determining the elements of a stereotype (Henwood et al. 1993:272).

4. For reviews of the literature on stereotype research, see Dovidio and Gaertner (1993); Ehrlich (1973:20–60); Hamilton and Trolier (1986); Stephan and Stephan (1993); and Wood and Chesser (1994).

5. Study results also may be affected by the method that is used. Ehrlich and Rinehart (1965) found that respondents who used an open-end method listed fewer traits, exhibited greater disagreement with one another, and constructed different stereotypes than those who used the usual checklist method.

6. The number of the item (usually one through seven) representing the greatest degree of closeness each person in a study is willing to accept with the members of a particular ethnic group is used to calculate the group's average social distance score.

7. Stephan (1985:613) noted that "discrimination . . . against out-group members" may occur even among groups whose members have been chosen randomly (called minimal groups).

8. See, for example, Deaux, Reid, Mizrahi, and Ethier (1995).

9. Several studies using "a picture-story format" found that, on average, both White and Black children show a pro-White, anti-Black bias (see, e.g., Williams and Morland 1976).

10. Many sociologists believe either that efforts to answer these questions move beyond the boundaries of sociology's scholarly domain (See and Wilson 1988) or that such research may undermine the victories that have been won against racist doctrines. As we explained in Chapter 5, however, heredity may play a large role in shaping individual differences within a given population but have nothing to do with differences among groups. Gordon (1978:23) stated this idea as follows: "A view of human behavior which leans in the direction of biological determinism for individual behavior is . . . not in the least incompatible with the idea of racial equality."

11. Many studies have shown that although frustration does create an emotional readiness to be aggressive, it will not be translated into action unless certain triggering "cues" are present in the situation (see, e.g., Berkowitz 1989).

12. The idea that people may "drain off" aggressive impulses by displacement is a popular one. This process is called *catharsis*.

13. Middleton (1976) compared White southerners with non-southerners and found that sociocultural factors are the most important determinants of the higher level of prejudice against Blacks in the South; that these same factors play the greatest role in creating anti-Black prejudice throughout the United States; but that psychological factors operate in similar ways within each region to produce different levels of individual prejudice.

14. For a review of studies of the attitude–behavior relationship see Schuman and Johnson (1976).

15. The median is the number that divides any set of numbers exactly in half, that is, the middle number.

16. The exact levels of a given attitude may vary with the wording of the questions. In regard to Whites' acceptance of residential desegregation, for instance, NORC used a question that elicited a lower approval response (Schuman, Steeh, and Bobo 1985:60).

17. For an important study of this more general attitudinal shift, see Williams, Nunn, and St. Peter (1976).

18. Kluegel (1990:513) noted that although the modern type of racism does not focus on genetic inferiority it still attempts to explain group differences in individualistic terms.

19. At the rates of change in effect between 1950 and 1960, the "gap" between White and non-White incomes "would not close until 2410" (Broom and Glenn 1965). See also Lieberson and Fuguitt (1967:188-200).

20. Some social-learning theorists believe attitudes never cause actions. Skinner (1974: 10) stated: "Many of the things we observe just before we behave occur within our body, and it is easy to take them as the causes of our behavior." For a critique of the institutional discrimination theory, see Butler (1978).

Japanese
Americans

The Japanese in America have faced severe racism. This family's home in Seattle, Washington was defaced while they were detained in a relocation center during World War II. However, the history of the Japanese Americans generally supports the idea that disadvantages based on racial distinctiveness are not necessarily permanent in American society.

*I am proud that I am an American citizen of Japanese ancestry. . . .
Because I believe in America. . . . I pledge to do her honor in all times
and all places.*

—Mike Masaoka

*To create a truly fulfilling identity, Asian Americans realize they must
redefine and articulate Asian American identity on their own terms.*

—Amy Tachiki

Our discussions of immigration to America, nativism, racism, and prejudice and discrimination showed that the less the members of a group have resembled the Anglo American ideal of an "American," the less acceptable they have been to the dominant group and the more prejudice and discrimination they have suffered. Groups that are socially, culturally, and physically most "distant" from the dominant group's notion of the ideal American have been considered to be the lowest in "assimilative potential" or even to be "unassimilable."

Of all the factors that affect a group's prospects, being classified by the dominant group as "non-White" has been the most troublesome. During the colonial period, Africans and American Indians were defined as standing outside of the developing Anglo American society. As other physically distinctive groups entered the territory of the United States, they also were viewed typically as being too distant from the American ideal to be included as full members of American society. They were therefore subjected to levels of prejudice and discrimination resembling those directed toward African and Native Americans. From this perspective, non-White people in America have had fewer opportunities and faced larger obstacles to material or worldly success than have White people. The opportunity for these groups "to climb the ladder of success" (i.e., to achieve secondary assimilation in the public sphere) has been lower from the first and has remained so.

Some Americans believe that this summary exaggerates and that the obstacles standing in the way of the success of the non-White groups were hardly different from those faced by their own forefathers. Many others will agree that non-Whites have faced the highest levels of prejudice and discrimination but will not agree that these barriers have been large enough to explain why African, Mexican, and Indian Americans have remained conspicuously outside the mainstream of American life. Most White Americans appear to believe that hard work, education, perseverance, and faith in the American dream are still the main ingredients of "success" in American society (Kluegel 1990: 513). From this vantage point, even those who suffer the highest levels of prejudice and discrimination should be able to succeed if they will only try hard enough. Their battle may be more difficult, the argument goes; but if they will work hard, opportunities will appear, and they will earn their place in American society.

The preceding contrast in types of explanations (one emphasizing differences in *the levels of discrimination* various groups have faced, the other emphasizing differences in *the levels of effort* put forth by various groups) ignores the many other factors we have mentioned that affect the rate of assimilation of minorities and is, therefore, too sharply drawn. The contrast nonetheless reflects real political differences in contemporary America and serves as a useful point of reference for our further consideration of the experiences of all non-White groups in America.

The contrast is especially prominent in discussions of the Japanese Americans. Although (as we discuss later) the largest non-White groups in America have been comparatively "unsuccessful," *materially speaking,* the Japanese Americans frequently have been singled out as "proof" that racially distinctive groups can "succeed" in America even in the face of high levels of discrimination. Many articles and books have proclaimed the Japanese Americans to be a "model minority," a non-White group that has overcome all obstacles through hard work and determination (Hosokawa 1969; Petersen 1971). In McWilliams's (1949:155) opinion, "no other immigrant group ever faced such difficulties as the Japanese encountered in this country" and "no group ever conducted themselves more creditably." Despite the odds, this view contends, in terms of many criteria of success, the Japanese have "made it" in America.

By 1976, for instance, the average (mean) number of years of education among Japanese Americans reached 13.2 years, a level still not attained by Whites in 1987 (12.7 years; Hirschman and Wong 1985:296). Similarly, among White Americans who were employed in 1976, 14.2 percent of the males and 15.3 percent of the females were in occupations classified as "professional, technical, and kindred workers." Among Japanese Americans, 21.4 percent of the males and 15.9 percent of the females were classified in these high-prestige occupations.[1]

Consider also the matter of comparative incomes. In 1980, the average (mean) income for Japanese American males was noticeably higher than for their majority-group counterparts ($17,905 versus $16,822; Hurh and Kim 1989:523).[2] An even more noticeable gap favoring Japanese Americans existed between the average family incomes of the two groups ($27,350 versus $20,800), though the size of this gap also may have reflected a larger average number of wage earners among Japanese American families (Hurh and Kim 1989:519).

Even so, some scholars wondered whether the comparatively higher incomes of Japanese Americans were as high as they should be, given their higher educational attainments and, perhaps, greater effort expended in a longer average work week. Stated differently, given these higher levels of "investment" among Japanese Americans, should not their earnings advantage have been even greater than it was?[3] When a number of relevant factors were taken into account, Hirschman and Wong (1984:597) found that the incomes of the Japanese Americans were about $2,000 below what they should have been according to their qualifications. This suggests that there still was considerable discrimination against them in the job market. Hurh and Kim (1989:523), in a similar analysis, found that Japanese Americans received 93 percent as much income as similarly qualified White Americans.

These arguments have been challenged by other research. Chiswick (1983:210–211), for instance, found that when adjustments were made for group differences in such things as education, experience, and the number of weeks worked per year, the annual earnings of White and Japanese American men were roughly equal. By 1995, however, several studies had shown that the average earnings advantage of Japanese American men and women had reached a level that was either equal to or slightly more than would be expected on the basis of their educational levels and other pertinent qualifications (Barringer, Gardner, and Levin 1995; Sakamoto and Furuichi, in press).[4] Nevertheless, even if job discrimination is no longer a major problem for Japanese Americans, the possibility that they still may suffer from other forms of discrimination leads some commentators to reject the "model minority" image (Lee 1990; Takaki 1991). They believe instead that the "success story" characterization is a self-serving stereotype through which the dominant group attempts to deflect attention away from continuing discrimination against the Japanese Americans and, more especially, to prove that the problems of Black Americans, Mexican Americans, and American Indians are due to a lack of effort rather than to discrimination (Hurh and Kim 1989:530; Tachiki 1971:1).

The Japanese Americans, then, present a puzzling and instructive picture. Despite their non-White racial identification, they appear in several important respects to have followed a path of assimilation resembling that of many of the second-stream immigrants who were arriving from Europe during the same period. They surely have not disappeared as a group, however, and there is today a continued questioning within the Japanese American community of its place in American society. Let us begin to explore this puzzle by examining some of the most important events that have affected the Japanese since their arrival in this country. We return later to questions concerning the types and extent of Japanese American assimilation.

Japanese Immigration and Native Reactions

Anti-Asian Sentiment

Even though the Japanese immigration to America was comparatively small (see Table 7.1), many factors combined to create the impression that the United States was in grave danger of being overrun by "hordes" of "Mongolians" and must be constantly on guard against "the yellow peril."[5]

Before 1868, the Japanese government did not permit its citizens to emigrate, and laborers ordinarily did not receive permission to travel abroad until 1884 (Ichihashi 1932:6).[6] Those granted passports before 1884 were mainly students who were expected to seek knowledge and come back home "so that the foundations of the Empire may be strengthened" (Ichihashi 1932:3). In 1890, there were only 2,039 Japanese in the entire country, but in 1891 about 1,500 Japanese immigrants reached the United States. This small but rapid increase, following as it did some forty years of anti-Chinese agitation, attracted the unfavorable attention of the San Francisco *Morning Call*. The *Call* launched a "crusade against Japanese contract labor" (Daniels 1969:20), claiming that

**TABLE 7.1 Japanese Immigration
to the United States, 1861–1994***

Years	Number
1861–1870	149
1871–1880	186
1881–1890	2,270
1891–1900	25,942
1901–1910	129,797
1911–1920	83,837
1921–1930	33,462
1931–1940	1,948
1941–1950	1,555
1951–1960	46,250
1961–1970	39,988
1971–1980	49,775
1981–1990	47,085
1991–1994	31,982
Total	494,226

Source: U.S. Immigration and Naturalization
Service, *1994 Statistical Yearbook,* 1996:
26–28.

*No record of immigration from Japan was
kept before 1861.

Japanese immigrants were taking work away from Americans. By 1905, anti-Asian hostility was focused on the Japanese. In that year, a war between Russia and Japan ended in a resounding victory for Japan. For the first time since the Europeans began colonizing the world during the fifteenth century, a "non-White" nation had defeated a "White" nation. In so doing, Japan established a reputation as a first-rank military power. The belief that the United States was in imminent danger of being swamped in a sea of human waves from the East was revived, and the hostility among California's working people that previously had been directed at the Chinese was now aimed at the Japanese.

Anti-Japanese Protest

The first large anti-Japanese protest meeting in California, organized in 1900 after labor unions gained partial control of the San Francisco city government (tenBroek, Barnhart, and Matson 1954:35), featured such prominent figures of the day as J. D. Phelan (later a U.S. senator) and E. A. Ross, a sociology professor at Stanford University. Phelan declared that "these Asiatic laborers will undermine our civilization" (tenBroek, Barnhart, and Matson 1954:35). He stated also, in a conspicuous display of poor judgment, that "the Chinese and Japanese are not the stuff of which American citizens can be made" (Daniels 1969:21). Ross advanced the familiar claim that Japanese immigration undercut native labor, a sentiment echoed in that election year by the platforms of both major political parties.

Five years later, a sustained campaign against the Japanese was launched. The most conspicuous forces initiating this campaign were, as in 1892, a newspaper and, as in 1900, organized labor. The newspaper was the respected *San Francisco Chronicle*. For nearly a year, the *Chronicle* ran "scare" headlines and page-one articles attacking Japanese immigration. In its first broadside, the headline read "THE JAPANESE INVASION, THE PROBLEM OF THE HOUR"; another headline said "THE YELLOW PERIL— HOW JAPANESE CROWD OUT THE WHITE RACE" (Daniels 1969:25). The paper repeated the claim that the Japanese immigration would become a "raging torrent" that would inundate the West Coast and pose an economic threat to native laborers.

The anti-Japanese barrage led to the formation of the Asiatic Exclusion League (tenBroek, Barnhart, and Matson 1954:35). This group, comprised primarily of labor union representatives, listed both economic and racial reasons for exclusion. The combined agitations of the *Chronicle* and the League were followed by a rapid increase in the number of incidents of interracial violence in San Francisco. Individual Japanese were attacked. Rocks and rotten eggs were thrown into Japanese places of business, and a boycott instituted against Japanese restaurants ended only after the restaurant owners agreed to pay for "protection." These incidents were accompanied by periodic demands that the board of education implement a school segregation plan. A year and a half after the League began its agitation, the board of education ordered all Japanese, Chinese, and Korean pupils to attend a separate school for Orientals.

The School Board Crisis

Since school segregation in San Francisco affected only a small number of pupils in only one city, we might expect that there would have been little more than local interest in it. Strangely, though, this conflict spiraled into a tense confrontation between the governments of the United States and Japan. After the segregation order went into effect, various reports concerning it were published in Tokyo newspapers, and the Japanese government filed an official complaint with President Theodore Roosevelt. President Roosevelt quickly announced his concern about the situation and authorized the use of armed forces, if necessary, to protect the Japanese. A few weeks later, the president moved to prevent local mobs from committing acts "which would plunge us into war" (Daniels 1969:39).

The school board crisis set into motion a long and complicated series of negotiations between the governments of the United States, Japan, and California. President Roosevelt wanted a solution that was not insulting to Japan and, at the same time, would restrict Japanese immigration. A compromise was achieved in two main steps during 1907 and 1908. In the first step, the school board repealed the school segregation resolution as the President issued an executive order to limit the entry of Japanese workers into the United States through Mexico, Canada, or Hawaii (Ichihashi 1932:244–245).

The second part of the compromise was the celebrated **Gentlemen's Agreement.** The agreement stated that, beginning in 1908, the government of Japan would issue passports to the United States only to non-laborers; laborers who lived in America but had been visiting Japan; the wives, parents, and children of those who had settled in America; and those who owned an interest in an American farm enterprise (Ichihashi 1932:246; Petersen 1971:43). Additionally, on its own initiative, the Japanese government curtailed the issuance of passports to Hawaii (which was now a U.S. possession) and to Mexico. Thus, about eighteen months after the school crisis had erupted, the Gentlemen's Agreement appeared to have limited the further immigration of the Japanese without insulting Japan.[7]

The Gentlemen's Agreement led to sharp reductions in the number of Japanese aliens admitted to the United States and Hawaii; and, for awhile, departures actually exceeded admissions (Petersen 1971:197). These drastic changes ended what has been called the "frontier period" of the Japanese experience in America (LaViolette 1945:10).

The "Picture-Bride Invasion"

As has been true of the vanguard of many immigrant groups, most of the Japanese who came to America before 1908 were single male sojourners who wished to "build a nest-egg" and return to the homeland (Montero 1980:104). The census of 1900 found that of the 24,326 resident Japanese, 985 were women (Glenn and Parreñas 1996:126); so the Japanese community in America at this time contained few families and the bare beginnings of ordinary institutional life. Since the Gentlemen's Agreement permitted those who were the wives of residents of the United States to enter, many of the men who decided to stay sent home to Japan for wives. This action was completely consistent with the Gentlemen's Agreement, but many Americans nevertheless saw it as treachery.

In Japan, marriages were more a union of two families than of two individuals and were arranged by a go-between who was respected by both families (Ichihashi 1932:293). Under normal circumstances, the partners would meet at a specified place and time, and the wedding would be conducted. But what was to be done when the partners were, literally, an ocean apart? A solution to this problem was the "picture-bride marriage" (Miyamoto 1972:226) whereby the prospective bride and groom exchanged photographs and, after the go-between's work was done, were married in a legal proxy ceremony. The bride then would sail for America to join her husband.

The emigration of Japanese women to the United States was greatly accelerated by this method. Glenn and Parreñas (1996:128) reported that "Between 1909 and 1923, 45,706 Japanese women entered the United States, of whom 32,678 . . . were listed as wives." Although many of these newcomers were not enthusiastic about their new lives, they had little to say in the matter (Chow 1994:186). A Mrs. Takagi, for instance, stated: "They just pick out your husband and tell you what to do" (Glenn and Parreñas 1996:129). Also, the brides often were so dismayed on meeting their husbands that they vowed to go "back on this very boat" (Glenn and Parreñas 1996:130). Additionally, most of the women found that their husbands lived in rural areas, frequently under harsh conditions (Gee 1994:56; Kikumura 1994:149). In these circumstances, the picture brides often led hard and lonely lives (Glenn and Parreñas 1996:131).

In any event, the arrival of so many women enabled the Japanese in America rapidly to establish families and communities. The ratio of Japanese men to Japanese women dropped from over 240 to 1 in 1900 to less than 2 to 1 in 1920 (Glenn and Parreñas 1996:132). As a result, most Japanese men were able to marry and thereby to gain not only wives but also extra adult laborers to help them make a living. As Glenn and Parreñas (1996:132) observed, any Japanese "woman arriving in the United States could expect to pull her weight economically." The main forms of employment outside the home were in agriculture and, as was true of Irish women, domestic service.

The "picture-bride invasion" angered many natives who simultaneously believed that the whole process was contrary to the Gentlemen's Agreement and that many more Japanese were arriving (and staying) than really were. In fact, during the 1911–1920 period, a large number of Japanese left the country (Ichihashi 1932:292). The arrival of the picture brides did, however, greatly reduce the imbalance between the sexes within the Japanese community in America and create the conditions necessary for building families and developing institutionally complete communities. By 1920, the Japanese, like so many other immigrant groups, had formed numerous small communities and subcommunities that recreated, in many ways, the institutions and culture of the homeland.

The Japanese Family and Community in America

Family and Community Cohesion

Many immigrant groups have been cohesive, had families that (at least formally) were dominated by the father, attached great importance to age, given preference to male children (especially the first born), and experienced a marked split between the first and second generations. But this cluster of characteristics was especially pronounced among the Japanese.

Consider the split between the generations. The different Japanese and Japanese American generations were so distinct from one another that they were identified by different names. The first-generation immigrants, the **Issei,** were those who arrived before the legal exclusion of 1924. The second generation, the **Nisei,** were American-born citizens who generally reached adulthood by the outbreak of World War II. The third generation, the **Sansei,** were born mainly following World War II; and the **Yonsei,** the fourth generation, are the children of the Sansei.[8]

The distinctiveness of the Japanese generations resulted primarily from the interruption of the immigrant flow caused by the Gentlemen's Agreement and then, later, by exclusionary legislation. After 1924, the Issei did not continue to increase in numbers through the arrival of more newcomers from Japan. Since nearly all young people of Japanese descent in America were Nisei, the peer and youth groups established within Japanese communities were comprised almost exclusively of youngsters who had been born in the United States; hence, the Nisei seldom encountered people who were recent migrants from the old country, and the old-country ways of the Issei stood in sharp contrast to the American ways of the Nisei.

The two-stage process through which the Issei immigration was halted generated special problems for them but did not prevent them from developing in America, as in Japan, highly interdependent and cohesive communities. Within the ethnic community, a person could receive help in locating a job, finding a place to live, or starting a business. One could also speak the native language, eat familiar foods, and relax among relatives and friends. The ethnic community also provided the Japanese some protection from the hostility of the surrounding society. As was true for other immigrant groups, the ethnic community was simultaneously a tool to assist the immigrant to adjust to the demands of the new setting and to sustain and embellish the way of life that had been left behind.

Several aspects of Japanese family and community life are of special importance in understanding their adjustment in America. As noted earlier, the traditional Japanese marriage was primarily a union of two families. The extended family unit thus created was, in turn, connected in numerous ways through other marriages to the larger community. An important effect of this pattern of interrelationships was that everyone in the community had important obligations to many others within the community. The Issei identified strongly with their homeland and were eager to reestablish this traditional pattern of family and community relationships and to transmit its sustaining values to the Nisei. Their open affection for Japan was frequently used against them in later years.

The Nisei were taught Japanese etiquette, which involved a high regard for obligation and authority. Children were expected to understand that they were members of a family and community and that each member had numerous duties and responsibilities. The parents were obligated to the children, but the children were expected to reciprocate. In this way, the children learned that the acts of each individual were of significance to the entire group (LaViolette 1945:19; Miyamoto 1972:228–229). In addition to the importance of politeness, respect for authority, attention to parental wishes, and duty to the community, the Issei also emphasized the importance of education, hard work, and occupational success. The main links between the extended family and the community grew out of the fact that people from the same areas of Japan tended to settle near one another in the United States. **Kenjin**—those from the same province—felt especially close to one another and were preferred as friends, neighbors, business associates, and marriage partners. These bonds were so strong that associations based on them, called **kenjinkai,** often were formed. But the purposes of the kenjinkai went far beyond social, business, and recreational activities. They published newspapers, acted as employment agencies, provided legal advice, gave money to needy members, and paid medical and burial expenses (Light 1974:283). They also frequently sponsored a form of financial assistance known as the **tanomoshi.** The tanomoshi was an organization through which money was pooled and then loaned in rotation to various members entirely on mutual trust (Light 1974:283; O'Brien and Fugita 1991:6).[9] The success of the tanomoshi illustrates the point that the Japanese brought with them "specific principles for creating social organizations" that were of great value in developing strong communities and pursuing worldly success (O'Brien and Fugita 1991:3).

Many of the functions of the kenjinkai were formalized in the Japanese Association, which "was the most important Issei group" (Kitano 1969:81). The Japanese Association provided numerous social and benevolent services, but its main objective was the protection of the Japanese community. The Issei worked through this association to keep the Japanese community "in line" and, thereby, to reduce friction with the Americans. They also used the association to obtain legal services and police assistance. Whenever the police were unresponsive, the Japanese Association could ask the Japanese consul to intervene in their behalf. Everything considered, the Japanese Association played an important role in establishing and maintaining traditional Japanese ways of life within the American setting and, consequently, of resisting cultural, primary, and marital assimilation (Kitano 1969:81–82).

Another important community-building association established by the Issei was the Japanese Language School (Kitano 1969:24–25; Petersen 1971:54–58). The Issei, like the parents of many other ethnic groups, believed that successfully transmitting the ideals of their culture required that their children understand the old-country language; so the main purpose of these schools was to teach Japanese to the Nisei. Although the schools were not very effective in their efforts to transmit the Japanese language, they did symbolize the desire of the Issei to assure their children a Japanese education and, simultaneously, to prevent them from becoming "too American" (Sone 1994). The schools also brought the Nisei together after public school hours and on Saturdays, thereby strengthening the social ties among them and decreasing their contacts with non-Japanese American children.

All of these factors combined to accentuate the differences between the Issei and Nisei. Each of the two generations was unusually homogeneous with respect to age, background, and general life experiences. The center of gravity within the Issei generation was the old country and its traditions; the Nisei, like most other second-generation groups, sought increasingly to break with the old ways.

Japanese Occupations and the Alien Land Laws

The first Japanese who came to America with their government's permission, the so-called "school boys," took part-time jobs to help pay the costs of their stay here. Most of these students worked as domestic servants; however, when the main body of Japanese immigrants began to arrive during the 1890s, these newcomers took a wide variety of jobs in railroad construction, canning, lumbering, mining, fishing, and seasonal farm labor. During the first decade of the twentieth century, however, the Japanese moved increasingly into agriculture, especially in California where they were most numerous. By 1908, agriculture was the leading form of employment among them (Ichihashi 1932: 162–163).[10]

As the Japanese became more conspicuous in agriculture, native Americans began to complain that the Japanese were acquiring too much land and were "taking over" food production. As usual, a persuasive charge against the Japanese was that they did not compete fairly. They were willing to work for less than White laborers and, occasionally, preferred payment in land rather than in wages. In this way, they were gradually gaining strength in agriculture and driving some of the natives out of farming.

The fear that the efficient Japanese would gradually acquire all of the farming land of California led to the passage of the Alien Land Law of 1913. This law did not specifically mention any nationality group. Instead, it prohibited ownership by those who were "ineligible to citizenship." This curious phrase rests on some equally curious facts about American naturalization law. When the first naturalization act was written in 1790, citizenship was made available to any "free white person." The Japanese initially were denied citizenship because when Hawaii was annexed in 1898, the United States recognized as citizens only people who had been citizens of Hawaii; and the Japanese had been denied citizenship in Hawaii (Petersen 1971:47). This denial of citizenship by the United States was challenged by Takao Ozawa, who described himself as "a true American," chose a wife educated in America, and spoke only English at home so his children would not learn Japanese (Takaki 1989:208). In 1916, Ozawa applied for American citizenship, but his application was denied; so he appealed to the U.S. Supreme Court. In 1922, in *Ozawa v. United States,* the Court ruled that although Ozawa had many fine qualifications he, nevertheless, was not White and not eligible for citizenship.

The discriminatory intent of the Alien Land Law was readily apparent in Japan and, once again, the Japanese government entered a vigorous official protest. As matters developed, the Alien Land Law had little effect on either the development of Japanese agriculture or the relations of the United States and Japan. The Issei soon learned to evade the law by registering their land in the names of their children or trusted American friends. More important, though, was that the outbreak of World War I (in which the United States and Japan were allies) sharply increased the need for agricultural workers. The Japanese were admirably suited to meet this sudden high demand. As a result, overt anti-Japanese activities in California were reduced. The traditional Japanese techniques of farming served them well. "Their skill and energy," wrote Iwata (1962:37), "helped to reclaim and improve thousands of acres of worthless lands throughout the state . . . and made them fertile and immensely productive." Even though they controlled only about 1 percent of California's agricultural land, the crops they produced were valued at about 10 percent of the state's total (Iwata 1962:37).

By 1920, it was obvious that the Gentlemen's Agreement had not stopped the growth of the Japanese population and that the Alien Land Law had not prevented them from increasing their land holdings. As agricultural products again became plentiful, the agitation against the Japanese (whether Issei or Nisei) again increased.

Exclusion

The exclusionists now shifted their attention to immigration restriction at the national level. And, as discussed in Chapter 5, the time was ripe for a national approach. The doctrine of White supremacy had become increasingly popular throughout the United States, as had the demand that the United States be protected against "the rising tide of color" through some form of federal restriction on immigration.

The main thrust of the national movement was toward a quota system rather than a system of exclusion. The Emergency Quota Act of 1921 not only established a quota for many countries but also recognized the validity of the Gentlemen's Agreement and exempted Japan from the system. Nevertheless, when the Immigration Quota Act of 1924 was passed, the Gentlemen's Agreement was unilaterally repudiated and Japan was denied a quota. These actions were taken even though the Japanese government was willing to accept a quota (since it applied to many other nations as well). The number of Japanese who would have been eligible for admission each year under the quota system was 100 (Daniels, Taylor, and Kitano 1991:xv).

Why did the United States single out Japan for international humiliation instead of assigning it a tiny quota? In a letter that summarized the understandings of the Gentlemen's Agreement, the Japanese government expressed its willingness to modify the agreement but warned that excluding the Japanese would be "mortifying . . . to the people of Japan" and would have "grave consequences" (Daniels 1969:101). U.S. Senator Henry Cabot Lodge viewed the latter phrase as a "veiled threat" against the United States and led the drive for an exclusion provision in the new immigration law.

The Japanese were very angry. The United States had, in their view, violated its own principles of equality and justice as well as the Gentlemen's Agreement. Although it is impossible to weigh fully the consequences of these events, some scholars have suggested that it was an important link in the chain of events leading to the Japanese attack on Pearl Harbor in 1941 (Kitano 1969:28).

The Second-Generation Period[11]

The cessation of Japanese immigration to the United States in 1924 and the continuing status of the Issei as noncitizens left them in a strange position. Like many others, they had come to America, established homes, started families, and filled various niches in the American economy. Indeed, in the latter respect, they had made quite a name for themselves. They were extremely industrious and by transferring many old-country skills had become prominent in agriculture and landscape gardening. But despite their obvious ability to adapt to American conditions, even in the face of the exaggerated hostility of the natives, their standing in this country at the end of the 1907–1924 "settlement period" was anything but secure. The second-generation period was one in which the Issei continued to build on the economic and community foundations established during the frontier and settlement periods.

By now many Issei men and women had established small businesses to serve other members of the Japanese community. Issei wives had assisted in these businesses and also found work in such jobs as food processing and garment making (Glenn and Parreñas 1996:133). As the Japantowns grew in San Francisco, Seattle, Los Angeles, and other cities, some professional jobs in midwifery and teaching also became available to Issei women. The goal of the Issei was to assist the Nisei to achieve the standing in American society to which their citizenship entitled them and also to adopt and exemplify the traditional virtues of Japanese society.

The Issei strongly approved of the Nisei attendance at public schools and constantly urged them to study hard and bring honor to the family name. The Nisei were encouraged to participate in American-style youth organizations through the formation of Japanese Boy and Girl Scout troops, YMCAs and YWCAs, and all-Japanese baseball and basketball leagues. Also, as the Issei themselves underwent some degree of cultural assimilation, American ways of doing things were introduced into the home, the ken-jinkai, and the Buddhist church. As the Nisei grew older, they frequently were embarrassed by their parents' English and were often ashamed of their own Japanese appearance and manners. They, of course, resented being teased by other American children about their physical features and were hurt and angered when they were called "Japs." As the Nisei became aware that their parents were not and could not become citizens, they sometimes used this point to emphasize the difference between themselves and their parents (Ichihashi 1932:350).

As the Nisei reached adulthood, many of them felt that the older organizations established by the Issei did not meet their special needs. Even though they were Americans, they faced the same sort of prejudice and discrimination that was directed against their parents. Job discrimination was a particularly galling source of worry and frustration (Hosokawa 1969:191, 489). During the 1920s, the Nisei began to establish protective groups similar to the Japanese associations founded by the Issei leading, by 1930, to an umbrella organization of Nisei—the Japanese American Citizen's League (JACL; Hosokawa 1969:194). The JACL represented the Nisei's determination to rise in American society and be accepted as equals. In addition to combating discrimination, the JACL gave attention to such conventional matters as getting out the Nisei vote, electing Japanese Americans to public office, and working to gain citizenship for the Issei (Hosokawa 1969:197–200). These efforts were not very effective; nevertheless, the JACL provided an important rallying point for the Nisei and accelerated their cultural assimilation (Kitano 1969:82).

By 1941, the Japanese American community had been developing for about fifty years. The Issei had been notably successful economically and in raising their families, despite the special hardships created by immigration restrictions and the denial of citizenship. The Nisei had undergone a high degree of cultural assimilation (mainly by substitution) and were striving for secondary assimilation. Some members of the third generation, the Sansei, were now on the scene. It is true that anti-Japanese activities continued to exist, especially during election years. But neither these hostile activities nor any of those prior to this period may easily be compared to the events in the months following December 7, 1941.

War, Evacuation, and Relocation

The aerial attack on Pearl Harbor led to a declaration of war against Japan, to the establishment of martial law in Hawaii, and to the quick arrest of 1,002 German, 169 Italian, and 370 Japanese "suspicious aliens" (Taylor 1993:45). It also provoked a renewed attack in many newspapers against all of the Japanese, aliens and citizens alike. Many of the old hate slogans were revived (e.g., "once a Jap, always a Jap") and there were rumors that the Japanese were planning extensive sabotage. It was said that the language schools had indoctrinated the Nisei in favor of Japan and that the other Japanese community organizations were fronts for Japanese patriotic fanaticism (tenBroek, Barnhart, and Matson 1954:93–94).[12] In the face of growing fears of an invasion of the West Coast, of espionage, and of sabotage, President Franklin Roosevelt issued Executive Order 9066 in February, 1942 authorizing the military commanders as a national-defense measure to prescribe military areas and to impose restrictions on the movements of all persons within those areas. Under this authority (supported by an act of Congress in March), Lt. Gen. John L. DeWitt, the commander of the Western Defense Command, issued a series of public proclamations and civilian exclusion orders beginning in March 1942. General DeWitt argued that the entire Pacific Coast was particularly vulnerable to attack, invasion, espionage, and sabotage, and that, for these reasons, certain groups of people would be excluded from some designated military areas as a matter of "military necessity." Under these orders, all people of Japanese ancestry, whether aliens or citizens, were required to leave the prohibited areas.[13]

The first destination of the evacuees was a group of fifteen "assembly centers." From the assembly centers, the evacuees were transferred to ten "relocation centers." This movement was started in March 1942 and was completed in November. In the process, more than 110,000 people of Japanese ancestry—more than 70,000 of whom were American citizens—were forced from their homes and imprisoned without warrants or indictments.[14] All of this presumably was required by "military necessity." The individuals involved were not accused of any specific acts of disloyalty or tried for any crime in a court of law. Why, then, was the mass evacuation and internment of the Japanese and Japanese Americans a "military necessity"?

One of the most revealing commentaries on this subject was General DeWitt's explanation of the decision to evacuate. The general wrote as follows:

> In the war in which we are now engaged racial affinities are not severed by migration. The Japanese race is an enemy race and while many second and third generation Japanese born on United States soil, possessed of United States citizenship have become "Americanized," the racial strains are undiluted. . . . It therefore allows that along the vital Pacific Coast over 112,000 potential enemies, of Japanese extraction, are at large today. There are disturbing indications that these are organized and ready for concerted action at a favorable opportunity. The very fact that no sabotage has taken place to date is a disturbing and confirming indication that such action will be taken (quoted by Rostow 1945:140).

DeWitt's argument that the absence of sabotage was evidence that it surely would occur was advanced also by the famous "liberal" columnist Walter Lippmann and the "liberal" Attorney General of California (and later Supreme Court Chief Justice), Earl Warren (Walls 1987:145–146). It appears, therefore, that a very large group of people—most of whom were citizens of the United States—were arrested and imprisoned without trials purely and simply because of their race. It was assumed that whereas people from other nations may become Americans, those of Japanese ancestry remain forever Japanese.

The national security questions raised here are complex. As we have seen, the Issei and Nisei were a highly organized, cohesive group. They had worked hard to maintain the Japanese language and traditional forms of family and community life. And since the Issei were ineligible for American citizenship, their ties with Japan were quite strong. Consequently, one may agree that the military threat to the West Coast in 1942 was real and that reason and prudence required that those of Japanese ancestry should be regarded in a special light. However, even if one were to agree that considerations of this type are reasonable, does it follow that the evacuation and relocation program was a suitable response?

Consider, for instance, the situation in Hawaii. There the Japanese population comprised over 37 percent of the total population, as compared to less than 2 percent of the population of the West Coast (Ogawa and Fox 1991:136). After a period of investigation, 1,118 Issei and Nisei were sent to the mainland for internment (Daniels 1991a:74). Those taken into custody in Hawaii, however, were arrested on the basis of individual actions and charges. There was no program to take people into custody on the basis of their racial or ethnic identity.

Consider, too, the way this problem was handled among the more than 1 million aliens of German and Italian descent. People included in this category had to abide by certain security regulations. They could not enter military areas, own or use firearms, or travel without a permit. If German or Italian aliens were suspected of disloyal acts or violated a regulation, they could be arrested. After a hearing, they could be interned, paroled, or released. As in Hawaii, cases were treated individually. Of even greater significance is that the security regulations did not apply in any way to *citizens* of German and Italian descent. It is difficult to escape the conclusion that "the dominant element in the development of our relocation policy was race prejudice, not a military estimate of a military problem" (Rostow 1945:142).

The Relocation Program

Approximately ten weeks after the attack on Pearl Harbor, the evacuation of the Japanese and Japanese Americans from the West Coast began. In January, Attorney General Biddle established zones that were prohibited to enemy aliens but stated there would be no "wholesale internment, without hearing and (consideration of) the merits of individual cases" (Leighton 1946:17). Throughout this period, numerous acts of hostility against the Japanese and Japanese Americans were reported: jobs were lost, credit was discontinued, signs appeared saying, "No Japs Allowed," and Japanese women were attacked by men pretending to be FBI agents. Despite these problems, the government apparently still did not intend to carry out a mass evacuation. Even after General DeWitt proclaimed portions of California, Oregon, Washington, and Arizona to be military areas, he was quoted as saying that "no mass evacuation is planned for Japanese" (Leighton 1946:34). Only a short time later, a mass evacuation was underway.

Understandably, many Japanese Americans could hardly believe it. Everything they had been taught about the American system of democracy argued against such a possibility. Even if every member of a person's family were convicted felons, each person still must be regarded as innocent until proven guilty. The strong belief in the American system and the disillusionment that accompanied the evacuation are reflected in the following comments by a farmer's son (Leighton 1946:27): "I was very confident that there would be no evacuation on a major scale . . . the American system of education . . . gave me faith that our government would not be moved by economic pressure and racial prejudice." The anguish and sense of betrayal expressed by this young man was shared, and possibly accentuated, among the Japanese who had been drafted for military service, as may be seen in a Nisei soldier's comment: "They are evacuating all the Japanese from the Coast and even trying to take away our citizenship. I don't know why I am in the Army. I want to see democracy as it is supposed to be, but this is getting just as bad as Hitler" (Leighton 1946:27).

The evacuation proceeded in two main stages spread over a period of approximately seven months. The first stage removed people from their homes to hastily prepared assembly centers in racetracks, fair grounds, and livestock exhibition halls (tenBroek, Barnhart, and Matson 1954:126). Japanese and Japanese Americans of both sexes and all ages were required to leave behind everything they could not carry. Many people sold their homes, businesses, and other possessions at "panic-sale" prices. Others stored their goods or simply left everything in locked houses hoping that they would be safe until their return. Both the economic costs and the costs in human misery and humiliation were staggering. Probably only those who have experienced it can appreciate fully the emotional impact that is created when proud families who are leading productive lives and planning for the future are forced from their homes, assigned identification numbers, and placed under guard with hundreds of others.

The experiences of the members of the Japanese communities of San Francisco and the Bay area were typical. Most members of these communities were moved by buses to the Tanforan racetrack located south of San Francisco (Taylor 1993:61).[15] Even if the planned modifications of the racetrack had been completed, it was hardly a fit place to house the nearly 7,800 people who were there at one time. They lived in barracks and horse stalls with little privacy. The new residents were shocked by the primitive conditions and the high fences, and many of them "stated later that their experiences at Tanforan were the most disturbing of the whole relocation period" (Taylor 1993:63–64).

Most of those detained in the assembly centers gradually were moved to one of the relocation centers. These centers were placed away from the coastal areas and in climates that were "either too hot or too cold, too wet or too dry" (Hosokawa 1969:352). They were in California (Manzanar and Tule Lake), Arizona (Poston and Gila River), Arkansas (Rohwer and Jerome), Idaho (Minidoka), Utah (Topaz), Wyoming (Heart Mountain), and Colorado (Granada).[16] The camps were not finished when the first evacuees arrived; so, in addition to facing various kinds of shortages and physical discomforts, the internees also had to do a substantial share of the construction work needed to complete the camps. Since the camps' officials were eager to distinguish the relocation program from the concentration camp and forced-labor programs of the Nazis, much of the official language was euphemistic. The internees were referred to as "residents," their barracks were called "apartments," and the term "relocation center" was a euphemism for concentration camp (Tussman 1963:210).

Let us briefly consider life in the camps, giving special attention to what was intended to be the largest of the camps (Poston), which was located near Parker, Arizona.[17]

Life in the Camps

The camps' administrators attempted to organize the camps along the lines of a typical, self-governing, American community. They hoped in this way to reassure the friendly aliens and, especially, the loyal citizens that the U.S. government recognized their rights and was concerned about their welfare. It was hoped, too, that the camp communities would soon be able to support themselves through farming and also to serve as an example of the differences between authoritarian and democratic responses to internal and external threats.

The evacuees at Poston faced numerous problems related to housing, water, food, and other necessities. The "apartments" were flimsily constructed and small. Sometimes as many as eight people lived in one room and were often humiliated by the lack of privacy (Houston 1994:168–169; Sone 1994:167–168). There was hardly any furniture. Mattresses were made of cloth bags stuffed with straw. The heat was intense in the summer, whereas winter temperatures occasionally fell below freezing. And then there were the armed guards and the barbed-wire fences. It is little wonder that many people felt betrayed at having been sent to such a place and, therefore, either actively resisted or failed to cooperate fully with the administration's plans. Nevertheless, a newspaper, police force, and fire department were established. A community council was elected, an irrigation canal was completed, gardens were planted, and various social activities were organized. By the end of August 1942, Poston's population had reached its peak of 17,814 people (Daniels, Taylor, and Kitano 1991:xxi). By then, the more optimistic members of the administration were hoping that Poston soon would approximate a typical American community.

There were still many underlying problems, however. For example, there were internal divisions within the administrative group. And among the evacuees there existed a strong difference of opinion concerning the desirability of cooperating with the administration. The conservatives, most of whom were Issei, did not trust the administration and resented having the Nisei in positions of authority. The liberals, most of whom were Nisei, were impatient with those who did not try to prove their Americanism. Many in this group were enjoying the new responsibilities and experiences camp life had made possible. As tensions mounted, there was an increase in stealing, name-calling, and violence. Some evacuees believed there were FBI informers among them, and some of the suspected informers were assaulted. By the middle of November 1942, distrust and anger were widespread among the residents of Poston. The dissatisfaction of the residents culminated in a demonstration and general strike in one of Poston's three units. After several days of negotiations, the Emergency Executive Council (comprised almost entirely of Issei) agreed to end the strike in return for the release of a man who had been arrested.

Although the strike in Poston ended on a cooperative note, many officials were discouraged by the course of events in Poston and in most of the other camps as well. For example, several weeks after the Poston strike, a riot at Manzanar resulted in the killing and wounding of some of the evacuees (Daniels, Taylor, and Kitano 1991:xx); and early in 1943, the evacuees at Topaz were incensed when a soldier on guard duty shot and killed James Wakasa, a man who had lived in America for forty years and had himself served in the Army during World War I (Taylor 1993:136–137). Consequently, the officials abandoned the idea of developing the camps as model communities. Instead, the decision was made to resettle all "loyal" evacuees outside the camps as soon as possible.

This new plan was strengthened when the War Department reversed an earlier stand regarding military service for the Nisei by announcing its intention to form an all-Nisei combat team. Eventually, more than 20,000 Japanese and Japanese American men and women were inducted following this change of policy. Many Nisei served in the Pacific theater as interpreters, interviewers of prisoners, code breakers, and translators (Johnson 1995). These young Americans, recruited mainly from the camps, were "'the eyes and ears' of the Allied Forces in the Pacific" (O'Brien and Fugita 1991:65). Most of the rest served in the 100th Battalion and the 442nd Regimental Combat Team. These units compiled an outstanding battle record in the European theater.[18]

The decisions to resettle the evacuees and to enlist the Nisei for military duty led to a program of clearance and recruitment. Each evacuee was asked to answer a questionnaire concerning his or her background and loyalty to the United States. This program came as a surprise to the evacuees and resulted in anxiety, confusion, and controversy throughout the camps. The focus of controversy—around which several important issues revolved—was question 28: "Will you swear to abide by the laws of the United States and to take no action which would in any way interfere with the war effort of the United States" (Broom and Kitsuse 1956:28)?[19] Many internees were unsure how to answer this question. They wondered how a simple "yes" or "no" answer would be interpreted. A "yes" answer might mean that they, or some member of their family, would be drafted into military service; a "no" might mean they would be sent to a special prison camp for disloyals.

These issues clouded the government's plan to grant leave clearances to the "loyal" Japanese (i.e., those who answered "yes") and to segregate the "disloyal" Japanese in a special camp (Tule Lake). For example, by November 1943—less than a year after the Poston strike—more than 18,000 people had been segregated at Tule Lake; however, there was ample reason to believe that many of those were not really disloyal.[20] Indeed, some loyal Japanese felt it was their duty as Americans to protest the violation of their rights by refusing to cooperate with the effort to draft them (O'Brien and Fugita 1991:67). Many loyal Japanese also refused to cooperate with the government's effort to release them from the camps. At first, thousands of internees, mostly Nisei, did leave when they were cleared; but the number who chose to leave rapidly declined. Newspaper reports of violence against some of those who had resettled caused many others to refuse to leave; hence, at the begining of 1945, nearly 80,000 people remained in the camps. About half that number were still in the camps as the government moved to close them in the summer of 1945. It seems reasonable to conclude, as a government report did, that the treatment of the Japanese in the United States during World War II had tended "to disintegrate the fiber of a people who had previous to evacuation, been unusually self-reliant, sturdy, and independent" (War Relocation Authority 1946; quoted by Broom and Kitsuse 1956:32).

Legal Issues

The primary legal issues raised by the evacuation and relocation program were addressed by the U.S. Supreme Court in three different cases. The first of these, *Hirabayashi v. United States,* reached the Court in June 1943, over a year after the relocation program was set into motion.

Gordon Hirabayashi was arrested, convicted, and jailed for violating General DeWitt's curfew order to stay in his place of residence between the hours of 8:00 P.M. and 6:00 A.M. Hirabayashi's appeal to the Supreme Court maintained that the curfew order represented an unconstitutional delegation of congressional authority to the military and that it should have applied to all citizens within the military areas, not just to those of Japanese ancestry (Ball 1991:176). In an unanimous opinion, the Court stated: "Distinctions between citizens solely because of their ancestry are by their very nature odious to a free people" (Tussman 1963:190) but ruled, nevertheless, that because the danger was great the curfew order had been appropriate (Tussman 1963:192). Although the opinion upholding the curfew was unanimous, Justice Murphy noted that the restriction on the Japanese Americans "bears a melancholy resemblance to the treatment accorded to members of the Jewish race in Germany" (Tussman 1963:197).

The second case, *Korematsu v. United States,* concerned primarily the constitutionality of the evacuation of the Japanese Americans from the West Coast. Fred Korematsu had been born in the United States, had never been out of the country, did not speak Japanese, and was not suspected of disloyalty. He attempted to avoid the order to leave his home, was convicted, and was given a suspended sentence. The Supreme Court upheld Korematsu's conviction. Justice Douglas concurred but "was distraught by his vision of thousands of citizens incarcerated without benefit of loyalty hearings" (Ball 1991:180). Unlike in *Hirabayashi,* however, the decision was not unanimous. Justice Roberts argued that Korematsu's constitutional rights had been violated. Justice Murphy stated that the exclusion was not a military necessity and fell "into the ugly abyss of racism" (Tussman 1963:213). Justice Jackson rejected the idea that a given act (in this case, refusing to leave home) could be a crime if committed by a citizen of one race but not by a citizen of another.

The reservations that plagued the Supreme Court's members in their deliberations concerning the curfew and the evacuation reached full force in their consideration of *Ex Parte Endo.* Like Fred Korematsu, Mitsuye Endo had been born in the United States, did not speak Japanese, and had committed no specific act of disloyalty. Endo challenged the right of the government to imprison her and other loyal Japanese Americans; and all of the justices agreed with her. Ms. Endo and all other loyal Americans were to be set free unconditionally. Justice Murphy, who had reluctantly agreed to the curfew and had rejected the evacuation, stated that the relocation program had been discriminatory and was "utterly foreign to the ideals and traditions of the American people" (Petersen 1971:90). In one critic's opinion, "One hundred thousand persons were sent to concentration camps on a record which wouldn't support a conviction for stealing a dog" (Rostow 1945:146).

The full effects on the Japanese and Japanese Americans of the devastating experience of evacuation, relocation, and resettlement are beyond exact calculation. No meaningful estimate may be made of the emotional costs suffered by the thousands of people who saw their hopes and aspirations destroyed and their families broken;[21] and although no one knows exactly the extent of the monetary losses, there can be no doubt that they were enormous. When in 1948 the Evacuation Claims Act was passed, the internees were paid about $37 million as restitution for their losses (Taylor 1991:166). A debate concerning the adequacy of this payment commenced, however; and in 1983 the Commission on Wartime Relocation and Internment of Civilians (CWRIC) issued a report stating that the total losses were "between $810 million and $2 billion in 1983 dollars" (quoted by Taylor 1991:166).[22] In 1988, after a long campaign for redress spearheaded by the JACL (Tateishi 1991), Congress passed a bill stating that a "grave injustice was done to both citizens and permanent resident aliens of Japanese ancestry" by the relocation program and that the relocation was a result of "racial prejudice, wartime hysteria, and a failure of political leadership" (Daniels, Taylor, and Kitano 1991:226). The bill agreed to award each of more than 60,000 surviving detainees a tax-free payment of about $20,000 dollars. The payments, accompanied by a formal apology by President George Bush, commenced in a public ceremony on October 9, 1990 (Daniels 1991b:219).[23]

Another form of restitution also occurred during the decades following World War II. In 1983, Fred Korematsu was formally cleared of the charges leveled against him in 1942. Accordingly, his conviction for refusing to obey a military order was overturned. Judge Marilyn Hall Patel, who presided, stated "that the government knowingly withheld information from the courts" and relied "on unsubstantiated facts, distortions and representations of at least one military commander whose views were seriously infected by racism" (Minami 1991:201). Then, in 1986, Gordon Hirabayashi won a court case establishing that government officials had withheld vital information during his trial in 1942. The court agreed that the government's claim that people of Japanese ancestry had been a threat to national security was false (Howery 1986:9).

From the vantage point of the present, we may look back and see that by the end of the second-generation period the Nisei (and many Issei as well) were strongly committed to American society and culture. Many of them embraced the goal of secondary assimilation and, perhaps also, of primary and marital assimilation. Their lives were suddenly thrown into disarray, however, in the aftermath of the attack on Pearl Harbor. They and their families suddenly were forced out of their homes and various normal pursuits, transported to inland prisons, and incarcerated. What were the effects of these catastrophic events on their subsequent adaptation to American society?

𝒥apanese American Assimilation

Cultural Assimilation

Our reasoning about rates of assimilation (in Chapter 2) showed that it is best to think in terms of several subprocesses, such as cultural assimilation (by substitution or addition), secondary assimilation, primary assimilation, and marital assimilation. We also saw (in Chapter 1) the necessity of taking into account certain important factors that usually influence the course of assimilation, such as the size of the immigrant group, the social distance between the immigrants and the host society, whether the group entered voluntarily, the timing of the immigration, and the goals of the immigrants. In the case of the Japanese in America, the factor of intergenerational differences also assumed an unusual importance.

Intergenerational Differences. First-generation groups ordinarily limit their contacts with people outside of the group mainly to economic matters, and this was true of the Issei; and, as is usual for such groups, the Issei wished to maintain and transmit their own heritage to the Nisei to prevent the development of a wide cultural gap between the generations. The Japanese language schools were designed to assist the Issei to achieve these goals. As noted previously, however, the language schools were not really very successful in these respects. Contacts with English-speaking children in the public schools influenced the Nisei, as it had other second-generation groups, to move toward cultural assimilation. Although the Nisei were restrained and "Japanesey" in the home, they favored the American pattern of behavior in school and other public settings. Additionally, the Issei were "ineligible to citizenship," whereas the children with whom the Nisei mainly associated were, like themselves, born in America. The halt in the flow of Japanese immigrants combined with these factors to create an unusually wide cultural gap between the Issei and Nisei.

Little has been said so far concerning the Sansei; but this third generation is of special importance in any effort to assess the rate of assimilation among Japanese Americans. According to the ideas of Park and Gordon, the Sansei should be more assimilated than the Nisei and both should be more assimilated than the Issei. The cultural assimilation of the Sansei should occur by substitution and should be close to the Anglo American pattern. The facts concerning cultural assimilation are far from complete and must be pieced together from several different sources. The evidence is generally based on studies of small samples, although some results from a national sample of Japanese Americans are available.

Several studies have found evidence that is consistent with the expectation that each succeeding generation will be more assimilated. Connor (1974:161) found that the Issei in his study were most likely to agree with statements reflecting traditional child-rearing ideas (e.g., "Parents can never be repaid for what they have done for their children"), the Nisei were intermediate in agreement, and the Sansei were least likely to agree. In a comparison of Nisei and Sansei, Feagin and Fujitaki (1972:18) found that although an individual's religious affiliation is a complicating factor, with Buddhism serving to support the traditional culture, some evidence showed that the Sansei were more culturally assimilated than the Nisei. To illustrate, the Nisei were more likely to be comfortable speaking Japanese and to do so regularly in the home than were the Sansei. They also felt more strongly than the Sansei the importance of maintaining Japanese customs and traditions. Matsumoto, Meredith, and Masuda (1973) found the general pattern of increasing cultural assimilation by generation among Japanese Americans in Honolulu and Seattle, though the strength of the pattern in the two cities was not identical. Kitano (1969:156–157) examined answers given by the members of the three generations to statements such as "Once a Japanese, always a Japanese" and, as expected, found that the Issei were most likely and the Sansei least likely to agree with the statements. In regard to some aspects of traditional beliefs, however, the expected pattern either was weak or did not appear. Finally, based on an analysis of data from a comprehensive national survey of the Issei, Nisei, and Sansei[24]—the Japanese American Research Project (JARP)—Woodrum (1978:80) found that, in terms of English proficiency and religious affiliation, the Nisei were more culturally assimilated than the Issei.

The findings of these studies are not totally consistent, but they strongly suggest—as expected under assimilation theory—that cultural assimilation was low among the Issei, higher among the Nisei, and highest among the Sansei.

The Sansei.   Are the Sansei "completely Americanized" as many Issei have said (Connor 1974)? Only two of the studies cited contain pertinent information. Connor (1974) found much less acceptance of traditional Japanese ideas among the Sansei than among the members of the other two generations, but he also found more acceptance of these ideas among the Sansei than among a sample of Anglo Americans. Kitano also found noticeable differences between the Sansei and the Anglo Americans in regard to certain beliefs and attitudes.

A revival of cultural nationalism among the Sansei, beginning during the 1960s, affords some further evidence that they have not completely abandoned their Japanese heritage and, at the same time, that the process of ethnogenesis may be at work. A major theme of this revival is that Japanese Americans should reject the Anglo conformity of the Nisei and actively promote some form of cultural pluralism in which the valued traditions of Japan, as modified by the American experience, may be sustained and elaborated. Those who champion this view are extremely critical of the older generations' willingness to "make the most of a bad situation and push ahead" (Fujimoto 1971:207) or, even worse, to focus attention on the presumably beneficial effects of the wartime relocation. They view the historical experience of the Japanese minority in America as being essentially like that of the Chinese, Koreans, and Filipinos and quite similar to that of Black Americans, Mexican Americans, and American Indians. As Ichioka (1971:222) stated in a critical review of Hosokawa's book *Nisei: The Quiet Americans,* "In this time of political, social, and moral crisis in America, old and new problems demand radical approaches, not tired orations. . . . We bid the old guard to retire as 'quiet Americans.'" Nevertheless, the nationalist tone of the 1960s and 1970s had subsided sufficiently by the mid-1980s to permit Kitano and Daniels (1988:71) to remark that "the Sansei and Yonsei . . . are the most 'American' of any Japanese group; many of them have never faced overt discrimination, and some have never had close ethnic ties or ethnic friends."

On the basis of our observations concerning the Sansei, we offer the following generalization: Their level of cultural assimilation by substitution is higher than that of the two preceding generations, but they still exhibit some elements of the traditional culture of Japan and are, in some cases, actively attempting either to revive their ancient heritage or to construct a specifically Japanese American identity.[25]

Given the comparatively high degree of cultural assimilation by substitution among the Nisei and Sansei, how far have these groups moved toward the American pattern in terms of the other main subprocesses of assimilation? We saw previously that the Japanese Americans have attained in some respects a high degree of secondary structural assimilation (e.g., in education, occupation, and income). We turn now to some further evidence on secondary assimilation.

Secondary Structural Assimilation

Organizational Membership.   In addition to a group's levels of education, occupation, and income, another indicator of secondary assimilation is membership in nonethnic formal organizations. Excellent evidence on organizational memberships for the Japanese Americans may be found in several studies based on the data gathered in the JARP study. For example, Levine and Rhodes (1981:78–79) found that among the Nisei who belonged to only one organization (not counting church), 58 percent belonged to a Japanese American group, whereas 42 percent did not. Even among "joiners" (Nisei who belonged to four or five organizations), 27 percent belonged to no Japanese organizations. The level of participation was lower still among the Sansei. Most of those in the third generation were not members of a Japanese organization. Among those who belonged to a noncollege organization, about half belonged to one that was not Japanese; and among the "joiners," most of the members' time was given to the nonethnic groups. Montero's (1980:60) analysis, also based on JARP data, showed that a majority of both the Nisei and Sansei (55 and 69 percent, respectively) who belong to groups name a non-Japanese group as their "favorite organization."

In a different study, Fugita and O'Brien (1985:989) reported that, excluding church membership, over 69 percent of their sample belonged to non-Japanese organizations and almost 53 percent were members of Japanese organizations. Fugita and O'Brien believed, however, that the level of Japanese American participation in ethnic organizations was still high in comparison to most other ethnic groups. They stressed that the participation of Japanese Americans in voluntary associations was especially high "in areas with a lower density of fellow ethnics," a finding that suggested these Japanese Americans made a special effort to be involved in the community (O'Brien and Fugita 1991:102)

Residential Assimilation.   Another important measure of the extent to which secondary assimilation is occurring for a given ethnic minority is the degree to which the group lives in desegregated residential areas. We emphasized previously that American ethnic groups always have tended to congregate in certain areas, as well as to be segregated, and that these areas frequently have become known as "their" parts of town; however, to the extent that an ethnic group's members accept either the Anglo conformity or pluralist models of adaptation, we would expect that as assimilation occurred they would leave their old neighborhoods and move into less separated neighborhoods, even if the initial separation was largely voluntary (Zhou and Logan 1991:388). This expectation is called the **theory of spatial assimilation** (Gross and Massey 1991:350). The initial residential segregation that was typical of European ethnic groups also characterized the residential patterns of Japanese Americans. In most cities of the West, those of Japanese heritage have been noticeably segregated from other groups. The extent of this segregation, however, has varied greatly among cities, reflecting the many factors that affect residential assimilation.

Sociologists frequently have studied the extent of residential segregation of different groups by calculating and comparing what are called **indexes of dissimilarity** (Taeuber and Taeuber 1964:29). The basic idea of an index of dissimilarity may be seen in an example: If 25 percent of the people in a given city were Japanese Americans, and if 25 percent of the people in each part of the city were Japanese Americans, this group would not be residentially segregated and the index of dissimilarity would be zero. On the other hand, if all of the city's Japanese Americans lived together, and there were no other ethnic groups represented among them, then there would be complete segregation and the index of residential segregation would be 100. This index, therefore, ranges from a low of 0 (no segregation) to a high of 100 (complete segregation). Index values above 60 are considered high, those below 30 are considered low, and those between 30 and 59 are considered moderate (Kantrowitz, cited by Denton and Massey 1988:804). Although this way of estimating residential segregation has faults, it is easy to understand and extremely useful.

Jiobu (1988:114) presented some valuable information on the residential segregation of Japanese Americans and the members of six other ethnic groups (each as compared to Whites) in the twenty-one Standard Metropolitan Statistical Areas (SMSAs) in California.[26] For the Japanese Americans, the average (mean) level of segregation (dissimilarity) was a moderate 46. The levels of Japanese segregation in the various SMSAs ranged from a high of 65 (in Visalia) to a low of 29 (in San Jose). In the largest SMSA, Los Angeles, the index for Japanese Americans was 54. The average level of segregation in the twenty-one SMSAs for Koreans, by comparison, was 69, and for Vietnamese the average was 76. In fact, the average level of segregation for the Japanese was the lowest among the seven groups included in the study. These findings indicate that Japanese Americans in California were more assimilated residentially than the members of the other comparison groups but were still moderately segregated from the dominant group.

Some additional information presented by Farley and Allen (1987:145) indicated that residential segregation among the Japanese is moderate throughout the United States. These researchers examined sixteen of the largest metropolitan areas in the United States and found that the average level of residential segregation in 1980 for all Asians combined was 43, ranging from a high of 54 in New Orleans to a low of 31 in Washington. Denton and Massey (1988) studied the relationship of residential segregation to educational, occupational, and income levels among the twenty SMSAs in the United States that contained the largest populations of Asians in 1980. The results, for all Asian groups combined, showed that as these groups have risen in socioeconomic status, the levels of segregation have been substantially and uniformly higher among the least educated than among the most educated members of the Asian groups (Denton and Massey 1988:811).

White, Biddlecom, and Guo (1993) examined a special census file to study the residential assimilation of seven Asian groups living in the fifty largest SMSAs in the United States. The results of this study confirmed the finding by Denton and Massey that higher levels of education were linked to higher levels of residential assimilation among all of the groups. They also found that all of the Asian groups tended to live in neighborhoods comprised primarily of Anglo Americans. They did not find however, as Jiobu had for California, that the Japanese had the highest level of residential assimilation among these groups. After taking into account (in addition to education and income) such factors as whether people were native or foreign born, were naturalized citizens, their age, and (if immigrants) the year in which they arrived, White, Biddlecom, and Guo (1993:110–111) concluded that the groups that had been in the United States longest (Japanese, Chinese, and Filipinos) were somewhat less assimilated residentially than the more recent arrivals. They suggested that this finding may reflect the earlier experiences of these groups in America.

Taken together, we conclude that these studies of organizational participation and residential segregation are largely consistent with our earlier conclusion based on Japanese attainment in income, education, and occupation. By each of these measures, a substantial amount of secondary assimilation has occurred among Japanese Americans.

Primary Structural Assimilation

If the Japanese Americans are participating more in "mixed" organizations (including schools and businesses) than in all-Japanese organizations, and if they live in relatively mixed neighborhoods, then presumably a foundation has been laid for the more "social" activities that indicate the occurrence of primary structural assimilation. The studies based on the national data from the JARP provide important evidence concerning the extent to which the Nisei and Sansei interact with people of Japanese and non-Japanese ethnicity. For instance, in answer to questions concerning their two closest friends, a majority of the Nisei (53 percent) and a large majority of the Sansei (74 percent) reported that at least one of their two closest friends was non-Japanese (Montero 1980:60; see also Fugita and O'Brien 1985:993).

Do Japanese Americans visit their neighbors more freely if they live in a mostly Japanese neighborhood? According to Levine and Rhodes (1981:83), "the Nisei are neighborly folk. Whatever the composition of their environs, about seven of every ten are on visiting terms with three or more neighbors." These findings suggest that the Nisei have reached a fairly high level of primary assimilation and (given the findings on the friendship patterns of the Sansei) that the Sansei are moving even further in that direction. This conclusion also is supported by the finding that 75 percent of the Nisei and 80 percent of the Sansei want their children to associate actively with Whites rather than sticking "pretty much with Japanese Americans" (Levine and Rhodes 1981:115).

Marital Assimilation

Marital assimilation, when completed, represents the end point among the subprocesses of assimilation we are studying. Intermarriage is of special importance "because it can be understood as both an indicator of the degree of assimilation of ethnic and racial groups and an agent itself of further assimilation" (Lieberson and Waters 1988:162).

Those who intermarry contribute to the blurring of ethnic boundaries. They increase the diversity of their respective ethnic groups and increase the range of ethnic identities that their children may assume. Some important factors that increase the rate of out-marriage are small group size, spatial nearness to other ethnic groups, low social distance between ethnic groups, a long period of time in the United States, and religious similarity (Alba and Golden 1986; Stevens and Swicegood 1987).

Although the importance of studying ethnic intermarriage is clear, the solution to some research problems is less so; and the interpretation of statistics on intermarriage requires caution. For example, when a marriage occurs between a member of the majority group and a member of a minority group, we ordinarily consider this to be evidence of marital assimilation by the partner from the minority group; however, if the friends of the married couple are drawn mainly from the minority group, if the couple lives in a neighborhood composed primarily of others in the minority group, and if the children of the marriage are raised in the culture of the minority group, are we still to call this assimilation? Consider also this situation: Minority-group members who marry out frequently select partners from other minority groups. Does this represent assimilation? "Does a woman," Spickard (1989:17) asked, "cease to be black or brown or yellow or white if she marries someone of another color?" Moreover, what constitutes an out-marriage? Is a marriage of a person who is part Irish and part German to a person who is part Irish and part Italian an in-marriage or an out-marriage? Finally, what conclusion should be drawn when the children of out-marriages identify themselves as members of two or more ethnic groups (Stephan and Stephan 1989)? With these questions in mind, let us examine the results of some studies on intermarriage among the Japanese.[27]

Except in Hawaii, interracial marriages of all kinds in the United States have been low. This is due in large part to the fact that many laws have defined the boundaries of races in terms of the criteria commonly used in the community—as distinct from direct evidence on genotypes—and prohibited marriages across those lines. Burma (1963) studied all forms of interethnic marriage in Los Angeles between 1948 and 1959 by analyzing information gathered from marriage licenses. The period studied by Burma was chosen because, before 1948, the laws of California prohibited intermarriages of Whites with members of another race (defined largely by color); and during 1959, it became illegal to require a marriage license to show an applicant's race.[28] The data of the study, therefore, reflect what was happening during a crucial time span in an area possessing a comparatively large Japanese American population. Out of more than 375,000 marriage applications, Burma counted over 3,000 that were interracial; and of these, 600 involved Japanese applicants (Burma 1963:163). His data showed that out-marriages involving Japanese Americans rose from approximately 11 percent of all out-marriages in 1949 to nearly 23 percent of the cases in 1959.[29]

Based on studies in Fresno and San Francisco reported by Tinker (1973), the trend in intermarriages between White Americans and Japanese Americans noted by Burma apparently continued, especially among the Sansei. Tinker found that in Fresno in the 1969–1971 period, half of all marriages involving Japanese Americans were out-marriages. A similar level of out-marriage also was discovered by Kikimura and Kitano in Hawaii for 1970 and in Los Angeles during 1971 and 1972. These authors concluded that various reports strongly suggest that out-marriages have become so frequent among Japanese Americans that the Sansei are as likely to marry outside the group as within it. Finally, Parkman and Sawyer (1967:597) compared intermarriage rates during the years 1928–1934 with those of 1948–1953 and found that the rate of Japanese out-marriage roughly tripled between the two periods.

The trend toward increasing marital assimilation among the Japanese Americans found in these geographically limited studies is generally confirmed by two broader studies. On the basis of JARP's national sample, Woodrum (1978:80) found that out-marriage became more common with each succeeding generation. Similarly, on the basis of a national public-use sample prepared by the U.S. Bureau of the Census, Gurak and Kritz (1978:38) analyzed intermarriage statistics for thirty-five ethnic groups and found that the Nisei have married out more frequently than the Issei.[30] They also found, however, that the Nisei who married out were less likely to marry a member of the Anglo American core group than were the Issei. Spickard (1989:119) noted that the in-termarriage rate for each Japanese American generation has been higher in areas where the Japanese-ancestry population was sparse.

Although the case is far from proven, it seems reasonable to say that the Japanese Americans have been moving rapidly in the direction of Anglo conformity assimilation in regard to each of the subprocesses we have examined. Despite the many unanswered questions, it is easy to see why the Japanese Americans frequently are mentioned as evidence that any group—regardless of their race, culture, or history of oppression—can move fully into the mainstream of American life, usually within three generations. It also is easy to see why controversy continues over the final outcome of this drama of association between two very different groups—the Japanese minority and the Anglo majority.

Much of the evidence suggests that Park's and Gordon's analyses are correct and that complete, or practically complete, Anglo conformity assimilation awaits Japanese Americans. Kitano and Daniels (1988:73) reported that the Sansei and later generations "overwhelmingly" accept interracial marriage. In their view, this belief "adds to the possible acceleration of assimilation" (Kitano and Daniels 1988:73). Some signs, however, point to a different direction. For one thing, even though overt discrimination against Japanese Americans is now comparatively low, O'Brien and Fugita (1991:104) found that over half of their Sansei sample believed that Japanese Americans continue to face discrimination. Kitano and Daniels (1988:74), similarly, noted that Japanese Americans are still physically visible and, therefore, are subject to certain kinds of limitations. For example, in television, movie, and stage productions, even Sansei who are highly assimilated culturally may still find they are asked to play roles such as an enemy soldier, a gardener, or a cook. Evidently, "the desired body type and physical image in America remains that of a Caucasian" (Kitano and Daniels 1988:74). And Hirschman and Wong (1985:304) cautioned that to some extent Japanese American success, particularly in education, may signify that the group is being denied opportunities along other lines. Educational success, in this view, is emphasized as the surest way to escape social and economic discrimination (Goleman 1990:B8).

In addition to the fact that those Japanese Americans who wish to pursue Anglo conformity may still face discrimination, we also have noted that pluralist goals may be rising within the Japanese American community. Family and community ties among Japanese Americans appear still to be strong and, especially among the Sansei, there has been a resurgence of pride and interest in their ethnic heritage. For these reasons, the prediction that the Japanese Americans will continue on the path toward Anglo conformity may be incorrect. As Levine and Montero (1973:47) stated, "there is little evidence that the subculture will soon wither away."

Japanese American "Success"

As we observed at the beginning of this chapter, the success of the Japanese in American society, especially in terms of education and occupation, has caused many people to wonder how they have been able to overcome the stigma of a non-White identity and to do so in a comparatively short time against such great odds. Speaking quite broadly, the scholarly theories presented to explain this phenomenon have focused primarily on what are called cultural and structural factors.[31]

The Cultural View

We stressed earlier that the Issei brought with them the traditional values of Japan. They believed, as have the members of many other groups, in the importance of hard work, thrift, education, occupational success, the pursuit of long-range goals, politeness, respect for authority, mutual trust, perseverance, and duty to one's parents and community. The latter belief was at the center of family life. Marriages created not just unions of couples but unions of families. The extended family units that were formed thereby were connected, in turn, in numerous ways to the larger community. An important effect of this pattern of interrelationships was that everyone in the community had important obligations to many others within the community. Each of the individual families was embedded within a highly organized network. Various traditions of organization, such as those leading to the formation of rotating credit groups, afforded a "cultural blueprint" that helped create community solidarity (O'Brien and Fugita 1991:3).

Value Compatibility.   Advocates of the cultural view have emphasized two ways in which the family and community values just described have contributed to the success of the Japanese in America. The first of these focused on the idea that there is "a significant compatibility (but by no means identity) between the value systems found in the culture of Japan and the value systems in American middle class culture" (Caudill and DeVos 1956:1107). The **value compatibility** argument is not that Japanese and American middle-class cultures are similar in general but rather that certain key values are common to these otherwise quite different cultures.

In a study of some 20,000 Issei and Nisei who were resettled in Chicago during World War II, for example, Caudill and DeVos (1956) found that the Nisei quickly moved out of menial, unskilled, and poorly paid jobs into semiskilled, service, and managerial jobs. They also moved out of the undesirable residential districts and into more expensive housing. They were accepted by employers, landlords, and neighbors and were praised as hard workers who showed respect for authority. From this perspective, the Nisei succeeded in Chicago because "All in all, Japanese reverence for hard work, achievement, self-control, dependability, manners, thrift, and diligence were entirely congruent with American middle-class perceptions" (Kitano 1969:76).

Family and Community Cohesion.   The discussion so far has rested on the assumption that the Issei were the bearers of the traditional values of Japan and that these values were transmitted substantially intact to the Nisei. This result, of course, is what one might expect within a closely knit family group. Recall, however, that the generation gap between the Issei and Nisei was larger in some important respects than has been true of many other ethnic groups in America. For example, the Issei could not become citizens of the United States, whereas the Nisei were citizens. And the Nisei rapidly turned to Christianity, unlike the Issei who in general remained Buddhists. Petersen (1971:202–207) contended that the differences between the Issei and Nisei led, in fact, to a high degree of intergenerational conflict over dating, courtship, marriage, and politics. He emphasized, though, that the various forms of adolescent rebellion of the Nisei were not translated into the kind of general social rebellion that often has occurred among second-generation immigrants. The Nisei usually were considered to be "good" boys and girls by their teachers, law enforcement officers, and social welfare officials. Nevertheless, the intergenerational conflict that did exist was sufficiently serious to make us wonder how the Issei were able to perform the task of value transmission. Miyamoto (1939; 1972) and Petersen (1971) argued that the transmission of the traditional values to the Nisei and Sansei was accomplished by the entire Japanese community. According to Miyamoto (1972:218), "the Japanese minority maintained a high degree of family and community organization in America, and these organizations enforced value conformity and created conditions and means for status achievement."

The emphasis on community solidarity in the transmission of values directs our attention to the high frequency with which other people in the Japanese community supported the efforts of particular parents. Kitano (1969:68) illustrated this point in a story of a Nisei child who broke his arm in an athletic contest. The child was told by a series of Japanese adults, including his scoutmaster, his parents, his doctor, and his schoolteacher, that "Japanese boys don't cry"; and he was praised when he did not cry. Incidents of this sort were a daily reminder to the Nisei that they were Japanese and that the entire community expected them to behave as their parents had instructed. From this perspective, the entire community molded the Nisei and prepared them for success in school and later life.

Has the Japanese American family continued to place a high value on education or has cultural assimilation served to reduce education's importance? Research by Schneider and others strongly supported the view that the value of educational achievement has continued at a high level among the children and grandchildren of the Nisei. In a study of East Asian students of Chinese, Japanese, and Korean heritage, Schneider and Lee (1990:360) combined information on the students' economic and cultural histories with information concerning their personal interactions with their parents, teachers, and other students. Based on in-depth interviews, Schneider and Lee (1990:370, 374) found that "East Asian parents tended to have clearer and higher educational expectations for their children than Anglo parents" and that these expectations "are transmitted through a cultural context in which education is highly valued."

In a later study comparing the educational achievements of more than 24,000 East Asian American and White American students, Schneider, Hieshima, Lee, and Plank (1994) specifically explored Japanese American values using evidence from in-depth interviews with Sansei parents and their Yonsei children. These authors found that in some respects the Yonsei were more similar to White students than to Chinese and Korean students, but they also found that "Japanese Americans, like other East-Asian groups, place a high intrinsic value on education" (Schneider, Hieshima, Lee, and Plank 1994: 347). The authors argued that the emphasis on education among Japanese Americans has been transmitted through the close relations of family members even though the families have become Americanized in some other respects.

Critique.   Few scholars have claimed that the culture of the Japanese has been irrelevant to their success in America. Still, as presented, the cultural view has attracted substantial criticism. We have alluded already to one of the most frequent complaints: When the achievements of the Japanese (or any other group) are recounted as a "success story," the story diverts attention from continuing discrimination and other problems that the group may have. It also may become a stereotype to be used by the majority as a "put-down" for other minorities, especially other non-White minorities (Okimoto 1971; Tachiki 1971). The majority may point to the Japanese and ask, "They have made it; why can't you?" The implied answer to the question is that if success is the result of possessing the "right" values, then the group is not transmitting the "right" values to its individual members. This implication places all of the blame for the "failure" of the group on the group itself. The opponents of cultural interpretations often state that such views "blame the victim" by asserting or implying that worldly success or failure is due mainly to differences in will power or effort (Ryan 1971).

Another related criticism is that the "success–values" argument "has been made with respect to every ethnic group that has achieved a notable degree of affluence" (Steinberg 1989:84). In addition to the Japanese, as we noted earlier, some other groups that frequently are cited as demonstrating the efficacy of success values are the Chinese, Cubans, East Asians, Greeks, Jews and Koreans.[32] Do all these groups possess the same constellation of values in the same degree? And do they differ from less successful groups only in this way? Steinberg (1989:87) summarized the requirements for an adequate analysis as follows: "Only by adopting a theoretical approach that explores the interaction between cultural and material factors is it possible to assess the role of values in ethnic mobility without mystifying culture and imputing a cultural superiority to groups that have enjoyed disproportionate success." *This important point must be kept in mind each time we discuss differences in group success in later chapters.*

The structural view includes attempts to explain group differences in terms of specific "material factors."

The Structural View

Discussions concerning the success of the Issei frequently note that despite their initial poverty they rapidly became established as the independent owners or operators of many small businesses and farms. Bonacich and Modell (1980:37–43) cited several studies showing that by 1930, even in the face of vigorous discrimination, the Japanese were concentrated in small, family-owned businesses, both as owners and employees. From this vantage point, the general question, "How did the Issei succeed?" may be stated more specifically: "How did the Issei become established in businesses?"

Several noncultural answers to this question have been proposed. Ikeda (1973: 498), for instance, argued that the Japanese who came from the less impoverished districts of Japan and had the highest literacy levels were the most successful in America. Daniels (1969:11–12) stated that the hostility of the Americans toward the Japanese made their employment prospects so uncertain that the Japanese were practically forced to use their skills on an independent basis. Still another suggestion was that the Japanese reached the West Coast just in time to fill some empty niches in the economy of a rapidly expanding new region (Modell 1977). Lieberson (1980:381–382) argued that the cessation of immigration from Japan decreased direct competition between the natives and Japanese and created the opportunity for the latter gradually to occupy special niches.

Middleman Minority Theory.   Another noncultural explanation of Japanese success is that they comprised a **middleman minority.** Such minorities, which have appeared throughout the world at different times in history, are referred to as "middlemen" because "they occupy an intermediate rather than low-status position" (Bonacich 1973:583). The **middleman minority theory** is based on the idea that sojourning is a necessary ingredient in the development of an intermediate economic position, and its application to the Japanese rests on the fact that initially they were sojourners (Bonacich 1973:585–588). Such groups typically concentrate in commerce and trade. The main reasons for this appear to be that sojourners are strongly motivated (1) to work hard and be thrifty in order to amass capital as quickly as possible, (2) to take risks in the hope of great gains, and (3) to concentrate their funds in lines of work that permit easy liquidation (Bonacich and Modell 1980:30). These characteristics promote high ethnic-group solidarity. Sojourners cultivate ties with other members of their own group and avoid strong ties with those in the host group; hence, when sojourners having the requisite skills are confronted by a hostile society, the chances are high that they will concentrate in small businesses and will cooperate closely in economic and all other matters (Cobas 1985).

The strong solidarity and economic cooperation of the Japanese, from this perspective, enabled them to cut costs in a number of ways and thereby to compete effectively not only with other small businesses but even with the giant firms that dominated the "center" of the American economy. Typically, the entire family worked long hours in the business without pay, and all earnings except those that were essential to life and health were "plowed back" into the business (Bonacich and Modell 1980:47). The businesses developed along these lines soon were able to provide employment for other

Japanese who also were willing to work long hours at low pay; such employees commonly accepted room and board as a part of their pay, which further reduced the cost of running the business. Community solidarity also led to cooperative agreements with kinsmen that created both **vertical** and **horizontal integration**. Through thrift and cooperation, the business holdings of the Japanese grew at a very rapid rate.

Dual-Economy Theory.   The middleman minority theory helps to explain not only the economic success of some immigrant groups, but also to explain how they provided the support their children needed in order to be able to enter that segment of the economy known as the **primary labor market**.[33] The primary labor market contains "good" jobs that are stable, offer chances for promotion, and have high wages and good working conditions. Workers in this segment of the economy receive earnings and promotions that are commensurate with their levels of education and skill. Most immigrants in the past, however, as well as large numbers of unskilled or undocumented contemporary immigrants, were unable to gain jobs that were in the primary labor market. These immigrants, instead, were forced into the **secondary labor market** which consists of "dead-end," poorly paid jobs. Even people who assimilate culturally or possess high levels of education or skill may be trapped in this segment of the economy and may be unable to move up occupationally. This line of reasoning, known as **dual-economy theory**, affords the point of departure for another explanation of the business success of certain immigrant groups.

Ethnic-Enclave Theory.   Although many groups in history may be described as having played the role of middlemen, Portes and Bach (1985:340) argue that the middleman theory "fits awkwardly" as a description of the experience of the Japanese Americans; and they also question its application to the experience of the Jews (who definitely were not sojourners) and of the Cubans in America. They prefer instead the **ethnic-enclave theory** (Wilson and Portes 1980). This theory is based on the idea that immigrant workers may be part of a special type of economy that provides unusual routes of upward mobility (Butler and Wilson 1988; Portes 1981; Wilson and Martin 1982). Such an economy, say its proponents, is not a middleman economy, though it may resemble one in some ways. It does not necessarily function as an intermediary between those in the upper and lower reaches of the economy; but it is based on community solidarity, the presence of a pool of disadvantaged ethnic workers, and vertical and horizontal integration. An **ethnic enclave** is a grouping of immigrants who organize a variety of business enterprises (Portes and Bach 1985:203).[34] Ethnic-enclave economies—for example, the ones developed by the Cubans in Miami and Los Angeles and the Japanese in Honolulu and Los Angeles (Logan, Alba, and McNulty 1994:717)—thus present a third kind of labor market in which immigrant workers only *appear* to be participating in a secondary labor market located at the economic "periphery" (Wilson and Martin 1982: 155). In fact, they occupy "good" jobs within the ethnic enclave resembling those in the "center" economy (Butler 1991:30).

A vigorous debate developed among specialists concerning the enclave theory (Portes and Zhou 1996; Sanders and Nee 1996), with some studies finding that ethnic solidarity did enable immigrant workers to enjoy advantages similar to those of participants in the primary labor market (e.g., Bailey and Waldinger 1991; Wilson and Martin

1982) and others finding contrary evidence (e.g., Gilbertson and Gurak 1993; Sanders and Nee 1987). The reason for an "enclave effect," when it appears, also has been a subject of debate. One explanation was based on a group's ability to gain a high level of control over markets (Jiobu 1988); another argued that enclaves provide a training system that reduces risks for both employers and employees (Bailey and Waldinger 1991).

Consequences of Issei Success.   We have seen that the Japanese business economy was destroyed by the relocation program during World War II and, although it was re-built in a modified form after the war, many of the Nisei found careers outside of the ethnic community. The high level of education among the Nisei opened up many opportunities within the mainstream economy; but then the Nisei were torn between their loyalty to the ethnic community and their desire to "get ahead" within the majority society (Montero 1980:85–86; 1981:835). There is some irony in the fact that the educational achievement that was so encouraged by the Issei and made possible by the solidarity of the Japanese community also has made it possible for the Nisei to leave the ethnic community entirely (Bonacich and Modell 1980:152). On the other hand, as Butler (1991:244) proposed, the Issei's hope that their children would experience economic mobility in the broader society may have been an important reason for the parents' great efforts in business. Indeed, this pattern appears to be typical of entrepreneurial minorities. Portes and Bach (1985:346) concluded in this regard that the progress made by the immigrants is "consolidated into educational and occupational mobility, within and outside the ethnic enclave, by later generations."

In keeping with this view, the trend toward increased occupational assimilation appears to be marked among the Sansei, though they still are prominent as entrepreneurs (O'Hare 1992:34; Taylor 1993:276–277). O'Brien and Fugita (1984; 1991) argued, however, that the increasing independence of the Sansei from the ethnic enclave does not necessarily mean that their Japanese ethnicity is of diminished importance to them. More likely, these changes may mean that the basis of ethnic identification has shifted from one of economic cooperation to one of psychological support; therefore, we should not conclude that the continued upward mobility of the Japanese necessarily will lead to the complete loss of Japanese identification and culture.

A Comparison of Success Theories

Our discussion has revealed a variety of factors that may help to explain the worldly success of the Japanese in America. They have lived by a code of values that encourages achievement; they have exhibited a high degree of community solidarity that may be rooted in the traditions of Japan and also in their economic adaptation to American society (whether as middlemen or participants in a dual economy or an ethnic-enclave economy); and they have used skills learned in Japan to fill special niches in the American economy. Each of these (and other) factors must be considered in an adequate explanation of Japanese achievement.

We must neither ignore nor exaggerate the role of culture in our attempt to understand the Japanese experience in America. An exclusive emphasis on cultural factors, as noted earlier, tends to promote "self-congratulatory sentimentalism" (Steinberg 1989:

87); but it also is true that situational and other "material" factors may be overemphasized. Most theorists agree that the success values and group pride of the Japanese have played an important role in the outcome. As Hirschman and Wong (1986:4) stated, "The introduction of structural determinants does not eliminate the role of cultural influences."

The facts of Japanese success in education, occupational standing, and income levels, if not their causes, are generally uncontested; but some Japanese American militants have expressed doubts about the human meaning of their success. Is the material success that has always lain at the center of the values of American society really a worthwhile goal for human beings (Takagi 1973:151)? In the view of some Japanese Americans, the answer to this question is "no"! Okimoto (1971:17) put it this way: "I doubt whether we have succeeded in any but the narrowest materialist definition of the word."

Evidently, these questions and observations plunge us headlong into the arena of conflicting value premises. They also illustrate in concrete terms the conflict between the ideology of Anglo conformity and such alternatives as cultural pluralism and separatism. Whether one prefers or rejects Anglo conformity, however, it is generally agreed that the experience of the Japanese Americans confirms the rule that non-White groups are especially subject to severe discrimination in the United States. It seems uncontested, too, that the Japanese Americans have been exceptional in the extent to which they have undergone cultural and secondary assimilation. There is further ample reason to believe that both primary and marital assimilation are well underway. Even though the evidence shows that the main trend for the Japanese Americans is toward full Anglo conformity, it still is possible that the contemporary revitalization of ethnic consciousness among the Japanese is more than a passing fad (Levine and Rhodes 1981:152–154). Some form of pluralism, which previously was most popular among the Issei, has found new adherents among the Sansei and Yonsei.

We now pursue some of these issues further through a consideration of the experience of Mexican Americans.

Key Ideas

1. Even though they have experienced unusually high levels of prejudice and discrimination, the Japanese Americans are an exception to the generalization that non-White minorities in the United States have not attained high levels of education, occupation, and income.

2. An analysis of a group that has not responded to very high levels of prejudice and discrimination in the usual ways may afford clues concerning why the usual responses arise and how they may be prevented.

3. The Japanese family and community in America have been highly cohesive.

4. Despite vigorous efforts to stop them, the Issei were very successful in small business enterprises, particularly in agriculture.

5. When Japanese nationals within the United States experienced discrimination, they could—and often did—turn to the Japanese government for assistance.

6. The Japanese generations in America have been unusually distinctive. This distinctiveness is largely due to restrictions on immigration in the Gentlemen's Agreement and the Immigration Act of 1924.

7. The evacuation and relocation program during World War II resulted in the imprisonment of more than 70,000 American citizens of Japanese origin and also about 40,000 legal resident alien Japanese without any charges, trials, or criminal convictions.

8. An effort was made to organize the Relocation Centers along the lines of a typical American community. This largely unsuccessful attempt widened further the gap between the Issei and Nisei but also increased both generations' familiarity with community organization and political participation.

9. Cultural assimilation has been comparatively low among the Issei, high among the Nisei, and higher still among the Sansei.

10. The Sansei have not completely replaced Japanese culture with Anglo American culture. Some evidence supports the idea that pluralism is gaining in popularity among them.

11. The Nisei and Sansei have moved substantially in the direction of secondary, primary, and marital assimilation.

12. More frequently than the Nisei, the Sansei have openly raised questions concerning the human costs of the worldly success of their group.

13. The history of the Japanese Americans generally supports the idea that disadvantages based on racial distinctiveness are not necessarily permanent in American society.

14. The cultural view of Japanese success in America stresses the role of their value system and traditional group solidarity. According to this view, Japanese achievement may be explained by the compatibility between certain key values within Japanese and middle-class American cultures and by various advantages stemming from Japan's tradition of group loyalty.

15. The structural view of Japanese success in America stresses the importance of various noncultural factors such as the kinds of skills they possessed, their level of literacy, the level of economic development on the West Coast at the time of their arrival, their role as a middleman minority, and their ability to establish ethnic enclaves and, through them, become dominant in certain markets.

16. An adequate explanation of any group's worldly success requires a consideration of both cultural and structural factors.

Key Terms

dual-economy theory   States that the American economy consists of a primary job sector at the center of the economy and a secondary job sector on its periphery.

ethnic enclave   A distinctive economic formation characterized by the spatial concentration of immigrants who organize a variety of enterprises to serve their own ethnic market and the general population.

ethnic-enclave theory   States that immigrant workers who live in an ethnically enclosed labor market may be part of a special type of economy that provides routes of upward mobility for workers who might otherwise be trapped in the secondary labor market.

Gentlemen's Agreement   An agreement between the United States and Japan in 1908 concerning the kinds of emigrants the Japanese government would permit to leave the country.

horizontal integration   Cooperative agreements among kinsmen who operate similar types of businesses.

index of dissimilarity   A measure of the extent to which groups differ from one another in regard to characteristics, such as places of residence, occupations, educational attainment, and income.

Issei   The first generation of Japanese immigrants.

kenjin   Japanese people from the same province.

kenjinkai   Associations based on provinces of origin.

middleman minority   A minority which occupies an intermediate economic position in a society.

middleman minority theory   States that groups occupying intermediate economic positions are strongly motivated to work hard, to be thrifty, to take economic risks, and concentrate their funds in businesses that may easily be converted into money.

Nisei   The Japanese American children of the Issei; the second generation of people of Japanese origin.

primary labor market   Contains stable, high-wage jobs permitting upward mobility.

Sansei   The Japanese American children of the Nisei; the third generation of people of Japanese origin.

secondary labor market   Contains unstable, low-wage jobs, with little prospect of upward mobility.

spatial assimilation theory   States that the members of minority groups move into neighborhoods with better schools, more expensive homes, and higher prestige as their socioeconomic status rises.

tanomoshi   An organization through which money is pooled and then loaned in rotation to various members.

value compatibility   The presence of key common values among otherwise different cultures.

vertical integration   Cooperative agreements among kinsmen who operate different kinds of businesses that provide supplies and help market products.

Yonsei   The Japanese American children of the Sansei; the fourth generation of people of Japanese origin.

Notes

1. These figures may be elevated by the inclusion of recent Japanese immigrants (Hirschman and Wong 1985:298).

2. The average income of Japanese American females in 1980 exceeded that of White American females ($9,979 versus $7,708); but the striking comparison here is between males and females rather than between the ethnic groups.

3. Whether the Japanese earn as much as they ought to earn given their qualifications is the subject of a highly technical debate among specialists (see, e.g., Barringer, Gardner, and Levin 1995:231–267).

4. Barringer, Gardner, and Levin (1995: 235, 265) emphasized that among Asian groups, only the Japanese and Asian Indians have reached parity.

5. The "yellow peril" originally referred to the alleged intention of the Chinese to conquer the United States through "peaceful invasion" (tenBroek, Barnhart, and Matson 1954: 19–29.)

6. For an exception see Marumoto (1972: 5–39).

7. A Canadian branch of the Asiatic Exclusion League was formed in Vancouver, B.C., in 1907. Later Canada concluded a gentlemen's agreement with Japan similar to Japan's with the United States (Sugimoto 1972).

8. Another frequently used generational term is *Kibei*—Nisei who were sent to Japan as children in order to receive a traditional Japanese upbringing. The term *Nikkei* refers to all people of Japanese ancestry.

9. The Chinese called rotating credit associations *hui*. The Japanese also used the names *ko* and *mujin* (Light [1972]1994:84–85).

10. The Japanese also had become prominent in rice farming in Texas (Walls 1987: 39–80).

11. Miyamoto (1972:220–221) called the 1907–1924 period the settlement period, and the 1924–1941 period the second-generation period.

12. The Nisei were vulnerable to the charge because Japan granted citizenship on the basis of kinship (the principle of *jus sanguinis*). The United States grants citizenship to those born within the country (the principle of *jus soli*).

13. For the effects of these orders on Italian Americans, see Fox (1990).

14. In 1940, there were about 127,000 Japanese and Japanese Americans in the United States. Of these, 47,000 were aliens and 80,000 were American citizens. Almost 90 percent of the total lived in California, Arizona, Oregon, and Washington (Thomas 1952:3).

15. Before the evacuation, Japanese people were urged to leave the military areas voluntarily. About 5,000 people did so (Taylor 1993: 60–61).

16. The Immigration and Naturalization Service also maintained at least fifteen "internment camps" in eight states. These smaller camps were designed to hold "potentially dangerous enemy aliens," among whom were included some Japanese (Walls 1987:175–176; Daniels, Taylor, and Kitano 1991:xvii).

17. The discussion of life in the Poston Relocation Center is based on the excellent study by Leighton (1946).

18. For a discussion of the role of Japanese Americans in World War II, see Hosokawa (1969:393–422). The 100th Battalion and the 442nd "Go For Broke" regiment "received

more than 18,000 individual and unit citations" (O'Brien and Fugita 1991:66).

19. Question 28 initially was: "Will you swear unqualified allegiance to the United States of America and . . . foreswear any form of allegiance to the Japanese emperor?" (Thomas and Nishimoto 1946:47). A "yes" answer to this question was impossible for most Issei because it would have left them "people without a country." Similar issues were raised by question 27 which asked if the respondent would be willing to serve in the armed forces.

20. More than 8,500 of those incarcerated at Tule Lake eventually were cleared.

21. For the human costs of these events, see Kitano (1991), Mass (1991), and Taylor (1993).

22. Taylor (1991:166) stated that a study commissioned by the CWRIC placed the losses, adjusted for inflation, at between $2.5 billion and $6.2 billion.

23. The initial payments were made "to a group of the oldest survivors, five of whom were older than 100 years of age" (Daniels 1991b:220).

24. An important purpose of this study, sponsored by the JACL and directed by Gene N. Levine of UCLA, was to understand how the successive generations of Japanese and Japanese Americans have adapted to American society. The researchers initially (1962–1966) gathered data on about 18,000 Issei living in the continental United States. Subsequently (1966–1967), Nisei and Sansei participants received mailed questionnaires or were interviewed by telephone.

25. This revitalization effort also involves constructing a broader identity that relates Japanese Americans to all other Asians and other non-White minorities.

26. The seven groups were Black, Chinese, Filipino, Japanese, Korean, Mexican, and Vietnamese. An SMSA consists of the population of a city containing at least 50,000 residents plus all contiguous, functionally related, nonagricultural counties.

27. Problems may arise from the way intermarriage rates are reported. Suppose that of ten marriages, there are six in which both partners are Catholic and four in which only one partner is Catholic. Since four of the ten marriages are mixed, the rate *for marriages* is 40 percent; however, since only four of sixteen individual Catholics are in a mixed marriage, the rate for *individuals* is 25 percent (Rodman 1965:776–778).

28. The races listed were: Chinese, Filipino, Indian, Japanese, Negro, White, and Other (Burma 1963:158).

29. Calculated from Table 6 in Burma (1963:163).

30. Gurak and Kritz found that thirty-one of the thirty-five groups in the analysis had higher out-marriage rates than the Nisei.

31. There is general agreement that "cultural" describes one side of this dichotomy; but several different terms are used to designate all the many factors we call "structural," including situational, contextual, and material (Bonacich and Modell 1980:29–30).

32. See, for example, Light (1972), McDowell (1996), Min (1996), Moskos (1980), Portes and Bach (1985), Rosen (1959), and Steinberg (1989), respectively.

33. Hachen (1992:39) defined labor markets as "arenas where people and jobs are matched."

34. The emergence of ethnic enclaves, according to Portes and Rumbaut (1990:21), depends on three conditions: (1) immigrants with a knowledge of business; (2) access to sources of capital; and (3) access to labor. In their opinion the first requisite is the most important.

Mexican Americans

From Colonized Minority to Political Activists

Mexican Americans originally entered the United States through force rather than through voluntary immigration. Continuous struggle, as indicated by the farm workers' protests, has been a conspicuous element of the Mexican American experience.

In spite of what many Anglo pioneers may have thought generally of Mexicans, most were careful to make the proper distinctions between different "types" of Mexicans. Mexican landowners were "Spanish" or Castilian, whereas Mexican workers were "half-breeds" or "Mexican Indians." The well-known aphorism explains the situation—"money whitens."

—David Montejano

. . .the Borderlands are physically present wherever two or more cultures edge each other, where people of different races occupy the same territory, where under, lower, middle and upper classes touch, where the space between two individuals shrinks with intimacy. I am a border woman. I grew up between two cultures, the Mexican (with a heavy Indian influence), and the Anglo (as a member of a colonized people in our own territory).

—Gloria Anzaldua

The preceding chapters highlighted the point that the population of the United States has been built up mainly by successive waves of immigrants from various parts of the world and that these immigrants, broadly speaking, entered this society voluntarily. In the case of the Mexican Americans,[1] however, we confront a second kind of situation. Unlike the Irish, Germans, Italians, Jews, Chinese, Japanese, and (except the American Indians) all other groups we have discussed, the Mexican Americans did not initially become "newcomers" to American society by leaving the old country and crossing oceans. Instead, like African Americans and American Indians, they originally became a part of American society through conflict and coercion. The southwestern or **"borderlands"** region of what is now the United States, in which the Mexican American population still is concentrated, was settled by people of Spanish-Mexican-Indian ancestry long before it was settled by Anglo Americans; and, along with the American Indians, the Mexican Americans entered the society through the direct conquest of their homelands.

Some observers believe this is a fact of overriding importance, a fact that makes totally inapplicable to the Mexican Americans the assimilationist ideas we have explored thus far. As Sanchez stated, "the Spanish Mexicans of the Southwest are not truly an immigrant group, for they are in their traditional home."[2] From this standpoint, the expectation that the experience of the Mexican Americans can be analyzed properly in terms of any or all of the three main ideologies of assimilation discussed previously is considered to be a serious mistake. It is rather argued that to understand the Mexican American experience we must employ an anti-assimilationist ideology and framework. What ideas does such a view contain?

The Colonial Model

The principal reasons to assume that something is wrong with a conventional assimilationist interpretation of the Mexican American experience may be most easily appreciated by considering again the predictions one would make on the basis of Park's race-cycle theory. The Mexican American group has now been in existence since 1848, quite long enough to have passed through the conflict and accommodation stages and to be well into the final stage of complete assimilation. In terms of our modification of Gordon's concepts, we should by now have witnessed a high degree of cultural and secondary assimilation and a substantial degree of primary and marital assimilation. In fact, however, the relations between Mexican Americans and Anglos[3] in the borderlands have been marked by repeated instances of "falling back" into the conflict stage of Park's cycle. Considering the length of time that has elapsed since 1848, the levels of most forms of assimilation strike many observers as unexpectedly low.

We have seen that different ethnic groups have tried, with varying success, to preserve and elaborate their cultures and have been, in varying degrees, the objects of prejudice and discrimination. We have seen, too, that there are good reasons to question whether **immigrant minorities** ever have assimilated in precisely the way Park's ideas would suggest. Nevertheless, we also have seen that as a guide to an understanding of the experience of many European groups in the United States—especially those from northern, western, and central Europe—the ideas of assimilationist theory are of considerable value. People of different heritages have been incorporated solidly into American society and have, for many purposes, come to view themselves mainly, if not exclusively, as Americans.

But how well would these ideas serve us if we wished to understand, say, interethnic relations in Africa? The **colonized minorities** of Africa generally have been in a very different situation from the immigrant minorities of the United States. In contrast to the more or less voluntary movement of the immigrant minorities to America, the colonized minorities of Africa generally were indigenous to the areas in which they resided and were forced to "join" the society of the colonizers. Furthermore, the colonized minorities of Africa typically were not numerical minorities. They had less power, of course, which is why we call them minorities; but by sheer weight of numbers they have been in a better position than immigrant minorities to maintain and elaborate their cultures in the face of the dominant group's efforts to establish its own culture as the only acceptable one (Blauner 1972:53).

The economic situation of the colonized minorities of Africa also has differed noticeably from that of the immigrant minorities in America. Although the American immigrant minorities usually have had to take whatever kind of work they could get, at least initially, they frequently have been able to move on to something more desirable and to exercise some degree of choice in what they would accept. Even their first jobs were likely to be ones that some Anglo Americans were doing or had done recently. The complaint that "they" are undercutting us economically and are taking "our" jobs away has been heard monotonously in America. But this kind of labor difficulty did not arise in the African colonies. There the indigenous populations usually were required to engage in only the hardest, most menial kinds of tasks. The better jobs were reserved for members of the dominant group. Ordinarily, the opportunity to move around and compete freely with the members of the dominant group did not exist or was very limited (Blauner 1972:55).

Under these conditions, the colonized minorities in Africa did not usually come to think of themselves as French or Dutch or English, and they did not typically move into the mainstream of the dominant group's social life. Instead, the colonized minorities of Africa looked forward to the day when the European invaders could be annihilated or forced to leave and return to their own countries. The cycle of race relations was not characterized by a steady movement forward out of the stage of accommodation into the final stages of assimilation. Rather, it was primarily a back-and-forth movement between the stage of accommodation and the prior stage of conflict.[4] In its main or "classical" form, which was witnessed repeatedly in Africa after World War II, this oscillation continued until the dominant White group, in most instances, was thrown out of power and the previously colonized minorities became majorities. In many of these cases large numbers of the dominant White group fled or were driven out of the country. The final stage of relations between dominant Europeans and colonized Africans, then, was a conflict (usually violent) followed by separation rather than an accommodation followed by assimilation. With these points in mind, Blauner (1994:159) argued that "the communities of color in America share essential conditions with third world nations abroad: economic underdevelopment, a heritage of colonialism and neocolonialism, and a lack of real political autonomy and power." Blauner added that colonization has taken different forms in the history of different American ethnic groups and that variations in time, place, and the manner of colonialization have affected the character of racial domination and the responses of the dominated group.

Several scholars have suggested that the kind of colonial racial relations existing between the invaders and natives in much of Africa affords a more understandable picture of the relations between Anglos and Mexican Americans than do the ideas of assimilationist theory. Moore (1970:464) stated that the concept of colonialism "describes and categorizes" the initial contacts of Mexicans and Americans. Blauner (1972:119) argued that "the conquest and absorption of the Mexican population is an example of classical colonialism." Acuña (1981:3) documented the colonization process of Mexican Americans in his book *Occupied America,* and stated that "the conquest of the Southwest created a colonial situation in the traditional sense."

Mexican Americans, in fact, may be viewed as a people who have undergone classical colonialism not once but twice. The Indians of Mexico were first subdued by the Spaniards. Then, after Mexico became an independent nation, a portion of her population was subjugated by another invader. As in the case of African colonialism, one group (first the Spaniards and then the Anglo Americans) invaded and occupied the territory of another group (the Mexicans). Thus, the original Mexican American population—what Alvarez (1985:37) called the **"Creation Generation"**—entered American society in a fundamentally different position from that of the Irish, German, or other ethnic minorities that were entering during the same period. "The Mexicans in the conquered territory," in Acuña's (1981:1) words, "became victims of a colonial process in which U.S. troops acted as an army of occupation."

The invaders have regulated closely the "place" within the dominant society of the conquered people, their descendants, and the more recent arrivals from Mexico. This regulation has been particularly apparent in the kinds of work that have been deemed suitable for people of Mexican ancestry. At the time of the American conquest, the former Mexican territories consisted of a landed Mexican elite, a number of Anglo merchants, a class of independent but impoverished Mexican rancheros, and an indebted Mexican working class. The Anglo elite frequently intermarried or became *compadres* ("god-relatives") with the landowning Mexican families (Montejano 1987:8–9). Over time and through a number of unscrupulous legal and illegal actions, many of the Mexican elite lost their land titles. In terms of the **colonial model,** those of Mexican ancestry were viewed as meeting the same need for cheap, controlled labor as had African slaves. They were expected to "occupy positions at the bottom of the occupational structure" that "no free domestic labor can be found to perform" (Portes and Bach 1985:12); they were expected to fill permanently the dead-end jobs of the secondary labor market with no prospect of moving into those jobs that permit people to be upwardly mobile (the primary labor market).[5]

Although the European groups we have discussed also displayed resistance to Anglo conformity, as is seen in the rise of cultural pluralism, the solidarity of the Mexican Americans generally has been more troublesome for the dominant group; consequently, the reactions of the Anglo Americans—particularly in Texas—involved more force, more overt coercion, and a generally higher level of ethnic discrimination and racism than usually was true in the case of European minorities. Given the differences in the histories of the groups, the colonial model proposes (in contrast to the **immigrant model**) that one should not expect the Mexican Americans to move into the mainstream of American life in three or four generations or to cease their existence as a profoundly distinctive group. One should expect, instead, that there will be constant tension in the direction of separation or even secession.

The colonial perspective, as we have discussed it, has existed and been applied to the Mexican American experience for many years, though the frequent and explicit application of this view may be specifically traced to the 1960s (Cuéllar 1970:149). As the protest activities of Black Americans during this period gathered momentum, Mexican American protests also became both more frequent and more visible. Many intellectuals within the group were critical in speeches and in print of the usual assimilationist interpretations of the condition of the Mexican Americans put forward by (mainly) Anglo American scholars. An important result of these efforts has been the emergence and diffusion of a body of scholarship (largely by Chicano writers) proposing an anti-assimilationist interpretation of the Mexican American experience. Chicano scholars emphasized not only the unity of the Mexican American people but also their relationship to the Spanish-Indian peoples of Mexico and Central and South America. Chicano movement activists of the 1960s revived the concept of Aztlan, an ancestral homeland of the Aztecs. The Mexican Americans living in the United States were seen to be part of a larger population, *La Raza,* that shared a very ancient and complicated heritage stemming not only from Spanish culture but also from the Aztec, Inca, Maya, and Toltec cultures. The Mexican American heritage, therefore, is a rich mixture of Indian and Spanish civilizations. Its heroes include not only such courageous fighters against Anglo imperialism as Joaquín Murieta and Juan Cortina but also the illustrious Montezuma, who fought against Spanish imperialism. Their history can also draw on the contributions of the scholars and scientists of the Indian high civilizations (Murguía 1989:9). Mexican American political activists argued that nationalism was the key to organizing *La Raza* to struggle against racism and exploitation. The idea was to unify all Chicanos to rebel against colonialism and to gain control of their communities and the institutions that affected their lives. Community control would result in more equitable policies and greater economic and political equality and would allow the Chicano community to safeguard its distinctive cultural identity (Barrera 1988:3).

We now have considered some of the ways that an anti-assimilationist perspective may differ from the more common assimilationist views, including cultural pluralism. Specifically, we have considered that three of America's minorities—American Indians, Mexican Americans, and Black Americans—have been forced to join American society and that two of these groups—the Indians and Mexican Americans—have been conquered in their own land and have undergone a process of colonization quite similar to that experienced by the native populations of Africa.[6] We have seen that in the case of the Mexican Americans, some version of the colonialist interpretation has for some time been preferred by many members of the group itself and that, more recently, the colonial model afforded a focal point around which much of the revisionist Chicano scholarship was organized. A few who supported the most radical point of view sometimes suggested that the most desirable solutions to the problems of the Mexican American group lay in the direction of separation or secession. More often, however, the main aim has been to combat Anglo conformity and to promote cultural pluralism.

Early Indian–Spanish Relations

To assess the competing claims of the assimilationist (immigrant model) and anti-assimilationist (colonial model) interpretations of the Mexican American experience, we begin with the landings of the Spaniards in Mexico during the second decade of the sixteenth century. Here, as in the case of the landings of the English in Virginia and Massachusetts approximately one hundred years later, a conquering European, Christian group established itself on lands previously occupied by indigenous American groups. In both instances, the dominant migrant group gradually expanded its frontiers to create an increasingly large colonial territory. The expansion of the English toward the west and of the Spanish toward the north were the processes that would one day bring these two enormous colonial developments together.

The specific course of colonial development in the English and Spanish territories differed in a number of significant aspects. For one thing, the two powers' entire approaches to colonization were different. We described in Chapter 3 the heavy reliance of the English on a private, profit-sharing method to promote exploration and colonization. The exploration and colonization of the Spanish territories, however, relied more strongly on the initiatives of the crown and the church. The Spanish monarchs were interested primarily in acquiring lands and precious metals, whereas the Roman Catholic Church wished to save the souls of the "heathens." The English, too, were interested at first in these very same things; but after a while it became clear that there was no gold and silver treasure on the Atlantic coast. So the efforts to Christianize the Indians proved to be largely futile.

These differences in colonization methods and experiences had one consequence of special importance for us: The relations between the conquering Europeans and the conquered Indians developed along significantly different paths in the two cases. As noted in Chapter 3, the relations between the English and the Indians became predominantly hostile and were interspersed with warfare. The Indians soon were considered to stand in a completely different relation to the developing society than the Dutch, Irish, or Germans. The policy of the Anglo Americans toward the Indians became one of exclusion and extermination. By and large, the Indians were forced to move west as the Anglo American frontier advanced.

The relations between the Spaniards and the Indians in Mexico also were frequently hostile, but the Spaniards were much more successful than the Anglo Americans in the matter of converting the Indians to Christianity, at least to many of its outward forms. Consequently, even though the Spaniards also took an enormous toll in human lives and misery, the cross as well as the sword marked the advance of the northern frontier of Mexico.[7] The policy of the Spaniards was to bring Christianized Indians into the colonial society they were building—peacefully, if possible, but by force if necessary. The place of the Indians in Mexican society, to be sure, was at the very bottom. They provided most of the manual labor that was needed to construct and maintain the *haciendas* and to exploit the riches of the earth. They were the *peons*, who were bound to the Spanish masters and the land in a form of human slavery; but they also were human beings and Christians, and they were accepted as an integral, if lowly, part of Mexican society.[8]

The Spaniards' policy of counting the Indians "in" rather than "out" led, during a period of three centuries, to a much higher degree of marital assimilation of the Indians with the dominant Europeans than was true on the eastern seaboard. Although the exact nature of this assimilation process lies beyond our scope, two things should be noted. First, just as the English subscribed generally to the Anglo conformity ideology of assimilation, the Spaniards adhered generally to an Hispano conformity ideology. The Indians were expected to do their very best to move toward a mastery of Spanish culture and ways of acting. Second, by the time Mexico achieved independence in 1821, the culture and population of Mexico nevertheless had become very much more "Indianized" than had the culture and population of the United States. Whatever may have been the intentions of the dominant Spaniards, the melting pot process of assimilation was more significant in Mexico than in the United States.

The Hispano–Indian society of Mexico and the Anglo American society of the United States came into direct and continuous contact after the Louisiana Purchase in 1803. The line of contact between these groups was exceptionally long and blurred. The treaty through which the United States secured Louisiana from France did not give a detailed description of the boundaries of the territory. This fact helped to create and maintain an almost constant state of tension along the frontier, first between Spain and the United States and then, later, between Mexico and the United States. Many Americans seemed to believe that Texas definitely had been included in the purchase; but the Spanish and Mexican governments disagreed. Many other Americans believed that it was the "Manifest Destiny" of their country to span the continent. In this way, a struggle began that led, by 1848, to the transfer of what we now know as the American Southwest from Mexico to the United States and to the creation of the Mexican American minority group. The incorporation of Texas into the United States was an important part of that story.

The Texas Frontier

The process through which the Mexican American group has emerged may be visualized more clearly by a consideration of some of the events that occurred in Texas after 1803. Spain's claim to the eastern portion of Texas was disputed openly by the United States until 1819, when Spain and the United States completed a treaty giving Florida to the United States and Texas to Spain. The treaty established the Sabine River as the boundary between Louisiana and Texas. Then, in 1821, Mexico's long struggle to gain independence from Spain was successful; and all of Spain's North American territories then came under the control of the new nation. As the Americans attempted to push their frontier westward, consequently, they became involved in conflicts with Mexico.

The Mexican government worried from the beginning that it might be unable to secure its long, sparsely populated northern frontier from the encroachments of the Americans. Many people in the United States did not accept the treaty agreements that had been concluded with Spain. Many southerners, in particular, were eager to expand the cotton industry into the rich lands of East Texas. Furthermore, the United States recently had been flexing its muscles in international affairs (e.g., the Monroe Doctrine) and was clearly in a stronger military position than the young Mexican nation. Also, the Americans generally did not hide the fact that they regarded themselves to be racially superior to the heterogeneous population of Mexico. The majority of Mexico's citizens were either Indians or Spanish Indians (*mestizos*). Basically, the heritage of the "pure" Spaniards was itself suspect in the Americans' minds because of the centuries of interaction between the Spaniards and various African populations (e.g., the Moors). Hence, racism played an important role in Mexican and American relations.

The Mexicans had some reason for optimism, however. They had established a form of government resembling that of the United States, and they hoped their northern neighbor would have a greater respect for the territorial integrity of a constitutional democracy than it had had for that of imperial Spain. In addition, the Mexican government decided to attempt to create a buffer zone between the two nations by colonizing Texas with Anglo Americans. In one sense, this plan would merely promote Anglo American dominance in the area; but since all of the Anglo American settlers were expected to become citizens of Mexico and members of the Roman Catholic Church, the

Mexican officials hoped to maintain control over them. They hoped that border relations would be improved and Texas would become a less tempting target for a forcible invasion.

This strategy ultimately failed. Less than fifteen years after Mexico gained her independence from Spain, Texas broke away from Mexico to establish still another independent republic. Nevertheless, a basis for *Tejano* and Anglo American immigrant cooperation was created and maintained by able leaders from both sides. Stephen F. Austin, the leader of the first group of Anglo American immigrants to Texas, was enthusiastic about the prospect of an independent Mexico and the development of Texas within it. He sincerely accepted Mexican citizenship and was a respected link between the native and immigrant groups. From the native Mexican side, such men as Ramón Músquiz and José Antonio Navarro worked energetically to assist the assimilation of the Anglo Americans into Mexican society. But the goodwill and substantially similar interests of the native and immigrant leadership in Texas did not extend to Mexico City. In a way, the central authorities fell victims to their own plan. The colonization program was so successful that by 1835 the Anglo American immigrants outnumbered the *Tejanos* by about five to one; hence, as the talk of revolution spread, most of those who favored it were, simply as a matter of numbers, Anglo Americans. When the revolution erupted, the Texan armies were comprised mainly of Anglo Americans; nevertheless, a large proportion of the native Mexicans in Texas believed that various actions of the central government had been unjustified. Kibbe (1946:33) estimated that as many as one-third of those who opposed the government of Santa Anna were *Tejanos*, and several *Tejano* units participated in the actual fighting during the Texas revolution (Barker 1943:333).[9]

After the defeat of Santa Anna in 1836, Texas was established as an independent nation. The conflict between Texas and Mexico did not stop, however. Most of the Texans believed the boundary between the two countries was the Rio Grande, whereas still others thought Texas extended beyond the river to the Sierra Madre mountains. The Mexican government, on the other hand, did not officially concede that Texas was lost to them. Even those in Mexico who did recognize that Texas was now independent believed the boundary was the Nueces River. As a result, the large tract of land between the Rio Grande and the Nueces River continued to be an active battleground. Although the *Tejanos* were a numerical minority, they were not yet treated systematically as an ethnic minority. An ethnic line of distinction did exist, but it was a blurred rather than a sharp line. Taylor (1934:21) described the situation as follows: "During the period of confusion some Texans were fighting with Mexicans . . . other Texans were committing depredations against both Texans and Mexicans, while Mexicans could be found on both sides." Gradually, however, friendships between the *Tejanos* and the Anglo American Texans became more difficult to maintain, and the relations between the groups became more strained. Anglo American Texans, in particular, increasingly failed to distinguish the *Tejanos* from Mexican nationals and came to regard the conflict in Texas as one of "Mexicans" versus "Americans" (Montejano 1987:26–30).

Many of the Anglo American Texans did, in fact, still regard themselves as Americans and were eager to have Texas join the United States. This goal was shared by many people within the United States. It is hardly surprising, therefore, that after only some ten years of independence, Texas agreed to become a part of the United States.

Conflict in the Borderlands

The annexation of Texas aggravated rather than ended the hostilities in the borderlands. President Santa Anna had warned in 1843 that "the Mexican government will consider equivalent to a declaration of war against the Mexican Republic the passage of an act for the incorporation of Texas with the territory of the United States" (Faulkner 1948:324). After the annexation, diplomatic relations between the two governments were broken off, and both sides prepared for war. Since the United States accepted Texas' claims concerning the boundary between the two nations, President Polk ordered General Taylor to occupy the land between the Nueces and the Rio Grande. The Mexicans, of course, considered this an invasion of their territory. In April 1846, a battle between Mexican and American troops occurred north of the Rio Grande; and, in May, President Polk asked Congress for a declaration of war against Mexico, claiming that Mexico "has invaded our territory and shed American blood on American soil" (Faulkner 1948:325). Abraham Lincoln was among those who did not accept this explanation. His own view was that the war was "unnecessarily and unconstitutionally commenced by the President" (Faulkner 1948:325).

Constitutional or not, "one of the most obviously aggressive wars in American history" was under way (Jordan and Litwack 1987:315). The conflict involved not only the disputed territory between Texas and Mexico but all of Mexico. General Taylor moved south of the Rio Grande to Monterrey; Colonel Kearny directed the conquest of New Mexico, Arizona, and California; and General Scott invaded at Vera Cruz and captured Mexico City. In February 1848, Mexico surrendered under the terms of the **Treaty of Guadalupe Hidalgo.** The treaty ceded to the United States nearly one-half of the territory of Mexico. The Rio Grande was established as the boundary of Texas. So the great bulk of the land that now comprises the southwestern region of the United States was acquired.[10] The "Manifest Destiny" of the United States to stretch from the Atlantic to the Pacific had now been achieved. The Spanish-Mexican-Indian group that was left behind as Mexico's northern frontier receded (75,000 to 100,000 people)[11] was now a conquered group. As individuals, they had the right either to "retain the title and rights of Mexican citizens, or acquire those of citizens of the United States" (Moquín and Van Doren 1971:246). Those who did not declare their intention to remain Mexicans automatically became citizens of the United States after one year. At this point, although they were U.S. citizens, they generally were viewed as a defeated and inferior people whose rights need not be taken too seriously (Griswold del Castillo 1990). They "gradually saw their property and influence dwindle as they faced . . . the flood of Anglo Americans" (Burner, Fox-Genovese, and Bernhard 1991:387).

In this way, the Mexican Americans became a minority within the United States. Their entry into the society was by conquest and, to repeat, was quite different from that of the Irish and Germans who were arriving in large numbers in the East during this very same period. The "Creation Generation" of Mexican Americans had not decided to leave their native land and go to the United States. They simply discovered one day that by a mutual agreement of the United States and Mexico (at gunpoint), the places where they lived were no longer in Mexico. In fact, to continue being Mexicans, they either had to leave their homes and move south of the new border established by the treaty or declare officially their intention to remain Mexican nationals within the United States. Acuña (1981:19) states that "About 2,000 elected to leave; most remained in what they considered *their* land."

The Treaty of Guadalupe Hidalgo did not end the physical violence between the Anglos and Mexican Americans within the borderlands. Although there is no accurate tabulation of the violent interethnic encounters that took place between individuals and groups, it has been reported that the number of Mexican Americans killed in the Southwest during the years 1850 to 1930 was greater than the number of lynchings of Black Americans during that same period (Moquín and Van Doren 1971:253). In Moore's (1976:36) opinion, "No other part of the United States saw such prolonged intergroup violence as did the Border States from 1848 to 1925."

If the treaty did not end the violence, it did mark the point beyond which those of Mexican descent were subordinated to the Anglo Americans. A system of ethnic domination and subordination had been born. We referred in Chapter 6 to an important explanation of how such systems arise. Recall that, as presented by Noel (1968), if one group has greater power than another, if there is competition for scarce resources, and if ethnocentrism is present, then a system of ethnic stratification invariably will arise. Our description of contacts between Mexicans and Americans in the borderlands strongly suggests that all three of these essential ingredients were present. The superior power of the Anglo Americans was demonstrated, of course, by the outcome of the war with Mexico. The desire of the Anglo Americans for the land, as we noted, was apparent for decades prior to the war. Though ethnocentrism was most conspicuous among the Anglo Americans, feelings of superiority existed on both sides. We see, therefore, that the Americans had ample incentives to compete with the Mexicans for Texas; they had the power to seize it if necessary, and they typically had a low regard for the Mexican people. Most Mexican Americans found themselves in a position in society not much better than that occupied by Indians and African Americans elsewhere in the United States. The combination of these ingredients created a highly unstable situation along Mexico's northern frontier, especially in the area of Texas.

The strip of land between the Nueces River and the Rio Grande was the staging area for many violent conflicts. Numerous "filibustering expeditions" were launched into this area by Anglo Americans in an attempt to extend U.S. territory even more deeply into Mexico. The traffic was not entirely one way, however. Between 1859 and 1873, the flamboyant Mexican leader Juan N. "Cheno" Cortina initiated a series of raids along the Texas border (Acuña 1981:33–37; Rosenbaum 1981:41–45; Webb [1935] 1987:173–193). Cortina, who was born near Brownsville, Texas, came prominently to attention in July 1859 in the first of a series of "**Cortina Wars.**" Cortina rescued a former servant from the Anglo American marshal in Brownsville who was reportedly mistreating her, and he was forced into open conflict with American authorities after wounding the marshal. Cortina brought together his men and captured Brownsville in an early-morning raid. For the next two months, Cortina's force remained in the area between Brownsville and Rio Grande City, burning, looting, and killing. During the following years, Cortina's daring exploits won him labels ranging from "cattle thief" to "champion of his race" (Lea 1957:159). Among the Mexican people, Cortina was immortalized as a border hero in several *corridos,* or ballads, about the border raids (Paredes 1958). These border conflicts provoked continuous, bitter confrontations with military and law enforcement authorities on both sides of the Rio Grande.

The interethnic violence in Texas reached a peak during the early 1870s, but the disorders subsided by 1875. The combined actions of the authorities on both sides of the Rio Grande led to a reduction of border raiding. Cortina was commissioned as a general in the Mexican army and was stationed far from the border in Mexico City. By 1878, after more than forty years of almost continuous friction and warfare, the Anglo Americans had established an uneasy control over the land between the Nueces River and the Rio Grande and over the Mexican American people who lived there.

The next three decades were relatively quiet along the Rio Grande. But if this period seemed to be one of accommodation, the hatreds and antagonisms smoldered at its very surface. Violent group conflict was always a possibility and was frequently a reality. Various incidents—shootings, lynchings, beatings, and so on—continued. Each incident usually led to some form of retaliation from the injured side, which only aggravated the matter further. Relations between the Mexican Americans and the Texas Rangers, in particular, were very poor (Acuña 1981:25–29). In the years to come, the Rangers increasingly were viewed by Mexican Americans as an official expression of hatred against them. The period of relative quiet was brought to an end by political and economic troubles. There was mounting opposition to the repressive regime of the dictator Porfirio Díaz, until he was overthrown by liberal revolutionaries in 1911. The new government was short-lived, however; and the following period of conflict kept the border in a state of agitation.

Angered by the diplomatic recognition of the new revolutionary Mexican government by the United States, Francisco "Pancho" Villa began attacking Americans. When Villa crossed the border, raided Columbus, New Mexico, and killed a number of Americans, President Woodrow Wilson sent General John J. "Blackjack" Pershing into Mexico to capture Villa. Pershing searched for Villa for nine months but returned home empty-handed. The years of revolution in Mexico and the border crossings by Villa and Pershing severely damaged the relations between Mexico and the United States. They also fanned the flames of distrust, hatred, and violence that had existed for so long between the Mexican Americans and Anglos. Quite clearly, the period of apparent accommodation between Mexican Americans and Anglos had ended.

The "reversion" to an earlier stage in Park's race cycle, that of intergroup conflict, is a dramatic illustration of the point that the experience of the Mexican Americans has differed fundamentally from that of the European minorities. The periodic eruption of organized conflict between Mexican Americans and Anglos poses a serious challenge to the central ideas of the assimilationist perspective and suggests that a perspective that includes the colonialist view may be more appropriate for analyzing the incorporation experiences of this group.

A defense of the assimilationist view of the Mexican American experience, however, concerns the question of *when* the analysis actually should begin. Although it is undeniable that the Mexican Americans were in the borderlands for more than three centuries before this territory was annexed by the United States, the critics of colonial theory are more impressed by a series of events that coincided with the peak of the second immigrant stream from Europe. These events laid the groundwork for arguing that the Mexican Americans, though initially Americans through conquest, are nevertheless similar in most essential respects to the Europeans of the second stream. We turn now to the basic ideas of this contention.

The Immigrant Model

How can a comparison of the Mexican Americans to the immigrants of the second stream be valid? The basic argument is this: Although the Mexican Americans occupied the Southwest long before the Anglos, comparatively few of them resided on the American side of the border prior to 1900. For nearly fifty years after the signing of the Treaty of Guadalupe Hidalgo, relatively few Mexican nationals moved to the United States with the intention of becoming permanent residents. An unknown but probably large number of people did move back and forth across the border in search of work. At this time, however, such movements were mainly informal; few records were kept. For one period, in fact, between 1886 and 1893, there are no official records of immigration from Mexico into the United States.

In a way, this is not so strange. The first major federal law restricting immigration was not enacted until 1882. America's policy had been to have an "open door" to the world, to encourage people to move to the United States and share the labors (and rewards) of developing the continent. Even when the attention of the nation did turn to immigration, the main focus of debate was the second immigrant stream and the "yellow peril" from Asia, not people from Mexico. After the Chinese Exclusion Act was passed and the Gentlemen's Agreement was put into effect, there still was little concern about the immigration of Mexicans. United States policy toward Mexico remained unrestrictive. The border patrol did not begin operations until 1924, and its first efforts to control immigration from Mexico, paradoxically, seem to have been directed primarily against the Chinese (Grebler, Moore, and Guzman 1970:519). Mexicans continued to cross into the United States legally and with ease. For most practical purposes, a Mexican national could enter the United States (at a small fee) simply by obtaining permission at a border station. Still, as had been true since the end of the Mexican–American War, the flow of legal immigrants was only a trickle. Less than 14,000 entrants were counted during the entire last half of the nineteenth century.

Beginning with 1904, however, the number of entrants from Mexico began to rise substantially (see Table 8.1 on page 206). The rapid expansion and growing scale of the agricultural, mining, transportation, and construction sectors of the southwestern economy required a massive infusion of labor. The official count during this period appears greatly to understate the actual rate at which Mexicans were entering and remaining in the United States. One official report estimated that "at least 50,000 'nonstatistical' aliens" arrived in "normal" years (Gómez-Quiñones 1974:84). Another estimate sug-

**TABLE 8.1 Mexican Immigration
to the United States, 1820–1994***

Years	Number
1820–1830	4,818
1831–1840	6,599
1841–1850	3,271
1851–1860	3,078
1861–1870	2,191
1871–1880	5,162
1881–1890	1,913
1891–1900	971
1901–1910	49,642
1911–1920	219,004
1921–1930	459,287
1931–1940	22,319
1941–1950	60,589
1951–1960	299,811
1961–1970	453,937
1971–1980	640,294
1981–1990	1,655,843
1991–1994	1,400,108
Total	5,969,623

Source: U.S. Immigration and Naturalization
Service, *1994 Statistical Yearbook,*
1996:26–28.

*No record of immigration from Mexico was
kept between 1886 and 1893.

gested the figure may have reached 100,000 (Bryan 1972:334). No one can be sure, of course, how many of those who entered in a nonimmigrant status then became permanent residents of the United States; but it seems certain that a great many did.

The sudden sizable flow of immigrants from Mexico during the first decade of the twentieth century was greatly exceeded during the second decade, but a still greater wave of Mexican immigrants came during the 1921–1930 period. From a purely official and numerical standpoint, then, the great period of Mexican immigration had hardly commenced when the peak of the new immigration was reached; and Mexican immigration did not crest until the second immigrant stream was nearly over.

During this period, the composition of the Mexican American population was transformed. Before 1900, most Mexican Americans either had been among those conquered in the Mexican–American War or were their descendants. From this standpoint, the Mexican immigrants of the period after 1900 were in many respects the first generation—entering more or less voluntarily—of what has become our nation's second largest minority. From this standpoint also, just barely enough time has passed to test the three-generations hypothesis in regard to those who arrived after 1900. The modern Mexican Americans are predominantly either Mexican nationals, who have entered the United States since 1900, or their descendants. From an assimilationist perspective, therefore, the reason they have seemed slow to assimilate is that Mexicans are comparatively recent immigrants. They are not, strictly speaking, people who "got here first"; and they have not had as long to adopt the "American way" as those who arrived in the United States before 1900. In short, the immigrant model downgrades the significance for the process of assimilation of the "historical primacy" of the Mexican Americans.

Alvarez (1985) argued that this application of the immigrant model is not valid. Even though, technically, those who have moved from Mexico to the United States since 1900 are "immigrants," is it reasonable to say that people have emigrated when they move from one side of a politically arbitrary (and mostly imaginary) border into a territory that previously had been a part of their homeland, with which they have maintained continuous contact, and in which their native culture still flourishes? Aren't such people more nearly "homecomers" than "newcomers"?

Alvarez (1985) presented two main reasons to consider that it is more accurate to say the people in this movement were migrants, rather than immigrants. First, it is hard to believe, he maintained, that the psychological impact of moving across the U.S.–Mexican border would be similar to that of leaving Europe for America. In most instances, the European immigrants realized that they were leaving the Old Country for a long time, possibly for good; that they would arrive in a very different and strange land; and that their children would grow up under quite new social conditions. Can the same things be said of the Mexican "immigrants"? Alvarez argued that there is little reason to suppose that most of those who participated in the "immigration" from Mexico during the early part of the twentieth century thought of themselves as moving irrevocably from an old, familiar environment into a new and alien one. Mexico and the United States are physically continuous and culturally overlapping countries. Urbanization and industrialization brought many Mexicans into Southwestern cities, such as San Antonio, Houston, El Paso, and Los Angeles, where the migrants established large ethnic *barrios.* Even at considerable distances from the border, Spanish has continued to be the primary spoken language of many Mexican Americans and numerous Spanish words and terms have found their way into the vocabularies of the Anglo Americans. In short, the presence of these familiar cultural elements almost surely has served further to modify the Mexican's "immigration" experience. It seems unlikely that they have felt unalterably separated from their native land, as have so many other immigrants. Rather it seems more likely that Mexicans have felt right at home in the Southwest and have not felt, or could more easily resist, the usual pressure that is placed on immigrants to become "Americans."[12]

A second reason offered by Alvarez for regarding those who moved from Mexico to the United States after 1900 to be simply migrants rather than immigrants stems directly from the colonial model itself. Whatever one may conclude concerning the attitudes and reactions of the post-1900 Mexican newcomers, the relationship of this group to the host society was still strongly influenced by the fact that the Creation Generation were a conquered people in their own land. Even if we assume that the Mexicans who came to the United States after 1900 did regard the change as large and permanent, and even if they did feel that they were foreigners in the United States, they still could not assume the "normal" status of immigrants. The host society did not distinguish between the "colonized" Mexicans and the "immigrant" Mexicans. The latter group could not function as immigrants because they were forced into the same kinds of jobs, housing, and subservience as the former. As Alvarez (1985:43) stated, "Socio-psychologically, the migrants, too, were a conquered people." From this perspective, Mexicans who came to the United States as part of the **"Migrant Generation"**—and even those who have come since 1930—merely joined the ranks of the existing colonized Mexican American minority (Alvarez 1985:39). From this standpoint, the similarities between Mexican "immigration" and European immigration are superficial.

Our comparison of the colonial and immigrant models shows that each emphasizes different aspects of the history of Anglo and Mexican American relations. Many of the most important facts are not in question. It is true, as is stressed in the colonial account, that (1) the Mexicans occupied the borderlands hundreds of years before the Anglo Americans arrived and, thus, may claim historical primacy; (2) the Anglo Americans, through the annexation of Texas and the Mexican–American War, forced Mexico to cede the Spanish Southwest; (3) the relations between the Mexican Americans and Anglos in the borderlands have been filled with more tension and conflict than usually has been the case for immigrant minorities; and (4) the processes of assimilation have not produced as much change among the Mexican Americans as one would expect to occur in an immigrant population during a period of over 140 years. But it also is true that the great majority of the Mexican American population is comprised of people who have entered the United States from Mexico since 1900 and their descendants. It may be possible, therefore, if one starts the analysis with the "Migrant Generation" of the early 1900s rather than with the "Creation Generation" of 1848, that the processes of assimilation may be operating among the Mexican Americans in a fairly "normal" way. To help evaluate these clashing interpretations, let us review some of the main features of the Mexican American experience since 1900.

Mexican Immigration and Native Reaction

We have seen that a combination of social turmoil in Mexico and economic opportunities in the United States led to a sharp rise in Mexican immigration during the first decade of the twentieth century.[13] The Mexicans' opportunities for work, as already stated, were mainly in the hard, dirty, and poorly paid jobs in railroading, mining, and agriculture. The work conditions experienced by large numbers of Mexicans and Mexican Americans in these three industries during the early portions of the twentieth century had a lasting effect on the Mexican American community. Railroad work, which was the main kind at first, helped to take significant numbers of Mexicans out of the Southwest into other parts of the United States. In many instances, railroad crews completed their jobs far from the border area and were forced to accept other jobs wherever they happened to be. Many Mexican American communities outside the Southwest started in this way (Gómez-Quiñones 1974:88; Kerr 1977:294).

Even more important in its effects was the way the Mexican labor force generally was organized. In each of these main industries, the work force was organized in gangs; frequently, the work gangs included all members of a family. This meant that entire families were intermittently on the move. The employers took advantage of this migrant labor force by providing temporary housing at high rents. To reduce their costs, the employers did not provide adequate sanitation or improve the facilities. The children of such families frequently engaged in unsafe, backbreaking labor and did not receive adequate schooling or health care. Additionally, migratory agricultural labor, which gradually became the primary source of employment for Mexican labor, is seasonal. Employers generally assumed and expected that the migratory Mexican workers would go "home" to Mexico when the work ran out.

The movement of Mexican labor into agricultural work was stimulated by America's entry into World War I. In California, the demand for workers in the citrus, melon, tomato, and other industries increased sharply, encouraging Mexicans to come across the border to perform these necessary tasks. The other southwestern states were similarly affected. Workers were needed in Texas to tend the cotton, spinach, and onion crops, while in Arizona, New Mexico, and Colorado, there was a shortage of workers to raise vegetables, forage crops, and sugar beets (Reisler 1976:77–100). From the beginning, these forms of labor were "seasonal, migratory, and on a contract basis" (Gómez-Quiñones 1974:89). To meet this increased demand for "stoop" labor, the Commissioner of Immigration and Naturalization approved, in 1917, some special regulations to permit Mexican farm workers to enter the United States in large numbers. Although the regulations soon were modified to permit temporary workers from Mexico also to fill jobs in railroad maintenance and mining, the "invasion" of agricultural work by both temporary and permanent immigrants from Mexico was the most prominent result.[14] The events of this period stamped into the public's mind a stereotype of the Mexicans and Mexican Americans as agricultural workers.

As noted previously, the increasingly large migration of Mexicans to the United States during this time was not a topic of general concern or debate. Even though the Mexican migration reached its peak in 1924—the same year in which the Immigration Act established the quota restrictions on European immigration and excluded the Japanese—the open door policy remained in effect for Mexicans. The new law, in fact, contained provisions that made it possible for a Mexican immigrant to work on the American side of the border during the day but to stay at his or her residence in Mexico during the night (Moore 1976:48). Moreover, as the open door began to close on people of many other nationalities, cheap labor from Mexico became even more attractive to employers in the United States; consequently, Mexican immigration jumped sharply during the 1920s both in absolute numbers and as a proportion of the total of all immigration to this country (Grebler, Moore, and Guzman 1970:64).

The mutual attraction of Mexican labor and American employers, however, began to subside shortly after the immigration restrictions on other nationalities went into effect. Both because the Mexican immigration became so large and the agricultural sector of the American economy went into a downturn, Mexican immigration now became a subject of national controversy. Predictably, the demand arose to extend the quota system established in 1924 to cover Mexicans. To support this demand, some of the restrictionists used racist stereotypes to support their claims that the Mexicans were socially undesirable. A Texas congressman referred to them as "illiterate, unclean, peonized masses" who are a "mixture of Mediterranean-blooded Spanish peasants with low grade Indians" (Moore and Pachon 1985:136). As things developed, however, no extension of the restrictive legislation was needed.

The flow of Mexican immigration was dampened in the late 1920s when the United States discontinued the practice of issuing permanent visas at the border stations and instead now required applicants to file at an American consulate.[15] Under these circumstances, many people preferred to cross the border illegally to avoid the cost of waiting at the border, as well as the possibility that they would not be admitted. Of course, once these undocumented people reached the United States, they were fugitives and were in no position to insist on ethical treatment or to stand upon legal rights. As a result, they frequently fell prey to the unscrupulous and discriminatory acts of labor contractors, employers, and underworld businesses. The life of the migratory or contract laborers also became harsher because they often were regarded with special hostility and suspicion by Mexican Americans as well as Anglo Americans, who feared that the uncontrolled entrance of Mexican laborers to the United States would depress working conditions.

The Great Depression

Although Mexican immigration appeared to be tapering off in the face of these control measures, a dramatic reduction in the flow followed the great financial crisis of 1929. The immediate and primary cause of this decline, of course, was the sharp reduction in employment opportunities. The prospects were so unattractive, indeed, that the Mexican immigration of 1931 fell below 4,000 for the first time since 1907. The annual number of new arrivals fell even further in the subsequent years of the 1930s and did not begin to recover noticeably until the beginning of World War II.

In addition to the fact that the Great Depression made the United States a less attractive destination for migrants, there was another development of special importance. Many groups and officials within the United States sought to decrease unemployment and the costs of government welfare by deporting Mexican aliens (Hoffman 1974). Some aliens, as in the previous periods, had returned voluntarily to Mexico when their jobs dried up, but many had not; and the border patrol increased its efforts to locate and deport people who had become public charges or were in the United States illegally. At the same time, the authorities in many American cities found that it was much less expensive to pay the transportation and other costs of sending people to Mexico than it was to maintain them on welfare rolls.[16] These combined national and local efforts to save money by "sending the Mexicans home" were in some ways a preview of the evacuation of the Japanese and Japanese Americans nearly a decade later. As in the case of the later "roundup" of the Japanese, little attention was paid either to the preferences of the evacuees or to their legal status (Moore and Pachon 1985:137). Mexicans who were naturalized citizens frequently were deported along with Mexican nationals. Many native Americans of Mexican ancestry were scrutinized closely and were intimidated by the prospect of **"repatriation."** In some cases, families were broken apart when the Mexican father was sent "home," while his American-born children remained behind.

The entire repatriation program emphasized to the Mexican American community just how vulnerable they were to the actions, sometimes whimsical, of government officials. In some instances, the deportations spread panic within the *barrios*. People became afraid that if they applied for relief they would be sent to Mexico. As a result, it is quite possible that many people who were eligible for relief did not apply. McWilliams (1972:386) indicated that more than 200,000 Mexicans left the United States during a twelve-month period of 1931–1932 alone, while Grebler, Moore, and Guzman (1970: 526) stated that the Mexican-born population of the United States declined during the 1930s from 639,000 to around 377,000. More important, though, than the sheer number of deportations is that American citizens of Mexican heritage were shown dramatically that they were not necessarily considered to be full-fledged citizens. As long as there was a shortage of cheap labor, the "Mexicans" were welcomed and praised as cooperative, uncomplaining workers; but when economic times were bad, American officials wanted the "Mexicans" to go "home."

The *Bracero Program*

There was little need for additional cheap farm labor in the United States until World War II created a new manpower emergency. This time, however, the "cooperative" Mexican labor force was not so easily pulled across the border. For one thing, the war also had created a labor shortage in Mexico; for another, Mexico's government was no longer persuaded that the United States was a "good neighbor." So instead of permitting an unrestricted out-migration of workers, Mexico agreed to allow *braceros* to enter the United States on certain conditions: They were to receive free transportation and food; they were not to be given jobs presently held by American residents; they were to receive guarantees concerning wages, working conditions, and living quarters; and only a limited number of *bracero* workers could be employed within a given year (McWilliams 1973:266). It was agreed, too, that specified Mexican officials could make inspections and investigate any complaints that might arise, and that the workers would be protected from discrimination (Reimers 1985:42–43). With these guarantees and protections, Mexican workers flocked to the *Bracero Program*. Between 1942 and 1945, more than 167,000 agricultural workers were recruited under the plan.[17]

The *Bracero Program* is of special interest for two reasons. First, it provided some experience for both Mexico and the United States concerning the problems of planning and regulating the back-and-forth movement of temporary workers between the two countries. At the very least, the results of the program showed how difficult the task is. For example, as World War II progressed, the employment opportunities for Mexican workers increased in the United States, and as they did, the flow of undocumented temporary workers also increased. Many Mexican workers found it to be much more convenient and less expensive to be undocumented aliens than *braceros*. The American employers—chiefly the growers and ranchers—also found that they could save time and money (and avoid "red tape") by hiring undocumented workers; consequently, in many cases, the undocumented workers and the *braceros* were receiving different wages and benefits while working together in the same fields (Grebler, Moore, and Guzman 1970:67). Needless to say, this situation produced many ambiguities. It also produced an increase in the border patrol's efforts to locate, arrest, and deport undocumented migratory workers. This effort reached its pinnacle during 1954–1955 in a highly publicized roundup called "Operation Wetback" (Reimers 1985:56). Even though hundreds of thousands of undocumented workers (and an untold number of legal entrants and American citizens) were sent to Mexico, many of them quickly came back to the United States either legally or, again, illegally.

The existence of a mixture of legal and undocumented temporary workers of Mexican descent has continued to raise questions about the status of the Mexican Americans in our society. Since they generally were defined as Mexicans by other Americans, Mexican Americans' sense of ethnic distinctiveness was intensified. The increased immigration reinforced Mexican cultural practices and the use of the Spanish language in Mexican American communities. The growing numbers of Mexican immigrants also heightened Americans' prejudices against Mexicans (Gutierrez 1995:39–68). The dominant group's frequent failure to distinguish Mexican Americans from Mexican nationals has been made easier by the presence of so many Mexican immigrants. Both groups are easily considered by many members of the dominant group to be especially suited for hard manual labor and to be unsuited to possess all of the rights and privileges of American citizens. The idea has been encouraged that Mexican Americans as well as Mexican nationals are "really" foreigners who may go "home" if they do not like conditions in the United States.

To complicate the picture still further, many members of the Mexican American community have been ambivalent about the presence of many new arrivals from Mexico. On the one hand, the newcomers are often welcomed because they serve in important ways to replenish and strengthen the prized and distinctive culture of the Mexican Americans; but, at the same time, they constitute a deep pool of reserve laborers who may be called on by employers to keep wages low or to resist the efforts of American citizens to form strong and effective labor unions. Even though the law requires that domestic workers be hired in preference to immigrant workers, employers frequently attempt to get around this requirement (Dunne 1967:48). In many cases, though, little effort in this regard is needed because the work is so hard and the wages are so low that few domestic workers will accept the jobs (Portes and Bach 1985:62). Another threat posed for Mexican Americans by the newcomers is that they afford a continuous excuse for the border patrol and many other official agencies to pry into the private lives of those who "look Mexican." For this reason, as in the days of the welfare repatriations, Mexican Americans still are much more exposed than most other Americans to the threat and the actuality of being deported illegally.

The *Bracero Program* was also of special interest because it gave the Mexican government a firm basis on which to protest acts of discrimination not only against their citizens in the United States but also against Mexican Americans (McWilliams 1973:269). For example, in October 1943, the Mexican government issued a formal protest "against the segregation of children of Mexican descent in certain Texas schools." The practice of establishing "Mexican schools" began in 1902 in Seguin, Texas. By 1930, 90 percent of the South Texas schools were segregated. By the early 1940s, separate schools for Mexicans existed throughout the state (Montejano 1987:160). The Mexican government was aware of many other incidents of discrimination, particularly in Texas. One of these occurred when Sergeant Macario Garcia, a winner of the Congressional Medal of Honor, ordered a cup of coffee in a cafe in Sugar Land, Texas, and was refused service. A fight developed, and Sergeant Garcia was arrested on a charge of aggravated assault (McWilliams 1973:261). In another incident, a Mexican American PTA group in Melvin, Texas, was refused a permit to use a community center building. These and many other cases of overt or probable discrimination against Mexican Americans, as well as Mexicans, led the Mexican government in 1943 to halt the *Bracero Program* in Texas. This action led Governor Coke Stevenson of Texas to make a goodwill tour of Mexico, to proclaim a good neighbor policy for Texas and to appoint a Good Neighbor Commission (McWilliams 1973:270). But these efforts, as well as some others on the local level, failed to satisfy the Mexican government, and the *Bracero Program* was not resumed in Texas during World War II.

The Zoot-Suit Riots

The problem of discrimination against Mexican Americans during World War II was by no means restricted to Texas. Certain events that took place in the Los Angeles, California, area during this period were at least equally alarming and may have had a more lasting effect on the relations of Anglos and Mexican Americans. At about the same time the Japanese were being evacuated and interned, the **Zoot-Suit Riots** were given wide publicity in the Los Angeles newspapers. According to Mazon (1984:1), the Zoot-Suit Riots, which occurred between June 3–13, 1943, "were not about zoot-suiters rioting, and they were not, in any conventional sense of the word, 'riots.' No one was killed. No one sustained massive injuries. Property damage was slight." These disorders may be described as a series of mob attacks by off-duty policemen, U.S. sailors, and other servicemen directed mainly at Mexican Americans who called themselves *pachucos* and wore zoot suits. The zoot-suit look included pants with full trousers and a waist extended high to the chest, a broad-shouldered jacket, long ducktail haircuts, and pointed shoes. Probably of greater importance though, the zoot suits flaunted the distinctiveness of being Mexican American, pride in the Mexican heritage, and resentment of the racism of the dominant group (Romo 1983:166). The zoot suit was an international phenomenon worn by street traders in London and associated with American gangsters. This dress style gained notoriety among fad-conscious adolescents and was popularized in Harlem among blacks. The Mexican American zoot-suiters, alien to both Mexican and American cultures and fluent in neither Spanish nor English, were the antithesis of the servicemen and were met with anger and shock by the dominant society.

The summers of 1942 and 1943 witnessed two particularly notable events involving zoot-suiters. The first of these centered on the mysterious death of a young Mexican American, José Díaz, following a fight between two rival gangs near an East Los Angeles swimming hole. The press coverage of this event was described by McWilliams (1973: 229) as "an enormous web of melodramatic fancy." The gravel pit near which the gang fight occurred was referred to as "The Sleepy Lagoon," and the newspapers emphasized that the case involved Mexican Americans. Twenty-two young men of a 38th-Street gang were arrested and charged with conspiracy to commit murder. Following a trial, called the **Sleepy Lagoon Trial,** that lasted several months, three of these young men were convicted of first-degree murder, nine were convicted of second-degree murder, five were convicted of lesser offenses, and five were acquitted (Romo 1983:166). The convictions were appealed by an organization of East Los Angeles citizens on the grounds that the trial had been conducted in a biased and improper way, in an atmosphere of sensationalism. The prosecution had played on the fact that the defendants were of Mexican heritage, had ducktail haircuts, and wore zoot suits. These improper tactics were criticized by the appeals court, which overturned the lower court's decision. After nearly two years of imprisonment, the defendents were released "for lack of evidence" (McWilliams 1973:231). Although this outcome was viewed as a great victory for justice and the Mexican American community, the fact still remains that seventeen young men served prison sentences for a crime they were not proven to have committed. Their crime, it seems, was that they were Mexican Americans.

The Sleepy Lagoon Trial, conducted as it was during the period of the Japanese internment and with generous press coverage, strengthened the impression held by many people that the Mexican Americans were "just naturally" criminals. The supposed natural link between Mexicanness and criminality seemed to receive official support shortly after the arrest of the Sleepy Lagoon defendants. Captain E. D. Ayres of the Los Angeles Sheriff's Office presented to the grand jury a report of the results of his investigation of what was considered to be the "problem of Mexican delinquency." Captain Ayres's suppositions, conclusions, and chain of reasoning sounded much like those presented by General DeWitt to justify the wartime treatment of the Japanese. In Captain Ayres's view, those of Mexican ancestry are more likely to engage in violent crimes than Anglos because such behavior is an "inborn characteristic." Anglo youths, said Captain Ayres, may use their fists or kick when they fight, but the "Mexican element" feels "a desire to use a knife or some lethal weapon . . . his desire is to kill, or at least let blood" (McWilliams 1973:234). Such opinions, presented by a police official during these tense days, could hardly have increased the dominant group's understanding of the underlying causes of the behavior of the *pachucos.* The answer lay in an entirely different direction. As noted by Sanchez (1972:410), the *pachuco* movement grew not out of the violent nature of the Spanish-speaking people but from the discriminatory social and economic situation in which the Mexican Americans lived. Nevertheless, the stereotype of the naturally violent *pachuco* gangster was apparently widely believed.

The publicity surrounding the Sleepy Lagoon Trial, the presentation of the Ayres Report, and numerous contacts between the police and *pachuco* fighting gangs prepared the way for the Zoot-Suit Riots (Mazon 1984). Mexican youths wearing zoot suits had gradually come to represent for many members of the dominant group an open defiance of constituted authority, and the zoot suit itself became a symbol of moral degradation; consequently, those who wore them appeared to many to be enemies of the state who needed to be "taught a lesson."

There had been some intermittent fighting during this time between the "zooters" and sailors and marines who were stationed near the East Los Angeles *barrio.* The servicemen considered the *pachucos* to be draft dodgers, and the Mexican Americans resented the servicemen's frequent visits to their neighborhood (Romo 1983:167). Widespread violence between the servicemen and the "zooters" began when a group of sailors was beaten up, allegedly by a gang of Mexican Americans, while they were walking through the *barrio* area. On the following night, about two hundred sailors "invaded" East Los Angeles in a caravan of some twenty taxicabs. On their way, they stopped several times to beat severely at least four Mexican American youths wearing zoot suits. In the following days, the local newspapers featured reports concerning violence (and threats of violence) between servicemen and "zooters." By June 7, the numbers of people engaged in the disorders had swelled into the thousands. Throughout all of this, the Los Angeles Police Department reportedly took few steps to curb the activities of the servicemen and, for the most part, seemed to avoid the areas in which violence was occurring until after the conflict was over. In some cases, the police simply followed along behind the servicemen to arrest the Mexican Americans who had been attacked! The disorders were not brought under control until the military authorities intervened. Servicemen were ordered to stay out of downtown Los Angeles and the *barrio,* and the order was enforced by the shore patrol and military police.[18]

There can be little doubt that many members of the Anglo American group subscribed to the theory of innate criminality among Mexican Americans and more or less openly approved of the efforts of the servicemen to "clean out" the "zooters." It seems clear, too, that the zoot suit itself became a hated symbol of Mexican American solidarity and defiance. In a large number of instances, the servicemen stripped the suits from their victims and ripped them apart. An official view of all this was illustrated dramatically when the Los Angeles City Council declared that it was a misdemeanor to wear a zoot suit (McWilliams 1973:245–250).

The repercussions of the Sleepy Lagoon Trial and the Zoot-Suit Riots were felt throughout the United States as well as abroad. The disorders were headline news in newspapers all over the United States. Zoot-suit and other race-related conflicts broke out in several other cities across the United States following the Los Angeles disorders. And just as the incidents of discrimination against Mexican Americans in Texas had led the government of Mexico to end the *Bracero Program,* the ambassador from Mexico asked for an official explanation of the Zoot-Suit Riots. The explanation—that there was no prejudice or discrimination against people of Mexican ancestry—was hardly convincing. The war effort of the United States had been damaged; the allies of the United States had been given yet another reason to wonder about the strength of this country's commitment to racial and ethnic equality; and the enemies of the United States had been given a powerful weapon of propaganda that they did not hesitate to employ.

The Mexican American Civil Rights Movement

During all this time, Mexican American youths (and even some noncitizen aliens) were subject to the wartime military draft in the United States (Scott 1974:134). Considering the level of discrimination against these young men at the time, they seemed more eager to serve and fight for the United States than might have been expected. As in the case of the Nisei, the displacements and humiliations experienced by the Mexican Americans during the early war years appeared generally to heighten their desire to prove their loyalty and worth rather than the reverse. As a result, a disproportionately high number of Mexican Americans served in the armed forces; also, like the Nisei, they comprised a disproportionately high share of the casualty lists and were frequently cited for their outstanding fighting qualities and contributions to the war effort. The first Congressional Medal of Honor awarded to a drafted enlisted man during World War II went to José P. Martinez of Los Angeles. Altogether, thirty-nine Mexican Americans received the Congressional Medal of Honor (Scott 1974:140). Although in the early days of the war Mexican American servicemen frequently had been shunned or harassed by other servicemen as disloyal, undisciplined *pachucos,* their valor earned them acceptance on equal terms.

On this basis, Mexican Americans fully expected their position in civilian life after the war to be far better than it had been before the war. Their return to civilian life, however, was marked by bitter disappointment. They found mainly that the prejudices and the various forms of discrimination they had encountered before the war remained. They still might be refused service in a restaurant, they still had difficulty obtaining work outside of the occupations that traditionally had been assigned to them, and they still saw that the young people of *La Raza* typically attended segregated schools (Scott 1974:141). The reality of the continuation of prejudice and discrimination against them came as a severe shock to many returning veterans. Despite their loyal and costly services to the country, they remained second-class citizens. This discovery jolted not only the Mexican American veterans but their friends and families as well. Since the entire Mexican American community was affected, an increased awareness of their collective problem as a minority group was stimulated. Hence, in the period since World War II— and especially the 1960s—Mexican Americans launched a distinct phase of the civil rights movement. This movement was marked by a sharp increase in organized political and protest activities by Mexican Americans in all of the main sectors of American life.

For roughly seventy-five years after the end of the war between Mexico and the United States, Mexican Americans in the Southwest contended with segregation in the public schools; segregation and discrimination in public facilities such as restaurants, movie theaters, swimming pools, and barbershops; primary election procedures that prevented them from exercising their right to vote; and discrimination in housing. They also suffered discrimination in the administration of justice that prevented them from serving on juries and treated violence against them as so common as to pass almost unnoticed (Garcia 1989:27). Mexicans had long protested discrimination in the United States through mutual-aid societies and the Mexican consulates, but a growing middle class of Mexican Americans began to think about integration into the American political system. The most famous and successful organization of Mexican Americans—the League of United Latin-American Citizens (LULAC)—was formed in 1929. LULAC emphasized both assimilation and the elimination of discrimination. Its leaders felt it was the duty of Mexican Americans to develop "true and loyal" citizens of the United States (Cuéllar 1970:143; Garcia 1989:30; Marquez 1987). LULAC members reaffirmed the need to maintain bilingualism, but voted English as the organization's official language and to exclude Mexican nationals. We should not be surprised to learn, however, that even with these principles and the presumably uncontroversial goal of developing "the best, purest and most perfect type of a true and loyal citizen of the United States of America" (Garcia 1989:31), LULAC aroused the fear in some Anglo Americans that the "Mexicans" were forgetting "their place."

The years of World War II brought significant changes in the Mexican American community. In the first place, as noted earlier, a large number of Mexican Americans served in the armed forces. This experience permitted them to work side by side with Americans from different regions of the country and from different socioeconomic origins. In the process, they learned a great deal about the opportunities and privileges that most American citizens took for granted. These veterans felt "completely American." As such, they were unwilling to think of themselves as "Mexican" or to accept the inferior status generally accorded Mexicans. As expressed by Alvarez (1985:44), they were more likely to argue, "I am an 'American' who happens to be of Mexican descent. I am going to participate fully in this society because, like descendants of people from so many other lands, I was born here." In short, they accepted the immigrant model.

The war years did more than solidify the servicemen's acceptance of American identity, however. The events of the war accelerated the movement of Mexican Americans into the cities. As a result, this traditionally rural population was brought into a more extensive and intimate contact with the Anglo Americans. Large numbers of these migrants were exposed to even more overt forms of discrimination than they had learned was customary—for example, the Zoot-Suit Riots. They learned in this way that the opportunities of the city, attractive though they were in many cases, were nonetheless severely limited for "Mexicans."

The combination of continued, and even increased, discrimination against Mexican Americans on the home front and the new expectations of the returning servicemen set the stage for the emergence of some new, more aggressive, political and social organizations following the war. In the immediate postwar years, one such organization, the Community Service Organization (CSO), was formed in California; another, the G.I. Forum, was formed in Texas. Both of these groups have sought to represent the interests of Mexican Americans on a wide social, economic, and political front (Allsup 1982). As the decade of the 1950s drew to a close, however, some Mexican Americans came to feel that organizations like LULAC, CSO, and the G.I. Forum were not pressing vigorously enough for equal rights. They thought, too, that the established organizations were not pursuing the correct strategy in the political arena. For these reasons, the Mexican American Political Association (MAPA), the Mexican American Youth Organization (MAYO), and the Political Association of Spanish-Speaking Organizations (PASO) were formed with the intention of putting direct pressure on the major political parties, including the nomination or appointment of their members to public office. A spectacular example of the success of this approach may be seen in the election of Mexican Americans to various offices in Crystal City, Texas.[19] These separate efforts were thought of as part of a larger movement, *La Causa* (Valdez 1982:271).

Another organization, The United Farm Workers Union (UFW), organized in California in 1962 by César Chavez and Dolores Huerta, was instrumental in publicizing the plight of Mexican Americans to a national public. Originally begun as an effort to gain collective bargaining rights and union recognition for Mexican American and Filipino farmworkers in California, the movement used nonviolent tactics and "emotionally charged ethnic symbols" such as a stylized black Aztec eagle flag and images of the Mexican Virgin of Guadalupe to attract members and publicity (Gutiérrez 1995:196). The UFW protested the use of undocumented Mexican workers to break strikes by American citizens and urged the repeal of the *Bracero Program*. This stand against immigration was criticized by other Chicano and Mexican American groups, and by the mid-1970s the UFW and other Mexican American organizations expressed solidarity on the immigration controversy arguing that many Mexican Americans would not be in the United States "if their fathers had not been illegal aliens" (Gutiérrez 1995:199). Many of the more conservative Mexican American organizations and the Chicano advocates became more united in the late 1970s as they focused on policies to regulate immigration. The groups feared that the negative feelings toward Mexican immigration would once again "open the door to discrimination against anyone who looked Latino" (Gutiérrez 1995:195).

In the late 1960s, Mexican American organizations turned to litigation as an instrument for political mobilization and incorporation. The Mexican American Legal Defense and Education Fund (MALDEF), established in 1967 by two attorneys, Pete Tijerina and Gregory Luna, with the help of the African American civil rights organizations and funding from the Ford Foundation, initiated an organized legal attack against the continued segregation of Mexican American students in schools. A series of cases were filed in the late 1960s and the 1970s demanding the desegregation of schools in the Texas cities of Houston, Dallas, El Paso, Del Rio, and New Braunfels, and in Portales, New Mexico, and Denver, Colorado. MALDEF also extended provisions of the Voting Rights Acts of 1965 and 1970 to the Mexican American community by challenging the political practice of using multimember voting districts that denied Mexican Americans representation in city and county elections in Texas and California. The *United States v. Texas Bilingual* case initiated by MALDEF in 1981 made Texas school districts implement bilingual programs and required the state to enforce the decision and evaluate the programs. In 1982 MALDEF won the *Plyler v. Doe* case in the United States Supreme Court, a decision that determined it was unconstitutional for school districts to deny a free public education to undocumented immigrant children. Extending the struggle for improved educational opportunities, MALDEF filed the *Edgewood v. Kirby* case in 1984 that, when it was finally won in 1991, reformed the Texas school finance system by making the distribution of money for schools more equitable. The *Edgewood* case moved more money toward school districts with a poor tax base and high concentrations of Mexican American youth. In 1992, MALDEF won the *LULAC v. Richards* case that declared the system of financing higher education in Texas unconstitutional. Although the decision was reversed by the Texas Supreme Court in 1993, the case resulted in changes in the ways all universities and professional schools were funded in Texas and doubled the budgets for universities serving geographic areas with high concentrations of Mexican American students. The efforts of MALDEF and other community-based organizations to serve as advocates for Mexican American interests, train leaders, and register voters have helped reduce structural barriers to assimilation. At the same time, these struggles have heightened the consciousness of Mexican Americans regarding their ethnic identity and sense of community.

We may summarize by saying that the prominent early Mexican American organizations moved in a gingerly way into the political arena. They took great pains to reassure the Anglo Americans that they did not intend to create a disturbance but only to make themselves and their ethnic brethren into "better" (i.e., more Anglicized) citizens. As time passed, however, different organizations were formed for the purpose of placing greater pressure on the dominant society in an effort to gain more nearly equal treatment. In this way, a renewed emphasis on cultural nationalism emerged as a central feature of the Mexican American movement beginning in the 1960s.

This emphasis on cultural nationalism has brought into sharp relief many of the issues that are of greatest interest to us here. What are the goals of the Mexican Americans within American society? How important is it to Mexican Americans that their culture be strengthened and developed? To what extent are the processes of assimilation affecting the distinctiveness and solidarity of the Mexican Americans? The answers to these and other similar questions help to answer the larger question: How useful are the colonial and immigrant models when applied to the Mexican American experience? We address these questions as we explore in Chapter 9 the intergenerational experiences and the cultural and structural assimilation of Mexican Americans.

Key Ideas

1. The relations between Mexican Americans and Anglos represent a second kind of intergroup contact. Like American Indians and African Americans, Mexican Americans originally became part of the United States through force rather than through voluntary immigration.

2. Some social analysts think a sequence of intergroup relations that is initiated through forced entry cannot be understood in terms of the theories of Anglo conformity, the melting pot, or cultural pluralism. They believe, instead, that a variation of colonial theory (e.g., internal colonialism) affords a more accurate picture of the relations between Mexican Americans and Anglos.

3. Colonized minorities, in contrast to immigrant minorities, usually remain in their homeland, are especially committed to the preservation of their native culture, and are prevented by the dominant group from moving about freely to compete for jobs with members of the dominant group. Under these conditions, the sequence of race relations does not move steadily "forward" toward full intergroup merger; it is characterized, rather, by a back-and-forth movement out of conflict into accommodation and back again into conflict. This sequence is interrupted by the expulsion or annihilation of one group or the other. Advocates of the colonial model dispute the claims of those who prefer the immigrant model.

4. The Spanish approach to colonization differed from that of the English. A key difference was that the Spanish included the Indians in the developing colonial society, whereas the English excluded them. As a result, the Indians of Mexico have moved much further toward full assimilation than have the Indians of the United States.

5. The Mexican American group emerged out of a long series of conflicts between the United States and Spain and between the United States and Mexico. Although the Texas revolution was not based on ethnic differences, the ethnic cleavage gradually deepened following Texas's independence. The Mexican American group emerged as a distinct minority group at the end of the Mexican-American War.

6. The Treaty of Guadalupe Hidalgo did not end hostilities between the Mexican Americans and Anglos in the borderlands. Continuous struggle, marked by intermittent open conflict, was a conspicuous element of border life well into the twentieth century.

7. Although the Mexican American group was created when the United States forcibly occupied the southwestern and western lands previously owned by Mexico, most of the present members of the group are not the descendants of that "Creation Generation." The Mexican American population of the United States has grown overwhelmingly through immigration from Mexico since the beginning of the twentieth century.

8. Since Mexican immigration reached its peak later than the peak of the second immigrant stream, many social analysts think of the Mexican Americans as having begun their stay in America near the end of that stream. The apparent slowness of the group to assimilate, therefore, may be due to the comparatively recent arrival of large numbers of immigrants in the United States.

9. Opponents of the immigrant model propose that Mexicans who move to the United States are better thought of as migrants rather than immigrants. From this viewpoint, the movement of Mexicans across an arbitrary political boundary into an area that is both geographically and culturally similar to their homeland is not to be compared to movements of Europeans across oceans into a country with a much different culture. Moreover, when Mexican nationals have reached the

United States, the members of the dominant group typically have greeted them with even higher levels of prejudice and discrimination than usually have been directed toward European immigrants.

10. Three widely publicized examples of dominant-group discrimination against Mexican Americans are the repatriations of the 1930s, the "Zoot-Suit Race Riots" in the 1940s, and "Operation Wetback" in the 1950s. In each of these cases, some officials of the dominant group demonstrated that they made no real distinction between Mexican American citizens and Mexican nationals. They also revealed their belief that all people of Mexican ancestry were innately inferior. As in the case of the evacuation and internment of Japanese Americans, many Mexican American citizens were illegally punished through deportation, intimidation, and physical assault.

11. The *Bracero Program* illustrates how the relations of the dominant group in America to its minorities may be altered by international events.

12. World War II and the Mexican Americans' active participation in it increased the group's commitment to full rights as American citizens and led many of its members to expect a sharp decline in prejudice and discrimination following the war. When the expected changes did not occur, the Mexican Americans demanded their civil rights. Those demands have been expressed in a higher degree of formal social and political organization, legal actions, and in sharp increase in interest in the goals of cultural pluralism.

Key Terms

barrios   Ethnic communities with large concentrations of Spanish-speaking residents. In the southwest region of the United States these residents are usually Mexican Americans and Mexican immigrants.

borderlands   The region, originally a part of Mexico, that stretches inland from the U.S.–Mexico border to include the southwestern United States.

Bracero Program   An agreement between the U.S. government and the Mexican government to allow Mexican agricultural laborers to work in the United States.

braceros   Mexican agricultural workers who came to the United States as part of the *Bracero Program*.

colonial model   A perspective that analyzes intergroup relations in terms of the ways colonization has affected racial domination and the responses of the dominated group. When applied to U.S. racial and ethnic relations, the model assumes that persons of color in America share many of the same experiences that conquered people in third-world nations have experienced.

colonized minorities   Ethnic groups, generally indigenous to an area in which they become minorities, who are forced to become a part of the society of colonizers. These minority groups did not "join" the United States voluntarily like immigrant minorities.

Cortina Wars   A series of border raids led by Juan Cortina, a Mexican leader. These raids heightened antagonisms between the United States and Mexico.

Creation Generation   The original Mexican population who became U.S. citizens as a result of the Treaty of Guadalupe Hidalgo.

immigrant minorities   A minority group that was created through voluntary immigration.

immigrant model   Argues that Mexican newcomers after 1900 came to the United States voluntarily and that the same assimilation processes that apply to other immigrants also should apply to Mexican Americans.

La Raza   A term used to refer to the Mexican American ethnic group.

mestizos   The mixture resulting from intermarriage of indigenous Mexican Indians and the Spanish.

Migrant Generation   The group of Mexicans who came to the United States between 1900 and 1930.

pachucos   Another term used to refer to the zoot-suiters, often associated with gang-related youth and youth rebellion against both Mexican and American cultures.

repatriation   The practice of rounding up and deporting Mexican-origin residents to Mexico. Both Mexican American citizens and immigrants were affected by the deportations.

Sleepy Lagoon Trial   A well-publicized trial of young Mexican Americans convicted of murder in Los Angeles. The case was eventually dismissed for lack of evidence and biased procedures.

Tejanos   The native Mexicans living in Texas when it broke away from Mexico to become an independent republic; also applied to all contemporary Mexican American Texans.

Treaty of Guadalupe Hidalgo   The treaty signed in 1848 between the United States and Mexico that ceded nearly one-half of the territory of Mexico to the United States. The Rio Grande was established as the boundary of Texas. Mexican citizens who resided in the territory were given the right to retain Mexican citizenship or acquire U.S. citizenship.

Zoot-Suit Riots   Confrontations between Anglo servicemen and Mexican American youths who wore distinctive outfits called zoot suits.

Notes

1. Probably no other American ethnic group has been more absorbed by the question "What shall we call ourselves?" The members of this group vary widely in their specific histories, geographical locations, and social characteristics; a term of identification adopted by one segment of the group may be considered inaccurate or offensive by others. In addition to *Mexican American*, the terms *Chicano, Latino, Latin American, Spanish American, Spanish speaking, Hispano, Spanish surname, Mexican origin*, and *Mexicano* have been prominent as identifiers. Each has a specific connotation that distinguishes it. Government documents often use the term *Hispanic;* but it refers not only to Mexican Americans but also to Puerto Ricans, Cubans, and others of Spanish ancestry. The term *Mexican American* appears to be the most widely accepted and is used in this text to refer to all those who trace their ancestry to Mexico. For discussions of terms of self-reference see Garcia (1981), Nostrand (1973), and H. Romo and R. Romo (1985:318–321).

2. George I. Sanchez, quoted by Grebler, Moore, and Guzman (1970:545).

3. The term *Anglo* refers to all non-Hispanic Whites.

4. Lieberson (1961:908) showed that this pattern has been typical in situations in which the migrant group has been dominant.

5. See Edwards, Reich, and Gordon (1975) for an influential statement of this view.

6. The terms *internal colonialism* and *third-world perspective* often are used to emphasize that there are differences between the experience of classical colonialism and that of non-White people in America (Blauner 1972: 54, 70). For discussions of the concepts of colonialism, internal colonialism, neocolonialism, and the situations to which they apply, see Barrera (1979:188–204) and Moore (1976).

7. Diseases also, as we will note again in Chapter 12, played a very important role in the conquest. Crosby (1972:52) stated in this regard that "we have so long been hypnotized by the daring of the conquistador that we have overlooked the importance of his biological allies."

8. Had the official policy of Spain been followed in general practice, the status of the Indians would have been higher. The Laws of the Indies, promulgated in 1542, stated that "Indians are free persons and vassals of the crown. . . . Nothing is to be taken from the Indians except in fair trade" (quoted in McNickle 1973:28).

9. Nine of the defenders killed in the Alamo were *Tejanos*.

10. An additional 54,000 square miles along the southern border of the New Mexico Territory was bought from Mexico in 1853. Moore and Pachon (1985:19) stated that "as it happened (and no Mexican thinks it accidental), the Gadsden Purchase . . . included some of the richest copper mines in the United States."

11. Pachon and Moore (1981) stated that there were around 75,000 Mexicans in the Southwest in 1848, whereas Griswold del Castillo (1990) estimated 100,000.

12. The rate of naturalization among Mexicans has been, in Moore's opinion, "extraordinarily slow" (Moore 1976:49; see also Moore and Pachon 1985:135).

13. For an analysis of some of the specific forces lying behind these broad currents, see Acuña (1981:194–206) and Barrera (1979:67–75).

14. Portes and Rumbaut (1990:17) point out that these "invasions" occur because employers in the host society are willing to hire new workers.

15. The consular officers began to apply strict standards to determine whether an applicant for a visa was likely to become a public charge in the United States (Moore and Pachon 1985:136).

16. Although Mexican labor had been brought to the United States initially to perform mainly rural tasks, by 1930 the majority of the Mexican-origin population lived in cities (see, e.g., R. Romo 1983).

17. Calculated from Table 4.3 in Grebler, Moore, and Guzman (1970:68).

18. These orders were given after the Mexican government protested and the U.S. State Department ordered the Navy to act (R. Romo 1983:167).

19. For accounts of the Mexican American movement in Crystal City, see Camejo (1973) and Gutiérrez and Hirsch (1973).

Mexican Americans

Identity and Incorporation

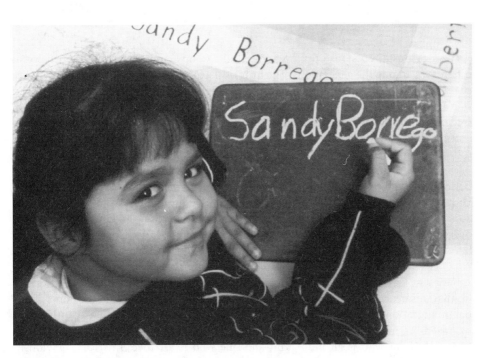

This Mexican American child is learning to write her name as Sandy, an Anglicized version of Sandra. Even if she and her parents value bilingualism, her family will have to struggle to maintain Spanish without strong community supports to do so.

. . . three institutions most clearly framed the experience of Mexican American adolescents and young adults . . . the family, the school, and the workplace. Each exposed young people to a different set of values and expectations which fostered an understanding of their own ethnic identity. . . . they were concerned with the balance between what was "Mexican" in one's past with what was "American" in one's present, they were concerned about the future and what the term "Mexican American" implied.

—George J. Sánchez

The idea that we only need one language leads to isolation and cultural arrogance. This type of thinking can lead to laws that exclude, prohibit and punish those who don't speak English. . . . It's happened before.

—Reynaldo Macias

Our previous discussions of immigrant ethnic groups emphasized the importance of differences among the generations. The historical experiences of the Mexican Americans presented in the previous chapter—as seen through the lenses of both the colonial and immigrant models—demonstrated how important intergenerational differences are in understanding the processes of intergroup relations. Chapter 7, concerning the Japanese and Japanese Americans, showed that the generations were sufficiently distinct to bear different names. This distinctiveness was caused mainly by the immigration pattern experienced by members of this group. Most of the Japanese immigrants came during a period of roughly three decades (1890–1920). Thereafter, the Japanese population of the United States grew almost totally by natural increase until after World War II. For the most part, Issei males had married only Issei females. The Nisei children, therefore, were overwhelmingly native Americans born of foreign parents. It was unusual for a Nisei to have only one parent who had been born in Japan.

This pattern, of course, has been common among nearly all immigrant groups to America, at least in the beginning. But among most other groups, the stream of foreign immigrants generally has continued in a fluctuating manner far beyond the point of initial immigration. In this way, the foreign-born and native generations have continued to be mixed. An important result of this process is that many native-born Americans have had one parent who is an immigrant and one who is a native American. Obviously, whether one has two foreign-born parents, one foreign-born parent, or two native-born parents may have a significant effect on the type and extent of one's own assimilation in America. Also, the proportional size of these different groups within an ethnic group surely is a significant matter. Both of these factors—the number of children of foreign, mixed, or native parentage and the proportion of the group that is foreign-born, mixed, or native—have played an especially important role in the Mexican American experience because the nativity and parentage categories in this ethnic group are unusually mixed. In fact, no other American ethnic group presents such a variegated picture of nativity and foreignness.

The pattern through which the Mexican American population has developed affects the study of intergenerational differences in important ways. For example, among all ethnic groups in America, the category "natives of native parentage" includes the third and subsequent generations. But since among the Mexican Americans this category includes the descendants of the original settlers as well as those who have migrated to the United States since 1900, it is a more diverse category for this group than for the others we have studied. Nevertheless, since the Mexican immigration of the twentieth century (including the undocumented immigration) has continued at a high level, a large majority of the natives of native parentage are the descendants of relatively recent migrants. Consider, too, that the closeness of the mother country and the frequent movements back and forth across the border by some members of each of the nativity and parentage groups call into question the easy assumption that each generation should be more assimilated than the preceding one. In fact, this is one reason why those who regard the Mexican Americans as a colonized minority believe that the intergenerational differences within their group will remain smaller than would be true for an immigrant minority. The crucial questions for us in this regard include the following: Is the Mexican American culture being renewed and invigorated among the third and subsequent generations? Do the children of native parentage exhibit levels of cultural assimilation that are consistent with the predictions flowing from the immigrant model? Has a new, emergent culture been formed?

As was true of our discussion of the Japanese Americans, the data needed to determine whether or in what ways the Mexican Americans are assimilating are far from complete. Although many different sources are of value, an indispensable body of information concerning this ethnic group has been compiled and tabulated by the U.S. Bureau of the Census. Let us consider certain problems in the use of these data as well as some of the major things they reveal.

Identification and Diversity

So far, we have referred to the Mexican Americans without attempting to define exactly who the members of this group are. Because the Mexican Americans are dispersed over a large geographical area, because they have come into American society both through conquest and through immigration, because their immigration has been heaviest during the twentieth century, and because legal immigration has been greatly exceeded by undocumented immigration, they are an extremely heterogeneous group. The difficulties of making accurate general statements about them may be illustrated by considering the efforts of the U.S. Bureau of the Census to identify the members of this group.

Before the 1930 census, people of Mexican origin were placed in the category of "Other"; but beginning in 1930, the enumerators were asked to classify people as "Mexican" on the basis of their "racial" characteristics. In 1940, the Census Bureau attempted to count the people who listed Spanish as their mother tongue. Both of these methods of identification were problematic. The first relied on the census takers' judgment, and the second included people from all Spanish-speaking countries. Still, these attempts did enable investigators to distinguish among the foreign born, natives of foreign or mixed parentage, and natives of native parentage.

In 1950, 1960, and 1970, the Census Bureau approached the identification of the Mexican Americans in still another way. Lists of Spanish surnames were drawn up, and Mexican Americans were identified as "white persons of Spanish surname." This way of identifying Mexican Americans also has been criticized. Many Mexican American women who marry non-Mexican husbands lose their Spanish surname, but not necessarily their Mexican American identity. Similar miscounts affect non-Hispanics who marry persons of Spanish surname. Adding to the problem, the names of some Mexican Americans were not listed as Spanish surnames. In the 1980 census, a special "origin or descent" question was asked that permitted people of Hispanic origin to classify themselves as "Mexican," "Mexican American," "Chicano," "Puerto Rican," "Cuban," or "other Spanish/Hispanic" (Bean and Tienda 1987:50). These categories, too, have been criticized as failing to reflect the increasing racial and ethnic diversity of the Hispanic population; so in a scientifically selected sample of the 1995 Current Population Survey (CPS) households were asked what categories and terminology they preferred. When asked about their preferred racial-group term, about 7.5 percent of the respondents chose "Hispanic" rather than "White," "Black," "American Indian," "Asian," or "Something Else." Twenty-eight percent of the respondents preferred "multiracial," suggesting that the 1980 categories did not capture the increasing number of mixed race or *mestizo* people in the United States. When asked about their preferred ethnic-group term, 58 percent of the respondents named "Hispanic" as compared to "Latino"[1] (12%), "Of Spanish origin" (12%), "Some other term" (8%), or "No one term" (10%).

Despite the imperfections in classifying and counting the Mexican American population, the Census Bureau reports have made possible a number of highly informative (if not completely exact) analyses concerning this ethnic group. For instance, we may now examine the changes that are occurring through time in the occupations, incomes, and levels of education among Mexican Americans and compare these to changes occurring among Anglo Americans. By comparison, we may determine broadly some of the ways in which the two ethnic groups are becoming more or less similar. The census tabulations also enable researchers to study generational changes among Mexican Americans. As useful as these comparisons are, though, they do not reflect completely the diversity that exists among the Mexican Americans. For this reason, we rely also on a number of other sources of information.

Consider some basic points about this large, diverse ethnic group. Although substantial Mexican American groups are to be found in several states outside the Southwest—mainly in Illinois, New York, and Florida—in 1980 approximately 83 percent of their members lived in the five southwestern states of Arizona, California, Colorado, New Mexico, and Texas (Bean and Tienda 1987:80); hence, the special reports of the Census Bureau focus entirely on the latter states. The reports show that the Mexican American population has increased at each census period both in absolute size and as a proportion of the total population. By 1993, this minority had increased to about 14.6

million people (U.S. Bureau of the Census 1995:51). California had the largest *number* of Mexican American residents, whereas New Mexico had the largest *proportion*. A non-southwestern state, Illinois, had the third-largest population of Mexican Americans (behind California and Texas).

Although in the early twentieth century Mexican Americans were concentrated in various farm and rural areas, by 1979 more than 80 percent of the Mexican American population was located in urban areas (Pachon and Moore 1981:116), with California having the highest proportion of urban dwellers and New Mexico having the lowest. The cities also differed in the absolute and relative sizes of their Mexican American populations. For example, in terms of absolute size, the most "Mexican" metropolitan areas in the United States are Los Angeles-Long Beach, San Antonio, Houston, and Chicago (Bean and Tienda 1987:150). In 1990, the majority of the residents in the following cities of the Southwest were Hispanic: El Paso (69%), Santa Ana (65.2%), and San Antonio (55.6%);[2] and some smaller metropolitan areas also have a decidedly visible Mexican American population and "atmosphere." Especially notable among these are Brownsville-Harlingen-San Benito, McAllen-Pharr-Edinburg, Corpus Christi, and Albuquerque. These facts highlight again two basic characteristics of the Mexican American group: It is very heterogeneous, and it is concentrated in the Southwest. Our generalizations about this group, therefore, must be even more tentative than for most other American ethnic groups. With these limitations in mind, we turn to a brief consideration of the main subprocesses of assimilation.

Mexican American Assimilation

Cultural Assimilation: English and Spanish

We have seen that ethnic groups in America, whether immigrant or colonized, typically have tried to maintain and elaborate their cultural heritages. The degree to which this has been true, however—as well as the group's success in doing so—has varied among ethnic groups. In regard to the maintenance of their heritage, the Mexican Americans have been one of the most successful ethnic groups in America. Consider again, for instance, what usually has happened in the important matter of language use.[3] Despite a great number of exceptions and local variations, the general pattern among American ethnic groups has been for the use of the ancestral tongue to diminish noticeably across the generations and for English to become the usual language among those in the third and subsequent generations.

Although it is not possible to state even roughly what proportion of the Mexican American population has, over the years, preferred to maintain their native culture, it seems likely that the proportion has been high in comparison to most other American ethnic minorities. Whether this is true or not, it is clear that they have been the primary contributors to the maintenance of the Spanish language in the United States over a comparatively long period of time. For example, the number of students with **limited English proficiency** enrolled in U.S. schools is growing; there was a 70 percent increase of such students from 1984 to 1992. Most of those students were immigrants or recent arrivals, but many were not. Forty-one percent of the children with limited English proficiency who are students in U.S. elementary schools were born in the United States. Almost three out of four of these limited English-speaking students in U.S. schools speak Spanish as their native language, and of those Spanish speakers, 40 percent were born in Mexico.[4] For this reason, Spanish is more likely to survive in the United States than any other foreign language.

The number of speakers of Spanish as a first language continues to increase in the United States, largely because of continued immigration. In 1990, for example, Spanish was the language of the home for more than 7 percent of the people in the United States and was more commonly used in the home than all other non-English languages combined (U.S. Bureau of the Census 1995:53). However, the longer Mexican immigrant children have been in the United States, the more likely they are to become monolingual English speakers.

Many factors determine when Spanish is no longer transmitted to the succeeding generation. The most important factor is whether the parents either speak English predominantly or teach their children English as their first language. Veltman (1988) estimated that there were some 4 million Hispanics in the United States who did not speak Spanish at all. Others are bilingual but speak mainly either Spanish or English. The propensity among Mexican Americans to abandon speaking Spanish varies with age, place of birth, length of time in the United States, whether a group is too small or scattered to resist outside pressures effectively, and the immigrants' income, gender, and education (Grenier 1985; Stevens 1992).

Only a few English-speaking Mexican American children will learn and maintain Spanish as a regularly spoken language. The children of recent immigrants learn English very quickly in the schools and by watching television and are less likely to be able to teach their own children Spanish. The majority of the monolingual Spanish speakers in the United States are recent immigrants, Spanish-speaking children who have not yet entered school, and the elderly. Veltman (1990) estimated that less than one-fourth of the grandchildren of immigrants will maintain Spanish as their first language. As incomes and levels of education increase, Mexican Americans are more likely to be fluent in English than in Spanish (Portes and Rumbaut 1990:213; Portes and Schauffler 1996).[5] Even highly educated parents who value bilingualism do not have much chance of transmitting the Spanish language to their children if they do not have strong community and social supports to do so (Portes and Schauffler 1996:8–29).

The high concentration of Mexican Americans at various points throughout the borderlands, the closeness of Mexico, the steady reinforcement by continuing immigration, and the availability of Spanish-language radio and television all help to maintain the frequent use of Spanish. Still, second-generation youths learn English quickly and often prefer to use it with their peers and siblings. A controversial method of maintaining the native language against the forces of assimilation is **bilingual education.** Although many immigrant groups have tried to teach their children their native language in the schools, bilingual education is often associated with Spanish-speaking groups because so many recent immigrants, as well as the Mexican Americans who were part of the "colonized" territories of the Southwest, speak Spanish.

Flashpoint 2: Bilingual Education

The debate over bilingual education in the public schools in the United States has provoked bitter political disputes throughout the nation's history. These debates have become especially heated in the 1980s and 1990s as using languages other than English and bilingual education have become targets of anti-immigration groups. For example, in 1996 eight bills were placed before Congress that would proclaim English as the only official language of the United States and outlaw bilingual education. Supporters of those bills asked, "Why should the 1 in 20 public school students in the nation who can't speak English be taught in their own language today when the immigrant children who entered school speaking only Italian or Yiddish or German a century ago managed to get along just fine (Celis 1995a:5)?" An immigrant parent from one of New York City's poorest neighborhoods argued, "What bothered me was that they place children in bilingual programs and keep them there for years and years. They aren't learning English."[6] This parent and others in her neighborhood filed a lawsuit against their school district claiming that bilingual education as structured in New York City did not work and might even inhibit the learning of English.

The question of bilingual education takes on even greater significance at a time when the new students in many school districts are increasingly immigrant children who do not speak English well. Despite a steady growth of federal funds for bilingual programs, bilingual education has reached only a fraction of the population for which it was intended. Moreover, very few of the funded bilingual programs have attempted to *maintain* the native language of the immigrant children served (Hakuta 1986:205). Still, opponents of bilingual education have vociferously argued that bilingual education impedes assimilation into American society, keeps immigrants from learning English, and represents a threat to the status of English and the ideals of Americanization.

The bilingual education debate is framed by two positions that reflect the Anglo conformity and the cultural pluralist models of assimilation. Anglo conformists argue that it is the responsibility of the schools to teach English and to promote assimilation by substitution. The pluralists counter that the schools should strive to recognize that children learn best in a language they understand and, that to maintain a strong nation, bilingual programs should strive to protect the language and culture of immigrant groups.

According to Headden (1995), opponents claim that "bilingual education has emerged as one of the dark spots on the grim tableau of American education" and while bilingual education began as a good idea, it "now needs fixing."[7] Opponents argue that bilingual programs are staffed by poorly trained teachers who themselves are struggling with English and that immigrant children are kept in these programs by self-serving administrators and teachers out to save their own jobs. They point out that the school dropout rates for Hispanics remain the highest of any ethnic group despite the fact that Hispanics have been the largest beneficiaries of bilingual education.

Those who support bilingual education protest that those who attack it know very little about it and, in fact, do not even know the definition or purpose of bilingual education. Clearly, *full bilingual education programs,* those that develop all skills in both languages and use English and the student's native language as media of instruction, are aimed at maintaining and developing both the minority language and English. Most American bilingual programs are *transitional* or *partial bilingual programs,* in part because many Americans view full bilingual programs and maintenance of the minority language as anti-assimilationist or separatist. Also, most bilingual education programs in the United States have been viewed as compensation for the educational disadvantage that a limited-English-speaking child experiences in the United States. In fact, supporters of bilingual education would agree that students wind up in bilingual classrooms who really need remedial help or because there is no room in regular classes. Many programs, therefore, are not representative of true bilingual education.

Pluralists view full bilingual programs as a way to maintain the pluralistic nature of the United States and as a way to encourage all children, including Anglo American children, to be bilingual. They claim that the United States has never really supported true language-maintenance bilingual programs. Let us look now at some of the controversies that have followed bilingual education in the United States.

Historical Perspectives.   The English colonists believed that America and its citizens should be defined by a common language. Of course they believed that English should be that common language. They argued that English reflected the democratic and traditional values brought from England and that immigrants became "real Americans" by speaking it. The upper- and middle-class colonists encouraged their children to learn Latin, French, or German; but bilingualism on the part of immigrants was frowned upon, considered poor social adaptation, and believed to indicate mental confusion and low intelligence (Portes and Schauffler 1996:433).

The 1848 constitution of California and the early laws of New Mexico required that all laws and regulations be written in Spanish and English. The Treaty of Guadalupe Hidalgo also gave Mexican citizens who became Americans the right to maintain their cultural traditions. Still, although speaking some foreign languages was admired, the speaking of Spanish was considered inferior. In San Francisco, Cosmopolitan Schools were established as early as 1867 in which particular attention was given to teaching German and French; but it was not until 1913 that Spanish was added to the curriculum, some forty-six years after the other European languages had been recognized (Kloss 1977).

In Texas in 1858, laws were passed declaring that English had to be the principal language in the public schools, despite the fact that many of the Mexican-origin children came to school speaking only Spanish. In New Mexico, Spanish had always been spoken. In 1930, for example, children from Spanish-speaking homes constituted one-half of the school enrollment there, but less than one-fifth of those who made it to the twelfth grade. Educator George I. Sanchez pointed out that "The use of standard curricula, books, and materials among these children is a ridiculous gesture" (cited in McWilliams 1945:133). Mexican migrant workers throughout the Southwest were "socially ostracized and sharply set apart from the resident white communities. All or most members of the families worked in the fields. Thus, most continued to speak Spanish, lived among their own group, and followed their own mode of living with few opportunities to become acculturated" (McWilliams 1945:119).

Departing from the position of earlier, more conservative, Mexican American organizations such as LULAC that emphasized learning English and assimilation, the Congress of Spanish Speaking Peoples (*El Congreso*), met in 1939 and issued a "Call to Action." *El Congreso* denounced theories of racial supremacy and rejected the concept of Anglo conformity. The members called for protection and expansion of the cultural rights of Spanish-speaking people and demanded the recognition of the bilingual-bicultural society that already existed in fact in the Southwest. Combating discrimination against Spanish speakers was a main goal; thus *El Congreso* advocated the censure of textbooks portraying Latinos as inferior, the increased teaching of the historical and cultural background of the Latino in the United States, and the recognition of Spanish as having a status equal to that of English. The members of *El Congreso* called for more Mexican teachers in American public schools and for bilingual education for children as a way to wipe out illiteracy (Sanchez 1993:247; Gutiérrez 1995:215–216).

Despite the call for bilingual education for Spanish-speaking children, much of the segregation of Mexican students throughout the Southwest was rationalized in terms of their presumed language "deficiency." For example, school officials argued that the segregation of Mexican children into "Mexican schools" would facilitate the learning of English and other subjects because the Mexican children would not have to compete with Anglo children. They also argued that segregation would allow special attention to the language difficulties of Mexican American children who entered school speaking only Spanish and that segregation would allow more time for Americanization (Garcia 1989:265–266). Quite to the contrary, many Mexican American parents and educators argued that both the school districts that segregated Mexican children and the courts of law that allowed the segregation to continue based on language differences were "confusing education with English" (Garcia 1989:267). Mexican parents presented the case that learning English could be accomplished more quickly in an integrated classroom with English-speaking peers. They also pointed out that the rest of education would suffer under segregation because the Mexican schools were overcrowded, poorly staffed, and inadequately funded. They argued that segregated schools would not make "good Americans" out of Mexican children.

Legal Developments.   Mexican American leaders and organizations identified school segregation as the most despicable form of discrimination practiced against Spanish-speaking children. As the debate over school segregation and language issues continued, schools neglected the academic performance of Mexican American students and, as a result, children learned neither English nor Spanish well. The compulsory school attendance laws were not enforced for Mexican children and local school officials channeled those who did attend into non-reading, pre-first grade classes or industrial and vocational education programs (San Miguel 1987:46–53).

In 1930, LULAC supported a group of Mexican parents in Lemon Grove, California, when the Anglo school board built a two-room building designated as the "Mexican school" and required all Mexican students to attend classes there. The appeals court upheld the school district's right to separate children based on "their English language handicaps"; but the San Diego Superior Court overturned the case arguing that segregation "deprived Mexican children of the presence of American children so necessary for learning the English language."[8]

Litigation against the segregation of Mexican American students continued (San Miguel 1987). LULAC assisted a group of Mexican American parents in Pearland, Texas, in their protest against a policy in which Mexican American students were forced to attend a dilapidated one-room, one-teacher Mexican school whereas Anglo students had a modern school plant. After several months of pressure and negative publicity, the Mexican American children were "invited" to attend school in the main building. LULAC also assisted several Mexican American families in challenging the practice of school segregation—in *Mendez v. Westminister School District*—claiming that Mexican American students in Los Angeles were being denied their constitutional rights by being forced to attend separate "Mexican schools." In 1946, the judge ruled that the practice of segregating children of Mexican descent was in violation of the equal protection clause of the Fourteenth Amendment. The court also agreed with one of the plaintiff's central arguments—that Spanish-speaking children learn English more readily in mixed than in segregated classrooms. Another point that the case affirmed was that children should not be grouped for special instructional purposes solely on the basis of racial origin or social background. The ruling was upheld by the appeals court, setting the stage for the famous desegregation case *Brown v. Topeka Board of Education* in 1954, which challenged the "separate but equal" policy of segregating African American children.

Although these court cases eliminated separate schools for Mexican Americans, many Mexican American students continued to be placed in segregated classes solely because of their inability to speak or understand English. Moreover, negative attitudes toward Spanish continued, and many Mexican children were punished or ridiculed for speaking their native language in the schools. Steiner (1969:209) documented incidents of children who were forced to kneel on the playground and beg forgiveness for uttering a Spanish word, to stand in the corner for using Spanish in the classroom, to go to "Spanish detention" for speaking their native language, and to endure paddling if they persisted in being "Spanish-speaking."

With the influx of Spanish-speaking Cuban refugees into Florida in the late 1950s and early 1960s, the Ford Foundation funded an experimental program in bilingual education in Dade County, Florida. The Coral Way Elementary School enrolled predominantly middle-income children and had equal numbers of American students and Spanish-speaking students. The 1963 Dade County Bilingual Program was designed to maintain the Cuban children's Spanish language skills as well as teach them English. The plan included English-speaking children who would also learn in Spanish. Talented bilingual teachers among the refugees in Miami were recruited to teach in the bilingual program. Subsequent evaluations of the program showed that both English-speaking and Spanish-speaking children improved their reading test scores and seemed to learn well in both languages (Hakuta 1986:194–198).

In the wake of the Dade County program's success and the Black civil rights movement that spread to the Southwest, Mexican American organizations demanded bilingual education for the large numbers of Mexican children who were failing in English-only classrooms. The passage of the Bilingual Education Act of 1968, Title VII (an amendment to the 1965 Elementary and Secondary Education Act) provided funds to promote research and demonstration programs in bilingual education. Seven-and-a-half million dollars were appropriated to stimulate innovative programs. The legislation targeted limited-English-speaking children from families with incomes below $3,000 per year (Hakuta 1986:198).[9] The bilingual education legislation made it possible for interested school districts to compete for funds for experimental programs, but districts were not obligated to implement bilingual education. The programs reached only a small proportion of the non-English-speaking children who needed bilingual instruction and emphasized the early elementary school levels, especially kindergarten through third grade.

The primary impetus for bilingual education came in the litigation of a 1974 Supreme Court case *Lau v. Nichols*. The *Lau* decision, based on the experiences of Chinese immigrant students in California, determined that the failure of the San Francisco school system to provide English-language instruction to Chinese students who did not speak English denied those students a meaningful opportunity to participate in the public educational program. The Court reasoned that merely providing the same facilities, textbooks, teachers, and curriculum for students who did not understand English was not equal treatment. The interpretive guidelines for the *Lau* decision published by the Office for Civil Rights indicated that the schools were required to "open up instruction" so that students who did not speak English could benefit. In the summer of 1975, the Office for Civil Rights offered specific remedies to school districts to help them comply with the *Lau* decision. The **Lau Task Force Remedies** recommended bilingual education as the best way to provide assistance to elementary school students with limited English proficiency.

Arguments Pro and Con.   Almost eight years after the *Lau* decision, the Texas Federal District Court mandated the phasing-in—starting in September of 1981—of a statewide kindergarten-through-twelfth-grade bilingual education program. Judge William Wayne Justice wrote in his decision that "unless [these children] receive instruction in a language they can understand . . . thousands of Mexican American children in Texas will remain educationally crippled for life." The Texas Education Agency and the State Board of Education opposed the decision claiming that "Bilingual education is a resegregation program."[10]

Although evidence clearly showed that the vast majority of bilingual programs were designed to mainstream children quickly into English-only classrooms, many opponents of bilingual education believed that the programs were designed to maintain the students' native languages. Hakuta (1986:226) argued that the strong negative opinions against bilingual education could not be caused by educational shortcomings in the programs because research has provided strong evidence that advanced bilingualism promotes academic achievement.[11] He proposed that the heated opposition to bilingual education was a result of the strong identification of "bilingual" with "Hispanic" and the association of bilingual education with the political mobilization of Hispanics.

In the 1980s, the administration of President Ronald Reagan attacked bilingual education and supported Anglo conformist programs that focused entirely on the development of English skills. Federal expenditures for bilingual education, adjusted for inflation, declined 48 percent during the 1980s, despite a 50 percent increase in the limited-English-proficient student population.[12] Leading the opposition to bilingual education was a movement for making English the official language of the United States.

In December of 1995, the U.S. Senate Governmental Affairs Committee heard testimony regarding a Senate bill to declare English the nation's official language and severely restrict the federal government's use of other languages. Advocates for language-minority groups protested that groups who opposed the English-only movement had been excluded from the hearings. Arguments for such legislation were that English as a national language was needed because there were some 323 languages now spoken within the borders of the United States, and bilingual education had denied English-speaking children access to schooling in English. Senator Ted Stevens, representing Alaska, testified that he was concerned that "California was becoming a Spanish-speaking state."[13] On August 1, 1996, after nearly six hours of emotional debate, the House approved a bill that would make English the official language of the United States. The debate, which has been a familiar one in history, was over the need to codify the use of English into law and over the importance of English as defining what it means to be an American. Supporters of the English-only legislation argued that the bill would encourage immigrants to learn English, give them a common bond with other Americans, and help them assimilate. They contended that pluralism in the United States was leading to dangerously segregated linguistic ghettos that the federal government accommodated with bilingual education and ballots in languages other than English. House Speaker Newt Gingrich cited the perils of linguistic pluralism and warned that if bilingual instruction continued it would lead to "the decay of the core parts of our civilization."

Critics of the legislation noted that the overwhelming majority of Americans already speak English well and that immigrants would be better served if Congress provided financing for English-language classes. Falcoff (1996)[14] claimed that the legislation represented "an irrational fear of Spanish." He noted that the United States is one of the world's major Spanish-speaking countries—producing important Spanish-language television and radio programs[15] and supporting a vigorous Spanish-language press. He pointed out that the fact that the United States has a large Spanish-speaking population does not mean that the country is likely to become linguistically divided. Most immigrants want to learn English because they see English as fundamental to economic and social advancement; young immigrants see English as the key to popular culture. Falcoff (1996) also noted that the persistence of Spanish in the United States reflects the uninterrupted flow of newcomers, rather than a resistance to assimilation.

The tensions displayed in these debates are similar to those that aroused the "Americanization" movement prior to the passage of the 1924 Quota Act when Anglo conformity and English language homogeneity were seen as essential for nationhood and collective identity. Immigrants were compelled to speak English as the prerequisite of social acceptance and secondary assimilation. Former President Theodore Roosevelt proclaimed shortly after World War I, "We have room for but one language here, and that is the English language; for we intend to see that the crucible turns our people out as Americans, and not as dwellers in a polyglot boardinghouse; and we have room for but one sole loyalty, and that is loyalty to the American people" (cited in Portes and Rumbaut 1990:184).

Bilingual education supporters have maintained a united front against the English-only movement, arguing that immigrants are the primary target of the campaign. They proposed a pluralistic compromise to the language restrictionists. They noted the status of Mexican Americans and Native Americans as colonized minorities and argued that indigenous languages, such as Spanish and Native American languages, which predated English on American soil, have a prior moral claim that other immigrant languages do not have and should, therefore, be exempted from any English-only mandate. They argued that those languages should be maintained, along with English, as part of the country's rich heritage.

The pursuit of Anglo conformity is not logically inconsistent with transitional versions of bilingual-bicultural education. Some Anglo conformists are willing to support bilingual-bicultural programs in the public schools for a comparatively short period of time. The aim of such programs is to act as a "bridge" between the culture of the home and the culture of the larger society. The expectation is that minority children will be most successfully "weaned" from the parent culture if their primary instruction is conducted in the language of the home. As usual under Anglo conformity doctrine, children taught in this way are expected, after a few years, to complete the crossover to the English language and Anglo American ways and to leave their ethnic cultures permanently behind. It is here that Anglo conformist and pluralist policies differ. Cultural pluralists may agree that bilingual-bicultural education should give children a full command of English and the customs and values of the dominant society. They will not agree, though, that the object of such an education should be to wean the children away from the parent culture. On the contrary, from the perspective of cultural pluralism, bilingual-bicultural education should ensure not only that minority children will master the dominant culture but also that they will be assisted to preserve and elaborate their heritages in a full and appreciative way.

These differences in the educational policies favored by Anglo conformists and cultural pluralists should dispel any notion that the debate between them is purely academic. The public schools in America, as traditionally operated, clearly are instruments of Anglo conformity. Furthermore, the implementation of an educational program that would genuinely meet the criteria of pluralism would require significant changes in U.S. educational institutions. The continued debate over bilingual education is really about who will define the dominant culture. Hakuta (1986) argues that bilingual-bicultural education openly acknowledges the legitimacy of non-English languages and cultures, and, as a consequence, appears to threaten the status of English and the dominance of Anglo Americans.

Long-Term Implications.

The continued political pressure for bilingual education and the growth of Spanish-language media afford strong evidence that cultural assimilation is not occurring among the Mexican Americans in the same way as it typically has among the European minorities. It is true, of course, that the older members of the group and those who are recent immigrants rely most heavily on Spanish; and it is true that this pattern has been common among many other ethnic groups. Linguists have noted that many third- and fourth-generation Mexican Americans speak only a popular variety of Spanish or mix Spanish and English in a style called **code-switching.**

These Mexican Americans may have a limited verbal Spanish repertoire, but they still take great pride in their language as a symbol of cultural identity (Peñalosa 1989).

The high degree of bilingualism among the Mexican Americans may illustrate the pluralist ideal of cultural assimilation by addition discussed in Chapter 2. The Mexican Americans, so far, may not be following the Anglo conformity pattern of cultural assimilation by substituting English for Spanish, though some scholars believe otherwise;[16] or, even if this switch is occurring, a change in only one cultural element (albeit a very important one) may not be sufficient to produce cultural assimilation in other respects. Keefe and Padilla (1987:16–18) present evidence showing that as language loyalty declines among Mexican Americans, loyalty to the Mexican heritage nevertheless continues.

More research along these lines must be conducted if we are to gain a better understanding of cultural assimilation. In addition, we need a more detailed picture of the views and day-to-day behavior of Mexican Americans, especially as these are expressed within the family.

Cultural Assimilation: Family Patterns

A vigorous, often heated, controversy also has swirled around the subject of the characteristics of the Mexican American family and **familism.** Most research on this topic has agreed that even the fourth generation retains aspects of Mexican culture, particularly the value of, and involvement in, large and local **extended families.** Much of the early research on Mexican American families tended to focus on the deviant aspects of the Hispanic culture, did not examine intragroup differences, and used frameworks that failed to capture adequately the change and strengths in Mexican American families.[17] For example, Mexican-origin families have been described as patriarchal, religious, cohesive, and traditional. Men, particularly older men, have been portrayed as regulating family life in a strict and austere way (much has been made of the notion of "**machismo**"), whereas women have been portrayed as subordinate, religious, and patient sufferers. Many critics of such portrayals have agreed with Williams's assessment that some influential scholarly works have been affected by the stereotypical definitions of Mexican Americans held by the majority group.

Williams (1990) conducted a valuable study of continuities and changes within the Mexican American family during the last several decades through in-depth interviews with seventy-five Mexican American couples of "working" and "business/professional" backgrounds. She gathered information on the way the important life-cycle events of birth, marriage, and death were handled in the period from the 1920s through the 1950s. These "traditional" patterns were then compared to "current" practices[18] to see whether changes had occurred in the rituals surrounding these important events. Her research showed that the cohesion of the extended family declined during the period under study, with funeral ceremonies remaining "as the last bastion for sustaining extended kinship arrangements" (Williams 1990:138).[19] The results showed, too, that the power of men declined during the decades studied.

Williams's findings were interpreted within a broad framework concerning the general effects of industrialization, urbanization, and bureaucratization on family life in America. She argued that during the last several decades Mexican American families (on the whole) have become more like Anglo American families but that this trend toward convergence does not mean that Mexican Americans are assimilating by "attempting to become like Anglos." Her thesis, instead, is that the groups are becoming more similar because both sets of families "are responding to major changes on the societal and global levels" (Williams 1990:148).

In another important study of family structure and ethnicity, Keefe and Padilla (1987) examined generational differences among Mexican Americans and also compared the family structures of Mexican Americans to those of Anglo Americans. The analysis was based on interviews and reinterviews with samples of Anglo and Mexican American respondents.[20] One major part of the research focused on the interactions of the respondents with their primary kin (parents, siblings, children) and secondary kin (other relatives) within and outside of the local community.

Among the many (and complicated) findings, three stand out. First, primary-kin ties were the most significant for both Anglos and Mexican Americans; Anglos, however, had fewer primary kin close at hand, and Mexican Americans maintained closer ties. Second, Mexican Americans were more likely than Anglos to have a local extended family and to maintain contact with relatives. These two findings lead to a third that is of special importance in relation to cultural assimilation: Even though Mexican Americans in the second and third generations appeared to be assimilating culturally in some important respects, the effect of these changes was to strengthen, rather than weaken, the extended family. The U.S.-born Mexican Americans have become highly urbanized and are exposed to many sources of family breakdown; but "The Chicano family," as Keefe and Padilla (1987:144) stated, "is far from being a declining institution."

A third important study of Mexican immigrant families looked at the ongoing processes of gender as they relate to migration and settlement (Hondagneu-Sotelo 1994). Hondagneu-Sotelo's California study, also using interviews, participant observations, and home visits with a small group of Mexican immigrant families, illustrates how the principles behind the models of assimilation presented in Chapter 2 may be tested against specific research findings. Her research found that many immigrants live and work in the United States for many years with dreams of eventually returning to Mexico. As time passes, they develop ties to jobs, financial institutions, churches, schools, friends, and neighbors, that connect them to the United States. Hondagneu-Sotelo found that migration patterns—whether a husband preceded his wife and children, intact families migrated together, or men and women migrated independently and then formed a family—made a big difference in assimilation patterns. She found that the immigration process did shape family relationships. When Mexican men migrated to the United States to work in the *Bracero Program*, the wives and daughters who remained behind assumed traditional male responsibilities. When families immigrated to the United States intact, the men and women arrived with cultural and ideological baggage, but as they began to take advantage of work opportunities and participate in their new communities, they reshaped traditional social relationships. For example, women worked outside the home for wages, men helped care for children, and children, who learned English in the schools, often exerted authority over family matters previously out of their control.

We conclude, therefore, that the kind of cultural assimilation we might expect on the basis of Park's and Gordon's theories—a substitution across-the-board of Anglo for Mexican American culture—seems not to be occurring. Movement toward assimilation in some respects has not been accompanied by changes in all of the other aspects of culture; however, if the ideas of assimilationist theories seem inadequate to explain what is occurring among the Mexican Americans, the ideas of colonialist theory also fall short. Although Mexican Americans reject many facets of Anglo American culture, the two groups appear nevertheless to be moving toward one another in some important ways which, as Williams (1990) maintained, may not mean that the former are adopting the culture of the latter. Mexican Americans appear to accept the necessity, if not the desirability, of secondary structural assimilation. Let us examine some facts in this regard.

Secondary Structural Assimilation

Our exploration of secondary assimilation among Mexican Americans focuses on their occupations, incomes, education, and residential location.

Occupations.   As noted previously, Mexican Americans have from the beginning played a distinctive role in the American labor force. By 1920, Mexican American workers were much more likely to be employed as farming, mining, or railroad laborers than in any other capacity. And they were far more likely to be found in these occupational pursuits than were Anglo American workers. This concentration in certain types of work was never, of course, complete. Especially since the beginning of World War II, Mexican Americans have been moving out of "their" customary occupations and into many different jobs that pay more and carry with them higher levels of pay and social prestige. For example, the proportion of native-born Mexican American men engaged in "professional" occupations rose steadily from more than 3 percent in 1960 to more than 11 percent in 1994 (Bean and Tienda 1987:328; U.S. Bureau of the Census 1995: 404).

A study of labor force participation among Mexican and Mexican American women in the U.S. Southwest showed that, historically, Mexican-origin women have had much lower labor force participation rates than their White and Black counterparts (Badar, Broman, Bokemeir, and Zinn 1995). In recent years, however, Mexican-origin women have been entering the labor force at an increasing rate. The authors argued that this pattern does not necessarily reflect increased cultural assimilation, since many of the women working outside the home maintained a high level of cultural identification, use of Spanish, and ethnic pride. They suggested that lower labor force participation for Mexican and Mexican American women was due to lower levels of education that limited job opportunities. According to one report on women of Hispanic origin in the labor force, just over one-third of the Mexican-origin women of twenty-five years and older had graduated from high school in 1980, and less than 13 percent worked in managerial and professional specialties (U.S. Department of Labor 1989). The Badar, Broman, Bokemeir, and Zinn study (1995) argued that Mexican American and Mexican women have entered the labor force in greater numbers because of increased unemployment among male heads of household. Additional factors, such as increased economic development in the Southwest, also resulted in greater opportunities for female employment outside the home. The study found that some cultural assimilation processes, such as learning English, opened up more job opportunities; but the majority of the Mexican American women who worked were employed in peripheral industries and secondary occupations, such as clerical service, agricultural work, health service, education, or manufacturing.

Thus, although some of the changes that have occurred are in the direction of occupational assimilation, some are not. For instance, the rate of increase in the proportion of Mexican American men working in the professions seen in the 1960s slowed noticeably during the 1970s. Moreover, although Mexican American men, as compared to Anglo men, experienced a relative gain in professional work between 1960 and 1980, the actual gap between the two groups increased slightly from 6.0 percent in 1960 (3.3 versus 9.3) to 6.4 percent in 1980 (5.7 versus 12.1) (Bean and Tienda 1987:329).[21] In addition, despite the higher rate of increase in professional employment among Mexican American males compared to Anglo males, the level of professional employment among Mexican Americans in 1980 still had not reached the Anglo level for 1960. The levels of professional employment among native-born women of both ethnic groups are generally higher, but a comparison of Mexican American and Anglo women leads to the same conclusions as for men (Bean and Tienda 1987:334–335).

Incomes. We should note also that even when Mexican Americans gain access to the more "desirable" occupations, they frequently are in the lower-paid positions within them. Combining this fact with the continuing differences between the occupational distributions of Anglos and Mexican Americans, we should not be surprised to find a continuation of income differences between the two groups. And this is, indeed, the case. Although Mexican Americans showed a steady improvement in incomes during the 1960–1980 period, the personal income for Mexican Americans hovered around 67 cents for each dollar received by Anglos.[22] This means that even during a period of rising occupational standing and increased incomes, the average (mean) income for Mexican Americans remained about two-thirds that of Anglos.

A somewhat different picture emerges, however, when median family incomes for 1980 and 1993–94 are compared. In 1980, Mexican American families received just over 66 percent as much as White families (Bean and Tienda 1987:346–347). By 1993–94, however, the family incomes of Mexican Americans had declined to around 60 percent as much as Anglo families (U.S. Bureau of the Census 1995:48, 51); therefore, despite a rise in the dollar income among Mexican Americans in the latter period, their relative position declined. Moreover, the absolute gap between the median family incomes of the two groups almost doubled between 1980 and 1993–94. We conclude, therefore, that although the real economic situation of the Mexican Americans may be improving gradually, the relative and absolute gaps between Mexican American and White families are still growing. Additionally, a much higher percentage of Mexican American than White families live in poverty (26 versus 9) (U.S. Bureau of the Census 1995:48, 51).

Whether people find it possible to move out of low-prestige, poorly paid jobs into more desirable jobs may depend to a considerable extent on the educational levels of the people involved. It is of special importance, therefore, to know whether the educational level of the Mexican American population has been increasing over time. Such increases would be expected if this ethnic group has been moving in the direction of secondary assimilation.

Education. Dramatic differences in educational levels between Hispanic and non-Hispanic groups have persisted over many years. Past research has emphasized that Mexican American children have faced severe discrimination in the schools and, as a consequence, have had lower achievement levels than Anglos (Fligstein and Fernandez 1985:164; Valdivieso and Davis 1988:6). Although Mexican Americans still lag far behind the Anglo population, the available evidence suggests strongly that they are becoming more assimilated in regard to education. Between 1960 and 1980, for example, the median level of education among Mexican Americans increased from 6.4 years in 1960 to 9.1 years in 1980. Among the native-born portion of the group, the average rose from 7.6 years in 1960 to 11.1 in 1980. The foreign-born group also showed a marked average increase from 3.6 years in 1960 to 6.1 in 1980. By 1987, the proportion of Mexican Americans completing four years of high school or more had risen to 46 percent, which was the highest level ever recorded, and the median level of education among those between 25 and 34 had reached 12.1 years (U.S. Bureau of the Census 1989:8). In addition, college completion more than doubled from 2.5 percent in 1970 to 6.3 percent in 1994 (U.S. Bureau of the Census 1995:157).

We must be cautious in interpreting these evidences of increases in schooling among Mexican Americans, however. Even though the successive generations of Mexican Americans seem to be achieving higher levels of education, one careful analysis (Bean, Chapa, Berg, and Sowards 1994) showed that within different age categories the third generation generally has not reached the educational level of the second generation. To illustrate, the mean level of education among second-generation males between the ages of 25 and 29 was 12.3 years, but among third-generation males the average was 12.2 years; similarly, among second- and third-generation females in the 25–29 age group, the mean levels of education were 11.9 and 11.7, respectively. These findings call into question the adequacy of the view, based on the overall statistics, that each generation of Mexican Americans is attaining a higher level of education than its predecessors.

Another study found similar patterns of lower achievement among third-generation Mexican Americans. Wojtkiewicz and Donato (1995) found that U.S.-born Mexicans with U.S.-born parents (the third or higher generation) were less likely to graduate from high school than Whites, but U.S.-born Mexican children with foreign-born parents (the second generation) were more likely to graduate from high school than Whites. They suggested that immigrant parents may pass on higher levels of motivation to their children than do native U.S. parents.

A problem that continues to be particularly prominent among Mexican American youths is the high rate at which they "drop out" (or are "pushed out") of school before reaching high school graduation. Female students tend to do better in school than males; Carter and Wilson (1993) reported that almost 63 percent of the Hispanic female students in 1992 graduated from high school compared to 52 percent of the Hispanic male students. An important factor affecting these levels is the frequency with which Mexican American children, particularly males, are required to repeat grades (Fligstein and Fernandez 1985:165).

From 1989 to 1992, Romo and Falbo (1996) followed the school careers of one hundred Mexican-origin youths whom their school district had designated as "at risk" of dropping out of school. Data included school records, questionnaires administered to each parent and teenager in their homes, and tape-recorded, transcribed interviews and participant observations with a subsample of twenty-six of the families. Only nineteen of the original hundred graduated at the end of their senior year. Romo and Falbo focused on the success stories of those youths who completed high school. The study revealed that the process of earning a high school diploma is a complex one, influenced by peer cultures, parental resources and education, the availability of effective school programs and policies, and strong parental support. They found that education was highly valued by all the students and their families; parents wanted their children to go to college, and students wanted to be doctors and lawyers, but by age twenty they had earned only a fraction of the credits needed to earn a high school diploma. In most of these families the mothers were primarily responsible for their children's education and, when these parents had limited schooling themselves, they were unable to help their children with school work. Many did not understand the school system and did not realize that their children were tracked into low-level courses. Few had the confidence to approach the school for help. Those who did often felt themselves at a disadvantage, particularly when staff members spoke only English. Students and parents reported experiencing frustration over the schools' unwillingness or inability to provide help, and many reported encountering hostility from teachers, counselors, or administrators. Many of the students who dropped out of school made rational decisions to leave a school system in which they had few alternatives but failure.

Poor high school graduation rates limit the number of Mexican American students who can go on to college. Moreover, tracking into low-level courses in high school may leave some Mexican American students who do go to college inadequately prepared for college-level work. Although there has been increased representation among undergraduates and college graduates, Hispanic students complete college at a lower rate than the general student population. Of those Hispanic students who go on to postsecondary education, most enroll in two-year institutions. This does not help their upward mobility significantly, since for most Americans the educational gateway to opportunity is a four-year college degree (LeBlanc Flores 1994).

The broad figures we have presented concerning the occupations, incomes, and educational levels of the Mexican Americans conceal many underlying differences of interest. For example, since Anglos, on average, have higher levels of education and hold better-paying jobs than Mexican Americans, some of the difference in median incomes is due to these factors. It is accurate to say, therefore, that some of the income inequality between the Mexican Americans and Anglos arises from the educational and occupational differences between the two groups.

We have mentioned that one way of assessing the extent to which the dominant group discriminates against minority groups is to calculate the pay of similar workers in different ethnic groups to discover whether it "costs" to be a member of a minority group.[23] For example, in 1959, the mean income of male Mexican American workers who had completed four years of college or more was $1,251 less than that of Anglo workers with the same level of education.[24] Similarly, Anglos who had completed less than eight years of school earned slightly more on average than Mexican Americans who had attended high school for up to three years. In other words, *as far as education alone* was concerned, it appears that Mexican Americans "paid a price" in the job market because of their group membership.

Before this conclusion is accepted, however, other factors affecting income must be considered. Since older, more experienced people generally have higher incomes, some of the income differences we have noted may be due to the experience differences between older Anglo and younger Mexican American workers. Our comparison, consequently, should be restricted at least to Anglos and Mexican Americans who have similar levels of education and are of similar ages. When the groups have been "matched" in several important respects, it is reasonable to suppose that any remaining income difference is due largely to discrimination. Using a similar method, Poston and Alvírez (1973:708) showed that in 1959, approximately $900 of the $1,251 difference between Mexican American and Anglo workers may have been a result of discrimination. Subsequent analyses (Cotton 1985; Poston, Alvírez, and Tienda 1976) found that the economic "cost" of being a Mexican American worker increased during the decade of the 1970s despite the increasing levels of education among Mexican Americans![25]

Residential Segregation.   As we noted previously, another important measure of the extent to which secondary assimilation is occurring for a given group is the degree to which that group lives in the same residential areas as the members of the dominant group. In most cities of the United States, Mexican Americans long have been, and still are, noticeably segregated, not only from Anglos but also from Blacks. However, the extent of this segregation, as we saw for Japanese Americans, varies greatly among cities and regions of the country. For example, the lowest regional index of residential segregation (dissimilarity) of Mexican Americans and Anglos in the United States in 1980 was 48.3 (the South) and the highest was 62.3 (the Northeast). Among ten metropolitan areas (SMSAs) having large Mexican American populations, the lowest level of residential segregation was 39.1 (Riverside, California) and the highest was 66.0 (New York City). Intermediate levels were found in such cities as Chicago (64.0), Los Angeles (61.1), San Antonio (58.9), and Houston (50.4) (Bean and Tienda 1987:174). The levels of residential segregation between Hispanics and Anglos in some smaller SMSAs having relatively large Mexican American populations include Fresno (45.4), Phoenix (49.4), and Corpus Christi (51.6) (Massey and Denton 1987:815–816). Most of these residential segregation indexes lie within the moderate range, though the average for the cities of the Southwest is higher than the average for the nation (Lopez 1981:53–54); hence, although there are large and important differences among cities, the typical situation is a moderate degree of Mexican American–Anglo residential segregation.

The extent to which Mexican Americans and Anglos are segregated residentially may be decreasing over time; if so, this would indicate that secondary assimilation is taking place. If, on the other hand, the level of residential segregation has remained unchanged for several decades or has increased, this would indicate strongly that a full merger of the ethnic groups is hardly just over the horizon. Massey and Denton (1987) calculated the changes in residential similarity between Hispanics and Anglos between 1970 and 1980 for sixty SMSAs.[26] Thirty-three of the SMSAs studied showed a decline in Hispanic–Anglo residential segregation, and the remaining twenty-seven showed an increase. More to the point, however, is that the changes in some of the SMSAs with a very high percentage of Mexican Americans showed an average increase. In thirteen SMSAs having more than 100,000 Mexican Americans who comprised at least 80 percent of the Hispanic population, an increase in residential segregation occurred in nine, and the average decline in the remaining four SMSAs was comparatively small (+5.4 versus –1.9).[27] Some findings for the period 1980 to 1990 suggest that this general pattern of residential segregation may have continued through that period (Harrison and Weinberg 1992).

To interpret these facts, it is helpful to have a standard of comparison. Although the extent of Black–White residential segregation will be discussed more fully in Chapter 11, we may note here that in 1980, the average Hispanic–Anglo index in the sixty SMSAs studied by Massey and Denton (1987:816) was 43.4, whereas the Black–White index was 69.4. Although Massey and Denton did not focus on Hispanics in their 1993 study of racial segregation, they noted that residential segregation of Hispanics generally begins at a relatively modest level among the poor and falls progressively as socioeconomic status rises. The researchers found that in the Los Angeles metropolitan area, the *poorest Hispanics* (with a segregation index of 64) were less segregated than the *most affluent Blacks* (whose score was 79).

The fact that Mexican Americans are less segregated from Anglos than Blacks and that poor Mexicans are less segregated than affluent Blacks is not due simply to socioeconomic differences between the two minority groups. The evidence points strongly to persisting racial discrimination and to the conclusion that segregation among Mexican Americans declines sharply with rising socioeconomic status, suburbanization, and the number of generations spent within the United States (Massey and Denton 1987:803, 819; Massey and Denton 1993:113–114). However, higher-status Blacks and suburban Blacks are as likely to live in a segregated neighborhood as are those who are less affluent (Clark and Mueller 1988; Massey and Denton 1993). It is probable, therefore, that rapid immigration of Mexicans to the United States has led, at least temporarily, to an increase in the relative size of the Mexican immigrant portion of urban communities and to a slowing of residential desegregration. The apparent increases in education, socioeconomic status, and suburbanization for those who are native born are consistent with the view that secondary assimilation in these respects is underway.

Primary Structural Assimilation

The evidence reviewed shows that, in general, Mexican Americans have been moving out of rural areas and into the cities, and that within the cities they are less segregated from Anglos than are Blacks. It shows, too, that Mexican Americans are more likely now to be working in jobs that previously were held almost exclusively by Anglo Americans. Each of these forms of secondary assimilation favors an increase in the amount of equal-status interaction that will occur between Mexican Americans and Anglos, and thereby raises the probability that friendships will develop across the ethnic line. We would expect, therefore, an increase in the number of Anglo–Mexican American friendships on the job, in the neighborhood, and among those of similar education and income. We also would expect more friendships to form between Anglos and Mexican Americans of native parentage than between Anglos and Mexican Americans of mixed or foreign parentage.

Friendship Patterns.   Although little is known concerning the trends in Mexican American–Anglo friendship formation, some valuable evidence was provided by the work of researchers in UCLA's Mexican American Study Project (Grebler, Moore, and Guzman 1970). The researchers gathered information on the friendships of Mexican Americans in three large cities during various periods of the respondents' lives. The study participants in Albuquerque, Los Angeles, and San Antonio were asked about the ethnicity of their friends when they were children, about the ethnicity of their present friends, and about the ethnicity of their children's friends. In all three cities, the participants reported that the extent of out-group friendship relations had increased through time (Moore 1970:134).

As expected, friendship patterns differed for those who lived in more or less desegregated neighborhoods, and they also varied by income levels. For example, in Los Angeles and San Antonio, the Mexican Americans who lived in neighborhoods having relatively few Mexican Americans (desegregated areas) were more likely to have predominantly Anglo friends than were those living in neighborhoods having a relatively large number of Mexican Americans (segregated areas). And, for the most part, those of higher income who lived in desegregated areas were more likely to have predominantly Anglo friends than were those of lower income (Grebler, Moore, and Guzman 1970:397). The income differences discovered within the desegregated neighborhoods, however, did not hold up within the segregated areas. People of higher income within the segregated areas were hardly more likely to report a predominance of Anglo friends than were those of lower income in those areas.

These findings from three cities representing main centers of Mexican American culture suggest that, with the passage of time, Mexican Americans decreasingly have only Mexican American friends. Although this generational trend is much more pronounced among those living in desegregated neighborhoods and among those of higher income, it suggests that if the occupational, educational, and residential assimilation of Mexican Americans continue, primary assimilation also will increase.

We emphasized previously that when a dominant and subordinate group are brought together by conquest, the groups frequently react to one another with greater mutual hatred and rejection than if the minority arose through immigration. For this reason, Mexican Americans frequently have been described as having a low assimilative potential. Despite the forces working toward ethnic separateness, however, we have seen that Mexican Americans and Anglos are in some respects coming closer together. Let us turn now to that "most infallible index" of assimilation—intermarriage (Kennedy 1944:331).

Marital Assimilation

Several studies of Mexican American intermarriage have been conducted, with the majority of them focusing on Los Angeles, Albuquerque, and San Antonio. Three main findings stand out. First, the occurrence of out-marriage for Mexican Americans is much lower in some places than in others. For instance, in the early 1960s, the rate of out-marriage was 20 percent in San Antonio (Alvírez and Bean 1976:285), 33 percent in Albuquerque, and 5 percent in Edinburg, Texas (Murguía and Frisbie 1977:384). Second, there has been a gradual long-term increase in the rate of out-marriage. For example, in a study comparing rate of out-marriage in San Antonio, Bradshaw and Bean (1970:393) demonstrated that the rate in 1850 was about 10 percent. One hundred years later, the rate had approximately doubled. This general trend may be seen even in some small, comparatively isolated communities that have a tradition of high levels of social distance. Cazares, Murguía, and Frisbie (1985:399), for instance, compared out-marriage rates for Mexican Americans in Pecos County, Texas, for the periods 1880–1960 and 1970–1978 and found that out-marriage (for marriages) had increased from about 4 percent for the early period to 15 percent for the later period. Some studies, however, show that the rise in out-marriages is not rapid or that a rise may be followed by a decline. In Corpus Christi, for instance, the rate hardly changed between the early 1960s and 1970s, rising from 15 to 16 percent (Alvírez and Bean 1976:383). By 1988, the rate had reached 18 percent (Sherwood 1988:D14). In Albuquerque, a rapid rise from 33 percent in 1964 to 48 percent in 1967 was followed by a sharp decline to 39 percent in 1971 (Murguía and Frisbie 1977:384), and in California there was a gradual decline from 55 percent in 1962 to 51 percent in 1974 (Schoen, Nelson, and Collins 1978).

The third main finding of interest here is that Mexican Americans who are natives of native parentage are more likely to marry out than are Mexican Americans of mixed parentage who, in turn, are more likely to marry out than are those born in Mexico (Grebler, Moore, and Guzman 1970:409; Moore and Pachon 1985:108). In short, whether one examines the overall out-marriage rates at different points in time or the rates for those in different generations, the main conclusion appears to be the same: Mexican Americans are moving slowly toward marital assimilation (Murguía 1982:50).

Whereas most research on Mexican American intermarriage has focused on individual characteristics—such as generational status, age, sex, and social class as predictors of intermarriage—Anderson and Saenz (1994) found that structural conditions can influence intermarriage independently of cultural values and individual preferences. They identified five major structural determinants of intermarriage: (1) opportunities for contact or the extent of segregation; (2) social differentiation (differences in education, income, or occupational prestige between ethnic groups, and the extent of such differences within a group); (3) ethnic-language maintenance (which affects the development of primary and secondary relationships); (4) group size (total population of an ethnic group in a particular area); and (5) an imbalance in the sex ratio (number of males per 100 females). Each of these factors either facilitated or represented barriers to favorable relations between Mexican Americans and Anglos, but three of these five conditions—opportunities for contact, status diversity within the ethnic group, and levels of Spanish-language maintenance—were *significant predictors* of out-marriage. Based on this research, Anderson and Saenz argued that we must consider a combination of structural- and cultural-level factors in order to obtain a more complete understanding of Mexican American assimilation.

Some writers believe the evidence on out-marriage supports the immigrant model. Mittlebach and Moore (1968:53) stated that in Los Angeles, at least, the rate of Mexican American out-marriage "is roughly that of the Italian and Polish ethnic populations in Buffalo, New York, a generation ago"; and in a reanalysis of these data, Schoen and Cohen (1980:365) agreed that the assimilation of the Mexican Americans "appears to be very much in the tradition of earlier American immigration." Barrera (1988) concluded (1) that a considerable amount of intermarriage is taking place; (2) that the rate has been increasing over time; (3) that it is strongly affected by generation and social class; and (4) that it is related to other indices of assimilation, such as language. Similarly, Penalosa (1970:50) concluded that many contemporary changes among Mexican Americans suggest that they are coming to resemble "a European immigrant group of a generation ago."

Mexican American "Success"

What does the evidence on the various forms of assimilation among the Mexican Americans tell us about the success with which they have adapted to American life? How, for instance, do they compare with the Japanese Americans? Although the Mexican Americans have been moving toward the American mainstream, they have not been as successful (from the perspective of Anglo conformity) as the Japanese Americans. In nearly every—if not every—aspect of assimilation, the Mexican Americans less nearly approximate the Anglo American ideal than do the Japanese Americans. They have not relinquished their culture as rapidly; they have not attained equal levels of occupation, education, and income; and they appear to be more segregated in their friendship and marital patterns. Why is this true?

This question lies at the very heart of the ideological issues we have discussed throughout this book. In some respects, the comparative "failure" of the Mexican Americans in terms of Anglo conformity may, with equal force, be seen as "success" from the perspective of cultural pluralism. The Mexican Americans have been more successful than the Japanese Americans in their efforts to maintain and develop their own distinctive heritage, the desirability of which seems clearly to be acknowledged by many Japanese Americans, particularly among the Sansei and Yonsei. Recall, though, that ideal cultural pluralism (as sketched in Chapter 2) calls for a high level of secondary assimilation, as does Anglo conformity; hence, in this regard, the Mexican Americans still have not reached the goal of ideal pluralism. The trick, of course, is to be successful in worldly ways without giving up the cultural, social, and marital spheres of group life. But what if worldly success can be purchased only through cultural assimilation by substitution, or taking on key aspects of the Anglo culture? What if the maintenance of the ethnic culture is itself an obstacle to the attainment of worldly success? These explosive questions have been in the forefront of the frequently bitter debate concerning public policies relating to the Mexican Americans.

Consider again, for example, the question of the use of Spanish in the schools. The dominant group insisted until the latter part of the 1960s that only English was the legal and proper language of instruction in the schools. Mexican American children have been said to suffer from a language "barrier" that must be "surmounted." From this point of view, teaching the children in Spanish only retards their assimilation into the mainstream of American life. Even when the desirability of bilingual education has been acknowledged, the curriculum usually has been designed to "phase out" Spanish as early as possible.

The underlying assumption for this pro-assimilationist view is that the possession of a Mexican heritage is a handicap in the modern world. From the Mexican American point of view, however, this assumption is simply a part of a broader struggle between the Mexican American and Anglo cultures. A frequent observation concerning classical colonialism is that oppressor groups not only conquer the territories of the groups they subordinate, but also that they attempt to destroy the native cultures as well; thus, many Mexican Americans consider the insistence that they give up Spanish and undergo full cultural assimilation by substitution to be an example of "cultural imperialism."

Mexican American scholars have launched a scathing critique of cultural explanations for the lack of success of Mexican Americans. For example, such concepts as "present orientation," "fatalism," and "familism" have been used by Anglo American scholars to label Mexican Americans as passive recipients of whatever fate may be thrust upon them. Such ideas, Romano (1968:24) contended, are simply social-science stereotypes that strengthen the popular notion among Anglos that Mexican Americans are largely responsible for their own unfortunate circumstances—a situation that can only be changed through full cultural assimilation by substitution. In a similar vein, Vaca (1970:26) argued that the attack on the values of Mexican American culture is only a mask for the Anglo conformity ideology. Cultural analysis, he said, presents a "vicious," "misleading," and "degrading" portrait of Mexican American culture. It is a portrait that distorts reality and implies that Mexican American culture should not continue to exist within contemporary American society. Williams (1990:22) pointed out that the characteristics noted in the earlier studies, such as *machismo* and familism, are common in many societies and therefore are not *particularly* characteristic of Mexican Americans.

Of greater importance, however, has been an increasing emphasis on noncultural explanations of the socioeconomic position of the Mexican Americans. We noted earlier, for example, that a substantial portion of the average difference between the in-comes of Mexican American and Anglo workers may be caused by discrimination. We noted, too, that documented and undocumented immigration to the United States has been intimately related to changing economic circumstances (Portes and Rumbaut 1990:14). And we emphasized that both Mexican immigrant workers and native Mexican American workers typically have entered a "dual" labor market in the United States. One set of jobs, historically "reserved" for Anglo workers, has offered good pay, security, and the possibility of advancement. The second set of jobs, into which "cheap" labor typically has been funneled, has consisted of the back-breaking, seasonal, and "stoop" work that Anglo workers ordinarily have refused to perform (Pachon and Moore 1981:118–119; Portes and Bach 1985:69). The latter jobs have offered little hope of advancement even when the workers were educated and experienced. When minority workers are routinely allocated to dead-end jobs, according to this line of criticism, no amount of "activism" or "future orientation" will lead to significantly improved economic circumstances.

As in the case of the worldly success of the Japanese Americans, our discussion strongly suggests that a strictly cultural explanation of the comparative "progress" of the Mexican Americans is inadequate. To assume that whatever problems the Mexican Americans have are the fault of their culture is to ignore the effects of structural factors that exist within the surrounding society. Both the critics of the cultural explanation and its defenders agree, of course, that Mexican American culture is different from Anglo American culture in certain respects (Moore and Pachon 1985:122–131). Indeed, were that not the case, all talk of Mexican American culture would be pointless; and it is the determination of many Mexican Americans to maintain a distinctive culture even if it is a source of conflict with the dominant group. But to agree that Mexican American culture is *different* is by no means to acknowledge that it is *deficient*. As Barrera (1979:180) argued, "The cultural apparatus of any people is so complex that presumably negative traits can always be found." But unless a bipartisan comparison is conducted of the "negative" and "positive" traits in both the dominant and subordinate groups, Barrera stated, no valid inferences concerning the relation of values to success are possible.

Most Mexican Americans seem to be determined to find a middle way wherein the "positive" features of their culture and their pride in *La Raza* will move side by side with increasing secondary assimilation, but many members of this ethnic group appear to have concluded that pluralism rather than Anglo conformity may provide a solution to the problem of cultural survival. They have rejected the value orientations analysis of their situation and are engaged in constructing a stronger, more nearly independent community.

The evidence we have reviewed concerning the cultural, secondary, primary, and marital assimilation of the Mexican Americans may be interpreted as lending partial support to either the immigrant or the colonial models. Neither interpretation seems to fit all the facts. Some scholars have argued we should replace both perspectives with models that stress the complexity and variability of the immigrant experience and the individuals' own influence and control over the "pace" and direction of their "adaptations" to American life. Some Mexican immigrants attempt to follow the Anglo conformist prescriptions for inclusion—learning English and becoming citizens while laying the Mexican heritage aside. Others, adhering to the pluralist model, maintain strong ties to the country of origin while becoming citizens or legal residents of the United States, persisting in their own cultural practices while selectively incorporating elements of Anglo culture (Gutiérrez 1996). Mexican Americans appear to be statistically, as they are in reality, both a conquered and an immigrant minority. We will return to this puzzle in Chapter 16.

Key Ideas

1. Language is an important element of cultural identity. In the United States, acquiring English-language skills has been viewed as a key measure of cultural assimilation. Most immigrant groups try to maintain their native language; however, this is very difficult to do over several generations without strong community support. Teaching English and the native language in the schools, or bilingual education, can help children learn both languages. Bilingual education has created heated debates over the status of English and other languages. Most educational programs in the United States are Anglo conformist in that they try to move immigrant children into English-only classes as quickly as possible (i.e., they advocate cultural assimilation by substitution).

2. Today, although Mexican Americans in general show higher levels of cultural, secondary, primary, and marital assimilation than they did in the past, it seems unlikely that the differences between Mexican Americans and Anglos will soon disappear. Increased immigration has heightened discrimination, segregation, Spanish-language maintenance, and cultural awareness. Assimilation in jobs and income, for example, is not occurring rapidly and, in fact, may have been halted during the 1970s and 1980s.

3. A popular explanation of the comparative lack of worldly success by Mexican Americans has focused on the way their values differ from those of Anglos. From this perspective, Mexican Americans must hasten to rid themselves of their culture if they wish to get ahead in American life. The value orientations approach has been vigorously attacked as a form of cultural imperialism that works in the service of the Anglo conformity ideology. Many social scientists, particularly Mexican American scholars, have identified a number of conditions, such as dominant-group discrimination and the traditional allocation of Mexican Americans to dead-end jobs, as the biggest barriers to secondary structural assimilation.

4. Neither the colonial model nor the immigrant model fits all the facts of the Mexican American experience. Their history includes both colonization and immigration, and an adequate account of their present and future social reality must reconcile these facts.

Key Terms

bilingual education   The use of two languages in teaching subjects other than a foreign language. Transitional bilingual programs teach subject matter in the students' native language until they can learn in English; partial bilingual programs teach oral skills in both languages, but make only limited use of instruction in the child's native language; and full bilingual programs aim at maintaining and developing both the minority language and English.

code-switching   The speaking style of switching back and forth from English to Spanish and vice versa. Code-switching is common among second- and third-generation Mexican Americans.

extended families   Families that include parents, children, grandparents, and other relatives or godparents. All family members usually do not live in the same household.

familism   An orientation in which the needs of the family are more important than the needs of the individual. Familism implies close reciprocal relationships among family members.

limited English proficiency   An inability to speak, read, or write English well enough to function in an English-speaking society.

machismo   A Spanish term referring to an attitude of masculine superiority and dominance. Stereotypes have portrayed Mexican males as being *macho* and Mexican families as patriarchal or dominated by a male father figure.

Lau Task Force Remedies   Guidelines interpreting the *Lau v. Nichols* decision that recommended bilingual education at the elementary school level for children with limited English skills.

Notes

1. A *CPS Supplement for Testing Methods of Collecting Racial and Ethnic Information: May 1995* (U.S. Department of Labor, Bureau of Labor Statistics, October 1995) reports more details of the census survey. Also, Murguía (1991) notes that the pan-ethnic terms *Latino* and *Hispanic* are different in connotation, with Latino coming from the Spanish language and suggesting cultural pluralism and cultural maintenance, and Hispanic coming from the English language and emphasizing assimilation.

2. These figures were taken from the Census Bureau web site from data ranking cities with 200,000 or more population.

3. For a broad discussion of the measurement of cultural assimilation, see Hazuda, Stern, and Haffner (1988).

4. Additional statistics regarding non-English-speaking students can be found in the report "Descriptive Study of Services to Limited English Proficient Students," (U. S. Department of Education, Office of the Under Secretary, Washington, D.C., 1993).

5. Research on language maintenance shows that Mexican Americans who live in segregated neighborhoods are likely to use Spanish more frequently than those who live in less "Mexicanized" neighborhoods. Similarly, immigrants who work mostly or exclusively with other recent immigrants and use Spanish in the work context maintain the language longer (see Portes and Schauffler 1996).

6. The Bushwick Parents' Organization filed suit against District 32 in Brooklyn, New York, in 1995, arguing that after three years of bilingual education, one-third of the bilingual students in that district scored lower on English-language tests than when they started (see Stern 1996).

7. Headden (1995) reported that most of the 6.7 million non-English-speaking people in the United States live in the Southwest, South Florida, and New York. Thus far, twenty-two states have enacted English-only laws, including California and Arizona, states with large numbers of non-English speakers.

8. The Lemon Grove case is described by Balderrama (1982).

9. In 1974 the Bilingual Education Act was amended to require evaluation of funded programs. The 1974 extension of the act expanded funding and clearly defined bilingual education as instruction in English, allowing instruction in the native language to the extent necessary for the child to progress effectively through the educational system (Fishman 1978:407).

10. Rosenberg (1981) provides a comprehensive review of the bilingual education legislation.

11. See Moran and Hakuta (1995) for an extensive review of research on bilingual education.

12. See "Immigrant Children and their Families: Issues for Research and Policy," in *The Future of Children: Critical Issues for Children and Youths* (National Research Council, Summer/Fall 1995):79.

13. A summary of this debate was reported by Crawford (1995).

14. Falcoff (1996:A11) argued that there are many divisive forces in American society, but language is not one of them. He claimed that the English-only legislation was led by hysterical "populist xenophobes."

15. Grebler, Moore, and Guzman (1970: 429) noted that U.S. Spanish-language radio stations play an important role in assisting people to maintain both their language and their ethnic identity. Over one-half of all foreign-language radio broadcasting in the United States is conducted in Spanish, and Spanish is the only foreign language that is used exclusively by any U.S. station.

16. See, for example, Fishman, "Language, Ethnic Identity, and Political Loyalty," cited by Moore and Pachon (1985:120).

17. For critiques see Williams (1990) and Zambrana (1995).

18. An important feature of this study is the researcher's care in constructing a standard to use for comparison.

19. Even here, though, some important changes occurred (Williams 1990:56).

20. The largest of three surveys included interviews with 626 respondents.

21. This seemingly paradoxical result arises because a low rate of increase when applied to a large number may yield a larger absolute increase than a higher rate of increase that is applied to a small number.

22. Calculated from Table 10.6 in Bean and Tienda (1988:368–369).

23. See, for example, Farley and Allen (1987:335–342); Poston and Alvírez (1973); Poston, Alvírez, and Tienda (1976); Siegel (1965); and Williams, Beeson, and Johnson (1973).

24. Calculated from Poston and Alvírez (1973:707, Table 1).

25. There also is evidence that among Mexican Americans, the "costs" are greater for those whose appearance is darker and more Indian than for those who are lighter, more "European-looking." For analyses and discussion see Massey and Denton (1993:113), Telles and Murguía (1990), and Telles and Murguía (1992).

26. The sixty SMSAs were the fifty largest SMSAs plus ten others having large Hispanic populations.

27. Calculated from Bean and Tienda (1988:150, Table 5.8) and Denton and Massey (1987:815–816, Table 3).

African Americans

From Slavery to Segregation

*"Jim Crow" refers to the laws passed by southern legislatures
that established a system of racial segregation that encompassed
every type of public facility ranging from water fountains to
schools and cemeteries.*

To those of my race who depend on bettering their condition in a foreign land . . . I would say "Cast down your bucket where you are."
—Booker T. Washington

The equality . . . which modern men must have in order to live is not to be confounded with sameness. On the contrary, in our case, it is rather insistence upon the right of diversity.
—W.E.B. Du Bois

The Negro must have a country and a nation of his own.
—Marcus Garvey

We seek . . . the inclusion of Negro Americans in the nation's life, not their exclusion. This is our land, as much as any American's.
—Roy Wilkins

The analyses of Chapters 8 and 9 revealed several important parallels between the history of the Mexican Americans and the history of many colonized peoples throughout the world. Chief among these is that, through conquest, the Mexican Americans lost lands to which they had had a long-standing claim. Initially, they did not enter the United States voluntarily; consequently, many members of this ethnic group have felt they are a conquered people in their own land.

Mexican Americans, of course, are not alone among American minorities in this respect. American Indians were undeniably natives in their own land, and they most assuredly have not become a part of American society either voluntarily or through immigration. As discussed in Chapter 2, the primary contacts between the two groups took place within a framework of conflict. Whereas the Indians were more interested in repelling the invaders than they were in becoming a part of their society, the Anglo-Americans were more interested in expelling or annihilating the Indians than they were in assimilating them. The overall result was that the Indians were forced off nearly all of the lands that the Europeans considered desirable.

With these ideas and examples as a background, we turn to a consideration of America's largest racial minority—Black or African Americans. Unlike the European minorities, African Americans did not migrate voluntarily, and unlike American Indians and Mexican Americans, they were not present on American soil when the English and Anglo Americans arrived. Like the Mexican American experience, therefore, the Black experience does not fit neatly either the colonial or immigrant perspectives. As a result, both viewpoints have been prominent in the arguments concerning the place and future of African Americans in American life.

The Period of Slavery

In Chapter 3 we learned that the first Africans to arrive in Jamestown in 1619 were purchased as bonded or indentured servants and, as such, were not in a significantly different status from that of the many White servants in the colony. We learned also that only gradually did the English, who were struggling to survive and to learn how to turn a profit for the colony's investors, shift from Whites to Blacks as the main source of cheap labor.

During the 1650–1700 period, however, changes in the laws and the methods of tobacco cultivation in the colonies led to the acceptance of Black slavery as the solution to the labor problem. The numbers of Black slaves then mounted rapidly as the practice of indenturing Whites declined. As being Black became, in Bennett's (1964:38) phrase, "a badge of servitude," the rules of servitude became much more restrictive. Black slaves had few legal rights and little hope of freedom. Slave women suffered a double burden of racial and sexual oppression. As Black workers, they were valued for their skills and physical strength; as women, they were expected to produce slave babies for sale or labor (Winegarten 1995:27). It is no wonder that individual flight and organized rebellion among the slaves increased during this time, as did the level of vigilance among the masters.

As discussed in Chapter 3, many Africans vigorously resisted enslavement. As they were transported through the terrifying and deadly "Middle Passage" to the New World, slaves sometimes overcame the crews and captured the ships on which they were imprisoned; and when no other forms of escape seemed possible, committed suicide. Resistance to slavery involved the use of every method imaginable and continued throughout the long period of American slavery. After the Underground Railroad was organized, the chances of escape greatly improved.[1] In addition, many challenged the institution of slavery with covert acts of resistance. Slaves worked more slowly, feigned illness or pregnancy, secretly learned to read, broke tools or destroyed property, injured themselves, or aborted their pregnancies to prevent their children from being born slaves (Winegarten 1995).

Despite efforts to force the return of runaway slaves, and the often cruel punishment of those who attempted to rebel, at least 200 insurrections, and possibly as many as 1,200, were planned between 1664 and 1860 (Jacobs and Landau 1971:100); and at least fifteen were actually carried out (Davie 1949:44). Three uprisings during the nineteenth century attracted widespread attention. Gabriel Prosser, a slave blacksmith, used the Bible to persuade other slaves that their situation was similar to that of the Israelites under the pharaohs and that God would help them to gain their freedom (Bardolph 1961:35). After a betrayal of the conspiracy brought the effort to a quick end, Prosser was captured and hanged. A second notable slave insurrection was organized in 1822 by Denmark Vesey. Vesey purchased his freedom in 1800 and used information he learned about the successful slave revolt in Haiti to inspire slaves in South Carolina to organize and rebel. Vesey and thirty-four slaves were hanged; others suspected as conspirators were deported from the United States (Ducas 1970:108). The most famous uprising was led by Nat Turner in 1831 in Virginia. Turner claimed to hear voices from heaven and to be "called" to free his people. A revolt began when Turner and a handful of followers killed all the Whites in his master's household. Altogether, they killed fifty-five White men, women, and children. After a six-week search for the rebels, Turner was captured and later hanged.[2]

The willingness of slaves to protest their treatment increased with the onset of the Civil War. As White Southerners became ever more fearful that the slaves would rebel, patrol laws were strengthened, slave rations and supplies were increased, and picket lines were doubled to discourage escape attempts. When the Union army invaded various portions of the Confederacy, slaves were encouraged to raise objections to the way they were treated. Consequently, many slaves refused to accept punishment, were insolent to their masters, assaulted Whites, informed for the Union armies, or joined the Union armies as recruits (Davie 1949:45). The legal system of slavery became more rigid than ever before. Still, there was no large-scale insurrection; the majority of the slaves remained faithful with some even fighting loyally beside their masters in the Confederate army.

The Impact of Slavery on Its Victims

Elkins (1968) and other scholars have argued that there was not still greater resistance on the part of the Black slaves because (1) the U.S. slave system was exceedingly oppressive, more so than the systems in Latin America; (2) this brutal system reduced human beings to a subhuman condition; and (3) these conditions generated extreme subservience and passivity among the slaves. It is not settled, however, that Black American slaves were as genuinely submissive as Elkins suggested nor that Black slavery in America was worse than any other kind. Mintz (1969:30–31), for example, pointed out that Spanish slavery in the West Indies was at least as bad as American slavery. Other sociologists and historians argued that Elkins's theory missed an important story of endurance and achievement (Billingsley 1968; Blassingame 1972). Using oral histories, slave diaries and letters, and other sources, these scholars emphasized the self-generative character of Black society under slavery and stressed the theme of a resilient slave culture. In contrast to the views that portrayed slaves as passive, Gutman stressed that the slaves actively charted their own course despite heavy restrictions placed upon them. Members of the slave community helped and protected one another, which in turn created a sense of cohesion and pride. They maintained words from the various African languages, established family networks that persisted despite slave codes that did not recognize slave families, created a slaves' religion that was a mixture of African and Christian beliefs, and passed on to their children variations of African folktales, music, and dance. Gutman (1975) found that large numbers of slaves and ex-slaves lived in long marriages and two-parent households. He argued that a common slave culture spread over the South derived from the cumulative slave experience and was maintained by extended kin groups and reciprocal social obligations.

The Profitability of Slavery.   Probably the most controversial attack on Elkins's thesis of the extreme subservience of the slaves was presented by Fogel and Engerman (1974) in the book *Time on the Cross.* Instead of viewing the slave system as purely repressive and psychologically destructive, Fogel and Engerman assembled evidence to show that slaves were effective workers who developed a much stronger family life, a more varied set of occupational skills, and a richer, more distinct culture than was previously recognized. The authors demonstrated that slave owners made many efforts to reward the slaves who worked diligently, and that, as a result, the typical slave was a vigorous and productive worker. In fact, because the masters gave careful attention to such matters as slave management, diet, family stability, bonuses, and promotions, the slaves were more efficient workers than either northern farm workers or free southern laborers (Fogel and Engerman 1974:192–209).

Fogel and Engerman's thesis touched off an intellectual firestorm because the work did not include a strong moral condemnation of slavery. For this reason, Fogel wrote a second book, *Without Consent or Contract* (1989),[3] to clarify his position. The second work included an afterword that addressed the problems of slavery. He argued that the system of slavery in the United States did not produce extreme subservience, as Elkins claimed, but did have a devastating effect on the lives of the slaves because of (1) the extreme degree of dominance required by the system; (2) the denial of economic and political opportunities; (3) the denial of citizenship; and (4) the denial of cultural self-identification. Fogel argued that although slaves were able to retain certain African customs, to modify the European religions they practiced, and to produce songs and folklore, the U.S. slave system resulted in virtually unrestrained domination of the slaves' personal lives.

The debates over slavery range over a very broad spectrum of issues as the controversies continue to catch the attention of historians and others. Most agree, however, that as slavery evolved, it became the principal factor controlling relations between Whites and Blacks in the United States. Of special importance has been the analysis of the contemporary effects of slavery and emancipation, to which we return later in this chapter and in Chapter 11. Of particular interest have been the effect of slavery on the contemporary African American family and on the course of upward mobility and assimilation of African Americans.

Immigrant or Colonized Minority?

The experience of Black people in America up to the time of the Civil War resembled, in some respects, that of both an immigrant and a colonized minority. African Americans were an "immigrant" minority in the sense that they had traveled from their native lands and entered the host American society as members of a subordinate group; unlike European immigrants, however, their subordinate position was not regarded as something temporary. African Americans also resembled a "colonized" minority in the sense that they had been physically "conquered" and, subsequently, had not been accepted as suitable candidates for full membership in the society of the conquerors; but they were not in their own land. The very structure of the relations between the native Whites and the "immigrant" but enslaved Africans was such that neither the immigrant nor the colonial perspective seems completely applicable.

Although some African Americans became highly assimilated culturally during the slave period, these cases were very unusual. Most Blacks were deliberately kept from learning any more of the White man's ways than was absolutely necessary and, as a result, little structural assimilation occurred during the long ordeal of slavery. Even the free Blacks were subject to a high degree of discrimination and were not readily accepted into the mainstream of American institutional life.[4] The classical solution of the colonized minority's dilemma—throwing the invaders out—was hardly possible; however, the goal of ending the domination of the Whites by leaving the United States and, perhaps, returning to Africa was the subject of serious discussion and concrete actions. The most notable example of a secessionist solution to the "Negro problem" during this period began when an organization called the American Colonization Society (founded in 1816) established the colony of Liberia for free Blacks on the west coast of Africa. The colony and its main settlement, Monrovia, grew slowly and, in 1847, was declared a republic.

Although Liberia still exists today as the second oldest Black republic in the world (after Haiti), the return of African Americans to this African state was not successful as a solution to American racial problems. Fewer than 3,000 colonists from America were present in the colony at the time it became a republic, and even some influential Black leaders in America who favored some kind of separatist solution—like Martin Delany— did not support the Liberian experiment.

Neither Assimilated nor Colonized.   While neither an assimilationist nor a colonialist interpretation seems truly congruent with the situation of the Blacks in America before the Civil War, it seems clear that the essential character of the relations between the races during that period is most nearly captured by the colonialist view. Blacks (whether slave or free) were not on the road to full assimilation. Their experience in America prior to the Civil War was in no important respect comparable to that of the colonial Dutch, Irish, or Germans. On the other hand, one can find significant parallels between the condition of the Blacks and the Indians. Both peoples had been subjected to a tremendous cultural shock. Their customary ways of living had been shattered. Their primary choices in life were reduced to extreme subordination, annihilation, or flight. As Blauner (1972:54) asserted, "Whether oppression takes place at home in the oppressed's native land or in the heart of the colonizer's mother country, colonization remains colonization."[5]

The relative superiority of the colonialist interpretation of the antebellum period does not assure us, however, that it is the proper tool for analyzing events in the twentieth century. We must also consider the Black experience in America since the Civil War.

Emancipation and Reconstruction

As the Civil War approached, the popularity of abolishing slavery waned. Lincoln himself favored deportation as a solution to the "Negro problem," and even after the war was underway, he stated clearly that his main purpose in fighting it was to save the Union rather than to affect the status of slavery. Moreover, many people in the North shared the opinion of White Southerners that Black people were naturally suited to servitude and should not be encouraged to seek equality. This opinion was sufficiently common during the early years of the war that Northern officers were generally unwilling to accept Blacks as soldiers. There were even reports of Northern officers who re-turned runaway slaves to their masters! This situation was altered, however, when Lincoln issued the **Emancipation Proclamation** on January 1, 1863. Among other things, the order proclaimed the slaves to be free and authorized the armed forces of the United States to enlist freedmen. Black regiments from Massachusetts, New York, and Pennsylvania were soon organized, and when the North began to draft military recruits, Blacks were included. Altogether, around 180,000 African Americans fought against the Confederacy, winning fourteen congressional medals of honor (Moskos and Butler 1996: 23). But, as usual, the inclusion of the Blacks did not mean they were treated equally. They did not at first receive the same pay as the White troops and Black regiments did a disproportionate share of the heavy labor (Litwack 1979).

Freed African Americans

Throwing off a lifetime of restraint and dependency and beginning to live like free men or free women was not an easy task. According to a former Confederate general, recently **freed Blacks** had "nothing but freedom" (Tindall 1984:671). By the end of the war, a **Freedmen's Bureau** had been established to assist all former slaves to assume their new status (Franklin and Moss 1988:208–210). There were between 3.5 and 4 million freedmen, and most of them had no way to earn a living (Davie 1949:21). Although the bureau labored under constant criticism until it expired in 1872, it made a substantial contribution to the welfare of the former slaves and of many White people as well.

The task of providing for the freedmen, however, was only a part of the broader task of rebuilding or reconstructing the economic and political systems of the South. In President Lincoln's view, the Southern states had never really left the Union; therefore, the job of reintegrating them did not require a massive reorganization. His Proclamation of Amnesty and Reconstruction in 1863 offered a pardon to nearly all Southerners who would pledge allegiance to the United States and agree to support the abolition of slavery. Lincoln's ideas concerning Reconstruction were bitterly opposed by the Radical Republican leaders in Congress. They argued that the Southern states should have the status of a conquered province and be forced to meet stiff requirements before being readmitted to the Union.

After the assassination of Lincoln in 1865, President Andrew Johnson adopted a Reconstruction plan similar to Lincoln's. By the end of 1865, the Thirteenth Amendment, which abolished the legal institution of slavery, had been ratified. All of the Confederate states had been recognized by the president, and all except Texas had held conventions and elected representatives and senators to Congress. But the end of slavery as a legal system did not end the subordination of African Americans. New Southern laws, called "Black Codes," severely restricted the rights of Blacks; and these laws gave the Radical Republicans the political leverage they needed to fight the president's program (Franklin and Moss 1988:206).[6] In response to the Black Codes, Congress passed the Civil Rights Act of 1866.

This law, based on the Thirteenth Amendment and passed over Johnson's veto, declared Blacks to be citizens of the United States, gave them equal civil rights, and gave the federal courts jurisdiction over cases arising under the act (Faulkner 1948:401).

Soon after this, Congress approved the Fourteenth Amendment which reaffirmed state and federal citizenship for persons born or naturalized in the United States and forbade any state to abridge the "privileges and immunities" of citizens. The amendment contained other provisions that have had far-reaching effects. It declared that states could not deprive any person of life, liberty, or property without "due process of law" or deny any person "the equal protection of the laws." These clauses of the Fourteenth Amendment have been applied in several civil rights cases involving minority group citizens (Tindall 1984:682–683).

Congress also passed four sweeping Reconstruction bills that divided the Southern states into five military districts, provided for elections in which the freedmen could participate equally, and required new constitutions that ensured all citizens the right to vote. An acceptable constitution and the approval of the Fourteenth Amendment were required for the readmission of a state to the Union. By 1870, all eleven former Confederate states were again represented in Congress.

Congressional Reconstruction infuriated the members of the old planter class and nurtured a hatred that was slow to die. In the elections creating the Reconstruction legislatures, 703,400 Black and 660,000 White voters were registered (Franklin 1961:80); for the first time, Black legislators were elected to public office. Among the Whites, many who were elected were "carpetbaggers" from the North and "scalawags" (Union loyalists) from the South. The composition of these conventions and the widespread bribery, fraud, and theft that became common in the governments established by them led quickly to charges that "Negro-carpetbag-scalawag" rule was the result of a "conspiracy to degrade and destroy the Southern way of life" (Franklin 1961:103). Such charges ignored certain pertinent facts. In regard to composition, only in South Carolina did Black legislators outnumber Whites, and only in Mississippi and Virginia did Northern Whites outnumber Southern Whites (Franklin 1961:102). In regard to honesty, the graft and corruption emerging within the Southern Reconstruction governments was often small by comparison with that occurring in the North during this same period. In Franklin's (1961:151) opinion, "the tragedy of public immorality in the Southern states was only part of a national tragedy." It should be said also that despite the unfavorable conditions under which they labored, the Reconstruction governments succeeded to some extent in placing political power in the hands of the common people. For the first time, many poor citizens, both Black and White, were able to vote and to participate directly in the affairs of government.

White Hostility

Many Blacks soon began to exercise the new freedoms granted by the Emancipation Proclamation, the Civil Rights Act, and the Reconstruction acts. The assertion of their rights violated the traditional "etiquette of race relations" that symbolized and helped to maintain the Whites' position of dominance.

The Whites developed direct, organized, secret methods to intimidate and punish Blacks who attempted to exercise their new rights or compete directly with them for jobs.

The most spectacular of the organizations attempting to force the Blacks back into their traditional servile position and, simultaneously, to restore political power to the Whites was the **Ku Klux Klan,** formed in 1866.[7] The Klan's purpose soon became the destruction of the Reconstruction governments and the return of Black people to their traditional subordinate status. The main tactics of the Klan involved mysterious incantations, cross burnings, and somber warnings delivered in full costume at night. When these methods seemed insufficient, house burnings, floggings, and murder were added. Women, as well as men, were Klan members. By the 1920s, perhaps half a million or more White Protestant women had joined the Women of the Ku Klux Klan (WKKK) and in some areas constituted a significant minority of Klan members (Blee 1991:2). Women of the Klan used traditions of community gatherings, kin networks, private relationships, children's auxiliaries, and social celebrations to circulate the Klan's message of racial, religious, and national bigotry. Blee argued that it was the integration of Klan beliefs and hatreds into the normal everyday life of White Protestants that made the Klan's power so devastating. The Klan quickly created a culture that promoted White racial privilege and a convenient "cover" for anyone (whether members or not) who wished to punish or intimidate Black people. Such tactics were so effective that Black people soon found it was safer to proclaim that politics was "White men's business." This protective reaction, adopted during the Reconstruction period, was to last for many decades.

As the Klan's campaign against Blacks became increasingly terrorist, some states and the federal government passed anti-Klan laws. Even some Klan members deplored the violence and felt that things had gotten out of hand. But the efforts to control the violence against Blacks and to prevent intimidation were not successful. The disputed presidential election of 1876 led in 1877 to the complete withdrawal of federal troops and the end of Reconstruction.

The Restoration of White Supremacy

Race relations in the South had been dramatically and irrevocably altered by the Civil War, emancipation, defeat, and Reconstruction. The successful campaign of the old planter class, with the aid of the poor Whites and many business people, to end Radical Republican Reconstruction and recapture political control of the South did not put everything back into its prewar place. Having succeeded in recapturing the state governments and bringing about the withdrawal of federal troops, the Whites wished to reestablish their dominance over the Blacks; as a part of this effort, they insisted the racial problem was a Southern problem that should be resolved by Southerners without "interference." The Northerners, in turn, had been left in a state of exhaustion by all the efforts that had gone into assuring the freedom and civil rights of Blacks. Their general response to the White Southerner's demands to be given a free hand, therefore, was to "wink and look the other way."

Economic Slavery

The economic and legal weapons used by the Whites to return the Blacks as nearly as possible to a condition of slavery are of considerable interest. On the economic side, "sharecropping" developed. This new system of agricultural production reduced many Whites as well as Blacks to a state resembling slavery. The planters still retained most of the productive land, but they generally were bankrupt. They had lost their slaves and generally were unable to pay wages for labor. Sharecropping worked in the following way: Banks and other lenders advanced money to the planters for a certain (usually large) share of the planter's next crop. The planters, in turn, advanced money and supplies to tenants for a certain share (also usually large) of their portion of the next crop. Although this system did permit the South's agricultural economy to resume production, it created a vicious cycle of borrowing and indebtedness. Because cotton was the cash crop in greatest demand, this method of financing also led to the overproduction of cotton and the rapid depletion of the soil's nutrients. Each of these elements helped to drive large numbers of landowners out of business.

The tenancy and sharecropping system worked to the disadvantage of practically everyone but the lenders. But it worked to the greatest disadvantage of the Black tenants. Many White landowners did not make public the exact records of the amounts they received for their crops or the amounts of credit they had extended to their tenants for food, clothing, and supplies during a given year. Since many tenants could neither read nor write, they had no effective way to challenge the owner's statement of what they were entitled to from the sale of the crop or what they owed the owner for supplies. Moreover, Black tenants soon learned they were in no position to insist that they be given an accurate statement of their earnings and debts. For a Black person even to hint that he or she was being cheated by a White was regarded by the Whites as the height of insolence and was sure to be punished; consequently, the tenants could do little or nothing when they learned, after the sale of the crops, that their backbreaking labor was to be rewarded by an increase in their debt. The tenants, especially the Black tenants, were kept by these devices in a condition hardly better than the slavery from which they presumably had recently escaped. The whole family, including women, children, and extended kin, worked to harvest enough crops to meet their obligations (Winegarten 1995:44, 47). When large numbers of tenants and owners could no longer earn a living in agriculture, they migrated to the cities.

Jim Crow Laws

The process of lowering the social standing of the Blacks from the pinnacle reached during Reconstruction involved legal as well as economic weapons. The primary areas of conflict for many years were the right to vote and segregation in public transportation. Following the Civil War, many railroad and steamship lines refused to permit Blacks to purchase first-class accommodations. And as a part of the Black Codes regulating the movements and privileges of the freedmen, Mississippi, Florida, and Texas each passed laws restricting the use of first-class railroad cars by Blacks (Woodward 1957:xiv–xv). The laws were the first of many **"Jim Crow"**[8] laws passed by southern legislatures to segregate Blacks from Whites. Later the term "Jim Crow" came to refer to the pattern of racial discrimination that resulted from state and local laws which required segregation in every type of public facility from schools to cemeteries. These first Jim Crow laws later were repealed; but as the quest to reestablish White supremacy grew, Jim Crow legislation began to reappear. At first, only the rights to vote and to use public transportation were affected. In time, however, every aspect of life—schooling, housing, religion, jobs, the courts, recreation, health care, and so on—was included.

The repeal of the first Jim Crow laws did not mean southern Whites were ready to accept racial equality in "social" matters. Even before the end of the Reconstruction period, in fact, both the churches and the schools had become almost completely segregated without any legislation whatever. Interracial violence was extremely common as Whites increasingly sought to prevent Blacks from exercising their rights as citizens. Also, during this period, the rate at which Blacks were being lynched by Whites rose dramatically (Frazier 1957:160).

Voting Restrictions

Gradually, the pressure mounted to separate the races in every way, to disfranchise the Blacks, and to place them in a position of complete subordination. In order to prevent Blacks from voting, schemes to circumvent the Fifteenth Amendment, which prohibited states from denying any person the vote on grounds of race, color, or previous conditions of servitude, were devised. In 1890, Mississippi changed the voting requirements in its constitution to reduce the number of Black voters; and during the next twenty-five years, all of the old Confederate states followed Mississippi's lead.

The methods employed relied on three main ideas, usually used in combination. In some states, voters were required to be able to pass "literacy" tests or to be property holders. In some states, the voters were required to pay a poll tax, usually months in advance of an election. And, in some states, the procedure for nominating people to office was restricted to Whites (the White primary) on the ground that the nominations were not elections and were, therefore, a "private" matter. These qualifications also had a deterrent effect on many White voters; however, several loopholes in the laws were created to decrease their effects on Whites. For instance, in order to meet the literacy test, a person might be required to show an "understanding" of some portion of the federal or state constitution. Since White officials were in charge of these "tests" and decided who had passed, only the people considered to be non-White were ever found to be "illiterate" and unqualified to vote.

Another technique to permit Whites only to evade the other voter qualifications was the notorious "grandfather clause." Under one type of grandfather clause, people could qualify as voters only if their ancestors had been eligible to vote in 1860 (Frazier 1957:157). Since few southern Blacks could meet this type of test, and many Whites could, a grandfather clause disqualified many more Blacks than Whites. Some idea of the efficiency of these methods may be seen from the records in Louisiana. In 1896, there were more than 130,000 Black voters; in 1904, there were less than 1,400 (Lawson 1976:14–15).

Despite economic, political, and social oppression, Black men and women resisted in a number of ways. They took their grievances to the Freedmen's Bureau. When attacked, some responded. They defied segregation and disfranchisement with lawsuits and civil disobedience. Black women joined organizations, such as the Woman's Christian Temperance Union and farmers' alliances, and they spoke publicly, attended meetings, and convinced the men in their families both to vote and how to vote (Winegarten 1995:81).

Separate But Equal

The other main focus of the segregationists' efforts—public transportation—led to a momentous decision by the U.S. Supreme Court affecting the civil rights of all Americans. In 1890, Louisiana passed a law requiring separate rail-car facilities for Whites and Blacks. The law stated that "all railway companies carrying passengers . . . in this state shall provide equal but separate accommodations for the white and colored races" (Tussman 1963:65). Under the law, Whites and Blacks were not permitted to sit together in a coach or a section of a coach. Criminal charges could be filed for a violation of the law.

In 1896, this law was challenged in the Supreme Court in the famous "separate but equal" case *Plessy v. Ferguson*. Plessy, who was stated to be "seven-eighths caucasian," had been ordered to leave a coach assigned to members of the White race and had refused to comply. He had been arrested and jailed for violating the law. The main legal point in Plessy's case was that he had been deprived of his rights under the Fourteenth Amendment to the Constitution. The majority of the Court argued that even though the amendment was intended to achieve the absolute equality of the races, no law could abolish social distinctions based on color.

The majority opinion was eloquently challenged by Justice Harlan, who argued that the Louisiana law was unconstitutional because it violated the personal freedoms of all of the people of Louisiana. It was the purpose of the Thirteenth, Fourteenth, and Fifteenth amendments to make the Constitution colorblind and to remove the race line from our system of government. But if a state could prescribe separate railway coaches, then it could also insist that Whites and Blacks must walk on opposite sides of the street or sit on opposite sides of the courtroom or be segregated in public meetings. By this reasoning, the state could require the separation in railway coaches of Protestant and Catholic passengers or of native and naturalized citizens.

Justice Harlan also believed that, in the long run, the decision would stimulate racial resentment and hatred. The real meaning of the Louisiana law, he argued, is that Whites consider Blacks to be so inferior that it is degrading to mingle with them in any way. The statute was not intended to guarantee that Blacks would not be forced to associate with Whites but that Whites would not be forced to associate with Blacks. Such an approach to race relations was a serious mistake, Harlan believed. "The destinies of the two races in this country," he wrote, "are indissolubly linked together, and the interests of both require that the common government of all shall not permit the seeds of race hate to be planted under the sanction of law" (Tussman 1963:81).

Harlan's fear that the result of *Plessy* would be the extension of racial segregation not only in railroad coaches but in many other spheres of life was clearly justified. Within three years, every southern state had adopted a law segregating the races aboard trains. By 1910, most of these same states had extended segregation to include the waiting rooms in railway stations; by 1920, racial segregation in the South (and a few adjoining states) had become the normal practice in almost every public matter. In time, signs proclaiming "Whites only" or "Colored" were displayed at drinking fountains, rest rooms, theaters, swimming pools, libraries, public telephones, bathing beaches, hospital entrances, restaurants, and so on. In many instances, the laws regulating the permissible behavior of the members of the two races stated exactly, in feet and inches, how far apart their separate entrances into public buildings or places of amusement must be and how close together they were allowed to sit or stand. Of course, in all of these situations, the separate facilities for Blacks were supposed to be equal to those for Whites. In fact, this was almost never the case. In only a few short years, the White southerners had succeeded by law in creating a rigid caste system. Once again, as in the period of slavery, Black people had no rights that White people were bound to respect.

In some ways, the Jim Crow system that emerged after 1890 was an even more efficient instrument of subordination than slavery had been. It is true that the Blacks under Jim Crow were no longer legally the property of the Whites, but then it is also true that the Whites no longer had as strong an incentive to be concerned about the welfare of Blacks. Under slavery, at least some Blacks were in close daily contact with some Whites, and those contacts were often friendly and compassionate (though it is easy to exaggerate this). The Jim Crow system made many forms of friendly and understanding contacts between the races practically impossible. Residential segregation *increased* as the Jim Crow system became more pervasive. Blacks increasingly were pressured into slum areas that were occupied solely by Blacks.

The system of enforced racial segregation also may have been as difficult to bear psychologically as slavery had been. During the period of slavery, a major source of emotional sustenance for Blacks was the hope, however faint, that someday they might be released from bondage. Emancipation, the Thirteenth, Fourteenth, and Fifteenth Amendments, and Reconstruction all seemed to fulfill this dim and ancient hope. Black people voted, were elected to office, moved about fairly freely, mingled with Whites in public places, and owned property. But the Supreme Court's decision in *Plessy* cleared the way for the rise of Jim Crowism and the virtual reenslavement of Black people in many southern and adjoining states. Although under the Jim Crow system Black people still retained significant freedoms, such as the right to attend schools (albeit inferior ones) and to own property, the laws permitted under *Plessy* practically neutralized the *intent* of the post–Civil War amendments to the Constitution.

We should note in passing that although legal segregation, with only a few exceptions, was established primarily in the South and in some border states, many forms of racial discrimination, including segregation, occurred in other parts of the country. Even in states that had enacted special civil rights laws attempting to guarantee the rights contained in the federal constitution, many discriminatory practices existed. For example, hotels were suddenly "filled" when Black guests tried to register, or theaters were "sold out" when Black patrons arrived. Cases have been reported in which Blacks were served "doctored" foods in restaurants to discourage them from returning (Davie 1949:290). Moreover, socially enforced residential segregation soon became the rule throughout the United States. The Jim Crow laws of the southern states helped create and strengthen a system of racial discrimination that went far beyond the extralegal discrimination that has been prevalent in many parts of the United States.

Migration and Urbanization

Immediately after the Civil War, some African Americans began to exercise their new freedom to move about. At first, this movement took place almost entirely within the South and consisted primarily of migration from the Atlantic seaboard to the more westerly states of the South and from rural areas into the cities. Increasingly, however, social and economic forces favored migration out of the South. As we have seen already, the newly created Jim Crow system reduced African Americans to second-class citizenship; and this legal attack was accompanied by economic woes. In the rural areas, crop failures, the boll weevil, and soil depletion were crippling the cotton industry. In the cities, many jobs that traditionally had been "Negro jobs" were either being displaced by machines or were being taken over by Whites. At the same time these "push" factors were operating in the South, the "pull" factors in the North were comparatively weak. For example, despite the need for labor in the industrializing areas, and despite the general hostility of employers toward foreign laborers, the hostility of both White northern workers and their employers against Black workers was even greater (Lieberson 1980:5, 383).[9] White immigrants feared they would lose their jobs if thousands of Blacks came north. Intensifying the hostility of White workers, some employers imported trainloads of Blacks from the South as strikebreakers when union members demanded higher wages (Farley and Allen 1987:111). Moreover, both federal immigration policies and the desires of southern leaders to maintain a cheap labor pool conspired to make it difficult for Blacks to take advantage of any opportunities that might have awaited them in the North. Black women sometimes migrated in larger numbers than their male relatives because they could find work more easily than men in the growing market for domestics, cooks, nursemaids, and laundresses (Winegarten 1995:47).

Conditions in the North changed sharply, however, with the outbreak of World War I. The war suddenly halted the supply of cheap labor that had been provided by European immigration, and it was stopped just at a time when the demand for labor to produce war materials was rising. Northern employers looked to the South for a new supply of cheap labor. Therefore, during the 1910–1920 period, more than a half million Black people headed north (Farley and Allen 1987:113).[10] This movement is of special interest not only because it was the largest mass migration of Blacks from the South up to that time, but also because it originated mainly in the Deep South rather than in the border states. Most of the migrants sought jobs in New York, Chicago, Philadelphia, and

Detroit. The Black population of these cities increased during the decade by nearly 750,000 (Frazier 1957:191). The newcomers found jobs in iron and steel mills, automobile construction, chemical plants, and other industrial settings. They received much higher wages than they were accustomed to in the South, and northern employers, for the most part, found them to be competent and easier to work with than immigrant laborers from foreign countries.

The urbanization of Blacks in the cities of the North, though greatly aided by industrial jobs and high wages, was hindered by the prejudice and discrimination of Whites. In the workplace, Whites struggled to prevent Blacks from gaining union membership and the better training and jobs that accompanied such membership. In the broader community, Whites fought to force Blacks into segregated neighborhoods. Prior to this time, Blacks, along with other poor people, had been concentrated in areas of low-rent housing; but if they wished to and could afford it, Blacks were able to live in various parts of the cities. Now, however, real estate agents catered to the preferences of Whites and "steered" Black customers into all-Black neighborhoods (Farley and Allen 1987:136–137). Increasingly, cities passed laws requiring Blacks and Whites to live in segregated areas, and in some places—conspicuously in East St. Louis and Chicago— bloody attacks on Black people took place (Farley and Allen 1987:115).

Just as the great migration of Mexicans into the United States in this century has caused many observers to believe the immigrant model applies to them, the great migration of Black Americans to the North also has been compared to the European immigrations. From this perspective, although Black Americans have been physically present within the United States for centuries, their entry into the American industrial economy as "immigrants" actually has been underway for little more than three generations; hence, even though their experience up to the time of World War I may properly be characterized as colonial, their experience since that time increasingly has resembled that of recent immigrants (Kristol 1972).

The end of World War I, an economic depression in the early 1920s, and the Great Depression of the entire decade of the 1930s greatly reduced the migration of southern Blacks to the North and West; but the movement was by no means stopped. The Black population of these regions continued to rise throughout the period and at a much faster rate than in the South. For example, during the two decades from 1920 to 1940, over twice as many Blacks left the South as had departed during the 1910–1920 period, while the Black population of the South rose only slightly (Farley and Allen 1987:113).

The next great surge of Black migration accompanied World War II. As in the case of World War I, many Blacks moved to the war plants in the cities of the North and West. Again, Chicago, Detroit, New York, and Philadelphia received large numbers of these migrants. By this time, however, the South also had become far more industrialized than previously; so many migrating Blacks moved to southern cities, such as Birmingham, Houston, Norfolk, and New Orleans. And for the first time, western cities such as Los Angeles, Portland, and San Diego drew sizable numbers of Blacks out of the South. The favorite single destination for Black migrants was Harlem in New York City. This Black community grew during the period under discussion into the largest urban Black population in the world (Davie 1949:100).

Although Jim Crow laws continued to dominate the lives of Black southerners, many had escaped to other regions of the country, had adjusted to life in urban areas, and were working in industrial occupations. These migrants were still subjected to many types of extralegal discrimination. Nevertheless, northern Blacks enjoyed a greater degree of formal and legal equality; and this legal advantage afforded a basis from which to launch an energetic, if excruciatingly slow, judicial and legislative offensive against all forms of discrimination affecting Blacks and—by extension—all other minority groups in America. This offensive, generally referred to as the civil rights movement, may be dated from the period in which Jim Crowism was becoming established in America.

The Civil Rights Movement

The Supreme Court's decision in *Plessy v. Ferguson* marks the point at which Black people in the South officially had lost the battle to retain most of the advantages won in the Civil War. As we noted, however, the decision in *Plessy* was not only a signal to the South that it might go ahead on a state-by-state basis to reduce Blacks to second-class citizens, it also was a ratification of many changes that already had occurred in the relations between the races. The level of White violence against Blacks had risen sharply, the doctrine of innate Black inferiority was gaining in strength (as discussed in Chapter 5), and many Blacks feared that to continue open resistance to White supremacy was foolhardy. Even before *Plessy* made it official, therefore, African Americans already had been forced into an inferior status, and some African American leaders had concluded that the wisest course of action was to accept the fact that Whites were not going to permit Black equality, at least not in the short run. The most influential statement of this view that Blacks should accept a new accommodation with Whites on the Whites' terms was voiced by the Black leader Booker T. Washington.

Separate and Subordinate

Born in Virginia of a slave mother and a White father, Washington had overcome extreme adversity to get an education at Hampton Institute, a post–Civil War missionary school. Washington used his education to establish Tuskegee Institute, one of the leading Black colleges. At the Atlanta exposition of 1895, Washington expressed the view in a speech called the **"Atlanta Compromise"** that Blacks should focus "upon the everyday practical things of life, upon something that is needed to be done, and something which they will be permitted to do in the community in which they reside." Washington's famous speech was carefully designed to assure White people that Blacks were ready to accept their inferior status in the political arena. He stated: "In all things that are purely social, we can be as separate as the fingers yet one as the hand in all things essential to mutual progress" (Washington [1895]1959:156). He argued further that Blacks were still too recently removed from slavery to take their place as equals among the Whites. He emphasized that Blacks must adopt an economic program of manual labor and self-help as the best means to win their full rights as citizens rather than engaging in political action. Needless to say, Washington's views were very flattering to Whites and were immediately praised by them. It has been reported that many of the White people who heard Washington's speech leaped to their feet in a standing ovation, while many Blacks in the audience sat silently weeping.

Washington became a celebrity almost overnight. Until his death twenty years later, he was the most influential and powerful spokesman for Black America. His views on race relations were central to the so-called Tuskegee point of view, which stressed appeasement of the Whites, segregation, and the importance of self-help. He presented both a program (the "gospel of wealth") and an organization (The National Negro Business League) to help attain it. At the center of his strategy was the development of Black business enterprise and economic solidarity among Blacks (Butler and Wilson 1988: 136–137).

The Niagara Movement

Washington's approach to the race question was widely accepted among Blacks as well as Whites, but some Black leaders bitterly criticized him for sacrificing education and civil rights for the acceptance of White conservatives. For example, in 1902, Monroe Trotter (1971:35) attacked Washington as a "Benedict Arnold of the Negro race." In 1903, W.E.B. Du Bois established himself as Washington's leading critic. Du Bois, the holder of a Ph.D. degree from Harvard University, called Washington's teachings propaganda that was helping to speed the construction of a racial caste system. In 1905, a small group of Black "radicals" under the leadership of Du Bois formed the **Niagara Movement** to express opposition to Washington's program. They disagreed with him emphatically on many major issues. Their "Declaration of Principles" stated that Black people should protest the curtailment of their political and civil rights. They pointed out that the denial of opportunities to Blacks in the South amounted to "virtual slavery." And they proclaimed their refusal to accept the impression left by Washington and his followers "that the Negro American assents to inferiority, is submissive under oppression, and apologetic before insults." In contrast to Washington's strategy of political submission coupled with economic development, the members of the Niagara Movement insisted that agitation and complaint was the best way for Blacks to escape the "barbarian" practices of discrimination based on race (Meier, Rudwick, and Broderick 1971: 58–62).

Given the time at which it was made, the Niagara Declaration seemed very radical. Jim Crowism was reaching full fruition. In the minds of most people, Blacks as well as Whites, the segregation of the races in the South would remain the "solution" to the race problem until the Blacks were able to "live up" to White standards and "earn" gradual acceptance as equals. It should be observed, though, that for all their differences the Washington "conservatives" and the Du Bois "radicals" agreed that Blacks should strive to establish economic independence, that they should join together to attempt to solve their problems, and that the ultimate goal of any strategy should be the full acceptance of African Americans as first-class citizens of the United States (Meier, Rudwick, and

Broderick 1971:xxvi). They disagreed sharply on whether the proper means to the attainment of their ends should be humility, subservience, and patience or an aggressive, indignant demand for the immediate recognition of their rights.

The NAACP.   The Niagara group was not large or immediately very influential, but its declaration revealed dramatically that not all Blacks accepted Washington's policies. More important, however, is that, in 1909, most of the Niagara group's members merged with a group of White liberals to form the National Association for the Advancement of Colored People (NAACP). The leaders of the NAACP opposed "the ever-growing oppression," "the systematic persecution," and the disfranchisement of Black people. They demanded that everyone, including Blacks, be given free public schooling that would focus on professional education for the most gifted—what Du Bois had earlier called "the talented tenth"—as well as industrial training for all who wished it; however, this goal could not be achieved unless Blacks received equal treatment under the law. Consequently, the NAACP adopted a legal and legislative strategy. It called on Congress and the president to enforce strictly the Constitution's provisions on civil rights and the right to vote, and it urged that educational expenditures for Black children be made equal to those for Whites (Meier, Rudwick, and Broderick 1971:65–66).[11]

The NAACP soon began to make its presence felt. As editor of the organization's official magazine, *The Crisis,* Du Bois was able to place his ideas before a large audience; in 1915, the organization's legal efforts helped to bring about a Supreme Court decision declaring the "grandfather clause" unconstitutional. After Booker T. Washington died later in that same year, the NAACP became the leading organization devoted to the civil rights of Black Americans.

At the very time of the inception of the NAACP, however, certain events were forcing many Blacks to conclude that no amount of legal action could guarantee them first-class citizenship. As a result, many cities became powder kegs of racial resentment and unrest.

Continued Racial Violence

Three types of interracial violence were prominent during this period. Lynchings, especially of Blacks by Whites, had been an important form of violence for several decades and were still a source of great concern. Although the Klan went through a dormant period in the early 1900s, the massive immigration from Europe, coupled with the nation's employment ills, revived it. In 1915, the Klan's leader, Imperial Wizard William Simmons, initiated a new era of hatred and intolerance. At the same time a widely shown film, *Birth of A Nation,* glorified the Klan as a group that had preserved the American South from uncivilized Blacks (Salzman 1992). Although the actual number of lynchings that were recorded was somewhat lower between 1910 and 1920 than in the two previous decades, the circumstances under which they occurred and the publicity they received led to more open and angry denunciations by Black spokespersons than in the past. Many lynchings were conducted in an especially sadistic way and in a carnival atmosphere. Some victims were tortured and burned at the stake, and some newspapers issued invitations to Whites to come to witness a lynching or a burning. Between the period from the emancipation to the Great Depression, about 3,000 Blacks were lynched in the American South (Beck and Tolnay 1990:526). Unsurprisingly, some militant Black leaders advocated armed resistance as a solution to these problems (Franklin and Moss 1988:318–321).

Another main form of violence during these years consisted of mob attacks by Whites on the property of Black people and on the people themselves. This type of violence was most common in the cities of the South. For the most part, in these outbreaks, Blacks were unorganized and defenseless, but in some cases they fought back. For example, in 1921 between fifty and seventy-five armed Blacks confronted a White mob of 1,500 to 2,000 people in Tulsa, Oklahoma. In the conflict that followed, over fifty people died and "the entire section known as Black Wall Street—more than one thousand homes and businesses—lay in ruins" (Butler and Wilson 1988:147). In several outbreaks in cities of the North, Blacks also organized and retaliated against Whites. The summer following the end of World War I was filled with such a large number of mob attacks by Whites, and so much blood was shed in the summer of 1919 that James Weldon Johnson (1968:304), head of the NAACP, referred to it as "the Red Summer." Approximately two dozen outbreaks occurred in American cities, and fourteen Blacks were publicly burned, eleven of them alive (Lincoln 1961:56). These conflicts were of the type usually described as race "riots."

The rise of White nativist sentiment expressed in the revival of the Ku Klux Klan and the lynchings, burnings, mob attacks, and race riots occurred during or immediately following World War I, a war that had been fought "to make the world safe for democracy." Since between 350,000 and 400,000 Black Americans had served during the Great War, the gap between the nation's lofty ideals and the actual conditions at home was not lost on many Blacks.

All of these elements combined following the war to give a large number of Blacks a new sense of racial identity. This **"Black Renaissance"** was visibly furthered by a group of writers and artists located in Harlem, among them Langston Hughes, Zora Neal Hurston, and Claude McKay. These writers generated poetry, novels, and newspaper columns that exalted Black pride, Black cultural expression, and Black exclusiveness. This renaissance, with its bristling spirit of protest, also generated an extreme form of **nationalism** that promoted separatism.

Separatism

Many Blacks were more convinced than ever before that the prospects of Black people in America were very poor. Under these conditions, the legalistic approach of the NAACP did not seem sufficiently direct or vigorous to many Blacks. In the minds of hundreds of thousands of Black Americans, the program offered by a new leader, Marcus Garvey, seemed the answer to a prayer.

Back to Africa.   Garvey, a dark-skinned man, was born in Jamaica in 1887. He came to the United States during World War I and organized the Universal Negro Improvement Association (UNIA). The UNIA's major long-range goal was to enable African Americans to leave the United States and settle in an independent nation in Africa. The philosophy of independence preached by Garvey appealed mainly to the lower-income, urban masses. Middle-class or professional and business people were offended by his attacks on them and their acceptance of White standards and by his contempt for those who had light-colored skin.

Garvey's heroes were men like Denmark Vesey, Gabriel Prosser, and Nat Turner who had promoted violent resistance to slavery. Somewhat ironically, his colonization program was inspired by "conservative" Booker T. Washington's autobiography *Up From Slavery*. Garvey admired Washington's emphasis on racial separation and self-help. Garvey's ideas concerning the eventual solution of America's racial problem, though, were radically different from Washington's. Whereas Washington saw separation as a tool to be used to gain eventual acceptance by White Americans, Garvey visualized the renunciation of American citizenship and the permanent separation of the two races. As Baker (1970:8) said, "Garvey's UNIA was an effort to have Black Americans vote with their feet."

The idea of recolonization, of course, was not at all new, but Garvey's "back to Africa" movement represented the first time a Black person had attempted to organize such a venture. Moreover, the effort came at a time when large masses of Black Americans were concentrated in urban ghettos and were ready to listen. Garvey (1970:25) lashed out at most Black leaders for "aping white people" and for exhibiting "the slave spirit of dependence." These so-called leaders, he said, were "Uncle Toms" who could not be trusted. He argued that the time had come for Blacks to be self-reliant, to have a country of their own in Africa. The purpose of the UNIA was to inspire "an unfortunate race with pride in self and with the determination" to take its place as an equal among races (Garvey 1968a:295).

Under Garvey's leadership, the UNIA established a number of Black-run business enterprises, including the Black Star Steamship Line. This line was intended to link Black people throughout the world and to provide the transportation they would need to return "home." The UNIA also established the Universal African Legion, the Black Eagle Flying Corps, the Universal Black Cross Nurses, and some other organizations designed to promote self-reliance and Black pride. These organizations—with their members dressed in smart uniforms—dramatized Garvey's ideas and attracted widespread attention and admiration. These tactics also earned him the enmity of most other influential Black leaders and the federal government.

Garvey's numerous enemies slowly closed in on him. Both the NAACP, which by comparison seemed "conservative," and the socialists under A. Philip Randolph agreed that Garvey must be stopped. They were assisted in their efforts by Garvey's own shortcomings as an administrator. In 1922, Garvey was indicted for mail fraud; in 1923, he was convicted and imprisoned in the federal penitentiary in Atlanta. One news magazine proclaimed "Garvey defeated Garvey." While the bulk of the Negro press approved of this end to Garvey's career, a White newspaper, the *Buffalo Evening Times,* noted that many White men who were greater offenders had received lighter sentences or no punishment for similar crimes (Cronon 1969:135). Although his sentence was commuted in 1927, Garvey was deported to Jamaica as an undesirable alien. After his deportation, the UNIA no longer had an inspiring leader; therefore, the influence of the largest mass movement among Black Americans to that date waned. The scandal and suspicion created by the trial, imprisonment, and deportation of Garvey led to a rapid decline of the UNIA. The organization's nationalistic message, though, has had an enduring influence among African Americans. It appealed to the masses, profoundly stirred the race consciousness of Blacks around the world, and served as a focal point for pride in African culture.

Two direct descendants of the UNIA have been very prominent. The first of these, the Lost Nation of Islam, came into existence less than five years after Garvey's deportation. The second, to which we turn later, did not arise until the mid-1960s.

Black Muslims.

The Lost Nation of Islam (or Black Muslim) group was launched by two inspiring leaders. The first of these, W. D. Fard, was a man of mystery. Little is known about him. He appeared in the Black community of Detroit in 1930 and then mysteriously disappeared just four years later. His primary doctrine was that the White race was the devil on earth, that African Americans were the lost tribe of Shebazz, and that the salvation of Blacks lay not in the White man's religion, Christianity, but in the Black's true religion, Mohammedanism (Lincoln 1961:72–80). Fard founded the Temple of Islam and assembled a devoted following. Chief among his disciples was Elijah Poole, who became known as Elijah Muhammad. After Fard's sudden disappearance in 1934, Elijah Muhammad assumed the leadership of the movement and took the title "Messenger of Allah" (Lincoln 1961:15–16).

The teachings of Elijah Muhammad, like those of Marcus Garvey, advocated race pride, self-help, and the separation of the races; however, his views differed from Garvey's in at least two important respects. First, although Garvey stated that Jesus had been Black and that Black people should renounce Christianity and its White symbolism, religion had been secondary to politics in the UNIA. Among the Black Muslims, however, religion has been the dominant element. They developed an extremely demanding moral code that forbade the use of tobacco or drugs, extramarital sexual relations, racial intermarriage, dancing, attendance at movies, participation in sports, laziness, lying, and a host of other things. Second, the political goals of the Black Muslim movement also differed from those of the UNIA. Garvey's main goals were to return Black people to Africa and Africa to Black people. Elijah Muhammad, however, was neither so explicit about his political objectives nor so determined to leave the United States. The Muslims have called at various times for a separate nation right here in the United States and have suggested that several states should be set aside for this purpose.

The most important difference between the Garvey movement and the Black Muslim movement, however, is that the latter has gradually gained in strength and influence over the years. The number of people who are officially members of the Black Muslim organization is unknown, but the effect of the movement extends far beyond its membership. Certainly, the teachings of Elijah Muhammad and his famous convert Malcolm X have been widely circulated within the United States and overseas. Many people who do not belong to the Muslim church or subscribe to all of its teachings nevertheless have developed respect for the Muslims' high standards and strict discipline. The Muslims have been notably successful in the rehabilitation of ex-convicts and drug addicts, and they have been successful in their efforts to build a strong economic base. The strict moral code and philosophy of economic independence have had an especially powerful appeal to the many Black people who reside in the urban ghettos of America. It has played a significant role in "revitalizing" the lives of many people who previously had given up in the face of seemingly overwhelming difficulties.

The importance of the Black Muslim movement cannot be measured solely in terms of its official size. After the collapse of the Garvey movement, it served as a valuable repository of Black separatist philosophy and as a continuing reminder to Black Americans that there was an alternative to the goal of "integration." In the 1990s, the Nation of Islam's leader, Louis Farrakhan, revived many aspects of the Garvey movement's Black pride and separatist ideology; and he organized a Million Man March in Washington, which we discuss in more detail in the next chapter.

Strategy, Tactics, and Conflict

The NAACP had maintained its legal warfare against discrimination throughout the period under discussion. But with the onset of the Great Depression in 1929, the association was increasingly criticized for its relative inactivity in economic matters. The Depression struck hard at all American workers, but its effects on Black workers were particularly devastating. Blacks had been systematically excluded from most units of the leading labor organization, the American Federation of Labor (AFL), and, as usual, they were "the last hired and the first fired."

These circumstances led to some significant changes in the organization, strategy, and tactics of African Americans. We noted previously, for example, the rise of the Black Muslims. Of interest, too, was the organization of a number of new protest groups whose main objective was more and better jobs for Black people. These organizations were part of a widespread effort to persuade African Americans to use their substantial economic power as a lever to improve conditions. The common slogan of these organizations, "Don't Buy Where You Can't Work," emphasized that their main weapons were the economic boycott and the picket line.

One of the new organizations to employ these direct-action tactics was the New Negro Alliance, Inc. The alliance grew out of a spontaneous protest occurring at a hamburger grill in Washington, D.C. (Bunche [1940]1971:122). This grill was located in a Black residential area and depended entirely on Black customers. In 1933, the Black workers at the grill were fired, and White workers were hired to replace them. Several onlookers were outraged by this act of blatant discrimination and formed a picket line at the grill. This tactic quickly led to the reinstatement of the Black workers. This form of protest was so successful that many other groups, including the NAACP, adopted it. The NAACP's new willingness to address the economic problems of Black people, however, continued to be secondary to its main focus on the issue of school segregation.

The beginning of World War II signaled the close of the Great Depression. The demand for labor rapidly increased as armaments production rose. The boom spread to construction, service industries, transportation, and other sectors of the economy; but the sudden increase in the demand for labor served mainly to put the huge force of unemployed Whites back to work. The main jobs that opened up for Blacks were as service workers and farm laborers (Myrdal [1944]1964: 409–412).

The continuation of conspicuous discrimination in the midst of still another global war "to make the world safe for democracy" enraged many African Americans. Two forms of discrimination were particularly galling: discrimination in war production and in the armed forces. Both of these areas involved federal dollars and, therefore, seemed to represent national policy. One leader, A. Philip Randolph, established in 1942 the March on Washington movement, which sought to organize millions of Black people. He argued that "mass power" used in an orderly and lawful way was "the most effective weapon a minority people can wield" (Randolph 1971a:230). Although the United States still had not entered the war at the time Randolph issued his first call to march, President Franklin D. Roosevelt was eager to prevent any large demonstration of unrest. In June 1941, the president issued an executive order (No. 8802) prohibiting racial discrimination in defense industries, in government, and in defense training programs. The order also established a Fair Employment Practices Committee (FEPC) to investigate possible violations of the order.

CORE: The Expansion of Nonviolent Protest.   The principle of nonviolent direct action had a broad appeal. Some leaders, however, felt that the March on Washington movement's application of the principle left much to be desired. Specifically, they objected to the exclusion of Whites from participation in the movement and to the absence of a program to prevent mass protest from becoming violent. Consequently, still another new protest organization, the Congress of Racial Equality (CORE), was formed to further the use of nonviolent direct action. CORE leaders were afraid that many embittered African Americans were ready to employ violence in a desperate attempt to force the dominant group to grant them civil and social equality. Bayard Rustin observed in 1942 that some Blacks had concluded it would be better to die to gain victory at home than to die on a foreign battlefield in defense of White Americans. He also reported that many Blacks even hoped for a Japanese victory "since it don't matter who you're a slave for" (Rustin 1971:236).

CORE's philosophy represented an attempt to apply the methods of Jesus and Gandhi to the race situation in America. It rested on the conviction that social conflicts cannot really be solved by violent methods, that violence simply breeds more violence, and that "turning the other cheek" has the power to shame the evildoer. This approach was later adopted and refined by Martin Luther King, Jr. The practical expression of these beliefs involved a carefully graduated set of steps. In a conflict situation, the first step was patient negotiation. If this effort failed, the next step was to attempt to arouse public opinion against the opponent's discriminatory actions. Only after these remedies were exhausted did CORE advocate the use of boycotts, picket lines, and strikes.

In addition to patient negotiations, agitation, and the use of labor's protest methods, however, CORE developed a new technique of nonviolent direct action. The technique's first use appears to have occurred in 1942 following an incident of discrimination in a cafe against two CORE leaders, James R. Robinson and James Farmer. After nearly a month of attempts to negotiate, the CORE leaders stated that unless the management agreed to talk with them, they would be forced to take some other course of action. About a week later, an interracial group of twenty-five people entered the restaurant and took seats. The White people among the group were served promptly, but the

Black people were not served at all; however, the White people did not eat. Instead, they told the manager that they did not wish to eat until their Black friends also had been served. The manager angrily refused; so the group simply continued to occupy a large number of the restaurant's seats. When customers who were waiting to be served saw they would be unable to be seated, they left. After a period of fuming, the manager had all of the protesters served. Thus ended successfully the first "sit-in," a technique of protest that became increasingly popular during the next two decades (Farmer 1971:243–246).

The protest tactics of organizations such as the March on Washington movement and CORE were only a part of the complicated interracial situation that existed in the United States during World War II. We saw previously that the tense early years of the war were marked by numerous open confrontations and violence between ethnic groups. We mentioned that Mexican American "zoot-suiters" had been attacked in Los Angeles and some other American cities; Mexican Americans in the armed forces had been discriminated against both inside and outside of the service. We have seen, too, that intense anti-Japanese sentiments supported the fateful evacuation and illegal internment of the Japanese from the West Coast. During this period, various forms of violence involving Blacks and Whites also erupted. Confrontations reminiscent of the "Red Summer" of 1919 occurred in Mobile, Alabama, in Beaumont and El Paso, Texas, in Philadelphia, Pennsylvania, and in Newark, New Jersey. The largest outburst took place in June 1943 in Detroit, Michigan. Racial tensions in Detroit had been building over a long period of time as both White and Black southerners moved there to work in the automobile industry. According to one account, twenty-five Blacks and nine Whites were killed, and more than 700 other people were injured (Osofsky 1968:420).

The Decline of Colonialism.   The Allies in World War II had fought not only against fascism but also, officially, against the doctrine of White supremacy. During the course of the war, large numbers of non-White peoples in the United States became aware that many people like themselves were fighting and dying to save the very nations that had been historically the main representatives of the White-supremacy theory. Certainly, the experiences of many men and women in uniform emphasized the disparity between the official principles of the United States and the actual practices within it. Throughout the military services, Jim Crow practices were common. And since many military training camps were in the South, Black servicemen faced segregation when they left the camps. They were frequently in danger of physical assault not only by local citizens but by officers of the law as well. For instance, a Black soldier was shot in Little Rock, Arkansas, because he would not tip his hat and say "sir" to a policeman. Another Black soldier was shot by two police officers because he had taken a bus seat reserved for a White in Beaumont, Texas (Rustin 1971:235). In Centerville, Mississippi, a sheriff obligingly shot a Black soldier in the chest merely because a White MP asked him to (Milner 1968:419). As the old colonial empires were dissolved following the war, and as new independent nations arose in their place, incidents such as those described became increasingly embarrassing to American leaders. How could the United States explain to the peoples of other nations the discrepancy between its ringing declarations of human rights and the treatment of its own minority groups at home?

Increased external pressures on the American government to attend to these conditions resulted in a series of important changes in official domestic policies. The patient legal work of the NAACP and the direct-action methods of the March on Washington movement and CORE had begun to show some dramatic results. For example, in 1948, as President Harry Truman and Congress considered the advisability of instituting a peacetime military draft, the leader of the March on Washington movement, A. Philip Randolph, took a strong stand against segregation in the armed forces. Randolph stated that unless the military services were desegregated, he would lead a nationwide campaign to encourage young people to refuse to enlist. He stated further, "I personally will advise Negroes to refuse to fight as slaves for a democracy they cannot possess and cannot enjoy" (Randolph 1971b:278). Later that year, President Truman acted to end all segregation in the armed forces of the United States (Osofsky 1968:465.)

Victories in the Courts

The NAACP's battle to end segregation in public education had gradually gained strength through an impressive series of court victories. As early as 1938, the Supreme Court ruled that the State University of Missouri was required to admit a Black applicant to its law school. Similar rulings were handed down in cases affecting the law school of the University of Oklahoma (1948), the law school of the University of Texas (1950), and the graduate school of the University of Oklahoma (1950). These rulings led to an all-out effort by the officials of segregated school systems to improve the facilities for Black students and, if possible, to make them physically equal to those for Whites. These victories also laid the groundwork in 1954 for one of the most important court cases in the history of the United States.

Brown v. Topeka Board of Education.   The *Brown* case differed from the other cases just mentioned in a very important respect. The earlier cases had not called into question the "separate but equal doctrine" approved in the Supreme Court's *Plessy* decision in 1896. Now, however, the Court brought this doctrine directly under review. The question of central importance was this: Even if the separate educational facilities for the minority group are equal in buildings, libraries, teacher qualifications, and the like, do these "equal" facilities provide educationally equal opportunities? The Court ruled that they do not. Chief Justice Warren, speaking for the Court, argued that to separate children "from others of similar age and qualifications solely because of their race generates a feeling of inferiority as to their status in the community that may affect their hearts and minds in a way unlikely ever to be undone. . . . We conclude that in the field of public education the doctrine of 'separate but equal' has no place. Separate educational facilities are inherently unequal" (Clark 1963:159). Segregation in public schools was unanimously held to violate the "equal protection" clause of the Fourteenth Amendment and, therefore, was declared unconstitutional. In a separate ruling on the same day, the Court also declared segregated schools to be a violation of the "due process" clause of the Fifth Amendment.

In its *Brown* ruling in May 1954 (*Brown I*), the Supreme Court recognized the difficulties that would be encountered in the effort to desegregate public schools; consequently, the Court issued another decision in 1955 (*Brown II*) on the question of *how* the transition from segregation to desegregation was to be achieved. The Court emphasized that variations in local conditions had to be taken into account in planning for the change and that the primary responsibility for the implementation of the 1954 ruling rested with local authorities and the lower courts. The Court insisted, however, that local school systems must "make a prompt and reasonable start toward full compliance" with its decision and racial discrimination in school admissions must be halted "with all deliberate speed" (Tussman 1963:45–46).

The *Brown* rulings ushered in a new era of hope among Blacks and of heightened resistance to "integration" among Whites. White citizens councils, described by some Blacks as "the Klan in gray flannel suits" (Osofsky 1968:479), were formed throughout the South to find ways to prevent school desegregation. The KKK itself underwent another revival. All of the old charges of the White supremacists were again brought forward. And many southern politicians searched frantically for the legal grounds needed to overturn the Court's school desegregation decisions. Although school desegregation was initiated promptly and successfully in many southern communities, the general intensity of White reactions to desegregation efforts began to make clear to Black Americans that change "with all deliberate speed" might, in fact, be very slow. The growing pessimism among Blacks was fueled by numerous incidents of intimidation and violence throughout the South.

An important episode in the struggle to desegregate the schools occurred in Little Rock, Arkansas, during the 1957–1958 school year. The Little Rock school board had gone to work on a school desegregation plan in 1954, almost immediately after the first *Brown* decision. While the board was developing its plan, the state officials of Arkansas were attempting to "nullify" the *Brown* decisions. The central feature of the Arkansas nullification plan was an amendment to the state constitution declaring the *Brown* decisions to be unconstitutional. Despite the stand by the official of the state, the school officials of Little Rock moved ahead to desegregate. Nine Black school children were selected to attend Central High School beginning in September 1957. On the day before school opened, the governor of Arkansas, without notifying the school officials, assigned units of the Arkansas National Guard to Central High School and declared the school "off limits" to Black children. When the nine Black students attempted to enter school the next day, the national guardsmen, on the governor's orders, prevented them from entering. Each day for the next three weeks, this performance was repeated. At the end of this time, President Eisenhower sent regular federal troops to Central High, and the students at last were admitted. Federal troops remained at the school for the rest of the school year, a year filled with tension and disturbances. The threat to law and order was so serious that by the end of the year the school board begged the courts to permit them to discontinue their plan.

These events raised some very serious questions. Could a state nullify a Supreme Court decision? Who was responsible for the chaos surrounding the effort to desegregate Central High? Should a desegregation effort be discontinued or delayed if it threatens to lead to racial conflict? The Court's rulings on these questions were unanimous.

No state can nullify a decision of the Court. The state of Arkansas, therefore, acted unconstitutionally in preventing Black children from attending Central High. Moreover, the actions of the governor and other officials of the state of Arkansas had been, in the Court's view, largely responsible for all of the turmoil surrounding the desegregation effort. The governor's actions had increased opposition to the desegregation plan and encouraged people to oppose it. Finally, the Court refused to accept the idea that desegregation attempts should be carried out only if no violence or disorder were threatened. The importance of public peace was recognized, of course, but Black children's rights to an equal education were not to be sacrificed in the name of law and order.

Despite the Court's unwavering stand on the correctness of its *Brown* decisions, it could not arrest the declining faith of many Black people in the law's unaided power to bring about a swift end to the many forms of racial discrimination they faced (of which school segregation was only one). The conviction grew that some further action was needed, something bolder and more direct. The "something bolder" produced a dramatic shift in the direction of the civil rights movement.

Key Ideas

1. Elkins argued that the slave system of the United States was more oppressive than the slave systems of Latin America, and that this system dehumanized the slaves, creating in them extreme subservience. Fogel and Engerman applied economic analyses to the study of slavery and determined that in a plantation economy, slaves were valuable property and, as such, were well treated and rewarded for productive work. The debate over the nature of the system of slavery and its impact continues. Scholars agree, however, that slavery had a profound effect on both slaves and owners and on the relations between Blacks and Whites throughout the United States.

2. Blacks resisted slavery in many ways, including escape, suicide, armed rebellion, legal challenges, and covert acts. Their resistance was met with harsh repression and even greater restrictions. Slaves often coped with slavery by submitting to its authority and finding other ways to preserve their families, culture, and identity.

3. After the Civil War, southern Whites were unwilling to accept the freed slaves as equals. The Whites developed a number of techniques to intimidate Blacks and to restore control of the southern governments to the Whites, including the organization of the Ku Klux Klan, a system of tenant farming, and voter restrictions. There was not, however, an extensive system of laws regulating the relations of the races. The Jim Crow system of legal segregation developed mainly between 1890 and 1920—during the period of the second immigrant stream. The development of the Jim Crow system was strongly encouraged by the Supreme Court's "separate but equal" doctrine in *Plessy v. Ferguson.*

4. As the Jim Crow system developed, African Americans organized to resist it and to claim their full rights as American citizens. The NAACP, the leading protest organization for decades to come, demanded full equality for Blacks and launched a legal battle to attain it.

5. Like Mexican Americans, African Americans appear to be, in some ways, a colonized and, in some ways, an immigrant minority. Up to the time of World War I, the Black experience was so marked by oppression that the colonial model seems quite apt. The great northward "immigration" of World War I, however, laid a foundation for arguing that African Americans resemble a recent immigrant group.

6. World War I was followed by numerous episodes of Black–White conflict and the emergence of a mass secessionist movement under the leadership of Marcus Garvey. Garvey emphasized race pride, self-help, and the unity of Black people everywhere.

7. During the Great Depression, African Americans began to adopt the boycott and other weapons of the labor movement as tactics to force equal treatment. The NAACP began to focus on the issue of school segregation.

8. The years during and immediately after World War II produced changes in federal policies aimed at reducing discrimination in employment, in schools, and in the armed forces. In 1948, President Truman ended all segregation in the military.

9. In 1954, the Supreme Court ruled in *Brown v. Topeka Board of Education* (*Brown I*) that public school segregation was unconstitutional and was psychologically damaging to the segregated children. In a second *Brown* decision *(Brown II)*, the Court declared that desegregation should occur with "all deliberate speed." Despite the Supreme Court's rulings, many state and local governments continued to resist desegregation.

# Key Terms

Atlanta Compromise   A term referring to a speech given by Booker T. Washington designed to assure White people that Blacks were ready to accept their inferior status in the political arena. Washington, a former slave, believed that Blacks should concentrate on agricultural and vocational training, areas where they could earn livings separate from Whites.

Black Renaissance   The emergence in the 1920s of Black writers, artists, and intellectuals in Harlem that resulted in an upsurge of Black pride and cultural expression.

Emancipation Proclamation   The freeing of all slaves in the "states in rebellion against the United States" that was brought about when President Lincoln signed the Emancipation Proclamation on January 1, 1863.

freed Blacks   Free persons of color who purchased their freedom, gained freedom as a result of the Emancipation Proclamation, or earned freedom for service in American wars. Some were freed by conscientious owners in their wills or in their lifetimes. Many freed Blacks were skilled artisans, farmers, or laborers. About half of the freed Blacks lived in slave states.

Freedmen's Bureau   A government agency set up in the War Department after the Civil War to issue provisions, clothing and fuel to "refugees and freedmen and their wives and children." The bureau was also authorized to rent land, negotiate labor contracts, provide medical care, and set up schools for the freed slaves.

Jim Crow   A term used to refer to laws that were passed, but then repealed, in the 1860s that segregated Whites and Blacks in public transportation, housing, work sites, restaurants, theaters, hospitals, playgrounds, public parks, swimming pools, organized sports, churches, cemeteries, and schools, to mention a few examples. In the 1890s these laws were revived and became even more extensive, supported by the *Plessy v. Ferguson* decision that laid down the "separate but equal" rule for the justification of segregation.

Ku Klux Klan   A secret organization of Whites formed in 1866. The KKK used intimidation, lynchings, and other terrorist tactics to keep Blacks in a subordinate position to Whites.

nationalism   Devotion to one's own nation that can include a desire for or advocacy of national independence. The Garvey movement promoted Black nationalism that emphasized Black cultural expression, Black pride, and exclusiveness.

Niagara Movement   The "radical" position led by W.E.B. Du Bois that criticized Booker T. Washington's position of submission and economic development. Du Bois emphasized agitation and complaint to gain the full acceptance of African Americans as first-class citizens. The Black leaders of the Niagara Movement joined with White liberals to form the NAACP.

Notes

1. Many freed Blacks participated actively in the abolitionist movement and in the Underground Railroad. David Walker, Martin Delany, and Frederick Douglass issued ringing denunciations of slavery. Sojourner Truth and Harriet Tubman also became famous as abolitionists. Tubman, "The Moses of Her People," is reported to have assisted 200 to 300 slaves to escape (Burner, Fox-Genovese, and Bernhard 1991:402). Perhaps as many as 100,000 slaves fled the South through the Underground Railroad (Franklin and Moss 1988:172).

2. The largest slave insurrection to take place in the United States occurred in Louisiana during 1811 and involved between 300 and 500 slaves. The rebels were engaged by a force of militia and regular troops and were rapidly defeated (Genovese 1974: 592).

3. In 1993 Fogel was awarded a Nobel Prize in Economic Science for his application

of economic theory and quantitative methods to the history of slavery.

4. Martin Delany described the situation in these words: "The slave is more secure than we; he knows who holds the heel upon his bosom—we know not the wretch who may grasp us by the throat" (quoted by Jacobs and Landau 1971:149).

5. The identification of colonization with extreme oppression, whether an actual colonial system is established or not, was explained by Wilson (1972:262) as follows: "Fundamental to the colonial model is the distinction between colonization as a process and colonialism as a social, political and economic system. It is the process of colonization that defines experiences which are common to many non-White people of the world, including Black Americans."

6. The Black Codes resembled the antebellum "Slave Codes," but in some states Blacks now could acquire, own, and sell property; enter into contracts; and be legally married (Jordan and Litwack 1987:378).

7. The name is based on the Greek word for circle (*kyklos;* Franklin and Moss 1988: 226).

8. During the 1830s, Thomas D. Rice, a White performer in blackface, presented a song that referred to Jim Crow. The term became a popular code word for the segregation of Black people (Jordan and Litwack 1987: 397).

9. The rise in European immigration during this period led to both increased racial and ethnic competition for jobs and the organization of labor unions to fight competition. The rise of labor unions increased "the rate of violence against blacks" (Olzak 1989:1328).

10. Jobs and higher wages "pulled" from the North; but the boll weevil's destruction of the cotton industry and increased violence against Blacks also "pushed" from the South (Tolnay and Beck 1992:104).

11. Another important organization, the National Urban League (1911), was an interracial effort to help Blacks who were migrating to the cities to find jobs and get established. The Urban League always has been considered more conservative than "protest" organizations like the NAACP.

African Americans

Protest and Social Change

The Million Man March, organized in 1995 by Minister Farrakhan, was a peaceful protest to emphasize family values and counter the negative images of Blacks that dominated media presentations. The March again raised the issue of Black nationalism.

Power concedes nothing without demand.

—Frederick Douglass

When you are forever fighting a degenerating sense of "nobodiness"—
then you will understand why we find it difficult to wait.

—Martin Luther King, Jr.

. . . while individual empowerment is key, only collective action
can effectively generate lasting social transformation
of political and economic institutions.

—Patricia Hill Collins

The Rise of Direct Action

Soon after the *Brown* decisions, there was a sharp increase in unemployment among African Americans. This decline in the economic circumstances of African Americans, coming as it did on the heels of great judicial victories, was particularly galling and decreased their faith in the value of changing laws. A more specific event, however, precipitated a new phase in the effort to ensure the civil rights of African Americans. On December 1, 1955, in Montgomery, Alabama, Mrs. Rosa Parks refused to yield her bus seat to a White person and was arrested. As the news of Mrs. Parks arrest spread, Black people in the city, at the urging of NAACP leader E. D. Nixon, began a boycott of the local buses. In less than a week, nearly all of the more than 40,000 Black citizens of Montgomery had rallied around the dynamic young pastor of the Dexter Avenue Baptist Church, Martin Luther King, Jr., in a massive boycott of the buses. At first, the boycott was intended to last only one day, but various incidents of harassment and intimidation by Whites led to a decision to continue the boycott indefinitely. This decision was followed by further acts of intimidation. For instance, on January 30, 1956, Martin Luther King's home was bombed; two days later, the home of E. D. Nixon also was bombed. On February 22, twenty-four Black ministers and fifty-five others were arrested for nonviolent protesting (King 1971a:297).

The confrontation between Blacks and Whites over segregation in Montgomery ended in the desegregation of the buses more than a year later. During that time, the bus boycott became a symbol of nonviolent protest throughout the world. Martin Luther King, Jr., became the leading spokesman for the philosophy of nonviolence and the most prominent figure in what rapidly became a new phase of the relations between Whites and Blacks in America. The events in Montgomery contributed to a growing conviction among Black Americans that, in King's (1964:80) words, "privileged groups seldom give up their privileges voluntarily." To promote the philosophy and practices of nonviolent protest, King founded the Southern Christian Leadership Conference (SCLC) in January 1957.

Increasing Militancy

The decade following the Montgomery bus boycott was filled with dramatic developments in American racial relations. Although the legal approach continued to play an
indispensable role, various forms of direct action became far more popular, especially
among young people. A sit-in by college students at a Woolworth's store lunch counter
in Greensboro, North Carolina, in 1960 set off a veritable chain reaction of student sit-
ins throughout the South. These events led rapidly to the formation of yet another organization devoted to nonviolent direct action, the Student Nonviolent Coordinating
Committee (SNCC). Although the members of the new organization accepted the philosophy of nonviolence espoused by CORE and SCLC and were clearly inspired by Martin Luther King, Jr., they believed their goals could not be pursued vigorously enough
within any of the existing organizations. The many lines of cleavage within the Black
community became prominent once again. The older organizations, such as the once
"radical" NAACP, were now regarded by many as "too conservative." Simultaneously,
however, the older organizations were being changed by the "radical" tactics of direct
action.[1]

Amidst charges of excessive "conservatism" and "radicalism," nearly all of the main
Black protest groups adopted some combination of legal and direct-action methods,
though the new organizations were in the vanguard (McAdam 1982; Morris 1984). In
this process, the entire civil rights movement became more militant. The battle cry
"Freedom Now!" gradually gained acceptance even among many Black "conservatives."
The NAACP, for example, sponsored many demonstrations during this period; and
CORE pioneered still another new protest tactic by conducting an interracial "Freedom
Ride" on a bus headed for New Orleans. Here, for the first time, White people joined in
the protest. This ride ended when the bus was fire-bombed in Alabama, but many
others were to follow (Burns 1963:55). The representatives of the different protest organizations found that whatever their legal rights were supposed to be, sit-ins, kneel-ins,
lie-ins, boycotts, picket lines, and freedom rides might each be met by mob violence,
tear gas, police dogs, arrests, jail terms, and, in some cases, by death.

The tempo of direct action increased during the spring of 1963. As the number of
demonstrations in the South reached a new high, the nonviolent technique was frequently used in the North as well. Two protests in 1963 stand out. The first of these took
place in Birmingham, Alabama, which was a symbol of southern White resistance to desegregation. A coalition of Black leaders under the direction of Martin Luther King, Jr.,
joined an ongoing nonviolent protest campaign in Birmingham. The protests began
with well-organized demonstrators going to jail for conducting sit-ins at lunch counters
(King 1964:60). Within a month, thousands of demonstrators, including King, had been
jailed and many others had been physically assaulted by police. Later, protesters were
met by police with clubs, high-pressure water hoses, cattle prods, and dogs. This attack
on unarmed, unresisting men, women, and children aroused enormous national and international support, leading to a truce with Birmingham's business leaders. It was
agreed that lunch counters, rest rooms, and other public places would be desegregated.
The Birmingham protests had demonstrated dramatically that "the theory of nonviolent
direct action was a fact" (King 1964:46).

A second outstanding protest of 1963 was a huge (approximately 250,000 people) March on Washington. Reviving the technique he had pioneered during the early years of World War II, A. Philip Randolph called for a massive protest march on the nation's capital to dramatize the problem of unemployment. The march captured the attention of the entire country. For millions of people, Martin Luther King, Jr.'s famous "I Have a Dream" speech encapsulated the aspirations of the civil rights movement. The march showed that the movement was beginning to look beyond direct-action protest toward a new focus on political action, beyond civil rights to a heightened concern for economic opportunity, and beyond appeals to the conscience of White people to a demand for equality.

The effects of the direct-action protests between 1956 and 1964 were mixed. In most states of the South, the protests had achieved rapid changes in desegregating restaurants, theaters, buses, hotels, and so on. Black men and women increasingly could expect to be served courteously; however, the protests had been less than successful in some states and had done little to bring about changes in segregated schooling, poor housing, and discrimination in law enforcement. Moreover, throughout 1964, instances of White violence increased. For example, three voter-registration workers (James Chaney, Andrew Goodman, and Michael Schwerner) were killed in Mississippi. Members of the KKK were suspected; and in 1967, seven of the suspects were convicted on civil rights charges (Bullard 1991:21–22).

Civil Rights Legislation

The escalation of violence by Whites weakened the allegiance of many Blacks to the philosophy of nonviolent resistance. As the limitations of direct action became apparent, Black leaders began to turn to different directions. The political pressure mounted by the March on Washington was increased through voter registration and "get out the vote" drives. With the strong support of President Johnson, President Kennedy's civil rights program was passed as the Civil Rights Act of 1964. This legislation prohibited discrimination in voting, public accommodations and facilities, schools, courts, and employment; however, official violations of the voting rights section of the law (Title I) continued in the South after the law was passed. In response to these violations, Martin Luther King, Jr. led a nonviolent demonstration in Selma, Alabama; and, shortly thereafter, Congress passed the Voting Rights Act of 1965. This law suspended all literacy tests for voters and permitted the federal government to station poll watchers in all of the states of the South (Osofsky 1968:570–581).

The legislation of 1964 and 1965 marked the end of official segregation in America. Yet something was clearly wrong. The laws had not, in fact, ended discrimination; and, like the direct-action demonstrations that preceded them, they had had little visible effect on conditions in the Black ghettos of the cities. After a decade of notable victories, there still was pervasive unemployment, underemployment, and poverty. Many Black neighborhoods were characterized by high "street" crime, poor health and sanitation, poor housing, inferior schools, poor city services, high divorce and separation rates, low access to "city hall," demeaning and inadequate welfare services, high prices for inferior goods and services, and poor relations with the police. What now was to be done? An answer from the past attained renewed popularity.

Black Power

We mentioned earlier that the *Brown* decisions encouraged most Black Americans to believe the end of school segregation and other forms of inequality was near. We saw, however, that these hopes were soon dampened by the strong evidence—as in Montgomery and Birmingham—that many Whites intended to resist the Court's rulings in every way possible, including the use of violence. The primary reaction among Blacks to the massive resistance of the Whites, as noted earlier, was nonviolent protest. This was not the only reaction, however. Not since the days of Marcus Garvey had so many Black Americans been ready to listen to those who doubted the possibility or desirability of "integration" and who urged, instead, some form of separation. The organization that was best able to capitalize on this renewed interest in a separatist solution was the Lost Nation of Islam (the Black Muslims).

The Black Muslims, as mentioned in Chapter 10, had been led since the mid-1930s by Elijah Muhammad. They had been hard at work during the intervening years but had not attracted many converts; however, during the late 1950s and early 1960s, they attracted many new converts and a great deal of attention from the mass media. A new and dynamic Muslim leader, Malcolm X, was a particularly effective advocate of the Black nationalist philosophy.

Renewed Black Nationalism.   Malcolm X, who substituted an "X" for the surname his grandparents had received from their slave master (Little), became the minister of the large Muslim temple in Harlem. Like his teacher, Elijah Muhammad, Malcolm X emphasized that Black people must organize to regain their self-respect and to assert their collective power. Consequently, he and his followers sought some form of separation from White America. If the U.S. government would not pay the costs of sending Blacks to Africa, then, Malcolm X argued, the United States should set aside some territory within its borders so African Americans could move away from the Whites. Malcolm believed that such a separate territory should be given as payment for the long period during which Black slaves worked without pay to help build America (Malcolm X and Farmer 1971:390).

Malcolm X was very interested in Africa and believed strongly that Black people throughout the world shared a similar destiny. In time, Malcolm and Elijah Muhammad came into conflict over various matters; and in 1964, Malcolm left Elijah's organization to found a rival Muslim group, the Organization of Afro-American Unity. The organization's charter emphasized the right of African Americans to defend themselves against violence in any way necessary (Malcolm X 1971). In addition to this "defensive" use of violence, however, some African Americans began to think in terms of attack. The most militant members of the group began to use the word "revolution" as more than a metaphor.

Violent Protests. The clearest evidence of a shift among some Blacks away from the acceptance of only "defensive" violence and toward the acceptance of "offensive" violence began to appear in 1964. For example, in July an off-duty New York City police lieutenant intervened in a dispute between some Black youths and a White man. When one of the youths attacked with a knife, the officer shot and killed him. Two days later, a rally called by CORE to protest the lynchings of civil rights workers in Mississippi led to a clash with police in which one person was killed. In the following days, a crowd attacked the police with Molotov cocktails, bricks, and bottles in the Harlem and Bedford-Stuyvesant areas of New York; the police responded with gunfire (National Advisory Commission 1968:36). Then, on a hot evening in August 1965, a California motorcycle patrol officer stopped a young Black man for speeding near the Watts area of Los Angeles. After the driver failed a sobriety test, he was arrested. The officer radioed for assistance while a large crowd of people gathered. When the prisoner's brother and mother arrived and began to struggle with the police, they too were arrested. As the police departed, the angry crowd threw stones at the police car (McCone 1968:608).

Rumors that the police had beaten the intoxicated driver, his family, and a pregnant woman spread throughout the area. Later, groups of Black people stoned and overturned some passing automobiles, beat up some White motorists, and harassed the police (National Advisory Commission 1968:37). The next evening, three cars were set on fire, snipers opened fire on the firefighters, and people began burning and looting stores and buildings owned by Whites. The burning, looting, and sniping then spread into the Watts area; and two city blocks on 103rd Street were burned out while firemen were held off by sniper fire (McCone 1968:615). Late in the day, the governor of California ordered nearly 14,000 national guardsmen into the area to restore peace. Burning and looting spread into other parts of southeast Los Angeles, and the fighting between rioters, police, and guardsmen continued for two more days.

The Watts area rioting was the worst in America since the 1943 outbreak in Detroit. Thirty-four people were killed; over 1,000 were injured; and more than 600 buildings were damaged or totally destroyed. The pattern of burning and looting strongly suggested that the Black rioters had intentionally focused their attacks on food, liquor, furniture, clothing, and department stores owned by White people.

The level of Black protest increased during 1966. According to the National Advisory Commission (1968:40), forty-three major and "minor disorders and riots" occurred during that year, including a new outburst in Watts. Two of the major disorders in Chicago and Cleveland involved extensive looting, rock throwing, fire bombing, and shooting at the police. In each case, the disorders and riots were preceded by a history of dissatisfaction among Blacks in regard to police practices, unemployment, inadequate housing, inadequate education, and many other things (National Advisory Commission 1968:143–144); and they were usually precipitated by some seemingly minor incident, frequently involving the police. For example, in Chicago, the rioting commenced after police arrested a Black youth who had illegally opened a fire hydrant in order to cool off with water.

The heightened militancy of many African Americans and their impatience with the rate of social change was dramatized in a speech delivered by Stokely Carmichael (Osofsky, 1968:629–636). Like many Black leaders before him, Carmichael, the chairman of SNCC, urged Black people to "get together" in their own behalf. He rejected the idea that Black Americans could "get ahead" through individual ambition and hard work. What was needed, he said, was "Black Power." The slogan "Black Power" was not completely new; neither were the ideas of race pride and self-help suggested by it; however, the use of this phrase at this particular time took on special significance. The phrase was vague enough to encompass a wide range of perspectives. It symbolized the frustration of many integrationists as well as Black nationalists. In the minds of many White people, though, the slogan was identified primarily with Black revolutionaries and separatist organizations.

The increasing willingness of African Americans, especially the young adults, to demand an immediate end to racial inequalities and to back their demands with violence, if necessary, ushered in still another phase in Black–White relations. Just as the legal approach had been made secondary by the advent of widespread nonviolent protests, the use of violent methods now moved to the fore. As in the earlier shift, organizations, leaders, and methods that had at first seemed "radical" now seemed "conservative" by comparison. The level of violence was escalated again during 1967, with most of the disorders occurring in July.[2]

The violent protests declined after 1968.[3] The most influential Black leaders had never accepted the principles of separation or violent protest. For example, shortly before his assassination on April 4, 1968, Martin Luther King, Jr. (1971b:586), argued that "the time has come for a return to mass nonviolent protest." In his view, nonviolence was more relevant as an effective device than ever before: "Violence is not only morally repugnant, it is pragmatically barren" (King 1968:585). Apparently, most African Americans soon accepted this assessment. By 1973, legal and political approaches to the solution of the problem of racial inequality had once again become the primary weapons of African Americans.

Declining Momentum.   Civil rights activities by African Americans during the 1970s and 1980s were, in Brisbane's (1976:575) words, "calmer, more sober, more conservative." Global economic and political problems during the 1970s thrust such issues as inflation and military spending to the forefront. These changes were joined in the 1980s by a shift to the political right during the administrations of Presidents Ronald Reagan and George Bush. These social and political trends were reflected in a decreased willingness by the dominant group to support the social spending that was needed to maintain the levels reached during the 1960s. Even though many other groups—including women, homosexuals, the elderly, and the physically handicapped—also organized to combat discrimination and gain equal rights, the 1970s and 1980s witnessed a "dramatic loss of momentum" (Tabb 1979:349). The U.S. Commission on Civil Rights (1981a:35) expressed concern that in such matters as school and job desegregation, police protection, voting rights, housing, and affirmative action, the federal government's civil rights enforcement effort was not adequately funded and coordinated. In some cases, according to the Commission (U.S. Commission on Civil Rights 1979a), changes in the laws have "aided and abetted the obstructionists." Numerous court rulings during the 1980s served to restrict the scope of effective minority action against civil rights violations. Even though the Civil Rights Act of 1991 reversed the effects of some rulings of the U.S. Supreme Court concerning discrimination in employment, the fact that the rulings had been made still increased the concern of many African Americans that their civil rights were in jeopardy.

Renewed Visibility of Black–White Conflict

There were numerous other signs in the 1980s that the gains of the 1960s and 1970s were under attack. Various incidents, often involving conflict with police officers, exploded into major urban riots. For instance, in Miami, Florida, three large disturbances took place during the 1980s. In 1980, eighteen people were killed and more than 400 were injured in the Liberty City section; in 1982, two people were killed and more than twenty-five were injured in the Overtown section; and in 1989, six people were injured and thirty buildings were burned, again in Overtown, after a policeman killed an African American motorcyclist (Reinhold 1992:A12). These and many other events were reminders that America's racial problems had not been solved.

These problems returned to national prominence and a higher place on the political agenda in 1991, after an African American man named Rodney King was arrested for traffic violations by four White Los Angeles police officers. The arrest was videotaped covertly by a nearby citizen. The videotape, run repeatedly on national television, showed Mr. King writhing on the ground while being kicked and beaten with batons by the officers. According to press and television accounts, most viewers, White as well as Black, thought that the arrest and beating of Mr. King was a clear case of police brutality; consequently, when the officers were tried more than a year later, the nation was "stunned" (as many newspapers reported) by the acquittal of all four officers on the charge of "assault with a deadly weapon" and of three officers on the charge of an "excessive use of force as a police officer."[4]

Major urban disorders erupted in several American cities, with the largest and most severe rioting of the twentieth century occurring in Los Angeles itself. The violence started in the Florence-Normandie area of South Central Los Angeles and spread southeast into Watts and north into Koreatown. As in the case of the Watts riots in the 1960s, Blacks were prominent among the rioters and non-Blacks were the main targets; but in this case, Hispanics also were prominent among the rioters, and Asians, principally Koreans (but also some Cambodians), were among the targets. City, state, and federal officials called for the rioting to end. Mr. King, in a halting yet eloquent appeal for peace, asked the crucial question: "Can we all get along?" Again, as in the 1960s, thousands of troops were rushed to the scene; and by the end of the first week in May, the explosion was over.[5] Estimates of the deaths and damage vary; but at least fifty-one people were murdered (*New York Times,* May 17 and August 13, 1992), hundreds more were injured, and burning and looting were responsible for millions of dollars in damage. Twenty-seven of the victims of the rioting were African American. Blauner (1996:167) noted that the racial violence after the King verdict "marked the first time since the

1960s that incidents of racial injustice against an African American . . . have seized the entire nation's imagination." Whites were almost as upset about the videotaped beating as Blacks. Almost 86 percent of White Americans disagreed with the jury's decision, were angered by the absence of African Americans from the jury, and did not believe the trial should have been held in the lily-white suburban venue of Simi Valley (Blauner 1996:168).

Whites were much less likely than Blacks, however, to see the arrest of King and the release of the officers as evidence of a larger pattern of racism in the United States. A TIME/CNN poll taken during this period made clear some of the differences between the views of African and White Americans concerning the state of race relations in the United States. Consider the answers to the following questions: "Have prejudice and discrimination against Blacks become more prevalent in recent years?"—54 percent of the Blacks and 31 percent of the Whites answered "yes" (Kramer 1992:41); "Would the verdict [in the King trial] have been different if the police and the man they had beaten had all been White?"—82 percent of the Blacks and 44 percent of the Whites answered "yes" (Lacayo 1992:32); "Which makes you angrier, the verdict or the violence that followed?"—twice as many Blacks as Whites said the verdict made them angrier, whereas almost three times as many Whites as Blacks said the violence made them angrier (Ellis 1992:28); and when asked to give "the reason for the jury's not-guilty verdict," 45 percent of the Blacks and 12 percent of the Whites said "racism" (Church 1992:25). Blauner (1996:169) emphasized that White Americans tend to view racial incidents as aberrations in American life, whereas African Americans believe that racism is a central part of American society.

The O. J. Simpson Trial

Four years after the trial of Rodney King's assailants, another spectacular trial divided the nation largely along racial lines and once again focused attention on racial relations. A popular and wealthy African American former professional football player and movie star, O. J. Simpson, was accused of murdering his former wife, Nicole Brown Simpson, and her friend Ron Goldman. Both Ms. Simpson and Mr. Goldman were White. The trial lasted nine months and was followed on television by millions of viewers throughout the United States and in other countries. Reactions to the trial seemed to be especially shaped by race, and sometimes by gender. Almost every opinion poll taken during the trial showed a gap of about 40 percentage points between the views of Blacks and Whites. Most Whites held fast to the belief that Mr. Simpson was guilty, while most Blacks maintained that he was innocent. The polls suggested that African Americans held a deep suspicion of the police and the criminal justice system. A verdict of "not guilty" was decided by a jury panel of nine Blacks, two Whites, and one Hispanic. Ten jury members were women and two were men.

The jurors, who had been sequestered for longer than any jury panel in California history, deliberated for less than four hours to reach their verdict. The testimony and racial attitudes of a witness for the state, police detective Mark Fuhrman, were key elements in the trial that fanned racial tensions. Detective Fuhrman had been interviewed on tape by an aspiring screen writer interested in urban police departments. In the tapes, which were played in court as evidence, the former detective used the word "nigger" more than three dozen times and talked about police officers who routinely perjured themselves, destroyed evidence, arrested people without probable cause, and beat confessions out of those they arrested. Many Black police officers did not see the attitudes expressed on the tapes as surprising or exceptional. Many White officers were upset by the tapes and said they did not reflect the views of most people in Los Angeles or in the police department.

Reactions to the trial among residents of Los Angeles and elsewhere also split along racial lines. On radio talk shows, Whites claimed the press and Black leaders were blowing the significance of the tapes and the extent of racial prejudice out of proportion. Blacks claimed that the tapes demonstrated the racism that African Americans experience almost daily. Blacks, because of negative experiences with police in their communities, believed that there was a police conspiracy to frame Mr. Simpson. The idea of a police conspiracy seemed bizarre to many Whites; but, as explained by the president of the Los Angeles Urban League, it seemed bizarre only because the police treat the members of the White and Black communities quite differently. Many Blacks view the police as "an occupying force" characterized by brutality and deep-seated racism.

When the verdict "not guilty" was read on October 3, 1995, the *New York Times* reported that 400 African American students at the historically black Morehouse College roared and cheered; Whites who stopped work to watch the jury decision on television responded with disbelief and anger. Both Blacks and Whites felt that the case exacerbated the already simmering ethnic and racial tensions in America, and numerous editorials appeared in newspapers throughout the United States commenting on the racial implications of the trial. Cornel West (1995:15), an African American professor at Harvard, stated that the Simpson verdict represented "the first time in history that a majority Black jury has wielded an apparatus of state power against the will of the nation's white citizenry."

The racial disagreement seen in these incidents (and dramatized in the riots) certainly shows that the long road of change traveled by African and White Americans since 1619 has not yet produced the levels of merger called for by the various ideologies of assimilation. Many African Americans are disappointed, angry, and bitter and do not believe that they yet have achieved equality as citizens. Even the new Black middle class has not overcome fully the barrier of racism. Hochschild (1995:115) attributed the continued elusive racial bias that African Americans face in the United States to "the permanence of racism." In her interviews with Blacks she found that despite the gains made in many areas, successful Blacks still contend with "inhospitable personnel officers, informal social ostracism, excessive penalties for mistakes, exclusion from communication networks, resistance from subordinates, assumptions about cultural and personal inferiority, lower ratings from bosses, and 'ghettoized' assignments."

In 1994, in the largest court case in the history of the public accommodations section of the 1964 Civil Rights Act, Denny's restaurant chain was ordered to pay millions of dollars to Black customers who were discriminated against in its restaurants. Employees testified that they were told to follow what were called "Blackout" policies to keep African American customers to a minimum, including actions taken against military officers, police officers, teachers, and government officials. Whites were seated ahead of Blacks; Blacks were seated in the rear of the restaurant and service to them was slow; Blacks were asked to pay before eating, were required to make minimum purchases, and were even sometimes "locked out" of the restaurants. These policies resulted in service so disrespectful to African Americans that it would be hard to deny racist intent (Kohn 1994).

Just a year earlier, a federal court approved one of the largest financial settlements in a class action race discrimination suit against another restaurant chain, Shoney's. Employees of Shoney's charged that the chain deliberately shunted Blacks into low-paying, low-visibility kitchen jobs, when it hired them at all, and clearly showed a preference for Whites (Smothers 1993:12). In 1994, the U.S. Department of Labor, the federal agency responsible for protecting workers' rights, also settled the largest race discrimination suit ever brought by government workers. African American employees claimed that they had been unfairly dismissed, demoted, or denied promotion in 1981, 1983, and 1984. The Justice Department also reached out-of-court settlements in 1995 with a number of banks accused of showing bias in lending to Blacks. The suit contended, among other things, that banks refused to allow African Americans to clear poor credit histories, an opportunity normally given to Whites. It also maintained that banks required Blacks to meet unnecessarily high standards to qualify for loans and denied Black applicants mortgages at a rate about five times the denial rate of White applicants (Holmes 1995:C1).

Another major discrimination case focused nationwide attention on Texaco, Inc., the fourteenth largest corporation in the United States (Eichenwald 1996). In November 1996, a Texaco executive released secretly recorded tapes of a meeting in which senior Texaco executives planned the destruction of documents requested in a Federal discrimination lawsuit. The tape recordings also showed the executives berating minority employees with racially insulting language. Six Texaco employees had previously sued the company alleging that Texaco fostered a racially hostile environment and systematically discriminated against minority employees in promotions. Newspaper editorials and comments from other minority employees noted that the only thing unusual about the Texaco case was that racism was reported. Although Texaco had anti-discrimination policies, equal opportunity programs, and appropriate channels for filing discrimination complaints in place, the White managers and executives operated by their own, often discriminatory, rules with little corporate oversight. Texaco's chairman and chief executive expressed dismay at the blatant racism captured on the tapes. Faced with threats of a national boycott of Texaco products, the corporation settled the discrimination suit by agreeing to pay damages to employees who claimed discrimination, raise salaries for Black employees, provide diversity training programs, and create an independent task force to oversee the changes. Farley (1996) pointed out that these continuing successful law suits about employment discrimination are indications of persistently unequal opportunities for African Americans in the job market, which result in a growing gap in earnings between Blacks and Whites.

Our sketch has shown that African Americans moved slowly and painfully out of slavery to citizenship and out of rigid segregation and the denial of equal rights to a legal and official form of equality. But the many evidences that "old-fashioned racism" has been replaced to some extent by "modern racism," and the widespread belief among

African Americans that the gains of the 1960s have been eroded, make the careful analysis of social and economic changes and trends all the more important. We turn, therefore, as we have previously in the cases of the Japanese and Mexican Americans, to the question of the extent to which assimilation has occurred between Black and White Americans.

African American Assimilation

Cultural Assimilation

Each ethnic group we have considered so far has faced the question, "As we adopt American culture, what shall become of our own culture?" We saw that, although there are important group differences in this respect, each group has made an effort to retain, transmit, and elaborate its heritage. The tendency of an ethnic group to attempt to adopt these strategies has been shown to be intimately related, among other things, to whether a group has entered the country voluntarily. As a rule, groups that have come into the United States voluntarily have been more willing to undertake cultural assimilation than have Mexican Americans and American Indians. From this perspective, we should expect that African Americans would have been very resistant to cultural assimilation. Even though they were separated from their homelands, the separation did not arise in any way from a dissatisfaction with life in the old country or the desire to start anew in another land; thus, like Mexican Americans and American Indians, Africans initially did not wish to undertake cultural assimilation. Apparently, however, they had little choice. Those who survived the horrors of being captured, bought, and transported to America were in an extremely poor position to retain, transmit, or elaborate their heritage. The entire system of American slavery was constructed, as noted in Chapters 3 and 10, to strip the slaves of their cultures, to destroy the link between Africans and their past, and to replace their cultures with ways of thinking and acting that were deemed appropriate for slaves.

It has become increasingly accepted that Black Americans succeeded, nevertheless, in constructing a distinctive culture based on their African roots. To illustrate, Levine (1977:6) found that a number of the characteristics of African cultures, such as the high praise given to verbal improvisation, have remained central features of Black American culture. Levine argued that it is a mistake to assume, however, that cultural elements must be unchanged in order to be derived from African traditions. In his view, "Culture is not a fixed condition but a process. . . . The question is not one of survivals but of transformations" (Levine 1977:5). Gutman (1976:212) also believed that some important continuities existed between the lives of the plantation slaves of the early nineteenth century and those of rural Mississippi Blacks in the third decade of the twentieth century.

The Moynihan Report. An incendiary implication of the view that the African heritage was totally destroyed during slavery is that the present culture of African Americans may be a "distorted" or "pathological" version of White American culture. One version of this belief argues that the transmission of such a "distorted" culture from one generation to the next gives rise to many of the problems facing African Americans to-day (e.g., poverty and unemployment, high street crime rates, and teenage pregnancy). The solution to these problems, from this perspective, is for African Americans to give up their "pathological" culture and adopt the standard American culture.

A well-known extension of this argument holds that the "deficiencies" of Black culture may be seen in the "breakdown" of the Black family. Although this view has been common, its direct political impact is generally traced to an explosive document prepared by Daniel P. Moynihan (1965) to help shape the federal government's War on Poverty. This document, commonly called the Moynihan Report, was based on the assumption that "at the heart of the deterioration of the fabric of Negro society is the deterioration of the Negro family" (Moynihan 1965:5). This "deterioration" was judged, in turn, to be the lasting result of the indescribable oppression experienced during slavery. Moynihan (1965:29–45) referred to a "tangle of pathology" in the Black family that resulted in lowered levels of education and school attendance, lowered income, lowered IQs, and high rates of arrest, delinquency, unemployment, and narcotics use. The Moynihan Report called for government action to enhance "the stability and resources of the Negro American family" (Moynihan 1965:48).

Notice that this analysis is consistent with Elkins's view, discussed in Chapter 10, that the modern problems facing African Americans are a lingering consequence of the extraordinary harshness of the slavery period. This perspective, many critics have noted, emphasizes the effects of past racism but ignores or minimizes the effects of present racism. In this way, the modern social problems of African Americans appear to result from *their* inability to take advantage of opportunities rather than from the majority's failure to expand opportunities. Many people think this view "blames the victim."

An Ethnic-Resource Model.

As the results of Moynihan's analysis became generally known, many scholars reacted angrily. Although his description of the severity of the effects of the slavery period was generally accepted, his conclusions concerning their modern effects were not. Critics attacked the idea that the problems of African Americans stemmed from the presumed weaknesses and failures of the Black family. They emphasized, instead, the many strengths, resources, and achievements of the Black family (e.g., Billingsley 1968; Jackson 1991; Rainwater and Yancey 1967; Wilkinson 1978). The work of these scholars supported an **ethnic-resource model** that suggested that cultural strengths have protected the Black family through the devastating effects of slavery and through more recent patterns of Black male unemployment. Cultural resources also have fostered adaptive marriage and family patterns that help families keep functioning through extreme hardships. Hill (1971), for instance, argued that Black families emphasize strong kinship bonds, hard work and ambition, and an equalitarian (rather than a "matriarchal") authority pattern. These elements buffer the deleterious effects of male unemployment and White discrimination. Moreover, accumulating evidence supports the idea that the extended family, rather than the nuclear family, is the proper unit of analysis for studies of the strengths and weaknesses of the Black family (Hatchett, Cochran, and Jackson 1991:49).

Gutman (1976:95–100) provided additional support for the ethnic-resource model. His analysis of slave marriages and families showed that despite the undeniable hardships and restrictions of slavery, Black slaves placed a high value on family stability and responsibility. A subsequent study comparing Black and White family structure in Philadelphia in 1850 and 1880 found that roughly three-quarters of the families in both groups consisted of two parents and their dependent children. The study found also that the households of former slaves were more likely than other Black households to be headed by couples (Furstenberg, Hershberg, and Modell 1985). Slavery surely narrowed the choices available to the slaves; but these downtrodden people were able, nonetheless, to create both an effective culture and a distinctive social identity that were rooted in, and transmitted by, families. These families struggled, with discernible success, to cope with the obstacles to family unity presented by the slave system. The presumption does not seem justified, therefore, that the contemporary problems of African Americans are mainly a reflection of their failure to develop a family pattern during slavery that was capable of transmitting "positive" values from one generation to the next. The net result of many studies has been to cast grave doubts on Moynihan's thesis that there is a "tangle of pathology" within Black families arising from a failure of African Americans to overcome the "disorganizing" effects of the slavery experience.

Contemporary Families.   What, however, has happened to Black and White family organization during the twentieth century? The 1990s have been characterized by heated political debates about "family values" and appropriate family forms that have drawn researchers' attention to changes occurring in American families. Tucker and Mitchell-Kernan (1995) looked at trends in African American family formation and the approaches scholars used in studying them. These researchers found, for instance, that the very rapid changes in Black families in marriage rates, divorce rates, household structure, women's labor force participation, and households with children in poverty are pervasive in families throughout American society. Today there are more births out of wedlock, more divorces, and more non-family living arrangements among *all* ethnic groups.

For example, the proportion of families headed by husbands and wives has declined in recent decades among both Blacks and Whites, although the decline among Blacks has received more notice (Eggebeen and Lichter 1991:803; Farley 1988:24–25). Families headed by husbands and wives comprised about 58 percent of White households and 33 percent of Black households in 1994. As the number of families headed by husbands and wives has declined, the number of children living in one-parent homes has risen. In 1990, 19 percent of all White children, 30 percent of all Hispanic children, and 55 percent of all Black children lived in one-parent homes (U.S. Bureau of the Census, March 1994). Blacks as a group were less likely to marry than either Whites or Hispanics, but this was not the case fifty years ago.

While these changes in family organization leave us still with the problem of attempting to understand the relative contributions of culture and living conditions in bringing them about, they do not, taken alone, support the view that Black family life is a "distorted" variant of White family life. In the view of most contemporary scholars of family life, Black Americans have for a very long time been in the process of constructing a resilient new culture based on their experiences in the past and in the present. They have responded in adaptive ways to economic and social changes beyond their control and in doing so have maintained a strong sense of cultural identity. We thus encounter again the process of ethnogenesis discussed in Chapter 4. Cultural assimilation involves more than the acceptance of new cultural elements and the rejection of old ones. It includes the creation of new elements of culture.[6]

The "Million Man March."

Two weeks after the O. J. Simpson verdict, African Americans used a public march with the theme of unity and the responsibility of Black men to their community to call attention to the needs of the Black family and to focus attention on Black pride and Black culture. The march was organized by Minister Louis Farrakhan, the controversial leader of the Nation of Islam. Some epithets used in media commentaries about the march denounced Farrakhan as a "Booker T. Washington conservative," "a Marcus Garvey black nationalist," an "anti-Semite," a "race-baiter," a "sexist," and a "homophobe." Some prominent Black leaders and organizations were unwilling to endorse or participate in the demonstration because of Mr. Farrakhan's role.

Others claimed that the media were trying to shift the focus from problems in the Black community to White anxiety and emphasized that the demonstration was about concerns much bigger than Mr. Farrakhan. The National Urban League president described the peaceful protest as the "largest family-values rally in the history of America." The march was seen by many as a way to counter the overwhelmingly negative images of Blacks, particularly Black males, that dominate the media. Attracting between 400,000 and 1 million Black males to Washington, D.C., and exceeding the turnout at the March on Washington in 1963, the Million Man March was said to celebrate the majority of Black men who work hard, support their families, and contribute to their communities. Glenn Loury, a conservative Black economist, claimed that the majority of Blacks are part of the middle and working classes, but that the 10 percent who are poor and have multiple problems have come to represent the entire Black community.[7]

Minister Farrakhan, one of the last speakers at the all-day rally, delivered a lengthy speech concerning inspiration, White supremacy, a conspiracy against Blacks in White America, and the need for Black nationalism. He criticized the dominant group for giving too little attention to the problems of Black teenagers in trouble, double-digit unemployment rates among Black workers, and Black families that are falling apart because they do not have adequate incomes. Additionally, he called for Blacks to practice "bootstrap capitalism." The appeal by Blacks to Blacks, with no clear role for White people, called for the regeneration of the Black family, Black pride, and strong African American role models.

The march was an acknowledgment of the reality of Black culture and the view that its development is a positive thing. The participants also clearly wished, however, to be an integral part of mainstream America—to have good jobs, better incomes, and strong families. As is true for many African Americans, the marchers were committed to both Black culture and mainstream culture—an option we have referred to as cultural assimilation by addition. Indeed, many scholars have suggested that Blacks and Whites of the same social class levels are more alike than different in their values, behavior, and family organization (e.g., Gordon 1964:173; Wilson 1980:140). We conclude, therefore, that although African Americans are not identical to middle-class Anglo Americans in culture, their level of cultural assimilation is high.

Secondary Structural Assimilation

There can be no doubt that since emancipation African Americans have moved in many important ways toward the goal of full secondary assimilation; however, it is equally clear that a number of gaps still exist between the levels of Whites and Blacks in such significant matters as jobs, income, education, and housing. Moreover, as we shall see, if contemporary trends continue, the differences in these areas will not disappear soon.

Occupations.   Whites, of course, always have been more heavily concentrated than Blacks in the higher-prestige, better-paying jobs, and they still are. For example, although the proportion of Black males in professional and managerial jobs increased almost sixfold between 1940 and 1980 (Farley and Allen 1987:264), their proportion in those top jobs was still lower than among White males in 1994.[8] The pattern among Black and White females was similar. Despite a more than threefold increase in professional jobs and a more than fivefold increase in jobs as proprietors, managers, and officials, Black women in 1980 had not reached the levels of White women in 1940, and they were less likely to be employed as professionals than White women or White men (U.S. Bureau of the Census, 1994). By 1994, the percentage of Black women in professional and managerial jobs had risen further but was still below that of White women in similar jobs (20.1 versus 31.1 percent). Two other points are of particular interest here. One is a dramatic change in the proportion of Black women working in domestic service. In 1940, 60 percent of the employed Black women were household workers. By 1984, only 5.9 percent of the employed Black women held such jobs. In the 1980s, the percentages of primary professional occupations held by Blacks of both sexes were teacher (9.7) and nurse (7.5) (Butler 1996:140).

The overall occupational distribution of Blacks has become more similar to that of Whites. Between 1940 and 1980, the index of occupational dissimilarity for Black and White males fell from 43 to 24, showing a large movement in the direction of occupational assimilation (Farley and Allen 1987:265).[9] This movement was not uniform within the various regions of the country, however. Studies based on a different measure of occupational assimilation showed that occupational inequality *increased* in the South during the 1940s and 1950s, but that, as Blacks moved out of the South, there were real improvements in employment opportunities during the 1970s (Burr, Galle, and Fossett 1991; Fossett, Galle, and Burr 1989). Cohn and Fossett (1995) suggested that variations in racial employment inequality can be attributed to factors such as regional differences in economic growth, size of the major firms doing the hiring, differing employer practices, and labor union strength.

Although the occupational "upgrading" revealed by these statistics is encouraging for those who favor secondary assimilation as a goal, five additional considerations are in order. First, since Blacks are more likely than Whites to occupy the lower positions of pay and prestige within each occupational category, occupational assimilation probably would still be incomplete even if the index of occupational dissimilarity were zero. Second, on the basis of detailed analyses of occupational data, Farley and Allen (1987: 270–274) found that the rate at which Blacks were moving into high-prestige jobs during the 1970s slowed during the 1980s. Third, rapid technological and economic changes, such as increasing automation and the transfer of unskilled jobs to other countries, are permanently displacing Black workers who are concentrated in the secondary labor market (Bowman 1991:159; Wilhelm 1983). Fourth, the basic reading and math skills of young Black male workers in the 1990s were not, on average, as well matched to changing patterns in the demand for labor as were the basic skills of young Whites who had the same years of schooling and lived in the same regions (Ferguson 1996:77). Finally, the apparent reductions in occupational inequality cited before are based on figures for Blacks who are a part of the employed labor force; but large numbers of Blacks are unemployed, underemployed, or are employed at substandard wages.

For most of the years between 1955 and 1975, the unemployment rate for Black males was roughly twice as high as for Whites; and after 1975, the gap widened. In 1994, approximately 13 percent of the Black population sixteen years and older was unemployed compared to 5.7 percent of the White population of the same age. Throughout this time, unemployment among Black teenagers was exceptionally high (Farley and Allen 1987:214, 238). Research suggests that since 1940 the economic status of older Black workers stabilized relative to Whites but that of younger workers deteriorated in the late 1980s and the 1990s (Cancio, Evans, and Maume 1996:551–554; Ferguson 1996: 78). Thus, although Black males are now more likely to get jobs that previously were "reserved" for Whites, they still are much less likely to get a job at all.

Incomes.   There has been a definite increase in Black incomes since the 1950s, both in dollars and in purchasing power, but there still are large gaps between the incomes of Blacks and Whites. Overall, the median incomes of Black families increased more rapidly during the 1980s than the median income of White families, but the overall gap between the two groups changed little during the decade (Barringer 1992:A1). In 1989, Black families received an average of 62 cents for each dollar White families received. In 1994, African American men working full-time, year-round earned a median income about 72 percent as high as non-Hispanic White men, and African American women earned a median income about 85 percent as high as non-Hispanic White women (U.S. Bureau of the Census, Department of Commerce NEWS, June 1996).[10]

These comparisons, taken together, suggest real increases in the incomes of African Americans but only a modest movement toward equality with Whites. Perhaps even more revealing is a comparison of the total average wealth (as opposed to annual incomes) of Black and White Americans. U.S. Bureau of the Census figures released in 1990 showed that the estimated median net worth of Black American households was about one-tenth that of White households ($4,169 versus $43,279; O'Hare, Pollard, Mann, and Kent 1991:30). Oliver and Shapiro (1995) argued that systemic economic barriers—such as historically low wages, discrimination in institutions, limited access to capital, the rise of suburbs, and the growth of inner-city ghettos—have impaired the ability of Blacks to accumulate wealth over the generations and have contributed significantly to Black and White inequality.

As shown in our comparisons of Mexican American and Anglo incomes in Chapter 9, the general figures we have presented conceal many specific differences of importance. For instance, women typically have lower incomes than men, and since a higher percentage of Black families are headed by women, a higher percentage of Black families are poor. To illustrate, the median family income of Black two-parent households in 1989 was about 3.3 times as high as the median for Black female-headed households ($31,757 versus $9,590; O'Hare, Pollard, Mann, and Kent 1991:20). Also, as in the case of the Mexican American–Anglo comparison, some of the differences in per capita incomes between Blacks and Whites is due to the higher educational levels of Whites. Once again, we see (as in Chapter 9) that to estimate the income "costs" of discrimination against a minority group, it is necessary to "match" the groups being compared in many important respects.

Through an approach of this type, Farley and Allen (1987:354) showed that in 1985, even when the employed workers of the groups were matched in several pertinent ways, there still was a substantial difference in earnings between Black and White males (over $3,000) that may have been the result of discrimination. This difference, moreover, represented the reversal of a trend toward greater similarity between the earnings of Black and White males that had been underway for four decades (Smith and Welch 1986); therefore, for Black men at least, it would appear that the effect of discrimination on earnings increased during the early 1980s. The results of the analysis for women, however, contained a surprise. To begin with, employed Black women earned an average of about $650 *more* in 1980 and about $800 more in 1985 than did White women; and had the Black women been identical to White women in the respects considered in this study, then the gaps *in favor* of Black women would have increased to around $1,100 in 1985; but as Hacker (1992:96) observed in a similar type of study, "The comparative status of women warrants only a muted cheer" because women of both races are underpaid. For Blacks of both sexes, however, educational gains (especially at the college level) appear to make a substantial difference in the incomes they receive (Smith and Welch 1978, 1986; Farley and Allen 1987:347). Because of the close relationship of education and income, estimates of Black progress in the area of income usually focus on changes in the level of education and on changes in patterns of schooling (e.g., desegregation). The following section looks at educational attainments of African Americans.

Education.   In *An American Dilemma*, Myrdal saw education as a solution to America's race problem. Education represented a vehicle for combating racist beliefs as well as a means of improving the material conditions of Blacks. Prior to emancipation, the vast majority of Blacks were given no formal schooling; consequently, changes in the level of education among African Americans since the Reconstruction period have been enormous. In 1870, 80 percent of African Americans were illiterate; in the same year, illiteracy among Whites stood at 12 percent. By 1970, these levels had fallen to approximately 4 percent of all Blacks over fourteen years old and to less than 1 percent for Whites of the same age group (Goff 1976:422). Race differences in illiteracy rates in the 1980s were negligible, even though the definition of literacy involved more complex functional literacy skills compared to the earlier measures, which were usually determined by the ability to sign one's name (Allen and Jewell 1996:174).

The absolute gains in years of school completed since the 1940s have been much greater for Blacks than for Whites. By the 1960s, racial differences in school enrollment were basically nonexistent (Allen and Jewell 1996:174); and, by 1990, 88 percent of

Blacks between five and twenty years of age were enrolled in school, compared to 89 percent of Whites in this age group. In 1992, there was no substantial difference between Blacks and Whites in the median number of years of school completed.

Students who drop out of high school face a more difficult road to success than their peers who finish high school or college. The school dropout rate is highest among students living in low-income families; and, as a consequence of poverty, a larger, but statistically insignificant, proportion of Blacks than Whites leave school before the completion of high school (McMillen, Kaufman, Whitener 1994:5–6). Overall, however, within low-, middle-, and high-income groups, there were few differences between the high school dropout rates of Whites and Blacks during the 1980s and early 1990s (McMillen, Kaufman, Whitener 1994:31).

This review of educational progress demonstrates that in terms of illiteracy, school enrollment, and dropping out of school, Blacks have achieved near parity with Whites. The findings show that the educational patterns of African and White Americans are moving in the direction of complete educational assimilation. These findings do not show, however, that the overall educational gap between Blacks and Whites has closed or will soon close. For instance, even though in 1994 the percentage of those who had completed only high school was slightly higher among Blacks than Whites (36.2 versus 34.5), and students from the two groups went on to college in equal proportions (17.5 percent), a substantially higher percentage of the White students graduated from college (15.1 versus 9.5); and, proportionally, more than twice as many Whites as Blacks obtained an advanced degree (7.9 versus 3.4) (U.S. Bureau of the Census 1995:158). Overall, the gap between the two groups in the percentage of those completing college doubled from 5 percent in 1960 to 10 percent in 1994.[11]

As in the case of income gains, Black progress in education, though real, is a part of a general increase within American society. Such an increase within a given group may or may not keep pace with that of the total population. As we have seen, even when a group's level is rising, the absolute differences between groups may actually widen. Also, the educational increases for African Americans do not necessarily pay off in comparable salaries. According to a 1993 Census Bureau report (Ross 1993), higher education translated into greater earning power for both Blacks and Whites; but Whites gained more.

Educational levels, of course, reveal little concerning educational quality. If, as the *Brown* decisions state, segregated schooling is damaging to those who are set apart, then the continuation of segregated schools reduces the quality of education for Blacks. From this standpoint, educational assimilation is incomplete as long as the schools are segregated or classrooms within desegregated schools remain segregated. Although a substantial amount of school desegregation occurred between 1968 and 1973, primarily because of court-ordered busing, many urban schools remained segregated despite court-mandated desegregation plans or voluntary actions. Although many minority students and White students benefited from desegregation remedies, the gains often came with high economic, educational, and personal costs—especially for Black and Hispanic children from low-income families who attended inner-city public schools (Heise 1996).

Residential Segregation.   The national trend is toward less segregation in many cities, but the historical development of metropolitan areas and local conditions within them affect the patterns. In some areas of the South, for example, housing patterns still reflect the effects of slavery and the plantation economy. In the antebellum South, the slaves and their families commonly lived in the backyards of the White masters (Taeuber and Taeuber 1969:48). Although Whites typically enjoyed superior dwellings, Blacks and Whites were found side-by-side in various parts of the cities (Farley and Allen 1987: 136–137); consequently, the level of residential segregation at that time was typically less than it is in most parts of the United States today. Even when the Jim Crow system of deliberate, legal segregation came into being between 1890 and 1920, the southern pattern of interracial housing was not much affected. In the "Southern Plan" of segregation (Pettigrew 1975:36), it was unnecessary to force Blacks into racially separate geographical areas. Both tradition and the Jim Crow system created such a vast social distance between the races that residential closeness did not threaten the respective social "places" of the two races. As African Americans began to stream out of the South during World War I, however, they entered northern states in which they were, in most respects, legally equal to Whites. Certain facts of northern life, nevertheless, prevented Blacks from dispersing throughout all parts of the cities.

There was, first of all, an economic barrier. Like the European immigrants before them, most Blacks could afford to live only in the least expensive areas of the cities. But also of great importance, as noted in Chapter 10, was that Black people faced an enormous amount of legal and extralegal housing discrimination. Even when African Americans had the money to afford housing outside of the ghettos, they usually were unable to purchase it (Jaynes and Williams 1989:145).[12]

Comprehensive, detailed studies of trends in housing segregation in the United States prior to 1940 are unavailable. Some studies of selected cities, however, suggest that residential segregation increased gradually from emancipation to World War I and then accelerated sharply until 1930 (Taeuber and Taeuber 1969:43–55). Using housing information published by the U.S. Bureau of the Census, Taeuber and Taeuber (1969: 32–41) calculated residential segregation indexes (indexes of dissimilarity) for 109 American cities during 1947–1960 and for 207 cities in 1960. Their analysis established two important points. First, the average level of residential segregation of Blacks and Whites in American cities by 1940 was very high in every region of the country. Second, although there was a slight decline in residential segregation between 1940 and 1960 in most of the 109 cities that were studied, the declines were usually small, and the patterns within the cities varied. For instance, some cities had an increase in residential segregation during one or both of the two decades studied.

What has happened to residential segregation in U.S. cities since 1960? Blacks have continued to move into the central cities, whereas Whites have continued to form suburban rings around them. This pattern has raised some questions about whether analyses of residential segregation should focus on metropolitan areas rather than on central cities and also has led to conflicting conclusions about the direction of residential segregation. Although some studies have found that during some periods the level of African American residential segregation has declined little or has remained about the same (Massey and Denton 1993:83; Van Valey, Roof, and Wilcox 1977:842), a number of other studies have shown that the efforts to reduce segregation in some American cities and metropolitan areas with large Black populations have been effective (Farley and Allen 1987:140–146; Farley and Frey 1994; Harrison and Weinberg 1992). Farley and Allen, for instance, have shown that among the twenty-five central cities with the largest Black populations, all but two (Philadelphia and Cleveland) experienced some decline in Black–White residential segregation between 1970 and 1980. Overall, declines occurred during the decade in twenty of the twenty-five cities. In a similar study of all metropolitan areas in the United States using 1990 data, Harrison and Weinberg (1992) found decreases in the residential segregation of Blacks in most of the metropolitan areas.[13] The declines were substantial in eighteen large areas, most of which were in Florida and Texas. During the entire period from 1960 to 1990, the average level of residential segregation of Blacks in American cities declined from a segregation index of about eighty-six to an index between sixty-four and sixty-nine, depending on the study.[14]

Farley and Frey (1994:32–33) found that, although segregation varied widely among cities, the segregation of Blacks remained much greater than that of Hispanics and Asians. The average segregation score in 1990 for Blacks was 20 points above the average score for Hispanics or Asians. Farley and Frey (1994) also identified four practices that exacerbated segregation: (1) mortgage lending policies were discriminatory; (2) Blacks who sought housing in White areas faced intimidation and violence; (3) suburbs developed strategies for keeping Blacks out, such as zoning laws, real estate agents who dealt only with Whites, and intimidation by the local police; and (4) federally sponsored public housing encouraged segregation.

The persistence of residential segregation has led to legal battles similar to those that have occurred in the effort to desegregate schools, jobs, voting, public accommodations, and other social arenas. For example, agreements among homeowners to sell their homes only to members of certain groups have been declared illegal,[15] rules requiring segregation in federally funded housing have been removed, and open-housing laws have been passed. And, in 1968, Congress passed the Fair Housing Act barring "racial discrimination on the part of any parties involved in the sale, rental, or financing of most housing units" (Farley and Allen 1987:139).[16]

It is clear that in the 1980s and 1990s, income and educational gains made by African Americans since World War II have not been translated commensurately into residential assimilation (Hwang, Murdock, Parpia, and Hamm 1985). High-status Blacks are much more likely than high-status Whites to live in "poorer, more dilapidated areas" that are "characterized by higher rates of poverty, dependency, crime, and mortality" (Massey, Condran, and Denton 1987:29). Many affluent Black families also choose to live in expensive all-Black suburbs (Dent 1992; O'Hare, Pollard, Mann, and Kent 1991:31). Massey and Hajnal (1995:539) proposed that segregation patterns in the United States have consistently evolved to minimize White–Black contacts, with only the level of segregation changing over time. They concluded that racial segregation in the United States resembles the apartheid system that previously existed in the Union of South Africa. In the United States, Blacks have been forced into segregated suburbs and channeled into segregated cities through institutionalized discrimination in the real estate and banking industries, racially biased public policies, and persistent White prejudice (Massey and Denton 1993). Farley and Frey (1994:33) noted that while racial attitudes have changed, with most Whites endorsing the *principle* of equal opportunities for Blacks in the housing market, Whites, nevertheless, were uncomfortable when numerous Blacks moved into their neighborhoods; and they were reluctant to move into predominantly Black neighborhoods.

In a study of Los Angeles, California, Bobo and Zubrinsky (1996) found, in a survey of the attitudes of Whites, Asians, Blacks, and Hispanics, that stereotypes of Blacks and Hispanics as being unintelligent, preferring welfare, and being hard to get along with were most consistently important among White respondents. For Whites, sharing residential areas with any subordinate group, but especially with Blacks, brought the threat of a loss of relative status advantages. The researchers concluded that Black–White separation was likely to continue, even in a diverse city like Los Angeles, because Whites viewed desegregation as undermining their superior status.

Our consideration of changes in occupations, incomes, educational levels, and housing patterns suggests that, on average, African Americans have been moving slowly during recent decades toward the patterns found among Whites, though there are significant differences in the experiences of males and females in these respects, and the movement toward assimilation was halted or slowed during the 1970s and 1980s. When compared to an ideal of complete secondary assimilation, all of the changes we have discussed are small. For this reason, most observers appear to agree with Farley (1988:24) that, although gains among Blacks "are widespread," Blacks "will not soon attain parity with whites."

Primary Structural Assimilation

The gains previously discussed show that Black–White relations in the United States are changing as the social and historical contexts of racial relations change, individuals' attitudes change, and younger people replace the older generation who experienced legal segregation. Many interactions between Blacks and Whites that were once infrequent, and often illegal, now occur with little notice (e.g., swimming, dancing, eating together, dating, mixed schools, churches, public transportation, and sports teams). Between 1964 and 1974, researchers at the University of Michigan's Institute for Social Research (1975:4) found an increase in contacts between Blacks and Whites in neighborhoods and on the job as well as in schools. The Michigan studies reported that the proportion of Whites who had no Black friends declined from about 80 percent in 1964 to about 60 percent ten years later. According to research compiled by the Committee on the Status of African Americans (Jaynes and Williams 1989), Blacks and Whites share a substantial consensus, in the abstract, on the broad goal of a desegregated and equalitarian society. Nearly 100 percent of Blacks surveyed in studies of racial attitudes endorsed the principles of school desegregation and free residential choice; they also reported that race would not be a deciding factor in their voting patterns. However, for Whites, these principles of equality are endorsed less when social contact is close, of long duration, frequent, and involves significant numbers of African Americans (Jaynes and Williams 1989:129–130). The committee concluded that race still matters greatly in attitudes and behaviors in the United States. There remains a reluctance on the part of Whites to live in racially mixed neighborhoods as Blacks and Whites are treated differently in many situations. There continues to be an awkwardness in interracial, interpersonal relationships. In the midst of closer ties in terms of culture, employment, and incomes, resistance to high levels of primary structural assimilation continues to be high.

For example, Schofield (1995) reported that evidence from a wide variety of situations, ranging from conflicts between youth gangs of different ethnic and racial backgrounds to racial incidents on college campuses, showed that serious problems still exist in intergroup relations. Because of pervasive residential segregation, children often have their first close and extended contacts with those from different racial and ethnic groups in school. Many of those relationships are no longer just between Blacks and Whites. With minority group members becoming an increasingly large proportion of the U.S. population, children in the schools are likely to encounter multifaceted, multiethnic situations. Schofield also emphasized the difference between mere desegregation, which results in a racially mixed environment, and true integration, which refers to positive relations among members of different groups. Schofield (1995:637) noted that because of anxiety and uncertainty about dealing with out-group members, resegregation or clustering in racially homogeneous groups results. As noted in an earlier study by Hallinan and Williams (1989) of over a million high school friendship pairs, only a few hundred cross-race friendships developed. In colleges and universities as well, it is common for Black students to form their own sororities, fraternities, and political organizations. The reasons usually given by Black students for the latter phenomenon is that "such activities make predominantly White campuses more hospitable" (Collison 1988:A39).

In a report on diversity at the University of California at Berkeley (Institute for Social Change 1991), group interviews with students were used to explore primary structural relationships. Black students reported that the environment they encountered on the campus was one in which racial and ethnic segregation was "everywhere" and they perceived subtle and pervasive racism. They felt that students were "categorized," "labeled," and "stereotyped" according to their perceived group identity. Black students coming from predominantly White high schools discovered that they were no longer the "token Black person," burdened with constantly explaining what it was like to be Black. They joined clubs and organizations that celebrated and affirmed their African American identity and culture. However, Black students also experienced new pressure from African Americans to make decisions about friends, social networks, and even who they would sit with at lunch, on the basis of race. Some felt ill at ease in the White community and not really accepted by their own group.

Black students from desegregated urban high schools or from predominantly Black schools had an easier adjustment to racially mixed social groupings. Many Black students were sensitive to their high visibility in mostly White classes at Berkeley and felt that they were the subjects of subtle discrimination by professors, teaching assistants, and other students. Many felt that ethnic and racial politics on the campus forced them to choose "what kind of Black" they were going to be—one who was committed to Anglo conformity, pluralism, or separatism. Many Black students said they associated mostly with other Black students where they were less likely to be rejected or stereotyped (Institute for Social Change 1991:30).

Presumably the changes in legal and social segregation that have occurred since the 1950s should have helped turn many of the increased personal contacts into friendships. In fact, this has happened; but, as shown by the studies cited above, as important as these reported changes are, they are modest in relation to the Anglo conformity ideal of complete primary assimilation.

Marital Assimilation

Interracial marriage—especially of Blacks with Whites—has long been a subject of interest. An understanding of this process, though, has been complicated by laws in many states prohibiting Black–White intermarriage, by differences in record-keeping procedures, and by a trend toward removing racial identifications from marriage records. In 1967, when the Supreme Court ruled that laws prohibiting interracial marriages were unconstitutional, sixteen states still had them. At that time, too, only three states (Hawaii, Michigan, and Nebraska) published official records on interracial marriages (Heer 1966:263). By 1976, the effort to remove racial identifications from marriage records had been successful in seven states and the District of Columbia (Monahan 1976:224). Also, the social practice of designating those with any Black ancestry as Black has meant that the children of interracial marriages are identified only as African American. When those children marry, efforts to determine the number of racial intermarriages are complicated further (McDaniel 1996).

Despite the technical problems created by these conditions, some excellent studies have been conducted.[17] Some of the main findings of these studies are that (1) out-marriages among Blacks have been much less common than out-marriages among other racial and ethnic groups; (2) the rate of Black–White intermarriage went up rapidly during the 1960s and nearly doubled in the 1980s and 1990s; (3) the rate of Black–White intermarriages is higher in the South than in the North, and highest in the West; and (4) the declining pool of Black males who are eligible as marriage partners has resulted in more Black families that are headed by women who have never married and has encouraged those who do marry to marry outside their racial group.

In a study of interracial marriages in Los Angeles during the years 1948–1959, Burma (1963:160) found that Black males were much less likely to marry out than were Japanese, Chinese, Filipino, or Native American males and that Black females were even less likely to marry out than were Black males. Even after all the turmoil and change of the 1960s, Blacks were still found to be the least likely of thirty-five different American racial and ethnic groups to marry out (Gurak and Kritz 1978:38). Lieberson and Waters (1988:173, 176) showed that although Black women seemed less likely to marry within their group than in the past, the probability of in-group marriages is still *very much* higher than among any of the twenty-one other groups included in their analysis. To be more specific, almost 99 percent of Black women in their first marriages had married Black men.

Even though the level of Black out-marriage is still extremely low when compared to other racial and ethnic groups, the rate of change has jumped noticeably since 1960. Monahan (1976) conducted a nationwide survey of Black–White intermarriage and found that the total proportion of mixed marriages rose from 1.4 per one thousand marriages in 1963 to 2.6 in 1970. By 1990, the rate was nearly 4 per one thousand marriages (Wilkerson 1991:A1). Throughout this period, the proportion of Black–White intermarriages was three to four times higher in the North than in the South, though the rate of increase was much faster in the South than in the North, and highest in the West. Altogether, the rates of intermarriage of African Americans and Whites nearly doubled over the years 1980–1996, but such behavior was still relatively rare. Only about 1 percent of African American women and 3 percent of African American men were interracially married (McDaniel 1996).[18]

In their analysis of data from the 1980 census, Lieberson and Waters (1988:176) found that although the first marriages of Black women under the age of twenty-five were still very likely to have been with Black men, the younger women were much more likely to have interracial marriages than older Black women. According to 1980 census data on interracial married couples, about 3 percent of the Black–White interracial couples were marriages of White husbands and Black wives; 10 percent of those interracial marriages were Black husbands and White wives; and 5 percent of the interracial marriages were Black spouses with spouses of backgrounds other than Black or White, such as American Indian, Japanese, or Chinese. Older Blacks were more likely than younger Blacks to wish to maintain their group boundaries and culture and, therefore, to oppose interracial dating. Better-educated Blacks and those with higher family incomes were less likely than other Blacks to oppose interracial dating and interracial marriages (Jaynes and Williams 1989:130).

In 1954, the National Opinion Research Center began asking those who participated in the General Social Survey how they felt about intermarriage.[19] At first only 4 percent of the White population approved of such a possibility. Since that time, responses to the intermarriage question have shown a steady movement up, but there has been less approval for intermarriage than for equity in jobs and for school desegregation. For example, in 1972 two in five Whites interviewed believed that intermarriages between Blacks and Whites should be illegal; this proportion fell to one White in five nearly two decades later (Wilkerson 1991:A1). In 1991, some 66 percent of the Whites polled in the General Social Survey still disapproved of racial intermarriage. A Gallup Poll in 1983 also found that 22 percent of Blacks expressed disapproval of interracial marriages (Schuman, Steeh, and Bobo 1985:75, 145). These considerations all suggest that the color line will be slow to shift (Spickard 1989:341).

Toward Pluralism.   Whether it is their intention or not, African Americans appear to be moving toward the goal of ideal pluralism. They appear simultaneously to be mastering Anglo American culture and developing their own distinctive culture; also their level of secondary assimilation is generally rising. Although Blacks and Whites seem to be coming together in cultural and secondary structural ways, they appear to be remaining largely apart in their private relations. W. E. B. Du Bois emphasized this African American duality or "double consciousness" in his 1903 book, *The Souls of Black Folk*. He wrote, "One ever feels his two-ness,—an American, a Negro; two souls, two thoughts, two unreconciled strivings. . . . He simply wishes to make it possible for a man to be both a Negro and an American, without being cursed and spit upon." The development of African American pluralism must not blind us to the continuing discrimination Blacks face in jobs, incomes, education, and housing. The remaining gaps in these areas give little assurance that the past separation of the races will not continue or deepen. Even contemporary middle-class Blacks "speak again and again of 'living in two worlds'" (McCarroll, McDowell, and Winbush, cited in Lacayo 1989:58). Feagin and Sikes (1994) have shown that, despite all of the legislation designed to prevent discrimination, middle-class African Americans still encounter a substantial degree of discrimination in public places. On the other hand, for those who seek pluralism, there is no assurance either that Black culture will survive the pressures of Anglo conformity or that the degrees of separation will not increase.

African American "Success"

We indicated earlier that in very broad terms a split long has existed between those who favor hereditarian explanations of group differences in worldly (or material) "success" and those who favor environmental answers. In our analysis, though, hereditarian answers have been shown to rest on invalid assumptions concerning races and racial membership; therefore, we have emphasized the split that exists between environmentalists who stress either cultural or structural explanations of differences among ethnic groups (i.e., those who attribute group differences primarily to the different norms, values, and motives of their members as compared to those who attribute group differences to such "material factors" as income differences and the many social forces that help create those differences). We have examined this pair of theoretical preferences in our discussions of the worldly success of the Japanese and Mexican Americans and also in our discussion of the controversy concerning the possible role of the Black family in the analysis of the modern social problems that are most prevalent among African Americans.

We turn now to a broader comparison of various ideas concerning the worldly "success" of African Americans.

Growing African American Affluence

A report by O'Hare, Pollard, Mann, and Kent (1991:29) showed that the number of affluent Blacks—those with yearly incomes of $50,000 or more—has grown substantially since the 1960s. In 1989, nearly one in seven Black families was affluent, compared with one out of every seventeen in 1967. The researchers explained this change as a product of the civil rights legislation that opened up opportunities in education and employment for Blacks and also of the economic expansion that followed the 1981–1983 recession. These middle-class adults are the first generation of African American children to benefit from desegregated schools, expanded higher-education opportunities, and equal employment laws. The children of the 1960s reached middle age in the 1980s and 1990s, the age when increased educational attainment begins to pay off financially. The report showed that the affluent Blacks are well educated (32 percent college graduates), own their own homes (77 percent), are in their prime earning ages (66 percent are age 35–55), are married (79 percent), and live in the suburbs. Like affluent White families, most Black families reach the $50,000-a-year income level by combining earnings from two or more family members. Less than 2 percent of Black single adults have personal incomes that could be considered affluent. Although these figures suggest that economic assimilation is occurring among this group of Black families, we have seen also that, overall, Blacks have lower participation in the labor force, higher unemployment rates, and greater percentages of single-parent households than Whites.

One interesting finding about successful Black women and men concerns tension between them. Black women professionals report that they feel pressure to be less successful because their accomplishments exacerbate White society's emasculation of Black men (Hochschild 1995:109); at the same time Black men complain that there is little in textbooks or the media about Black fathers who are present in their families. There are gender differences, too, in the job market. For example, among Black college faculty, accountants, executives, and middle-class magazine readers, more men report racial discrimination in hiring but more women report racial discrimination in advancement; also while as many Black women as men have professional jobs, well-educated Black men have always earned more than well-educated Black women (Hochschild 1995: 110–112). Wilkinson (1996:297) pointed out, however, that although gender does contribute significantly to social inequality, sex and gender are less potent forces in the lives of African Americans than class or race.

The "Culture of Poverty" Explanation

During the 1960s, the "culture of poverty thesis," attributed initially to anthropologist, Oscar Lewis (1965), became a popular explanation for the persistence of poverty among families in general. The basic idea of the culture of poverty thesis is that poor people develop particular patterns of values and ways of coping with their difficulties and pass these patterns down essentially intact from one generation to the next. Such values and behavior, according to this thesis, prevent poor people from taking school seriously or from working hard when they get a job; the poverty of one generation breeds and ensures the poverty of the next. Unless the poverty cycle is broken, this thesis states, children of such families are destined to learn the same "defective" pattern of behavior exhibited by their elders.

Most of the research conducted to determine whether poor people do, as the culture-of-poverty thesis claims, possess a distinctive culture has not supported this idea.[20] For example, the belief that poor Black males do not take seriously the matter of getting and keeping jobs has been vigorously challenged by Liebow (1967:64–65), who maintained that what looks like a "present orientation" to the middle-class observer is, in fact, a "future orientation." The poor Black worker is no less aware of the future than is his or her middle-class critic; but, Liebow said, these two people are looking at very different futures. The Black worker is facing a future "in which everything is uncertain except the ultimate destruction of his hopes and the eventual realization of his fears" (Liebow 1967:66). Thus, Liebow argued, when a poor Black man squanders a week's pay it is not because he is unconcerned with his future. He does so precisely because he is aware of the future and its dim prospects.

Many critics of the culture of poverty thesis have seen it (along with the Moynihan thesis) as an elaborate way to shift the responsibility for social change away from the White majority and onto the shoulders of the minority, saying something must be wrong with *them*. The implication of this is clear: Black people must relinquish their own culture and become more like White Americans.

An "Underclass"?   Many observers have expressed the fear that the most disadvantaged of the inner-city dwellers, the "hard-core" poor, Whites as well as Blacks, are becoming so separated from the rest of the society that there is a danger they will become a permanent "underclass." Hochschild (1995:250–260) presents strong evidence that, for perhaps the first time in American history, a group of poor Blacks have become so alienated that they threaten the existence of stable communities. She contended that most poor Blacks have continued to pursue the American dream of "success" through legitimate hard work and have rejected succeeding financially through drug sales, gaining concessions through protest and violence, or withdrawing from all effort. But, she warned, there is no reason to expect society's "luck" in these respects to last if the discrepancy between their hopes for success and the realities they face each day continues to grow.

A Selective Mobility Explanation

In 1978, sociologist William J. Wilson wrote a controversial book, *The Declining Significance of Race,* based on the thesis that race as a factor affecting socioeconomic status was diminishing.[21] Stated briefly, the reasoning behind this thesis is as follows: Throughout the long years between the beginnings of African American slavery and the end of World War II, practically all Blacks, professionals as well as the poor, were members of an oppressed lower caste. Under these conditions, Black people's racial affiliation rather than their economic circumstances determined their chances for occupational advancement; therefore, the inequalities between Blacks and Whites were, strictly speaking, *racial* in nature. Since World War II, however, the United States has seen the creation of a significant Black middle class, as discussed earlier, among whom occupational advancement depends more on *class* location than on racial membership. The result is a growing cleavage *within* the Black community in which socioeconomic classes have become more visible (Wilson 1978:2–4; see also Featherman and Hauser 1978:381–382). In short, well-educated Blacks increasingly have opportunities for occupational advancement that are similar to those of Whites, whereas the uneducated members of all groups, including Whites, increasingly descend into a growing population of multiracial poor.

Wilson's conclusion that the life chances of Blacks had more to do with their economic class position than with their day-to-day encounters with Whites angered many scholars and stirred a debate that has not yet been settled.[22] At the time of the publication of *The Declining Significance of Race,* the Association of Black Sociologists (ABS) published a denunciation (*Footnotes,* December 1978:4) of the book and accused Wilson of omitting significant facts "regarding the continuing discrimination against Blacks at all class levels," of misinterpreting some of the facts presented, and of drawing unwarranted conclusions. The ABS members were "outraged over the misinterpretation of the Black experience" and "extremely disturbed over the policy implications" of the book. Wilson, of course, was aware that in such matters as public school education, residential segregation, and full political participation, racial antagonism was still very much alive. He also recognized that older Black workers, due to the historic effects of discrimination, did not earn the same incomes as Whites. His argument, however, was that as younger talented and educated Blacks entered the labor market in competition with Whites, the racial barriers to advancement would be largely eliminated (Wilson 1980:177).

Wilson (1987) expanded his analysis of the ghetto poor[23] in another controversial book, *The Truly Disadvantaged.* He acknowledged that, despite the Great Society programs of the 1960s, the proportion of Black births occurring outside of marriage and the proportion of Black families headed by women had both risen. He also acknowledged that welfare dependency, violent crime, and increased joblessness among Blacks had reached "catastrophic proportions" (Wilson 1987:21). In Wilson's view, problems such as poverty, unemployment, street crime, and teenage pregnancy cannot be explained fully as simple consequences of either culture or discrimination. He stated that explanations must include "societal, demographic, and neighborhood variables," and argued that "the sharp rise of Black female-headed families is directly related to increasing Black male joblessness" (Wilson 1987:30, 105). In a third important book, *When Work Disappears,* Wilson (1996) proposed that many of the problems in the inner-city neighborhoods are fundamentally a consequence of the disappearance of work. Wilson acknowledged that cultural factors do play a role, but he argued that the loss of blue-collar jobs, the relocation of other jobs to the suburbs, the lack of locally available training and education, and the dissolution of government and private organizations that once supplied job information and employment opportunities have had devastating effects on the Black urban poor and their families.

We have seen in this brief summary that many questions concerning the "success" of African Americans are still unanswered. How one interprets these persistent differences in levels of achievement—as a consequence of lesser abilities, biases, an oppositional culture, differences in family income or education, barriers of social class, regional economic changes, or differences in cultural capital—has implications for policies that facilitate assimilation. Some of the evidence reviewed so far shows that in the important areas of occupations, income, and education, racial differences have declined substantially. These findings show that as a group African Americans *are* succeeding in some ways and that the gains *are* significant. But we also saw that in some ways the gaps between the achievements of Blacks and the rest of the population are growing. It is possible, as Wilson contended, that better-educated Blacks have taken advantage of the opportunities created by the civil rights movement and have moved out of the inner cities, leaving behind an increasingly visible group of poor Blacks.

The Entrepreneurial Option

We noted in Chapters 4 and 7 that many minority groups, both within the United States and throughout the world, have reacted to dominant-group hostility by becoming middleman minorities or by developing a secure economic base within an ethnic enclave. We may now wonder: To what extent have Black Americans relied on self-employment as a response to hostility? O'Hare (1992:34) reported that while the number of Black-owned firms was less than 15 per 1,000 population, the comparable figures for some other minorities were as follows: Korean Americans more than 102; Asian Indian Americans about 76; Japanese Americans 66; and Cuban Americans about 63.[24] The figures also showed, however, that the number of Black-owned businesses grew in the years 1972–1987 from over 187,000 to over 424,000 (O'Hare, Pollard, Mann, and Kent 1991: 26). Nevertheless, this mode of adaptation to out-group threat was still comparatively low among African Americans. Why was this true?

Lieberson (1980:381–382) listed several important factors to be considered in comparing the economic success of Asian Americans and African Americans, including a greater opportunity for "Asian groups to occupy special niches," an even higher level of hostility by Whites toward Blacks than Asians, and the higher level of economic competition presented to Whites by Blacks. Portes and Bach (1985:45–48) described various explanations of group differences in business success and concluded, as stated previously, that one way "up" is the development of an ethnic-enclave economy whose component firms function in ways that resemble those at the "center" of the economy rather than those at the "periphery." They agreed with Frazier (1957) that to develop an enclave economy a group must possess "'a tradition of enterprise' based primarily on experience in 'buying and selling'" (Portes and Bach 1985:46). In a comparison of Cuban-owned and Black-owned businesses in Miami, Wilson and Martin (1982:155) found that "the black business community appears to be merely an extension of the periphery economy" while the Cuban community had created an enclave economy.

The question of the business success of African Americans has been analyzed further by Butler (1991, 1996). A major objective of Butler's analysis was to challenge the belief that African Americans do not have a strong tradition of business and self-help. He argued (1) that beginning during the colonial period, a noticeable segment of the African American population followed an entrepreneurial path similar to that of the middleman minorities; (2) that a substantial Black middleman economy was constructed before 1900; but that (3) with the development of the Jim Crow system, segregation forced Black business development to detour from the usual path of middleman groups and to develop, instead, as a **truncated middleman minority** (Butler 1991:143, 228). As the Black entrepreneurs were separated from White consumers, they became dependent on "Protected markets in personal services catering to other Blacks" (Boyd 1991:411). Butler found that African American individuals became entrepreneurs and professionals within the Black community because they were cut off, or truncated, from the main business districts of America as a result of segregation. Racism forced them to do business exclusively within their own group. He argued that the modern-day descendants of Black Americans who engaged in business have inherited a philosophy of life and a way of adapting to extreme hostility resembling that of the descendants of other middleman minorities, and with similar socioeconomic consequences (Butler 1991:258, 314). Yet despite the racism that prevented them from continuing as middlemen, Butler (1996:145) found that there was "really no difference between the offspring of African Americans today whose parents, grandparents, and great-grandparents adjusted to America by self-help and the offspring of other self-help ethnic groups."

An important consequence of this historical pattern, Butler argued, is that African Americans have followed two routes to worldly success in American society, the immigrant model of assimilating into the mainstream and the entrepreneurial route as a truncated middleman minority. The first route to success, described in our discussion of the secondary assimilation of the new Black middle class, resembles what one would expect on the basis of the immigrant model (Butler 1991:242–244). Despite the extremely high levels of discrimination against them, the new arrivals in the northern and southern cities, like many immigrants before them, worked hard to establish themselves in the society's mainstream and to make a place in the world for their children. Many third- and fourth-generation descendants of this group are now "making it in America." The second route to success, in Butler's view, stems from a strong, misunderstood, and underestimated tradition of business enterprise among African Americans. He stated that, with appropriate adjustments for new conditions, the example of the truncated middleman minority may afford a blueprint for adjustment for many of those African Americans who do not wish to follow, or are unable to follow, the immigrant model (Butler 1991:322).[25]

All of the arguments presented concerning the worldly success of African Americans are hotly contested and are of great public importance. As we emphasized previously, positions taken in the public debate over what should be done to promote the assimilation of minority groups are closely connected to competing social policy views. Liberals, generally, stress the role of past and present discrimination and other structural factors in creating and maintaining group differences. Conservatives, on the other hand, focus strongly on the role of cultural differences as important causes of group differences in success. Wilson (1991:1) argued that his approach transcends the "simplistic either/or notions of culture versus social structure" by showing some of the links between these notions. Butler (1991:324), too, argued that his approach "is neither conservative nor liberal" but rather one that encourages African Americans to consider "a path which has been followed for centuries by oppressed and outcast groups."

Regardless of the extent to which increases in the worldly success of African Americans depend on changes in Black culture, on a greater similarity of opportunities, or on "the dynamic interplay between ghetto-specific cultural characteristics and social and economic opportunities" (Wilson 1987:18), it is probable that this issue will continue to animate political debates for some time to come. The disagreement over the question of the causes of African American success remind us that social-scientific theories and evidence frequently suggest certain practical steps that may be taken to solve social problems. It reminds us, too, that the various ideologies of group adjustment lie just beneath the surface of public debate over what should be done regarding the assimilation of minority groups.

In Chapter 12, we will consider the relationship of these issues to the experience of the American Indians.

Key Ideas

1. Massive resistance by Whites to the *Brown* decisions was met by a sharp increase in the use of nonviolent protest tactics by African Americans. Racial confrontations in southern cities such as Little Rock, Montgomery, Greensboro, and Birmingham crumbled the structure of Jim Crow segregation in public places and accommodations and paved the way for the passage of the Civil Rights Act of 1964 and the Voting Rights Act of 1965.

2. The slow pace of social change led many African Americans to shift their protest strategies from nonviolence to "offensive" violence. The years 1967 and 1968 were the peak years of violent protests; but violent outbursts, as well as large peaceful demonstrations, occurred in the 1970s, 1980s, and 1990s as a consequence of continued experiences of racial injustice.

3. A scholarly and public debate continues over the nature of African American culture and its influence on the assimilation process of African Americans. It seems accurate to say that African Americans have developed and possess a distinctive culture of their own but that they, like Mexican Americans, are moving toward an additive form of cultural assimilation.

4. African Americans, especially females, appear to be moving toward secondary assimilation in jobs. There also has been secondary assimilation in incomes, again especially among females; but the trend among males slowed during the 1970s. The evidence on the education gap also is mixed, with the overall trend pointing toward educational assimilation (especially through high school); but there are several indications of slowed change in desegregated schooling because of residential segregation. Very slow change is occurring in the sphere of residential segregation.

5. While the rate of primary and marital assimilation has increased markedly, the total amount of these forms of assimilation is still very low. Therefore the separation of Blacks and Whites (at present rates of change) will remain for a long time to come. The continued primary and marital separation of Whites and Blacks, along with the visible changes in cultural and secondary assimilation, suggests that Blacks are moving toward the goal of cultural pluralism.

6. Although the hereditarian thesis concerning African American achievement is still debated, public policy since the 1950s has been more affected by a disagreement within the ranks of environmentalists. The comparatively high achievement of Japanese Americans in the sphere of secondary assimilation and the comparatively low achievement of Mexican Americans and Blacks in this regard have been interpreted by some to be a consequence of particular values found within their cultures. The culture of poverty thesis maintained that most Blacks possessed and transmitted to their children values that were obstacles to success. Research focusing on cultural resources, rather than deficits, has shown that African American culture has adapted to cope with the devastating effects of slavery and has been a

resilient source of support. Other research has pointed to structural changes in job opportunities, mobility patterns, and majority-group discrimination as continuing, important barriers to minority-group achievement.

7. Business enterprise has been a source of economic advancement for African Americans since before they gained their freedom from slavery. Entrepreneurship is increasing rapidly among African Americans, though this mode of adaptation to out-group threat is still comparatively low. The role of self-help and Black institutions in the lives of African Americans has received renewed scrutiny.

Key Terms

ethnic-resource model   A theoretical perspective that emphasizes the strengths, resources, and achievements fostered by ethnic cultures rather than deficits.

truncated middleman minority   The disruption (or cutting off) of the middleman minority tradition among African Americans by the rise of Jim Crow segregation.

Notes

1. During this period, many new organizations came into being. Jaynes and Williams (1989:186) reported that more than 1,100 organizations were founded between 1965 and 1987.

2. The major disorders involved a combination of four factors: (1) many fires, looting, and reports of sniping; (2) more than two days of violence; (3) large crowds; and (4) the use of National Guard and federal forces along with local law enforcement agencies.

3. Some observers believe the peak was reached later (see, e.g., Feagin and Hahn 1973: 105–106).

4. In a TIME/CNN poll 79 percent of the White and 78 percent of the Black respondents said they expected a verdict of guilty (Church 1992:23). Two of the officers also were acquitted on charges of "filing a false police report" and one was acquitted as an "accessory after the fact to a felony."

5. Disorders in some other places, for example, Las Vegas, Nevada, continued for some time thereafter. According to Johnson (1992:

A10), violence erupted on 16 of the 18 nights following April 30.

6. An excellent illustration of this process is the establishment of the Kwanzaa holiday period by Mavlana Ron Karenga. The seven-day holiday is celebrated each year, beginning on December 26. Each day is devoted to one of the seven cardinal principles of the Black Value System (Monsho 1988).

7. Karen de Witt, "Black Men Say the March in Washington Is About Them, Not Farrakhan" (*New York Times,* October 15, 1995:12).

8. The proportion of Black males in professional and managerial jobs compared to Black females in similar jobs was 14.5 versus 29.3 percent (U.S. Bureau of the Census, 1994).

9. See Chapter 8 for a description of indexes of dissimilarity.

10. See U.S. Bureau of the Census, Department of Commerce 1996, Table 8. *Total Money Income in 1994 of Persons 15 Years Old and Over, by Sex, Region.* These census tables do

not include information about the employment status of the persons included in the median income figures.

11. To illustrate, in 1960, 3.1 percent of the
Black population and 8.1 percent of the White
population had completed college. At that
time, therefore, 5 percent more Whites than
Blacks had completed college. By 1994, even
though the percentage of Blacks who completed college had risen to 12.9, the gap between the groups had increased to 10 percent.
The percentage of Whites completing college
had by then reached 22.9 percent (Bureau of
the Census 1995:157).

12. Do Black Americans prefer to live in
segregated housing? A series of national polls
shows that they do not, and that their preference for desegregated housing is rising (Farley
and Allen 1987:150–155; Jaynes and Williams
1989:143).

13. We thank the authors for sending us a
copy of their report. We also thank Teresa A.
Sullivan for calling the study to our attention.

14. Harrison and Weinberg (1992) reported
the higher figure; Farley and Frey (1994) reported the lower figure. The segregation scores
for Black Americans among 25 of America's
largest metropolitan areas in 1990 ranged from
a low of 44 in Anaheim-Santa Ana to a high
of 89 in Detroit (O'Hare and Usdansky 1992:
7).

15. Such agreements are called restrictive
covenants.

16. Schuman and Bobo (1988:295) found
that some of the opposition to open-housing
laws may reflect a general opposition to federal coercion, but they found also that "personal prejudice against blacks" is an important
element. Bobo and Zubrinsky (1996) found
a general openness to integration among
Whites, but concluded that ongoing patterns
of individual and institutional discrimination
in the housing market still contribute to high
levels of residential segregation.

17. For references to this literature, see
Monahan (1976:223–231); Tucker and Mitchell-Kernan (1995).

18. The female out-marriage rate is higher
for every other racial and ethnic group (Mc-
Daniel 1996). White Americans have very high
rates of ethnic intermarriage, but there is a
strong tendency to select out-group spouses
who are also White.

19. The National Opinion Research Center
and the Gallup Poll both use a series of questions posing hypothetical social settings that
vary in racial composition. Respondents are
asked to indicate whether they would take part
in such settings.

20. See, for example, Jaynes and Williams
(1989:540–544).

21. This argument has appeared in several
different analyses during the past century.
For incisive comments concerning a number
of these, see Wilhelm (1983:117–119) and Boston (1988:1–21).

22. See for example, the debate in *American
Sociological Review* (August 1996). Cancio,
Evans, and Maume, Jr., (1996) analyzed the effect of race on earnings among young workers
who, in Wilson's view, should experience little
discrimination. The study showed that the
proportion of the racial gap in hourly wages
due to discrimination *increased* between 1976
and 1985. The authors rejected Wilson's thesis
and contended that the government's retreat
from anti-discrimination initiatives resulted
in organizational discrimination that contributed to racial inequality in earnings.

23. Wilson (1991:6) adopted the term
"ghetto poor" in an effort to shift attention
away from the debate over the term "underclass" and toward a focus on research issues.

24. The level of self-employment among
non-Hispanic Whites was just over 67.

25. Butler (1996:156) found that many of
the top 100 Black enterprises are quite new; 47
percent were founded in the 1970s and 21 percent in the 1980s. A sizable number of those
enterprises serve the entire business community, not just the Black community. Butler also
pointed out that as these middlemen gain economic stability, they send their children to
college to become professionals and managers.

Native Americans

The First Americans

The desire of Whites for more land led to continuous friction with the Indians and ultimately to the transfer of enormous tracts of land to the Whites. Although many land transactions were conducted in good faith, many involved deception, fraud, and violence.

*We told you a little while ago that we had an uneasiness on our minds,
and we shall now tell you what it is; it is concerning our land.*

—Mohawk speaker, Albany Congress, 1754

The thinking Indian . . . asks that he be treated as an American.

—Society of American Indians

*For the sake of our psychic stability as well as our physical well-being
we must be free men and exercise free choices.*

—Clyde Warrior

*The Indian people are going to remain Indians
for a long time to come.*

—Melvin Thom

They were called "the vanishing Americans." After three centuries of contact with Europeans, the Indians who populated what is now the continental United States had declined in number from at least 2 million to less than one-eighth of that (Snipp 1989: 10, 63). Diseases, bullets, alcoholic beverages, and industrial civilization had taken their appalling toll. Whole tribes, bands, or nations—perhaps fifty altogether—had disappeared (Spicer 1980a:58). Although the extent of the depopulation from the diseases brought to the New World varied considerably among different tribes and locations, McNeill (1976:190) estimated that, overall, more than 90 percent of the Indian population was decimated by epidemic diseases.[1] Deneven concluded in this regard that "the discovery of America was followed by possibly the greatest demographic disaster in the history of the world" (quoted by Snipp 1989:15).

At the time of the American Revolution, the Indian population still may have been large enough for a unified stand by the tribes to have brought the colonization effort to a halt; but the swelling population in Europe created an enormous emigration to America. The developments in machine technology radically altered the terms of the competition between the Americans and the Indians and set the stage for the military conquest of the West during the last half of the nineteenth century. This conquest seemed to spell the end for the Indians as bearers of distinctive cultures. In fact, as stated earlier, many tribes *have* vanished. But by 1996, the government of the United States still recognized 318 tribes in the forty-eight contiguous states (Nagel 1996:14) and 226 Alaskan tribes (NARF 1994), while additional Indian groups sought official recognition. Hence, the American Indians have failed to "vanish" as anticipated. Instead, their population has *increased* rapidly so that today the Indians are one of the fastest growing groups within the United States. Their amazing increase during the twentieth century has produced a population that may be approaching in size the one existing in 1600.

The number of Native Americans increased eightfold from 1900 to 1990, with much of the growth occurring in the decades after 1960. From a low point in 1900 of 237,196, the Native American population grew to 523,591 in 1960 and to 1.88 million in 1990 (Nagel 1996:5). During this time traditional Native American culture, along with Indian popular culture, has thrived. Forty-eight Indian newspapers and newsletters are published by Indian tribes or organizations; and efforts are being made by tribal leaders to restore lost languages by encouraging the use of native languages (Nagel 1996:15, 47). Although many languages have completely disappeared, more than 150 Indian languages are still in use, not counting dialects (Stewart 1977a:501). Moreover, American Indians "were not and have not become a single . . . people justifying a single label . . . as most Americans believe" (Spicer 1980a:59). The tribes represent a great many people with different cultural backgrounds, different historical experiences, and different senses of identity. The tribes have, however, had to make numerous accommodations over time, which we will discuss in this chapter and in Chapter 13.

In Chapters 2 and 3, we examined briefly the relations between some of the coastal tribes and the English during the seventeenth century in order to help explain the origin of the Anglo conformity ideology and to illustrate the scope of its application. Now we enlarge our inquiry to trace in broad outline some of the key events, people, and social processes that help to explain the present circumstances of the diverse people called "Indians."

The English Penetration of the Continent

Decades before the English founded Jamestown and Plymouth, French explorers and fishermen were active along the St. Lawrence waterway and the eastern coast of Canada. The main interest of both the French and the English soon became the valuable pelts the Indians would trade for items such as guns, alcoholic beverages, clothing, and costume jewelry.

The French and Indian War

French fur trappers, explorers, and priests rapidly expanded their alliances with various Indian tribes and extended French claims to the entire Mississippi River Valley and portions of the Gulf Coast. The English at this time were making alliances with Indians such as the Iroquois who could supply pelts either as trappers or as "middlemen" between the English and the tribes still further west (Nash 1974:93, 99).

The relationship between the Iroquois and the English increased England's ability to compete for the western fur trade, but it also had other consequences. The Iroquois, in search of pelts, invaded the lands of rival Indian tribes, some of whom were the trade allies of the French. These invasions led to bloody conflicts among the Indians, to enormous changes in the relative sizes and strengths of various tribes, and to a wide variety of changes in the cultures of all the tribes in contact with the French and English. During most of the next one hundred years, the English depended either on the assistance or the neutrality of some or all of the powerful Five Nations of the Iroquois.[2]

Even though the English traders frequently were "despised and held in great Contempt by the Indians as liars and Persons regarding nothing but their own Gain" (McNickle 1973:38–39), and even though the French government adopted as its official policy the view that interracial mixing was desirable (Nash 1974:104), the English had two advantages of dealing with the Indians: As they offered the Indians higher prices for their furs, their trade goods also were of a higher quality than those the Indians could get from the French.[3] Nevertheless, the sharp business practices of the English traders and land speculators created frictions; and the Iroquois became ever more contemptuous of the English and their culture. For instance, in 1744 in answer to an invitation to send some of their young men to be educated in Virginia, the Iroquois replied, "If the English Gentlemen would send a Dozen or two of their children to Onondaga, the great Council would take care of their Education, bring them up in really what was the best Manner and make men of them" (Nash 1974:260).

The showdown between France and England came in the French and Indian War, which was fought mainly between 1754 and 1761.[4] During the first years of this conflict, the Iroquois were primarily neutral, though the Mohawks sometimes supported the English and the Senecas sometimes supported the French. However, after the English attacked with a large fighting force, the Iroquois threw their full weight to the side of the English (Nash 1974:267–268). When the war ended, an avalanche of new settlers poured into the Ohio Valley.

At this moment, an Ottawa chief named Pontiac and an Indian evangelist called the Delaware Prophet attempted to convince the Indians that they should give up the White man's trade goods, return to the old ways, and create an intertribal military organization to combat the Whites (Josephy 1961:110–112). Pontiac gained the support of many tribes such as the Hurons, Potawatomis, and Chippewas. Starting with a siege of Fort Detroit in May 1763, warriors from many tribes commenced an attack against the English; and as the fighting spread, the frontier was hurled back toward the Atlantic coast. When Pontiac learned that the French, Spanish, and English had signed a treaty in Europe, he sued for peace.[5]

Anglo American–Indian Policies

The Proclamation of 1763

Pontiac's uprising failed to drive the English out of North America, but it did serve as a final argument for those in England who believed the colonies should be required to follow a uniform policy toward the Indians. Such a policy, the Proclamation of 1763, was promulgated by the king. This important proclamation declared that (1) all land west of the crest of the Appalachian mountains was "Indian Country"; (2) any settlers west of the Appalachians who had not acquired a legal title to their land from the Indians must return to the colonies; and (3) all future land purchases from the Indians must be conducted in public meetings attended by representatives of the king (McNickle 1973:43). This act recognized that the government of England was obligated to attempt to control trade between the Indians and the colonists and, in particular, was obligated to prevent the swelling colonial population from invading Indian Country. But there were too many colonists and too few soldiers and Indians. There was no way for the English to prevent the colonists from moving onto Indian lands and taking possession of them by fair means or foul.

The proclamation nevertheless established a pattern that the Continental Congress later adopted. An early note from Congress to the Iroquois during the American Revolution stated, "Brothers! This is a family quarrel between us and Old England. . . . We desire you . . . not join on either side, but keep the hatchet buried deep" (McNickle 1973:49). Then, in 1787, the proclamation's lead was followed further in the famous Northwest Territory Ordinance which promised that, "The utmost good faith shall always be observed toward the Indians; their lands and property shall never be taken from them without their consent: and their property, rights, and liberty, they shall never be invaded or disturbed, unless in just and lawful wars authorized by Congress" (Jackson and Galli 1977:3).

Congress, however, was no more successful in regulating contacts with the Indians than the English had been. George Washington lamented that the frontiersmen, "in defiance of the proclamation of Congress . . . roam over the Country on the Indian side of the Ohio, mark out Lands, Survey, and even settle them. This gives great discontent to the Indians" (Prucha 1962:35).

Enforcing the Treaties

As president, Washington set out to establish "a firm peace" based on the "principles of justice and moderation" (Prucha 1962:41). His main tool was a series of laws (Trade and Intercourse Acts) to enforce the treaties already concluded with the major tribes of the North and South, as well as all future treaties that might be made. The existing treaties with such tribes as the Iroquois, Delawares, Wyandots, Chippewas, Shawnees, and Choctaws were being widely violated. The basic problem was "the presence of . . . tribesmen in the path of aggressive and land-hungry whites" (Prucha 1962:3).

Consider, for example, some of the events following the Greenville Treaty of 1795 through which twelve Indian tribes ceded around 50 million acres of Ohio to the United States. As usual, the Indians received a certain quantity of goods and a promise of future annual payments for their land; and, also as usual, a line was drawn on the map to separate Indian Country from White Country. As the White population in the Ohio Valley grew, however, many traders and settlers tried to gain concessions from the Indians beyond the established frontier line; and, as in the past, one of their major trade offerings to the Indians was liquor. Huge quantities of liquor were given to the Indians in return for their land and other possessions. The effects were felt by the Indians throughout the

Northwest Territory. Josephy (1961:147) stated that "almost overnight large segments of once proud and dignified tribes became demoralized in drunkenness and disease."

A new leader, Tecumseh, and his brother, Tenskwatawa (the Shawnee Prophet), came forward at this time to resume Pontiac's call for the Indians to turn away from the White man's way, reject the trade goods that destroyed their independence, and unite to prevent the Whites from acquiring any more land. In a meeting with Governor (later president) William Henry Harrison, Tecumseh argued: "No tribe has a right to . . . Sell a country! Why not sell the air, the clouds and the great sea, as well as the earth? Did not the Great Spirit make them all for the use of his children?" (Josephy 1961:155).

Harrison flatly rejected Tecumseh's view of landownership and made it clear that he would continue to make treaties and acquire Indian lands.[6] Tecumseh, therefore, continued to meet with the leaders of other tribes to urge them to join him in a pan-Indian uprising against the United States. Although Tecumseh was eloquent, most of the older chiefs were not convinced they should now become the allies of some of their traditional Indian enemies. Many also were receiving annual gifts from the Whites and were reluctant to give these up.

Soon after a battle between Tecumseh's warriors and Harrison's forces on Tippecanoe Creek, the War of 1812 between England and the United States began. Tecumseh threw all of his weight into the conflict on the side of the English. Perhaps if the English won the war, he reasoned, then the rights of the Indians would be respected; but if the United States won, he believed, "it will not be many years before our last place of abode and our last hunting ground will be taken from us, and the remnants of the different tribes . . . will all be driven toward the setting sun" (Josephy 1961:163). The English lost the war; Tecumseh lost his life in battle; and the Indians never again had the active support of a European power against the United States.

Indian Removal

Legal Issues

In 1802, the state of Georgia ceded the western portion of its lands to the United States in return for a promise that the federal government would extinguish the land claims of the Cherokee Indians in Georgia (Hagan 1971:54). To fulfill the agreement, the federal government, through a series of treaties, forced the Cherokees to give up almost 60 million acres of land. This pressure on the Cherokees was particularly ironic because these Indians were making a determined effort to adjust to the Whites' ways and were widely celebrated as one of the most "civilized" of all the tribes. The Cherokees were organized as a loosely federated republic. They had a written constitution, a bicameral legislature, and an appellate judiciary. One of their members, Sequoyah, devised a system based on syllables that permitted the Cherokee language to be written; and this invention led to the spread of literacy among them (Spicer 1980a:84). Nevertheless, in 1828–1829, on the basis of the agreement of 1802, Georgia annexed the Cherokees' land and tried to force upon them the laws of Georgia. The Cherokees protested Georgia's claim to jurisdiction over their tribe in two cases argued before the United States Supreme Court: *Cherokee Nation v. Georgia* (1831) and *Worcester v. Georgia* (1832). The judgments in these cases, with Chief Justice John Marshall speaking for the Court, established the basic principles that have guided the Indian policies of the United States ever since (McNickle 1973:52).

These cases dealt with different aspects of a basic question: Are Indian tribes sovereign nations? The main issue in *Cherokee Nation* was whether an Indian tribe, like other foreign nations, has the constitutional right to bring a court action against a state. The Supreme Court ruled that the Cherokee tribe was not a foreign nation and, therefore, could not sue Georgia. Chief Justice Marshall stated that Indians "are acknowledged to have an unquestionable . . . right to the lands they occupy" but concluded that Indian tribes "may more correctly . . . be denominated domestic dependent nations" (Chaudhuri 1985:24).[7] This ruling, while agreeing that Indian tribes are **sovereign nations,** nevertheless placed limits on their sovereignty.

The main issue in *Worcester* was whether Georgia could pass laws that superseded the laws of the Cherokees. On this score the Court ruled in favor of the Indians. "The Cherokee Nation," Marshall wrote, "is a distinct community, occupying its own territory . . . in which the laws of Georgia can have no force" (Bordewich 1996:46). This decision established the principle that although tribal sovereignty has limits, the remaining sovereignty is great indeed. Tribal powers included the right to make treaties, to be protected from state encroachments, and to enjoy certain basic immunities with respect to the United States (Chaudhuri 1985:23, 26). Taken together, the *Cherokee Nation* and *Worcester* rulings conveyed an ambivalent view of the limits of tribal authority that has continued down to the present.[8]

The Indian Removal Act.   Even though the Cherokees won in the *Worcester* case, they had the bad fortune to do so while Andrew Jackson was president. Jackson favored a policy of forcing the Indians to move west of the Mississippi, and as president he sponsored the Indian Removal Act of 1830. This act was designed to force all of the Indians in the southeastern states to move west of the Mississippi. Jackson ignored the Supreme Court's rulings and made it clear that he would enforce the Indian Removal Act.[9] During the next six years, Jackson concluded ninety-four treaties with the Indians to induce them to move to new homes in Indian Territory (now Oklahoma) in order to make room for White settlers who were eager to move onto Indian lands. All of the usual tactics, including bribery, threats, and misrepresentation, were employed by the Whites to bring these treaties into existence. Even though many of the Indians' White friends saw **removal** as a way to help protect the Indians from the Whites, the Indians no longer believed the government's promises (Lurie 1982:138). When Jackson sent a message saying that the Indians were to receive "an ample district west of the Mississippi River . . . to be guaranteed to the Indian tribes as long as they shall occupy it," the leaders of the Chocktaws replied: "The red people are of the opinion, that in a few years the Americans will also wish to possess the land west of the Mississippi" (McNickle 1973: 72).

The Indians were given no choice. The removal process, which continued into the 1840s, is widely regarded as one of the most dishonorable chapters in American history. Removal shattered the lives of tens of thousands of Indians who owned their own homes, earned their living through farming, and sent their children to school as did their White neighbors. Despite this level of cultural assimilation, they did not receive the protection of the federal government. The Indians felt that the United States had violated its own principles of fairness and justice. One appeal to the conscience of the citizens of the United States read as follows: "Our cause is . . . the cause of liberty and justice. It is based upon your own principles, which we have learned from yourselves; for we have gloried to count your Washington and your Jefferson our great teachers" (Josephy 1961:179).

The Trail of Tears

Faced with the calamity of losing the last of their ancestral grounds, some Indians decided to fight; others sought protection through the courts; but in the end, nearly all of them were moved hundreds of miles along what has become known as "The Trail of Tears."[10] The "Five Civilized Tribes" in the Southeast played the central role in a tragedy that "may well exceed in weight of grief and pathos any other passage in American history" (Mooney, quoted in Van Every 1971:30). After lengthy negotiations, further legal battles, promises of "perpetual" land grants in Indian Territory, and agreed annual payments, four of the Civilized Tribes—the Choctaws, Creeks, Chickasaws, and Cherokees—all agreed to move.[11] The ordeal of removal took about twenty years, during which more than 15,000 people died of famine and disease along the way (Spicer 1980a: 84–86).

The fifth Civilized Tribe—the Seminoles—refused to move. The Seminoles had fought against the United States in the War of 1812 and again in 1818 when Andrew Jackson invaded Florida in a move against the Spanish. The Seminoles were angry over the deceptive practices that had been used in attempting to arrange their removal to the West. Another source of resistance stemmed from the fact that many Black slaves had fled from the United States and were now living among the Seminoles. Consequently, in 1835, after some Seminoles killed an Indian agent and attacked a group of soldiers, the Seminole War erupted. The war lasted nearly seven years, led to the deaths of between 1,500 and 2,000 American soldiers, and cost the United States at least $20 million (Josephy 1968:324).

By the early 1840s, approximately a hundred thousand Indian people had been moved from their homes east of the Mississippi into Indian Territory. While most of these refugees had come from the southeastern portion of the United States, such tribes as the Delawares, Kickapoos, Miamis, Ottawas, Peorias, Potawatomis, Sacs, Foxes, Shawnees, and Wyandots also were removed from their homes in the North and East and sent to Indian Territory. The only large tribes of Indians to remain in the Northeast were members of the Iroquois League; however, even among the Iroquois, elements of the Cayugas, Oneidas, and Senecas were moved to Indian Territory (Spicer 1980a:61).

The great influx of people into Indian Territory created numerous new problems. The United States had pledged to provide rations, weapons, and tools; but these necessities frequently did not arrive or did not arrive in sufficient quantities. The United States had promised protection against the "wild tribes" who already lived in or near Indian

Territory, and this promise also was not kept. The Comanches, Osages, and Pawnees, for example, were outraged that the newcomers were moving into their territory, competing with them for buffalo, and generally interfering with their established ways of living. As the buffalo became more difficult to find, these Plains tribes raided the livestock of the Indian refugees, and the newcomers were forced to defend themselves (Hagan 1971: 85–87).

By the latter part of the 1840s, only scattered fragments of many tribes remained east of the Mississippi River; by this time, wagon trains from the United States were crossing Indian Country headed for Oregon. The soldiers garrisoned in a line of forts running from Canada to Mexico were expected to keep unlicensed traders and travelers out of Indian Country, and to protect the eastern Indians from the Indians of the Plains. After gold was discovered in California, the tribes could not be protected from this westward movement. Finally, it was becoming clear that the idea of drawing a line on the map to give the eastern portion of the country to the Whites and the western portion to the Indians could not work. White traders, hunters, trappers, farmers, ranchers, and miners could not be kept on the eastern side of the frontier line. Nevertheless, many western Indian tribes still fought for control of their homelands. Their resistance has given modern people much of the imagery, romance, legend, and tragedy associated with the saga of "the winning of the West." But behind the saga lies the reality that already had been experienced by the Indians of the East in the previous two hundred years. Treaties with individual tribes were followed by the encroachments of White frontiersmen. The encroachments led to attacks, and the attacks led to retaliation. No matter how valiantly the Indians fought, they were outnumbered and outgunned. In a span of less than four decades, the experience of the western tribes recapitulated that of the eastern tribes.

Plains Wars and Reservations

The Horse–Buffalo Economy

The Plains Indians who faced the forts and frontiersmen of the United States practiced a way of life that has captured the imagination of people throughout the world. Consider the familiar image of the Indian warrior: He is dressed in fringed and beaded buckskins, mounted on a dashing charger, wearing a war bonnet of flowing eagle's feathers. This image, which is frequently held of all Indians, derives principally from the cultures of the Plains tribes, especially those of the Sioux (Dakota or Lakota). Moreover, this complex of traits, also including certain styles of dancing and singing, has been most influential in the popular pan-Indian culture of modern Indian Americans (Wax 1971:149).

This exciting style of life, which has had such a profound influence on non-Indians and Indians alike, began to take shape near the beginning of the eighteenth century when the Indians acquired horses and firearms from the Spanish. Until then, the Plains had not been a very hospitable place to live, so the human population had been small.[12]

As the Indians near the Plains learned the arts of horsemanship, two important cultural changes occurred. First, many tribes began to mold their entire way of life around the use of the horse and the buffalo. Mounted and with guns, the Indians now found the buffalo to be not only a reliable source of food but also a source of materials for housing, clothing, tools, and many other useful articles (Lurie 1982:133). Under these new conditions, many tribes deserted their previous localities to take up a nomadic existence. Some tribes were lured onto the Plains; others were pushed onto the Plains by the "domino effect" of the westward expansion of the French and English colonizers.

Increased Intertribal Warfare.   The competition among the tribes for hunting grounds frequently led to conflict, while the scarcity of horses led to a conflict-filled pattern of raiding and theft. Fighting skill and prowess in war were highly valued as warfare became a central feature of the Plains culture. The young men clamored for opportunities to "count coup"—to touch the living members of hostile tribes. The more numerous and daring the warrior's coup, the higher his social status in the tribe (Hagan 1971: 106).

The development of the horse–buffalo and war complexes is well illustrated by the Arapahos, Blackfeet, Cheyennes, Comanches, and Crows, among others; but no tribes exceeded the Sioux as examples of the new lifestyle. At the end of the seventeenth century, three major divisions of the Lakota-speaking peoples (Teton Sioux, Yankton Sioux, and Santee Sioux) lived in the forests of what is now Minnesota. As the Chippewas, who were allied with the French in the fur trade, moved into the territory, the Lakotas moved westward to invade the lands of tribes such as the Cheyennes, Crows, and Pawnees. Spicer (1980a:92) noted that the Lakotas became the dominant peoples of the northern Plains and the most thoroughly adapted as horse-riding buffalo hunters. Various bands among the Tetons—for example, the Brulés, Oglalas, Miniconjou, and Hunkpapas— were particularly respected for their horsemanship and feared for their fighting abilities.

When the Whites began to cross the Plains, the tribes were "in the very midst of their great cultural fluorescence and were formidable and enthusiastic warriors" (Lurie 1982:139). But the Whites' diseases immediately took a terrible toll. In 1837, the population of the Mandans, one of the few farming tribes of the Plains, fell from around 1,600 to less than 100 (Hagan 1971:94; Wax 1971:32–33). Over a period of years, cholera and smallpox took about one-half of the Crow tribe's 4,000 people (Spicer 1980a:93); and in 1849, the Pawnees lost a fourth of their population to diseases (Hagan 1971:94). These catastrophes were intensified by the rapid depletion of the buffalo. White hunters slaughtered the herds, making it much more difficult for the Indians to maintain a proper diet.

Soon after the signing of the Treaty of Guadalupe Hidalgo, Oregon, New Mexico, Utah, Kansas, and Nebraska were organized as territories, and California was admitted to the Union as the thirty-first state. Each of these steps stimulated traffic across Indian Country, bringing about increasing contacts and conflicts between Indian and White people. To regulate these interactions, the army quickly extended to the western Indians the tried-and-true system of treaties and reservations that had been so successful in dispossessing the Indians of the East. At Fort Laramie a treaty was signed in 1851 in which approximately ten thousand Plains Indians agreed to permit the wagon trains of the

Whites to cross their territory (Brown 1973:68). In return, the United States agreed to make annual payments of food and other supplies and also to provide protection from the White people traveling west. In the same year, the Santee Sioux ceded most of their territory in return for a guaranteed reservation on the Minnesota River (Josephy 1968: 336). Shortly thereafter, several other Plains tribes ceded over 90 percent of their lands and accepted reservations (Hagan 1971:98).

Violations of the Treaties

As had been true in the East, the government failed to prevent violations of the treaties by Whites and to provide the rations and supplies guaranteed to the Indians. These failures led to renewed and expanded conflicts. As a result, the thirty-year period during and following the Civil War was a time of frequent, widespread warfare between Indians and Whites. The events of many of these conflicts were well publicized and dramatized both at the time of their occurrence and subsequently. The names of the Indian war chiefs and their White opponents became well known. One need only mention chiefs such as Red Cloud, Sitting Bull, Gall, Crazy Horse, Spotted Tail, Chief Joseph, Little Crow, Cochise, Geronimo, Little Wolf, and Quanah Parker or White military leaders such as Kit Carson, Philip Sheridan, William Sherman, George Crook, Alfred Terry, O. O. Howard, John Gibbon, and George Custer to be reminded of the blood that was spilled across the West during these years.

The end of the Civil War brought a renewed effort by the Whites to build roads and railroads across Indian Country. To protect caravans passing through the Sioux lands, the federal government attempted to complete a treaty with them that would grant a trainload of presents and an annual payment of supplies thereafter. At the very time the treaty was being negotiated, however, the army sent a regiment of troops into Sioux country to build a chain of forts along the Powder River. The Sioux, led by the Oglala Chief Red Cloud, were enraged by this action and broke off the negotiations. Red Cloud gathered the warriors of the various Sioux tribes and sought the assistance of the Arapahos, Cheyennes, and even his enemies, the Crows. After several months of guerrilla warfare, a small group led by Crazy Horse lured a detachment of soldiers under Captain William Fetterman into a trap. All eighty-one soldiers were slain.

After this battle, called the Fetterman Massacre by the Whites, the U.S. government sent several commissions to meet with Red Cloud and the other Sioux chiefs. Red Cloud refused to meet with the commissions. The Oglala chief demanded that the soldiers be withdrawn from the forts along the Powder River. Finally, in 1868, the forts were abandoned and both sides promised to keep the peace. The Treaty of 1868 established the Great Sioux Reservation, comprising most of what is now North and South Dakota.

The Battle of Little Bighorn. The peace did not last long. White miners violated the Treaty of 1868 by moving into the sacred Black Hills to mine gold. The Sioux were infuriated by this renewed invasion of their land and protested strongly to Washington. The government replied by offering to buy or lease the Black Hills so the gold could be mined. The Indians refused to permit mining on any basis; so the government decided

to dispossess them by force. All of the tribes in the area were ordered to report to the reservation agencies; but large groups of Sioux led by Sitting Bull, Crazy Horse, and their allies refused to report. In addition, numerous "treaty" Indians left their reservations to join the "hostiles"; so in 1876, Generals Crook and Terry and Colonels Gibbon and Custer were ordered into Sioux country to "whip the hostiles" into submission (Brown 1972:367–372; Josephy 1968:340).[13]

On June 25, 1876 Custer marched on a Sioux and Cheyenne encampment. This advance may have been precipitated by Custer's belief that the Indians would flee as soon as they saw the approaching troops. His main concern was to prevent the Indians' escape. The Indians, however, had decided to make a stand and had amassed an army of between 1,000 and 2,500 warriors, depending on whose estimate one accepts.[14] As his Seventh Cavalry units approached the village, Custer divided the cavalrymen into three groups and attacked.[15] Custer's detachment was soon surrounded by warriors led by Crazy Horse, Two Moon, and Gall.[16] Every member of Custer's group was killed, and the remaining two groups of the Seventh Cavalry suffered heavy losses.

The stunning victory of the Indians over the U. S. army on the Little Bighorn River was, in fact, one of the last gasps of a people fighting frantically to preserve their independence. Some of the warriors who helped to destroy Custer's units on the Little Bighorn were survivors of one of Custer's earlier surprise attacks, the slaughter of a group of Southern Cheyennes on the Washita River. Still others were the friends or relatives of Indians who were murdered in a battle referred to as the Sand Creek Massacre—an event described by General Nelson A. Miles as the "foulest and most unjustifiable crime in the annals of America" (Hagan 1971:108).

Such atrocities by White people against Indians did nothing to still the outburst of anger among Whites as the news of "Custer's last stand" spread. The federal government claimed the Indians had violated the Treaty of 1868 and, therefore, must now cede to the Whites all rights to the Black Hills and the Powder River country. The Indians were told that if they did not agree, their rations would be discontinued and they would be sent south to Indian Territory. Without the rations supplied at the agencies, many Indians would starve, and none of them relished the thought of being forced to move far away from their beloved Black Hills. With great reluctance, Red Cloud and Spotted Tail signed the agreement and then were placed under virtual arrest on their reservations in Nebraska.

Gradually, the chiefs of most of the other Sioux tribes signed the new agreement to give up the Black Hills. Sitting Bull, however, had taken his people and fled to Canada. Crazy Horse's people spent the winter of 1876–1877 searching for food and fighting soldiers. When General Crook sent word to Crazy Horse that he could have a reservation in the Powder River country if he would surrender, the great Sioux war chief marched into the Red Cloud Agency in Nebraska to become a reservation Indian (Brown 1972: 290–294).[17]

With the surrender of Crazy Horse and, later in the same year, the surrender of Chief Joseph and his Nez Perces, armed Indian resistance to American dominance in the territory acquired from Mexico had nearly ended. Several other famous confrontations occurred during the next ten years, including an "escape" by the Northern Cheyennes from Indian Territory, the so-called Ute War, and the last-ditch efforts of the Apaches in the Southwest. Irresistibly, however, the forces of the rapidly industrializing American giant stripped away the means whereby an open fight could be sustained. After the buffalo had been slaughtered, the Indian population had declined precipitously, primarily as a result of disease and famine.[18] Most of the surviving Indians had been assigned to reservations and, under military guard, were required to live on them. No further military resistance could be offered. The words of Chief Joseph's widely publicized surrender speech reflected the situation in eloquent, tragic phrases: "Our chiefs are killed. . . . It is cold and we have no blankets. The little children are freezing to death. . . . Hear me, my chiefs. I am tired; my heart is sick and sad. From where the sun now stands, I will fight no more forever" (Josephy 1961:339–340).

From Separatism to Anglo Conformity

We have seen that from the earliest days of the American republic, the primary thrust of the official policy of the federal government embodied the idea that Indians and Whites should be kept apart. This policy was responsible for the sharp distinction that was created between Indian Country and White Country. Ultimately, it also led to the great expansion of the reservation system. Throughout this time, however, many people had doubted the wisdom of separatism and had urged instead that the Indians be assisted to become "civilized"; consequently, a secondary, seemingly contradictory thrust of official policy embodied the idea that the Indians could "be absorbed into American society" if they were given the tools, animals, seeds, and information needed to become farmers (Prucha 1962:214). The Indian Trade and Intercourse Act of 1793 empowered the president to "promote civilization" among "friendly Indians" and to expend $20,000 a year for two years for this purpose (Jackson and Galli 1977:63). Various additional laws continued this policy until 1819, after which time the amount of the annual "civilization fund" was reduced to $10,000; but the payment was then placed on a permanent basis.

The Bureau of Indian Affairs

The actual work of administering these activities relating to the Indians had been entrusted to the Secretary of War in 1789. Secretary John Calhoun, in 1824, created a new agency which he named the Bureau of Indian Affairs (BIA). Among the duties of the head of the bureau was "the administration of the fund for the civilization of the Indians" (Jackson and Galli 1977:43). The work of the BIA commenced immediately, although until Congress approved the plan, the duties assigned to the head of the BIA were still legally the responsibility of the Secretary of War. In the Trade and Intercourse Act of 1834, the BIA was authorized, and the Commissioner of Indian Affairs was placed atop an organization that has exercised "immense power . . . over the lives and property of the Indian people" from that time to this (Deloria 1972:52).[19]

At the bottom of the BIA's hierarchy of authority were the Indian agents and sub-agents. These were the employees who lived on the reservations and were responsible for distributing annuities (either in money or goods) and for carrying out the program to civilize the Indians. As increasing numbers of Indians became dependent on the BIA and its agents, the question of the relationship between the federal government and the Indian tribes grew more perplexing. The idea that the tribes were separate nations and could remain so began to give way to the idea that the Indians were "wards" of the government, and the government was their "guardian." Simultaneously, the idea that no further treaties should be signed with Indian tribes grew in popularity.

The End of Treaty Making

Whether or not new treaties should be signed with the Indians was decided, oddly enough, in the Appropriations Act of 1871. A rider to this act stated that Indian tribes would no longer be recognized as powers "with whom the United States may contract by treaty" (Hertzberg 1971:3–4). All treaties previously established would continue in force, but all new arrangements between the federal government and the tribes would be decided by Congress through legislation rather than by negotiation.

This sweeping change in the legal status of the Indian tribes greatly strengthened the hand of those who thought the government's traditional separatist policy should be discontinued. If Indian tribes were not sovereign nations and could not negotiate treaties, then why should they continue to live on reservations apart from other people? Land speculators and potential settlers wondered why the Indians should continue to occupy more land than they were "using"; political conservatives, forgetting the agreements to pay the Indians for their earlier land cessions, wondered why the government should continue to pay out "doles" to support the Indians; and reformers wondered if the "civilizing" process would not be hastened if the reservations were divided up so each family would have its own specific plot of land. Thus, both greed and humanitarian concern combined in support of legislation to break up the reservations, end the established policy of separatism, and institute a policy of Anglo conformity.

The legislative battle over this issue was heated and prolonged. Critics of the plan to divide the reservations into individual allotments of land argued that it would "despoil the Indians of their lands and . . . make them vagabonds" (McNickle 1973:81). Advocates of the plan, in contrast, argued that the allotment of reservation lands to individuals would help instill in the Indians a pride of ownership, encouraging them to give up their tribal past and adopt the American way of life.

The Dawes Act

The break with the past came in February 1887 with the passage of the General **Allotment** (Dawes) Act. The law provided for surveying the reservations and dividing the land into tracts which then were to be allotted to the members of the tribes in parcels of various sizes. Any land left over after each tribal member had received his or her allotment would be declared "surplus" and could be sold to the United States. The money a tribe might receive for the sale of surplus land would be held in trust by the United States Treasury. The interest from the funds could be used to support activities that would hasten the movement of the tribes toward Anglo conformity. If, after a twenty-five-year trial period, an individual allottee had proven to be capable of managing his or her own affairs, that person could receive a "certificate of competency," a title to his or her land, and citizenship. At this point, presumably, the Indian would have become a well-motivated, self-reliant farmer and, therefore, would be no longer a ward of the federal government (McNickle 1973:82–83). If the plan worked, the tribal life of the Indians would be disrupted, and the individual members of the tribes would be transformed into American citizens.[20]

Did the Indians who received individual parcels of land adopt the White model and become self-sufficient farmers? Generally, they did not. The main effect of the Dawes Act was to transfer most of the plots of land held by individual Indians into the hands of White people. As the opponents of the act had feared, the desire of the Whites for land and the Indians' ignorance of American law led to widespread deceit and fraud in real estate transactions. During the period 1887–1934, the Indians lost over 87 million acres of land—approximately two-thirds of their collective holdings before the passage of the Dawes Act (Jackson and Galli 1977:95). Most of the land that remained to the Indians was arid and barren. It was predominantly land that White people did not want.

Another important effect of the Dawes Act was to increase the power of the BIA and its control over the Indian people. In order to carry out the provisions of the act, the BIA had to hire more people and have them intrude in unprecedented detail into the lives of the Indians. For instance, the BIA was charged with developing membership rolls for the recognized tribes in order to determine who was and was not eligible for government services (Snipp 1989:33). In order for the allottees to farm their lands, for example, irrigation systems sometimes were needed; so the BIA entered into the contracting business. Some allottees were physically unable to farm their lands; so the BIA arranged for the lease of the lands and for the investment of the collected funds. In doing these and many other things, the agents of the BIA exercised decision-making powers that traditionally had been the prerogatives of the chiefs and the tribal councils. Even the rations to which the Indians were entitled could be withheld if BIA agents felt the Indians were not moving satisfactorily toward Anglo conformity.

The Dawes Act was the centerpiece of the general effort to bring the Indians into the mainstream of American society. Recall that this was the early period of the second immigrant stream, with its heightened nativism and renewed emphasis on the importance of the Anglo conformity assimilation of foreign elements within the American population. The Dawes Act strengthened various policies that were designed to force upon the Indians the culture of the dominant group and, at the same time, to destroy their cultures.

Indian Education

The forces that helped move the U.S. government to adopt an Indian policy favoring Anglo conformity were also at work in the field of education. The attempt to "civilize" the Indians had always included educational programs. Schools for this purpose had already been established in colonial times. But as the nineteenth century advanced and the Indians increasingly were confined to reservations, building and operating Indian schools became an important function of the BIA. At first, the BIA established two kinds of reservation schools—day schools and boarding schools. Students who did well in the day schools, which were located near the students' homes, became candidates for "advancement" out of their homes and into the boarding schools. The boarding schools removed Indian children from their families and increased their exposure to the English language and Anglo American ways of thinking and acting. Yet, in time, the conviction grew that something further was needed "to equip the Indians with necessary competencies and to update them to their changed situation in the world" (Jackson and Galli 1977:75). The Indian child, it was argued, needed to be removed not only from the family but from the reservation as well. To accomplish this, the off-reservation boarding school came into existence.

The BIA authorized Richard H. Pratt, an army officer, to convert an abandoned army barracks at Carlisle, Pennsylvania, into a boarding school for Indians. The Carlisle School, thus founded in 1879, definitely was based on the Anglo conformity ideology. Pratt believed the Indians' heritage should be replaced with the skills and attitudes of the larger society; and the best way to do this, he thought, was permanently to remove Indian children from their tribal surroundings (Hertzberg 1971:16–17; Hoxie 1984:54–60). Pratt also developed the "outing system." Under this system, students from Carlisle attended the public schools while living in the homes of selected American families. In this way, each Indian child might be separated not only from his or her family and tribe, but from all other Indians as well.

In the decades following the passage of the Dawes Act, the BIA expanded the off-reservation boarding school system. The curriculum at the off-reservation schools was mainly a mixture of the "three Rs" and a number of vocational arts and crafts. These schools represented an intensive effort to transform Indian children into assimilated citizens of the United States.

The Ghost Dance and Wounded Knee

The attempt to "civilize" the Indians through education was intimately bound up with various programs to Christianize them. Beginning with the early contacts among the English and the Indians, missionary schools were established and supported by various Christian groups. By 1819, the missionary effort was so well established that when Congress appropriated the "civilization fund" the president approved grants of money to some missionary societies to assist in their educational work (Jackson and Galli 1977: 69). The primary effort of the missionary schools was not simply to teach the Indians but to convert them; and to be satisfactorily converted, the Indians were expected to give up all vestiges of their native religious beliefs and practices. This goal of the missionary schools also was adopted by the government-supported schools as a part of their general Anglo conformity policy. Any sign that reservation Indians were not accepting Christianity or, worse yet, were retreating from Christianity, was viewed with suspicion.

The Whites' fear of a resurgence of Indian religious beliefs and practices was revealed by a tragic and infamous episode in the winter of 1890. During the latter part of
the 1880s, a spiritual revival called the Ghost Dance religion swept over the Plains. This
religion, like several others of the time, promised the Indians that by practicing certain
rituals, dances, and songs, they could harness the supernatural power of their ancestors
and thereby cause the White people to vanish from the earth. The dead people of all
Indian tribes would be resurrected, the buffalo would return to the Plains, and the land
would resume its original splendor.

The Messiah of the Ghost Dance religion, Wovoka, was a member of the Paiute
tribe of Nevada. He urged Indians of all tribes to participate in the Ghost Dance, to lead
good lives, and to await peacefully the promised day of the resurrection of the ancestors.
The rituals and ideas of the Ghost Dance combined Christian and indigenous elements.
For example, the Messiah taught that "you must not fight. Do right always" (Brown 1972:
409). At the same time, the Indians wore special Ghost Shirts that many believed to be
bulletproof.

The Ghost Dance reached the Sioux in the fall of 1890 and quickly spread on the
reservations. Ghost dancing rapidly became so common that "almost all other activities
came to a halt" (Brown 1972:409). The strange behavior of the Indians frightened the
Whites. Calls went out for military protection and the arrest of the Ghost Dance leaders.
One of the leaders to be arrested was Sitting Bull, the famous medicine chief of the
Hunkpapa Sioux. Sitting Bull had returned to the United States from Canada almost ten
years earlier, had become a celebrity while touring with "Buffalo Bill" Cody's Wild West
Show, and was now living with his people at the Standing Rock Reservation. Shortly
after the order went out, Sitting Bull was arrested and, in a tragic sequence of events, was
killed by two of the Indian officers who took him into custody.

Another leader to be arrested was a Miniconjou named Big Foot. When the news
of Sitting Bull's death reached Big Foot, he and about 350 others, most of whom were
women and children, fled toward Red Cloud's Pine Ridge Reservation. On the way, he
was apprehended by units of the Seventh Cavalry (Custer's former regiment) and was
ordered to go to an army tent camp at Wounded Knee Creek, South Dakota. The
Indians camped that night at Wounded Knee. The soldiers were deployed all around
the Indian camp, with their big guns placed on high ground overlooking the entire
area. The next morning the army commanders ordered the warriors, most of whom
wore Ghost Shirts, to turn in their guns and other arms. According to some reports,
one young warrior raised his rifle over his head and fired. The reaction of the soldiers
was immediate. A withering blast of rifle fire, soon followed by the shells of the big
guns, cut through the surrounded and practically defenseless Indians (Brown 1972:
413–418). At the end of the "battle," at least 40 percent of the Indians were dead (Spicer
1980a:93).

The death of Sitting Bull and the U.S. army's actions at Wounded Knee snuffed
out the Ghost Dance religion and, with it, the hope of the rebirth of tribal independence. It became clear to the Indians that the Ghost Shirts could not stop bullets. The
carnage at Wounded Knee, which occurred in the year that the frontier officially was
declared closed, has served ever since as a symbol of the appalling quality of European–

Indian relations in the period from 1607 to 1890. For almost three centuries, the White people had encroached upon the Indians' lands and had insisted either that the Indians be driven away or be made over in the image of White people. The Indians' resistance to either of these demands frequently had led to attempts to annihilate them.

Cycling Between Anglo Conformity and Cultural Pluralism

As the twentieth century approached, the policy of Anglo conformity was in full sway. The Indian population had declined to less than 240,000, their lands were being allotted and sold, and many thought the end of the "Indian problem" was in sight; however, one conspicuous legal barrier still prevented the Indians from participating fully in the mainstream. Since few Indians were citizens, they were in legal limbo; they "were prisoners of war when no state of war existed" (McNickle 1973:91). As a show of gratitude to the thousands of Indians who had volunteered to fight in the American armed forces in World War I, Congress passed the Indian Citizenship Act in 1924. Many Indians feared, however, that this was yet another of the Whites' tricks to escape their treaty obligations and detribalize the Indians.

Some Indian voters, nevertheless, soon became involved in political matters. Their activities helped to initiate a thorough analysis of the effects of the federal government's trusteeship of the Indian people. The results of this analysis, known as the Meriam Report, were published in 1928.[21] The report showed in detail that the land allotment policy had failed in its basic purpose. Individual allotments had not aided the Indians to overcome the problems of ignorance, poverty, and disease and to move into the American mainstream. On the contrary, by the time the Meriam Report was undertaken, most of the Indian allottees had lost control of their lands and, in the process, their best chance to become self-sufficient. In the meantime, the tribes that had continued to live on unallotted reservations actually had been fairly successful in giving individuals the responsibility of using specified plots of land for their own support. Paradoxically, the "magic" of individual ownership appeared to be working best among the Indians who owned their lands communally. This difference may have arisen because, unlike the allottees, the individual proprietors of tribal lands could not sell them (Jackson and Galli 1977:99).

The Indian Reorganization Act

The Meriam Report came at a time when many people were calling for a radical change in the government's approach to Indian affairs. This call was answered by the Indian **Reorganization** Act (IRA), or Wheeler-Howard Act, of 1934. By this act, the federal government abandoned the effort to require the Indians to adopt the dominant group's lifestyle and embraced instead a pluralist policy. Generally speaking, the new policy sought to assist (not force) the Indians to "lead self-respecting, organized lives in harmony with their own aims and ideals, as an integral part of American life" (McNickle 1973:93). More specifically, the IRA restored the right of the Indian tribes to govern themselves *provided* they were willing to adopt the American model of representative democracy. The IRA also permitted the Indian tribes to organize themselves as corporate business enterprises.[22]

In addition to stimulating democratic self-government and an active participation in the American business economy, the IRA also aimed to encourage Indians to maintain and develop their identities as Indians. Under the policies of the Dawes Act, all things Indian had been denigrated or suppressed. Indian children in the government schools had not been permitted to wear long hair, to dress in their tribal costumes, to engage in tribal rituals, or to speak their native languages. There was a constant fear that the newly civilized youngsters would "go back to the blanket" (Hertzberg 1971:18). The new policy no longer viewed Indian tribal life as something totally incompatible with contemporary American life. Instead, the Indians were encouraged to develop their languages, renew their skills in arts and crafts, revive and have the opportunity to transmit their ancient rituals and ceremonies, and participate in community life on an equal footing with other Americans.

The reorganization of most of the Indian tribes under the provisions of the IRA did not launch a dramatic increase in their educational level and standard of living; however, the management of Indian affairs definitely took a new direction. Programs were initiated to enable the Indians to recover some of their lost lands. Loan funds were established to help finance a college education for qualified Indian students and to help new Indian corporations to develop and market new products or exploit the reservations' natural resources. More than in any previous period of their lives on the reservations, Indians began to participate in the planning and execution of the various programs that were intended to assist them.

Throughout this period of reform, however, the BIA was still very much in control of reservation life. The Bureau still received the annual appropriations from Congress, of course; and its scope now was expanded to include certain new duties such as assisting the tribes to organize representative governments, some of which appeared to represent the interests of the BIA more than those of their respective tribes. The BIA also continued to play a strong role in the determination of tribal memberships and the administration of justice; consequently, many Indians disliked the IRA and did not approve of the way it was administered. Despite the efforts of many people, a large discrepancy was maintained between the ideals of the IRA and the realities of Indian life.

The "Termination" Policy

The champions of the Anglo conformity policy regained the upper hand during the two administrations of President Eisenhower. In 1953, Congress adopted a resolution, House Concurrent Resolution 108, declaring that the Indians "should be freed from Federal supervision and control" (Bahr, Chadwick, and Day 1972:485). To set the Indians "free," HCR 108 suggested that all laws and treaties then binding the United States to the Indians should be nullified. This new policy, which became known as **"termination,"** seemed to be a direct assault on the idea that the Indians were entitled to payments and services for the land they had ceded to the government through treaties.[23] The Indians viewed this change as another shocking example of a unilateral action by the government to avoid completing its part of the treaty bargains (Svensson 1973:32).[24]

Congress hoped the termination policy would get the government "out of the Indian business" (Spicer 1980b:119). The termination of the services to a tribe could occur only if the tribe were sufficiently assimilated, willing to sever its ties with the federal government, and able to survive economically with local and state help. Few tribes were found to meet these standards.

The termination experience of the Klamath tribe of Oregon illustrates why the policy was so unpopular among Native Americans. The Klamaths, with a tribal membership of around two thousand people, owned nearly 1 million acres of land containing forests valued at approximately $50,000 per person (McNickle 1973:106). The government's plan gave the tribal members, many of whom did not understand the alternatives, no more than three years to decide what to do with their collective wealth. They could either form a corporation to manage their property or they could sell the land and timber and divide the money among the members of the tribe. Either way, the government's trusteeship would be terminated.

The issue was settled by a tribal vote in favor of selling and dividing the money. It was understood by the Klamaths that the federal government would buy their land, establish a national forest, and pay each member of the tribe $43,500. As matters developed, the government disbanded the Klamath Tribal Council and ended the trust relationship but certified only a fraction of the tribe's members as "competent." Ten years later over one-half of the members had not received their payments and continued to be wards of the government. The main result of termination for them was the destruction of tribal government and the disorganization of tribal life (Spicer 1980a:106). This policy, according to a U.S. Senate report, created a high level of personal disorganization among the Klamaths (McNickle 1973:107). It also increased poverty and deepened further the Indians' distrust of the federal government in general and the BIA in particular. The experience of many other tribes that were terminated paralleled that of the Klamaths (Peroff 1981).[25]

By the end of the second Eisenhower administration, it was apparent that the termination policy, as had been true of the earlier allotment policy, would not liberate the Indians to participate fully in the mainstream of American life. Both of these policies sought to end abruptly the special relationship of the Indians to the U.S. government; they served, in fact, only to take away from the Indians the resources they needed to create the very independence the policies tried to enforce.

It is vital to note here that the resistance of the American Indians to the termination policy did not mean they wished to continue forever as dependents of the federal government. Most Indians endorsed the IRA goal of "the ultimate disappearance of any need for government aid or supervision" (McNickle 1973:93), and they surely wished to be free of the interference and regulation of the BIA. But, in addition to the understandable fear that termination would deny them their treaty entitlements, there was the even greater fear that an abrupt end to their special status would mean an end to tribal life and their existence as Indians. The policy of termination did not take into account the strong wish among American Indians to fashion a mode of participating in American society that would not sacrifice their distinctiveness as Indians.

Governmental actions to effect termination had been brought to a standstill by 1961.[26] As the War on Poverty came into being, the termination policy, in Deloria's (1985c:251) words, "simply evaporated." Indians began to participate in various new government programs designed to expand their role in planning and controlling their own destiny. Near the end of the decade, President Johnson affirmed the right of Indians "to remain Indians while exercising their rights as Americans" (McNickle 1973:124); and in 1968, the Indian Civil Rights Act was passed. President Nixon, in 1970, attacked the idea that the federal government had the right to terminate unilaterally its special relationship to American Indians. The goal of national policy, the president said, must be to encourage self-determination among the Indians and "to strengthen the Indian's sense of autonomy without threatening his sense of community" (Jackson and Galli 1977:134). He also called for the renunciation of HCR 108. The intent of this presidential message was enacted into law by Congress in 1975 with the passage of the Indian Self-Determination and Educational Assistance Act. This act established a new relationship between the tribes and the federal government which, Olson and Wilson (1984: 204) stated, represents "the greatest victory for pan-Indian activists in American history." A Federal Acknowledgment Program, under which terminated and unrecognized tribes may apply for federal recognition, was adopted in 1978.

Pan-Indian Responses and Initiatives

Protest Organizations

After the federal government terminated its Anglo conformity policy and returned to the pluralist policy implicit in self-determination, American Indian political organization and activity reached an unprecedented level. Throughout historic times, as we have seen, the basic social unit in Indian life has been the tribe. The Indians generally were not organized at a level above the tribe, and when they were—as in the Powhatan, Wampanoag, and Iroquois Confederations—the organizations were loose. One's loyalty to the tribe still was primary. The Indians, nevertheless, did realize the advantages of acting together in broader groups. The efforts of such men as Metacom, Pontiac, Tecumseh, and Sitting Bull serve to remind us that the idea of organizing to resist the common foe is not new. As noted earlier, however, intertribal enmities and factionalism within the various tribes helped to prevent any of these efforts from achieving lasting success. Gradually, the Indians were divided, defeated, and concentrated on reservations. By the time the Indians' treaty-making powers were revoked in 1871, the federal government had assumed complete control of their lives.

As the last pitiful remnants of the previously proud and self-sufficient tribes were forced onto the reservations, various "friends of the Indians," most of whom represented Christian groups, began to agitate in their behalf. The early 1880s produced a number of actions intended to ameliorate the conditions among the Indians. The Women's National Indian Association was formed to protest the forced removal of the Ponca Indians to Indian Territory. A stinging indictment of the way the United States had treated the Indians, *A Century of Dishonor,* was published by Helen Hunt Jackson. When the Indian Rights Association was formed, a series of annual conferences to coordinate various efforts to assist the Indians also was instituted at Lake Mohonk, New York (Hertzberg 1971:20). Since all of these groups were formed by White people, their ideas, of course, of what would be good for the Indians molded the various programs and projects that were undertaken by them.

Recall that the activities of such well-meaning groups and individuals were partly responsible for the passage of the Dawes Act in 1887. At a time when the question of how to dissolve foreign elements into the main body of American society was becoming ever more pressing and the Anglo conformity ideology was gaining greater strength, the idea that the Indians could best be assimilated by forcing them to abandon their ancient heritages and adopt the culture of the dominant society seemed to many of the White supporters of the Indians to be quite humane and sensible. Few Whites thought to consult the Indians to see what *they* thought or wanted. Nevertheless, the Indians did have opinions and, as mentioned earlier, the Five Civilized Tribes led a lobbying effort to prevent the passage of the Dawes Act, which managed to limit its application for a time.[27]

The Society for American Indians.   The various strategies of the Whites, whether friends or foes, to civilize the Indians gradually helped to create a comparatively large group of Indians who were highly educated in the White fashion. These Indians moved easily between the White and Indian worlds. They also usually had friends and acquaintances in more than a single tribe. Many Indians in this bicultural position believed that their people must recognize that the White-dominated industrial American society would destroy all things Indian unless the Indians joined together, accepted the reality of the changed conditions, and attempted to fashion a new "Indian identity beyond the tribe and within the American social order" (Hertzberg 1971:300). Representatives from this Indian elite came together during the early years of the twentieth century to attempt to devise a plan through which Indians could become full participants in American society. In 1911, on Columbus Day in Columbus, Ohio, an organization was founded exclusively by and for Indians. The Society for American Indians (SAI) adopted a constitution to promote "the advancement of the Indian in enlightenment," "citizenship among Indians," and "the right to oppose any movement which may be detrimental to the race" (Hertzberg 1971:80).

Among the leaders of the new organization were several people who were well known and respected in both the Indian and White worlds. Dr. Charles Eastman (Ohiyesa), a Sioux, learned to read both English and Lakota as a child. He later graduated from Dartmouth and Boston University Medical School and was a physician at the Pine Ridge Reservation at the time of the Wounded Knee Massacre. Dr. Carlos Montezuma (Wassaja), the fiery Apache, worked his way through the University of Illinois and the Chicago Medical College. He practiced medicine at several Indian reservations, at Carlisle, and in Chicago. Dr. Arthur Parker (Gawasowannah), a Seneca, graduated from high school in White Plains, New York, and was educated as a Presbyterian minister and as an anthropologist. He became famous for his studies of the Iroquois. Although the leaders of the SAI shared the stated objectives of the organization, they differed in certain ways that later led to friction among them. Like many other Americans of the period, the SAI leaders spoke in terms of the melting pot metaphor. Their opinions ranged, in fact, between pluralism and Anglo conformity (Hertzberg 1971:39–57, 63, 156, 195).

The active life of the SAI was approximately thirteen years. The organization gradually came to represent two principal goals: the abolition of the BIA and the extension of citizenship to all Indians. The first of these seemed so nearly impossible to many of the members that it became a point of vigorous disagreement. The latter goal, as we have seen, was attained in 1924. The importance of the SAI, however, went beyond its specific accomplishments. The SAI demonstrated that some Indians were interested in organizing to pursue Indian goals within the framework of American society. The idea that Indians could adjust to the dominant society was now seen as a foundation on which to erect intertribal cooperation and to build a pan-Indian identity.

After the decline of the SAI and the passage of the IRA, the impulse to construct a pan-Indian organization at the national level was weakened. As a part of President Franklin Roosevelt's "New Deal," the IRA promised the American Indians a new set of options, including various opportunities to take command of their own tribal affairs. Further organizational efforts seemed unnecessary. The experiences of many Indians during World War II, however, and the gradual rise in congressional opposition to the pluralist philosophy underlying the IRA, led once again to the formation of a national pan-Indian organization.

The National Congress of American Indians (NCAI).

The NCAI was formed in 1944 by a group of World War II veterans. Like the Mexican American and Black veterans of the war, these men were exposed to many different influences as they traveled around the country and abroad. They came to believe that, as citizens of the United States who had risked their lives defending the country, they were entitled to equal treatment and a "fair shake" in economic matters. They were unwilling simply to return to the reservations to live under the authority of the BIA or to be relegated quietly to the slums of the cities. The NCAI wished to promote the interests of all Indians but, simultaneously, to permit each tribe to pursue its own particular objectives within the framework of its agreements with the United States. When the termination policy was initiated, the NCAI was in the forefront of the opposition. They certainly did not like the BIA's interference in their lives, yet they feared that any marked change was likely to make matters worse. The fight against termination, therefore, became a focal point of NCAI activities during the 1950s.[28]

This was a time of intellectual and spiritual ferment among American Indians. Many war veterans and their children were completing high school and entering college in unprecedented numbers (Steiner 1968:31). As had been true a half-century earlier for the men who founded the SAI, these new young intellectuals were uncertain of their place in American society. Were they leaving their tribal lives irrevocably behind to enter the American mainstream? Were they to return to the reservations when their formal education had ended? Or were they to shuttle back-and-forth in a kind of no-man's land?

The New Tribalism

A young Navajo, Herbert Blatchford, and some of his friends at the University of New Mexico invited their parents to visit with them in 1954 to consider their questions. The elders told the students that they should complete their education in White ways and then bring their knowledge back to the reservations (Steiner 1968:33). From this beginning, a small group of American Indian university students commenced to organize and struggle to formulate a new policy in Indian affairs. The new policy they created—variously called the new **tribalism,** tribal nationalism, or Red Power—was given its first full expression in 1961 following a very influential gathering, the American Indian Chicago Conference. As a part of the new policy, the underlying issue of Indian sovereignty has been debated in many court cases relating to tribal land claims, water rights, fishing and hunting rights, religious and burial rights, and contract disputes (*NARF Legal Review* 1991, 1992). In some cases the Indians have won; in other cases they have lost; and many cases are still in the courts.

The Chicago Conference.   The American Indian Chicago Conference, attended by representatives from more than sixty tribes, started as a convention of the "Indian establishment" comprised of influential tribal leaders and noted students of Indian life (Olson and Wilson 1984:158–159). Several uninvited young intellectuals also were there. In addition to Herbert Blatchford, Mel Thom (Paiute), and Clyde Warrior (Ponca), nine others were present. These young people grew increasingly impatient with what they saw as the excessive caution of their elders. They formed a Youth Caucus, began to participate actively in various committee meetings, and finally played a major role in drafting the Declaration of Indian Purpose issued by the conference. Shortly after the conference, the Youth Caucus met again—this time in New Mexico—and established a new pan-Indian organization, the National Indian Youth Council (NIYC). The NIYC, made up mostly of young, urban Indians, became the first of the Indian activist organizations formed during the civil rights era. The group's slogan "For a Greater Indian America" reflected its intertribal and Indian nationalist stance (Nagel 1996:129).

The Declaration of Indian Purpose stressed the Indians' "right of sovereignty," their agreement with Chief Justice Marshall's view that treaties with Indian tribes are binding, their determination to maintain their identity, and their need for technical assistance to regain "the adjustment they enjoyed as the original possessors of their native land" (Bahr, Chadwick, and Day 1972:485–486). These points represented a broad base of agreement between the members of the older NCAI and the newer NIYC. The two organizations diverged, however, on the matter of tactics. The NIYC wished to become more active in pressing Indians' claims; but the older leaders opposed any direct confrontation, such as a sit-in, because such behavior was "un-Indian." They did not consider American Indians to be just another minority group demanding to be treated like all other Americans. The younger leaders, however, considered their fight to be in some ways a part of the larger fight between the dominant society and all other oppressed groups; and they argued that, along with the other non-White groups, "Indians must exercise their rights" (Steiner 1968:304).

Fish-ins.   In 1964, the young militants got their first chance to apply their ideas. The Supreme Court of the State of Washington nullified eleven federal treaties that had guaranteed the fishing rights of the Indians in that state. The Makah tribe, which included Bruce Wilkie, a founder of the NIYC, called upon the NIYC to organize a protest concerning the loss of these fishing rights. The NIYC's president, Mel Thom, agreed to lead a nonviolent protest action.

At first the conservative leaders of the twenty-six tribes in Washington did not favor a protest. They feared that by violating the court's order they might go to jail, which is "undignified" and not "the Indian way." Nevertheless, in March 1964, several hundred Indians representing different tribes gathered for a fish-in on the Quillayute River. The fish-in idea spread rapidly. American Indians from all over the United States rushed to the Northwest to support the Washington State tribes. The idea also was elaborated. There were "Treaty Treks," "Canoe Treks," and war dances to protest restrictions on Indian fishing rights. The fish-ins were the precursors of the national Red Power movement, and the legal issues protested in fish-ins continued into the 1990s in court battles. In addition to forcing an eventual legal victory for Native American fishing rights, the fish-in movement provided a training ground for Red Power activists in other parts of the United States. The movement also taught the Indian activists that an alliance of tribal and pan-Indian organizations and collective action could be quite powerful in redressing grievances (Nagel 1996:162).

The next several years were marked by a sharp increase in organized Indian actions to protest various conditions or violations of civil rights. Most of these actions were conventional, nondisruptive efforts to improve the lives of American Indians; however, the number of actions involving direct nonviolent confrontations increased dramatically. For example, in 1969, a group of 89 young Indians, identifying themselves as "Indians of all Tribes,"[29] seized Alcatraz Island in an effort to "hold on to the old ways" (*Indians of All Tribes* 1971:200; James 1986:230). They took this action on the basis of a federal law that gave the Indians the right to reclaim lands that were no longer being used. The number of protesters on the island ranged from 1,000 to the 15 that federal marshals removed in June of 1971. Although the demonstration did not achieve the avowed purposes of establishing title and a pan-Indian cultural center, the occupation of Alcatraz did succeed "in dramatizing the Native American demand for self-determination, tribal lands, and tribal identities" (Olson and Wilson 1984:170). Many Indians saw the occupation of Alcatraz and the steps that followed as a major turning point in awakening Indian ethnic pride and restoring dignity to a people who had been depicted as powerless and subjugated victims of history (Nagel 1996:133).

The American Indian Movement.   Propelled by the events at Alcatraz, the American Indian Movement (AIM) was established in Minneapolis, Minnesota, in 1970. This militant new body quickly grew into a national organization that argued for Indian sovereignty, insisted on the protection of the Indians' treaty rights, and challenged the validity of the tribal governments formed under the IRA (Bonney 1977:215). AIM's first major action, organized in 1972 in cooperation with some other Indian groups, was a protest march in Washington, D.C., called "The Trail of Broken Treaties." This protest climaxed with a six-day seizure and occupation of the BIA's offices (Olson and Wilson

1984:171). Then, in 1973, to protest violations of the Sioux Treaty of 1868, AIM members led by Russell Means and Dennis Banks seized Wounded Knee village on the Pine Ridge Reservation. The occupation of Wounded Knee, which lasted for seventy days, led to an armed face-off that attracted widespread media attention. The occupation ended when federal officials agreed to send a team of investigators to discuss the problem of broken treaties (Kifner 1979; Olson and Wilson 1984:172–174).[30] In the next few years there were several long- and short-term occupations. Many of these occurred on reservations and involved tribal factions associated with AIM or urban tribal members (Bonney 1977:215–217). Throughout the 1980s and into the 1990s, AIM remained a force in American Indian activism, organizing and participating in protests over land and grazing rights, the rights of tribes to sell cigarettes without state or federal taxes, and over athletic team Indian mascots, gestures, logos, and slogans. Although the tradition of active protest fostered by AIM has remained a salient force in the struggle for Indian civil rights, many of the AIM leaders either have been repressed by local and federal law enforcement agencies or their proposals have been incorporated into official policies. The result has been less direct-action protest and more attention to legal action.

Games of Chance.   An illustration of the jurisdictional conflicts between particular Indian tribes and outside legal entities concerns the operation of games of chance. During the past two decades, Indians increasingly turned to **gaming** as a source of income (*Americans Before Columbus* 1992:3); and as matters developed, by 1994 there were more than 160 tribes throughout the country with gambling businesses that were generating an estimated 6 billion dollars per year (Bordewich 1996:108). The gaming industry, thus, has become a very important source of money and jobs on many Indian reservations and has been referred to as "the new buffalo economy."

A conflict developed when federal legislation, the Indian Gaming Regulatory Act, stated that certain types of gambling could be offered on the Indian reservations only if they were legal in the state outside of the reservation; details were to be worked out with the state government. One of the difficulties the Indians faced was that in many instances the state officials were unwilling to grant the permission that was needed to operate specific games; and matters grew worse after new federal rules went into effect in 1992. For example, the new rules placed electronic gambling machines in the category that required the Indians to gain the approval of state officials. Officials in the state of Arizona refused to permit the Yavapai-Apache Indians to continue offering some popular games that had been producing an estimated 1.4 million dollars per year in revenue for the tribe. The Indians refused to discontinue the games on the ground that the state had refused to negotiate in good faith (*Americans Before Columbus* 1992). The day after the new rules took effect, agents of the FBI raided several reservations across Arizona to seize game machines; but at one of the sites, they were blockaded by a group of Indians, and a five-hour standoff ensued. The governor of Arizona negotiated an agreement with the tribal chairman, and declared a ten-day "cooling-off" period (*New York Times* May 13, 1992). The FBI raids triggered angry reactions throughout the Indian nations. Mr. Tim Giago, the editor of *The Lakota Times*, was quoted as saying, "The Indian nations are sick and tired of being treated like children. . . . Why in hell should these lands need the state's permission[?]" (Johnson 1992).

A similar dispute occurred in New Mexico when eleven tribes continued to operate casinos despite the fact that the State Supreme Court and three federal appeals judges had ruled that the gambling pacts the tribes signed with a former governor were illegal. Two Indian pueblos threatened to block federal and state highways through their land if they were forced to close the casinos. The Indian leaders argued that as sovereign nations[31] the tribes should deal directly with the U.S. government; they insisted that the gaming act gave too much power to the states. Nine of the tribes signed an agreement with U.S. Attorney John J. Kelly, in which the tribes agreed not to block federal projects and the government agreed the casinos could remain open. A female Hispanic judge of the Federal District Court, Martha A. Vazquez, ruled in 1996 that the agreement was invalid but that gambling could continue while the case was appealed (Johnson 1996:A12). These jurisdictional conflicts, and other similar events, illustrate the efforts of the tribes to define and enlarge the area within which they may determine the direction of their own lives.

Sovereignty for Alaskan Tribes.   For three decades, the Alaskan Indians, with the legal assistance of the Native American Rights Fund, tried to convince the federal government that Alaskan Indians should have tribal status, as do many other U.S. Indians. The state of Alaska and various oil companies opposed this designation claiming that Indian Country was terminated by the passage of the Alaska Native Claims Settlement Act in 1971. The Alaskan Indians sought tribal status because it would allow them to tax nonmembers and corporations on tribal land and give the tribes the authority to exercise the governing powers needed to provide social services and keep the peace. It also would entitle them to a government-to-government relationship with the United States and eligibility for various federal services. The Alaskan Indians had little doubt that the 226 tribes in Alaska could provide proof that they are "modern-day successors to historically sovereign bands of Native Americans," which is required for tribal status. To do so individually, however, would have meant hiring lawyers, historians, and anthropologists on a tribe-by-tribe basis, which would have been prohibitively expensive. Since the U.S. Supreme Court has ruled repeatedly that when either the executive branch or Congress has recognized a tribe, the courts must defer to their judgment, an official of the executive branch decided to act. All that was required was for an authorized person to publish a list that recognized that Alaskan tribes had the same status as Indian tribes in the other forty-eight states. The Assistant Secretary of the Interior for Indian Affairs, Ada Deer, a Menominee Indian woman, did precisely that. In October 1993, Deer published a list of federally recognized tribes in Alaska, which was a critical step toward eliminating discrimination against Alaskan Indians and in promoting tribal sovereignty in Alaska (*NARF Legal Review* 1994).

Issues and incidents such as these have served to heighten the American Indians' awareness of their shared characteristics and, thus, to promote the emergence of a new concept of "Indianness." An important, but in some ways fragile, framework of agreement has developed from these beginnings. On the one hand, this framework sometimes appears to be "only a thin veneer over reservation communities deeply divided by competing groups who often work at cross purposes" (Buffalohead 1986:270);[32] but, on the other hand, it has enabled the Indians to act in concert to protect their treaty rights and enlarge the powers of their tribal governments. Many of the reservations hold some of the richest resources in the United States, including coal, oil, gas, forests for logging, and water rights. In the past, the tribes have gotten only minimal profits from leases or contracts negotiated on behalf of the Indians by the BIA for rights to these resources. Many tribes have banded together to hire their own lawyers, to negotiate more profitable contracts, or to form companies of their own to extract the resources on their reservations themselves. In 1976, twenty-two tribes formed the Council of Energy Resource Tribes (CERT) which has grown in membership to forty-three tribes. CERT advised the Laguna Pueblo to decline $191,000 for a pipeline right of way and then helped the tribe negotiate a $1.5 million dollar contract (Snipp 1986:469).

Immigrant or Colonized Minority?

As noted in Chapters 8 and 9, the Mexican Americans originally entered the United States as a conquered group in their own homeland. In Chapters 10 and 11 we saw that, although Black Americans did not remain in their homeland, they nonetheless may be described as a conquered group. American Indians clearly entered American society as members of conquered groups; and like the Mexican Americans, their homelands were invaded and occupied by outsiders. The colonization of their lands was followed by political and economic domination and by numerous efforts to exploit their labor (Jacobson 1984).

In our consideration of the contemporary Mexican Americans, we argued that the large migration of Mexicans to the United States since 1900 affords a basis for applying the immigrant model to that group. Similarly, our consideration of Black Americans focused on their large twentieth-century migration since 1915 from the rural South to the urban-industrial North. In both cases—while acknowledging the earlier condition of these groups as conquered peoples—one may make the case that applying the immigrant model to them advances our understanding of contemporary events. Given the special relationship of the American Indians to the federal government and the continuation of reservation and tribal life, however, is there any basis whatsoever for considering American Indians to be similar to the immigrant minorities?

An attempt to apply the immigrant model to Indians may be farfetched. The possibility of such an application rests on the consequences of rural-to-urban migrations. In 1887, when the Dawes Act was passed, nearly all Indians lived on the reservations or in rural communities. By 1980, more than half of the Native Americans had left the reservations and were living in cities and towns. By 1990, however, all of the fifteen largest reservations, with the exception of Pine Ridge (which is one of the poorest places in the nation), had experienced increases in population growth that exceeded what is possible from natural increases. Some of the largest reservations experienced substantial growth—with the Navajo reservation up almost 37 percent, Fort Apache up 43 percent, the Osage and Blackfeet reservations up 38 percent each, and Fort Peck up 35 percent (Snipp 1992:19). These population increases suggest in-migration to the reservations. The net result is that there are still proportionally fewer Americans in Indian Country—reservations, trust lands, Alaska Native villages and lands near reservations—than there are in cities and urban areas; but the patterns suggest that an increasing number of Indians are returning to their cultural heritage.

As we saw, many "friends of the Indians" argued that the passage of the Dawes Act would help the Indians to become independent farmers; but we saw also that the law actually caused many Indians to lose their land, frequently leaving them with no alternative but to move to nearby towns or more distant cities. In the process, their ties with those who remained on the reservations were weakened; they were forced to take urban jobs, usually as unskilled workers; and they were required to take into account in their daily lives the language, ideas, manners, and ways of acting that predominated in the urban centers. Under such circumstances, some Indians, especially those who attended the boarding schools, moved rapidly in the direction of cultural and secondary assimilation. Many others clustered together in small enclaves where they clung uncertainly to the bottom rung of the economic ladder. In both cases, however, the urban Indians were subjected to the same broad forces of modernization as their contemporaries who were reaching the cities from Europe, Asia, Mexico, and the rural South.

Until the onset of World War II, the proportion of the Indians who lived mainly or permanently in urban centers was comparatively small; however, during the war, the number of Indians moving to towns and cities increased sharply. Approximately 40,000 Indians were attracted to the cities, primarily on the West Coast, by the new employment opportunities created by the war. The migration was stimulated, too, because many of the approximately 25,000 Indians who were drafted into the armed forces were stationed in or near cities (Stewart 1977b:524).[33] At the end of the war, approximately 80,000 Indians lived in urban places (Spicer 1980b:110).

The primary surge in the urban Indian population, however, came after that time. Despite the hopes aroused by the IRA, at the war's end most reservation Indians were still living under conditions of grinding poverty. Their populations were increasing more rapidly than their economies could support, while unemployment on the reservations was extremely high. These were among the circumstances that helped to move the federal government toward the policy of termination, with its underlying ideology of Anglo conformity. Rather than attempting more vigorously to develop the reservations and strengthen tribal life, the BIA launched a new program to help Indians "relocate" in cities. This kind of assistance to Indians was by no means new, but the effort became much more important after 1950 when Dillon S. Meyer, the man who directed the program to relocate the Japanese and Japanese Americans during World War II, became the Commissioner of Indian Affairs (Officer 1986:122). In 1952, the **relocation** idea became the foundation for a greatly expanded nationwide effort called the Voluntary Relocation Program.

The relocation program included various types of job training, counseling, and job creation. Indians who were selected for the program were provided transportation to a designated Employment Assistance Center in cities such as Chicago, Los Angeles, and Denver; and since the program's directors wished to make it difficult for the Indians to return home, they usually were sent to cities fairly far from their reservations. The idea of solving the "Indian Problem" by forcing the Indians into the mainstream again became dominant; so the relocation program and the termination program reflected, to some extent, the same general ideological climate. The message communicated to the Indians was "either conform to the Anglo way and move several hundred miles away from the reservation or stay . . . and live at substandard levels" (Bahr 1972:408). Between 1953 and 1972, more than 100,000 American Indians were settled in American cities under the relocation program. In addition, during the same period of time, more than 200,000 other Indian people moved away from their reservations without help from the program.

The tremendous growth of the urban American Indian population within the last five decades affords a basis for arguing that, like Mexican Americans and Black Americans, Indians too are now on the road to higher levels of assimilation. Implied also is the belief that as Indians become more urbanized they will move more fully into the mainstream. Price (1972:438) stated the case in this way: "Conditions in the city lead the Indian away from tribal patterns. The reservation offers a very narrow range of occupational, religious, political, and recreational alternatives. The range of possible choices is vastly increased in the city."

The urban areas offer many more opportunities for Indians to assimilate than do the rural reservations; however, one additional point concerning the urban experience of Indian Americans should be mentioned. Many Indians who *reside* in cities do not, in a certain social sense, *live* there. Some Indians, as Bahr (1972:408) expressed it, are only temporary migrants who "raid" the city, "take" city resources, and then return to the reservation or small off-reservation community to "live." This practice resembles that of the "birds of passage" and "sojourners" we noted among various American immigrant groups, but the nearness of the reservations and the strength of the tribal ties may mean that the intention to return home is more easily put into practice by Indians than by the members of most other groups. This particularly may be the case of the urban Indians who plan to return to the reservations when they retire from their city jobs. Even Indians who are not temporary migrants or do not plan to return to the reservation permanently may still maintain a strong sense of Indian identity and may do everything in their power to relate themselves to urban life as Indians.

Although research has shown shifts to English language usage, growing urbanization, and rising levels of education and income—all classic indicators of assimilation—researchers have reported evidence of ethnic resurgence. There has been an increase in the extent to which people select an Indian ethnic identification in U.S. Bureau of the Census counts; Indian ethnic organizations have grown in number and have been increasingly active in civil rights litigation; and there have been social and cultural revitalizations on the reservations as well as in urban Indian communities. These points and others are amplified in our consideration in Chapter 13 of the extent to which American Indians have been affected by the main subprocesses of assimilation.

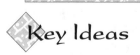

Key Ideas

1. France, England, Spain, and Holland each attempted to gain control of portions of North America. Prior to the American Revolution, the conflict was waged mainly between France and her Indian allies, England and her Indian allies, and the In-

dian tribes that at any given moment refused to form an alliance with either of these European powers. The greater numbers of the English and the timely support of the Iroquois led to the defeat of France and her allies.

2. Pontiac's uprising was an intertribal effort to stop the westward expansion of Anglo American society. It showed the power of a concerted Indian resistance and led the King of England to issue the Proclamation of 1763. This important document laid the foundation for the separatist Indian policies adopted later by the new American republic.

3. Land-hungry traders, settlers, and politicians devised numerous methods to persuade the Indians to sell or cede their lands. Although many land transactions were conducted in "the utmost good faith," many also involved deception, fraud, bribery, and threats of violence. The pressure of the Whites on the Indians led to continuous friction and the transfer of enormous tracts of land to the Whites.

4. Like Pontiac before him, Tecumseh attempted to form a pan-Indian military alliance to stop the advance of the Whites. Tecumseh's plan included many more tribes spread over a much larger area. It was the most ambitious military effort ever attempted by the Indians.

5. The Indian Removal Act led to the forced evacuation to Indian Territory of most of the Indians east of the Mississippi River.

6. During the eighteenth and nineteenth centuries, the Plains Indians had developed a way of life based on the horse, the buffalo, and raiding. The removal of the eastern Indians to Indian Territory and the movement of White Americans across the Plains precipitated several decades of bitter, tragic, and widely publicized warfare between the western Indians and the Americans.

7. The U.S. government continued the system of making treaties with Indian tribes until 1871. In that year, Congress declared that the United States would honor all existing treaties but would no longer recognize the tribes as treaty-making powers. By this time, most of the tribes had been assigned to reservations and placed under the direct supervision of the Bureau of Indian Affairs.

8. Through the General Allotment (Dawes) Act of 1887, the federal government abandoned its long-standing policy of separatism and adopted a policy of Anglo conformity. The Indians were to be forced to accept "civilization" and enter the mainstream of American life. The Meriam Report showed that few Indians became independent, self-sufficient farmers under the provisions of the Dawes Act. The main effects of the act were to place most of the Indians' lands in the hands of White people and to increase the levels of poverty among the Indians.

9. The Indian Reorganization Act of 1934, which replaced the Dawes Act, was based on the ideology of cultural pluralism. The Indians were encouraged to remain Indians and to participate as fully as they wished in the life of the broader society. The "termination" policy of the 1950s represented a brief return to the Anglo conformity policy. The Indian Self-Determination Act of 1975 marked the resumption of a policy of cultural pluralism.

10. A number of national pan-Indian organizations have been formed to promote the interests and welfare of American Indians. These organizations have been based on varying ideologies of adjustment, and some have taken on active protests; but in general they have expressed the wish that the American Indians be permitted to retain their cultural heritages.

11. Many groups of Native Americans have actively worked to renew their status as recognized tribes and have taken legal steps to affirm their tribal sovereignty. The sovereign status of the Alaskan tribes has been recognized. The emphasis on sovereignty and self-determination has resulted in conflicts between tribal and state governments over the power to control fishing rights, taxes, gaming, and liquor trafficking.

12. Since the middle of the twentieth century, American Indians have migrated in large numbers to urban areas, and they are now predominantly an urban people. The urban Indians appear to be moving more rapidly toward cultural assimilation than are those on the reservations. This observation affords a basis for attempting to interpret the contemporary experience of the Indians in terms of the immigrant model; however, among both reservation and off-reservation Indians, cultural addition is more conspicuous than cultural substitution.

Key Terms

allotment   The process of assigning parcels of Indian community land to individual land owners.

gaming   A broad term that encompasses a number of forms of gambling including such things as Bingo, slot machines, card games, and dice games.

relocation   A voluntary program initiated by the BIA in 1952. The aim of the program was to encourage Indians to move from the reservations to the cities and to adopt Anglo conformity.

removal   U.S. government policies that forced Indians to move from the lands they had originally inhabited to assigned reservations in Indian Territory.

reorganization   The Indian Reorganization Act (1934) that reaffirmed tribal autonomy and encouraged Indian tribes to form their own democratic governments, organize tribal business enterprises, and revive tribal religions, languages, and cultures.

sovereign nations   The Indian tribes have a government-to-government relationship with the U.S. government. Possessing sovereignty gives Indian tribes special privileges, such as making tribal laws, not paying federal or state taxes, establishing their own schools, and forming their own governments. Court rulings have limited tribal powers, and conflicts have arisen over relationships between tribal governments and state governments.

termination   The process by which the U.S. government declared that Indian groups that were sufficiently assimilated would no longer be considered Indian tribes. Terminated tribes no longer qualified for payments and services for the land they had given up to the government under treaties.

tribalism   Identification with an individual Indian tribe. Tribalism may also refer to efforts to gain greater tribal autonomy and stronger tribal governance and self-sufficiency.

Notes

1. The Indian population of the United States may be defined as people who identified their race as American Indian, Eskimo, or Aleut in the 1990 census (Snipp 1989:58). There were 1.96 million people in this category of whom 1.88 million were classified as "American Indian."

2. During this period, the Tuscaroras were driven out of the South and were accepted into the Iroquois League. The League then became the Six Nations of the Iroquois.

3. Of special significance in this regard was the higher quality of English rum (Nash 1974: 252–255).

4. In Europe this conflict was known as the Seven Years' War.

5. In 1769, Pontiac was killed by a Peoria Indian whom he believed to be a friend (Josephy 1961:128).

6. During the entire treaty-making period, which lasted for nearly a century, the White Americans concluded 645 treaties with various Indian tribes (Jackson and Galli 1977:26).

7. Justice Marshall went on to describe the relation of the Indians to the United States as "that of a ward to his guardian" (Jackson and Galli 1977:59). The use of the term *ward,* with its implication of dependency and close supervision, later created numerous problems for the Indians.

8. A third, earlier, ruling by Marshall (*Johnson v. McIntosh*) denied that Indians had title to the land they occupied, confusing matters still further (Chaudhuri 1985:24–25).

9. Legend insists that on hearing about the decision in *Worcester,* Jackson retorted, "John Marshall has made his decision. Now let him enforce it!"

10. The term *The Trail of Tears* originally applied specifically to the removal experience of the Cherokees. Since then it has become generalized to describe the entire removal process.

11. About a thousand Cherokees fled from Georgia to North Carolina where they established a separate tribe. The contemporary Eastern Band of the Cherokees, their descendants, still live in North Carolina.

12. Some of the sedentary farming tribes, such as the Mandans and Hidatsas, lived along Plains rivers before the rise of the horse–buffalo complex.

13. Although Custer was at this time a Lt. Colonel, he had held the rank of brevet (temporary) Major General during the Civil War. He continued thereafter to expect people to address him as "General" and, in fact, most did. The literature on Custer and his conduct of the battle of the Little Bighorn is large and controversial. See Connell (1984); Graham (1953); and Scott and Connor (1986).

14. Dr. Charles Eastman (Ohiyesa) estimated the former figure and Lieutenant (later General) Godfrey estimated the latter (see Graham 1953:97, 151).

15. Custer's command included about 650 cavalrymen, 145 infantrymen, and 40 "Ree" (Arikara) Indian Scouts (Connell 1984:383).

16. Some other chiefs present at the battle were Low Dog, Crow King, Hump, and Iron Thunder. Sitting Bull was a medicine chief rather than a war chief; so he was not on the battlefield.

17. The government showed no sign of keeping its promise to Crazy Horse, and he soon became unhappy and troublesome. General Crook attempted to have him arrested. Crazy Horse resisted and was killed on September 5, 1877 (Josephy 1961:306–309).

18. In 1860, it was estimated that there were approximately 20 million buffalo on the Plains. In 1890 there were fewer than six hundred.

19. The BIA was transferred in 1849 from the War Department to the Department of the Interior.

20. The Five Civilized Tribes organized Indian protests against the Dawes proposal. As a result, the Dawes Act was not applied to the Five Civilized Tribes, the tribes of Indian Territory, or to the New York Indians (Hoxie 1984:72). Later, in the Curtis Act, the government dissolved the governments of the tribes that had refused allotment. Thereafter, tribal chiefs were appointed by the president.

21. Meriam et al. (1928).

22. At first, about two-thirds of the tribes that held elections voted to accept the IRA (Wax 1971:57). Later, the right of self-government was extended even to the tribes that voted against the IRA.

23. The ominous word *termination* does not appear in the resolution (Officer 1986:114).

24. Public Law 280, passed during the same summer, also had an important effect on the status of American Indians. PL 280 extended to certain states jurisdiction over civil and criminal matters on federal Indian reservations, thus attacking the principle of sovereignty established in *Worcester* (Svensson 1973:33–34).

25. The Menominees were restored to their tribal status in 1974 through the passage of the Menominee Restoration Act.

26. One hundred and nine bands and tribes had been terminated by this time (O'Brien 1985:44).

27. A council of Indians representing nineteen tribes in Indian Territory sent to the president of the United States a resolution attacking the Dawes Act as follows: "Like other people, the Indian needs . . . some governmental organization of his own . . . in order to make true progress in the affairs of life. This peculiarity in the Indian character is elsewhere called patriotism, and the wise and patient fashioning . . . of which alone will successfully solve the question of civilization" (Hertzberg 1971:9).

28. An important legislative victory for the NCAI was the establishment of an Indian Claims Commission in 1946 to hear cases involving damages to Indian tribes. By the time this program ended in 1978, 285 tribal claims had been settled (among 850 filed; Olson and Wilson 1984:137, 142).

29. See Nagel (1996:131–141).

30. Most discussions of this event have interpreted it as an Indian–White confrontation. Some scholars, however, view it primarily as a struggle between traditional and nontraditional Indians (Holm 1985:137–144).

31. The issue of sovereignty has raised concerns about individual rights. Bordewich (1996:314) quoted Ramon Roubideaux, a lawyer who is a member of the Rosebud Sioux Tribe, as arguing that sovereignty "is just a mask for individuals who rob people of their rights as U.S. citizens."

32. In the matter of gambling casinos, for example, there is intertribal and intratribal conflict as well as conflict between the tribes and state and federal officials (*Americans Before Columbus* 1992).

33. The most famous of the veterans were the "code talkers" (most of whom were Navajos) whose native languages were not understood by enemy interceptors (Jacobson 1984:167).

Native Americans

A Struggle to Maintain Political and Cultural Pluralism

Many groups of Native Americans have worked to renew their status as recognized tribes and to affirm tribal sovereignty. These efforts have resulted in conflicts between tribal and state governments over the power to control fishing rights, taxes, and economic enterprises such as gaming.

American Indians changed when it was necessary for their survival, but they have adjusted in ways that have allowed them to preserve their most valued traditions and lifestyles.

—C. Matthew Snipp

All cultures must depend on their younger generations to keep perpetuating age-old traditions. . . . They are the future leaders of our tribal people and in many ways are helping to keep our traditions alive. The work we are doing in the court room and in the state and federal legislatures is not just for our clients—the Native peoples of this country—but it is also for ourselves, our children, and our children's children.

—Native American Rights Fund

Throughout American history, federal Indian policy has shifted between the desire to segregate the Indian people and the desire to assimilate them. By negotiating treaties with Indian tribes, placing Indians on reservations away from Anglo Americans, and encouraging separate tribal governments, U.S. policies have promoted separatism. Over-all though, some form of assimilation has been the most prominent policy. Recall that: (1) the U.S. government altered the Indians' status as sovereign nations in 1871 and began treating them like other subordinate minority groups; (2) the General Allotment Act tried to eliminate tribal land bases and make individual Indians on the reservations into land-owning farmers and ranchers; (3) the BIA schools promoted English-only education and forced some Indian children to attend boarding schools away from their families; (4) the relocation of some Indians from the reservations to urban areas weakened their ties to the cultures of the reservations; and (5) the forced "termination" of services to some tribes and the denial of tribal status to many groups of Indians threatened to extinguish tribal life. How successful have the various assimilationist efforts been in promoting the cultural and structural assimilation of Native Americans?

The struggles of the American Indians have occurred in the reverse order from that of nearly all other American ethnic groups.[1] Groups who came from overseas, whether voluntarily or involuntarily, started with no political or cultural rights and mainly have attempted to gain political and cultural equality with the majority; Indians, in contrast, started with their own nations and have gradually lost much of what they had to the advancing Anglo American group. Since most Indian tribes have long been separate political entities, they have been forced to struggle to maintain their own institutions and beliefs in the face of tremendous racism and governmental policies of forced assimilation.

Chapter 12 suggested that, despite the pressures, the levels of each form of assimilation among American Indians are, in general, comparatively low. Indeed, as we saw,

354

the Indians have clung tenaciously to their tribal heritages and presently are struggling to amplify a pan-Indian identity and to renew tribal sovereignty. Also suggested in the previous discussion of the migration of Indians to urban areas is the view that the reservations are the repositories of the traditional cultures and that, therefore, the Indians who remain on the reservations are likely to live in a more traditional way and to be more successful in preserving their tribal heritages than are off-reservation Indians. Ideally, therefore, to assess the levels of cultural, secondary structural, primary structural, and marital assimilation of the American Indians, one would wish to be able to state the current level of each type of assimilation among each of the distinct Indian groups, taking into account the differences between reservation and off-reservation residents within each tribe. Such a complete approach cannot be attempted here. Rather we must rely on general comparisons that tend to submerge the important differences that exist among the tribes and a few examples chosen to illustrate some contemporary variations among the tribes.

Cultural Assimilation

Who is an Indian? In the previous chapters, we have discussed the difficulty of classifying the members of various ethnic groups. Similarly, the issues raised by the efforts to identify Native Americans also are complex. Tribal classifications are important because they have been used over the years to decide who was entitled to government rights and privileges and who was not (Barringer 1993).

For many years, the federal government attempted to define the American Indian population based on the concept of **blood quantum**[2] levels. In the nineteenth century, as discussed in Chapter 5, scientific ideas concerning race and racial differences were based on the ancient belief that "races" are sharply distinguishable genetic categories and that both physical and cultural traits are transmitted "through the blood" from one generation to the next. The presumed "amount" of blood that a person possessed from a particular race determined the degree to which that person would resemble and behave like others of similar biological background. For example, **full-blood** Indians were presumed to have the full measure of physical and social characteristics ascribed to Indians. Individuals with one White and one Indian parent were "half breeds" or **mixed-bloods** and were expected to have one-half of the physical and social characteristics of each parent. The Bureau of Indian Affairs used this blood quantum method to identify members of the Indian population. BIA officials calculated that if both parents were "pure" Indian, the blood quantum of their children was 100 percent. The children of racially mixed marriages were presumed to have some calculable fraction of "Indian blood," such as three-fourths, one-half, or one-eighth.

The blood quantum method is still used in some situations. For example, a one-fourth blood quantum is the minimal requirement for receiving some government services, such as medical care on the reservations. On this scale, a large number of tribal governments use one-sixteenth to one-half blood quantum criteria for determining tribal membership (Snipp 1989:34). Bordewich (1996:73) noted that Indians quite commonly speak about being "seven sixteenths Blackfeet or fifteen thirty-seconds Cheyenne." He also said that the Pequots of Connecticut have arbitrarily defined their late-nineteenth century great-great-grandparents as "full-blood" for the purpose of tribal enrollment. As the relationship between the blood quantum approach and the ideas of scientific racism have been clarified, Native American activists increasingly have challenged the racist assumptions underlying blood quantum tests of Indianness (Nagel 1996:244). Indeed, the terms *full-blood* and *mixed-blood* frequently refer to a person's cultural commitment rather than to some presumption concerning his or her biological ancestry.

Amidst controversies over how to determine who is a member of the various ethnic and racial groups, the federal government adopted **self-identification** as the method of classification for the Census Bureau and for most other agencies. As a result, changes in the ways that Native Americans have classified themselves are believed by demographers to be among the most important sources of the rapid growth of the Indian population. For example, the Indian population counted in the census increased more than fivefold in the three decades following 1950 (Passel and Berman 1986). Eschbach (1995) carefully analyzed birth and death rates and migration patterns and determined that the unexpected growth in the Native American population indicated that a large proportion of persons of mixed descent are now identifying themselves as Indian. These increases in the Indian population have occurred in urban areas as well as on the still largely segregated reservations. The reality that the population has not diminished as tribal members have learned English and intermarried has challenged the idea based on the assimilation models that the Indian population would decrease over time.

Nagel and Snipp (1993) proposed that ethnogenesis is occurring among Native Americans.[3] They argued that in response to reduced numbers and various threats to their survival, some tribes have combined, resulting in the disappearance of some groups, the growth of other groups, and the creation of multitribal composite communities. The formal recognition of some groups and not others as Indian tribes by the federal government has also forced Indians to reorganize, with some reservation tribes adopting tighter, more exclusionary membership rules and non-reservation tribes adopting looser, more inclusionary rules. For many Indians, the process of ethnogenesis has meant that the pan-Indian "nationality," which we discussed in Chapter 12, has become a new ethnic identity. Nagel and Snipp (1993:212) found that in 1910 only 8 percent of American Indians failed to report a tribal affiliation, but by 1980 almost one-quarter of the Americans who reported their race to be Indian failed to designate a tribe. Some of this ethnogenesis has occurred because of federal policy makers' tendency to treat the culturally varied Native American groups simply as "Indians." The increasing urbanization of the American Indian population also has provided a basis for pan-Indian identification. Eschbach (1995) suggested that having an Indian heritage has come to convey a positive status that it formerly did not have, which has encouraged many people of mixed descent now to claim their Indian heritage.

The experiences of the Native Americans provide good examples of the complexities of the processes of assimilation. As we noted in Chapter 12, this group represents almost 550 diverse cultural tribes and officially recognized groups that have survived wars and policies aimed at their annihilation. The processes through which the Indians have moved toward becoming sovereign states and toward developing a pan-Indian identity illustrate the changing nature and dynamics of ethnic relations in the United States. Let us look more closely at the operation of these processes.

Language Maintenance

At the time of first contact with Europeans, at least 200 and, perhaps as many as 1,200, languages and dialects were spoken by the Native American tribes.[4] By 1990, less than one third of those identifying themselves as American Indians spoke a language other than English, and fewer than 3 percent spoke no English at all. Although some of the tribes have managed to maintain their languages and are teaching them in reservation schools, many Indian languages are now extinct. For example, the Narragansetts of New England and the Luisenos of California have not spoken their native languages for at least a century. In addition to the languages that are no longer used, several other Indian languages may be nearing extinction. The Sac and Fox Indians of Oklahoma, for instance, are mainly English speakers. Among the Omahas, less than 10 percent of those under the age of forty speak only the native tongue. By 1980, in fact, in only one census region of the country (the Mountain States) did a majority of the Indians (62 percent) speak their native language in the home. The next highest region of native language use was in the west north-central region (21 percent) (Snipp 1989:176).

Although for the most part Indian children have been forced to learn English, and many of the Indian languages have disappeared as the elders of the tribe die, a number of different Indian languages are used in varying degrees on a daily basis. In some cases, these languages are spoken by a majority of the tribal members who usually also speak English, Spanish, or French. For example, most Oklahoma Cherokees, Iroquois, and Penobscots are bilingual. Furthermore, many Indians also speak more than a single Indian language or Indian dialect. In some cases, where the Indian languages already are in general use within a tribe, the number of native language speakers is growing. Among the Navajos—the largest reservation tribe in the United States—a majority of those on the reservation use the mother tongue in the home. Now that the Indians have control of the curriculum in the schools on the reservations, Navajo is also a language of instruction in the Rough Rock School and the Navajo Community College. Among the Apaches and many other tribes there is a renewed interest in learning and using the mother tongue (Olson and Wilson 1984:202–204; Nagel 1996:194–198).

What, then, are the general prospects for the survival and growth of the Indian languages? Since, presumably, a language community is easier to maintain in comparative isolation, we should expect Indian languages to fare better on or near reservations; and since children are more likely to be affected by exposure to alien languages than are adults, we should expect older people to report a greater use of an Indian language. An analysis by Gundlach and Busch (1981) showed that Indians who were twenty-five years or older were more likely than those under twenty-five to report that an Indian language was used in their home when they were children. This finding was true for both reservation and off-reservation Indians; however, the percentage who reported an Indian mother tongue was much higher for both age groups among the reservation Indians.

Snipp's (1989:178) analysis confirmed that native language speakers are generally found in non-metropolitan and reservation areas. For instance, in the east south-central region of the country, around 90 percent of the Indians living on or near a reservation speak a native language in the home, whereas in the same region only about 5 percent of those in metropolitan areas do so.

Snipp (1989:180) also reported some interesting findings concerning age differences in language use. Older people were more likely than children to be among those who speak a native language but little English, though the proportions in both cases were low. Among those between the ages of sixty-one and seventy, for instance, around 5 percent spoke little English. Among those between the ages of eleven and twenty, less than 2 percent spoke little English. Of special interest is the finding that young people were slightly *more* likely than older people to speak a native language and also to be fluent English speakers.

These data suggest that, although those who live on or near reservations and in non-metropolitan areas are more likely to have an Indian mother tongue than those who live in metropolitan areas, English is nevertheless the primary language of most American Indians. They also indicate, however, that approximately 25 percent of the Indians are fluent in both English and a native language, and that the younger people are slightly more likely to be bilingual than the older. As far as languages alone are concerned, then, the Indian cultures seem very unlikely to disappear within the next generation or two. The actual conditions among American Indians may well be more nearly consistent with the pluralist conception of cultural assimilation (i.e., by language addition) than with the Anglo conformity conception (i.e., by language substitution). The critical point here, of course, is the extent to which American Indians continue to become or remain bilingual and multilingual.

Although language is an extremely important part of culture, there also are other significant cultural elements that may continue, be modified, or die whether a native language exists or not. For example, religious preferences and ceremonies, housing styles, hair and dress styles, recreational patterns, and so on also reveal whether, or to what extent, one way of life has been added to or exchanged for another.

Indian Religious Freedom

Our historical sketch in Chapter 12 has shown that an enormous effort has been made by many different religious bodies to Christianize the Indians. The resulting pattern of religious affiliations is very complex. Many American Indians have accepted Christian beliefs, many practice both Christian rites and those of an Indian religion, and many adhere solely to an Indian religion. In the latter case, as we saw in the Ghost Dance religion, some elements of Christianity also may be included. In many cases, an adherence to Christian or native religious ways parallels a person's general level of "Indianness" which, in turn, tends to be related to whether a person is considered to be a "full-blood" or "mixed-blood." In general, "full-bloods" are culturally more conservative, more likely to live on a reservation, and more likely to practice an Indian religion.

Several native religions among American Indians are closely identified with particular tribes. The Silas John religion of the Apaches and the Handsome Lake (or Longhouse) religion of the Iroquois are illustrative. Probably the best known, and certainly the most controversial of the Indian religions is practiced by members of the Native American Church (NAC). The NAC is a pan-Indian religious movement that is nevertheless closely related to traditional tribal life (Hertzberg 1971:239). Its religious beliefs are compatible in several important respects with those of most Christian denominations. The church emphasizes brotherly love, close family ties, self-reliance, and the avoidance of alcohol. The controversial element, however, arises from the ritual use by NAC members of peyote as a formal part of the sacrament. Peyote contains several psychedelic substances. Therefore a number of state governments have declared the use, possession, or transportation of peyote by Indians for traditional religious purposes illegal. The NAC prohibits recreational use of the drug (Wax 1971:142–144), but numerous Indians practicing this religion have been arrested for their religious use or possession of peyote.

In addition to the NAC, a variety of Christian denominations and native religions may be found among most Indian tribes. For example, the Comanches are mainly members of the Methodist and Dutch Reformed churches, but a substantial number also belong to the NAC or practice their tribal religion; the Kiowas are divided among the Catholic, Methodist, Episcopal, and Baptist churches, as well as the NAC; the Pawnees include Catholics, members of the NAC, and adherents to their tribal religion; and the Sioux are mainly Episcopalians, Catholics, or members of the Church of God. They, too, include many members of the NAC and their tribal Yuwipi cult. In many cases, individual American Indians belong to more than one religious organization (Spicer 1980a:88–92). This crisscross pattern of religious experiences and affiliations frequently has been the basis of conflict within some tribes. The Nez Perces, for instance, long have been split between rival Presbyterian and Catholic groups, whereas the Prairie Band of the Potawatomis have been torn between conservatives, who adhere largely to the native religions, and liberals who are mainly Christians (Spicer 1980a:79, 95). In a unique blending of traditions, the Our Lady of Guadalupe Church on the Zuni Indian Reservation has combined the religious icons of the Catholic religion with large murals of more than two dozen life-sized kachinas, the spirit beings of Pueblo culture. The Catholic church has officially acknowledged a need to respect the cultural traditions of the Zuni who want to worship God in a way that is familiar to them (Niebuhr 1995).

The various religious factions have been united, however, in coalitions to protect Native American religious freedom. For many Indians, even those who are Christians, traditional religion and ceremonies are the essence of Native American culture. Congress passed a joint resolution called the "American Indian Religious Freedom Act" in 1978, but the U.S. Supreme Court ruled in the case *Employment Division of Oregon v. Smith* in 1990 that the First Amendment of the Constitution does not protect the religious use of peyote by Indians.

This situation led to a pan-Indian effort in support of new legislation to guarantee religious freedom to Indians (*NARF Legal Review* 1994). The Native American Cultural Protection and Free Exercise of Religion Act was introduced in 1994 by Senator Inouye of Hawaii. The legislation allowed the religious use of peyote by Indians and offered protection for Native American cultural and religious sites, the cultural and religious rights of Native American prisoners, and the cultural or religious use of eagle feathers and other animals or plants by Native Americans in religious ceremonies. The Indians were concerned about some forty-four sacred sites that were threatened by tourism, development, and resource exploitation. Additionally, many Native American prisoners were denied access to Indian spiritual leaders and denied the opportunities to practice their religions, despite the fact that other prisoners had access to priests, ministers, rabbis, and other religious leaders. Finally, Native Americans faced criminal prosecution if they were found in possession of eagle parts or feathers due to the Bald and Golden Eagle Protection Act.

The proposed legislation[5] permitted the use of lawfully obtained eagle feathers and provided for the protection of the free exercise of religion by Native Americans. The right of Indians to use peyote in religious services became law in 1994, and in that same year President Clinton relaxed a provision of the Endangered Species Act to meet demands from Indian leaders that they be permitted to gather eagle feathers and carcasses used in religious ceremonies. The sacred site component of the bill met resistance from legislators concerned that the legislation would be extended to non-Indian-land-based religious claims. The legislation that was passed, however, required federally funded institutions and government agencies to return Indian skeletons, grave goods associated with Indian burials, and other sacred and culturally significant articles to those Indian tribes and individuals with a justified claim to them. Opponents of the legislation requiring the return of Indian remains argued that because of emerging techniques for analyzing skeletal material, scientific knowledge of early American diseases, diet, and settlement patterns would be lost if the artifacts were not available for study. Some compromises have been reached; many of the artifacts have been returned to the proper tribes; and an increasing number of Indian scholars have assumed important roles in museums that were formerly Anglo dominated (Washburn 1995:252–256).

Traditions

The variety and complexity that exists among American Indians in regard to language and religion extends to every other sphere of life. In many cases, the members of a given tribe may live in a manner that is largely indistinguishable from that of their White neighbors, although even in such cases of high cultural assimilation, certain distinctive Indian elements may still be present. For example, Lorraine Canoe, a Mohawk Indian, has lived in Brooklyn for more than thirty-five years; but she considers the Mohawk reservation her real home.[6] She was born there and hopes to return when she retires. In the time she has been in New York, she has tried to return to the reservation for as many ceremonies as she can. She takes a nine-hour bus trip to the reservation for about half of the thirteen annual ceremonies and spends her summer breaks there. She owns a house on the reservation where her two grown daughters live. She cooks traditional boiled corn bread and brings one of her favorites—deer meat—back from the reservation. Although her daughters grew up in New York, they moved back to the reservation because they preferred the more traditional life and relaxed pace.

The split lives of urban Indians and variety of cultural "mixes" also extends to differences within various tribes. Consider the Oklahoma Cherokees, for example. This non-reservation group is located principally within a five-county region of northeastern Oklahoma, and the people who are considered, or consider themselves to be, Cherokees vary markedly in culture. The Cherokee tribe, with over 300,000 members in 1990, was the largest American Indian tribe (U.S. Bureau of the Census 1995:50). Wax (1971: 92–93) distinguished broadly between the "tribal Cherokees" and those "of Cherokee lineage." The tribal Cherokees live in old, distinctively Cherokee communities that have Cherokee names, and among these groups the main language of the home and church is Cherokee. Those of Cherokee lineage, however, may maintain only the most superficial connection with their heritage. They may have no social relationships with the tribal Cherokees, may live entirely in the White way, and may be unable to speak Cherokee. This same general pattern of variation within specific tribes may be found throughout the United States.

Consider the case of the Pequots, a 260-member Connecticut tribe. After 350 years of dispersion, most of its language, important ceremonial dances, and other traditions have disappeared. After the tribe introduced big-stakes gambling, it became enormously wealthy. In an effort to reconstruct an Indian culture, the tribe used some of its millions in profits to stage a major powwow that drew about 1,200 American Indians from all over North America to compete for prizes in sharing their traditional dances, skills, and songs (Johnson 1993:16). The Pequots said that they planned to observe the other tribes and borrow and adapt what they could in an effort to construct a culture of their own.

What, then, are we to conclude concerning the cultural assimilation of American Indians? First, all tribal cultures have been drastically changed by their long period of contact with the dominant American culture;[7] hence, a large majority of American Indians today speak English as one of their languages and exhibit greater or lesser degrees of acceptance of Anglo American ways. Second, the number of people who bear a particular Indian culture has, in many cases, either stabilized or now is increasing. Third, in addition to the maintenance and elaboration of the many tribal cultures, pan-Indian culture continues to develop. Although traditional rivalries and factionalism are still prominent, these increasingly are being subordinated to the larger concerns that affect all American Indians. Simultaneously, Indian people are emphasizing ways in which the many tribes share certain values.

American Indian Ethnic Renewal

There are many forces both inside and outside the American Indian communities that have promoted pan-Indian identity. Many have objected to the emergence of "Indian" as an ethnic group identifier, arguing that it reduces the experiences of Native Americans, who are tribal sovereign nations, to the status of immigrant ethnic groups who have no rights to sovereignty or nationhood (Nagel 1996:8). As we saw in Chapter 12, however, the activism of the 1960s convinced many Indian leaders that they had much in common with other minority groups. They increasingly thought of themselves as "Indians," as well as members of their tribal groups. Ironically, many of the policies aimed at assimilation, such as Indian education, political and economic development of the reservations, urban relocation, and settlement of land claims, led instead to increases in Indian ethnic identification and an Indian ethnic resurgence (Nagel 1996:115). Let us look at some of those processes.

Pan-Indian Identity. The boarding schools often provided young Indians with their first opportunities to interact with members of other tribes and to identify similarities in values. The Carlisle School in Pennsylvania tried to bring students from different tribes together to teach them English and citizenship skills. In doing so, English became a language Indian students could use across tribes. The school also produced marriages across tribes, which strengthened mixed tribal identity. Indians educated in these schools became some of the first pan-Indian leaders (Nagel 1996:116). Pan-Indian values—which Steele (1982:287) called "the informal credentials of 'Indianness'"—included such things as an acceptance of obligations to the extended family, the importance of mutual aid among Indians, noninterference in the affairs of others, a reverence for nature, and pride in a knowledge of Indian languages.

Service in the military was another experience that contributed to both the assimilation of Indians into U.S. society and to the development of a pan-Indian identity. To others in the military who knew little about tribal differences, the Pequots, Sioux, Navajos, Cherokees, and Mohawks became simply "Indians." After World War II, many Indians used their G.I. benefits to pursue additional education and, in the process, gained a better understanding of the common Indian problems of poverty and unemployment.

When tribes pursued legal claims in court, many of the petitions involved more than one tribe and required many occasions of intertribal contact and cooperation. Additionally, the publicity of the Red Power civil rights movement and the political organization required to participate in the massive federal programs of the Great Society in the 1960s combined to mobilize members of many different tribes as "American Indians." As the urban Indian population grew, pan-Indianism increased in importance. Active all-Indian associations formed in the urban areas containing large Indian populations. The Bay Area American Indian Council of San Francisco, representing around one hundred tribes, and the Chicago American Indian Center, also representing nearly one hundred tribes, became prominent examples of this trend (Spicer 1980a:113). Additionally, numerous all-Indian powwows, dances, and ceremonies, such as the annual American Indian Exposition at Anadarko, Oklahoma, encouraged American Indians to travel and associate with one another.

Finally, the maintenance of the tribal cultures and the development of a pan-Indian culture both serve to assure that the American Indians will have the option to remain American Indians even as they continue to assimilate the dominant culture. As Stewart (1977a:521) observed, "eventually, Indian cultures may fade away"; but, in the meantime, "Indians believe they can function with competence in modern society as Indians."

Secondary Structural Assimilation

The long period of conflict with the dominant society, the unwillingness of most tribes to adopt the dominant American ways, and the continuation of prejudice and discrimination into the present all have conspired to keep the Indians from participating equally in the educational, occupational, and financial systems of American society. For many decades, American Indians have lived in poverty, been ravaged by poor health and early death, and been inadequately clothed and sheltered. American Indians long have been, as Josephy (1971:15) stated, "the poorest of the poor."

No simple statistical accounting can do justice to the suffering the Indian peoples have endured. The authors of a 1969 report of the U.S. Senate's Special Subcommittee on Indian Education (Josephy 1971:168) commented on this point as follows:

> We are shocked at what we discovered. . . . We have developed page after page of statistics. These cold figures mark a stain on our national conscience, a stain which has spread slowly for hundreds of years. They tell a story . . . but they cannot tell the whole story. They cannot . . . tell of the despair, the frustration, the hopelessness, the poignancy, of children who want to learn but are not taught; . . . of families which want to stay together but are forced apart; or of . . . children who want neighborhood schools but are sent thousands of miles away to remote and alien boarding schools.

Education

If we consider a bit further the matter of schooling, two points stand out. First, there have been some definite increases in the educational levels of Indians during recent years; but, second, their educational attainments still lag noticeably behind those of Whites. For example, by 1989 more than 65 percent of all Indians over the age of twenty-four had completed twelve years or more of schooling; at the same time, more than 79 percent of the comparable White population had completed the same level of education (U.S. Bureau of the Census 1995:48, 50). Following a cohort of students from eighth to twelfth grade through 1992, the National Center for Education Statistics (1994) found that Native Americans had a 19.9 percent dropout rate compared to a 12.7 percent rate for Hispanics, a 9.6 percent rate for Blacks, and a 6.1 percent rate for Whites. As we have seen in some of our comparisons of Mexican and Black Americans with Whites, the rates of increase in college attendance have been higher among Indians than among Whites, but the absolute size of the gap between the groups has grown. The high percentages of high school and college dropouts among the Indian population has lowered young people's expectations of completing school. Bordewich (1996:286) quoted the Dean of Students at Haskell College at Lawrence, Kansas (formerly the Indian School, Haskell Institute) as saying, "Not long ago a kid came to me and said he wanted to drop out of school. I asked him why. He said, 'Because that's what Indians do.'"

We emphasized previously that the range of social variation among Indians is wide and that this point certainly applies to differences in educational attainment. Probably the most noticeable differences are between those who live in nonmetropolitan or reservation areas and those who live elsewhere; but there also are large differences between the young and the old. In general, for both sexes, those who live in cities and are young attain the highest average levels of education. For example, among metropolitan Indians older than twenty-four years who live in various regions of the country, the percentage of those with twelve or more years of education ranges, roughly, between 57 and 71 percent, whereas among those in nonmetropolitan areas the range is 37 to 60 percent. When people of different ages who live in various regions and have completed twelve or more years of education are compared, the range for those between the ages of twenty-five and thirty (including both sexes and both types of residential location) is, roughly, 71 to 79 percent, and for those over seventy the range lies between 13 and 29 percent (Snipp 1989:196–198).

There are substantial educational differences, too, among those who are over twenty-four and reside on one of the sixteen largest reservations. To illustrate, in 1970 almost 36 percent of those over twenty-four on the Wind River Reservation (WY) graduated from high school, whereas less than 13 percent graduated on the Papago Reservation (AZ). In 1980, these levels were over 39 and 25 percent, respectively. During the decade, however, the relative ranking of the reservations changed. In 1980, the Fort Peck Reservation (MT) had the highest proportion of graduates (almost 50 percent), while the Rosebud Reservation (SD) had the lowest (almost 20 percent) (Snipp 1989:202–203).

These figures attest to a general and rapid rise in the educational levels of Indians—levels that now approximate those of Mexican and Black Americans—but they tell us nothing concerning the quality of the schooling Indians receive, nor do they answer the question, "What does the educational experience of Indian children mean to them?" One devastating answer to that question may be found in the most extensive study of American education, the famous Coleman Report (1966). This study revealed that in answer to the question, "How bright do you think you are?" Indian children ranked themselves below all other groups.

We referred earlier to the schools operated by the BIA and their role in the attempt to force the Indians to adopt Anglo conformity. In the early days of this system, a comparatively small number of children attended the public schools. Now, however, over two-thirds of the Indian children attend public schools. The role of some of the government-operated schools has changed markedly. Many Indians now view the BIA reservation schools as their best chance to mold Indian education along the lines they desire. In some instances, when the BIA has attempted to close reservation schools, the Indians have protested and stopped the closings (Washburn 1973:103–104).

Lack of adequate funding, however, has seriously threatened the ability of the reservation schools to provide an adequate education. Despite a decade of efforts to improve the school for Pueblo children on the San Felipe Indian Reservation, Indian parents are deserting it for the public school in Algodones, six miles away (Barringer 1990). As a result, the tribal council, the sovereign tribal government, is pressuring parents to keep their children on the reservation; tribal elders accuse those who leave of disloyalty and disrespect and call them "Anglo." The parents respond that they want their children to adapt to the world outside of the reservation and express concerns about their children's opportunities to learn English, to do well academically, and to find good jobs if they attend the reservation school. Since state and federal funding for schools is based on enrollment, each student who "defects" to the public schools drains $2,500 from the Pueblo elementary school. In 1982, the reservation school enrolled 350 children. In 1990, with barely 300 children remaining, the reservation school had lost 15 percent of its budget, and had had to cut art, music, and physical education programs. The parents want their children to learn the best of both worlds—the reservation culture and "the English way." But those who enroll their children outside the reservation fear that the tribal elders will later deny them petitions for land or a building permit or a job with the tribal government; they also worry that they are going against tribal traditions that have kept the community intact over the years through wars, displacement, and Anglo intrusion. The federal government's cuts in education have influenced the decline in reservation schools. For example, although the BIA is required to finance tribal schools at the same per student average as the states they are in, most Indian schools are not equally funded. In South Dakota, the BIA in 1995 spent $2,900 on each high school student on the reservation while the state spent an average of $3,350 for each student in public schools outside the reservation (Brooke 1995).

The trend toward greater tribal control of the content and style of their children's education has extended into higher education with the establishment of such institutions as the Navajo Community College (mentioned earlier), the Lakota Higher Education Center, Sinte Gleska College (*Newsweek* 1973:71–72), and Little Big Horn College (Bordewich 1996:286). The first tribal college opened on the Navajo reservation in Arizona in 1968, and in 1994 throughout the United States there were twenty-six reservation colleges enrolling more than 16,000 Indian students. These tribal institutions began as community colleges granting associate degrees; but now three of them, including Sinte Gleska, offer four-year bachelor's programs and have recently expanded to offer master's degrees. Although the continued movement of the American Indians toward higher levels of educational attainment seems almost certain, one may well doubt whether the remaining gap between the Indians and the dominant group will close rapidly.

Occupations

Along with higher levels of education, the jobs of Indians who are employed have become more like those of the dominant group; but, both on and off the reservations, unemployment among Indians is high and economic hardship is common among them. The overall unemployment rates among males and females between the ages of twenty-one and twenty-five, for instance, have crossed 18 percent and 14 percent, respectively; and these rates are substantially below the ones for males and females between the ages of sixteen and twenty (more than 25 and 21 percent, respectively). The levels of unemployment on the reservations are even more unfavorable than the overall pattern; and on all of the sixteen largest reservations, the rate increased during the 1970s. To illustrate, at the Pine Ridge Reservation (SD), the unemployment rate rose between 1970 and 1980 from over 16 percent to nearly 36 percent. The reported level of unemployment on the Pine Ridge Reservation in 1995 was 75 percent and Shannon County, South Dakota, where the Pine Ridge Reservation is located, was the poorest county in the nation (Brooke 1995). These increases in unemployment occurred during a period when the number of people in the labor force also was increasing, suggesting that the increasing education and skill levels of the Indians were not matched by employment opportunities on the reservations (Snipp 1989:220, 226, 227).

One way that some 113 tribes have created jobs, as discussed earlier, is through the establishment of casinos and gaming on the reservations. Their advantage in this area is sovereignty which permits the suspension of many local, state, and federal laws on Indian territory. Reservations have no sales or property tax; so they can sell cigarettes, gasoline, and other items for low prices and can offer activities, like gambling, that are not permitted off the reservations. Gaming, in fact, has been described as "the best thing to happen to New Mexico Indians in four centuries of Spanish and American Dominance."[8] The gaming industry in New Mexico, which employs more than 3,000 people, has generated more that $200 million in revenue a year, and has reduced unemployment in the Sandia Pueblo in New Mexico to 2 percent.

Some tribes have used the profits from their casinos for other development projects. Consider the following: The Eastern Band of Cherokees earned about $850,000 per year between 1982 and 1992 and spent the money on government services for tribal members; the Santee Sioux helped tribal members buy homes or cars or go back to school; the Yankton Sioux's casino employed over 175 tribal members, about 80 percent of whom had been unemployed (*Americans Before Columbus* 1992); the Oneidas spent 9 million dollars to extend the Green Bay, Wisconsin, water and sewer system to the reservation (Bordewich 1996:109); the Morongo reservation just north of Palm Springs, California, employed more than 140 people in their bingo business and planned to develop a major desert resort; the 200 members of the Shakopee Mdewekantan tribe expected 1994 payments to exceed $500,000 for each member (Johnson 1994); and the Pequots, mentioned earlier, have employed 11,000 workers and made sufficient profits to fund sixteen restaurants, two hotels, a museum, a theater, a second casino, and—for all who can demonstrate that they are at least one-sixteenth Pequot—guaranteed employment, health care, child care, and educational expenses from kindergarten through graduate school (Pollack 1996).

Not all tribes have been successful in their gambling businesses, however. Many who have attempted gaming have struggled with conflicts among tribe members who oppose it because of the social impact. For example, some Oglalas oppose a casino because the gaming compact with the state gives South Dakota criminal jurisdiction over non-tribe members on the reservation. That, traditionalists argued, was an issue of treaty rights that Sioux warriors died for (Judson 1994). Other tribes have been exploited when they contracted with outside companies to run their gambling enterprises. Moreover, as more tribes initiate gaming businesses, they sometimes end up competing with one another. Still, the opportunity to become economically successful in the gaming business has made it possible for some tribes to buy back sacred lands they lost years ago and for others to invest in housing, hospitals, schools, roads, and other social services lacking on the reservations.

The gaming income also has allowed tribes to accumulate capital to diversify reservation economies that have long relied on government payments and subsidies. The Indian Business Association, a tribal trade group, now represents some 5,000 companies (Johnson 1994:10). The Southern Utes in Colorado have bought a gas-drilling company so they can extract their own gas resources rather than leasing the land to non-Indian businesses. The Navajos have organized an oil company. The Sioux on the Cheyenne River Reservation have begun raising bison, which are lower in fat and cholesterol than beef, and have found a market outside the reservation among health-conscious non-Indians. Indians have also financed Indian-run radio stations. Along the same lines, the Pine Ridge Sioux have published the first national Indian newspaper, *Indian Country Today,* that has a circulation of over 20,000. The newspaper employs thirty full-time employees, most of them Indian.

Tribes like the Arapaho on the Wind River Reservation in Wyoming, where there are not enough customers to make gaming work, have turned to tourism (McInnis 1994:4). In 1988, the Arapaho placed several tribal businesses into a trust. The small businesses—including a convenience store, a truck stop, a laundromat, and a construction company—provide eighty-five jobs and generate $7.5 million in annual revenues. The tribe also has plans for a reservation tour service. The Nez Perce Indians, a tribe that was forced from their land in Joseph, Oregon, in 1877, are being recruited to return by the White residents of the area who see the tribe as a potent economic resource (Egan 1996). The area has suffered economically as timber mills have shut down and the cattle industry has declined. Indian cultural events, such as powwows, have become a big tourist attraction, and the White town leaders have joined with the Nez Perce tribal leaders to invest in a Nez Perce cultural center. The tribe has also bought 10,000 acres of land along a creek in the area where their famous chief, Young Joseph, was born. The tribe will manage the land for hunting and fishing. Egan notes that the Whites see the return of the tribe as an economic plus, but the tribe sees it as a homecoming.

An obstacle to entrepreneurship among the Native Americans has been the lack of a capitalist tradition, which was seen as an "Anglo way of doing things." Until recently, there have been few residents on the reservations with experience as business managers and few with college experience (McInnis 1994:4). That pattern seems to be changing. The number of Indian-owned businesses increased 64 percent between 1982 and 1987 (Fost 1996). For example, the Laguna Indians in New Mexico have started manufacturing plants on the reservations. Laguna Industries employs 350 people and has contracts with the U.S. Department of Defense as well as several large companies. Although tribal elders hope that opportunities for jobs on the reservations will encurge young people to stay, these industries have not solved all the problems on the reservations. Unemployment continues to run as high as 35 percent on the Laguna Reservation.

Among those Indians who have jobs, the pattern of employment has become more similar to the dominant White pattern. In 1970, for instance, roughly 64 percent of White females and 43 percent of Indian females were employed in nonmanual jobs. By 1980, these figures had become 70 percent and 56 percent, respectively. Among males, the comparable figures were 41 and 22 percent (1970) and 45 and 28 percent (1980). We should also note that employed female and male Indians in both 1970 and 1980 were more likely to hold nonmanual jobs than were Black Americans (Snipp 1989:231).

Another way in which the jobs of Indians differ from those of Whites is that Indians are more likely to be employed by federal, state, or local governments. Indian employment by governmental agencies rose between 1970 and 1980 from around 24 percent to over 28 percent, whereas the employment of Whites by governments rose only slightly to remain between 15 and 16 percent. Blacks have become more similar to Indians in this respect. During this same period, government jobs for Blacks increased from about 15 percent to about 27 percent (Snipp 1989:238).

Although Indians still are plagued by high unemployment and the accompanying economic hardships, and although their general pattern of employment more nearly resembles that of Blacks than of Whites, there is clear evidence that their increasing educational levels do lead to higher-paying, higher-prestige jobs. In 1980, for example, 59 percent of Indian females and 55 percent of Indian males who had received a college education were employed in managerial and professional jobs, while an additional 28 percent of the females and 18 percent of the males in this group held technical, sales, and administrative support jobs (Snipp 1989:246). It is true, nonetheless, that Indians have much more difficulty translating high school graduation into college attendance than do Whites. Snipp (1989:190) calculated that among every additional one hundred White high school graduates, an additional forty-one people graduate from college; but among Indians, one hundred additional high school graduates produces only twelve additional college graduates. Furthermore, there is some evidence that the probability that an Indian between the ages of twenty-five and thirty will have completed four or more years of college is now *lower* than for those between the ages of thirty-one and seventy (Snipp 1989:200).

Incomes

The improved educational and employment levels of Indians have been accompanied by some improvement in income levels. As an example, in 1970, on average, for each dollar earned by White families, Indian families received 57 cents, which was less than 90 percent of the comparable figure for Black Americans (U.S. Bureau of the Census, *American Indians,* 1973); but, by 1979, on average, Indian family income had risen to 66 cents for each dollar earned by Whites, which was at that point, slightly *higher* than the median family income of Blacks compared to Whites (60 cents per dollar). The proportion of Indian families below the poverty line (27 percent) also has declined to a point below that of Blacks (31 percent), but both of these groups still have much larger proportions of poor families than do Whites (9.4 percent) (U.S. Bureau of the Census 1995:48, 50).

Nevertheless, by many measures American Indians are the poorest ethnic group in the country (Johnson 1994). Of the ten poorest U.S. counties in the 1990 census, four were Indian lands in South Dakota. Many Indian families on the reservations still live in shacks and must haul water in pickup trucks. Sandefur and Sakamoto (1988:79) noted that American Indians may appear to have a higher average income than Blacks; however, since Indians are more likely to live in traditional family households (couples with children) than either Blacks or Whites, their higher family income may reflect the efforts of more wage earners.

Life Chances

Health care is an area in which the efforts to close the gap between Indians and Whites appears to be having marked success. To illustrate, consider the change in the infant mortality rates among American Indians. From 1950 to 1983, this sensitive indicator of the general health level of a population declined from an extremely high 82 infant deaths per 1,000 Indian births per year to about 11 deaths per 1,000 births (Snipp

1989:352).[9] This large decline within such a short period of time is remarkable. Not only was the American Indian infant mortality rate rapidly approaching the White level (9.7 per 1,000 in 1983), it had fallen below the rate for Black Americans in 1992 (16.8) (U.S. Bureau of the Census, 1995:91).

The improvement in infant mortality, as important as it is, does not mean that the general health and mortality experience of American Indians is no longer a matter of concern. Indians still are much more likely than all Americans combined to die fairly early in life. Davis, Hunt, and Kitzes (1989:271) reported that in 1982, "37 percent of the deaths among American Indians occurred before age 45, compared with 12 percent of deaths in the same age group in the U.S. population." Indians also still suffer a disproportionate number of deaths from causes that reflect broader problems faced by Indians. For example, although accidental deaths among them have declined dramatically since 1970, Indians still are roughly twice as likely to die in an accident as are members of the general population; and suicide rates among Indians, though also lower than in 1970, are still roughly 25 percent higher than the rate for all Americans (U.S. Department of Health, Education and Welfare, *Health, United States, 1979,* 1980:12, 16); and Indian teenagers are about four times as likely to attempt suicide as are other teens (Brasher 1992). Indians also are about twice as likely to be murdered, four times as likely to die of alcoholism, and nine times as likely to die of tuberculosis as are other Americans (Snipp 1989:355–358). As is true of the American population as a whole, however, Indians are more likely to die of heart disease than of any other single cause (Rhoades et al. 1988:622).

The statistics concerning the status of American Indians in various areas of life may be viewed, from different perspectives, either as encouraging or discouraging. If one emphasizes the recency of serious attention to the development of the reservations and to integrating Indians into urban life and industrial occupations, then the size of the "lags" in these areas may be viewed in some ways as being relatively low. But when the "lags" are seen absolutely—in terms of life chances and human privation—it is evident that much remains to be done. Even though it may now be true, after many decades of effort, that Indians, collectively, are no longer the "poorest of the poor," it also is true that they still are far from having the standard of living enjoyed by Whites and still "are one of the most disadvantaged racial/ethnic groups in the United States" (Sandefur and Scott 1983:44).

Primary Structural Assimilation

Throughout the centuries, Indians and Whites have enjoyed few opportunities to be genuinely friendly. Some members of each group, of course, have had large numbers of friends within the other group; but the ordinary state of affairs has been for most of each Indian's friends to be other Indians of the same tribe.

Given the long history of conflicts between Indian and European peoples, and given the effort to contain the Indians by segregating them in Indian Country and on reservations, this outcome is hardly surprising. The historically low level of primary assimilation among the Indians has been extended into the present. Reservation Indians, both by choice and circumstance, are unlikely to have very many contacts with non-Indians. Urban Indians, on the other hand, may have numerous opportunities to form friendships with non-Indians in schools and colleges, at work, in various social organizations, and in their neighborhoods. How do Indians react to these possibilities?

Some valuable information on this question was presented by Ablon (1972) in a study of American Indians who lived in the San Francisco Bay Area. Most of those studied had come to the area under the BIA's relocation program. Ablon interviewed fifty-three Indians concerning many aspects of their lives in the city, including such things as who their early social contacts in the city were, how those contacts were made, whether they preferred Indian or White friends, how they felt about themselves, and so on. She found, first, that the Indians most frequently established their social contacts at gatherings sponsored by various intertribal organizations founded by or for Indians. The next most common form of early contacts was with friends or relatives from the reservations. The Indians reported that after they had been in the city for a while, they had an increasing proportion of their social contacts with people from work and in their neighborhoods. Most of the Indians stated they had White friends as well as Indian friends; however, in all of these contexts, their friendships with Whites tended to be superficial. Only three of fifty-four Indians who participated in the study stated they had more White than Indian friends.

Ablon (1972:422–423) argued that two prevalent attitudes among the Indians toward Whites are suspicion and a fear of rejection. Whites who attempt to be friendly toward the Indians are suspected of wishing to take advantage of them, while the Indians fear that the Whites will look down on them if they learn the details of the Indians' poverty-stricken reservation lives or their tribal beliefs. Moreover, aside from their reasons for wishing to avoid Whites, Indians have a strong, positive wish to be with other Indians. This view accords with One Feather's (1986:171) observation that "the people who moved to urban areas formed their own Indian communities. Indian centers became a focal point for the people that lived in cities."

As usual, of course, we should expect that the behavior pattern just described would vary among the tribes. In a study of Indians in Los Angeles—the city containing the largest American Indian population—Price (1972) compared the members of the three major tribal groups in the city (the Navajo, Sioux, and Five Civilized Tribes). He found that the Navajo were least likely to establish extratribal ties to life in the city, and the members of the Five Civilized Tribes were the most likely to do so. The Sioux were intermediate. For example, 64 percent of the Navajo, 33 percent of the Sioux, and 26 percent of the members of the Five Civilized Tribes revealed that they "associate entirely or mostly with Indians" (Price 1972:437). In general, the Navajo also maintained the strongest ties to the reservations, while the members of the Five Civilized Tribes maintained the weakest ties. From these findings, Price (1972:436) argued that the Navajos probably would "shift over time to patterns of life exemplified by the Five Civilized Tribes."

While the occurrence of such a shift would imply a parallel increase in primary assimilation for those involved, there is little reason to suppose that urban American

Indians will soon reach a point at which associations with other Indians will become unimportant. Liebow (1989:67) found in Phoenix, for instance, that the Indians there—representing many tribes—"have set about self-consciously creating a collective identity that is primarily tied to their adoptive metropolitan home." As Price (1972:439) noted, "the great majority of Indians in the city clearly are ideologically and emotionally affiliated with pan-Indianism." The maintenance or growth of this commitment among American Indians may well exert a continuing pressure against full primary assimilation.

Marital Assimilation

The romantic courtship and marriage of John Rolfe and Pocahontas during the earliest years of the Jamestown Colony did not foretell a high level of marital assimilation of the Indians into the society of the English. Although we lack the information needed to discuss these matters precisely in the present, much less in the distant past, it appears that until recently the levels of marital assimilation among the Indians have been low. This condition is what we would have expected on the basis of our discussion of the generally low levels of primary assimilation. To be sure, various circumstances have produced higher levels of intermarriage at some times and places than others. For example, during the early years in the southern colonies, where White women were scarce and Indian women were plentiful, there were numerous White male–Indian female marriages. According to Nash (1974:282), Thomas Bosomworth, who was a chaplain in the Georgia colony, "found it respectable to marry a Creek woman . . . and many others followed his example."

As in the case of Black Americans, of course, the actual levels of sexual relations between Indians and Whites always have been higher than the rates of legitimate intermarriage; consequently, the level of intermixture after almost four centuries of contact is quite high. The proportion of Indians who were considered to be full-bloods in the 1980s varied among the tribes and was, in general, higher on the reservations than in the cities. In both locations, however, only a minority among the American Indians now qualify as full-bloods, and many millions of Americans who do not profess an Indian identity claim some degree of Indian ancestry. We should note again that the terms *full-blood* and *mixed-blood* frequently refer to a person's cultural commitment rather than to their biological ancestry. Large numbers of mixed-bloods in the past and present have been, or now are, "completely Indian" in the way they think of themselves and live. On the other hand, some biological full-bloods have adopted the White man's way of life and have been regarded by themselves and other Indians as no longer Indian. Our claim that, in the past, the levels of Indian–White intermarriage have been low, therefore, is based only on those marriages in which one of the partners considers himself or herself to be an Indian. Most instances in which one partner acknowledges some degree of mixed ancestry are not counted as examples of Indian–White intermarriage.

Roy (1972:233), for instance, found that among twenty-eight Spokane Indian couples living on a reservation, twenty marriages in which both partners were Indians included at least one member who was not considered to be a full-blood. Roy (1972:233)

did note, however, that "people with a high percentage of Indian ancestry tended to select mates with a high percentage of Indian ancestry," suggesting some relationship between the Indians' cultural and presumed biological identities. A subsequent study of
the Spokane Indians by White and Chadwick (1972:246) found that urban Indians were
more likely than reservation Indians to consider their identities to be mainly a matter of
ancestry. The explanation of this finding appears to be that urban Indians suffer more
discrimination because of their physical appearance and, therefore, feel "Indian" if they
look "Indian."

Eschbach (1995:95–96) found that the lowest proportion of those who were intermarried were in the states with large Indian populations who lived in enclave communities. The range of Indians in mixed marriages varied from 16 percent intermarried in
the Southwest to 82 percent intermarried in the Midwest. The younger Indians generally
had higher intermarriage rates than older Indians, but the same regional differences
persisted for the young couples. One of the dilemmas in intermarriages is whether the
children will be identified as Indian or non-Indian. Nationally, only 47 percent of the
children in intermarried families are assigned the race of their Indian parent. The as-
signment of identity to children also varies by region, with 73 percent of the children
born to intermarried couples in Oklahoma assigned Indian descent, whereas only 33
percent of the children born to intermarried couples in the Northeast are assigned Indian descent at birth. Eschbach (1995:96) speculates that whether or not parents in
mixed marriages assign Indian descent to their children depends on the political and
economic importance of Indian identity in the area and the amount of discrimination
and ethnic conflict between Indians and others the parents have experienced. Eschbach
concludes that Indians in mixed marriages will continue to identify as Indian as long as
that identity is available to them *and* is socially valuable.

Despite the paucity of research on Indian intermarriage, we do know that the levels of marital assimilation among Indians appear to have risen sharply in recent times.
Between 1960 and 1970, the proportion of Indian husbands who married non-Indian
wives rose from 15 percent to 33 percent, and the proportion of Indian wives who married non-Indian husbands rose from over 24 percent to 39 percent (Heer 1980:519). By
1990, Eschbach (1995:93) found that nationally 59 percent of married Indians were
married to non-Indians. Taken at face value, these findings suggest a strong surge
among American Indians toward the mainstream of society. Given all of our other findings, however, it seems possible that the apparently large increase in intermarriage may
be "related to an increased desire among persons with mixed White and Indian ancestry
to identify themselves as Indian Americans" (Heer 1980:519), as we mentioned earlier.
Adding to this view are the findings of Passel and Berman (cited by Sandefur and McK-
innell 1986:348) that as many as 358,000 people in the United States changed their self-
identification from White to Indian during the 1970s. Bordewich (1996:66) quoted an
administrator of the BIA as saying, "There are a lot of just plain old Americans who
want to belong to an ethnic group of some kind. . . . [A]t this point in time a lot of
people want to be Indian."

Many tribes have been forced to expand their definition of who is an Indian because of the increased rate of out-marriage (Nagel 1996:245). For example, Sandefur

and McKinnell (1986:357) showed that in states that traditionally have had large numbers of people who define themselves as Indian (states where pressures toward marrying within the ethnic group presumably are strong), 37 percent of the Indian men marry women of different races. Out-marriage is even higher in states that traditionally have had comparatively small Indian populations. In these states, about 62 percent of the Indian men marry women of other races.

These broad generalizations, of course, leave many questions unanswered. Are the rates of intermarriage among some tribes remaining steady or falling in contrast to the general trend? Are the rates of intertribal intermarriage increasing and, if so, what is the social and cultural significance of these changes? These and other questions invite further study. For the moment, however, we must be content to note that the rates of Indian–White intermarriage appear to have risen sharply, which may signify an historic change in the relations of the two groups.

American Indian "Success"

We have noted that since the time of the first contacts in North America, some European peoples have attempted to "civilize" the Indians; however, the primary approach of the Whites throughout most of the centuries since then has been to attempt to separate the two groups of people. The Indians, for their part, have responded in a complementary fashion. Some of them have more or less willingly accepted "civilization," but far more common has been the attempt to remain apart, to accept only certain elements of European culture, and still to maintain their traditional ways of life.

Until the end of the nineteenth century, the Indians experienced only sporadic pressures to "succeed" within American society, but with the passage of the Dawes Act in 1887, the United States government adopted as its official and exclusive policy a program to force them to accept the ways of the dominant society. This change, as mentioned earlier, did not cause the Indians to alter their traditional policies. If they could not regain their lost lands and means of subsistence, then they still wished at least to become "dependent domestic nations"—self-governing groups within the boundaries of American society.

Once again, perhaps more sharply than previously, we see an illustration of the close link between a group's ideology and the question of assessing its success within American society. Even though the tribes have varied in their willingness to accept certain elements of White culture, there can be little doubt that the central impulse among the Indians has been to resist being drawn into American society. From this perspective, any step toward assimilation that involved the substitution of White for Indian ways has represented some measure of failure.

Although it has seemed clear to most White Americans that their civilization—at first agrarian but now urban-industrial—is superior and worth adopting, the Indians have largely disagreed. To a considerable extent, American ethnocentrism has been matched by Indian ethnocentrism. The Indians' conviction that their way is best has been bolstered by the increasing problems confronting industrial civilization. Problems relating to air and water pollution, soil erosion, energy exhaustion, ecological imbalance, and widespread feelings of loneliness and powerlessness are all interpreted by many Indians, and some non-Indians as well, as a sign of the impermanence and inferiority of White culture. From this perspective, the Indians always have had a great deal to teach the Whites about life, and now, soon perhaps, the Whites will be forced to listen. Deloria (1972:506) argued the point as follows: "At the present time everyone is watching how mainstream America will handle the issues of pollution, poverty, crime and racism when it does not fundamentally understand the issues. . . . It just seems to a lot of Indians that this continent was a lot better off when we were running it."

The outcome of the American Indians' struggle against the worldly success of White society is presently unclear. They appear now to have become predominantly an urban people, but many hope that "tribalism can be incorporated with modern technology in an urban setting" (Deloria 1972:506). This hope is counterbalanced, however, by the unquenched fear that the ancient tribal values will be lost before they can become ascendant. As Deloria (1981:149) stated subsequently: "While tribal traditions provide a bulwark against the consumer society, continued contact may well mean the end of Indian uniqueness in a world increasingly homogenized. The pervasive fear of Indians is that they will in the years ahead move from their plateau of small nationhood to the status of another ethnic group in the American melting pot."

We have described in several of the preceding chapters some of the dramatic changes that have occurred in American racial and ethnic relations during recent decades. In Chapter 14, we will consider further some of the ways White Americans have reacted to these changes, and we will also present additional information concerning the new immigration.

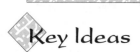

Key Ideas

1. The Indian population is increasing in number, contrary to what each of the assimilation models would predict. This may be due to an increasing number of persons of mixed Indian heritage identifying themselves as Indian.

2. Pan-Indian identity occurs when Indians see themselves as having common "Indian" bonds with members of other tribes. This identity represents assimilation by addition in situations where Indians maintain a strong tribal identity. It may become assimilation by substitution when tribal identity no longer prevails. As the boundaries of identity expand, "Indian" becomes a term to identify an ethnic group.

3. The movement of American Indians toward secondary assimilation in education, occupations, incomes, and health care has been very rapid during recent decades,

especially among urban Indians. Despite the rapid rates of change, however, the Indian averages still lag behind those of American society in general, and many reservations have high levels of poverty and unemployment. On average, however, the income levels of Indians have come to approximate those of Blacks and Mexican Americans. The average educational level among the American Indians now is higher than among Mexican Americans, and the rate of infant mortality among Indians is lower than among Black Americans.

4. Tribal sovereignty has given American Indians opportunities to create their own laws, schools, and businesses on the reservations. Gaming has brought increased wealth to a number of reservations and has allowed them to use the profits to diversify the economies on the reservations and promote traditional cultures. However, some reservations do not have the geographic location to succeed at gaming and have turned to entrepreneurship. They have established small businesses in tourism, provided services on the reservations, and built manufacturing plants. Some of these endeavors have created conflicts among the traditional and the more assimilated tribe members. Sovereignty also has created conflicts with state governments.

5. Historically, primary and marital assimilation of the Indians into White society have been low. Although the levels of primary assimilation may be rising somewhat faster in the cities than on the reservations, the levels still appear to be generally low. Marital assimilation, on the other hand, appears in recent years to have risen sharply. This puzzling finding suggests either that the levels of primary assimilation also are rising sharply or that the higher rates of intermarriage represent the assimilation of the Indians' spouses into Indian society.

6. Since the end of official separatism in the nineteenth century, the dominant society has alternated between Indian policies of Anglo conformity and cultural pluralism. Throughout this time, the Indian tribes as a whole have rejected the dominant culture and have defined success mainly in terms of tribal and cultural survival. From the perspective of an ability to maintain identities, cultures, and forms of organization that are distinct from that of the dominant group, the American Indians have been very successful.

Key Terms

blood quantum   Is presumed to indicate the degree to which a person is of Indian ancestry and is a key concept used, historically as well as currently, in administrative definitions of who is an American Indian. The concept was based on the ancient idea that hereditary characteristics are transmitted through the blood and, therefore, that the "amount of blood" a person possessed from a particular race determined physical characteristics and social behavior. This concept was central in the eugenics movement.

full-blood   A person who is believed to have no non-Indian "blood" or ancestry.

mixed-bloods   Persons who identify themselves as Indian but are recognized socially to have some non-Indian ancestry.

self-identification   Allows individuals to determine their own racial or ethnic identification. Self-identification is now used in federal census counts and is believed to be a factor in the rapid growth of the Indian population.

Notes

1. See Rothenberg (1995:290–294).

2. For an excellent discussion of the "blood quantum" approach to racial identification, see Snipp (1989).

3. Nagel and Snipp (1993) used the term *ethnic reorganization* to describe the process whereby an ethnic minority redefines its ethnic group boundaries and social structure.

4. See, e.g., Jordan and Litwack (1987:2); (Nagel 1996:115).

5. See *NARF Legal Review* (Summer/Fall 1994).

6. See the *New York Times* article by Kleinfield (1995:A9).

7. Snipp (1989:20) observed that since the White man's diseases generally preceded the actual arrival of many White people, the "traditional" tribal societies that were found by the Whites *already* had been markedly altered.

8. See Johnson (1996:24).

9. These figures reflect only the experiences of the approximately 850,000 American Indians who in 1980 lived within the boundaries of the eighty-eight service units of the Indian Health Service (IHS).

The New Immigration

The third stream of immigration to the United States may surpass the numbers of immigrants in the second stream. The new immigration has included many refugees and undocumented immigrants. Here, a boatload of Chinese illegal aliens are denied entry into the United States.

It doesn't take much to become a refugee.
Your race or beliefs can be enough.
—UNCHR wall poster, Bangkok

Well, how does a nation of no one culture, no one language,
no one race, no one history, no one ethnic stock continue
to exist as one, while encouraging diversity?
—Michael Novak

Ethnic diversity is an opportunity rather than a problem.
—Andrew M. Greeley

No one wants to be a Know-Nothing.
Yet uncontrolled immigration is an impossibility.
—Arthur M. Schlesinger, Jr.

The experiences of the Japanese Americans, Mexican Americans, African Americans, and Native Americans reveal some of the social consequences of the main types of intergroup contact at different periods in American history. The Japanese immigrated voluntarily during the second great immigrant stream; their immigration was halted by the Immigration Act of 1924; but they were able to resume immigration after 1952. The Mexican American ethnic group was created through conquest but has been prominent in both the second and, especially, the third great immigrant streams. African Americans were a part of the colonial immigration but, since the overwhelming majority came as slaves, they certainly did not enter the country voluntarily. The Native Americans were subjected to the rule of Europeans and their descendants over a long period of time. Our discussion reviewed a number of ideas concerning the factors that have encouraged or discouraged the members of these groups to adopt or reject one or another of the ideologies of intergroup relations discussed in Chapter 2. We turn now to a further consideration of the way domestic and international events since 1965 have combined to stimulate a "new"—and third—great immigrant stream and to affect various reactions among Americans to this immigration.

In Chapter 4, we summarized the main features of the new immigration, noting especially its rapid increase in size and also the diversity of the groups that comprise it. For the first time in U.S. history, most of the immigrants have come from non-European countries (see Figure 4.3). In the present chapter, we expand these themes but devote special attention to one refugee group within the third stream—the Vietnamese.

The circumstances surrounding the entry of the Vietnamese into the United States were such that a substantial effort was made to assist in their adjustment to American life. For that purpose, a number of analyses of that process have been conducted.[1] Because good information on the various Vietnamese generations has been collected and analyzed, and because the Vietnamese were the largest refugee group of the third stream, we will examine their adaptation to American life in some detail.

This chapter concludes with a discussion (1) of some events that indicate an increase of racism and nativism in reaction to this most recent heavy immigration and (2) a brief examination, in Flashpoint 3, of some of the salient issues of the contemporary debate over immigration policy.

Changes in the Laws and the Immigrant Stream

In the first dozen years following World War II, the U.S. government adopted a number of new immigration policies affecting refugees and also altered its basic immigration law. The new law, passed in 1952, was the Immigration and Nationality Act (INA). This law continued national-origins quotas for the nations of the Eastern Hemisphere and, consequently, was severely criticized by those who wished to do away with that approach; but the law also provided that members of all races could become citizens, eliminated gender discrimination in admissions, introduced special-preference designations for people who had talents or skills that were needed in the United States, and increased the number of relatives of citizens and permanent residents who could be brought into the country above the quota restrictions.

A second basic change occurred in 1965 when Congress passed the Immigration and Nationality Act Amendments (INAA). This law rejected the principle first adopted in 1921 that immigration quotas should be based on one's nationality. The total number of immigrants who could be admitted annually was raised to 290,000, an annual ceiling of 120,000 entries was set for the Western Hemisphere, an annual ceiling of 170,000 was set for all countries in the Eastern Hemisphere, and each country in the Eastern Hemisphere was limited to no more than 20,000 visas per year. The law also established a new preference system that aimed to reunite family members, permit certain professional and skilled workers to enter the country, and provide a place of asylum for refugees.

The combined effects of these and other immigration laws passed between 1945 and 1965 contributed to three important sociocultural characteristics of the new immigrant stream that distinguish it from the first and second streams. First, hundreds of thousands of refugees have entered the United States since 1945. Second, the racial and ethnic composition of the new immigration has been decidedly different from the first two streams, with the majority of immigrants originating in non-European countries. And third, the high level of undocumented entrants among the new immigrants has been unprecedented.

Refugees: An International Issue

The expulsion of people from their lands of residence is nothing new, of course; but the problems associated with international refugee movements have increased steadily since the seventeenth century. As the world became organized into nation-states and the human population skyrocketed, governments increasingly sought to control the composition of their populations by welcoming the members of some groups and driving out others. This tendency increased until, by the twentieth century, the problem of what to do with the rising number of refugees became an important international question. The "refugee problem" of the latter half of the twentieth century has been created by internal and international conflicts in which millions of people have fled from their homelands fearing for their lives. These people have sought to resettle in other countries primarily because they believed it was necessary in order to avoid execution, imprisonment, or persecution for political reasons rather than to improve their economic or religious opportunities.

Many people who were displaced by World War II or were refugees from communist countries were admitted to the United States under provisions of the Displaced Persons Act of 1948, which created 220,000 spaces above the immigration quotas for European victims of the ravages of the war. Additional numbers of nonquota immigrants were permitted under the Refugee Relief Act of 1953 (Abrams 1984:109). After the Hungarian Revolution of 1956, large numbers of the defeated anti-communist "freedom fighters" sought admission to the United States. President Eisenhower set a precedent by admitting thousands of Hungarians above Hungary's quota by granting them asylum under the "parole" authority (Reimers 1985:26).

The parole provision also was used by President John F. Kennedy in 1961 to allow the entry above the quota of the anti-communist Cuban refugees who fled following Fidel Castro's revolution (Reimers 1985:27). Additionally, following the failed Bay of Pigs invasion of Cuba, the Migration and Refugee Assistance Act of 1962 granted refugee status to resident Cubans and provided financial and other assistance to aid in their resettlement within the United States. During the remainder of the 1960s and throughout the 1970s, wars in Vietnam and other parts of Indochina created millions of new refugees who sought to establish new lives in other countries. The Refugee Act of 1980 aimed to establish a "systematic procedure for the admission and effective resettlement of refugees of special humanitarian concern to the United States" (U.S. Immigration and Naturalization Service 1996:A.1–18). Altogether, more than 780,000 Cubans and 725,000 Indochinese whose lives were disrupted by military and political upheavals have become a part of the population of the United States (Kitano and Daniels 1988:138; U.S. Immigration and Naturalization Service 1996:28). During the 1990s, wars in the former Soviet Union, Bosnia, Rwanda, and other locations throughout the world continued to displace people from their homes and create new refugees, many of whom have sought asylum in the United States.

The staggering increases in the numbers of refugees in the world and the efforts of displaced people to gain admission to the United States have generated serious tensions between Americans' desire to limit immigration, on the one hand, and the traditional idea that the United States is an asylum for oppressed people, on the other (Bernard

1980:495).[2] The periodic admission of refugees outside of the normal quota limits has left us uncertain whether such additional newcomers demonstrate, in Glazer's (1985:3) words, "our openness and generosity, or our simple incapacity to forge a national policy on the key question of who shall be allowed to become an American."

Increasing Diversity

The changes contained within the INAA of 1965, in combination with economic and political problems in third-world countries, stimulated a sharp increase in the volume of immigration from Mexico, Central America, the Caribbean, South America, and Asia and altered the sociocultural composition of the immigration flow that had commenced immediately following World War II. These changes in the new immigrant stream became more pronounced in the following decades of the twentieth century with the largest numbers of newcomers coming from Mexico. The other leading countries of origin have been, in order, the Philippines, Korea, China (including Taiwan), India, the Dominican Republic, Vietnam, and the countries of Central America (U.S. Immigration and Naturalization Service 1996:28). In addition, around 400,000 new immigrants have arrived from the countries of Africa since 1965.

These latest newcomers have exhibited a much wider variety of social, educational, and occupational backgrounds than those in the previous immigrant streams, greatly increasing the sociocultural diversity of the United States. Both the INA of 1952 and the INAA of 1965 included preference categories for those who had scarce job skills. These provisions have enabled a sizable group of professionals to join the third stream. To illustrate, in fiscal year 1994 among the immigrants admitted who listed a previous occupation, nearly one-third described themselves as having worked either in "Professional speciality and technical" or in "Executive, administrative, and managerial" jobs. People in these categories came from all over the world, but almost three-fourths of them were from Asia and Europe (47 percent and 27 percent, respectively) (U.S. Immigration and Naturalization Service 1996:68–69).[3] In the same year, more than one-fifth of those admitted with a stated occupation were listed in the category "Operator, fabricator, and laborer." These workers, too, came from all over the world; but their origins were more concentrated in the Western Hemisphere, with over 50 percent of them coming from Mexico and the countries of the Caribbean.

Speaking very generally, the Hispanics of the third stream, on average, have been of comparatively lower educational levels and possessed mainly blue-collar work skills (resembling, in this way, the immigrants in the previous streams); and the Asians, on average, have been more highly educated and possessed white-collar work skills (Cué and Bach 1980:262, 266; Kitano 1981:129, 132, 134). We can hardly overemphasize, however, that the labels "Hispanic" and "Asian" are umbrella terms each of which treats as a unit several groups that differ from one another markedly and also are internally variegated.

Economic Adaptation and Settlement Patterns. Following Castro's successful communist revolution in Cuba, the upper and middle classes were adversely affected; so many industrialists, landowners, managers, and professionals soon left for the United

States (Portes 1969:506). The entrepreneurial success of many of these highly skilled first-wave immigrants has attracted widespread notice. In Miami's "Little Havana," for example, "Cuban-owned firms went from 919 firms in 1967 to 8,000 in 1976 to 28,000 today. Most average 8.1 employees but include factories employing hundreds of workers" (Portes and Rumbaut 1990:21–22).

In contrast to the Cuban refugees who first emigrated following the revolution, the later immigrants from Cuba have consisted mainly of people of lower occupational and educational standing (Bean and Tienda 1987:28–29; Cué and Bach 1980:263–264; Massey 1981:59).[4] This pattern, in which the earlier refugees have higher levels of occupational skill than those who come later, was found also among the Vietnamese; and for much the same reason. The first-wave refugees of both Cuba and Vietnam were mainly members of political and educational elites who were unseated by revolutionary movements, whereas the later refugees were "people of more modest backgrounds" (Rumbaut 1996:318).

High levels of education or previous occupational attainments, however, often do not assure that immigrants will occupy similar positions within the United States. Kim (1980:604) presented as a typical example the experience of a former government administrator who worked in a service station while his wife worked in a garment factory. After working six- or seven-day weeks, they saved enough money to buy a small business and, eventually, were able to buy a home. Kelly (1977:179) reported cases in which the director general of the South Vietnamese Ministry of the Interior was employed working in yards, an air force colonel was delivering newspapers, a medical doctor was a dishwasher, and the chief of staff of the South Vietnamese army was a waiter.

An important economic response of some highly educated members of the new immigrant groups to the difficulty of resuming their former occupations is to establish small specialized businesses, as did the members of several groups in the first and second streams. Many Koreans who have professional backgrounds, for instance, have been unable to move into mainstream employment that requires English proficiency; so they have started businesses instead. The large Koreatowns in Los Angeles and New York have been built in this way.[5] Although the Koreans have established many different kinds of businesses, non-Koreans probably are most familiar with their work as greengrocers (Kim 1987:230). Many Asian Indians, too, are self-employed. They are especially prominent as owners or operators of convenience stores, stationery shops, and motels and hotels (McDowell 1996:C1; Mogelonsky 1996:133).

In discussions of the new Chinese immigrants, some observers distinguish between two main groups—characterized by Kwong (cited by Chow 1996:121) as the "downtown" and the "uptown" Chinese. The downtown Chinese are mainly those who have "settled in or near Chinatowns where they could easily find jobs in ethnic businesses," get along primarily in a Chinese language, and find inexpensive housing. In contrast, the uptown Chinese consist primarily "of better-educated professionals, businessmen, top financial managers, and former government officials" (Chow 1996:121). The high educational and occupational levels among the new immigrant Chinese have reinforced a "model minority" stereotype of upward mobility established earlier by the Chinese Americans. By 1980, more than 40 percent of the Chinese had completed college, attended graduate school, or completed a doctoral degree as compared to 18 percent of White Americans.[6] Similarly, by 1980 more than 41 percent of Chinese men and 26 percent of Chinese women were employed in executive and professional jobs as compared to about 27 and 23 percent of White men and women, respectively.[7]

The immigrants of the third stream also have been more diverse in their places of destination than were the immigrants of the first two streams. Although some states that traditionally have received large numbers of immigrants, such as New York, have continued to be popular destinations, some additional states and regions of the country have received a large proportion of the third-stream immigrants. The Vietnamese refugees, for instance, were intentionally resettled by the government in various parts of the country. They are concentrated mainly in California, Texas, Pennsylvania, and Louisiana (Montero 1979:8; Wright 1980:511). The Cubans, who also were intentionally resettled in different parts of the United States, have migrated in large numbers to southern Florida and southern California. Cubans remain in sizeable numbers, however, in northern metropolitan areas with large Spanish-speaking populations. Koreans are concentrated in Los Angeles, New York, and Chicago; and East Indians are concentrated in California and New York (Mogelonsky 1996:133). The majority of Mexicans have settled in the border states of the Southwest, particularly in California and Texas (Perez 1980:257; Portes and Rumbaut 1990:46).

Sociocultural Diversity. The members of some of the new immigrant groups have entered the country with a greater knowledge of English and of American folkways and mores than the average members of other first-generation groups. Filipinos typically read and speak English in addition to Spanish or one or more native languages like Tagalog or Ilocano. Following the Spanish–American War in 1898, the Philippine Islands became an American possession (Fifield and Romulo 1962:341). The United States then established a colonial government which set about to Americanize the islanders. The chief tool of Americanization (in addition to military force) was a new system of schools staffed with American teachers who required the use of English in the classroom.

Some observers consider Filipinos to be "the most 'Westernized' of Asian Americans" (Cariño 1996:297); and, as is true for most Asian groups in America, the Filipinos of the new immigration have a high average level of education. For instance, in a comparison of the percent of people within nine ethnic groups who had completed college, Barringer, Gardner, and Levin (1995:172) found that, in 1980, more than twice as many new immigrant Filipinos as Whites had completed college and that, overall, Filipinos ranked second in this respect among the nine groups (behind Asian Indians).[8] The Asian Indians of the new immigration, too, typically are highly westernized. English is an official language of India (along with fifteen other languages) and is widely used as a "common medium of communication" (Jensen 1980:296).[9] As is true of the Philippines, the Westernization of India (and Indians' knowledge of English) may be traced to a long history of colonial occupation by rival European powers, among whom Britain became dominant over two centuries ago. Both Filipinos and Asian Indians have shown a lower inclination than the other groups to form distinct ethnic enclaves but rather have tended to disperse more widely both geographically and economically (Takaki, cited by Barringer 1991:A9).

Time of Arrival.   Still another source of diversity among the new immigrants stems from the length of time the members of each group have been represented in significant numbers within the American population. Substantial numbers of Mexicans, Chinese, Japanese, and Filipinos reached the United States before 1924. Although the range of differences in education, social class, and job skills within these groups was large, most of the nineteenth- and early twentieth-century immigrants from these groups were fairly similar to one another. They were mainly manual laborers with little education. Nevertheless, despite high levels of prejudice and discrimination against them and imbalances in the numbers of men and women, these groups weathered the initial difficulties and successfully established families and lasting communities in different parts of the United States.

As we have seen, however, the representatives of these groups in the third immigrant stream (though still exhibiting a wide range of social characteristics) have tended on average to be of much higher initial educational and skill levels than were their compatriots from the earlier period. In addition, the descendants of the earlier immigrants are now highly assimilated culturally and structurally into American society, and—as shown in our discussions of the Japanese and Mexican Americans—there is strong evidence that primary and marital assimilation among them is underway. As a result, the new immigrants from these groups are able to take advantage of the established institutional and social life of the stable ethnic communities that already exist within American society. At the same time, there is often some hostility between the old-timers and the newcomers that may create problems for both groups. Even when these divisions are not a source of problems, they may limit interactions between members of the old and new groups. In any event, the presence of third-, fourth-, or even later-generation descendants of the earlier immigrants, alongside the new immigrants and their children, creates a much more diverse ethnic situation within these groups, and within the United States as a whole, than existed before 1965.

Several of the new immigrant groups, however, have found few co-ethnics awaiting them in the United States. There were very few Koreans in the United States, for instance, until the Korean War started in 1950. During the next fifteen years, approximately 21,000 Koreans—nearly all of whom were refugees, war brides and their children, or orphans—were admitted; and in the next four decades, more than 700,000 new immigrants arrived from Korea (U.S. Immigration and Naturalization Service 1996:27–28). Bolstered by natural increase, the Korean American population had reached 837,000 by 1990 (U.S. Bureau of the Census 1995:53). A very similar pattern developed also for people from the Dominican Republic and the other Caribbean countries, El Salvador and the other countries of Central America, and India. Thirty years after the passage of the INAA, hundreds of thousands of people from each of these countries were residents of the United States.

Although our discussion may suggest that the various immigrant groups of the third stream are fairly homogeneous, that is seldom the case. As is true of the Japanese Americans, Mexican Americans, African Americans, and Native Americans, the new immigrant groups also may be quite heterogenous. For instance, important sociocultural differences exist between the ethnic Vietnamese and the ethnic Chinese of Vietnam (Bach and Carroll-Seguin 1986:402). Desbartes (1986:414, 416) found that the ethnic

Vietnamese were substantially more likely than the ethnic Chinese to understand English, to have attended a university, to be Catholic, and to work in higher-prestige occupations. The ethnic Chinese were more likely to be in business than the ethnic Vietnamese.

The addition to the American population of so many people from so many different countries has altered the ethnic landscape of the United States, affecting practically every aspect of life ranging from the foods Americans eat to the languages that are spoken in the schools to the variety of religions that are practiced. Whether these changes are, on balance, a boon or a bane has become a widely debated subject throughout the country. The topic of undocumented or illegal immigration has received special attention.

Undocumented Immigrants

Although the family reunification and refugee provisions of the INAA were viewed as liberalizing the law, labor certification procedures made the entrance of many types of workers more difficult. For example, many of the people who wished to enter the United States to work have been delayed or excluded because they were unable to find a job in advance (as required by law); consequently, many of these workers have found ways to enter without acquiring the proper papers. Such undocumented or illegal immigrants have been at the center of much of the contemporary controversy over immigration. Debates rage over several questions including the following: How many illegals are in the country? What are their effects on American society? What policies toward them should be adopted?

There is controversy, too, over the proper terminology to be used in referring to these newcomers. The term "illegal immigrant" may suggest unfairly that the typical undocumented worker is a person of criminal tendencies who schemes to remain permanently in this country, but many observers believe the undocumented worker is generally "positively self-selected in terms of ambition and willingness to work" (Portes and Rumbaut 1990:11) and is usually a person who is seeking honest work. The undocumented worker also frequently is a sojourner and may soon return to his or her home.

The multiple entrances and exits of particular workers has established a cyclical migration flow that has complicated the problem of estimating how many undocumented immigrants are actually in the country at a given time. News stories frequently have raised the specter of an "invasion" of undocumented immigrants and have suggested that there could be as many as 15 million such persons in the United States; but, based on several studies employing different research methods, Massey (1981:61) concluded that in 1980 there were probably no more than 4 million undocumented immigrants and that around 60 percent of those were from Mexico. Significant numbers of undocumented immigrants also come from Canada, Central America, the Caribbean nations, Europe, and Asia (Lapham 1996:58). More recent efforts to estimate the number of undocumented immigrants in the United States have led to the conclusion that in 1980 there were almost certainly no more than 4 million and there may well have been no more than 1.5 million (Bean and Tienda 1987:119–120).

In any event, the widespread *perception* has been that undocumented immigration is a very important problem and that something must be done to bring it under control. For example, in 1979 the Federation for Immigration Reform (FAIR) sued the Bureau of the Census to prevent the count of illegal aliens from affecting congressional reapportionment; and during the early years of the 1980s, Congress repeatedly debated various immigration reform proposals. The usual issues occupied the attention of the legislators. The immigrants were said to be displacing U.S. workers, lowering wages, undermining working conditions, destroying the rule of law, and receiving social service benefits for which they did not qualify (Papademetriou 1987:325).

Immigration Reform

After years of controversy, a sweeping new Immigration Reform and Control Act (IRCA) was passed in 1986. The objective of the new law was to reduce the flow of undocumented immigration to the United States; but it also granted a general amnesty to bring about the legalization of all undocumented permanent residents who had lived in the United States since 1982 (Bean, Vernez, and Keely 1989:59). It spelled out various ways in which aliens could become legal residents, the types of penalties that could be applied to the employers of undocumented workers, and the procedures employers should follow in order to use foreign agricultural laborers. It also required that all newly hired workers present documents (such as a driver's license or a birth certificate) to prove that they are eligible for employment, and it authorized funds to be used to reimburse the states for some of the costs of legalization (Keely 1989:161–170). This complicated law's effects are difficult to assess. One analysis concluded that the law has been effective in reducing the flow of undocumented immigrants (Bean, Espenshade, White, and Dymowski 1990: 153), while a different analysis questioned whether there had been a significant reduction (Massey, Alarcon, Durand, and Gonzales 1987:320–321).

Another major overhaul in immigration policy was the Immigration Act of 1990. Included in this act was an increase in total immigration, changes in the grounds for exclusion and deportation, revisions in the requirements for naturalization, the creation of new temporary worker categories, and increased enforcement activities (Immigration and Naturalization Service 1994:A.1–21).

Our discussion so far has shown that the increasing numbers of refugees seeking asylum in the United States, the growing numbers of workers wishing to migrate to this country, and various changes in American immigration laws (especially the 1965 INAA) helped create a dramatic shift in the countries of origin of American immigrants and in the immigrants' social and economic backgrounds. The sharp increases in the volume of American immigration since the 1960s and the changed racial and ethnic composition of this third immigrant stream once again focused national attention on questions concerning the role of immigrants in American life and on the processes and ideologies of group adjustment discussed in Chapter 2. Moreover, even though this large contemporary immigration so far has been smaller in size, compared to the total U.S. population, than the first and second immigrant streams, it still has revived many of the same "immigration fears" and responses that were prominent during the earlier periods (Brimelow 1995; Simon 1985; Waldinger 1984:219). Many of the old concerns about America's ability to absorb the newcomers, and the willingness of the newcomers to be absorbed, have resurfaced. Also revived by the third stream have been fears that some of the new-comers may be inherently inferior to native Americans and may in time "degrade" our population. By the time of the presidential election campaign of 1996, these issues once again had assumed a prominent place in national debate (Pear 1996:A9). We will pursue these matters further in Flashpoint 3 later in this chapter.

The Vietnamese

We noted that the third immigrant stream has contained a disproportionately large share of refugees. Thousands of Hungarian and Cuban refugees were admitted to the United States during the 1950s, but only 335 emigrants from Vietnam entered during that period (U.S. Immigration and Naturalization Service 1996:27). However, the situation changed noticeably between 1961 and 1970 as America became more deeply in-volved in the war in Vietnam; and it increased dramatically after 1975 when American participation in the war ended (see Table 14.1).

Vietnam's contact with the West began in the sixteenth century when Vietnam was an independent country. Three centuries later, in 1863, it became an unwilling colony of France (Montero 1979:16; Morse and Hendelson 1972a:262–263). Our previous discus-sions of the relationship between colonized minorities and dominant invaders would lead us to expect that the French invasion probably resulted in long-term conflict, and it

TABLE 14.1   Vietnamese
Immigration to the United States,
1951–1994*

Years	Number
1951–1960	335
1961–1970	4,340
1971–1980	172,820
1981–1990	280,782
1991–1994	110,300
Total	468,577

Source: U.S. Immigration and Naturalization Service, *1994 Statistical Yearbook,* 1996: 26–28.

*There was no separate listing for Vietnam before 1951.

did. Following World War I, two opposing groups of Vietnamese nationalists were orga-nized, one communist and the other anti-communist; but both groups aimed to end foreign domination of Vietnam (Morse and Hendelson 1972a:263).

The Thirty Years War in Vietnam: 1945–1975

France lost control of Vietnam during World War II; but after the war, with U.S. and British support, the French came back. Eight years of bitter struggle led to the end of French rule and the Geneva Agreements of 1954 whereby Vietnam was partitioned into North and South Vietnam at the seventeenth parallel. People were allowed to choose whether they wished to live in the North or the South. In response, between 800,000 and 1 million Vietnamese (most of whom were Catholics) migrated from the North to the South (Kelly 1977:13; Morse and Hendelson 1972b:317).

After South Vietnam was established as a separate republic (with U.S. backing), a group called the National Liberation Front (the Vietcong) launched a guerrilla war within South Vietnam, supported by North Vietnam. As the United States continued to support South Vietnam, President Lyndon Johnson ordered a military buildup in 1963 that led the United States into a full-scale war with both the Vietcong and the regular military forces of North Vietnam (the Vietminh).

Although the war centered on Vietnam, it also included Cambodia (Kampuchea) and Laos. In the process, hundreds of thousands of people were uprooted. Rumbaut (1996:318) stated that in South Vietnam "about a third of the population was internally displaced during the war," in Laos "about a third of the Hmong population had been uprooted by combat," and in Cambodia "as many as a quarter of its people may have died." Villages became battlefields, and the residents fled to escape death or mutilation (Kelly 1977:13). In the United States, the combined effects of the civil rights protests, anti-war protests, and opposition to the protesters produced turmoil. In 1969, President Nixon began to withdraw U.S. troops. Nevertheless, U.S. participation in the war drag-ged on for another six years. It ended suddenly in 1975 when the South Vietnamese army collapsed within the space of a few weeks under the combined attacks of the Viet-cong and Vietminh (Wright 1980:509).

The War and the Boat People

The fighting in Southeast Asia continued after the Americans left with increasing num-bers of people searched for places of refuge. Communist governments were established in Vietnam and in Laos. The new Laotian government waged war against the Hmong people of the mountain regions and harassed the Chinese Laotians who dominated the merchant and professional occupations. As a result, thousands of Laotians fled to neigh-boring Thailand.

At the same time, an insurgent group in Cambodia toppled the American-backed Cambodian government. Cambodia had been heavily bombed by Americans during the early 1970s and hundreds of thousands of people had been driven from their homes. Now, on top of that tragedy, the new ruler of Cambodia, Pol Pot, instituted a shocking relocation and slaughter which, in the words of Kitano and Daniels (1988:147), "ended with the murder of at least one million Cambodians by Cambodians and the forced relocation of many others."[10] This carnage ranks among the leading disasters of human history. More than 100,000 Cambodians fled to Thailand and were joined later by an additional 150,000 Cambodians who were victims of famine. Most of these people were jammed into refugee camps that the Thai government had erected along the border (Strand and Jones 1985:19–21, 34).

Conditions in Vietnam were still very unsettled. The government of Vietnam was involved in the conflicts in Cambodia and Laos and also was engaged in border conflicts with China. In addition, Vietnam was pressing to restructure its economy along communist lines. As a part of the latter effort, large numbers of people who were engaged in private business or the professions (including many of the ethnic Chinese) were subjected to various reprisals;[11] consequently, tens of thousands of people were gripped by panic and fled from the country by sea in frail, untrustworthy boats.

Thousands of people had used small boats in 1975 to reach rescue vessels waiting off the coast of Vietnam. But this time there were no rescue vessels waiting, and the refugees were far from certain they would arrive safely at any destination. Many overloaded boats were swamped; the motors on many others failed at sea; and perhaps as many as 80 percent of the boats were attacked by pirates (Kitano and Daniels 1988:141). Even the refugees who succeeded in reaching land often were physically attacked, killed, or forced back to sea (St. Cartmail 1983:87–97).

There is no exact count of the Boat People. St. Cartmail (1983:89–90) estimated that by 1982, more than 493,000 people had arrived by boat in countries of first asylum. More than 200,000 more may have drowned or died of other causes in their attempt to find safety. Some 300,000 were accepted, temporarily, by Malaysia, Hong Kong, Indonesia, and Thailand. By 1981, at least 197,000 of the Boat People had been accepted by the United States (Strand and Jones 1985:9); but many thousands of other people were still awaiting new homes.

Refugee Resettlement

Most of those coming to America during the 1960s were the wives and children of U.S. citizens; but as the end of the war approached, the U.S. government announced that some refugees from Vietnam would be evacuated and resettled in the United States. As the communist troops approached Saigon in April of 1975, a hastily arranged and panicky evacuation of more than 60,000 Vietnamese was set into motion. Most refugees were flown to the Philippines and then to a holding center at Guam (Kelly 1977:30). Amidst the chaos of the evacuation, an additional 70,000 Vietnamese people left the country on their own initiative (Wright 1980:509). One way or another, approximately

130,000 refugees quickly reached U.S. territory. These were only the vanguard of the more than 2 million refugees who have fled from Vietnam, Cambodia, and Laos since then (Rumbaut 1996:316).

The United Nations High Commission for Refugees (UNHCR) mobilized to assist in solving the human problems generated by the crisis in Southeast Asia. Several countries agreed to accept refugees, but the countries that agreed to receive the largest number were those believed to be most responsible for the debacle—the United States and France. By 1992, more than 1 million Southeast Asian refugees "had been resettled in the United States, 750,000 in other Western countries" while many thousands were still in refugee camps in Asia (Rumbaut 1996:319).

The first refugees to reach the United States were admitted under the federal government's parole authority, which had been used earlier for Hungarian and Cuban refugees. The existing laws and authority were supplemented in 1975 by the Indochina Migration and Refugee Assistance Act, which provided funds to pay for the transportation and resettlement of the refugees. A permanent Refugee Resettlement Program was put into place in the Refugee Act of 1980.

President Gerald Ford assigned the responsibility for managing the evacuation to the Interagency Task Force for Indochinese Refugees (IATF). The IATF set up the initial receiving station at Guam and four mainland refugee camps in California (Camp Pendleton), Pennsylvania (Fort Indian Town Gap), Arkansas (Fort Chafee), and Florida (Eglin Air Force Base) to carry out the task of assisting the refugees to begin life anew in the United States. The main purpose of the camps was to assist the newcomers, in Kelly's (1977:2) phrase, to make "the transition from refugee to immigrant."

The Refugee Camps

In the camps, the refugees received security interviews and physical examinations and were assigned to living quarters in a tent or barracks. Then they were registered with one of nine voluntary agencies that had contracted with the IATF to find individual or group sponsors who would "assume fiscal and personal responsibility for the refugee families for a period of up to two years" (Montero 1979:26). The average cost of resettling a family was around $5,600, most of which was borne by the refugees' sponsors (Montero 1979:24, 28).[12] For this reason, most refugees were sponsored by groups rather than by individual Americans.

The first of the four original mainland refugee centers, at Camp Pendeleton, California, opened on April 29, 1975, the day before Saigon fell. By December of that year, approximately 130,000 people had been released from the reception centers into the United States. Over 121,000 of these had been matched with sponsors through the efforts of the voluntary agencies, while the remainder had been released after proving they did not require assistance (Strand and Jones 1985:33). The camps provided temporary shelter, food, clothing, and medical care for the refugees. They also provided child-care classes, college placement services, English language training, and instructions concerning how to handle some typical problems the refugees would encounter in their new home. Later on, the various sponsors of the refugees continued to provide life's necessities, help them find jobs, and enroll their children in schools (Kelly 1977:83–89; Montero 1979:27).

In this way, Vietnamese refugees were dispersed (though unevenly and in the face of some criticism) to every state in the United States. California received more than one-third of the refugees, while Texas, Pennsylvania, Louisiana, Virginia, Washington, and Florida (in that order) together received another one-third. The remaining refugees were scattered throughout the country, ranging from a few thousand in Illinois, New York, and Minnesota, to less than a hundred in Vermont and Wyoming (Montero 1979: 8).

Has this massive program of evacuation and resettlement succeeded in enabling the Vietnamese to become established in America?

Vietnamese American Assimilation

Recall that among the most important factors that may influence the rate of assimilation for a particular group are its members' command of English, their educational levels, their work skills, the extent to which the group organizes along family and ethnic lines for mutual aid and support, and the economic conditions in the host society at the time the group arrives. Although all of these factors may come into play simultaneously, they represent different aspects of the assimilation process and will be more or less prominent at various times. Our very brief summary only illustrates the refugee's experiences and begins, as before, with cultural assimilation.

Cultural Assimilation.   The extent to which English is used and understood by the members of an immigrant group is the key indicator of the occurrence of cultural assimilation within the group. Immigrants need to know the language in order to communicate effectively with those around them, find and keep jobs, arrange for places to live, and, in general, negotiate their way through a new and strange society. The central questions to be raised here, then, are: How proficient were the Vietnamese refugees in the English language at the time of their arrival? To what extent has their level of English proficiency risen since then? Information concerning the Vietnamese refugees' command of English was gathered in several studies of differing scope. We draw on two of these to illustrate the main points.

The *first study*, by Montero (1979), described and analyzed a series of studies conducted under the sponsorship of the U.S. Department of Health, Education, and Welfare (HEW) following the opening of the four mainland resettlement camps in 1975. The HEW reports included data on the entire population of refugees who went through the camps between 1975 and 1977 and from five special surveys that were conducted to ascertain how well the refugees were adapting to American life.[13]

In four surveys, the participants were asked whether the members of their household could understand, speak, read, and write English "not at all," "some," or "well." For example, one survey[14] revealed that among the refugees who were released from the resettlement camps within a few months, around 18 percent said they could under-stand, speak, read, and write English "well"; another 9 percent said they could not do these things "at all."[15] It appears, therefore, that the majority of people between these extremes (roughly 73 percent) had "some" ability to understand, speak, read, and write English.

The English proficiency of the resettled Vietnamese apparently rose rapidly within the first two years after their arrival. Survey five, conducted in 1977, found that those re-porting they could understand or speak English "well" had risen to 34 percent and those reporting they could read or write English "well" had risen to about 30 percent. At the same time, those saying they could not understand, speak, read, or write English "at all" had fallen to between 2 and 4 percent; hence, it seems that between one-fifth and one-third of the Vietnamese refugees who fled to the United States after the fall of Saigon ei-ther had a good command of English or rapidly acquired it.

The *second study*, conducted by Caplan, Whitmore, and Choy (1989:39), focused on two sample surveys of Boat People from Cambodia, Laos, and Vietnam. The sample contained 690 Vietnamese households in five locations within the United States.[16] The initial and current levels of the refugees' competence in English was assessed by using three measures of reading, speaking, and performance. The researchers found that in more than one-third of the Vietnamese households "the majority of adults knew at least some English when they arrived" (Caplan, Whitmore, and Choy 1989:31). By the time the interviews were conducted, there had been substantial improvements in the ability of the refugees to conduct their daily affairs in English.[17] Although the two studies we have cited concerning the English language skills of the Vietnamese are not strictly com-parable, a cautious reading of the combined findings of these studies suggests that no less than one-third of the Vietnamese refugees, and possibly more, were fairly proficient English-speakers within five years of their arrival in the United States.

Secondary Structural Assimilation.   Our principal indicators of secondary as-similation among Vietnamese Americans are education, occupation, income, and resi-dential segregation. We examine each of these briefly.

Information on the *educational level* of the Vietnamese refugees was gathered as a routine part of each person's induction into the resettlement camps. The general result of the statistics released by the federal government shows that "nearly 50 percent of the heads of household have at least a secondary school education, and more than 25 per-cent are college and university graduates." The average (median) educational level of the Vietnamese refugees by 1980 was approximately fourteen years (Jiobu 1988:92), which equaled the educational level of White Californians. Recall, however, that the refugees who arrived in the United States immediately following the evacuation in 1975 were more highly educated on average than the Boat People who came after 1978 (Caplan, Whitmore, and Choy 1989:24).

Of special interest in regard to educational assimilation, however, is the experience of the children of the refugees. Caplan, Whitmore, and Choy found that almost three-fourths of the Vietnamese refugees' children had overall grade point averages in the A or B grade range; and on the standardized California Achievement Test, over 60 percent scored in the top half (Caplan, Whitmore, and Choy 1989:70). These findings suggest that the secondary assimilation of the second generation should be comparatively rapid.

What *jobs* did the Vietnamese perform in their homeland? As one might expect of the members of the first wave, there was a strong representation of doctors, managers, and other professionals. Indeed, the largest single category was comprised of those who engaged in professional, technical, and managerial pursuits (24 percent) (Montero 1979: 23). In this regard, the first wave refugees compared favorably with the other main Asian groups and exceeded the level of White Americans (Barringer, Gardner, and Levin 1995: 198–199). Montero (1979:43–44) showed that the employment rate among male heads of household rose from 68 to 95 percent between surveys one and five, while the employment rate among female heads of household rose from 51 to 93 percent. Caplan, Whitmore, and Choy (1989:53) found that unemployment declined rapidly from about 88 percent shortly after the refugees' arrival to about 28 percent after forty months in the United States. These findings suggest rapid secondary assimilation.

Another point of note, which we already have encountered, is that the occupational talents and skills exercised by the refugees in their native land frequently did not carry over directly into the American setting. The fifth HEW survey, for instance, showed that although 95 percent of the male heads of household and 93 percent of the female heads of household had found some kind of employment, the kinds of jobs they held often were of lower pay and prestige than the jobs they had held in Vietnam (Montero 1979:38–44).[18] Moreover, refugees were consistently less likely to be in the labor force than were most Americans (Bach and Carroll-Seguin 1986:401).

It is not surprising, therefore, to find that the *incomes* of the Vietnamese were not as high as those of workers in many other groups and that they considered money problems to be of special importance. Strand and Jones (1985:134–135) reported that among twenty problem areas, the Vietnamese ranked "not enough money" as of greatest importance. Montero (1979:51) found that the annual median incomes of refugee households was about 70 percent that of the U.S. average. Barringer, Gardner, and Levin (1995:266) stated that the "Vietnamese consistently displayed incomes as low as, or lower than, blacks and Hispanics." By 1990, however, the labor force participation level of the Vietnamese was almost equal to that of the United States as a whole (Rumbaut 1996:324). It appears, therefore, that the Vietnamese have found a place in the American occupational structure and have achieved a fairly high level of economic self-sufficiency.[19]

The last of the four indicators of secondary assimilation under review is *residential assimilation*. As noted in Chapter 7, Jiobu (1988:107–148) presented a thorough analysis of ethnic group residential assimilation. The main finding of this study for our present purpose is simply that the Vietnamese were highly segregated. Their average level of residential segregation was 76. For comparison, the level of the Japanese, was 46 (Jiobu 1988:114).

Primary Structural Assimilation. We noted previously that immigrant groups to America commonly have considered the welfare of the family to be more important than the freedom and development of the individual. Discussions of the Vietnamese have emphasized that the family is "an entity by itself, an irreducible value and the only way of life for the Vietnamese" (Phung thi Hanh, quoted by Haines 1988:3). This value has been apparent in the efforts made by the resettled Vietnamese to maintain contacts with family members and compatriots in other parts of the country. In many cases, they have moved from their initial locations to other places having larger Vietnamese populations, particularly to California. While family reunification provided the primary impetus for this migration, some of the movement has been stimulated by the efforts of Vietnamese leaders to help reorganize the community within the new social context (Kelly 1977:202). This regrouping to achieve family and community cohesion has resembled the earlier formation of ethnic enclaves by Chinese and Japanese immigrants of the late nineteenth and early twentieth centuries (Montero 1979:61) and of Cubans in the last half of the twentieth century.

The focus of the Vietnamese on the maintenance and reunification of their families and community, along with the great demands of cultural and secondary assimilation, presumably has left them with little time or inclination to establish and develop primary relationships with native Americans; but little systematic information concerning this process is available. The Vietnamese have associated closely with their resettlement sponsors, of course, and an unknown number of lasting friendships may have emerged from these relationships. The relationship between the American sponsors and the Vietnamese, however, was mainly one in which the dominant Americans were working to bring an end to the financial responsibilities of sponsorship (Kelly 1977:159). Such arrangements did not encourage the formation of the friendly, equalitarian types of relationships that we have described as primary.

Marital Assimilation.   Given the brief period of time the Vietnamese have been in the United States, the extent to which they arrived in family groups, and their apparently low level of primary assimilation, there is little reason to expect a high level of marital assimilation among them. It is true that many of the first Vietnamese to come to the United States during the 1960s were the spouses of Americans; but this group is now a very small proportion of the total Vietnamese American population. Our interest centers on how much out-marriage has occurred among the entire group.

Excellent evidence on this point comes from Jiobu's (1988:159–162) analysis of 241,102 couples. Of the eight ethnic groups represented in this study,[20] the Vietnamese had a very low rate of intermarriage and the lowest rate observed in the comparisons. We conclude, therefore, that the rate of out-marriage among these refugees within the United States has been, so far, extremely low.

Conclusion.   The Vietnamese appear to be undergoing fairly rapid cultural assimilation. Their knowledge of the English language and of American society appears to have been high at the time they arrived (though much lower than that of the Filipinos and Asian Indians) and to have increased noticeably during their early years here. Of special importance is that the children of the Boat People are reported to be succeeding very well in American schools (Caplan, Choy, and Whitmore 1992).

The high initial educational and occupational levels of the Vietnamese adults did not, however, prevent them from undergoing rapid downward mobility as they moved into American society; consequently, their income levels have been comparatively low.

Residential segregation among the Vietnamese has been high despite the efforts of the American government to disperse them throughout the population. Indeed, the Vietnamese, like so many before them, have worked hard to construct their own distinctive communities and institutions; and they may have done this in the face of above-average levels of psychological distress and family conflict.[21] Primary and marital assimilation among the Vietnamese Americans appear still to be low.

On the basis of the available evidence—and despite the unquestionably unique experiences of this group of people—the Vietnamese appear to be following a sequence of adaptation to the American setting that will produce results resembling those found among the other Asian American groups we have considered.

The unfolding experience of the Vietnamese in America has much to teach us about the human meaning of immigration and adaptation to new circumstances. It invites us to examine the skills and resources of new immigrants, which we have done in a cursory fashion. But it also invites us to examine the kind of welcome that new immigrants receive and to reflect on America's capacity and willingness to continue to serve as a place of asylum for at least some of the world's dispossessed people.

Resurgent Racism and Nativism

In Chapters 4 and 5 we saw that native resistance to immigration rose as the volume of each of the first two great immigrant streams increased. At both times many natives feared the country was in danger of being "taken over" or "inundated" by "hordes" of foreigners. During the period of the first stream, the nativists responded by forming organizations (such as the Know-Nothings) that backed legal restrictions on the rights of the foreign born. They also promoted prejudice against all Catholics, as well as the racist idea that the Irish were an inherently inferior people.

During the period of the second stream, nativist xenophobia, bolstered by the White supremacy theories and arguments of scientific racism, led to the exclusion of Asians and the creation of immigration quotas aimed particularly at southern and eastern Europeans. Large variations in the immigrant flow heightened native fears concerning the economic impact of the immigrants and the ability of the country to absorb the newcomers.

The successful restrictive legislation of the 1920s led to a long-term decline of both popular concern about immigration and of the activities of nativist groups. So the early years of the third immigrant stream produced little nativist reaction at the national level. Indeed, as seen in the efforts to help various groups of refugees and in the removal of the national-origins principle from America's immigration law in 1965, the helping hand America extended to newcomers during this period was firm and generous. The social turbulence and rapid change of the 1960s and 1970s, however, joined with the rapid rise and altered composition of the third immigrant stream after 1965 to generate a heightened awareness of ethnicity within the United States that is reminiscent of the peak periods of the first and second immigrant streams. As before, natives have viewed the rapidly changing social conditions with apprehension. Public opinion polls conducted between the 1960s and the 1990s showed a steady increase in the percentage of those who believed that immigration into the United States should be decreased (Mydans 1993:14). As in the earlier periods of high immigration, nativist reactions have coincided with, and in various ways been intertwined with, an increase in the prominence of racist ideas and organizations.

Hate Groups and Hate Crimes

The changes in immigration law during the 1980s and 1990s have been accompanied by a rise in the activities of White supremacist organizations. Newspaper and magazine articles increasingly have chronicled the nativist and racist activities of various branches of the Ku Klux Klan (e.g., the Invisible Empire, Knights of the KKK), neo-Nazi organizations (e.g., National Alliance, Aryan Nations, Christian Identity movement), and "skinhead" groups (e.g., the Hammer Skins, United White Skinheads).[22] Literally hundreds of additional groups espousing White supremacy and hatred toward minorities and immigrants have been organized.[23]

Hate crimes against the persons and property of the members of various ethnic groups and those who are thought to be foreign appear to have spiraled upward during the 1990s.[24] Numerous reports of harassment, vandalism, and assaults aimed at Jews and various Asian groups have appeared.[25] Between 1990 and 1993, violent hate crimes within the United States were reported to be at record levels (Southern Poverty Law Center 1994:1). Many of these incidents were cases of majority-group members attacking minority-group members, but many of them also were instances in which members of minority groups attacked the members of other minority groups or members of the majority.

Consider a sample from 1993 alone. In that year a Black man "miraculously survived" an attack in Florida after "he was doused with gasoline and set afire by White assailants"; in San Francisco, a Black man was shot to death by several White men who "shouted racial slurs at him"; a Cambodian immigrant was beaten to death in Fall River, Massachusetts, by a group of about a dozen men; in Pomona, California, a Black teenager was charged with murder after shooting an Hispanic youth to death because of his race; a White youth in Winston-Salem, North Carolina, died of injuries suffered when he was beaten by two Black teenagers; and in a highly publicized hate crime, Colin Ferguson, a Black man, went on a shooting rampage on a New York commuter train, killing seven people (six White and one Asian American) and wounding seventeen others (Southern Poverty Law Center 1994:4–5).[26] Large numbers of similar bias-motivated attacks also were reported for 1994 and 1995 (Southern Poverty Law Center 1995:13–19; 1996:7–23).

During the 1970s and 1980s, the proliferating hate groups gradually adopted a much more militant stance. Several White supremacist leaders, calling themselves "Patriots," expanded the range of targets for hatred to include the federal government and its officials. They called for the overthrow of the government and the creation of a new, separate, all-White homeland. In 1978, William Pierce, an anti-Semite who has described Hitler as the "greatest man of our era," published *The Turner Diaries*. This fictional account of a White revolution has become "a handbook for White victory" (Southern Poverty Law Center 1996a:37; 1996c:5, 6). In the early 1980s, Louis Beam, a leader of the Texas Knights of the KKK, and William Potter Gale, a leader of the radical White supremacy group Posse Comitatus, established guerrilla warfare training camps in preparation for an expected "race war" (Southern Poverty Law Center 1996a:38, 40). Since then, hundreds of private militia groups, many of them with racist doctrines and ties to other racist groups, have been organized (Southern Poverty Law Center 1995: 1–15). The organizational bonds among these groups have been strengthened by their sophisticated use of the internet (Cooper 1995:14; Sheppard 1995:A1).

In 1987, the KKK leader Louis Beam was among a group of White supremacists who were indicted, but acquitted (by an all-White jury), for plotting "to overthrow the government . . . bomb federal buildings, sabotage railroads, and poison water supplies"; Posse Comitatus leader W. P. Gale was convicted of "plotting to kill a federal judge and IRS officials" (Southern Poverty Law Center 1996:36, 38). In 1992, Randy Weaver, an Identity movement member and fugitive from justice, became a militia hero when his son and wife were killed by federal agents in a standoff at Ruby Ridge, Idaho; and in 1993, the anti-government anger escalated further when eighty members of the Branch Davidian group died in a fire in Waco, Texas, after a prolonged confrontation with federal authorities. In 1995, Identity movement follower Timothy McVeigh was arrested and charged in the deaths of 169 people in the bombing of the federal building in Oklahoma City. Roy (1995:9) estimated that by 1995 about 25,000 people were active in the White supremacist movement.

All of these events occurred against a backdrop of growing native resentment of the rising volume and ethnic composition of the new immigration. These concerns played a role, during the 1980s, in violent episodes in Texas between Vietnamese immigrants and native fishermen (supported by the KKK) in regard to coastal fishing rights. They also may have contributed to violence and unrest in Miami, the port of entry for many refugees and undocumented aliens from Cuba and Haiti, and to the violence directed toward Koreans and Cambodians in the Los Angeles riots in May 1992.[27] They surely have contributed to a rising concern among natives about maintaining the continued dominance of the established culture.

As becomes obvious from the mentioned hate crimes, many natives fear, as they have at various times in the past, that immigrants, documented and undocumented alike, (1) damage the country's economy and (2) will prove to be unassimilable. Each of these fears has contributed to increasingly strident calls for the reduction and restriction of immigration.

Flashpoint 3: Is Immigration Good for America?

In 1980, an ecologist and an economist wagered $1,000 in a debate between what *New York Times* reporter John Tierney (1990:52) called the "doomsters and the boomsters." The issue was whether the world's growing human population was running out of natural resources. The ecologist (and "doomster") Paul R. Ehrlich, a professor at Stanford, argued in his book *The Population Bomb* that population growth is a great evil and will produce overcrowding, diminished resources, and food shortages. The economist (and "boomster") Julian Simon, a professor at the University of Maryland, argued that a growing population is a good thing because a larger population will contain a larger number of people with creative ideas. Their discoveries "will ultimately mean a cleaner environment, a healthier humanity, and more abundant supplies of food and raw material for everyone" (Tierney 1990:53). Simon's view was that other factors, such as a country's economic structure and political institutions, were more important to social well-being than the number of people. After both professors carefully watched increases in the population and the scarcity of five key resources for ten years, Professor Simon, the "boomster," won the bet. Yet Ehrlich's doomsday idea that overpopulation will lead to a global catastrophe has continued to attract the most attention.[28]

A similar concern, whether America's increasing population is good or bad, has framed the current discussions about immigration. The increasing size of the new immigration has aroused nativist, xenophobic opposition, as in the past, and generated a furious debate between immigration "boomsters" and "doomsters."

Proposition 187.   Election day 1994 had a special meaning to Californians. For many years, California had been the state documented immigrants named most often as their intended destination (U.S. Immigration and Naturalization Service 1996:63). California also seemed to be the destination of the largest group of undocumented immigrants; so on the ballot in the election of 1994 was a hotly contested proposal, known as Proposition 187, that sought to discourage undocumented immigration by depriving such immigrants of many vital public services. If the proposal passed, public school teachers would be required to verify that students who were enrolling for the first time were citizens and, if they were not, to report them to the authorities; undocumented immigrants would be barred from attending publicly supported colleges and universities; they would be ineligible for all public health services except emergency care, and clinic doctors would be required to report them to the authorities; most state welfare benefits for the children of undocumented immigrants would be eliminated; and all state and local law enforcement agencies would be required to verify the residency status of any person who was arrested and *suspected* of being in the country illegally (Ayres 1994b:1; Noble 1994:A17).

The debate surrounding the election was filled with charges and countercharges concerning the need for, and probable effects of, Proposition 187. Supporters of the measure argued that undocumented immigrants were driving down wages and straining the capacity of public services. California's Governor Pete Wilson, for instance, maintained that California had to take action to try to force the federal government to control the "invasion" of illegals (Ayres 1994a:12). Wilson stated that "We can no longer allow compassion to overrule reason" (Rohter 1993:4).[29] His opponent in the race for the governorship, Kathleen Brown, appeared to agree that the federal government should stop undocumented immigration but believed that the necessary laws already were in place and that the proposed measure would be unconstitutional (Ayres 1994a:

12). Many doctors and teachers throughout California were outraged that they would be required to become state law enforcement agents and that innocent children would be deprived of schooling and health care.

Many opponents of 187 attacked the idea that immigrants drive down wages; they argued that immigrants improve the U.S. economy. Others argued that the main motivation behind the proposal was xenophobia, not economics. Opponents cited the economist, Julian Simon—the man who won the debate referred to earlier—whose research showed that immigration produces an overall economic benefit. Simon had found, considering the United States as a whole, that immigrant families generally paid more in taxes than they received in public services (Lewis 1994:A15); and Jeffrey S. Passel of the Urban Institute was quoted as saying that places receiving "immigrants during the 1980s generally did better in terms of wage growth than places that didn't" (Rohter 1993:4).

The Mexican government cautiously entered the debate arguing that the "discussions surrounding the proposition too often had 'racist and xenophobic' overtones and unfairly blamed Mexican citizens for American problems" (Ayres 1994a:12). Bill Ong Hing, a specialist in immigration history and law, expressed the view that "for most people, economics is a diversion. Underneath it is race" (Lewis 1994:A15). Despite the numerous legal, ethical, and ideological objections raised against it, when the votes were counted, Proposition 187 had been approved by a decisive majority (about 60 percent). Opponents of the measure immediately mounted a constitutional challenge.

Both sides in the Proposition 187 controversy argued that a 1982 decision by the U.S. Supreme Court, *Plyler v. Doe,* supported their position. In *Plyler* the Court ruled against a Texas law that allowed public schools either to deny schooling to children who had not been "legally admitted" to the United States or to charge a fee for permitting them to attend public schools. The opponents of 187 emphasized that the Court had held unanimously that the equal protection clause of the Fourteenth Amendment "'extends to anyone, citizen or stranger' who is within a state's boundaries." Proponents of 187 argued that the 5-to-4 ruling meant that the children of undocumented immigrants were not guaranteed "the same education offered to all other children in Texas" (Noble 1994:A17).[30]

The day after the passage of 187, Superior Court Judge Stephen R. Pollack issued a restraining order blocking the enforcement of the cutoffs in educational and health service benefits mandated by Proposition 187 until further hearings were held on its constitutionality. Supporters of 187 nevertheless continued to work to assist various sympathetic groups in other states to get similar measures onto their ballots as immigration gained the attention of an increasingly large national audience (Ayres 1994b:20). In some states however, such as Texas, the opponents of 187 were able to prevent such a development.

Alien Nation?   The effort to lift immigration issues to a higher place among the nation's priorities had been underway for some time before the vote on Proposition 187. For example, over two years earlier Peter Brimelow, a senior editor of *Forbes* magazine and an immigrant from Britain, published a widely discussed cover story in the magazine *National Review* titled "Time to Rethink Immigration?" (Brimelow 1992). He stated—as opinion polls showed many people believe—that the United States *has* lost control of its borders and *is* being inundated by immigrants; and that immigration to the United States either should be sharply curtailed or stopped outright. Brimelow (1995) subsequently expanded his arguments and presented them in the book *Alien Nation*.[31]

Two questions may serve as a point of departure for our brief examination of the very volatile and complex issues at the center of the immigration debate. Is immigration *economically* desirable? Is the United States *capable of absorbing* so many ethnically diverse new immigrants?

The Economic Question. Whether the economic benefits of immigration outweigh its costs is hotly debated.[32] Do immigrants take jobs away from citizens and depress wages? Do the public services they use cost more than they pay in taxes? Specialists take opposite sides on these questions, and their research findings are often contradictory.[33] Huddle (1993), for instance, in a study based on data from Los Angeles County, concluded that immigrants cost the country's taxpayers more than $42 billion dollars each year. In a detailed critique of Huddle's work, however, Passel (1994) concluded that there is no evidence that immigrants cost the United States more than they contribute in taxes. According to his calculations, in fact, the immigrants of the third stream generate a surplus of at least 25 to 30 billion dollars per year. Similarly, Urban Institute economists Thomas Muller and Thomas Espenshade (1985) stated in a report on the effects of immigration to Los Angeles County that immigrants did not increase the aggregate level of unemployment among non-Hispanic White Californians or among Blacks. Immigrants took the lowest-level jobs, pushing the citizen workers up the economic ladder. The authors found evidence that although some natives were displaced from low-wage jobs by immigrants, many others gained from the presence of a larger population. They noted further that Hispanic immigrants did reduce the wages of some low-wage jobs; but they argued that many of these jobs would have been lost anyway to Asian countries or Mexico, where wages were even lower, if the companies had not hired immigrant workers in the United States.

Two other studies, one of the impact of Mexican immigrants on California's economy by demographers George Vernez and Kevin F. McCarthy (1990) of the Rand Corporation, and one by Michael Fix and Jeffrey S. Passel (1994) looking at data from geographical areas of different sizes, reported similar findings. Both of these studies suggested that immigration increased the number of jobs without any serious long-run displacement of native-born workers. Most of the immigrants took jobs in agriculture and low-paying industries. The researchers did find, however, that the immigrants' willingness to work at low wages kept wages depressed for some U.S. residents, particularly low-skilled workers in stagnant local economies with high concentrations of immigrants.

Brimelow (1995:168) recognized that immigration may increase the total number of jobs in the society; but he emphasized the point that some groups of natives, nevertheless, may be placed at a disadvantage by immigrants. He argued that Black Americans are such a group and referred to Booker Washington's arguments against immigration in his "Atlanta Compromise" speech (Brimelow 1995:173–175). After the Civil War, when immigration to the United States expanded enormously, Black leaders such as Washington expressed concern that immigrants were taking jobs that rightfully should go to Black Americans. From 1900 to 1935, African American newspapers strongly endorsed proposals to ban Mexican immigrants from the United States and supported the deportation roundups of Mexican workers. Black leaders warned that Greek, Italian, Mexican, and Asian immigrants would steal jobs from Black Americans (Fuchs 1990: 296).

The study by Muller and Espenshade (1985), however, showed that the presence of Mexican immigration may have facilitated upward job mobility among Blacks, especially in public service employment. These researchers found that Black Americans had higher-average educational and occupational levels than Mexicans and argued that the jobs performed by the members of these two groups were complementary rather than competitive. Muller and Espenshade did find some competition—particularly between low-skilled Black men and immigrants—in food service, retail trade, hotel service, and building maintenance (Muller and Espenshade 1985:102). In contrast to the views on immigration held by post-bellum leaders like Booker Washington, African American leaders in the 1980s used the immigration issue to build a coalition with Mexican American leaders to urge Congress to approve the legalization of undocumented immigrants.[34]

Brimelow (1995:151) attacked the view that immigrant families, as Simon (1989) put it, "are a good investment." Brimelow agreed that before the upsurge of the new immigration in the 1970s and 1980s, "immigrants earned more, and went on welfare less, than native-born Americans."[35] Then, based primarily on the work of George J. Borjas (e.g., 1990; 1994a)—an economist and an immigrant from Cuba—Brimelow (1995:146) presented the following argument: By the early 1990s, the welfare participation of immigrants *"was, on average, higher than native-born Americans (9.1 percent vs. 7.4 percent)"* (emphasis his). He noted, however, that according to Borjas's conclusion, when *refugee* households are removed from the calculation, the gap between the native born and immigrants was reduced to 0.4 percent (Brimelow 1995:150); but he did not present Borjas's further conclusion that immigration produces, overall, a definite (though comparatively small) economic benefit for the United States (between 6 and 20 billion dollars annually) (Borjas 1994b:3).[36]

Borjas (1994a:29) also showed, however, that the wages earned by immigrants, when compared to those of natives, declined in the 1970s (by 9 percent) and again in the 1980s (by 15 percent), suggesting that the immigrants who arrived later were less skilled and unlikely ever to reach parity with natives.[37] Borjas (1994b:20) argued that the American welfare system was attracting low-skill immigrants and that the economic benefits from immigration could be substantially increased if U.S. immigration policy were changed so that only skilled immigrants were admitted. A report issued by the U.S. Council of Economic Advisors, however, suggested that immigrants are not heavy users of public services. The report maintained that undocumented immigrants use even fewer resources than legal immigrants because they are younger, have fewer dependents, and are deterred from applying for welfare benefits. This report did agree, however, that immigrants, especially undocumented immigrants, do make substantial use of public health and education services because those services are easier to access (Bouvier 1986: 31).

A middle ground between the "boomsters" who believe continued immigration is basically good for America and the "doomsters" who believe continued immigration is a luxury that America can no longer afford was proposed by sociologist Frank D. Bean (1993:1F). Bean suggested that whether the effects of immigration are mainly positive or mainly negative depends on the economic conditions of the country. "In good economic times," Bean stated, "immigrants may be helpful, in bad times harmful." He cautioned, though, that realistic immigration policies should take into account the continuing rapid increase of the world's population and the rising immigration potential thereby created. From this viewpoint, Bean (1993:5F) concluded that "unless the country soon starts to generate more new and well-paid jobs, it may be wise to devise policies to slow unskilled immigration during periods of stagnant economic growth."

Vernez and McCarthy (1996) added that the existing studies prove little more than that most recent immigrants have low incomes and that families with low incomes contribute less in taxes than families with high incomes. The researchers stated that the previous studies of the costs and benefits of immigration were not really comparable because the data available on the immigrants' use of public services and the amount of taxes they paid were inadequate. Vernez and McCarthy (1996:45–46) concluded that the earlier studies focused on short-term policy issues such as how much immigrants contribute to or cost society in a given year rather than examining long-term issues such as the overall effects of population growth, the environmental costs of sustaining a growing population, and the development of the U.S. economy.

The Ethnic Absorption Question.   We argued in Chapters 2 and 3 that the basic framework of American society and culture was established during the colonial period primarily by people from England, with numerous borrowings and innovations; and that Anglo conformity became the accepted, semi-official pattern that immigrants were expected to adopt. Nevertheless, this conception of Americanism, while dominant, has never been accepted by all who were citizens and identified themselves as Americans; and, as we have seen, it has been periodically challenged but, to this point, never overturned. We have seen, too, that the dominance of Anglo conformity has been based on "the ability and willingness of an Anglo elite to stamp its image on other peoples coming to this country" (Schwarz 1995:62). And, as we stated earlier, non-White people were never considered to be eligible for admission to the dominant group precisely *because* they were not White.

Since the 1960s, however, Anglo conformity increasingly has been challenged by the pluralist belief that *people of every racial and ethnic group may become "100 percent Americans" without changes in their physical appearance or a complete substitution of Anglo American ways for those of their own cultures.* As stated by President Franklin D. Roosevelt, "Americanism is a matter of the mind and heart; Americanism is not, and never was, a matter of race and ancestry" (Schlesinger 1992:37).

The pluralist conception of Americanism did not sit well with Brimelow. He recited the well-publicized news that, if the present rates of change continue, the White majority in America will become a numerical minority at some point in the future. For example, the U.S. Bureau of the Census's projections (given the rates of change then current) showed that by the year 2050 the White majority will have declined to 52 percent of the total American population (U.S. Bureau of the Census 1995:19).[38] Brimelow (1995:63) illustrated these projected changes in a chart, ominously titled "The Pincers." The chart showed the White majority to be shrinking as it is squeezed between an increasingly large upper "claw" closing from the top (representing Asians, Blacks, and Other immigrants) and an increasingly large lower "claw" (representing Hispanics) closing from the bottom. Given Brimelow's consternation over the prospect that America is "browning," one may understand why Simon, among others, charged that Brimelow's "arguments are nothing but a facade for anti-foreign and racist feelings" (Simon 1993:27).

Reflecting Simon's perspective that greater diversity provides the country with more options and opportunites for cross-ethnic alliances, a special report prepared by Barone (1995) for *U.S. News and World Report* found that Americans' opinions regarding the issues surrounding immigration and also concerning personal values, did not follow ethnic and racial lines. The article claimed that because of diversity, people's racial or ethnic identification is not a reliable indicator of their views. Issues such as crime, economic threats, the role of government, abortion, and other matters were more likely than ethnic or racial group identification to determine one's alliances.

Brimelow (1995:9, 216) agreed that America has been "unusually assimilative" and that "the American experience with immigration has been a triumphant success"; but he doubted that America can successfully absorb the contemporary stream of newcomers unless its immigration policies are sharply altered. He maintained that the existing immigration policies are "bringing about an ethnic and racial transformation of America . . . with no particular reason to expect success" in absorbing the newcomers. We must at least have a lull, he said, similar to the ones that took place in the periods 1776–1815 and 1924–1965 to give the processes of assimilation time to work.

We close this brief consideration of the contemporary immigration debate with two last questions. First, does increased immigration lead to separatism? On the "doomster" side of the argument, Brimelow's answer to the question was "yes." He argued that unless there was a lull in the immigration flow, the United States would lose its underlying unity and be **Balkanized.** He agreed that Asian and Hispanic (but not Black) immigrants *might* assimilate easily, but he doubted it (Brimelow 1995:271–274); and he concluded that the probable negative consequences of allowing the new immigration to continue greatly outweighed the probable positive consequences. On the "boomster" side of the argument, Simon stated that immigration increases "*diversity* . . . foods eaten, ethnic festivals celebrated, types of schools operated privately, foreign-language newspapers published" but does not threaten the nation's unity because "this is variation *around* the mainline, rather than an alteration of the central traditions of national life" (1993:28).

Second, given that America's immigration laws were overhauled twice between 1986 and 1990, would still further changes in the laws greatly affect the course of the new immigration? One perspective suggests that the social forces that sustain the present phase of the third stream require that we think in broader terms. As Vernez (1993: 4) put it, immigration's benefits "have not all of a sudden disappeared" but, instead, the concurrent changes in a global complex of economic, social, and demographic factors have combined to make us more aware of immigration's downside. American ethnic groups are competing for jobs, not only with one another, but also with workers throughout the world. This perspective cautions that individual countries can no longer affect the global factors that regulate the ebbs and flows of modern immigration simply by changing from one set of fixed policies to another (Massey, Alarcon, Durand, and Gonzales 1987:320–321). Immigration must be managed in a flexible way that responds to changing global circumstances.

The vigorous debate over the new immigration and the ethnic diversity that it helps create in the United States illustrates the continuing conflict between the ideologies of Anglo conformity, cultural pluralism, and separatism in American life. The rising consciousness of ethnicity that was stimulated by the civil rights movements of the 1960s and 1970s and the size and ethnic composition of the third immigrant stream have added to the heterogeneity of American society. Whether this increasing diversity is, on balance, desirable or undesirable has been the focus of a vigorous, often highly emotional debate that centers on alternative visions of what kind of country America ought to be. The appeal of pluralism as the preferred route to Americanization has been greatly enhanced by the increasing diversity of the United States, but the danger that pluralism may slide into separatism also has risen, accompanied by an increase in racism and nativism within the United States.

These struggles over ideology, as well as the material benefits that may follow the success of one view over another, have encouraged increases in the interethnic hostilities that always, to some extent, have imperiled America's ability to move toward a truly pluralistic society. What can be done to lower the levels of intergroup hostility? Chapter 15 suggests some answers.

Key Ideas

1. The new immigration (or third immigrant stream) was set in motion by economic and political changes that occurred throughout the world and was given added impetus by changes in the immigration policies of the United States in 1965. The volume of the new immigration has reached, and may surpass, the numerical levels recorded at the peak of the second stream. The new immigration has consisted mainly of people from Mexico, other nations of the Western Hemi-

sphere, and Asia. Many of these newcomers have been refugees seeking asylum in the United States.

2. The new immigration has greatly increased the racial and ethnic diversity of the United States. Not only are there significant differences in appearance, culture, education, and skills between the native Whites and the majority of the new immigrants, but also there are significant differences between the new immigrant groups themselves and, additionally, between the newcomers of several groups and their American co-ethnics.

3. The Vietnamese have been an especially visible refugee group, both because they have been the largest refugee group of the twentieth century and because of the chain of events that led them to flee from Vietnam. The collapse of South Vietnam in 1975 led to a large evacuation of Vietnamese people and to the resettlement of many of them in the United States.

4. The sudden emigration of the Vietnamese combined with the U.S. government's resettlement program created a unique immigration experience for this group of people.

5. The cultural assimilation of the Vietnamese appears to be taking place rapidly. Although their secondary assimilation may be occurring slowly, there are reasons to believe it gradually will accelerate and reach a high level. Primary and marital assimilation appear to be very low.

6. There were many indications during the 1980s and early 1990s that xenophobia and racism in the United States were rising. White supremacist organizations proliferated during this period. They also established strong links with many groups of people who have expressed anger with the immigration, tax, and policing policies of the United States government and have formed militia groups for "self-defense." Many of those involved in the militia movement also expressed high levels of race hatred and some were preparing for a "race war." The rise in xenophobia and racism also was evident in a sharp increase in the number of assaults against the members of some racial and ethnic groups by the members of other groups.

7. Xenophobia and racism also have contributed to the increasing notice given immigration problems and policies in national political debate. California's Proposition 187, which was strongly approved by the state's voters in 1994, focused national attention on questions concerning undocumented immigrants. What effect do such immigrants have on the economy? Should undocumented immigration be controlled? What steps to control undocumented immigration are effective, humane, and constitutional? Experts generally agree, despite heated debate, that the overall economic effect of all immigration, including undocumented immigration, is either somewhat beneficial economically or makes little difference. Some experts believe, however, that immigration policies that differ from those adopted in the INAA in 1965 would lead to an increased economic benefit.

8. Regardless of the economic consequences of immigration, however, many members of the dominant group are concerned about the "browning of America." This concern brings to the forefront questions regarding the meaning of the term *American* and to whom it may be applied. The issues that are raised by these questions highlight the importance of the competing visions of what America should be that are captured in various ideologies of intergroup relations, some of which we have identified and discussed in this book—Anglo conformity, the melting pot, cultural pluralism, and separatism.

Key Terms

Balkanize   To divide into small states that are hostile to one another.

Notes

1. Rumbaut (1996:320) stated that "the 1975 refugees . . . may be the most closely studied arrival cohort in U.S. history."

2. This tension was illustrated also in a pathetic incident, known as "the Voyage of the Damned." Over 900 Jews attempted to escape from Germany in 1939 aboard a cruise ship bound for Havana. After the ship was denied permission to dock in Havana, it attempted to land in Florida. The United States enforced its quota law, and the ship returned to Germany. Most of the Jews on board lost their lives in Nazi concentration camps.

3. These percentages were calculated from Table 20 in the U.S. Immigration and Naturalization Service 1996:68–69.

4. This group, known as the "Marielitos," consisted of approximately 130,000 refugees who were brought from the Cuban port of Mariel in 1980 by a flotilla of boats organized by Cuban Americans.

5. According to Illsoo Kim (1987: 230) "Koreatown" is a "district where Jewish landlords and Indian, Pakistani, Chinese . . . and other non-Asian merchants intermingle" with Korean businessmen.

6. Calculated from Barringer, Gardner, and Levin (1995:Table 6.1, 172).

7. Calculated from Barringer, Gardner, and Levin (1995:Table 7.1, 198–199).

8. The nine groups were: Asian Indian, Black, Chinese, Filipino, Hispanic, Japanese, Korean, Vietnamese, and White.

9. Chief among these are Hindi, Bengali, Punjabi, Urdu, Gujarati, and Tamil.

10. Some writers present much higher estimates of the numbers murdered, see, for example, St. Cartmail (1983:90); Strand and Jones (1985:21).

11. For example, "reeducation programs," confiscations of property, and conscriptions to forced labor.

12. These grants provided $2,500 or more to assist in the resettlement of most families (Kelly 1977:133).

13. The sample surveys were conducted in five waves by telephone with random samples of Vietnamese household heads in various American communities (Montero 1979:33–55). The household heads reported information on all of the members of their households (Montero 1979:35).

14. This was the second survey. It was based on interviews of a national probability sample "of all refugees who had left the camps on or before October 15, 1975" (Montero 1979:35).

15. Calculated from Table 4.6 in Montero (1979:48).

16. The five locations were Boston, Chicago, Houston, Orange County (California), and Seattle.

17. For example, the percent of refugees who felt able to use English to shop for food rose from 32 to 92 percent and to be a salesperson rose from 6 to 23 percent (Caplan, Whitmore, and Choy 1989:220).

18. Vietnamese workers were substantially less likely than Filipino, Chinese, Korean, and Japanese workers to hold the types of jobs held by White workers (Jiobu 1988:87).

19. Caplan, Whitmore, and Choy (1989:77) found that "arrival English" played a very important role in economic advancement.

20. The eight groups were: Black, Chinese, Filipino, Japanese, Korean, Mexican, Vietnamese, and White.

21. Studies focusing on the psychological and interpersonal consequences for the Vietnamese created by the shock of a rapid, unplanned entry into the United States and a sharp downturn in economic standing have found widespread psychological distress, depression, and marital conflict among the refugees (see, e.g., Rumbaut 1996:328–330).

22. This classification of groups and the examples are from Southern Poverty Law Center, *Klanwatch Intelligence Report* (March 1994: 15–17).

23. According to Bullard (1991:59), "there were more than 350 known white supremacist groups in the United States" in 1991.

24. The Southern Poverty Law Center (1995:7) cautions that "Statistics on hate crimes are unreliable, because many bias-motivated crimes are not reported to law enforcement, and monitoring . . . varies from state to state."

25. See, for example, Mura (1992); Mydans (1992); U.S. Commission on Civil Rights (May/June 1992:3); U.S. Commission on Civil Rights (March/April 1992:1).

26. Some hate attacks by Whites have been against other Whites (Southern Poverty Law Center 1994:5).

27. Black American unrest in Miami and Los Angeles undoubtedly reflects other important causes such as police–community relations, as discussed in Chapter 11.

28. Tierney (1990:80) quoted Simon as complaining that "As soon as one predicted disaster doesn't occur, the doomsayers skip to another."

29. Immigration issues have divided political conservatives. See, for example, Gramm (1996:A10); Hutchison (1996:A10); Wilson (1996:A15).

30. In 1996, the Platform Committee of the Republican Party proposed that the "birthright guarantee" of the Fourteenth Amendment be abolished (Pear 1996:A9).

31. The book was widely reviewed (see, e.g., Richard Bernstein, "The Immigration Wave: A Plea to Hold It Back," *New York Times,* April 19, 1995:B2). For a critical commentary, see Bernard A. Weisberger, "A Nation of Immigrants," in Kromkowski (1995:40–52).

32. See, for example, Bouvier and Gardner (1986) and Cornelius (1982).

33. For example, if immigrants *throughout the country* pay federal taxes that are either greater than or equal to the full costs of the public services they receive, then the net economic result of immigration is either to increase the nation's per capita income or leave it unchanged; however, because federal dollars do not necessarily return to the states in which they are generated, the per capita income of the citizens *of some states* with large immigrant populations may suffer a decline in per capita income. Passel (1994) warned that researchers must make assumptions about immigrant behaviors, the availability of services, and other components of the equations and that those assumptions are often biased.

34. A poll conducted by the *New York Times* in 1986 showed that 44 percent of Blacks polled believed that immigrants "take jobs from Americans." Yet, 77 percent responded that "new immigrants would be welcomed in their neighborhoods" (Fuchs 1990:308–309).

35. Brimelow (1995:152) referred only to "cash programs like Aid to Families with De-

pendent Children, Supplementary Security Income, and other general assistance" and not
"to other means-tested programs, like Medic-
aid, Earned Income Credits, housing subsidies, food stamps."

36. Brimelow (1995:152–153) did present
an earlier hypothetical calculation by Borjas
showing that, given certain assumptions, native-born taxpayers were losing 16 billion dollars annually.

37. A study by the Rand Corporation confirmed Borjas's findings and also showed that
of all immigrant groups, Mexican immigrants
earned the lowest wages (Pelofsky 1996:D6).

38. This was the "middle series" projection.
The "highest" and "lowest" projections were
56 and 50 percent.

Reducing Prejudice and Discrimination

There are many ways to reduce prejudice and discrimination. Intergroup contacts can be effective if those involved are of similar social status and are engaged in cooperative, enjoyable, and mutually significant activity.

How can you change the opinions of men?
—Marcus Aurelius

*Privileged groups rarely give up their privileges
without strong resistance.*
—Martin Luther King, Jr.

*In our society, affirmative action is, among other things,
a testament to white goodwill and to black power.*
—Shelby Steele

*. . . institutionalized injustice demands
institutionalized compensation.*
—Paul W. Taylor

In the preceding chapters, we have reviewed many events of America's racial and ethnic history, some more infamous than others. The review has illustrated mainly the pervasiveness of prejudiced opinions and discriminatory actions aimed by the members of the most powerful group in the society at racial and ethnic groups possessing little power. Although the dominant group has long wished to convert the ideas of Anglo conformity into the law of the land—to *require* that everyone become Americanized along the lines they prefer—the *official* policy of the country in the long run always has rejected this approach as "un-American."

In Chapter 6, we noted Myrdal's ([1944]1964:3–4) view that most Americans accept, in principle, what he called "the American Creed" of equal access to justice and opportunity. If so, then Americans believe that prejudice and discrimination are morally wrong and, ideally, should be eliminated—that America is, in President Lincoln's eloquent words at Gettysburg, "a new nation, conceived in Liberty, and dedicated to the proposition that all men are created equal." Our review of the past has shown, of course, that the words "all men" were not thought by many people at that time to include non-Whites and women; nevertheless, this and other similar statements have provided a steady reproach to the national conscience and a moral basis for civil rights action.

In our review of theories of prejudice and discrimination, we saw that many people assume that ethnic prejudice is the sole or principal cause of discrimination and that, if we wish to reduce discrimination, we must find and alter the causes of prejudice. We saw further, though, some evidence to suggest that discrimination stems not only from prejudice but also has other roots. Our discussion of institutional discrimination, for instance, emphasized that if a person is unjustly denied an opportunity at one time—perhaps entry into college—then the person's lack of qualifications later will provide a seemingly "fair" basis for refusing to hire that person for a job which requires a college education. The employer who refuses to hire may, in fact, harbor little prejudice; but he or she nevertheless will have been a part of a chain of discrimination that has worked to deny someone an equal opportunity. Discrimination of this type is unlikely to be reduced by attacking the prejudices of individuals. This example suggests a fundamentally different view of the problem: Prejudice and discrimination are embedded within a larger sociocultural system, which to some extent affects both prejudice and discrimination *separately* through various proximate causes, and to some extent acts on both prejudice and discrimination *through* the other.

Theory and Practice

The various types of theories of prejudice and discrimination we have reviewed are important sources of ideas concerning possible ways to attack these social—and if we accept the American Creed, also moral—problems. There is not, however, a simple one-to-one correspondence between the theories and the various strategies of social change. A cultural transmission theory of prejudice may suggest to one person that we should give first priority to attacking racial and ethnic stereotypes by removing them from children's school books. But the same theory may suggest to another person that stereotypes may be attacked more effectively by requiring children from different groups to attend the same schools. These examples suggest that one's general theory of social organization and change—whether one is a consensus or a conflict theorist (as discussed in Chapter 2)—will have an important effect on the strategies of change one prefers. Since most Americans are consensus theorists, perhaps without realizing it, the most common suggestions for reducing prejudice and discrimination focus on the reduction of prejudice through various educational methods reflecting the cultural transmission, group identification, and personality theories. Remedies that frequently are proposed include courses in schools to combat group stereotypes, sensitivity training for professionals who deal with different racial and ethnic groups (e.g., teachers, police officers), books and films that portray sympathetically the plight of oppressed peoples, personal counseling for people who are filled with ethnic hatreds, and "get-togethers" that enable the members of different groups to become acquainted. A more vigorous consensual approach may counsel minority-group members to become informed concerning public affairs so they may know which political candidates to support and how to participate effectively in the political life of the country. Generally speaking, people who prefer a consensual approach tend to advocate methods of change that are gradual in their effects and are not likely to result in open conflicts between groups.

Many other Americans, in contrast, are conflict theorists—again perhaps without realizing it. They may have little faith in efforts to alter people's prejudices, believing that such an approach is too slow, too uncertain, or too idealistic. Conflict theorists prefer to focus on the reduction of discrimination (rather than prejudice) through methods derived mainly from the situational pressures, group gains, and institutional discrimination theories. They are likely to advocate litigation to force changes in unfair laws and organizational rules, organizing and participating in militant political groups, and, if these steps fail, to engage in organized protest. Discrimination, they argue, can be reduced effectively only by changing the society's organization—its structure—and to accomplish that, one must use group power and confrontation. These advocates tend to prefer legal, political, and protest methods that promise rapid social changes even though the risk of intergroup conflict may increase.

This broad pattern of theoretical and strategic preferences has been reflected in the studies that have been conducted in this field. Most studies have focused on the reduction of prejudice through the use of various educational approaches. Gradually, however, the focus of attention has shifted toward the reduction of discrimination, especially through changes in laws—by litigation, political participation, and organized social protest. We will illustrate these methods briefly, giving the most attention to the educational and legal approaches. We also comment briefly on increases in the political participation of minorities through electoral politics and organized social protest.

The Educational Approach

Cognitive Approach

Many people believe that individual prejudice and discrimination reflect a lack of knowledge and, therefore, that everyone should receive more education. This view rests on the belief that the more years of education people receive, the less likely they are to accept ethnic stereotypes or to express the wish to hold people of a different ethnicity at a great social distance. Fortunately for all who favor rational discourse in the treatment of human problems, there is considerable evidence to back up this belief. In general, the more educated people are, the lower their prejudice levels appear to be.

A more specific version of the view that knowledge begets tolerance is that the more people learn about intergroup similarities and differences, the less likely they are to accept stereotypes, and the less prejudiced they will be (Hewstone and Brown 1986: 10–12). As people gain more knowledge about the members of other groups, it is assumed, they will be more likely to respect the members of those groups and cooperate with them. Regrettably, it is easy to overestimate the beneficial effects of a largely informational or **cognitive approach** to the problems of intergroup hostility.

To illustrate, if the cognitive approach is a powerful method of reducing prejudice, then we would expect that in settings where large numbers of highly educated people come together—such as in colleges and universities—there would be high levels of interethnic harmony. Unfortunately, however, as minority enrollments in American colleges and universities rose during the 1980s and 1990s, so did the levels of interethnic hostility on many campuses. The faculties and students at a large number of colleges and universities were embroiled in often bitter debates concerning such things as the introduction of new courses focusing on racial and ethnic relations, recruitment of minority faculty members, new facilities to accommodate the growing numbers of students representing one ethnic group or another, and the creation of new departments and programs focusing on ethnic studies. And, as we discuss later, hostilities were increased over affirmative action in hiring and admissions. In addition, there were numerous incidents on campuses in which students exchanged ethnic slurs (or "hate speech"), defaced one another's property and, occasionally, engaged in open confrontation and conflict. Various political disagreements erupted. For example, White students who opposed curriculum changes were often charged with racism, a charge they deeply resented. They, in turn, often charged that the free and open discussion of important issues was being suppressed. Such disappointing evidence of the limited tolerance of ethnic-group differences existing among these young, well-educated people probably came as no surprise to the many scholars whose research had shown that although high levels of education and low levels of prejudice were correlated, the connection was not usually strong (see, e.g.,Taylor, Sheatsley, and Greeley 1978:45) and that "stereotypic beliefs are extremely resistant to change" (Pettigrew and Martin 1989:186).

In response to the ethnic tensions on their campuses, many colleges and universities instituted various kinds of programs to increase intergroup understanding and tolerance. Probably no other university experienced a greater degree of ethnic change in the composition of its student body during the 1980s than the University of California at Berkeley. Within that decade, the undergraduate student body "shifted from 66 percent white . . . to 42 percent white" (Institute for the Study of Social Change 1991:1). Asian students soon became the largest single group, but no group was now a majority. In addition to creating a rich social setting within which "students from differing backgrounds" could learn from one another, the dramatic change led to "disillusion, conflicts, tensions and retreat around issues of race and ethnicity" (Institute for the Study of Social Change 1991:1); consequently, the university initiated the Diversity Project "to find out, up close, how undergraduate students" experienced "the new racial and ethnic diversity of the campus" (Institute for the Study of Social Change 1991:7). The project's researchers interviewed Native American, Asian American, African American, Chicano/Latino American, and White American students concerning their experiences and views, and then published many valuable findings and insights. We describe here only one of the findings.

Seventy percent of the students agreed that they would "like to meet more students from ethnic and cultural backgrounds that are different from my own" (Institute for the Study of Social Change 1991:13); but, the researchers found, this agreement did not mean the same thing to students from different groups. White students were mainly interested in interpersonal contacts, while the members of all other groups were more interested in participating in special courses, programs, and activites that promote intergroup understanding. This finding shed light on what seemed to be a growing, seemingly contradictory, trend. At the same time the campus increasingly was being Balkanized around friendships, dating, parties, and so on, there appeared also to be a growing number of interethnic academic and professional organizations on the campus. Such a development is consistent with the idea that many minority-group members preferred to have primary relationships mainly with other members of their in-groups but were interested in expanding the scope of their secondary relationships to the members of out-groups. Although many White students interpreted the in-group preferences of the minority students as evidence of a growing separatism, this pattern of preferences is consistent with the idea that the minority-group students were seeking a pluralist solution to the new dilemmas of campus life.

Although the cognitive approach is useful, and may become more so as more is learned about how to implement it, many researchers and practitioners feel that it must be supplemented by noncognitive methods such as the **vicarious experience approach.**

Vicarious Experience Approach

Instead of simply imparting specific facts to people, a program of intergroup education may be based on films, plays, television productions, biographies, novels, and other modes of communication that present the members of all groups in a sympathetic way (Allport 1958:454). This approach attempts to "speak to the heart rather than to the head." The underlying premise here is that exposure to such materials may help people recognize and appreciate the humanness of the members of all groups and, thus, reduce the tendency for people to draw sharp boundaries between "them" and "us." Participants in such programs are encouraged to "take the role of the other," or to "walk awhile in the other person's shoes." Such a vicarious experience, it is assumed, should lead prejudiced people—members of minority groups as well as the majority—to see the world through the eyes of others and, thereby, to stimulate changes in attitudes and behavior.

Several criticisms of the vicarious experience approach have been advanced. Prejudiced people frequently do not interpret accurately a film or book that runs counter to their prejudices. They may pay greatest attention to side issues and ignore the central point. Also the effectiveness of a film or some other dramatic presentation in reducing prejudice depends greatly on the skill with which the "message" of tolerance is presented. Some presentations actually create a "boomerang" effect in which prejudices are heightened instead of diminished (Brown 1986:224). And one may reasonably argue that it is unrealistic to assume that something as superficial as a film or a book may seriously disrupt a deep-seated ethnic prejudice or lead to tolerant behavior.

An interesting attempt to test these ideas was conducted by Middleton (1960). One group of students was shown the award-winning commercial film *Gentleman's Agreement,* while another group of students was not shown the film. *Gentleman's Agreement* attempts to convey the message that anti-Semitism is despicable and is perpetuated significantly by people who succumb to situational pressures to discriminate. The primary findings were that (1) on average, the anti-Semitic sentiments of those who saw the film were significantly reduced, and (2) even though the film did not focus on anti-Black prejudice, there also was some reduction in this regard; hence, this study supported the idea that deeply ingrained ethnic prejudices may be reduced by a particular kind of vicarious experience.

Intergroup Contact

So far, we have considered two main approaches to increasing the intercultural knowledge of prejudiced people: (1) exposing them to accurate information, especially concerning ethnic out-groups and (2) assisting them "to place themselves in the other person's shoes." So far as attitude change is concerned, the informational approach generally appears to be weaker than the more emotional approach using novels, plays, films, and so on; but little evidence exists that either approach leads to permanent reductions in prejudice or to much change in behavior. It seems that other methods are required if much change is to be effected.

One of the most common suggestions for improving intergroup relations is that people should "get together" so they may establish communications, participate in various joint activities, and discuss their differences (Olson and Zanna 1993:145). When people do things together, they have the opportunity to judge the members of other groups on the basis of their individual merits, rather than on stereotypes. These ideas gave rise to the **contact hypothesis** (Allport 1958:250–261), which has been stated as follows by Ellison and Powers (1994:385): "contact, particularly close and sustained contact, with members of different racial and ethnic groups promotes positive, tolerant attitudes toward those groups."

The idea that contact is an important avenue to the reduction of prejudice is certainly consistent with much everyday experience. Early students of the contact hypothesis concluded that declines in prejudice are most probable if the people involved are of equal social status, if they are working cooperatively on something, if their activity is supported by people in positions of authority, and if the activity involves a relatively high level of intimacy (Stephan 1987:14). Intergroup contacts occurring under other circumstances, in contrast, may leave prejudices unchanged or intensify them. For example, children involved in school desegregation programs may become more prejudiced unless parents, teachers, school administrators, and local elected officials make strong public declarations supporting desegregation (Robinson and Preston 1976:911) and classroom activities are organized appropriately (Aronson and Gonzalez 1988:304–307).

Studies of intergroup contacts have been conducted in various social settings with various types of data. Numerous factors in addition to those we have listed have been shown to influence the outcome of contacts between the members of dominant and subordinate groups.[1] Our discussion focuses on several studies of intergroup contacts among people in schools and in a variety of other settings as revealed in national surveys.[2]

Intergroup Contact in Schools.   Studies of intergroup contact in schools have been concerned with a number of topics such as academic achievement and self-esteem, as well as with interracial attitudes and behavior. Although the effects of contact in each of these respects is a matter of considerable practical importance, we are interested here in interracial attitudes and behavior.[3]

One important review of evidence relating to the contact hypothesis in desegregated schools was conducted by St. John (1975). St. John's (1975:67–68) summary stated that, "for either race positive findings are less common than negative findings.... Sometimes desegregation is reported to have ameliorated the prejudice of Whites but intensified that of Blacks, sometimes the reverse." She noted, however, that the conditions under which contact was theoretically expected to lead to changes in attitudes were seldom fully realized in actual desegregation programs; and that when such conditions were met, the results were more promising.

This conclusion received general support from the results of subsequent studies of the long-term effects of desegregation (Hawley and Smylie 1988:284–285; Stephan 1986: 196; 1988:19). Gerard and Miller (1975), conducted a well-designed study of approximately 20,000 children's choices of friends, school-work partners, and play partners in the elementary schools of Riverside, California. Although the observed attitude changes led to "little or no real integration ... during the relatively long-term contact situation" (Gerard, Jackson, and Conolley 1975:237), studies covering still longer periods of time have shown that Blacks who have attended desegregated schools are more likely than other Blacks to attend college, to work in integrated settings, and to live in desegregated housing (Stephan 1988:19).

The results of studies of the type reviewed so far led some scholars to suggest that much more attention should be given to the actual school and classroom conditions under which children meet (Mercer, Iadicola, and Moore 1980:294; St. John 1975: 122). For instance, the equality of statuses among children within a desegregated classroom was often more apparent than real (Schofield and Sagar 1979:169–173; Schofield 1986:82). Even in small groups in which children were expected to work cooperatively to accomplish a given task, White children frequently were more active and influential than minority-group children (Cohen 1980:253–256). This finding led to systematic efforts to understand how the status rankings of the larger society were imported into the classroom and to devise various strategies to alter these rankings; and several techniques have been developed to foster interdependence and cooperation among students in the classroom (Brown 1986:615–620; van Oudenhoven 1989:208–213). For instance, a group of students may be assigned a task that can be completed only when the specific contribution of each member is included; or minority-group students may be taught a particular skill which they, in turn, teach to the majority-group students. These and other classroom methods that strive to produce equal-status contacts were reviewed by the Committee on the Status of Black Americans (Jaynes and Williams 1989:81) and found to be effective in helping to reduce inequalities of status in classrooms.

Systematic efforts also have been devoted to understanding the extent to which the social-psychological processes that result in same-race friendships operate in situations of interracial contacts within schools. A study of friendship pairs conducted by Hallinan and Williams (1989:76), referred to earlier, found that children who form cross-race friendships are likely to be in frequent contact and to be similar in their attitudes, values, and statuses.[4]

National Surveys.   Even though studies of attitude changes in residential and school settings have not always found that interracial contact led to more favorable attitudes, they nevertheless have provided considerable support for the idea that favorable changes are likely to occur under the conditions specified by the contact hypothesis. These conditions are unusual, however. As noted by Sigelman and Welch (1993:782) Blacks and Whites "often have only minimal contact and typically do not interact as social equals." For this reason, some researchers have wondered "whether contact *per se* fosters positive racial attitudes *in general*" (Ellison and Powers 1994:386).

In one study based on a national survey, Jackman and Crane (1986) found little difference between the racial attitudes of Whites who had Black friends and those who did not; however, in an analysis of a biracial national survey, Sigelman and Welch (1993: 792–793) found that Blacks who had interracial friendships and Whites with interracial neighborhood contacts experienced a decrease in the extent to which they perceived hostility between the races. And in a study based on a national sample of Black Americans, Ellison and Powers (1994:395) found that "blacks who report having close white friends express more favorable views of whites and race relations than those who lack such friends." They concluded that, although casual interracial contacts have little direct effect on Black's opinions of Whites, such contacts are nevertheless important because they increase the chance that close interracial friendships may develop (Ellison and Powers 1994:396).[5]

The evidence we have reviewed on the capacity of contact to reduce intergroup prejudice and discrimination is mixed. Obviously, intergroup contacts may not be hailed as *the* way to reduce prejudice; but, like the other educational methods we have considered, it surely has its place. The main point of the contact hypothesis generally has been supported by research: Under appropriate conditions, personal contacts between majority- and minority-group members can lead to reductions in prejudice (Stroessner and Mackie 1993:83). The method seems to work best when people are "in the same boat"; but even under typical conditions, contact sometimes leads to reduced antipathy (Amir 1976; Ellison and Powers 1994).

Our review has shown that educational methods may reduce prejudice and, possibly, discrimination. It also has shown that in the effort to alter people's behavior, "shaping situations" may be "more successful than direct attempts to change such deeply held attitudes as racism" (Pettigrew and Martin 1989:190). To what extent can social situations be shaped through changes in rules and laws?

The Legal Approach

The Laws and the Mores

For more than a century, one of the most prominent features of interethnic conflict in America has been the effort to control intergroup relations through laws and judicial decisions. This approach always has received a substantial amount of support in America, at least at the verbal level. As we have stressed, Americans generally endorse the ideals of freedom and equality of opportunity. They also frequently wish to have laws that help strengthen these ideals. In practice, however, Americans seem generally to couple the statement "There ought to be a law" with a low degree of respect for law (Myrdal [1944]1964:14).

Opponents of the legal approach frequently point out that laws, especially those attempting to control behavior relating to personal preferences, may inadvertently make matters worse. To support this view, people often cite the failure of the Prohibition experiment in America. Prohibition not only failed to prevent the manufacture, sale, and use of alcoholic beverages but seemed, instead, actually to have encouraged it. Prohibition created a "backlash." Much the same sort of thing has accompanied efforts to increase the legal restraints on the use of other drugs and on such things as prostitution. The same result may occur outside the arena of personal tastes. As we have seen, stricter rules on immigration have helped create greater numbers of undocumented immigrants.

Among social scientists, the view that unpopular legislation is doomed is usually traced to Sumner's analysis of the folkways and mores. His commentary on the effects of the laws passed during the Reconstruction period following the Civil War is frequently quoted: "Vain attempts have been made to control the new order by legislation. The only result is the proof that legislation cannot make mores" (Sumner [1906]1960:81). Despite appearances, Sumner believed that if laws were skillfully framed and rationally planned, then some portions of conduct could be altered; and, he believed that if conduct were altered, then changes in thought and feeling would follow (Ball, Simpson, and Ikeda 1962). Nevertheless, Sumner's work has been interpreted by many readers to mean "that social change must always be glacier-like in its movement and that mass change in attitudes must precede legislative action" (Roche and Gordon 1965:332).

There certainly is a large element of good sense in this argument. Quite clearly, as Sumner emphasized, the "stroke of the pen" does not produce changes in the morality of people; however, as this viewpoint ordinarily is understood, an important reservation should be noted. It assumes that attitudes are the wellspring of action. But our analysis has shown that even when people's "hearts are not in it," new ways of acting may lead people to change their minds because "Behaving differently . . . often precedes thinking differently" (Pettigrew 1971:279). Contemporary sociological thought generally agrees with a statement by Martin Luther King, Jr. (1962:49): "While it may be true that morality cannot be legislated, behavior can be regulated"; consequently, "the habits, if not the hearts, of people are being altered every day by Federal action."

Additionally, despite Sumner's emphasis on the general resistance of the mores to change, he also stressed that under some circumstances changes occur rapidly. One of these circumstances arises when two or more sets of conflicting mores exist simultaneously within a society. This conflict generates a "strain toward consistency," and the law may tip the balance in one direction or the other. In modern societies, in particular, the law seldom is required to stand alone against a monolithic set of opposing mores. More often, the law chooses between competing moral codes (Berger 1968:219).

We noted earlier that racial and ethnic prejudices among White Americans appear to have declined markedly during the last several decades. Of special interest here is that a strong majority of Whites in all regions of the country now agree that Black children should attend school with White children; however, a large majority of those who say they accept the ideal of desegregated schools also reject the most prominent method used to achieve this objective: "busing" (Bobo 1988:88).

School Busing

The use of buses to transport children between their homes and schools began in the United States several decades before buses were used for the purpose of desegregating schools. During the earlier period, busing was widely hailed as a progressive tool to ensure that children—particularly rural children—would not be denied an education because they lacked transportation. During this period, busing frequently was used to *maintain* school segregation.

Recall that the establishment of dual school systems became widespread as the Jim Crow system of segregation came into being in the South following *Plessy v. Ferguson* in 1896. It soon became obvious that the separate schools being established for Black, Asian, and Mexican children were not truly equal to those being established for Whites; so, minority communities began to organize to fight Jim Crow. By the 1930s, the National Association for the Advancement of Colored People (NAACP), the League of United Latin American Citizens (LULAC), and other minority-group organizations had selected segregation in education as the primary target of their efforts to expand the application of civil rights to minority citizens.

A series of court victories concerning segregation in graduate and professional education led to *Brown I* and the end of legal school segregation, though not to actual school desegregation. A number of school districts in the South and the District of Columbia did begin to comply in 1955, but "massive resistance" to desegregation in some states followed *Brown II* in which the Supreme Court stated that compliance must take place "with all deliberate speed." Consequently, "ten years after *Brown* only 1.2 percent of the nearly 3 million Black students in the 11 Southern States attended school with White students" (United States Commission on Civil Rights 1976:4).

One might well argue that this evidence shows the futility of a legal approach to social change, but such a conclusion would be premature. Consider two complicating factors. First, the *Brown* decision was extraordinary in its scope. It led not only to a national effort to desegregate schools, but also to the formal desegregation of every institution in American life. Such sweeping changes would have been difficult to effect under any circumstances, but in this case the difficulties were increased because many people thought the Court had exceeded its authority. In any event, *Brown's* place in American life remained ambiguous until, with the Civil Rights Act of 1964, Congress validated the prohibition of racial discrimination. In the process, Congress created many official tools that could be used to help combat racial discrimination.

The second complicating factor is that, after the Civil Rights Act was passed, the Court began to move with great vigor to desegregate schools. "Desegregation no longer progressed painfully from test case to test case" Glazer (1987:78) stated, "It moved rapidly as every school district in the South was required to comply" with the law. In 1966, the Department of Health, Education, and Welfare (HEW) began to require statistical evidence that desegregation was occurring. Between 1968 and 1973, the U.S. Supreme Court ruled that school systems could no longer have schools that were primarily for Whites or for minorities; that busing might be used, where necessary, to eliminate segregation; and that busing could be used to bring about school desegregation outside of the South (Schuman, Steeh, and Bobo 1985:35–36).[6] The busing of children to schools was nothing new in American life; but never before had it been adopted by the courts as a means to ensure racial desegregation. This step initiated a prolonged and bitter controversy.

The objections to busing for the purposes of desegregation have been numerous. Indeed, it is difficult to find people of any group who positively like busing and think it is the best conceivable way to improve education. Although Whites increasingly have agreed that their children should attend schools with minority-group children, their opposition to busing has remained high. A survey conducted in 1972 found that 87 percent of the White people questioned were opposed to busing. Over ten years later another survey found that 79 percent still were opposed to it. Busing is more highly regarded among Blacks, but the level of opposition to it was, and has remained, fairly high. In 1975 and 1977, more than half of the Black respondents were opposed (Schuman, Steeh, and Bobo 1985:78, 147). Some critics in both races emphasize that busing wastes time and money, exposes children to unnecessary risks, and takes children away from their neighborhoods. Others argue that, in any event, desegregation has "failed."[7]

Since our present discussion concerns the relation of law to social change, the broad claim that desegregation has "failed" is of special interest. Is it true that the orders of the courts and the other steps taken by the federal government under the Civil Rights Act have "failed?" If we take as our criterion compliance with official orders to dismantle legal systems of discrimination, the answer to this question is "no." The U.S. Commission on Civil Rights (1976:77–88) analyzed the role of the courts and the responsible executive agency (HEW) in effecting desegregation. The commission's study found that among 615 school districts, 84 percent were desegregated between 1966 and 1975. Some 59 percent of the districts reported that either the courts or HEW had provided the most important impetus to desegregate. During the period of heaviest intervention by legal bodies (1968–1972), the racial segregation of school children declined sharply in the South (to 46 percent) while remaining nearly constant in the North and West (29 percent) (Farley 1978; Jaynes and Williams 1989:75). By 1980, 70 percent of Black students were attending schools in which at least 5 percent of the students were White (Stephan 1988:8). It is evident that, although many children still attended predominantly segregated schools in 1980, a substantial amount of desegregation of the public schools had taken place. It also is clear that most of this change occurred after 1967, mainly as a result of court orders and busing (Farley 1975:22; Orfield 1982:1). By the school year 1990–91, only four of the nation's forty-four largest urban school districts "had *not* implemented a school desegregation plan" (Heise 1996:1095). Armor's (1995) review of the evidence (cited by Heise 1996:1100) showed that "mandatory desegregation plans generate more racial balance . . . than voluntary plans."

Even if one accepts the contention that court orders and busing succeeded in dismantling *legally* segregated school systems, however, numerous other questions remain. May it not be true, for example, that the law's success in dismantling Jim Crow in education has not achieved the larger purposes that the supporters of desegregation envisioned? Many people question, as we noted earlier, whether simply having children of different races within the walls of the same school necessarily, or even generally, leads to the intended changes in attitudes, behavior, and intellectual development. As St. John's (1975) review of evidence showed, children may or may not relinquish prejudiced attitudes, depending on the operation of many other factors. Some critics go even further to argue that placing minority-group children in schools where most of the students are White may have deleterious effects. Indeed, in Wilkinson's (1996:27–28) view, forced "public school integration and the associated demolition of the black school has had a devastating impact on" the "self-esteem, motivation to succeed . . . respect for adults and academic performance" of African American children.

Those who believe, nevertheless, that the patterns of school desegregation created through busing are on balance desirable, must face another question: Can school desegregation be maintained in the face of continued resistance to residential desegregation? For a long time now, Whites have moved more rapidly to the suburbs than Blacks and other minorities. This trend has created many metropolitan districts that increasingly resemble White rings around a non-White core. The U.S. Supreme Court ruled (*Milliken v. Bradley*) that it will not approve desegregation plans that attempt to cross school district lines to encompass an entire metropolitan area. For this reason, the large reductions in desegregation that were achieved within many American cities may be reversed by resegregation (Celis 1995b:A1); thus, the issue of the continuation of school segregation is intimately linked to housing segregation.

The extent to which the trend toward resegregation reflects the "normal" forces of spatial mobility or was accelerated by school desegregation (so-called "White flight") has been the subject of considerable debate and research.[8] Studies of the problems of desegregating housing show that White residents begin to leave a neighborhood if the number of Black residents exceeds 8 percent of the total and that a "tipping point," beyond which all (or nearly all) Whites will leave is reached when the percentage of Black residents "is somewhere between 10 and 20 percent" (Hacker 1992:37). There are conspicuous exceptions, and we need to know much more about them.[9] In some cases, racially balanced neighborhoods remain stable, but in other cases Blacks elect to construct all-Black neighborhoods. As long as these conditions remain in place, the end of legal (*de jure*) segregation in education will not assure the end of actual (*de facto*) segregation. How the legislatures and courts will view resegregation remains to be seen.[10]

Flashpoint 4: The Affirmative Action Debate

The words **affirmative action** have a benign, uplifting, ring; in fact, they have become "fighting words." The formal end of Jim Crow and the enactment of the civil rights legislation of the 1960s did not create true equality of conditions between the dominant group and various subordinate groups. The achievement of true equality required more than the simple absence of discrimination because, as expressed by President Lyndon B. Johnson, "You do not take a person who for years has been hobbled by chains, and liberate him, bring him up to the starting line, and then say, 'You are free to compete with all the others'" (quoted by Hacker 1992:119). Economist, author, and columnist Thomas Sowell (1977:114), who became an outspoken critic of affirmative action, agreed, stating that "If a firm has engaged in racial discrimination for years, and has an all-white work force as a result, then simply to stop explicit discrimination will mean little." Needed, instead, was "a positive policy of nondiscrimination" (Richard Nixon, cited by Robinson and Spitz 1986–87:86).

Such a policy was set forth by President John F. Kennedy in 1961 in Executive Order 10925. This order stated that the government would encourage "equal opportunity for all qualified persons" through "positive measures" (Robinson and Spitz 1986: 87–86). Federal contractors were required to "take affirmative action that applicants are employed . . . without regard to their race, creed, color, or national origin" (Benokraitis and Feagin 1978:10).[11] *Qualified* minority-group members were to be included in the pool of applicants for jobs and federal contracts. This order played a pivotal role in shifting governmental policy away from the assumption that the cumulative effects of past discrimination may be removed simply by adopting neutral policies and toward the assumption that some **preferential** or **compensatory treatment** of the victims of discrimination is required.

During the 1960s and 1970s, affirmative action programs were brought into general use, but criticism mounted; and by the 1980s and 1990s, these programs had come under fierce attack. To illustrate, in the mid-1990s, Ward Connerly, a successful businessman and a member of the University of California Board of Regents led a fight to end affirmative action in university admissions. As chairman of a group called the California Civil Rights Initiative, he also played an active part in forcing a state-wide referendum on affirmative action (Ayres 1996:A1).[12] Another opponent of affirmative action, Shelby Steele (1990:113), a Professor of English, stated in his book *The Content of Our Character* that Blacks "now stand to lose more from it than they gain." And Glenn C. Loury, a professor of economics, also expressed skepticism of affirmative action and, additionally, of the entire effort to attack the problems of minorities "through civil rights strategies or racial politics" (Loury 1986:188).

Why would three outstanding and successful men such as Connerly, Steele, and Loury—all of whom are Black Americans—take vigorous public stands against a government policy that was adopted in an effort to benefit, among others, people who by social definition are members of *their* group? These opponents of affirmative action argued along different lines; but they agreed that granting racial preferences, in Loury's (1986:194) words, "can actually destroy the good that is being sought on behalf of those initially unequal." These men were hardly alone in their dissatisfaction. In a 1995 poll, conducted by *Time/CNN*, 66 percent of the *Black* respondents agreed that affirmative action "sometimes or frequently discriminates against whites" (Lacayo 1995:39).[13]

Affirmative action grew in the years after 1961 through the various actions by presidents, Congress, and the courts. It also was extended to include women and the members of some minority groups other than Black Americans. Although a brief treatment cannot grasp the legal and moral complexities of this debate, we will refer to a few key events in its development and to some of the basic issues it has raised.

Development of Affirmative Action.

The legal foundation for Executive Order 10925 was laid by a long series of earlier presidential orders. For example, as the United States prepared for entry into World War II, President Franklin D. Roosevelt announced—in response to a threat by A. Philip Randolph, a Black civil rights leader, to lead "an 'all-out' thundering march on Washington"—that the policy of the federal government was the "full participation in the defense program by all persons, regardless of race, creed, color, or national origin" (Roosevelt [1941]1968:400). President Harry S. Truman expanded President Roosevelt's program to ensure fair employment practices, and President Dwight D. Eisenhower issued an order requiring contractors to avoid discrimination in all business matters (Benokraitis and Feagin 1978:9). Although overt discrimination declined, Black workers still were very underrepresented in federally funded jobs and still were among "the last hired and the first fired."

The 1960s brought significant changes in these conditions. Title VII of the Civil Rights Act of 1964 banned "discrimination by employers or unions" and authorized "the Attorney General to sue" if he believed there was discrimination in employment (Osofsky 1968:372). The law also established an Equal Employment Opportunity Commission (EEOC), enabled the government to bring school desegregation suits, and set financial penalities for violations. Federal compliance officers increasingly required that affirmative action plans incorporate specific "goals" and "timetables" that produce "results."[14]

Early Legal Challenges.

Throughout this period, various lawsuits concerning discrimination in education and employment came before the courts. A particularly important case, *Griggs v. Duke Power Co.*, was decided by the U.S. Supreme Court in 1971. Duke Power Company required applicants for a job or a promotion who did not have a high school diploma to pass a written test—one that Whites passed more frequently than Blacks. The plaintiffs argued that the test was unfair because it was not designed to test the specific abilities that were needed to perform the various jobs in question. The defendants argued that the test was fair because the same test was given to all job applicants. The Supreme Court sided with the plaintiffs and ruled that employers must give tests that measure the abilities and skills that are pertinent to the job for which an application is being made; and that tests that routinely lead to higher failure rates among the members of minority groups—i.e., have a **disparate impact**—are suspect. This decision placed on employers the burden of proving that their procedures were fair; and it strengthened the argument that apparently "neutral" and "fair" procedures might, nevertheless, be deemed to be discriminatory if they consistently produced unequal results.

Although none of the government actions we have reviewed required affirmative action in education, the similarities of the problems of discrimination in education and employment brought together the conflict over principles in the two institutional arenas. In 1972, Congress amended Title VII to extend coverage to educational institutions (Glickstein 1977:23). Though it may seem ironic, the application of affirmative action procedures has been fought as bitterly in the field of higher education as in any other segment of our society. One example is the famous and far-reaching U.S. Supreme Court case *Regents of the University of California v. Bakke* (1978). Allan Bakke, a White applicant to the medical school at the University of California at Davis, argued that he had been discriminated against by the university because the medical school had established a quota for minority applicants. Although Bakke's grades were higher than those of some minority applicants who were admitted to the school, Bakke twice was denied admission.

The Court ruled, in a complicated, closely contested decision, that Bakke was correct. The medical school, the ruling said, could give some consideration to the race of an applicant and could set a "goal" for the number of minority admissions, but it could not establish a rigid numerical quota. The difference between a goal and a quota, in principle at least, is that a goal may be reached by showing "evidence of good faith and positive effort" and involves no lowering of standards of merit and ability (Pottinger 1977: 44). Quotas, on the other hand, may be reached only by hiring a certain number of people in each target group even if the usual standards of merit and ability suffer. Critics maintain that, in practice, "numerical goals" are indistinguishable from quotas (Hook 1977:88).[15]

Some Salient Issues.

The lines of argument surrounding affirmative action in employment and desegregation in education converged and, together, presented American society with a divisive ideological and moral dilemma. On the one hand, with the *Brown* decisions, and the passage of the civil rights laws of 1964 and 1965, American society had fulfilled its formal political commitment to the civil equality of all persons without regard to "race, color, religion, sex, or national origin"; but, on the other hand, in the economic sphere, as well as in other social realms, these actions had not removed the effects of past discrimination.

The continuation of the effects of past discrimination (and of present discrimination as well) fostered the belief, as we have seen, that something beyond simple neutrality, something "affirmative," was required to compensate the victims of discrimination so they would be in a position to achieve economic equality. But how, critics asked, can America claim to be a just society if it abandons the historic ideal of appraising each individual only on his or her merits? When a White person is denied a job or admission to a professional school in order to make room for someone who was treated unjustly in the past, is this a moral act of compensatory treatment or an immoral act of **reverse discrimination**?[16] For many Americans, these are inflammatory and exceedingly complicated questions.[17]

Critics of affirmative action often cite the language of the Civil Rights Act of 1964 to show that affirmative action is unlawful and is, in fact, reverse discrimination. The Civil Rights Act stated that the law shall not "be interpreted to require any employer . . .

to grant preferential treatment to any individual or to any group because of race, color, religion, sex or national origin because of an imbalance" in percentages or the total number of employees (Todorovich 1975:13). Critics say that it is contradictory and morally indefensible to require that employers engage in affirmative action while simultaneously avoiding discrimination because affirmative action necessarily involves discrimination (Pottinger 1977:42).

Defenders of affirmative action reply that the courts have stated repeatedly that there is no contradiction in these requirements and that affirmative action is not reverse discrimination. They point out that preferential treatment may not be used unless it is first shown that there has been discrimination in the past, against either a particular individual or an entire group of people. A neutral policy is legally required, they say, unless discrimination has existed in the past and has not been overcome (Glickstein 1977: 26; U.S. Commission on Civil Rights 1981a:15–37). For example, the continuation of Jim Crow segregation into the 1960s established the grounds for many later claims. One ruling stated that unless "affirmative relief against continuation of the effects of past discrimination" is permitted, the purposes of the Civil Rights Act of 1964 would be completely nullified (Glickstein 1977:15). In rebuttal, Steele (1990:114) said that, in practice, past discrimination frequently is assumed rather than proven.

Another line of argument presented by critics of affirmative action maintains that the relief afforded is intended to be only temporary. In upholding affirmative action in the *Bakke* decision, Justice Blackmun expressed his hope that such a policy would be unnecessary "within a decade at the most" (quoted by Graham 1992:51). Connerly (1996: 11) acknowledged that affirmative action "has its roots in the American passion for fairness" but went on to say "it was not meant to be permanent." In a similar vein, Berman (1996:19) stated that "as a temporary program for blacks and women, affirmative action remains defensible." Proponents of affirmative action, in contrast, say that its continuation is necessary until equality is attained in order to prevent a slide back into rampant discrimination.

Later Legal Challenges.   Following the *Griggs* ruling in 1971, there was a sharp increase in the number of successful lawsuits that relied on statistical evidence to show that certain employment practices had a disparate impact on minority workers. To avoid the costs of lawsuits, many employers began voluntary affirmative action programs. For eighteen years, the *Griggs* ruling appeared to be settled national policy; however, in 1989 the U.S. Supreme Court ruled in *Ward's Cove Packing v. Antonio* that employers no longer were required to shoulder the burden of proof in disparate-impact cases. Instead, plaintiffs were given the burden of showing that the practices they wished to challenge were discriminatory (Greenhouse 1989:D6). This ruling contributed to a widespread concern among affirmative action's supporters that many of the anti-discrimination programs of the preceding twenty-five years were in danger of being revoked.

This concern was heightened by *Hopwood v. Texas,*[18] a case that many observers thought might become a direct test of the *Bakke* ruling. Four White students who had been denied admission to the University of Texas's Law School in 1992 sued the university alleging that their grades and test scores were above those of some minority students who had been admitted to the school, that they had been denied their right to equal protection of the law, and that, therefore, they were victims of reverse discrimination. When the case came to trial, U.S. District Judge Sam Sparks noted that the problem of segregated schools in Texas "is not a relic of the past" and that Texas's schools at all levels have "a history of state-sanctioned discrimination" (Sparks 1994:4, 5). The University of Texas's Law School, for instance, was ordered by the U.S. Supreme Court in 1950 (*Sweatt v. Painter*) to admit the plaintiff, Mr. Heman M. Sweatt, an African American, and to open its admissions procedures to other minority students. Judge Sparks ruled in *Hopwood* that the plaintiffs, as they claimed, had been denied the equal protection of the law because the law school used two separate and different admission processes for White and minority students. He ruled that the plaintiffs were entitled to reapply for admission; but that the law school was not required to admit them (Sparks 1994).[19] The plaintiffs then took their case to the Fifth Circuit Court of Appeals in New Orleans.

In a ruling affecting Texas, Louisiana, and Mississippi, a three-judge panel of the Fifth Circuit ruled against the University of Texas, saying, contrary to *Bakke,* that the university's use of race as a factor in admissions was not constitutional (Smith 1996:29). The panel said that the university had given preferential treatment to "blacks and Mexican Americans . . . to the detriment of whites and non-preferred minorities" (Smith 1996:2). The circuit court stated, however, that although the use of race as a factor in admission is prohibited, that it was constitutional to consider such factors as an applicant's "ability to play the cello, make a downfield tackle . . . or relationship to school alumni" (Smith 1996:29). The university then appealed to the U.S. Supreme Court to overturn the Fifth Circuit's decision; but the Supreme Court refused to hear the case because, by then, the University of Texas Law School had changed its admissions procedures.

At about the time the affirmative action plan of the University of Texas's Law School was struck down, the U.S. Office of Civil Rights announced that a seven-year investigation of the affirmative action plan of the University of California at Berkeley had shown that their plan did not discriminate against Whites and was constitutional (Applebome 1996:A8). The opposing conclusions in these two important cases left college and university administrators throughout the country uncertain about how to select students for admission and whether or how to conduct affirmative action programs.

While the nation waited for the U.S. Supreme Court to hand down a definitive ruling that would affirm or overturn *Bakke,* numerous efforts to halt affirmative action were underway throughout the country. A number of state legislatures were considering proposals to end affirmative action; the governing boards of universities in various parts of the country followed California's lead and voluntarily reconsidered affirmative action; and in several states, efforts similar to California's were underway to force a general referendum on affirmative action (Honan 1995). The many attacks being mounted on affirmative action again suggested that preferential policies might soon end—a suggestion given added impetus by some additional major decisions of the U.S. Supreme Court that narrowed the rights of minorities in several areas.[20]

Effectiveness of Affirmative Action.   An important consideration in attempting to assess affirmative action programs is "Do they 'work'?" Robinson and Spitz (1986–87: 88) cited several large-scale studies showing that affirmative action has "proven its effectiveness in increasing the employment of minorities and women while producing positive business results." And a review of studies conducted by the Committee on the Status of Black Americans (Jaynes and Williams 1989:319) concluded that, "while we cannot determine with the available data the precise numerical effect of antidiscrimination programs, the evidence does show positive effects." Steele (1995:A15), however, considered "affirmative action to be one of the least evaluated social policies in American history" and charged that "we justify the policy by vague ideals like 'diversity'" which makes it "unaccountable for any results it may have." Sowell (1977:130) maintained that even if affirmative action programs do "here and there" help someone get a job or be admitted to college, the general effect of such programs has been to hamper the progress of Black Americans.

Sowell's argument seems strained in the light of changes in the American workforce following the introduction of affirmative action. In a comparison of census data gathered in 1970 and 1990, Hacker (1996:27) showed that by 1990 the majority of American workers were White women, Asians, and Black women and that White men workers comprised about 47 percent of the total, down from about 57 percent in 1970 (Hacker 1996:26).[21] For the most part, Black men "made smaller gains than members of those other groups"; but Black men, nevertheless, were somewhat more likely in 1990 than in 1970 to be physicians, lawyers, professors, journalists, and computer analysts. They were much more likely to be electricians and sheet metal workers but slightly less likely to "have jobs of any sort" (Hacker 1996:27). In Lacayo's (1995:40) opinion, affirmative action programs have become vulnerable, in part, because of their success; without such programs "it's unlikely that African Americans—or women—would have been able to open up such White male bastions as big-city police and fire departments." And without such programs, White males would have many fewer competitors to threaten their dominance in the workplace.

Morality of Affirmative Action.   In the minds of many opponents of affirmative action programs, most of the arguments we have reviewed are really beside the point. The main point for many people, as we noted earlier, is that even if affirmative action "works," the central question concerns the fairness, justice, or morality of exacting compensation for past wrongs from some people now living, many of whom do not approve of discrimination and have not themselves knowingly engaged in discrimination. Many people, therefore, conclude that affirmative action is reverse discrimination. The issues raised here, however, are more complex than they may appear. We consider very briefly one counter-argument to illustrate the difficulties.

James W. Nickel sought to show that the compensatory treatment of victims of discrimination only *appears* to be reverse discrimination and *is* morally justifiable. Nickel stated the issue roughly as follows: The reverse discrimination argument is that past discrimination against Blacks was wrong because it made the "mistake of treating a morally irrelevant characteristic [skin color] as if it were relevant" (Nickel 1995:3); hence, when Blacks (and others) are given preferences, the society, in Steele's (1990:115) eloquent phrasing, is "reburdened . . . with the very marriage of color preference (in reverse) that we set out to eradicate. The old sin is reaffirmed in a new guise." Nickel maintained that this argument *seems* to be sound but actually is flawed. If Blacks now are given compensation in the form of special opportunities, he argued, it is not because they have dark skins (which was and still is a morally irrelevant characteristic) but because under slavery they were members of a group that was a legally designated object of discrimination whose badge of membership was in part, and still is, the color of their skins. Past discrimination, not skin color, is the relevant moral element; and past discrimination is the wrong that now needs to be righted through preferential treatment (Nickel 1995:4).

Nickel's analysis revealed a previously hidden aspect of the reverse discrimination view, but it most assuredly did not end the argument. Several readers of his commentary responded with analyses of their own, and a complicated and lively debate ensued (Cahn 1995). The main point to be made here is this: Although it seems obvious to many people who, with Glazer (1987:xviii), assume "that affirmative action is wrong in principle" and can be defended only on other grounds, the reverse discrimination viewpoint—the bedrock of the moral attack on affirmative action—is itself questionable.

A Final Consideration.   Although Glazer (1987:xviii) opposed affirmative action, he nevertheless presented an important reason for having it. "The great argument for affirmative action," he said, is "the condition of the Black population of the United States." As we have seen, Blacks, women, and the members of some other groups today occupy many more positions in our society that command high prestige and income than they did before affirmative action was put into place; and, if affirmative action were dismantled, what backup policy promises to continue even to attempt to help level the playing field? In Hacker's (1996:29) opinion, "Affirmative action has been our most successful policy for bringing citizens of slave descent into the main currents of national life." We must recognize that if affirmative action is discontinued, we may, as Hacker warned, "be taking a long step away from racial equity and parity." That step away may lead to an ironic result: The abolition of affirmative action could lead to "an increase, not a decrease, in the kind of black demands for reparations and mandated percentages of the action that whites find so annoying" (Lemann 1995:62).

Legal Approaches: Conclusion

We conclude our review of legal approaches to the reduction of prejudice and discrimination by noting that these approaches are consistent with the thinking of all who emphasize the possibility and importance of direct methods of controlling discrimination, even though there are some important differences in the methods preferred by different theorists. Some who advocate direct-control methods, for instance, may place heavy emphasis on educational programs aimed at shaping situations while others, such as the institutional discrimination theorists, may focus more attention on the way organizational rules are administered and on the laws passed by legislative bodies. Our discussion of affirmative action illustrates the point that the rules governing hiring and firing, admission into prestigious graduate and professional programs, and eligibility for various licenses and certificates play an enormously important role in the day-to-day lives of everyone in our society. Institutional discrimination theorists argue that strategic changes in the countless "laws" of the large bureaucracies of modern society are necessary before any attitudinal changes that may have taken place can be made effective.

Political Participation

Consensus Approach: Electoral Politics

Another approach to reducing prejudice and discrimination that is advocated by consensus theorists is participation in electoral politics. Members of minority groups are urged to inform themselves concerning public issues, vote in elections, lobby legislators to support or vote against various proposals, join political parties, and become candidates for political offices. During the twenty-five years following the end of the Civil War, African Americans voted actively in elections and held many political offices, but with the onset of the Jim Crow system their participation fell sharply in the South. This condition lasted until after World War II, when returning war veterans began organizing for equal rights and full participation in U.S. society. They were joined by Mexican American and Native American activists. Since that time, minority group members have been elected to public offices in increasing numbers and, also, to offices that previously were denied to them. Numerous American cities now have, or have had, African or Mexican American mayors, council members, and school board members. Native Americans have formed effective political and legal groups to lobby for their interests. One state, Virginia, has had an African American governor; and one distinguished African American, General Colin Powell, was actively sought by the Republican Party in 1996 to be its presidential or vice presidential candidate. African and Mexican Americans have served as Cabinet members and in other high posts within the federal government.

An indication of the magnitude of the increase in minority-group participation in electoral politics in general is revealed by examining some of the changes among African Americans, as presented by Jaynes and Williams (1989:230–244). For example, the percent of southern Blacks who were registered to vote rose dramatically from about 3 percent in 1940 to about 67 percent in 1970. For the next 18 years, the level of southern Black registration ranged between 53 and 67 percent. As Black voter registration rose, so did the number of Black elected officials—and much more in the South than in the other regions of the country. In 1941, there were 33 elected Black officials in the United States, and 20 of those were in the north-central region. By 1985, there were 6,016 elected Black officials, and over 63 percent of these (3,801) were in the South. During those same years, the number of Black members in the U.S. House of Representatives rose from 1 to 20, the number of state senators rose from 3 to 90, and the number of state representatives rose from 23 to 302. Between 1941 and 1986, the number of Black judges in the United States rose from 10 to 841. As their voting mass has grown, African Americans have become the swing vote in numerous local, state, and federal elections. President Bill Clinton, for example, was elected in 1992 with less than 45 percent of the popular vote nationally but with more than 90 percent of the African American vote. Reverend Jesse Jackson's efforts to register Black voters and his extraordinary performance as a vote-getting presidential candidate in 1980 and 1984, helped to elect in 1992 forty African Americans to the U.S. Congress (Dentler 1996:33).

Mexican Americans, too, have always been active politically in mutual-aid societies, trade union movements, and political clubs; but their relative concentration in the southwestern United States has affected their political visibility and has led policy makers to think of Hispanic concerns as simple variations of Black problems (Moore and Pachon 1985:176). The Voting Rights Act passed in 1975 extended to Hispanics the protection and benefits that the 1965 act provided to Blacks. Throughout the 1980s, as court cases replaced at-large elections with single-member districts, major voter registration drives increased the number of Mexican American voters and increased their voting-bloc strength. Still, much of the research on Hispanic voting patterns shows that the majority of the Hispanic adults do not participate in electoral politics (Tomás Rivera Center 1996:21). Many Hispanics are foreign born or recent immigrants who lack citizenship and cannot vote or participate politically.[22] The 1994 general election, however, demonstrated that Hispanic voters can be mobilized around issues of importance to them such as Proposition 187, discussed in Chapter 14, and bilingual education, discussed in Chapter 9. From 1988 to 1992, Hispanic voting in the presidential elections increased sharply in California (37.2 percent) and Arizona (31.1 percent) and noticeably in Illinois (11 percent) and Texas (8.5 percent). As expected, the increased number of Hispanic voters has led to an increase in the number of Hispanic elected officials at all levels of government.

All of the minority groups have shown an increased reliance on bureaucracies and the courts to achieve their political goals. There is a growing influence of Washington-based Asian, African American, Mexican American, and Native American lobby groups and a growing representation of these groups in national policy debates affecting their communities. Even though minorities still are underrepresented in many important decision-making positions, there can be little doubt that during the last half of the twentieth century their ability to affect public policy in important ways has increased substantially.

Conflict Approach: Organized Social Protest

Our discussion of various methods of reducing prejudice and discrimination has rested thus far mainly on the underlying assumption of consensus theory—that the majority's levels of prejudice and discrimination may be reduced with relatively little disharmony or open intergroup conflict. The usual expectation of those who favor education, intergroup contact, the passage of laws, and affirmative action is that, grumbling and complaining aside, the majority gradually, and for the most part peacefully, will respond to these programs of change by becoming more tolerant and inclusive. A further assumption is that as the majority's prejudice and discrimination decline, opportunities for the members of minorities will open up and that, after some unspecified period of time, the minorities will become "equal" to the majority. Intergroup tensions, according to the consensus view, will have been reduced with only moderate "dislocations" and "adjustments" along the way. This assumption, which is consistent with the expectations of the ideologies of Anglo conformity, the melting pot, and cultural pluralism, has been sharply challenged by conflict theorists, among whom minority-group members may be highly represented.

Although nonviolent public protest also, strictly speaking, is consistent with the three assimilation ideologies, subscribers to assimilationist views tend to frown on such actions and to emphasize that other approaches are likely to be more successful. Conflict theorists, in contrast, consider such actions to be absolutely necessary. It is argued that equality will never be given freely by the majority. The majority is much more likely, in this view, to reduce its levels of discrimination in the face of a boycott, a strike, a sit-in, or an outburst of violence than in response to the usual kinds of educational programs or even to laws prohibiting discrimination. Indeed, the majority may be unwilling to adopt laws of this type unless it is pressured to do so by organized protest groups.

From this vantage point, it is possible to claim that whenever the legal approach does succeed it is largely due to the power of protest groups, often groups comprised of minority-group members. Although educational programs, interracial contacts, and antidiscrimination laws may be desirable, from the conflict perspective these steps always must be only a part of a larger program consisting of militant ethnic organizations that pose a constant threat of confrontation with the majority.

In the preceding chapters, we have seen many instances in which ethnic minorities have organized to further their interests and protect themselves from dominant-group hostility. The Irish and Germans of the colonial and first great immigrant streams, for example, created numerous ethnic organizations that served these purposes. The Chinese, Italians, Jews, and Japanese of the second immigrant stream also organized for their mutual benefit and protection; and we have traced in greater detail the lengthy efforts of Black, Mexican, and Native Americans to develop effective protest organizations and methods of protest.

We also have seen that it is crucial to distinguish between nonviolent and violent protest, though the distinction sometimes breaks down as nonviolent efforts inadvertently spill over into violence—often when nonviolent protesters themselves are attacked. Whether the nonviolent or violent forms of protest are the most effective in gaining concessions from the majority represents an important theoretical dividing line. Many who accept nonviolent conflict as a necessary part of social change are totally opposed to the use of violence and believe that it is, in fact, counterproductive. For example, even though the ultimate goals sought by Martin Luther King, Jr. and Malcolm X were similar, these men disagreed sharply on what methods were most likely to succeed. King believed that violence was always wrong and would impede the progress of those who use it. Malcolm X, in contrast, strongly supported "defensive" violence and, at times, seemed to endorse "offensive" violence as well. This kind of division almost surely may be found among the conflict theorists within every minority group in America.

All efforts to reduce discrimination and to attain a social standing that is acceptable to the minority, conflict theorists believe, must involve some intergroup disharmony, tension, and open protest of some kind. Even the most educated Black Americans, Hacker (1996:29) asserted, "have no illusions that bias has been eradicated and they know that without external pressure they would not be where they are."

What will be the outcome of the interethnic struggles and efforts to learn to live together that now are underway in our society? Chapter 16 suggests some answers.

Key Ideas

1. Prejudice and discrimination are related to one another in a circular fashion. Discrimination may be reduced by attacks on prejudice, and prejudice may be reduced by attacks on discrimination; however, declines in prejudice are not necessarily translated into reductions in discrimination, and vice versa.

2. Theories of prejudice and discrimination suggest ways to attack these problems. Consensus theorists prefer to attempt to work primarily on reducing prejudice by focusing on its theoretical causes and to do so through strategies that are likely to generate little social conflict. Conflict theorists prefer to attempt to work primarily on reducing discrimination by focusing on its theoretical causes and to do so through strategies of protest that lead to open confrontations and social conflict, though not necessarily violent conflict.

3. One important form of intergroup education, the cognitive approach, consists of presenting people with information concerning out-groups; another, the vicarious experience approach, assists people "to take the role of the other" through books, plays, films, and so on. Both of these methods appear to be useful but not powerful methods of reducing prejudice. The vicarious experience approach, which attempts to stir people's emotions, seems to be somewhat more effective than the cognitive approach.

4. Intergroup contacts may be effective in reducing prejudice if the people involved are of similar social status and are engaged in a cooperative, enjoyable, and mutually significant activity. Under other circumstances, intergroup contacts may lead to increased prejudice; but even casual contacts create the opportunity for friendships to form.

5. Many forms of discrimination may be reduced directly rather than by attempting first to alter people's prejudices. The passage and strict enforcement of anti-discrimination laws, even when these laws are not popular, may bring about rapid changes in behavior. Although requiring individuals not to discriminate may boomerang and lead to increases in discrimination and prejudice, under many circumstances it does not. Furthermore, once people's discriminatory behavior has been altered, their prejudices often decline.

6. Prejudice and discrimination are embedded within a larger sociocultural system, which to some extent affects both prejudice and discrimination *separately* through various proximate causes, and to some extent acts on both prejudice and discrimination *through* the other. Since prejudice and discrimination to some extent form a mutually reinforcing circle, it is best to attack them simultaneously. The exclusive or preponderant attention given in the past to attempting to reduce discrimination by first reducing prejudice, rather than by attempting directly to reduce discrimination, is unwarranted.

7. Affirmative action is one of the most important and controversial methods of attacking discrimination. At the heart of a heated national controversy is the issue of whether employment or admissions to educational and training programs may take race and ethnicity into account without also compromising the nation's commitment to the ideal of equal treatment. Opponents of affirmative action maintain that departures from policies of neutrality that grant preferential treatment to minority-group members amount to reverse discrimination. Supporters of affirmative action deny that it is reverse discrimination and maintain that it is the most effective policy yet developed for bringing minority-group members into the American mainstream.

8. Although America's contemporary policies and noblest ideals assume that prejudice and discrimination may be sharply reduced through education, political participation and the passage of laws, history shows that changes in dominant–subordinate relations typically have required the organized protest of minorities. While organized protest necessarily involves intergroup tension, effective conflict may be limited to boycotts, strikes, lobbies, and other nonviolent tactics.

Key Terms

affirmative action Policies and programs that go beyond neutrality by seeking out and encouraging *qualified* minority-group members and women to become a part of the pool of applicants for openings and opportunities in schools, training programs, employment, contracting, and various other competitive settings.

cognitive approach Methods of reducing prejudice and discrimination that rely on developing an educated citizenry and also provide specific information to counter myths and stereotypes concerning various racial and ethnic groups.

compensatory (preferential) treatment   Awarding preferred standing or additional opportunities for contemporary social and economic advancement to the designated members of various racial, ethnic, and gender groups that have been subjects of past discrimination.

contact hypothesis   The idea that interracial and interethnic contacts, particularly close and sustained contacts under conditions of equality and cooperation, will promote mutually positive, tolerant attitudes and friendly relations among the members of those groups.

disparate impact   Consistently unequal outcomes among groups that are produced by various selection procedures used in admission to educational and training programs, in hiring and promotion, or in trying to assure equal access to social and economic opportunities. Disparate results may arise either from treating equal groups unequally or from treating unequal groups as if they were equal.

reverse discrimination   The belief that all or some members of the dominant group unjustly pay the direct and indirect costs of compensatory treatment.

vicarious experience approach   Methods of reducing prejudice and discrimination by creating opportunities for others to share indirectly the experiences of those who are objects of prejudice or discrimination. This may be done through the use of films, plays, television productions, biographies, novels, and other forms of communication.

otes

1. Some prominent factors are competition, voluntary interaction, similarities in beliefs and values, and the way various types of information-processing biases influence perceptions (Barnard and Benn 1988:126; Stephan 1985:643).

2. Two other areas of special research interest are desegregation in the armed services (see, e.g., Moskos and Butler, 1996) and in the workplace (see, e.g., Allen 1986; Pettigrew and Martin 1989).

3. A review of the literature by Stephan (1988:13, 16) supported the conclusion that in the short run "desegregation leads to small improvements in black reading achievement" and that in the long run "blacks who have attended desegregated high schools are more likely to finish high school, attend college, earn higher GPAs while in college, and are . . .

less likely to drop out of college than blacks who attended segregated high schools."

4. These researchers found in another study that even though interracial friendships are rare, they are almost as stable as same-race choices (Hallinan and Williams 1987:662).

5. In a later study, Powers and Ellison (1995) pursued the important issue of whether favorable attitudes result from interracial contact or lead to interracial contact. They found no reason to reject the idea that contact leads to more favorable attitudes.

6. These rulings were *Green v. County School Board of New Kent County* (1968); *Swann v. Charlotte-Mecklenburg County Board of Education* (1971); and *Keyes v. School District No.1, Denver, Colorado* (1973).

7. Orfield (1978) presented arguments against a number of these claims.

8. For reviews and interpretations of the findings, see Armor (1980; 1995); Jaynes and Williams (1989:83).

9. See, e.g., Richardson (1992:A13); Ton (1992:A14).

10. The courts at this time appear to be moving in the direction of accepting the claims of school systems that they have met the requirement that legal segregation be ended and that resegregation is largely a reflection of voluntary, individual decisions (see, e.g., Kunen 1996).

11. Positive government actions to combat discrimination, though not called "affirmative action," occurred well before the 1960s. The Wagner Act of 1935, for instance, required both the cessation of discrimination and positive actions to reinstate some workers with back pay (Sowell 1977:114).

12. The proposition stated that: "The state shall not discriminate against, or grant preferential treatment to, any individual or group on the basis of race, sex, color, ethnicity, or national origin in the operation of public employment, public education, or public contracting" (Hacker 1996:21). It was the "brainchild of two academics, Thomas Wood and Glynn Custred" (Lacayo 1995:40).

13. Seventy seven percent of the White respondents agreed with the statement.

14. By 1971, an affirmative action plan was defined as "a set of specific and result-oriented procedures to which a contractor commits himself to apply every good faith effort" (Benokraitis and Feagin 1978:13).

15. Some other important Supreme Court cases during this period that attempted to define the meaning and scope of affirmative action were *United Steelworkers v. Weber* (1979), *Fullilove v. Klutznik* (1980), and *Firefighters v. Stotts* (1984). The first two cases expanded the scope of affirmative action, but the third narrowed it. In *Weber* the Court ruled that it was legal for a training program to have a quota on the number of Black trainees; in *Klutznik*, it permitted federal programs to require that 10 percent of their money be set aside for minority contractors; but in *Stotts*, it decided that

during a time of job layoffs, the jobs of newly hired Black workers could not be saved by firing White workers with more seniority (Finsterbusch and McKenna 1986:187).

16. Some commentators reject the use of this term on the grounds that there could be reverse discrimination only if the previous victims were to become the dominant group and enforce institutionalized discrimination against the present dominant group. From this viewpoint, the compensatory treatment granted under affirmative action is a miniscule concession and can hardly be said to reverse the positions of the dominant and subordinate groups.

17. An excellent exploration of the difficult moral issues that are posed by these questions is in the outstanding contributions in Steven M. Cahn, (ed.), *The Affirmative Action Debate* (New York: Routledge, 1995).

18. The four plaintiffs were Douglas Wade Carvell, Kenneth Elliott, Cheryl J. Hopwood, and David Rogers.

19. Judge Sparks noted in a preliminary hearing that he was "troubled" that a part of the law school's admission procedure in 1992 had involved comparing the credentials of minority candidates only with those of other minority candidates (Graves 1993:B1).

20. In *Adarand Constructors, Inc., v. Peña,* the attorney for Adarand argued successfully that "the Transportation Department's policy was an unlawful set-aside based on race" (Johnson and Stone 1996:33). In another case, the Supreme Court agreed with White plaintiffs in Georgia's eleventh Congressional District that the district had been drawn unconstitutionally to create a Black majority. The Court ordered that the district's lines be redrawn and that a new election be held (Mauro and Watson 1996:36). In *Missouri v. Jenkins,* the Kansas City School District and the State of Missouri asked to be relieved of a massive, long-term, and very expensive desegregation plan even though the test scores of the Black children were still below the national average (Greenhouse 1995:3; Greenhouse 1996:A1). The Court agreed and relieved the city and

state of the responsibility of continuing the plan (Johnson and Stone 1996:33).

21. Calculated from Table C (Hacker 1996: 26).

22. In the United States as a whole, 44 percent of Latino adults are not U.S. citizens and, thus, cannot register and vote. Partly in response to the anti-immigrant sentiment of Proposition 187 and the English-only movement, Latinos have applied for naturalization in record numbers. For example, the number of immigrants applying for citizenship more than doubled in 1996 compared to the usual rate of naturalization over a twelve-month period (Tomás Rivera Center 1996:250).

The Future of Ethnicity in America

Each of these students represents a different country, but all are Americans and deserve equal opportunities to achieve secondary assimilation. A democratic and peaceful America will require further reductions in prejudice and discrimination.

For the third generation, the . . . ethnic cultures . . . are now only an ancestral memory . . . to be savored once in a while in a museum or at an ethnic festival.

—Herbert J. Gans

The American nationality is still forming: its processes are mysterious, and the final form, if there is ever to be a final form, is as yet unknown.

—Nathan Glazer and Daniel P. Moynihan

The social changes triggered by the civil rights movement and the ethnic diversity of the third great immigrant stream combined to increase sharply the ethnic-group consciousness of people throughout the United States, natives and immigrants alike. These social forces stimulated a renewed national debate over the problems of cooperation and conflict among people of different racial and ethnic backgrounds and, also, over the future of intergroup relations in America. Will the White ethnics of the first and second immigrant streams follow the path of the colonial Scotch-Irish and Germans and become an unidentifiable part of the American mainstream? Will non-Whites follow the path of the colonial Whites but at a slower rate? Will some form of pluralism be accepted by all groups, even the Anglo Americans, thus encouraging many groups to maintain and elaborate their distinctive heritages?

In Retrospect

We have considered many factors that affect whether, to what extent, and the rate at which the members of a given racial or ethnic group have been included within our society. We also have reviewed the historical sequences within which these factors operated to create the contemporary patterns of dominant–subordinate group relations. At the outset of our analysis, we tentatively adopted the three-generations process as a standard of reference. The basic idea of the three-generations process is that the members of the dominant group generally have expected newcomers to follow the path toward Anglo conformity and, ideally, to reach that goal no later than the third generation. Our review has shown, however, that by this standard, very few, if any, American groups have reached full Anglo conformity assimilation in the expected period of time. Even the colonial Scotch-Irish and Germans did not undergo primary and marital assimilation within three generations.[1] Indeed, it still may be possible at the turn of the twenty-first century to find some distinctive patterns of behavior among some of the descendants of these colonial immigrants. For example, a number of people in the United States still report that they are of Scotch-Irish ancestry and that this identity plays a significant role in their lives. Others take pride in being descended from people who came to America in the *Concord* (the German "*Mayflower*") in 1683. These groups, therefore, may be said to have at least a nominal sense of ethnic identity other than American and may, in this respect, be said to "persist" as distinctive ethnic groups (Lieberson and Waters 1988: 13–14).[2] Additionally, as the concept of ethnogenesis reminds us, if the conditions were right, it still is possible that these traces of group identity could serve as the foundation for some sort of ethnic-group revival or mobilization.

It is true, nonetheless, that the present levels of merger between the colonial immigrant groups and the Anglo American core are so high as to be virtually complete, and it is very likely that extremely high levels of merger were reached before the end of the nineteenth century. Since the colonial Scotch-Irish and Germans began entering in force during the early part of the 1700s, we may say that the full Anglo conformity assimilation of a northwestern European group in America may occur in less than 200 years, possibly in less than 150 years. Although this estimate extends the three-generations idea to as many as six or eight generations, it gives evidence that for all practical purposes, the Anglo conformity merger of some groups does occur, as Park said, "eventually." Moreover, if one adopts the cultural pluralists' definition of full assimilation, it is likely that the colonial immigrants approximated *that* goal in three generations.

Turning from the colonial immigrants to those who formed the first immigrant stream, we find little to alter the conclusions just reached. Many of the descendants of these immigrants have been in this country for as long as six generations, and very few have been here less than three. The levels of cultural and secondary assimilation that have occurred between them and the Anglo American core is unquestionably high, though not necessarily as high as that of the colonial immigrants. The first-stream immigrant Irish and Germans in New York, for instance, still may be more distinguishable than their colonial counterparts (Glazer and Moynihan 1964); but there is no reason to suppose that the first-stream immigrants are less assimilated at this point than the colonials were after a similar period of time. On the contrary, there is every reason to suppose that with the further passage of time these nineteenth-century immigrants will move toward higher levels of Anglo conformity. Again, this judgment must be tempered with the realization that a number of events could revive and strengthen the ethnic bonds that still exist, new ethnic groups might arise from the remnants of the old, and large concentrations of particular immigrants will form strong ethnic communities that will help to maintain their ethnic group.

The status of the White ethnics of the second immigrant stream, however, continues as a topic of contemporary debate. Why after three, or in some cases, four generations are these groups still, or again, so much in evidence? Are the White ethnics "on the threshold of disappearance" (Dinnerstein and Reimers 1975:140), or will their group allegiances continue to play an important role in the future (Greeley 1971:167)?

Curiously, the prediction that the White ethnics will "soon disappear" is not necessarily inconsistent with the prediction that these groups will "continue to be significant for some time to come." It all depends on what these phrases mean. In historical terms, "soon" may easily mean another generation or two; and "continue to be significant" may mean a level of merger similar to that presently exhibited by the nineteenth-century Irish and Germans. Such considerations show clearly why *it is essential for those who make forecasts in this regard to be specific about the types and levels of intergroup merger and also the time periods that are envisioned.*

White Ethnic Assimilation

Let us explore these issues briefly through some comparisons of the immigrants of the first and second streams with each other and with the members of the host American group. Our discussion draws heavily upon (and greatly simplifies) the illuminating research of Alba (1985; 1988), which focuses on Italian Americans as "a strategic test case," of Lieberson and Waters (1988), which compares a number of different White ethnic groups, and of Waters (1990), which examines the meanings people attach to ethnic identities. Following our usual order, we consider some evidence relating to cultural, secondary, and marital assimilation.[3]

Cultural Assimilation

As discussed in Chapter 4, the Italian immigrants of the second stream did not seem to be good prospects for Anglo conformity assimilation. They were, comparatively speaking, poor, illiterate, unskilled sojourners. Their continued allegiance to the family and the Italian community and their suspicion of American education combined to maintain a high level of ethnic distinctiveness well beyond the decline in immigration after 1924. As Alba (1988:141) stated: "By the end of the 1930s . . . the group's . . . cultural and occupational background would seem to have doomed Italian Americans to a perpetual position of inferiority and separateness in American society."

The changes that have taken place since then, however, have not confirmed that expectation. In regard to cultural differences, for instance, Alba (1985:135; 1988:146–147) marshaled evidence from the General Social Surveys of the NORC for the years 1975–1980 to compare certain values of the Italian Americans with those of a group of White Anglo-Saxon Protestants (often called WASPs). When such factors as the respondent's sex and age, the education and occupation of his or her parents, and the region of the country in which the person now lives or was raised were taken into account, Italian Americans were found to be very similar to WASPs. To illustrate, they did not differ significantly in their opinions on abortion, feminism, premarital sex, adultery, homosexuality, and divorce. Two items that suggested the Italians still had a greater allegiance to their families were that they were more likely than WASPs to reside where they had grown up, and they more frequently agreed that children's elders should teach them what is right. Still, in Alba's (1988:153) opinion, "among virtually all White ethnic groups, one can observe a progressive, if gradual, dampening of cultural distinctiveness."

Secondary Assimilation

How do the descendants of five northwestern European groups of the first immigrant stream and four south-central-eastern European groups of the second immigrant stream compare with one another on such measures of secondary assimilation as occupation, education, and income? We draw upon, and simplify, the analyses of Lieberson and Waters (1988) and Alba (1988).

Occupations.   Our previous discussions showed that such factors as the skills immigrants have brought with them, their time of arrival in the United States, and the geographical location of their points of entry have resulted in higher and lower concentrations of different groups in particular occupations. For example, in 1900, male Irish immigrants were more than four times as likely to be policemen or firemen than were other White males in the work force (Lieberson and Waters 1988:124); and, please recall, during this period Irish women were far more likely than Jewish or Italian women to work as domestic servants. Now, an important question of interest to us here is this: Have the earlier patterns of occupational concentration and avoidance continued into the latter part of the twentieth century? For each of thirteen ethnic groups examined by Lieberson and Waters, there has been a "leveling" of their characteristic occupational patterns, but there still were some "significant remnants" of the patterns found for 1900. "In general," they wrote, "there is a reduction of the distinctive ethnic occupational dispositions found in 1900 for immigrant men. This is to be expected under normal assimilative processes. However, these early immigrant occupational patterns still have significant vestiges 80 years later" (Lieberson and Waters 1988:127). But in a general comparison of the occupational distributions of Italians and WASPs conducted by Alba (1985:122–123), no significant overall difference was found when the groups were matched for age, place of residence, and family background.

Education.   The immigrants of the first two streams also differed from one another in their average levels of education, with those from the first stream showing much higher levels of literacy. Has this distinctiveness been maintained? Lieberson and Waters (1988:112–115) compared the changes among twelve groups, and the results for these groups were clear. The educational differences among the groups had declined sharply. This conclusion was consistent with Alba's (1988:145) detailed comparison of the extent to which Italian Americans and WASPs had attended or completed college. For example, among both second- and third-generation Italian men and women born after 1950, the levels of college attendance and graduation were very similar to those of WASPs of the same age. This similarity represented a large change from the differences found when earlier age groups—for instance, those born between 1915 and 1935—were compared.

Income.   Direct census information on the income differences of the various ethnic groups for the early decades of the century is not available; however, on the basis of estimates of some group differences in income, Lieberson and Waters (1988:140–142) believed there was little reason to think that the earlier pattern of inequalities exists today. Indeed, they found that by 1980 the first-stream groups did not have an income advantage over the second-stream groups. Therefore, in regard to three crucial indicators of secondary assimilation—occupation, education, and income—the level among European-ancestry groups appears to be high.[4]

Marital Assimilation

Turning now to intermarriage, the findings support three important conclusions. First, the trends among Italians and all White groups taken together show that in-group marriages have declined (Alba 1988:149–152; Lieberson and Waters 1988:197). For example, Italian men who were born before 1920 were much less likely to marry out than Italian men who were born after 1949. The pattern among Italian women was similar.

Second, because of the increase in intermarriages among White ethnics, the number of European-ancestry people in the United States who are products of ethnic intermarriages has grown steadily larger (relatively as well as absolutely). Among Italian Americans, for instance, the proportion of those who are children of intermarriages has risen from around 6 percent in the over-sixty-five age group to over 81 percent in the under-five age group.

Third, people whose parents and grandparents had not married out still were somewhat more likely to choose mates from their own ethnic group than were those whose parents or grandparents had married out.[5] In short, although the marital assimilation of Europeans and their descendants is well underway, it is still incomplete.

An Interpretation

On the basis of these considerations, the following speculations about the White ethnic experience seem reasonable. The White ethnics of the new immigration have not disappeared in three generations, but neither did the colonial or old immigrants.[6] As Neidert and Farley (1985:849) concluded, "if assimilation means that third-generation ethnic groups will be indistinguishable from the core English group," then these groups still have not assimilated; however, they went on to say, "if assimilation means that ethnic groups are neither favored nor at a disadvantage in the process of occupational achievement, then there is strong evidence to support the theory."

Although three generations may be long enough to permit a high degree of cultural and secondary assimilation among White European groups, the remaining forms of assimilation may take much longer. Even when the host and immigrant groups are similar in race and culture, full Anglo conformity assimilation may require as many as eight generations. On the assumption that the members of the second immigrant stream are moving toward an Anglo conformity merger with the dominant group, then they should become less distinctive as time goes on. Within three more generations, they may be no more distinctive than the nineteenth-century Irish and Germans are now.

Perhaps, given another two generations beyond that, they may be no more distinctive than the colonial Irish and Germans are now.

In short, the sheer fact that the second-stream groups are in some respects still distinguishable after three generations is not really too surprising. The expectation that they would vanish as distinctive groups *has rested on a misunderstanding of the inter-group relations of the past*. Since the speed of Anglo conformity assimilation among the colonial and first-stream immigrants has been much slower than is generally recognized, the belief that the merger of the second-stream immigrants with the host group is unusually slow has not yet been put fully to the test. Indeed, on the basis of the evidence we have reviewed, one can argue that the speed with which the second-stream Euro-peans have assimilated culturally and in the secondary arena constitutes, in Greeley's (1985) phrase, an "Ethnic Miracle." Somewhat paradoxically, pluralist *principles* appear to have been gaining force as actual *ethnic differences* among Whites have been, as Stein-berg (1989:254) argued, "on the wane." In his view, the United States has "never before . . . been closer to welding a national identity out of the melange of ethnic groups that popu-lated its soil."[7] Perhaps, to use Alba's (1985; 1988) engaging expression, the White ethnics are entering the "twilight" of their ethnicity. The evidence we have presented favoring this view may be bolstered still further by some additional evidence presented by Lieber-son (1988b). Although the U.S. Bureau of the Census discouraged people from giving the response "American" to the ancestry question in the 1980 Census, 13.3 million people (nearly 6 percent of the population) could not, or would not, specify any other ancestry (Lieberson 1988:171).

As applied to ethnicity, however, the twilight metaphor has one flaw. Except in cer-tain seasons in certain latitudes, earthly twilights give way to nightfall; but, according to Alba (1985:162), the twilight of ethnicity "will not in the near future, and may never, turn into night." Even if ethnicity among Europeans and their descendants is moving to-ward, or has reached, a point beyond which it no longer will serve reliably as an authen-tic basis for group cohesion and economic support, valued ethnic identities nevertheless may serve as social insulation—what Handlin called "contexts of belonging"—to pre-vent the anonymity and bewilderment that frequently develops among people within urban-industrial settings.[8] What may survive is a new form of ethnicity that Gans (1985) referred to as **symbolic ethnicity**. Symbolic ethnicity arises "as the functions of ethnic cultures and groups diminish and identity becomes the primary way of being ethnic" (Gans 1985:434). Gans predicted that this form of ethnicity, especially when it also reflects religious differences, may easily persist into the fifth and sixth generations and beyond. Waters (1990:166) also argued that symbolic ethnicity "will continue to characterize the ethnicity of later-generation whites." In her view, symbolic ethnicity has a strong appeal to White Americans because it helps to reduce the tension between the individual's desire to be, simultaneously, both special and a part of a community (Wa-ters 1990:147–150). An identification with an ethnic group carries for Whites many re-wards and few penalties; for non-Whites, however, "the consequences of being Asian or Hispanic or black are not symbolic. . . . They are real and hurtful" (Waters 1990:156).[9]

Whether the continuation of White ethnic distinctiveness and identity will be the central focus of everyday life or an expression of "a nostalgic allegiance to the culture of the immigrant generation" (Gans 1985:435) remains to be seen. Either way, however, one would expect a continued prominence of White ethnicity in American life for at least one or two more generations and a continued or growing acceptance of cultural pluralism as the principal view of the way immigrants and their descendants should become Americanized.

The Non-White Experience.

While this conclusion seems reasonable in regard to the White ethnics of the second immigrant stream, how well does it fit the situation of non-White Americans? Recall that some observers have interpreted the conflict between the Anglo American and non-White American ethnic groups in terms of the colonial model. Under this interpretation, the initial relations between a dominant group and a colonized group establishes a pattern that does not lead toward conformity to the dominant group's way of life. Rather, this pattern leads to attempts by the minority to end colonization through the establishment of a separate nation, either by overthrowing the dominant (usually invading) group or by leaving the territory altogether. The dominant group, for its part, prefers either that the colonized minority leave the territory or assimilate culturally while remaining apart and subordinate in all other ways. Since, in this view, both the dominant group and colonized minority resist the full merger of the groups, one would expect the continuation of friction among them, resulting, after numerous conflicts, either in separation or secession.

The main criticisms of the colonial model rest on efforts to show that some non-White groups (e.g., Japanese Americans) have achieved a high level of cultural and secondary assimilation and that the recent historical experiences of Mexican, Black, and Indian Americans resemble in some essential ways those of the second-stream immigrants from Europe. This argument—based on the immigrant model—does not claim that the immigration experience of the Japanese and the migration experiences of the other groups are identical to that of European immigrants. The non-White groups have faced, as Kristol (1972:205) conceded, "unique and peculiar dilemmas of their own," whereas Lieberson (1980:383), in an extensive analysis of the differences between Blacks and second-stream immigrants, concluded that "the situation for new Europeans in the United States, bad as it may have been, was not as bad as that experienced by blacks at the same time."

From this standpoint, most Blacks in the northern cities have not yet been there more than three generations; and although they have met less favorable conditions and greater discrimination there than previous immigrants, their future experiences may nevertheless, in highly important ways, resemble those of the White ethnics. Indeed, we saw evidence in Chapter 11 that many Black Americans, following the expansion of opportunities beginning in the 1960s, already have attained practically the same average levels of education as their White peers. This finding suggests the interesting (if debatable) idea that Black Americans who have reached maturity since the 1960s have only recently been accorded the levels of opportunities that were available to European immigrants a century ago.

The immigrant model does not deny the validity of the colonial model as an interpretation of some of the experiences of non-Whites in America (e.g., slavery, the conquest of the Indians and Mexican Americans, the Japanese relocation centers). It does assert, however, that in different ways the non-Whites are moving toward some form of assimilation, perhaps cultural pluralism, and are moving away from separation and secession. From the standpoint of national unity, the immigrant model is evidently more optimistic than the colonial model. Which of these views, then, gives us the best basis for forecasting the probable course of race relations in the United States? As we have seen, the answer to this question is still a matter of keen debate. But it is possible, as frequently happens, that the wrong question has been asked. Since the histories of Black, Mexican, Japanese, and Indian Americans contain certain elements that may justify either the colonial or the immigrant view, we may conclude (as people frequently do in such arguments) that both views are to some extent correct. This is really not a very satisfactory conclusion, however; so let us consider an alternative view that may help place the facts of conquest and assimilation in a new light.

Consequences of Colonization and Immigration: An Alternative View

We have stressed throughout that the conditions surrounding the initial contact between groups are extremely important in understanding the subsequent course of their relations. We have observed in general that (1) a conquered minority is likely to be hostile for a long period of time and to have separatist and secessionist tendencies, and (2) an immigrant minority is likely to exhibit hostility for a shorter period of time and to prefer some form of assimilation. There is a substantial amount of evidence, drawn from racial and ethnic contacts throughout the world, to support these basic generalizations. It is their strength, indeed, that sustains the debate over the colonial and immigrant models. The alternative view we consider does not question the accuracy of these basic generalizations. It emphasizes, instead, (1) differences in the social characteristics of colonized and immigrant minorities during the early stages of their formation and (2) that the basic generalizations refer to probabilities rather than to certainties. Our alternative view presents a dynamic merger of elements found in the immigrant and colonial models.

Early Stages of Ethnic-Group Formation

Consider the hypothetical (but realistic) situation of the people living in a small, independent, society that is soon to be conquered by an invading power. They have their own set of social institutions for dealing with life's problems: their own forms of government, religion, making a living, conducting family life, and raising children. They do not seek, wish, or need to join, or become part of, some other society. This circumstance provides the motive force for prolonged resistance to an invader.

If such a society is invaded and overpowered by outsiders, it may be taken into the invading society as an entire unit. If so, it is no longer an independent society; it is now a *colonized group* within an alien society. Since such groups already are complete social units at the time they enter the host society, their relationship to the host is mainly political. The group's members may "remain firmly embedded . . . in a web of familiar relationships" (Francis 1976:169).[10] This new ethnic group is a "viable corporate unit" (Francis 1976:397) that is able—if permitted to do so—to "continue functioning in the host society in much the same way" as it had before being conquered (Francis 1976: 170). The members resent being subordinate and, rather than seeking equal treatment with the majority, wish to restore their former existence as a separate group. They, therefore, are more likely to resist vigorously any efforts the host society may make to bring about any aspect of assimilation. Their primary goal is to escape the unsought and unwanted control of the invaders.

Immigrant Groups.   The conditions leading to the formation of an ethnic group by immigrants are quite different. The members of this type of ethnic group are, at the outset, completely dependent on the host society for the satisfaction of all their needs, economic as well as social. There are no established ethnic institutions; therefore, there is no existing web of familiar relationships. Although a group of people sharing a number of cultural characteristics have assembled in the same location, a community of people who possess a sense of common ethnicity remains to be formed within the host society. The group's potential members possess little in the way of resources and cannot continue to function as they did in their previous society. The social pattern the immigrant group develops represents a mixture of the cultures of the parent society and the host society. It is identical to neither but is in some sense a variety of each (Francis 1976:223).[11] The members of an immigrant ethnic group are less likely than those in a colonized group to resent the majority and are more likely to seek to be treated as equal to the majority. They, therefore, are more likely to be willing than those of a colonized ethnic group to undergo at least some aspects of assimilation (Francis 1976:397).

An Important Implication.   Since ethnic groups that come into being as a result of conquest and colonization often are complete social units from the beginning,[12] an important objective of such groups generally is to hold what they still have while attempting to recover what has been lost. This is why the *relationship of the colonized minority* to the society's majority is *likely* to be adversarial and characterized by vigorous resistance to assimilation. Since the dominant and subordinate groups' main concerns in this type of relationship usually center on issues involving continuing on together as a single unit, we refer to it as a **centrifugal relationship.** In contrast, ethnic groups that come into being as a result of immigration usually are formed within the host society and must rely to a considerable extent on the social institutions they find there. An important goal of the immigrant ethnic group, therefore, is to organize for mutual assistance and protection in order to assist its members to combat discrimination and gain equality with the majority in such important areas as jobs, education, and political participation. The *relationship of the immigrant minority* to the host society, therefore, is *likely* to be one of restrained resistance to some aspects of assimilation combined with active efforts to achieve secondary assimilation. Since the dominant and subordinate groups' main concerns in this type of relationship usually center on finding mutually satisfactory ways to bring the groups together, we refer to it as a **centripetal relationship.**

A Dynamic View of the Colonial and Immigrant Models

Let us now apply this reasoning to the debate over the colonial and immigrant models. Although colonized minorities are *likely* to resist assimilation and to be receptive to separatist ideologies, and although immigrant minorities are *likely* to accept some aspects of assimilation and be receptive to assimilationist ideologies, these outcomes are not inevitable. A centrifugal relationship *may* arise through immigration and a centripetal relationship *may* arise through conquest. Knowing whether a group has entered a society by conquest or immigration provides an important clue concerning the *type of relationship* that *probably* was formed between an ethnic group and a majority group. As useful as this information is, it nevertheless may lead us to miss a central point: In cases either of conquest or of immigration, the fundamental issue is whether a given group actually *did* form with the majority group a centrifugal or a centripetal relationship. It is *the result* of contact rather than *the events initiating* it that has the greatest effect on the subsequent relations of the dominant and subordinate groups.

The distinction we have drawn between two types of relationships that may develop between ethnic groups and dominant groups (centrifugal and centripetal) helps to clarify another point that is hidden in the debate over the colonial and immigrant models. Regardless of the type of relationship that is formed at the time of the original contact between two groups, this situation is not necessarily fixed for all time. The concept of ethnogenesis, which we have encountered at various points in our analysis, directs attention to an extraordinarily important phenomenon: Although the boundaries between racial and ethnic groups may appear to be highly stable lines that signify fixed, naturally occurring biological and cultural differences among groups, the importance of these boundaries may wax or wane depending on many external factors.

We have seen, for instance, that as the members of immigrant groups become more numerous or more highly concentrated in a particular area, competition arises between the natives and the newcomers for "the same valued resources (e.g., housing, jobs, other kinds of rewards)" and that this situation is likely to lead the members of both groups to organize to further their own interests (Olzak 1986:18). Such situations may cause people whose ethnic identities and attachments originally were weak to place a higher value and emphasis on them than in the past. A strong line of division may develop between "them" and "us" where no line or only a weak line previously had existed. Conversely, strong lines of division may weaken when some external factor, perhaps an attack from outside that threatens the survival of both groups, alters the situation.

These considerations support the idea that the boundaries of racial and ethnic groups that are accepted at any given time may be altered by changing circumstances. See (1986:224) has stated the matter succinctly: "the salience of ethnic identity is situationally determined." The groups of people who are thought of as "them" or as "us" may form and re-form, join and split, depending on the situation; hence, a centrifugal relationship may, at a later time, be transformed into a centripetal relationship. In addition, regardless of the original contact situation, many groups seek, or have thrust upon them, broad identities that previously did not exist. This aspect of ethnogenesis may be seen in the emergence of new identities such as Asian, Hispanic or Latino, and, from an earlier time, American Indian, that bring together groups with separate identities that may vary widely in sociocultural characteristics. This view of the long-range outcomes of contact between dominant and subordinate groups, therefore, is more dynamic than the view of either the colonial or immigrant models.

Some Applications of the Alternative View

What does this alternative view tell us about the present and probable future relations of Whites and non-Whites in America? Consider, for example, the Mexican Americans.

Mexican Americans

This group clearly was created through conquest. The fact of conquest itself, however, is not so crucial to our understanding of the present and future condition of this dominated group as is the fact that, at the time of the Treaty of Guadalupe Hidalgo, Mexican Americans already possessed a fully developed set of social institutions. They did not seek to enter into the life of the dominant society and did not depend on its economy or other institutions for the satisfaction of life's needs; consequently, their initial relationship to Anglo American society was centrifugal.

This relationship was essentially unchanged until well into the twentieth century. Nevertheless, as the forces of industrialization and urbanization became strong in the Southwest, not only Mexican Americans but Mexican nationals as well began to move into the American economy. The vast social changes accompanying the immigration of large numbers of Mexicans to the United States did not mean that Mexican Americans had somehow stopped being a colonized minority or that the history of conquest between them and the dominant group could be erased or disregarded. These changes meant, rather, that this group was beginning the prodigious transformation from a centrifugal to a centripetal relationship with the dominant group. Ethnogenesis was occurring, and a new ethnic group was being born—one that fused sociocultural elements deriving from the Creation Generation, the second- and third-stream immigrants, and the dominant society. Despite the efforts of many, probably most, Mexican Americans to resist this transformation, this process predominated throughout the twentieth century.

Since the end of World War II, the majority of Mexican Americans have moved into urban settings and have become dependent on the industrial economy for their livelihoods. At the same time, they increasingly have accepted their status as American citizens and have expected and demanded that they be accorded the rights and privileges of other Americans. In short, their relationship to the dominant group now is centripetal. It is this fact, rather than the movement of large numbers of Mexicans to the United States since 1910, that justifies the expectation that Mexican Americans now are moving toward the American mainstream. Most Mexican Americans appear to desire "the best of both worlds." While this statement of the group's goal is somewhat vague, the specific demands presented in its behalf (even by militants) generally imply an acceptance of cultural pluralism.[13] It seems likely that this perspective will continue to gain support in the years to come.

This judgment concerning the goals of Mexican Americans must be accepted only tentatively. While they now mainly wish to have the same rights and privileges accorded to the members of the dominant group, they may not continue to cherish this goal. The proximity to Mexico and the continuation of discrimination against people of Mexican origin within the United States are forces that favor the possibility that they will give up on assimilationist goals and seek some other social arrangement. Unless these citizens are permitted to advance (as compared to the dominant group) in income, education, political participation, health care, police protection, and housing, they may at some point reject pluralism and seek separatist or secessionist solutions instead. As noted in Chapter 9, Mexican Americans are having more difficulty than Blacks and Indians in gaining occupational prestige that is commensurate with their educational levels (Neidert and Farley 1985:848), and there is little reason to suppose they will continue to bear the burden of this inequity perpetually. In addition, the hostility of the dominant group to the large undocumented immigrant population—most of which is from Mexico—helps maintain centrifugal tendencies. On the one hand, undocumented people are unable to assimilate legally into the economic and political life of the society; but, on the other hand, they do assimilate into the familial and social networks that lie at the core of Mexican American life and identity. Still, it seems improbable that the social forces favoring a return to a centrifugal relationship will prevail. Even less probable, however, is that the Mexican Americans soon will embrace Anglo conformity. There is every reason to believe that Mexican Americans will remain, and will wish to remain, a distinctive ethnic group within American life for several generations to come.

Native Americans

Like Mexican Americans, Native Americans clearly entered this society through conquest; and their many separate societies afford myriad illustrations of the formation of centrifugal relationships. The various Indian societies obviously were viable social units before they were conquered. Afterward, the Indians did not desire to be treated as citizens; they preferred instead to be permitted to reconstruct their own independent societies. Most tribes have steadfastly resisted assimilation into the dominant society for more than three centuries. Since they became citizens in 1924, however, the Indians have shown increasing signs of being transformed into one, loosely federated, ethnic group with a centripetal relationship to the majority. Like most other Americans, they have been unable to resist completely the pressures of urbanization, industrialization, and bureaucratization. To a much greater extent than generally is recognized, as stated earlier, the Indians have moved into urban centers in search of employment. They have not, though, readily broken their ties to the reservations or to other members of their tribes within the cities. In general, their movement toward the status of a typical immigrant group has not been as great as among the Mexican Americans, although—as noted previously—there are wide differences among the various tribes in this regard. The tribes generally are quite cool toward the prospect of full Anglo conformity; they continue to be ambivalent about secondary assimilation, and they continue to resist all efforts to terminate their treaty rights. Nonetheless, they seem to continue to move toward the goal of being admitted into American society on an equal footing with other citizens while maintaining the right to live as Indians.

African Americans

Although African Americans were not conquered in their homeland, as were Mexican Americans and Indians, there can be little question that under slavery this group was cruelly treated and endured unbelievable suffering. These facts surely do suggest strong parallels between their experiences and those of Mexican Americans and Native Americans. We may, therefore, with considerable justification, view African Americans as a colonized minority; however, and this is crucial, *they did not form a centrifugal relationship with the dominant group.* How could they? At the time of enslavement, they represented many different nationalities and did not share a common culture or set of social institutions. In America, they were not independent of the host society; they were heavily dependent on it. Indeed, even the formation of an inclusive ethnic group and culture was greatly hindered by the slave system, with its vigilance and deliberate interference with the efforts of the slaves to communicate with one another and to organize. Only slowly and with great effort were the African slaves able to construct institutions of their own within the host society. This process, if not its rate of change, resembled the experience of many other immigrant groups.

Our sketch of African American history in Chapters 10 and 11 does not furnish the evidence needed to determine just how popular the various ideologies of group adjustment—ranging from Anglo conformity to secession—have been. We know only that their popularity has varied through time. Even without systematic evidence—and with all due respect to Garveyism—it seems safe to say that, during most of the present century, Blacks have been mainly divided between cultural pluralism and Anglo conformity (Jaynes and Williams 1989:195). The NAACP, the Urban League, CORE, the March on Washington movement, SCLC, and many other organizations have centered their efforts on improving jobs, education, income, housing, health care, and so on (i.e., on increasing secondary assimilation). Since these goals are common to both Anglo conformity and cultural pluralism, it is not clear which of these ideologies has been most favored.

The decade of the 1960s brought about noticeable changes in the perspectives of Black Americans. They increasingly doubted that Anglo conformity was a desirable goal and that cultural pluralism was feasible; separatist ideas again gained a more sympathetic hearing. Separatist sentiments seemed to decline during the 1970s and 1980s, but some signs of a revival began to appear in the 1990s. The continued inability of many Black Americans to gain better jobs, housing, police protection, and representation in the councils of government—especially among the ghetto poor described by Wilson (1987)—is sure to strengthen the hand of separatists (Lieberson and Waters 1988:155; Neidert and Farley 1985:848). In any event, African Americans will continue to be a distinctive group within American society for many additional generations.

Some Tentative Conclusions

Given these interpretations, we offer the following tentative conclusions. The main line of ideological debate among Whites concerns cultural pluralism. The strength of Anglo conformity is greater among WASPs, while the strength of pluralism is greater among the White descendants of the second-immigrant stream. Support within either group for separatism or secessionism is low, though there are some signs of rising support.

The picture is different when Whites are compared to non-Whites, but not drastically so. There is definitely some support within both White and non-White groups for separatism, with the strongest support being among the Whites. For instance, many Whites want Blacks to be kept out of their neighborhoods and feel they have the right to keep them out (Schuman, Steeh, and Bobo 1985:97; Taylor, Sheatsley, and Greeley 1978: 269). Also, during the 1990s, White separatist propaganda proliferated, coinciding with an increasingly visible tendency among separatists to talk of establishing an "Aryan homeland" (Reiss 1995:A11). Within both the White and non-White groups, however, the predominant preference of each group in regard to the other group appears to be a pluralist arrangement, though controversy surrounding residential desegregation is intense.[14]

The generally high support for cultural pluralism among both Whites and non-Whites with respect to the other suggests that a foundation is being constructed for a broad agreement on ethnic-group goals. Although the popularity of separatism may not be ignored, pluralism has emerged as the chief alternative to Anglo conformity in American thought concerning racial and ethnic relations. This point is frequently obscured by criticisms of assimilationist theory. For example, many critics conclude their attacks on assimilationist theory by advocating cultural pluralism. Despite its rejection of full Anglo conformity, cultural pluralism (we have tried to show) is best understood as a form of assimilation that is competing for acceptance within American society as a legitimate and equivalent alternative goal.

To insist that Anglo conformity and cultural pluralism are both legitimate forms of assimilation, however, may obscure another important point. We must emphasize again that the differences between these two are by no means trivial. Quite different social policies and tactics of change are sometimes suggested by these two assimilationist ideologies. One of the clearest illustrations of this point is the example of bilingual-bicultural education. Most people who favor Anglo conformity are opposed to programs of bilingual-bicultural education. Pluralists, on the other hand, want to pass on their family's language and culture; and they want the public schools, that they help support, to assist in their efforts.

Another example of the different social policies preferred by Anglo conformists and cultural pluralists may be found in the controversy surrounding the preservation of ethnic neighborhoods. Anglo conformists tend to view with suspicion the continuation of White ethnic neighborhoods beyond three generations. People who live there and struggle to maintain a distinctive ethnic culture are considered to be something less than "real" Americans. These citizens, Anglo conformists tend to believe, should be strongly encouraged by government policies covering such things as VA and FHA loans, urban renewal, and highway construction to move out of their neighborhoods and disperse throughout the cities, as expected under the spatial mobility hypothesis.

Many members of non-Anglo ethnic groups take a very different view of the matter. To them, the ethnic neighborhood does not represent a restraint on assimilation. It represents, rather, the way in which a group of people have chosen to express their Americanism. The neighborhood is a source of social morale and is the main link through which the individual is "plugged into" the society. The individual receives social and psychological support from family and friends in the neighborhood. The destruction of an ethnic neighborhood, therefore, does not necessarily signify the end of an alien culture and the complete adoption of American culture. It may signify, instead, the destruction of a specific way of being an American.[15] It is not surprising, therefore, that many White ethnics, Latinos, and Blacks object to the assumption by government officials that their old ethnic neighborhoods are slums or that these groups oppose policies that further the deterioration of ethnic communities.

This brief comparison of the social policy preferences of Anglo conformists and cultural pluralists should suffice to show that they do indeed differ—and in ways that most Americans consider to be of great importance; however, their disagreements, though large and significant, take place primarily within a mutually accepted economic and political framework. This does not mean that cultural pluralists are uncritical of the American economic and political system, nor does it mean that the conflicts arising between Anglo conformists and pluralists in this connection are minor. What it does mean is that cultural pluralists believe the operating principles of American life afford, in Glazer's (1972:174) words, "enormous scope for group diversity."

It is true, as our historical review illustrates, that official discrimination has occurred against many of the ethnic groups in the United States, especially against the non-White groups. But our courts and legislatures have declared (even if slowly) that all of these acts are opposed to America's basic principles. Slavery was, at last, ended; the relocation of the Japanese was declared illegal; African, Native, and Japanese Americans have become citizens; and discrimination on the basis of race, color, and national origins has been declared unconstitutional (Glazer 1972:175). The basic faith of the cultural pluralists is that the consensus on the principles of American economic and political life does not require a capitulation to the will of the dominant group. Even though the amount and severity of dominant-group discrimination in our history must give even an optimist pause, the main ethnic-group conflicts of the past have been settled on the side of the rights of minorities. Stated differently, the "tyranny of the majority," which Tocqueville ([1835]1988:250) warned might be the fatal flaw of democracy, has, so far, been forestalled; and cultural pluralists believe the institutions of this nation are sufficiently flexible to permit this pattern of intergroup acceptance to continue.

The right to maintain a pluralist pattern, however, does not ensure a group's actual success in doing so. Regardless of the desire of a group's members to have "the best of both," it may still be true, as discussed in Chapter 1, that the forces behind the historical shift away from tradition and toward modernity gradually will erode the distinctiveness of the ethnic groups in American society. Will these groups, as Park's race cycle theory states, eventually be "melted" into the dominant society?

Our analysis supports two basic conclusions. First, America's shift from an agrarian to an urban-industrial society has made it extremely difficult for ethnic groups to maintain or revive a centrifugal relationship with the majority. During this century, Mexican Americans have come to resemble an immigrant minority more than a conquered minority. Because of the sovereignty rights guaranteed to many American Indian tribes by treaties, they are in a stronger position than any others to resist assimilative pressures and to maintain an unusually high level of separation, if they so desire. Even so, many individual Indians have married out of their ethnic group and have moved into the mainstream of the society; those who remain on reservations increasingly live in a manner that resembles the main forms of American life.

Our second conclusion, however, is that the continuation of various levels of group distinctiveness among the descendants of the colonial, first-stream, and second-stream immigrants from Europe demonstrates that industrialization does not inevitably undermine racial and ethnic groupings (See and Wilson 1988:236). While many groups have undergone a high degree of cultural and secondary assimilation within three generations, the third and subsequent generations frequently have experienced a renewed interest in revitalizing their ethnic heritages and ties. Given sufficient time, nevertheless, even the maintenance of the levels of separation endorsed by pluralists may succumb to the homogenizing pressures of an advanced industrial civilization. No one knows how long such an outcome might take; but unless there are catastrophic changes in the world order, it seems almost certain that ethnic distinctions among Whites will disappear earlier than the distinctions between Whites and non-Whites. Taking history as our guide, and given the continuous possibility of ethnic rejuvenation under favorable circumstances, some of the White groups could sustain themselves for many additional generations, especially symbolically; and the disappearance of the sociocultural distinctions between Whites and non-Whites could take centuries.

These two conclusions suggest a third. While maintaining a high level of sociocultural distinctiveness may seem "obsolete" in modern societies, cultural pluralism is compatible with an urban-industrial society. Indeed, as most critics of Anglo conformity fondly note, America's great industrial might could not have been developed without the enormous contributions of its racially and ethnically diverse population. And many citizens think America's ethnic diversity strengthens its democratic institutions which, as we noted in Chapter 2, are rooted in political pluralism. Although the continued existence of racial and ethnic minorities may from time to time pose a problem for national unity, racial and ethnic groups also may help to sustain a sense of individual and social purpose for many Americans.

More pressing, though, than the problems of national unity that may be posed by the existence of racial and ethnic cleavages is the continuing failure to afford an equal opportunity for secondary assimilation to every American who wishes it. As Wrong (1977:488) stated, we must "increase the opportunities for individuals to escape from their ethnic communities, if they so wish, and improve the levels and quality of living in the ethnic communities themselves." Increasing the individual's opportunities to leave the ethnic community or remain within it requires additional reductions in the existing levels of racial and ethnic discrimination. Needed also are further, genuine, reductions in racial and ethnic prejudices. We must learn, as Voltaire urged, to "pardon reciprocally each other's folly." Each of these measures reflects the best traditions and highest aspirations of the American people.

Key Ideas

1. The occurrence of full Anglo conformity assimilation has been much slower than is generally recognized. Although many *individuals* have achieved this type of merger with the dominant group within three generations, very few *groups* have done so; however, a virtually complete merger has occurred for practically all White ethnic groups within eight generations. Given the continued dominance of an Anglo-based majority, groups from the countries of the second immigrant stream are unlikely to disappear entirely for perhaps four additional generations and may continue symbolically for many years to come. The European immigrants of the third stream probably will follow the pattern that has characterized those of the first and second streams.

2. Since no non-White group has experienced full Anglo conformity assimilation, no one knows whether this process can occur; however, some non-White immigrant groups (e.g., Japanese Americans) have experienced high levels of pluralism, especially at the cultural and secondary structural levels, showing that under some circumstances this assimilationist goal may be approximated by non-Whites within three generations.

3. Colonized and immigrant minorities typically establish different types of relationships with dominant groups. Colonized minorities usually have arisen from previously intact societies and typically have sought to maintain their group's distinctiveness and independence rather than to be accepted as equal members of the dominant society. Ethnic groups arising from immigration form within the host society and serve, among other things, to assist the group's members to attain equal treatment.

4. The concept of ethnogenesis may help to explain why heavily oppressed groups like Mexican Americans, African Americans, and Native Americans whose initial contacts with the dominant American society were, or were similar to, those of classical colonialism may nonetheless adopt cultural pluralism or Anglo conformity as goals. For example, although the initial relationship of Mexican Americans to the majority group arose through conquest, their subsequent experiences have, for the most part, transformed them into the type of ethnic group that typically arises through immigration. However, even though cultural pluralism is now widely accepted among Mexican Americans, the continuation of discrimination against them could fuel latent separatist tendencies.

5. Like the Mexican Americans, the Indian tribes were conquered and formed a centripetal relationship to the majority. Although there has been substantial variation among the tribes, some groups have shown a definite movement toward the acceptance of cultural pluralism. An increased resistance to this movement by the dominant group, however, could easily halt it and strengthen the movement among Indians for greater autonomy.

6. The main line of division between WASPs and Whites of the second immigrant stream concerns assimilationist ideology. Anglo conformity is stronger among the former, and cultural pluralism is stronger among the latter.

7. Whites are likely to express a higher level of separatist sentiment with respect to non-Whites than with respect to other Whites. The main line of division within the White and non-White groups with respect to the other group lies between those who favor cultural pluralism or some alternative.

8. In many cases, Anglo conformity and cultural pluralism, though both ideologies of assimilation, lead to noticeably different social policies and tactics of change.

9. America's shift from an agrarian to an urban-industrial society has made it extremely difficult for ethnic groups to maintain or restore a centrifugal relationship with the majority. A pluralist pattern of life, however, may persist within contemporary American society for many generations.

10. Although the maintenance of ethnic groups may pose a problem for national unity, they also may help to give meaning and purpose to people's lives.

11. The failure to grant equal opportunity to achieve secondary assimilation is a far more serious problem for America than the existence of ethnic divisions. Higher levels of secondary assimilation among minorities requires further reductions in the levels of prejudice and discrimination.

Key Terms

centrifugal relationship   The type of relationship that usually is formed between a conquered group and the conquering group. It is characterized by conflict and by efforts on the part of the subordinate group to free itself from the dominant group.

centripetal relationship   The type of relationship that usually is formed between an immigrant group and the host society. It is characterized by a desire on the part of the subordinate group to achieve equality with the dominant group in the secondary structural sphere coupled with restrained resistance to some forms of assimilation.

symbolic ethnicity   An ethnic identity that does not serve as an organizing focus for an individual's life or livelihood and does not require frequent interactions with, or deep commitments to, co-ethnics. This form of ethnicity arises "as the functions of ethnic cultures and groups diminish and identity becomes the primary way of being ethnic."

Notes

1. The Germans, in particular, maintained their language and other cultural elements well beyond that time (see Chapter 3).

2. Whether people who report a particular ancestry actually are of that ancestry is, of course, a different issue (see, e.g., Lieberson and Waters 1988:22-25).

3. We are even less able here than usual to present evidence concerning primary assimilation. No analysis of changes in primary relations among ethnic groups since the beginning of the twentieth century is available. We may presume, however, that the observed levels of secondary and marital assimilation in any given case may serve as a reasonable basis for conjecture concerning the probable levels of primary assimilation.

4. In an earlier study based on information from NORC, Greeley (1985:272) found that although the family income of Italian and Polish Catholics was not as high as that of Irish and German Catholics, all four Catholic groups were above the British Protestants and the national average for American Whites.

5. Some of these conclusions rest in part on inferences based on differences in age cohorts in 1980. The information that would be needed for direct comparisons with earlier periods is unavailable.

6. Many *individuals* have lost their ethnic identities. The speculations here refer entirely to groups.

7. An apparent paradox, discussed by Alba and Golden (1986:218), is that although the rates of intermarriage have gone up, the tendencies toward intermarriage appear to have remained stable. The authors observed that the rates have risen because the tendencies to marry out are higher in the mixed-ancestry groups and because these groups have increased in size.

8. Quoted by Herberg (1960:43).

9. Waters (1990:155–164) argued further that people who experience ethnicity as a trait which they may either choose to ignore or to accentuate may greatly underestimate the extent to which an ethnic identity creates obstacles in American society for those who are racially distinctive. As a result, being "an ethnic" may reduce, rather than increase, a White person's understanding of the problems facing non-Whites.

10. Francis refers to this type of ethnic group as a primary ethnic group.

11. Francis refers to this type of ethnic group as a secondary ethnic group.

12. In cases in which the invader has conqured only a portion of the conquered group's territory, the members of the invaded group who are now cut off from the main body of the society may still possess a full complement of institutions and be able to continue as if they were a whole society.

13. For example, one presentation of the aims of the Chicano movement stressed the need for various forms of education and the recognition of Chicano culture by the dominant group. The list of priorities adopted by the first convention of La Raza Unida Party included improvements in the areas of jobs, education, housing, health, and the administration of justice (Forbes 1973:292–294). La Raza Unida's goals also included, however, such separatist policies as community control of law enforcement, the schools, and the economy.

14. Bobo and Zubrinsky (1996:904) suggested that high levels of Black residential segregation are likely to continue even in large, ethnically diverse urban areas because many Latinos and Asians also hold negative stereotypes of Blacks and, like Whites, resist residential desegregation.

15. The disappearance of ethnic neighborhoods does not necessarily mean the ethnic community has dissolved (Parenti 1967:717–726).

References

Ablon, Joan. "Relocated American Indians in the San Francisco Bay Area: Social Interaction and Indian Identity." In Howard M. Bahr, Bruce A. Chadwick, and Robert C. Day, eds, *Native Americans Today,* 412–428. New York: Harper & Row, 1972.

Abrams, Franklin. "Immigration Law and Its Enforcement: Reflections of American Immigration Policy." In Roy Simon Bryce-Laporte, ed, *Sourcebook on the New Immigration,* 27–35. New Brunswick, N.J.: Transaction Books, 1980.

———. "American Immigration Policy: How Strait the Gate?" In Richard R. Hofstetter, ed., *U.S. Immigration Policy.* Durham, N.C.: Duke University Press, 1984.

Acuña, Rodolfo. *Occupied America,* 2nd ed. New York: Harper & Row, 1981.

Adamic, Louis. *A Nation of Nations.* New York: Harper and Brothers, 1944.

Adams, Romanzo. "The Unorthodox Race Doctrine of Hawaii." In E. B. Reuter, ed., *Race and Culture Contacts,* 143–160. New York: McGraw-Hill, 1934.

Adorno, T. W., Else Frenkel-Brunswik, Daniel J. Levinson, and R. Nevitt Sanford. *The Authoritarian Personality.* New York: Harper and Brothers, 1950.

Alba, Richard D. *Italian Americans.* Englewood Cliffs, N.J.: Prentice-Hall, 1985.

———, ed. *Ethnicity and Race in the U.S.A.* New York: Routledge, 1988.

———. "Italian Americans: A Century of Ethnic Change." In Silvia Pedraza and Rubén G. Rumbaut, eds., *Origins and Destinies: Immigration, Race, and Ethnicity in America,* 172–181. Belmont: Wadsworth Publishing Company, 1996.

Alba, Richard D. and Reid M. Golden. "Patterns of Ethnic Marriage in the United States." *Social Forces* 65 (September 1986): 202–223.

Allen, Walter R., and Joseph O. Jewell. "The Miseducation of Black America: Black Education Since *An American Dilemma.*" In Obie Clayton, Jr., ed., *An American Dilemma Revisited: Race Relations in a Changing World,* 169–190. New York: Russell Sage Foundation, 1996.

Allport, Gordon. *The Nature of Prejudice.* Garden City, N.Y.: Doubleday, 1958.

Allsup, Carl. *The American G.I. Forum: Origins and Evolution.* Center for Mexican American Studies Monograph no. 6. Austin, Tex.: University of Texas Press, 1982.

Alvarez, Rodolfo. "The Psycho-Historical and Socioeconomic Development of the Chicano Community in the United States." In Rodolfo O. de la Garza, Frank D. Bean, Charles M. Bonjean, Ricardo Romo, and Rodolfo Alvarez, eds., *The Mexican American Experience,* 33–56. Austin, Tex.: University of Texas Press, 1985.

Alvírez, David, and Frank D. Bean. "The Mexican American Family." In C. H. Mindel and R. W. Habenstein, eds., *Ethnic Families in America: Patterns and Variations,* 271–292. New York: Elsevier North-Holland, 1976.

Americans Before Columbus. Albuquerque, N.Mex.: National Indian Youth Council, 1992.

Amir, Yehuda. "The Role of Intergroup Contact in Change of Prejudice and Ethnic Relations." In P. A. Katz, ed., *Toward the Elimination of Racism,* 245–308. New York: Pergamon Press, 1976.

Anderson, Robert N., and Rogelio Saenz. "Structural Determinants of Mexican American Intermarriage, 1975–1980." *Social Science Quarterly* 75 (June 1994): 414–429.

Applebome, Peter. "2 Decisions Reflect Bitter Conflict Surrounding University Affirmative Action Policies." *New York Times* (March 22, 1996): A8.

Armor, David J. *Forced Justice: School Desegregation and the Law.* New York: Oxford University Press, 1995.

———. "White Flight and the Future of School Desegregation." In Walter G. Stephan and Joe R. Feagin, eds., *School Desegregation,* 187–226. New York: Plenum Press, 1980.

Aronson, Elliot, and Alex Gonzalez. "Desegregation, Jigsaw, and the Mexican-American Experience." In Phyllis A. Katz and Dalmas A. Taylor, eds., *Eliminating Racism,* 301–314. New York: Plenum Press, 1988.

Ayres, B. Drummond, Jr. "A Ballot Proposition Gives Voters the Opportunity to Influence National Immigration Policy." *New York Times* (September 25, 1994a): 12.

———. "Anti-Alien Movement Spreading in Wake of California's Measure." *New York Times* (December 4, 1994b): 1.

———. "Fighting Affirmative Action, Leader's Race Looms Large." *New York Times* (April 18, 1996): A1.

Bach, Robert L., and Rita Carroll-Seguin. "Labor Force Participation, Household Composition and Sponsorship among Southeast Asian Refugees." *International Migration Review* 20 (Summer 1986): 381–404.

Bachman, Jerald, and Patrick M. O'Malley. "Black-White Differences in Self-Esteem: Are They Affected by Response Styles?" *American Journal of Sociology* 90 (November 1984): 624–639.

Badar, Christine Velez, Clifford L. Broman, Janet L. Bokemeier, and Maxine Baca Zinn. "Labor Force Participation Among Mexican and Mexican American Women in the Rural and Urban Southwest: A Comparative Study." *Latino Studies Journal* 6 (January 1995): 68–91.

Bahr, Howard M. "An End to Invisibility." In Howard M. Bahr, Bruce A. Chadwick, and Robert C. Day, eds., *Native Americans Today,* 404–412. New York: Harper & Row, 1972.

Bahr, Howard M., Bruce A. Chadwick, and Robert C. Day, eds., *Native Americans Today.* New York: Harper & Row, 1972.

Bailey, Thomas, and Roger Waldinger. "Primary, Secondary, and Enclave Labor Markets: A Training Systems Approach." *American Sociological Review* 56 (August 1991): 432–445.

Baker, Ross K., ed. *The Afro-American.* New York: Van Nostrand Reinhold Company, 1970.

Balderrama, Francisco E. *In Defense of La Raza: The Los Angeles Mexican Consulate and the Mexican Community, 1929 to 1936,* 58–61. Tucson, Ariz.: University of Arizona Press, 1982.

Ball, Harry V., George Eaton Simpson, and Kiyoshi Ikeda. "Law and Social Change: Sumner Reconsidered." *American Journal of Sociology* 57 (March 1962): 532–540.

Ball, Howard. "Judicial Parsimony and Military Necessity Disinterred: A Reexamination of the Japanese Exclusion Cases, 1943–44." In Roger Daniels, Sandra C. Taylor, and Harry H. L. Kitano, eds., *Japanese Americans: From Relocation to Redress,* Revised Edition, 72–74. Seattle, Wash.: University of Washington Press, 1991.

Baltzell, E. Digby. *The Protestant Establishment.* New York: Vintage Books, 1964.

Bardolph, Richard. *The Negro Vanguard.* New York: Vintage Books, 1961.

Barker, Eugene C. "Native Latin American Contributions to the Colonization and Independence of Texas." *Southwestern Historical Quarterly* 46 (April 1943): 317–335.

Barnard, William A., and Mark S. Benn. "Belief Congruence and Prejudice Reduction in an Interracial Contact Setting." *The Journal of Social Psychology* (February 1988): 125–134.

Baron, Harold M. "The Web of Urban Racism." In Louis L. Knowles and Kenneth Prewitt, eds., *Institutional Racism in America,* 134–176. Englewood Cliffs, N.J.: Prentice-Hall, 1969.

Baron, Robert A. *Human Aggression.* New York: Plenum Press, 1977.

Barone, Michael. "The New America." *U.S. News and World Report* (July 10, 1995).

Barrera, Mario. *Race and Class in the Southwest.* South Bend, Ind.: University of Notre Dame Press, 1979.

———. *Beyond Aztlan: Ethnic Autonomy in Comparative Perspective.* South Bend, Ind.: University of Notre Dame Press, 1988.

Barringer, Felicity. "Pueblo Parents Feel Generation Gap." *New York Times* (October 24, 1990): B9.

———. "Immigration Brings New Diversity to Asian Population in the U.S." *New York Times* (June 12, 1991): A1.

———. "White-Black Disparity in Income Narrowed in 80's, Census Shows." *The New York Times* (July 24, 1992): A1, A10.

———. "Ethnic Pride Confounds the Census." *New York Times* (May 9, 1993): E3.

Barringer, Herbert R., Robert W. Gardner, and Michael J. Levin. *Asian and Pacific Islanders in the United States.* New York: Russell Sage Foundation, 1995.

Bean, Frank D. "Immigration Combatants Overlook the New Reality." *Houston Chronicle* (August 29, 1993): F1, F5.

Bean, Frank D., Jorge Chapa, Ruth Berg, and Kathryn Sowards. "Educational and Socio-demographic Incorporation Among Hispanic Immigrants to the United States." In Barry Edmonston and Jeffrey S. Passel, eds., *Immigration and Ethnicity: The Integration of America's Newest Arrivals,* 73–100. Washington, D.C.: Urban Institute Press, 1994.

Bean, Frank D., Thomas J. Espenshade, Michael J. White, and Robert F. Dymowski. "Post-IRCA Changes in the Volume and Composition of Undocumented Migration to the United States: An Assessment Based on Apprehensions Data." In Frank D. Bean, Barry Edmonston, and Jeffrey S. Passel, eds., *Undocumented Migration to the United States,* 111–158. Santa Monica, Calif. and Washington, D.C.: Rand Corporation and The Urban Institute, 1990.

Bean, Frank D., and Marta Tienda. *The Hispanic Population of the United States.* New York: Russell Sage Foundation, 1987.

Bean, Frank D., George Vernez, and Charles B. Keely. *Opening and Closing the Doors.* Santa Monica, Calif. and Washington, D.C.: Rand Corporation and The Urban Institute, 1989.

Beck, E. M. "Discrimination and White Economic Loss: A Time Series Examination of the Radical Model." *Social Forces* 59 (September 1980): 148–168.

Beck, E. M., and Stewart Tolnay. "The Killing Fields of the Deep South: The Market for Cotton and the Lynching of Blacks, 1882–1930." *American Sociological Review* 55 (August 1990): 526–539.

Benedict, Ruth. *Race: Science and Politics.* New York: Viking Press, 1961.

Bennett, Lerone, Jr. *Before the Mayflower,* rev. ed. New York: Penguin Books, 1964.

Benokraitis, Nijole V., and Joe R. Feagin. *Affirmative Action and Equal Opportunity: Action, Inaction, Reaction.* Boulder, Colo.: Westview Press, 1978.

Berelson, Bernard, and Patricia J. Salter. "Majority and Minority Americans: An Analysis of Magazine Fiction." *Public Opinion Quarterly* 10 (Summer 1946): 168–190.

Berger, Morroe. *Equality by Statute,* rev. ed. Garden City, N.Y.: Doubleday, 1968.

Berkowitz, Leonard, ed. *Roots of Aggression: A Re-examination of the Frustration-Aggression Hypothesis.* New York: Atherton Press, 1969.

Berkowitz, Leonard. "Frustration-Aggression Hypothesis: Examination and Reformulation." *Psychological Bulletin* 106 (July 1989): 59–73.

Berman, Paul. "Redefining Fairness." *New York Times Book Review* (April 14, 1996): 18–19.

Bernard, William S. "Immigration: History of U.S. Policy." In Stephan Thernstrom, Ann Orlov, and Oscar Handlin, eds., *Harvard Encyclopedia of American Ethnic Groups,* 486–495. Cambridge, Mass. The Belknap Press, 1980.

Bernstein, Richard. "The Immigration Wave: A Plea to Hold It Back." *New York Times* (April 19, 1995): B2.

Billingsley, Andrew. *Black Families in White America.* Englewood Cliffs, N.J.: Prentice-Hall, 1968.

Blassingame, John W. *The Slave Community: Plantation Life in the Antebellum South.* New York: Oxford University Press, 1972.

Blau, Zena Smith. *Black Children/White Children.* New York: Free Press, 1981.

Blauner, Robert. *Racial Oppression in America.* New York: Harper and Row, 1972.

———. "Colonized and Immigrant Minorities." In Ronald Takaki, ed., *From Different Shores: Perspectives on Race and Ethnicity in America,* 2nd ed., 149–160. New York: Oxford University Press, 1994.

———. "Talking Past Each Other: Black and White Languages of Race." In Karen E. Rosenblum and Toni-Michelle C. Travis, eds., *The Meaning of Difference,* 167–176. New York: McGraw-Hill, 1996.

Blee, Kathleen M. *Women of the Klan: Racism and Gender in the 1920s.* Berkeley, Calif. and Los Angeles: University of California Press, 1991.

Blumer, Herbert. "Industrialisation and Race Relations." In Guy Hunter, ed., *Industrialization and Race Relations: A Symposium.* London: Oxford University Press, 1965.

Bobo, Lawrence. "Group Conflict, Prejudice, and the Paradox of Contemporary Racial Attitudes." In Phyllis A. Katz and Dalmas A. Taylor, eds., *Eliminating Racism,* 85–114. New York: Plenum Press, 1988.

Bobo, Lawrence, and Camille L. Zubrinsky. "Attitudes on Residential Integration: Perceived Status Differences, Mere In-Group Preference, or Racial Prejudice?" *Social Forces* 74 (March 1996): 883–909.

Bodnar, John. *The Transplanted.* Bloomington, Ind.: Indiana University Press, 1985.

Bogardus, Emory S. "A Social Distance Scale." *Sociology and Social Research* 17 (January-February 1933): 265–271.

———. *Social Distance.* Yellow Springs, Ohio: Antioch Press, 1959.

Bolino, August C. *The Ellis Island Source Book.* Washington, D.C.: The Catholic University of America, 1985.

Bonacich, Edna. "A Theory of Ethnic Antagonism: The Split Labor Market." *American Sociological Review* 37 (October 1972): 547–559.

———. "A Theory of Middleman Minorities." *American Sociological Review* 38 (October 1973): 583–594.

———. "Abolition, the Extension of Slavery, and the Position of Free Blacks: A Study of Split Labor Markets in the United States, 1830–1863." *American Journal of Sociology* 81 (November 1975): 601–628.

———. "Advanced Capitalism and Black/White Race Relations in the United States: A Split Labor Market Interpretation." *American Sociological Review* 41 (February 1976): 34–51.

Bonacich, Edna, and John Modell. *The Economic Basis of Ethnic Solidarity.* Berkeley, Calif.: University of California Press, 1980.

Bonney, Rachel A. "The Role of AIM Leaders in Indian Nationalism." *American Indian Quarterly* (Autumn 1977): 209–224.

Bordewich, Fergus M. *Killing the White Man's Indian.* New York: Doubleday, 1996.

Borjas, George J. *Friends or Strangers: The Impact of Immigration on the U.S. Economy.* New York: Basic Books, 1990.

———. *Assimilation and Changes in Cohort Quality Revisited: What Happened to Immigrant Earnings in the 1980s?* Cambridge, Mass.: National Bureau of Economic Research, Inc., #4866, (September, 1994a).

———. *The Economic Benefits From Immigration.* Cambridge, Mass.: National Bureau of Economic Research, Inc., #4955, (December, 1994b).

Boston, Thomas D. *Race, Class, and Conservatism.* Boston: Unwin Hyman, 1988.

Boswell, Terry E. "A Split Labor Market Analysis of Discrimination Against Chinese Immigrants, 1850–1882." *American Sociological Review* 51 (June 1986): 352–371.

Bouvier, Leon F., and Robert W. Gardner, "Immigration to the U.S.: The Unfinished Story." *Population Bulletin* 41 (November 1986): 30–31.

Bowman, Phillip J. "Joblessness." In James S. Jackson, ed., *Life in Black America,* 156–178. Newbury Park, Calif.: Sage Publications, 1991.

Bradshaw, Benjamin S., and Frank D. Bean. "Intermarriage Between Persons of Spanish and Non-Spanish Surnames: Changes from the Mid-Nineteenth to the Mid-Twentieth Century." *Social Science Quarterly* 51 (September 1970): 389–395.

Brasher, Philip. "High Risk of Suicide Found in Native American Youths." *Austin American-Statesman* (March 25, 1992): A4.

Brigham, Carl C. *A Study of American Intelligence.* Princeton, N. J.: Princeton University Press, 1923.

———. "Intelligence Tests of Immigrant Groups." *Psychological Review* 37 (March 1930): 158–165.

Brimelow, Peter. "Time to Rethink Immigration?" *National Review* 44 (June 22, 1992): 30–46.

———. *Alien Nation.* New York: Random House, 1995.

Brisbane, Robert H. "Black Protest in America." In Mabel M. Smythe, ed., *The Black American Reference Book,* 537–579. Englewood Cliffs, N.J.: Prentice-Hall, 1976.

Broman, Clifford L., Harold W. Neighbors, and James S. Jackson. "Racial Group Identification Among Black Adults." *Social Forces* 67 (September 1988): 146–158.

Brooke, James. "In the Budget Talk from Washington, Indians See the Cruelest Cuts of All." *New York Times* (October 15, 1995): 10.

Broom, Leonard, and Norval D. Glenn. "When Will America's Negroes Catch Up?" *New Society* (March 25, 1965): 6–7.

Broom, Leonard, and John L. Kitsuse. *The Managed Casualty.* Berkeley and Los Angeles: University of California Press, 1956.

Brown, Dee. *Bury My Heart at Wounded Knee.* New York: Bantam Books, 1973.

Brown, Roger. *Social Psychology,* 2nd ed. New York: The Free Press, 1986.

Bryan, Samuel. "Mexican Immigrants on the Labor Market." In Wayne Moquin and Charles Van Doren, eds., *A Documentary History of the Mexican Americans,* 333–339. New York: Bantam Books, 1972.

Bryson, Bill. *The Mother Tongue: English and How It Got That Way.* New York: William Morrow and Company, Inc., 1990.

Buffalohead, W. Roger. "Self-Rule in the Past and the Future: An Overview." In Kenneth R. Philp, ed., *Indian Self-Rule,* 265–277. Salt Lake City, Utah: Howe Brothers, 1986.

Bullard, Sara, ed. *The Ku Klux Klan: A History of Violence and Racism,* 4th ed. Montgomery, Ala.: Klanwatch, The Southern Poverty Law Center, 1991.

Bunche, Ralph J. "The Programs, Ideologies, Tactics, and Achievements of Negro Betterment and Interracial Organizations," Unpublished Memorandum, 1940. In August Meier, Elliott Rudwick, and Francis L. Broderick, eds., *Black Protest Thought in the Twentieth Century,* 2nd ed., 122–131. Indianapolis, Ind. and New York: Bobbs-Merrill, 1971.

Burma, John H. "Interethnic Marriage in Los Angeles, 1948–1959." *Social Forces* 42 (December 1963): 156–165.

———. "A Comparison of the Mexican American Subculture with the Oscar Lewis Culture of Poverty Model." In John H. Burma, ed., *Mexican Americans in the United States,* 17–28. Cambridge, Mass.: Schenkman, 1970.

Burner, David, Elizabeth Fox-Genovese, and Virginia Bernhard. *A College History of the United States,* Vol. 1. St. James, N. Y.: Brandywine Press, 1991.

Burns, W. Haywood. *The Voices of Negro Protest.* New York: Oxford University Press, 1963.

Burr, Jeffrey A., Omer R. Galle, and Mark A. Fossett. "Racial Occupational Inequality in Southern Metropolitan Areas, 1940–1980: Revisiting the Visibility-Discrimination Hypothesis." *Social Forces* 69 (March 1991): 831–850.

Butler, John Sibley. "Institutional Racism: Viable Perspective or Intellectual Bogey." *Journal of the Black Sociologist* 7 (Spring-Summer 1978): 5–25.

———. *Entrepreneurship and Self-Help Among Black Americans.* Albany, N.Y.: State University of New York Press, 1991.

———. "Myrdal Revisited: The Negro in Business, the Professions, Public Service, and Other White Collar Occupations."In Obie Clayton, Jr., ed., *An American Dilemma Revisited: Race Relations in a Changing World,* 138–168. New York: Russell Sage Foundation, 1996.

Butler, John Sibley, and Kenneth L. Wilson. "The American Soldier Revisited: Race Relations in the Military." *Social Science Quarterly* 59 (December 1978): 451–467.

———. "Entrepreneurial Enclaves: An Exposition into the Afro-American Experience." *National Journal of Sociology* 2 (Fall 1988): 127–166.

Cafferty, Pastora San Juan, Barry R. Chiswick, Andrew M. Greeley, and Teresa A. Sullivan. *The Dilemma of American Immigration.* New Brunswick, N.J.: Transaction Books, 1983.

Cahn, Steven M., ed. *The Affirmative Action Debate.* New York: Routledge, 1995.

Camejo, Antonio. "Texas Chicanos Forge Own Political Power." In Livie Isauro Duran and H. Russell Bernard, eds., *Introduction to Chicano Studies,* 552–558. New York: Macmillan, 1973.

Cancio, Silvia A., T. David Evans, and David J. Maume, Jr. "Reconsidering the Declining Significance of Race: Racial Differences in Early Career Wages." *American Sociological Review* 61 (August 1996): 541–556.

Caplan, Nathan, Marcella H. Choy, and John K. Whitmore. *Children of the Boat People: A Study of Educational Success.* Ann Arbor, Mich.: University of Michigan Press, 1992.

Caplan, Nathan, John K. Whitmore, and Marcella H. Choy. *The Boat People and Achievement in America.* Ann Arbor, Mich.: The University of Michigan Press, 1989.

Cariño, Benjamin V. "Filipino Americans: Many and Varied." In Silvia Pedraza and Rubén G. Rumbaut, eds., *Origins and Destinies: Immigration, Race, and Ethnicity in America,* 293–301. Belmont, Calif.: Wadsworth Publishing Company, 1996.

Carmichael, Stokely. "Black Power" (Chicago: Student Nonviolent Coordinating Committee, 1966); reprinted in Gilbert Osofsky, ed., *The Burden of Race,* 629–636. New York: Harper & Row, 1968.

Carmichael, Stokely, and Charles Hamilton. *Black Power.* New York: Vintage Books, 1967.

Carter, Deborah J., and Reginald Wilson. *Minorities in Higher Education. 1992 Eleventh Annual Status Report.* Washington, D.C.: American Council on Education, 1993.

Caudill, William, and George DeVos. "Achievement, Culture, and Personality: The Case of the Japanese Americans." *American Anthropologist* 58 (December 1956): 1102–1126.

Cavalli-Sforza, L. Luca, Paolo Menozzi, and Alberto Piazza. *The History and Geography of the Human Gene.* Princeton, N.J.: Princeton University Press, 1994.

Cazares, Ralph B., Edward Murguía, and W. Parker Frisbie. "Mexican American Intermarriage in a Nonmetropolitan Context." In Rodolfo O. de la Garza, Frank D. Bean, Charles M. Bonjean, Ricardo Romo, and Rodolfo Alvarez, eds., *The Mexican American Experience,* 393–401. Austin, Tex.: University of Texas Press, 1985.

Celis, William 3rd. "The Answer Is Either 'Sí' or 'No Way.'" *New York Times* (October 15, 1995a): 5.

———. "Study Finds Rising Concentration of Black and Hispanic Students." *New York Times* (December 14, 1995b): A1.

Chaudhuri, Joyotpaul. "American Indian Policy: An Overview." In Vine Deloria, Jr., ed., *American Indian Policy in the Twentieth Century,* 15–33. Norman, Okla.: University of Oklahoma Press, 1985.

Chiswick, Barry R. "An Analysis of the Earnings and Employment of Asian-American Men." *Journal of Labor Economics* 1 (April 1983): 197–214.

Chow, Esther Ngan-Ling. "The Feminist Movement: Where Are All the Asian American Women?" In Ronald Takaki, ed., *From Different Shores: Perspectives of Race and Ethnicity in America,* 2nd ed. New York: Oxford University Press, 1994.

———. "Family, Economy, and the State: A Legacy of Struggle for Chinese American Women." In Silvia Pedraza and Rubén G. Rumbaut, eds., *Origins and Destinies: Immigration, Race, and Ethnicity in America,* 110–124. Belmont, Calif.: Wadsworth Publishing Company, 1996.

Church, George J. "The Fire This Time." *Time* (May 11, 1992): 18–25.

Clark, Kenneth B. *Prejudice and Your Child,* 2nd ed. Boston: Beacon Press, 1963.

Clark, Kenneth B., and Mamie K. Clark. "The Development of Consciousness of Self and the Emergence of Racial Identification in Negro Preschool Children." *Journal of Social Psychology* 10 (November 1939): 591–599.

———. "Racial Identification and Preference in Negro Children." In Eleanor E. Maccoby, Theodore M. Newcomb, and Eugene L. Hartley, eds., *Readings in Social Psychology,* 602–611. New York: Henry Holt, 1958.

Clark, W. A. V., and Milan Mueller. "Hispanic Relocation and Spatial Assimilation: A Case Study." *Social Science Quarterly* 69 (June 1988): 468–475.

Clayton, Obie, Jr., ed. *An American Dilemma Revisited: Race Relations in a Changing World.* New York: Russell Sage Foundation, 1996.

Cobas, José A. "A New Test and Extension of Propositions from the Bonacich Synthesis." *Social Forces* 64 (December 1985): 432–441.

Cohen, Elizabeth G. "Design and Redesign of the Desegregated School." In Walter G. Stephan and Joe R. Feagin, eds., *School Desegregation,* 251–280. New York: Plenum Press, 1980.

Cohn, Samuel, and Mark Fossett. "Why Racial Employment Inequality Is Greater in Northern Labor Markets: Regional Differences in White-Black Employment Differentials." *Social Forces* 74 (December 1995): 511–542.

Cole, K. C. "Innumeracy." In Russell Jacoby and Naomi Glauberman, eds., *The Bell Curve Debate,* 73–80. New York: Times Books, 1995.

Cole, Stewart G., and Mildred Wiese Cole. *Minorities and the American Promise.* New York: Harper and Brothers, 1954.

Coleman, James S., et al. *Equality of Educational Opportunity.* Washington, D.C.: U. S. Department of Health, Education and Welfare, 1966.

Collison, Michele N.-K. "A Seldom-Aired Issue: Do Black-Student Groups Hinder Campus Integration?" *Chronicle of Higher Education* 35 (October 5, 1988): A35.

Connell, Evan S. *Son of the Morning Star.* San Francisco: North Point Press, 1984.

Connerly, Ward. "Up From Affirmative Action." *New York Times* (April 29, 1996): A11.

Connor, John W. "Acculturation and Family Continuities in Three Generations of Japanese Americans." *Journal of Marriage and the Family* 36 (February 1974): 159–165.

———. "Changing Trends in Japanese American Academic Achievement." *The Journal of Ethnic Studies* 2 (1975): 95–98.

Conzen, Kathleen Neils. "Germans." In Stephan Thernstrom, Ann Orlov, and Oscar Handlin, eds., *Harvard Encyclopedia of American Ethnic Groups,* 405–425. Cambridge, Mass.: The Belknap Press, 1980.

Cook, James. "The American Indian Through Five Centuries." *Forbes* (November 1981).

Cooley, Charles H. "Genius, Fame, and Race." In Russell Jacoby and Naomi Glauberman, eds., *The Bell Curve Debate,* 417–437. New York: Times Books, (1897) 1995.

Cooper, Abraham. "Spreading Bigotry Via Internet." *Civil Rights Journal* 1 (Fall 1995): 14–15.

Cornelius, Wayne A. "America in the Era of Limits: Migrants, Nativists, and the Future of U.S.-Mexican Relations." *Working Papers in U.S.-Mexican Studies* 3. University of California, San Diego: Center for U.S.-Mexican Studies, 1982.

Cotton, Jeremiah. "More on the 'Cost' of Being a Black or Mexican American Male Worker." *Social Science Quarterly* 66 (December 1985): 867–885.

Crane, Paul, and Alfred Larson. "The Chinese Massacre." In Roger Daniels, ed., *Anti-Chinese Violence in North America,* 47–55. New York: Arno Press, 1978.

Crawford, James. "Congress Hears English-only Legislation." *News Reports and Analyses.* University of California, Santa Barbara: UC Linguistic Minority Research Institute, December 1995.

Crevecoeur, J. Hector St. John. "Welcome to My Shores, Distressed European." In Moses Rischin, ed., *Immigration and the American Tradition.* Indianapolis, Ind.: Bobbs-Merrill, 1976.

Cronon, Edmund David. *Black Moses.* Madison, Wis.: The University of Wisconsin Press, 1969.

Crosby, Alfred W., Jr. *The Columbian Exchange.* Westport, Conn.: Greenwood Press, 1972.

Cué, Reynaldo A., and Robert L. Bach. "The Return of the Clandestine Worker and the End of the Golden Exile: Recent Mexican and Cuban Immigrants in the United States." In Roy Simon Bryce-Laporte, ed., *Sourcebook on the New Immigration,* 257–269. New Brunswick, N.J.: Transaction Books, 1980.

Cuéllar, Alfredo. "Perspective on Politics." In Joan W. Moore, ed., *Mexican Americans,* 1st ed., 137–156. Englewood Cliffs, N.J.: Prentice-Hall, 1970.

Curran, Thomas J. *Xenophobia and Immigration.* Boston: Twayne Publishers, 1975.

Daniels, Roger. *The Politics of Prejudice.* New York: Atheneum, 1969.

———. *The Decision to Relocate the Japanese Americans.* Philadelphia: J. B. Lippincott, 1975.

Daniels, Roger, ed. *Anti-Chinese Violence in North America.* New York: Arno Press, 1978.

———. "The Forced Migrations of West Coast Japanese Americans, 1942–1964: A Quantitative Note." In Roger Daniels, Sandra C. Taylor, and Harry H. L. Kitano, eds., *Japanese Americans: From Relocation to Redress,* rev. ed., 72–74. Seattle, Wash.: University of Washington Press, 1991a.

———. "Redress Achieved, 1983–1990." In Roger Daniels, Sandra C. Taylor, and Harry H. L. Kitano, eds., *Japanese Americans: From Relocation to Redress,* rev. ed., 219–223. Seattle, Wash.: University of Washington Press, 1991b.

Daniels, Roger, Sandra C. Taylor, and Harry H. L. Kitano, eds. *Japanese Americans: From Relocation to Redress,* rev. ed., Seattle, Wash.: University of Washington Press, 1991.

Davie, Maurice R. *Negroes in American Society.* New York: McGraw-Hill, 1949.

Davis, Sally M., Ken Hunt, and Judith M. Kitzes. "Improving the Health of Indian Teenagers—A Demonstration Program in Rural New Mexico." *Public Health Reports* 104 (May-June 1989): 271–278.

Day, Robert C. "The Emergence of Activism as a Social Movement." In Howard M. Bahr, Bruce A. Chadwick, and Robert C. Day, eds., *Native Americans Today*, 506–532. New York: Harper & Row, 1972.

De Witt, Karen. "Scores on SAT Edge UP," New York Times News Service. *Austin American-Statesman* (August 27, 1992): A1, A11.

Deaux, Kay, Anne Reid, Kim Mizrahi, and Kathleen A. Ethier. "Parameters of Social Identity." *Journal of Personality and Social Psychology* 68 (February 1995): 280–290.

DeFleur, Melvin L., and Frank B. Westie. "Verbal Attitudes and Overt Acts." *American Sociological Review* 23 (December 1958): 667–673.

Degler, Carl N. "Slavery and the Genesis of American Race Prejudice." In Donald L. Noel, ed., *The Origins of American Slavery and Racism*, 61–80. Columbus, Ohio: Charles E. Merrill, 1972.

del Castillo, Richard Griswold. *The Treaty of Guadalupe Hidalgo: A Legacy of Conflict*. Norman, Okla.: University of Oklahoma Press, 1990.

de lo Earza, Rodolpho O., Frank D .Bean, Charles M. Bonjean, Ricardo Romo, and Rodolfo Alvarez, eds. *The Mexican American Experience*. Austin, Tex.: University of Texas Press, 1985.

Deloria, Vine, Jr. *Custer Died for Your Sins*. New York: Avon Books, 1969.

———. "This Country Was a Lot Better Off When the Indians Were Running It." In Howard M. Bahr, Bruce A. Chadwick, and Robert C. Day, eds., *Native Americans Today*, 498–506. New York: Harper & Row, 1972.

———. "Native Americans: The Indian American Today." *The Annals: America as a Multicultural Society* 454 (March 1981): 139–149.

———, ed. *American Indian Policy in the Twentieth Century*. Norman, Okla.: University of Oklahoma Press, 1985a.

———. "The Evolution of Federal Indian Policy Making." In Vine Deloria, Jr., ed., *American Indian Policy in the Twentieth Century*, 239–256. Norman, Okla.: University of Oklahoma Press, 1985b.

Dennis, Henry C. *The American Indian 1492–1976*. Dobbs Ferry, N.Y.: Oceana Publications, 1977.

Dent, David J. "The New Black Suburbs." *The New York Times Magazine* (June 14, 1992): 18–25.

Dentler, Robert A. "The Political Situation and Power Prospects of African Americans in Gunnar Myrdal's Era and Today." In Obie Clayton, Jr., ed., *An American Dilemma Revisited: Race Relations in a Changing World*. New York: Russell Sage Foundation, 1996.

Denton, Nancy A., and Douglas S. Massey. "Residential Segregation of Blacks, Hispanics, and Asians by Socioeconomic Status and Generation." *Social Science Quarterly* 69 (December 1988): 797–817.

Desbartes, Jacqueline. "Ethnic Differences in Adaptation: Sino-Vietnamese Refugees in the United States." *International Migration Review* 20 (Summer 1986): 405–427.

Diner, Hasia. "Erin's Children in America: Three Centuries of Irish Immigration in the United States." In Silvia Pedraza and Rubén G. Rumbaut, eds., *Origins and Destinies: Immigration, Race, and Ethnicity in America*, 161–171. Belmont, Calif.: Wadsworth Publishing Company, 1996.

Dinnerstein, Leonard, and Frederic Cople Jaher, eds. *The Aliens*. New York: Appleton-Century-Crofts, 1970.,

Dinnerstein, Leonard, and David M. Reimers, eds. *Ethnic Americans*. New York: Dodd, Mead, 1975.

Dobzhansky, Theodosius. *Mankind Evolving*. New Haven, Conn.: Yale University Press, 1962.

Dollard, John. *Caste and Class in a Southern Town*, 3rd ed. Garden City, N.Y.: Doubleday, 1957.

Dollard, John, Leonard Doob, Neal Miller, O. H. Mowrer, and R. R. Sears. *Frustration and Aggression*. New Haven, Conn.: Yale University Press, 1939.

Dovidio, John F., and Samuel L. Gaertner. "Stereotypes and Evaluative Intergroup Bias." In Diane M. Mackie and David L. Hamilton, eds., *Affect, Cognition, and Stereotyping,* 167–193. San Diego, Calif.: Academic Press, Inc., 1993.

Doyle, Bertram W. *The Etiquette of Race Relations in the South.* Chicago: University of Chicago Press, 1937.

Drury, D. W. "Black Self-Esteem and Desegregated Schools." *Sociology of Education* 53 (April 1980): 88–103.

Du Bois, William E. B. *The Souls of Black Folk* [1903]. Reprinted in *Three Negro Classics.* New York: Avon Books, 1965.

Ducas, George, ed. with Charles Van Doren. *Great Documents in Black American History.* New York: Praeger, 1970.

Dunn, L. C., and Theodosius Dobzhansky. *Heredity, Race and Society.* New York: The New American Library, 1964.

Dunne, John Gregory. *Delano.* New York: Farrar, Straus & Giroux, 1967.

Easterbrook, Gregg. "Blacktop Basketball and *The Bell Curve.* In Russell Jacoby and Naomi Glauberman, eds., *The Bell Curve Debate,* 30–43. New York: Times Books, 1995.

Easterlin, Richard A. "Immigration: Social Characteristics." In Stephan Thernstrom, Ann Orlov, and Oscar Handlin, eds., *Harvard Encyclopedia of American Ethnic Groups,* 476–486. Cambridge, Mass.: The Belknap Press, 1980.

Eckberg, Douglas Lee. *Intelligence and Race.* New York: Praeger, 1979.

Edwards, R. C., Michael Reich, and David M. Gordon. eds. *Labor Market Segmentation.* Lexington, Mass.: D. C. Heath, 1975.

Egan, Timothy. "Expelled in 1877, Indian Tribe Is Now Wanted as a Resource." *New York Times* (July 22, 1996): 1, A9.

Eggebeen, David J., and Daniel T. Lichter. "Race, Family Structure, and Changing Poverty Among American Children." *American Sociological Review* 56 (December 1991): 801–817.

Eichenwald, Kurt. "Texaco Executives, On Tape, Discussed Impending Bias Suit." *New York Times* (November 4, 1996): A1.

Ehrlich, Howard J. *The Social Psychology of Prejudice.* New York: Wiley, 1973.

Ehrlich, Howard J., and James W. Rinehart. "A Brief Report on the Methodology of Stereotype Research." *Social Forces* 44 (December 1965): 171–176.

Ehrlich, Paul R., and S. Shirley Feldman. *The Race Bomb.* New York: Ballantine Books, 1977.

Elkins, Stanley M. *Slavery,* 2nd ed. Chicago: University of Chicago Press, 1968.

Ellis, David. "L.A. Lawless." *Time* (May 11, 1992): 26–29.

Ellison, Christopher G., and Daniel A. Powers. "The Contact Hypothesis and Racial Attitudes among Black Americans." *Social Science Quarterly* 75 (June 1994): 385–400.

Elson, R. M. *Guardians of Tradition.* Lincoln, Nebr.: University of Nebraska Press, 1964.

Embree, Edwin R. *Indians of the Americas.* New York: Collier Books, 1970.

Eschbach, Karl. "The Enduring and Vanishing American Indian: American Indian Population Growth and Intermarriage in 1990." *Ethnic and Racial Studies* (January 1995): 89–107.

Falcoff, Mark. "Our Language Needs No Law." *New York Times* (August 5, 1996): A11.

Farley, Reynolds. "Racial Integration in the Schools: Assessing the Effect of Governmental Policies." *Sociological Focus* 9 (January 1975): 3–26.

———. "Three Steps Forward and Two Back? Recent Changes in the Social and Economic Status of Blacks." In Richard D. Alba, ed., *Ethnicity and Race in the U.S.A.,* 4–28. New York: Routledge, 1988.

———. The New American Reality: *Who We Are, How We Got Here, Where We Are Going.* New York: Russell Sage Foundation, 1996.

Farley, Reynolds, and Walter R. Allen. *The Color Line and the Quality of Life in America.* New York: Russell Sage Foundation, 1987.

Farley, Reynolds, and William H. Frey. "Changes in the Segregation of Whites from Blacks During the 1980s: Small Steps Toward a More Integrated Society." *American Sociological Review* 59 (February 1994): 23–45.

Farmer, James. *Freedom—When?* New York: Random House, 1965, 60–62. Reprinted in August Meier, Elliott Rudwick, and Francis L. Broderick, eds., *Black Protest Thought in the Twentieth Century,* 2nd ed., 183–202. Indianapolis, Ind. and New York: Bobbs-Merrill, 1971.

Faulkner, Harold Underwood. *American Political and Social History,* 5th ed. New York: Appleton-Century-Crofts, 1948.

Feagin, Joe R. "Indirect Institutionalized Discrimination." *American Politics Quarterly* 5 (April 1977): 177–200.

Feagin, Joe R., and Nancy Fujitaki. "On the Assimilation of the Japanese Americans." *Amerasia Journal* 1 (February 1972): 13–30.

Feagin, Joe R., and Harlan Hahn. *Ghetto Revolts.* New York: Macmillan, 1973.

Feagin, Joe R., and Melvin P. Sikes. *Living with Racism: The Black Middle-Class Experience.* Boston: Beacon Press, 1994.

Featherman, David L. and Robert M. Hauser. *Opportunity and Change.* New York: Academic Press, 1978.

Feldstein, Stanley, and Lawrence Costello, eds. *The Ordeal of Assimilation.* Garden City, N.Y.: Anchor Press/Doubleday, 1974.

Ferguson, Ron F. "Shifting Challenges: Fifty Years of Economic Change Toward Black-White Earnings Equality." In Obie Clayton, Jr., ed., *An American Dilemma Revisited: Race Relations in a Changing World,* 76–111. New York: Russell Sage Foundation, 1996.

Fifield, Russell H., and Carlos P. Romulo. "Philippines." *The World Book Encyclopedia,* vol 14, 332–344. Chicago: Field Enterprises Educational Corp., 1962.

Finsterbusch, Kurt, and George McKenna, eds. *Taking Sides: Clashing Views on Controversial Social Issues,* 4th ed. Guilford, Conn.: The Dushkin Publishing Group, 1986.

Firebaugh, Glenn, and Kenneth E. Davis. "Trends in Antiblack Prejudice, 1972–1984: Region and Cohort Effects." *American Journal of Sociology* 94 (September 1988): 251–272.

Fishman, Joshua. "Bilingual Education: What and Why?" In Margaret A. Lourie and Nancy Faires Conklin, eds., *A Pluralistic Nation: The Language Issue in the United States,* 407–416. Rowley, Mass.: Newbury House Publishers, Inc., 1978.

Fix, Michael, and Jeffrey S. Passel. "Immigration and Immigrants: Setting the Record Straight." Washington, D.C.: The Urban Institute, May 1994.

Fligstein, Neil, and Roberto Fernandez. "Educational Transitions of Whites and Mexican-Americans." In George J. Borjas and Marta Tienda, eds., *Hispanics in the U.S. Economy,* 161–192. Orlando, Fla.: Academic Press, 1985.

Flynn, James R. "Massive IQ Gains in 14 Nations: What IQ Tests Really Measure." *Psychological Bulletin* 101 (March 1987): 171–191.

Fogel, Robert W. *Without Consent or Contract.* New York: W. W. Norton and Company, 1989.

Fogel, Robert William, and Stanley L. Engerman. *Time on the Cross: The Economics of American Negro Slavery.* Boston: Little, Brown, 1974.

Footnotes. "ABS Statement Assails Book by Wilson." (December 1978): 4.

Forbes, Jack D. *Aztecas Del Norte.* Greenwich, Conn.: Fawcett, 1973.

Fossett, Mark A., Omer R. Galle, and Jeffrey A. Burr. "Racial Occupational Inequality, 1940–1980: A Research Note on the Impact of the Changing Regional Distribution of the Black Population." *Social Forces* 48 (December 1989): 415–427.

Fossett, Mark A., Omer R. Galle, and William R. Kelly. "Racial Occupational Inequality, 1940–1980: National and Regional Trends." *American Sociological Review* 51 (June 1986): 421–429.

Fost, Dan. "American Indians in the 1990s." In John A. Kromkowski, ed., *Annual Editions:Race and Ethnic Relations 96/97,* 101–105. Guilford, Conn.: Dushkin Publishing Group, 1996.

Fox, Stephen. *The Unknown Internment: An Oral History of the Relocation of Italian Americans during World War II.* Boston: Twayne Publishers, 1990.

Francis, E. K. *Interethnic Relations.* New York: Elsevier, 1976.

Franklin, John Hope. *Reconstruction.* Chicago: University of Chicago Press, 1961.

Franklin, John Hope, and Alfred A. Moss, Jr. *From Slavery to Freedom,* 6th ed. New York: Alfred A. Knopf, 1988.

Frazier, E. Franklin. *The Negro Family in the United States.* Chicago: University of Chicago Press, 1939.

———. *The Negro in the United States,* rev. ed. New York: Macmillan, 1957.

Fredrickson, George M. "Toward a Social Interpretation of the Development of American Racism." In Nathan I. Huggins, Martin Kilson, and Daniel M. Fox, eds., *Key Issues in the Afro-American Experience,* 240–254. New York: Harcourt Brace Jovanovich 1971.

Frethorne, Richard. "The Experiences of an Indentured Servant, 1623." In Frederick M. Binder and David M. Reimers, eds., *The Way We Lived,* 35–37. Lexington, Mass.: D. C. Heath, 1988.

Fuchs, Lawrence H. "Reactions of Black Americans to Immigration." In Virginia Yans-McLaughlin, ed., *Immigration Reconsidered: History, Sociology, and Politics,* 293–314. New York: Oxford University Press, 1990.

Fugita, Stephen S., and David J. O'Brien. "Structural Assimilation, Ethnic Group Membership, and Political Participation Among Japanese Americans: A Research Note." *Social Forces* 63 (June 1985): 986–995.

Fujimoto, Isao. "The Failure of Democracy in a Time of Crisis." In Amy Tachiki, Eddie Wong, Franklin Odo, and Buck Wong, eds., *Roots: An Asian American Reader,* 207–214. Los Angeles: The Regents of the University of California, 1971.

Funderburg, Lise. "Boxed In." *New York Times* (July 10, 1996): A15.

Furstenberg, Frank, J., Jr., T. Hershberg, and John Modell. "The Origins of the Female-Headed Black Family: The Impact of the Urban Experience." *Journal of Interdisciplinary History* 6 (Autumn 1985): 211–233.

Galton, Francis. *Hereditary Genius.* London: Macmillan, 1869.

Gans, Herbert J. "Symbolic Ethnicity: The Future of Ethnic Groups and Cultures in America." In Norman R. Yetman, ed., *Majority and Minority,* 4th ed., 429–442. Boston: Allyn and Bacon, 1985.

———. "Deconstructing the Underclass: The Term's Danger as a Planning Concept." *Journal of the American Planning Association* 56 (Summer, 1990): 271–277.

Garcia, John A. "Yo Soy Mexicano . . . : Self-Identity and Sociodemographic Correlates." *Social Science Quarterly* 62 (March 1981): 88–98.

Garcia, Mario T. *Mexican Americans.* New Haven, Conn. and London: Yale University Press, 1989.

Gardner, Howard. "Scholarly Brinkmanship." In Russell Jacoby and Naomi Glauberman, eds., *The Bell Curve Debate,* 61–72. New York: Times Books, (1897) 1995.

Garrett, Henry E. "Comparison of Negro and White Recruits on the Army Tests Given in 1917–1918." *American Journal of Psychology* 58 (October 1945): 480–495.

Garvey, Amy Jacques. *Garvey & Garveyism.* London: Collier-Macmillan Ltd., 1970.

Garvey, Marcus. "An Appeal to the Conscience of the Black Race." In Gilbert Osofsky, ed., *The Burden of Race,* 290–295. New York: Harper & Row, 1968a.

———. "Declaration of Rights of the Negro Peoples of the World." In Gilbert Osofsky, ed., *The Burden of Race,* 296–302. New York: Harper & Row, 1968b.

Gee, Emma. "Issei Women: 'Picture Brides' in America." In Maxine Schwartz Seller, ed., *Immigrant Women,* rev., 2nd ed., 53–59. Albany, N.Y.: State University of New York Press, 1994.

Genovese, Eugene D. *Roll, Jordan, Roll.* New York: Pantheon Books, 1974.

Gerard, Harold B., Terrance D. Jackson, and Edward S. Conolley. "Social Contact in the Desegregated Classroom." In Harold B. Gerard and Norman Miller, eds., *School Desegregation: A Long-Term Study,* 211–214. New York: Plenum Press, 1975.

Gerard, Harold B., and Norman Miller. *School Desegregation: A Long-Term Study.* New York: Plenum Press, 1975.

Geschwender, James A. "Explorations in the Theory of Social Movements and Revolutions." *Social Forces* 47 (December 1968):127–135. Reprinted in James A. Geschwender, ed., *The Black Revolt.* Englewood Cliffs, N.J.: Prentice-Hall, 1971.

Geschwender, James A., Rita Carroll-Seguin, and Howard Brill. "The Portuguese and Haoles of Hawaii: Implications for the Origin of Ethnicity." *American Sociological Review* 53 (August 1988): 515–527.

Gibbs, Jack P. *Control: Sociology's Central Notion.* Urbana, Ill. and Chicago: University of Illinois Press, 1989.

Gilbert, G. M. "Stereotype Persistence and Change among College Students." *Journal of Abnormal and Social Psychology* 46 (April 1951): 245–254.

Gilbertson, Greta A., and Douglas T. Gurak. "Broadening the Enclave Debate, The Labor Market Experiences of Dominican and Colombian Men in New York City." *Sociological Focus* 8 (No. 2 1993): 205–220.

Glazer, Nathan. "America's Race Paradox." In Peter I. Rose, ed., *Nation of Nations,* 165–180. New York: Random House, 1972.

———. *Affirmative Discrimination,* 1st and 2nd eds. Cambridge, Mass.: Harvard University Press, 1975 and 1987.

———. ed. *Clamor at the Gates.* San Francisco: Institute for Contemporary Studies, 1985.

Glazer, Nathan, and Daniel Patrick Moynihan. *Beyond the Melting Pot,* 1st and 2nd eds. Cambridge, Mass.: MIT Press, 1964 and 1970.

Glenn, Evelyn Nakano, and Rhacel Salazar Parreñas. "The Other Issei: Japanese Immigrant Women in the Pre-World War II Period." In Silvia Pedraza and Rubén G. Rumbaut, eds., *Origins and Destinies: Immigration, Race, and Ethnicity in America,* 125–140. Belmont, Calif.: Wadsworth Publishing Company, 1996.

Glenn, Norval D. "White Gains from Negro Subordination." *Social Problems* 14 (Fall 1966): 159–178.

Glickstein, Howard A. "Discrimination in Higher Education." In Barry R. Gross, ed., *Reverse Discrimination,* 14–18. Buffalo, N.Y.: Prometheus Books, 1977.

Goff, Regina. "Educating Black Americans." In Mabel M. Smythe, ed., *The Black American Reference Book,* 410–452. Englewood Cliffs, N. J.: Prentice-Hall, 1976.

Gold, Steven J., and Bruce Phillips. "Mobility and Continuity among Eastern European Jews." In Silvia Pedraza and Rubén G. Rumbaut, eds., *Origins and Destinies: Immigration, Race, and Ethnicity in America,* 182–194. Belmont, Calif.: Wadsworth Publishing Company, 1996.

Goleman, Daniel. "Probing School Success of Asian-Americans." *New York Times* (September 11, 1990): B5.

Gómez-Quiñones, Juan. "The First Steps: Chicano Labor Conflict and Organizing, 1900–20." In Manuel P. Servín, ed., *An Awakening Minority: The Mexican Americans,* 2nd ed., 79–113. Beverly Hills, Calif.: Glencoe Press, 1974.

Gordon, Milton M. *Assimilation in American Life.* New York: Oxford University Press, 1964.

———. *Human Nature, Class, and Ethnicity.* New York: Oxford University Press, 1978.

Gossett, Thomas F. *Race: The History of an Idea in America.* Dallas, Tex.: Southern Methodist University Press, 1963.

Gould, C. W. *America, A Family Matter.* New York: Scribner's, 1922.

Gould, Stephen Jay. *The Mismeasure of Man.* New York: W. W. Norton & Company, 1981.

———. "Curveball," *The New Yorker* (November 28, 1994): 139–149.

Graham, Hugh Davis. "The Origins of Affirmative Action: Civil Rights and the Regulatory State." In Harold Orlans and June O'Neill, eds., *Affirmative Action Revisited, The Annals* (September 1992): 50–62.

Graham, W. A. *The Custer Myth.* Harrisburg, Pa.: The Stackpole Company, 1953.

Gramm, Phil. "Who's a Nincompoop on Illegal Immigration?" *New York Times* (July 15, 1996): A10.

Graves, Debbie. "Judge: UT must fight admission lawsuit." *Austin American-Statesman* (October 22, 1993): B1.

Grebler, Leo, Joan W. Moore, and Ralph C. Guzman. *The Mexican-American People.* New York: The Free Press, 1970.

Greeley, Andrew M. *Why Can't They Be Like Us?* New York: E. P. Dutton, 1971.

———. *That Most Distressful Nation: The Taming of the Irish Americans.* Chicago: Quadrangle Books, 1975.

———. "The Ethnic Miracle." In Norman R. Yetman, ed., *Majority and Minority,* 4th ed., 268–277. Boston: Allyn and Bacon, 1985.

Green, James A. "Attitudinal and Situational Determinants of Intended Behavior Toward Blacks." *Journal of Personality and Social Psychology* 22 (April 1972): 13–17.

Greenhouse, Linda. "Supreme Court Civil Rights Rulings Follow Reagan's Conservative Line." *Austin American-Statesman* (June 11, 1989): D6.

———. "Detours on the Road to Legal Precedents." *New York Times* (February 12, 1995):3.

———. "In Supreme Court's Decisions, A Clear Voice, and a Murmur." *New York Times* (July 3, 1996): A1.

Grenier, Gilles. "Shifts to English as Usual Language by Americans of Spanish Mother Tongue." In Rodolfo O. de la Garza, Frank D. Bean, Charles M. Bonjean, Ricardo Romo, and Rodolfo Alvarez, eds., *The Mexican American Experience,* 346–358. Austin, Tex.: University of Texas Press, 1985.

Gross, Andrew B., and Douglas S. Massey. "Spatial Assimilation Models: A Micro-Macro Comparison." *Social Science Quarterly* 72 (June 1991): 347–360.

Gundlach, James H., and Ruth C. Busch. "Reservation Residence and the Survival of Native American Languages." *Current Anthropology* (February 1981): 96–97.

Gurak, Douglas T., and Mary M. Kritz. "Intermarriage Patterns in the U.S.: Maximizing Information from the U.S. Census Public Use Samples." *Public Data Use* (March 1978): 33–43.

Gutiérrez, David G. *Walls and Mirrors: Mexican Americans, Mexican Immigrants, and the Politics of Ethnicity.* Berkeley and Los Angeles: University of California Press, 1995.

———. *Between Two Worlds: Mexican Immigrants in the United States,* xviii. Wilmington, Del.: Scholarly Resources Inc., 1996.

Gutiérrez, Armando, and Herbert Hirsch. "The Militant Challenge to the American Ethos: 'Chicanos' and 'Mexican Americans.'" *Social Science Quarterly* 53 (March 1973): 830–845.

Gutman, Herbert G. *The Black Family in Slavery and Freedom, 1750–1925.* New York: Pantheon Books, 1976.

Hachen, David S. "Industrial Characteristics and Job Mobility Rates." *American Sociological Review* 57 (February 1992): 39–55.

Hacker, Andrew. *Two Nations.* New York: Charles Scribner's Sons, 1992.

———. "Goodbye to Affirmative Action?" *New York Review of Books.* (July 11, 1996): 21–29.

Hagan, William T. *American Indians.* Chicago: The University of Chicago Press, 1971.

Haines, David W. "Kinship in Vietnamese Refugee Resettlement: A Review of the U.S. Experience." *Journal of Comparative Family Studies* 19 (Spring 1988): 1–16.

Hakuta, Kenji. *Mirror of Language: The Debate on Bilingualism.* New York: Basic Books, Inc. 1986.

Hallinan, Maureen T., and Richard A. Williams. "The Stability of Students' Interracial Friendships." *American Sociological Review* 52 (October 1987): 653–664.

———. "Interracial Friendship Choices in Secondary Schools." *American Sociological Review* 54 (February 1989): 67–78.

Hamilton, Alexander, James Madison, and John Jay. *The Federalist Papers.* New York: New American Library, 1961.

Hamilton, David L., and Tina K. Trolier. "Stereotypes and Stereotyping: An Overview of the Cognitive Approach." In John F. Dovidio and Samuel L. Gaertner, eds., *Prejudice, Discrimination, and Racism.* Orlando, Fla.: Academic Press, Inc., 1986.

Handlin, Oscar. *Race and Nationality in American Life.* Garden City, N.Y.: Doubleday, 1957.

Hansen, Marcus Lee. *The Problem of the Third Generation Immigrant.* Rock Island, Ill.: Augustana Historical Society, 1938.

———. *The Atlantic Migration 1607–1860.* Cambridge, Mass.: Harvard University Press 1945.

Harrison, Roderick J., and Daniel H. Weinberg. "Changes in Racial and Ethnic Residential Segregation, 1980–1990." U.S. Bureau of the Census, Racial Statistics Branch, Population Division, 1992 (mimeographed).

Hatchett, Shirley J., Donna L. Cochran, and James S. Jackson. "Family Life." In James S. Jackson, ed., *Life in Black America,* 46–83. Newbury Park, Calif.: Sage Publications, 1991.

Hauser, Robert M. "The Bell Curve." *Contemporary Sociology* 24 (March 1995): 149–153.

Hawley, Willis D., and Mark A. Smylie. "The Contribution of School Desegregation to Academic Achievement and Racial Integration." In Phyllis A. Katz and Dalmas A. Taylor, eds., *Eliminating Racism,* 281–297. New York: Plenum Press, 1988.

Hazuda, Helen P., Michael P. Stern, and Steven M. Haffner. "Acculturation and Assimilation Among Mexican Americans: Scales and Population-Based Data." *Social Science Quarterly* 69 (September 1988): 687–706.

Headden, Susan. "One Nation, One Language?" *U.S. News and World Report* (September 25, 1995): 38–42.

Heer, David M. "Negro-White Marriage in the United States." *Journal of Marriage and the Family* 28 (August 1966): 262–273.

———. "Intermarriage." In Stephan Thernstrom, Ann Orlov, and Oscar Handlin, eds., *Harvard Encyclopedia of American Ethnic Groups,* 513–521. Cambridge, Mass.: The Belknap Press, 1980.

Heise, Michael. "Assessing the Efficacy of School Desegregation." *Syracuse Law Review* 46 (1996): 1093–1117.

Heiss, Jerold, and Susan Owens. "Self-evaluation of Blacks and Whites." *American Journal of Sociology* 78 (September 1972): 360–370.

Henwood, Karen, Howard Giles, Justine Coupland, and Nikolas Coupland. "Stereotyping and Affect in Discourse: Interpreting the Meaning of Elderly, Painful Self-Disclosure." In Diane M. Mackie and David L. Hamilton, eds., *Affect, Cognition, and Stereotyping,* 269–296. San Diego, Calif.: Academic Press, Inc., 1993.

Herberg, Will. *Protestant-Catholic-Jew.* Garden City, N.Y.: Doubleday, 1960.

Herrnstein, Richard J. "IQ." *Atlantic Monthly* 228 (September 1971): 43–64.

Herrnstein, Richard J., and Charles Murray. *The Bell Curve: Intelligence and Class Structure in American Life.* New York: The Free Press, 1994.

Herskovits, Melville J. *The American Negro: A Study in Racial Crossing.* New York: Alfred A. Knopf, 1928.

———. *The Myth of the Negro Past.* Boston: Beacon Press, 1958.

Hertzberg, Hazel W. *The Search for an American Indian Identity.* Syracuse, N. Y.: Syracuse University Press, 1971.

Hewstone, Miles. "Contact is not Enough: An Intergroup Perspective on the 'Contact Hypothesis.'" In Miles Hewstone and Rupert Brown, eds., *Contact and Conflict in Intergroup Encounters,* 1–44. Oxford: Basil Blackwell Ltd., 1986.

———. "Intergroup Attribution: Some Implications for the Study of Ethnic Prejudice." In Jan Pieter van Oudenhoven and Tineke M. Willemsen, eds., *Ethnic Minorities,* 25–42. Amsterdam: Swets & Zeitlinger B.V., 1989.

Hewstone, Miles and Rupert Brown. *Contact and Conflict in Intergroup Encounters.* Oxford: Basil Blackwell Ltd., 1986.

Higham, John. *Strangers in the Land: Patterns of American Nativism 1860–1925.* New York: Atheneum, 1963.

Hill, Robert B. *The Strengths of Black Families.* New York: Emerson Hall Publishers, 1971.

Hing, Bill Ong. *Making and Remaking Asian America Through Immigration Policy, 1850–1990.* Stanford, Calif.: Stanford University Press, 1993.

Hirschman, Charles. "America's Melting Pot Reconsidered." In Ralph Turner and James F. Short, Jr., eds., *Annual Review of Sociology,* 397–423. Palo Alto, Calif.: Annual Reviews Inc., 1983.

Hirschman, Charles, and Morrison G. Wong. "Socioeconomic Gains of Asian Americans, Blacks, and Hispanics: 1960–1976." *American Journal of Sociology* 90 (November 1984): 584–607.

———. "Trends in Socioeconomic Achievement among Immigrant and Native-Born Asian-Americans, 1960–1976." In Norman R. Yetman, ed., *Majority and Minority,* 4th ed., 290–304. Boston: Allyn and Bacon, 1985.

———. "The Extraordinary Educational Attainment of Asian-Americans: A Search for Historical Evidence and Explanations." *Social Forces* 65 (September 1986): 1–27.

Hochschild, Jennifer L. *Facing Up to the American Dream: Race, Class, and the Soul of the Nation.* Princeton, N. J.: Princeton University Press, 1995.

Hoffman, Abraham. *Unwanted Mexican Americans in the Great Depression: Repatriation Pressures 1929–1939.* Tucson, Ariz.: University of Arizona Press, 1974.

Holm, Tom. "The Crisis in Tribal Government." In Vine Deloria, Jr., ed., *American Indian Policy in the Twentieth Century,* 135–154. Norman, Okla.: University of Oklahoma Press, 1985.

Holmes, Steven. "A Matter of Perspective in a Lending-Bias Suit," *New York Times* (October 11, 1995): C1.

Holt, Jim. "Skin-Deep Science." In Russell Jacoby and Naomi Glauberman, eds., *The Bell Curve Debate,* 57–60. New York: Times Books, 1995.

Honan, William H. "Admissions Change Will Alter Elite Campuses, Experts Say," *New York Times* (July 22, 1995): Y9.

Hondagneu-Sotelo, Pierrette. *Gendered Transitions: Mexican Experiences of Immigration.* Berkeley and Los Angeles, Calif.: University of California Press, 1994.

Hook, Sidney. "The Bias in Anti-Bias Regulations." In Barry R. Gross, ed., *Reverse Discrimination,* 88–96. Buffalo, N.Y.: Prometheus Books, 1977.

Horn, Miriam, "The Return to Ellis Island." *U.S. News & World Report* (November 21, 1988): 63.

Horowitz, Donald L. *Ethnic Groups in Conflict.* Berkeley, Calif.: University of California Press, 1985.

Horton, John. "Order and Conflict Theories of Social Problems as Competing Ideologies." *American Journal of Sociology* 71 (May 1966): 701–713.

Hosokawa, Bill. *Nisei: The Quiet Americans.* New York: William Morrow, 1969.

Houston, Jeanne Wakatsuki. "Shikata Ga Nai—This Cannot Be Helped." In Maxine Schwartz Seller, ed., *Immigrant Women,* rev., 2nd ed., 167–171. Albany, N. Y.: State University of New York Press, 1994.

Howery, Carla B. "Update on Human Rights Cases." *Footnotes,* American Sociological Association (November 1986): 9.

Hoxie, Frederick E. *A Final Promise: The Campaign to Assimilate the Indians, 1880–1920.* Lincoln, Nebr.: University of Nebraska Press, 1984.

Huddle, Donald. *The Costs of Immigration.* Carrying Capacity Network. Revised July, 1993.

Hurh, Won Moo, and Kwang Chung Kim. "The 'Success' Image of Asian Americans: Its Validity and Its Practical and Theoretical Implications." *Ethnic and Racial Studies* 12 (October 1989): 512–536.

Hughes, Michael, and David Demo. "Self Perceptions of Black Americans: Self-Esteem and Personal Efficacy." *American Journal of Sociology* 95 (July 1989): 132–159.

Hutchison, Kay Bailey. "Who's a Nincompoop on Illegal Education?" *New York Times* (July 15, 1996): A10.

Hwang, Sean-Shong, Steven H. Murdock, Banoo Parpia, and Rita R. Hamm. "The Effects of Race and Socioeconomic Status on Residential Segregation in Texas, 1970–80." *Social Forces* 63 (March 1985): 732–747.

Hyman, Herbert H., and Paul B. Sheatsley. "Attitudes Toward Desegregation." *Scientific American* (July 1964): 16–23.

Ichihashi, Yamato. *Japanese in the United States.* Palo Alto, Calif.: Stanford University Press, 1932.

Ichioka, Yuji. "Nisei: The Quiet Americans." In Amy Tachiki, Eddie Wong, Franklin Odo, and Buck Wong, eds., *Roots: An Asian American Reader,* 221–222. Los Angeles: Regents of the University of California, 1971.

Ikeda, Kiyoshi. "A Different 'Dilemma,'" *Social Forces* 51 (June 1973): 497–499.

Indians of All Tribes. "We Must Hold on to the Old Ways." In Alvin M. Josephy, Jr., ed., *Red Power,* 197–201. New York: American Heritage Press, 1971.

Institute for Social Research. "Cross-Racial Contact Increases in Seventies: Attitude Gap Narrows for Blacks and Whites." *ISR Newsletter* (Autumn 1975): 4–7.

Institute for the Study of Social Change. *The Diversity Project: Final Report.* Berkeley, Calif.: University of California, November 1991.

Iwata, Masakazu. "The Japanese Immigrants in California Agriculture." *Agricultural History* 36 (January 1962): 25–37.

Jackman, Mary R., and Marie Crane. "'Some of My Best Friends Are Black. . . : ' Interracial Friendship and Whites' Racial Attitudes." *Public Opinion Quarterly* 50 (Winter 1986): 459–486.

Jackson, Curtis E., and Marcia J. Galli. *A History of the Bureau of Indian Affairs and Its Activities Among Indians.* San Francisco: R & E Research Associates, Inc., 1977.

Jackson, James S. ed., *Life in Black America.* Newbury Park, Calif.: Sage Publications, 1991.

Jacobs, Paul, and Saul Landau, eds., *To Serve the Devil,* vol. 1. New York: Vintage Books, 1971.

Jacobson, Cardell K. "Internal Colonialism and Native Americans: Indian Labor in the United States from 1871 to World War II." *Social Science Quarterly* 65 (March 1984): 158–171.

Jacoby, Russell, and Naomi Glauberman, eds., *The Bell Curve Debate.* New York: Times Books, 1995.

James, Lenada. "Activism and Red Power" (comment). In Kenneth R. Philp, ed., *Indian Self-Rule,* 229–231. Salt Lake City, Utah: Howe Brothers, 1986.

Jaynes, Gerald David, and Robin M. Williams, Jr., eds., *A Common Destiny.* Washington, D.C.: National Academy Press, 1989.

Jensen, Arthur R. "How Much Can We Boost IQ and Scholastic Achievement?" *Harvard Educational Review* 39 (Winter 1969): 1–123.

———. "Race and the Genetics of Intelligence: A Reply to Lewontin." In N. J. Block and Gerald Dworkin, eds., *The IQ Controversy,* 93–106. New York: Pantheon Books, 1976.

Jensen, Joan M. "East Asians." In Stephan Thernstrom, Ann Orlov, and Oscar Handlin, eds., *Harvard Encylopedia of American Ethnic Groups,* 296–301. Cambridge, Mass.: The Belknap Press, 1980.

Jiobu, Robert M. *Ethnicity and Assimilation.* Albany, N.Y.: State University of New York Press, 1988a.

———. "Ethnic Hegemony and the Japanese of California." *American Sociological Review* 53 (June 1988b): 353–367.

Johnson, Dirk. "Mob Violence Continues in Las Vegas." *New York Times* (May 19, 1992): A10.

———. "Economies Come to Life on Indian Reservations." *New York Times* (July 3, 1994): 1,10,11.

———. "A Migration Created by Burden of Suspicion." *New York Times* (August 14, 1995): A6.

Johnson, George. "Indians Take On the U.S. in a 90's Battle for Control." *New York Times* (February 11, 1996): E6.

———. "Indian Casino in New Mexico Is Forced to Close." *New York Times* (September, 26, 1996): A12.

Johnson, James Weldon. "Description of a Race Riot in Chicago." In Gilbert Osofsky, ed., *The Burden of Race,* 304–309. New York: Harper and Row, 1968.

Johnson, Kevin, and Andrea Stone. "High Court Loosens Desegregation's Grip." In John A. Kromkowski, ed., *Annual Editions: Race and Ethnic Relations 96/97,* 32–33. Guilford, Conn.: Dushkin Publishing Group, 1996.

Johnson, Kirk. "Rich, but Not in History, Connecticut Pequots Sponsor Cultural Powwow." *New York Times* (September 19, 1993): 16.

Jones, Maldwyn Allen. *American Immigration.* Chicago: The University of Chicago Press, 1960.

———. *Destination America.* New York: Holt, Rinehart and Winston, 1976.

———. "Scotch-Irish." In Stephan Thernstrom, Ann Orlov, and Oscar Handlin, eds., *Harvard Encyclopedia of American Ethnic Groups,* 895–908. Cambridge, Mass.: The Belknap Press, 1980.

Jordan, Terry G. "The 1887 Census of Texas' Hispanic Population." *Aztlan* 12, no. 2 (1981): 271–277.

Jordan, Winthrop D. "Modern Tensions and the Origins of African Slavery." In Donald I. Noel, ed., *The Origins of American Slavery and Racism,* 81–84. Columbus, Ohio: Charles E. Merrill, 1972.

Jordan, Winthrop D., and Leon F. Litwack. *The United States,* 6th ed., vol. 1. Englewood Cliffs, N.J.: Prentice-Hall, 1987.

Josephy, Alvin M., Jr. *The Patriot Chiefs.* New York: Viking Press, 1961.

———. *The Indian Heritage of America.* New York: Alfred A. Knopf, 1968.

Judson, George. "Not 'The Last' But an Official Tribe, Mohegan Indians Now Want Casino." *New York Times* (March 24, 1994): A12.

Jussim, Lee, Thomas E. Nelson, Melving Manis, and Sonia Soffin. "Prejudice, Stereotypes, and Labelling Effects: Sources of Bias in Person Perception." *Journal of Personality and Social Psychology* 68 (February 1995): 228–246.

Kamin, Leon. "Lies, Damned Lies, and Statistics." In Russell Jacoby and Naomi Glauberman, eds., *The Bell Curve Debate,* 81–105. New York: Times Books, 1995.

Kamphoefner, Walter D. "German Americans: Paradoxes of a 'Model Minority'." In Silvia Pedraza and Rubén G. Rumbaut, eds., *Origins and Destinies: Immigration, Race, and Ethnicity in America,* 152–160. Belmont, Calif.: Wadsworth Publishing Company, 1996.

Karlin, Jules Alexander. "The Anti-Chinese Outbreak in Tacoma, 1885." In Roger Daniels, ed., *Anti-Chinese Violence in North America,* 271–283. New York: Arno Press, 1978.

———. "The Anti-Chinese Outbreaks in Seattle, 1885–1886." In Roger Daniels, ed., *Anti-Chinese Violence in North America,*103–129. New York: Arno Press, 1978

Karlins, Marvin, Thomas L. Coffman, and Gary Walters. "On the Fading of Social Stereotypes: Studies in Three Generations of College Students." *Journal of Personality and Social Psychology* 13 (September 1969): 1–16.

Katz, Daniel, and Kenneth W. Braly. "Racial Stereotypes of One Hundred College Students." *Journal of Abnormal and Social Psychology* 28 (October-December 1933): 280–290.

Keefe, Susan E., and Amado M. Padilla. *Chicano Ethnicity*. Albuquerque, N. Mex.: University of New Mexico Press, 1987.

Keely, Charles. "Immigration Policy and the New Immigrants, 1965–1975." In Roy Simon Bryce-Laporte, ed., *Sourcebook on the New Immigration*, 15–25. New Brunswick, N.J.: Transaction Books, 1980.

———. "Population and Immigration Policy: State and Federal Roles." In Frank D. Bean, Jürgen Schmandt, and Sidney Weintraub, eds., *Mexican and Central American Population and U.S. Immigration Policy*, 161–178. Austin, Tex.: The Center for Mexican American Studies, 1989.

Kelly, Gail Paradise. *From Vietnam to America*. Boulder, Colo.: Westview Press, 1977.

Kennedy, Ruby Jo Reeves. "Single or Triple Melting-Pot? Intermarriage Trends in New Haven, 1870–1940." *American Journal of Sociology* 49 (January 1944): 331–339.

Kerr, Louise Año Nuevo. "Mexican Chicago: Chicano Assimilation Aborted, 1939–1952." In Melvin G. Holle and Peter d'A. Jones, eds., *The Ethnic Frontier: Group Survival in Chicago and the Midwest*, 293–330. Grand Rapids, Mich.: Eerdmans, 1977.

Kibbe, Pauline R. *Latin Americans in Texas*. Albuquerque, N. Mex.: University of New Mexico, 1946.

Kifner, John. "At Wounded Knee, Two Worlds Collide." In David R. Colburn and George E. Pozzetta, eds., *America and the New Ethnicity*, 79–90. Port Washington, N.Y.: Kennikat Press, 1979.

Kikumura, Akemi. "Once You Marry Someone It Is Forever." In Maxine Schwartz Seller ed., *Immigrant Women*, rev., 2nd ed., 149–154. Albany, N.Y.: State University of New York Press, 1994.

Kim, Hyung-chan. "Koreans." In Stephan Thernstrom, Ann Orlov, and Oscar Handlin, eds., *Harvard Encylopedia of American Ethnic Groups*, 601–606. Cambridge, Mass.: The Belknap Press, 1980.

Kim, Illsoo. "The Koreans: Small Business in an Urban Frontier." In Nancy Foner, ed., *New Immigrants in New York*, 219–242. New York: Columbia University Press, 1987.

King, James C. *The Biology of Race*. New York: Harcourt Brace Jovanovich, 1971.

King, Martin Luther, Jr. "The Case Against 'Tokenism.'" *The New York Times Magazine* (August 5, 1962): 11ff.

———. *Why We Can't Wait?* New York: New American Library, 1964.

———. "The Use of Nonviolence." In Gilbert Osofsky, ed., *The Burden of Race*, 522–526. New York: Harper & Row, 1968

———. "Our Struggle for an Interracial Society Based on Freedom for All." In August Meier, Elliott Rudwick, and Francis L. Broderick, eds., *Black Protest Thought in the Twentieth Century*, 2nd ed., 291–302. Indianapolis, Ind. and New York: Bobbs-Merrill, 1971a.

———. "We Still Believe in Black and White Together." In August Meier, Elliott Rudwick, and Francis L. Broderick, eds., *Black Protest Thought in the Twentieth Century*, 2nd ed., 584–595. Indianapolis, Ind. and New York: Bobbs-Merrill, 1971b.

Kitano, Harry H. L. *Japanese Americans*. Englewood Cliffs, N.J.: Prentice-Hall, 1969.

———. "Asian-Americans: The Chinese, Japanese, Koreans, Filipinos, and Southeast Asians." *The Annals* 454 (March 1981): 125–138.

Kitano, Harry H. L., and Roger Daniels. *Asian Americans*. Englewood Cliffs, N.J.: Prentice Hall, 1988.

Kleinfield, N. R. "Urban Indians Yearn for Lives They Left Behind." *New York Times* (January 3, 1995): A9.

Klineberg, Otto. *Negro Intelligence and Selective Migration.* New York: Columbia University Press, 1935.

———. "Mental Tests." *Encyclopedia of the Social Sciences,* vol. 10, 323–329. New York: Macmillan, 1937.

———. "Pictures in Our Heads." In Edgar A. Schuler, Thomas Ford Hoult, Duane L. Gibson, and Wilbur B. Brookover, eds., *Readings in Sociology,* 5th ed., 631–637. New York: Thomas Y. Crowell, 1974.

Kloss, Heinz. *The American Bilingual Tradition.* Rowley, Mass.: Newbury House Publishers, Inc., 1977.

Kluckhohn, Florence. "Dominant and Variant Value Orientations." In Clyde Kluckhohn, Henry A. Murray, and David M. Schneider, eds., *Personality in Nature, Society, and Culture,* 2nd ed., 342–357. New York: Alfred A. Knopf, 1956.

Kluegel, James R. "Trends in Whites' Explanations of the Black-White Gap in Socioeconomic Status, 1977–1989." *American Sociological Review* 55 (August 1990): 512–525.

Kohn, Howard. "Service with a Sneer." *New York Times Magazine* (November 6, 1994): 43–81.

Kramer, Michael. "What Can Be Done?" *Time* (May 11, 1992): 41.

Kraut, Alan M. *The Huddled Masses: The Immigrant in American Society, 1880–1921.* Arlington Heights, Ill.: Harlan Davidson, Inc., 1982.

Kristol, Irving. "The Negro Today Is Like the Immigrant of Yesterday." In Peter I. Rose, ed., *Nation of Nations,* 197–210. New York: Random House, 1972.

Kromkowski, John A., ed. *Annual Editions 95/96: Race and Ethnic Relations.* Guilford, Conn.: Dushkin Publishing Group, 1995.

———, ed. *Annual Editions: Race and Ethnic Relations 96/97.* Guilford, Conn.: Dushkin Publishing Group, 1996

Kunen, James S. "The End of Integration." *Time* (April 29, 1996): 39–45.

Lacayo, Richard. "Between Two Worlds: African American Middle Class." *Time* (March 13, 1989): 58–68.

———. "Anatomy of an Acquittal." *Time* (May 11, 1992): 30–32.

———. "A New Push for Blind Justice." *Time* (February 20, 1995): 39–40.

Lai, H. M. "Chinese." In Stephan Thernstrom, Ann Orlov, and Oscar Handlin, eds., *Harvard Encyclopedia of American Ethnic Groups,* 256–261. Cambridge, Mass.: The Belknap Press, 1980.

Lapham, Susan. "Census Bureau Finds Significant Demographic Differences Among Immigrant Groups." In John A. Kromkowski, ed., *Annual Editions: Race and Ethnic Relations 96/97,* 55–59. Guilford, Conn.: Dushkin Publishing Group, 1996.

LaPiere, Richard T. "Attitudes vs. Actions." Social Forces 13 (December 1934): 230–237.

LaViolette, Forrest E. *Americans of Japanese Ancestry,* Toronto: Canadian Institute of International Affairs, 1945.

Lawson, Stephen F. *Black Ballots: Voting Rights in the South, 1944–1969.* New York: Columbia University Press, 1976.

Layzer, David. "Science or Superstition." In Russell Jacoby and Naomi Glauberman, eds., *The Bell Curve Debate,* 653–678. New York: Times Books, 1995.

Lea, Tom. *The King Ranch,* vol. 1. Boston: Little, Brown, 1957.

LeBlanc Flores, Judith. "Facilitating Postsecondary Outcomes for Mexican Americans." *EDO-RC-94-4* (September 1994).

Lee, Everett S. "Negro Intelligence and Selective Migration: A Philadelphia Test of the Klineberg Hypothesis." *American Sociological Review* 16 (April 1951): 227–233.

Lee, Moon. "Asian Americans Don't Fit Their Monochrome Image." In John A. Kromkowski, ed., *Race and Ethnic Relations: Annual Editions 95/96,* 128–129. Guilford, Conn.: Dushkin Publishing Group, 1995.

Leighton, Alexander. *The Governing of Men.* Princeton, N.J.: Princeton University Press, 1946.

Lemann, Nicholas. "Taking Affirmative Action Apart." *New York Times Magazine* (June 11, 1995): 36–66.

Lerner, Richard M., and Christie J. Buehrig. "The Development of Racial Attitudes in Young Black and White Children." *Journal of Genetic Psychology* 127 (September 1975): 45–54.

Levine, Gene N., and Darrel M. Montero. "Socioeconomic Mobility among Three Generations of Japanese Americans." *Journal of Social Issues* 29, no. 2 (1973): 33–47.

Levine, Gene N., and Colbert Rhodes. *The Japanese American Community.* New York: Praeger, 1981.

Levine, Lawrence W. *Black Culture and Black Consciousness.* New York: Oxford University Press, 1977.

Lewis, Anthony. "The Politics of Nativism." *New York Times* (January 14, 1994): A15.

Lewis, Oscar. *La Vida.* New York: Random House, 1965.

Leyburn, James G. "Frontier Society." In Leonard Dinnerstein and Frederick Cople Jaher, eds., *The Aliens,* 65–76. New York: Appleton-Century-Crofts, 1970.

Lieberson, Stanley. "A Societal Theory of Race and Ethnic Relations." *American Sociological Review* 26 (December 1961): 902–910.

———. *A Piece of the Pie.* Berkeley, Calif.: University of California Press, 1980.

———. "Unhyphenated Whites in the United States." In Richard D. Alba, ed., *Ethnicity and Race in the U.S.A.,* 159–180. New York: Routledge, 1988.

Lieberson, Stanley, and Glenn V. Fuguitt. "Negro-White Occupational Differences in the Absence of Discrimination." *American Journal of Sociology* 73 (September 1967): 188–200.

Lieberson, Stanley, and Mary C. Waters. *From Many Strands.* New York: Russell Sage Foundation, 1988.

Liebow, Edward R. "Category or Community? Measuring Urban Indian Social Cohesion with Network Sampling." *Journal of Ethnic Studies* 16 (Winter 1989): 67–100.

Liebow, Elliot. *Tally's Corner.* Boston: Little, Brown, 1967.

Light, Ivan H. *Ethnic Enterprise in America.* Berkeley: University of California Press, 1972.

———. "Kenjin and Kinsmen." In Rudolph Gomez, Clement Cottingham, Jr., Russell Endo, and Kathleen Jackson, eds., *The Social Reality of Ethnic America,* 282–297. Lexington, Mass.: D. C. Heath and Co., 1974

———. "Ethnic Enterprise in America: Japanese, Chinese, and Blacks." In Ronald Takaki, ed., *From Different Shores: Perspectives of Race and Ethnicity in America,* 2nd ed., 82–92. New York: Oxford University Press, 1994.

Lii, Jane H. "Week in Sweatshop Reveals Grim Conspiracy of the Poor." *New York Times* (March 12, 1995): 1.

Lin, Keh-Ming, Laurie Tazuma, and Minoru Masuda. "Adaptational Problems of Vietnamese Refugees: Health and Mental Health Status." *Archives of General Psychiatry* 36 (August 1979): 955–961.

Lincoln, C. Eric. *The Black Muslims in America.* Boston: Beacon Press, 1961.

Linn, Lawrence S. "Verbal Attitudes and Overt Behavior: A Study of Racial Discrimination." *Social Forces* 43 (March 1965): 353–364.

Linton, Ralph. *The Study of Man.* New York: Appleton-Century-Crofts, Inc., 1936.

Lippmann, Walter. *Public Opinion.* New York: Harcourt, Brace, Jovanovich, 1922.

Lipset, Seymour Martin. *The First New Nation.* New York: W. W. Norton & Co., 1979.

Littlefield, Alice, Leonard Lieberman, and Larry T. Reynolds. "Redefining Race: The Potential Demise of a Concept in Physical Anthropology." *Current Anthropology* 23 (December 1982): 641–655.

Litwack, Leon F. *Been in the Storm So Long: The Aftermath of Slavery.* New York: Vintage Books, 1979.

Lobel, Sharon Alisa. "Effects of Personal Versus Impersonal Rater Instructions on Relative Favorability of Thirteen Ethnic Group Stereotypes." *Journal of Social Psychology* 128 (February 1988): 29–39.

Locklear, William R. "The Celestials and the Angels." In Roger Daniels, ed., *Anti-Chinese Violence in North America,* 239–256. New York: Arno Press, 1978.

Loehlin, John C., Gardner Lindzey, and J. N. Spuhler. *Race Differences in Intelligence.* San Francisco: W. H. Freeman, 1975.

Logan, John R., Richard D. Alba, and Thomas L. McNulty. "Ethnic Economies in Metropolitan Regions: Miami and Beyond." *Social Forces* 72 (March 1994): 691–724.

Lohman, Joseph D., and Dietrich C. Reitzes. "Note on Race Relations in Mass Society." *American Journal of Sociology* 57 (November 1952): 240–246.

Lopez, Manuel Mariano. "Patterns of Interethnic Residential Segregation in the Urban Southwest, 1960 and 1970." *Social Science Quarterly* 62 (March 1981): 50–63.

Lopreato, Joseph. *Italian Americans.* New York: Random House, 1970.

———. *Human Nature and Biocultural Evolution.* Boston: Allen & Unwin, 1984.

Loury, Glenn C. "Beyond Civil Rights." In Kurt Finsterbusch and George McKenna, eds., *Taking Sides: Clashing Views on Controversial Social Issues,* 4th ed., 188–194. Guilford, Conn.: The Dushkin Publishing Group, 1986.

Lurie, Nancy Oestreich. "The American Indian: Historical Background." In Norman R. Yetman and C. Hoy Steele, eds., *Majority & Minority,* 3rd ed., 131–144. Boston: Allyn and Bacon, 1982.

Lutz, Donald S. "The Changing View of the Founding and a New Perspective on American Political Theory." *Social Science Quarterly* 68 (December 1987): 669–686.

Lynwood, Carranco. "Chinese Expulsion from Humboldt County." In Roger Daniels, ed., *Anti-Chinese Violence in North America,* 329–340. New York: Arno Press, 1978.

MacLeish, Archibald. *A Time to Act.* Boston: Houghton Mifflin, 1943.

Malcolm X. "Malcolm X Founds the Organization of Afro-American Unity." In August Meier, Elliott Rudwick, and Francis L. Broderick, eds., *Black Protest Thought in the Twentieth Century,* 2nd ed., 412–420. Indianapolis, Ind. and New York: Bobbs-Merrill, 1971.

Malcolm X, and James Farmer. "Separation or Integration: A Debate." In August Meier, Elliott Rudwick, and Francis L. Broderick, eds., *Black Protest Thought in the Twentieth Century,* 2nd ed., 387–412. Indianapolis, Ind. and New York: Bobbs-Merrill, 1971.

Maldonado, Lionel, and Joan Moore, eds. *Urban Ethnicity in the United States,* 51–71. Beverly Hills, Calif.: Sage Publications, 1985.

Marumoto, Masaji. "'First Year' Immigrants to Hawaii & Eugene Van Reed." In Hilary Conroy and T. Scott Miyakawa, eds., *East Across the Pacific,* 5–39. Santa Barbara, Calif.: American Bibliographical Center-CLIO Press, 1972.

Marquez, Benjamin. "The Politics of Race and Class: The League of United Latin American Citizens in the Post–World War II Period." *Social Science Quarterly* 68 (March 1987): 84–101.

Mass, Amy Iwasaki. "Psychological Effects of the Camps on Japanese Americans." In Roger Daniels, Sandra C. Taylor, and Harry H. L. Kitano, eds., *Japanese Americans: From Relocation to Redress,* rev. ed., 159–162. Seattle, Wash.: University of Washington Press, 1991.

Massey, Douglas S. "Dimensions of the New Immigration to the United States and the Prospects for Assimilation." In Ralph J. Turner and James F. Short, Jr., eds., *Annual Review of Sociology* 7 (1981): 57–85.

Massey, Douglas, Rafael Alarcon, Jorge Durand, and Humberto Gonzalez. *Return to Aztlan: The Social Process of International Migration from Western Mexico.* Berkeley, Calif.: University of California Press, 1987.

Massey, Douglas S., Gretchen A. Condran, and Nancy A. Denton. "The Effect of Residential Segregation on Black Social and Economic Well-Being." *Social Forces* 66 (September 1987): 29–56.

Massey, Douglas S., and Nancy A. Denton. "Trends in the Residential Segregation of Blacks, Hispanics, and Asians: 1970–1980." *American Sociological Review* 52 (December 1987): 802–825.

―――. *American Apartheid: Segregation and the Making of the Underclass.* Cambridge, Mass.: Harvard University Press, 1993.

Massey, Douglas S., and Zoltan L. Hajnal. "The Changing Geographic Structure of Black-White Segregation in the United States." *Social Science Quarterly* 76 (September 1995): 527–542.

Mathews, Linda. "More Than Identity Rides On a New Racial Category." *New York Times* (July 6, 1996): 1.

Matsumoto, Gary M., Gerald M. Meredith, and Minoru Masuda. "Ethnic Identity: Honolulu and Seattle Japanese-Americans." In Stanley Sue and Nathaniel Wagner, eds., *Asian-Americans,* 65–74. Ben Lomand, Calif.: Science and Behavior Books, 1973.

Mauro, Tony, and Tom Watson. "Court Grows Critical When Race, Law Intersect." In John A. Kromkowski, ed., *Annual Editions: Race and Ethnic Relations 96/97,* 36–37. Guilford, Conn.: Dushkin Publishing Group, 1996.

Mazon, Mauricio. *The Zoot Suit Riots: The Psychology of Symbolic Annihilation.* Austin, Tex.: The University of Texas Press, 1984.

McAdam, Doug. *Political Process and the Development of Black Insurgency, 1930–1970.* Chicago: University of Chicago Press, 1982.

McCarthy, John, and William Yancey. "Uncle Tom and Mr. Charlie: Metaphysical Pathos in the Study of Racism and Personal Disorganization." *American Journal of Sociology* 76 (January 1971): 648–672.

McConahay, J. B. "Modern Racism, Ambivalence, and the Modern Racism Scale." In Dovidio and Gaertner, eds., *Prejudice, Discrimination, and Racism,* 91–125. Orlando, Fla.: Academic Press, 1986.

McCone, John A. "The Watts Riot." In Gilbert Osofsky, ed., *The Burden of Race,* 608–621. New York: Harper & Row, 1968.

McDaniel, Antonio. "The Dynamic Racial Composition of the United States." In Obie Clayton, Jr., ed., *An American Dilemma Revisited: Race Relations in a Changing World,* 269–287. New York: Russell Sage Foundation, 1996.

McDowell, Edwin. "Hospitality Is Their Business: Indian-Americans' Rooms-to-Riches Success Story." *New York Times* (March 21, 1996): C1.

McFee, Malcolm. "The 150% Man, A Product of Blackfeet Acculturation." In Howard M. Bahr, Bruce A. Chadwick, and Robert C. Day, eds., *Native Americans Today,* 303–312. New York: Harper & Row, 1972.

McKee, James B. *Sociology and the Race Problem: The Failure of a Perspective.* Urbana and Chicago: University of Illinois Press, 1993.

McInnis, Doug. "At Wind River, Cautious Steps Toward Capitalism." *New York Times* (November 6, 1994): 4F.

McLemore, S. Dale, and Ricardo Romo. "The Origins and Development of the Mexican American People." In Rodolfo O. de la Garza, Frank D. Bean, Charles M. Bonjean, Ricardo Romo, and Rodolfo Alvarez, eds., *The Mexican American Experience,* 3–32. Austin, Tex.: The University of Texas Press, 1985.

McMillen, Marilyn M., Phillip Kaufman, and Summer D. Whitener. *Dropout Rates in the United States: 1993,* U.S. Department of Education, National Center for Education Statistics, Office of Educational Research and Improvement NCES 94–669. Washington, D.C.: U.S. Government Printing Office.

McNeill, William H. *Plagues and Peoples.* Garden City, N.Y.: Anchor Books, 1976.

McNickle, D'Arcy. *Native American Tribalism.* London: Oxford University Press, 1973.

McWilliams, Carey. *Brothers Under the Skin.* Boston: Little, Brown, and Co., 1945.

———. *California: The Great Exception.* New York: A. A. Wyn, 1949.

———. "Getting Rid of the Mexicans." In Wayne Moquin and Charles Van Doren, eds., *A Documentary History of the Mexican Americans,* 383–387. New York: Bantam Books, 1972.

———. *North from Mexico.* New York: Greenwood Press, 1973.

Mead, George Herbert. *Mind, Self, and Society.* Chicago: University of Chicago Press, 1934.

Meier, August, Elliott Rudwick, and Francis L. Broderick, eds. *Black Protest Thought in the Twentieth Century,* 2nd ed. Indianapolis, Ind. and New York: Bobbs-Merrill, 1971.

Meister, Richard J., ed., *Race and Ethnicity in Modern America.* Lexington, Mass.: D. C. Heath, 1974.

Mercer, Jane R., Peter Iadicola, and Helen Moore. "Building Effective Multiethnic Schools." In Walter G. Stephan and Joe R. Feagin, eds., *School Desegregation,* 281–307. New York: Plenum Press, 1980.

Meriam, Lewis, et al. *The Problem of Indian Administration.* Washington, D.C.: Brookings Institution, 1928.

Merton, Robert K. *Social Theory and Social Structure,* rev. ed. Glencoe, Ill.: The Free Press, 1957.

Metzger, L. Paul. "American Sociology and Black Assimilation: Conflicting Perspectives." *American Journal of Sociology* 76 (January 1971): 627–647.

Middlekauff, Robert. "The Assumptions of the Founders in 1787." *Social Science Quarterly* 68 (December 1987): 656–668.

Middleton, Russell. "Ethnic Prejudice and Susceptibility to Persuasion." *American Sociological Review* 25 (October 1960): 679–686.

———. "Regional Differences in Prejudice." *American Sociological Review* 41 (February 1976): 94–117.

Miller, Adam. "Professors of Hate." In Russell Jacoby and Naomi Glauberman, eds., *The Bell Curve Debate.* New York: Times Books, 1995.

Miller, Neal E. "The Frustration-Aggression Hypothesis." *Psychological Review* 48 (July 1941): 337–342.

Mills, C. Wright. *The Power Elite.* New York: Oxford University Press, 1956.

Milner, Lucille B. "Letters from a Segregated Army." In Gilbert Osofsky, ed., *The Burden of Race,* 414–420. New York: Harper & Row, 1968.

Min, Pyong Gap. "The Entrepreneurial Adaptation of Korean Immigrants." In Silvia Pedraza and Rubén G. Rumbaut, eds., *Origins and Destinies: Immigration, Race, and Ethnicity in America,* 302–314. Belmont, Calif.: Wadsworth Publishing Company, 1996.

Minami, Dale. "*Coram Nobis* and Redress." In Roger Daniels, Sandra C. Taylor, and Harry H. L. Kitano, eds., *Japanese Americans: From Relocation to Redress,* rev. ed., 200–202. Seattle, Wash.: University of Washington Press, 1991.

Mintz, Sidney W. "Slavery and Emergent Capitalisms." In Laura Foner and Eugene D. Genovese, eds., *Slavery in the New World,* 27–37. Englewood Cliffs, N.J.: Prentice-Hall, 1969.

Mittlebach, Frank G., and Joan W. Moore. "Ethnic Endogamy—The Case of Mexican Americans." *American Journal of Sociology* 74 (July 1968): 50–62.

Miyamoto, S. Frank. *Social Solidarity Among the Japanese of Seattle.* Seattle, Wash.: University of Washington Press, 1939.

———. "An Immigrant Community in America." In Hilary Conroy and T. Scott Miyakawa, eds., *East Across the Pacific,* 217–243. Santa Barbara, Calif.: American Bibliographical Center-CLIO Press, 1972.

Modell, John. *The Economics and Politics of Racial Accommodation: The Japanese of Los Angeles, 1900–1942.* Urbana, Ill.: University of Illinois Press, 1977.

Mogelonsky, Marcia. "Asian-Indian Americans." In John A. Kromkowski, ed., *Annual Editions: Race and Ethnic Relations 96/97,* 132–138. Guilford, Conn.: Dushkin Publishing Group, 1996.

Monahan, Thomas P. "An Overview of Statistics on Interracial Marriage in the United States, with Data on Its Extent from 1963–1970." *Journal of Marriage and the Family* 38 (May 1976): 223–231.

Monk, Maria. "Few Imaginations Can Conceive Deeds So Abominable as They Practiced." In Moses Rischin, ed., *Immigration and the American Tradition.* Indianapolis: Bobbs-Merrill, 1976.

Monsho, Kharen. "Kwanzaa Celebrates Community of Blacks." *Austin American-Statesman* (December 16, 1988): F2.

Montejano, David. *Anglos and Mexicans in the Making of Texas,* 1836–1986. Austin, Tex.: University of Texas Press, 1987.

Montero, Darrel. *Vietnamese Americans: Patterns of Resettlement and Socioeconomic Adaptation in the United States.* Boulder, Colo.: Westview Press, 1979.

———. *Japanese Americans: Changing Patterns of Affiliation Over Three Generations.* Boulder, Colo.: Westview Press, 1980.

———. "The Japanese Americans: Changing Patterns of Assimilation over Three Generations." *American Sociological Review* 46 (December 1981): 829–839.

Moore, Joan W. *Mexican Americans,* 1st and 2nd eds. Englewood Cliffs, N.J.: Prentice-Hall, 1970 and 1976.

———. "American Minorities and 'New Nation' Perspectives." *Pacific Sociological Review* 19 (1976): 447–467.

———. "Is There a Hispanic Underclass?" *Social Science Quarterly* 70 (June 1989): 265–284.

Moore, Joan W., and Harry Pachon. *Hispanics in the United States.* Englewood Cliffs, N.J.: Prentice-Hall, 1985.

Moquín, Wayne, and Charles Van Doren, eds. *A Documentary History of the Mexican Americans.* New York: Bantam Books, 1971.

Moran, Carol E., and Kenji Hakuta. "Bilingual Education: Broadening Research Perspectives." In James A. Banks and Cherry A. McGee Banks, eds., *Handbook of Research on Multicultural Education,* 445–462. New York: Macmillian Publishing, 1995.

Morganthau, Tom, Marcus Mabry, Frank Washington, Vern E. Smith, Emily Yoffe, and Lucille Beachy. "Losing Ground." *Newsweek* (April 6, 1992): 20–22.

Morison, Samuel Eliot. *The Oxford History of the American People,* vol. 1. New York: New American Library, 1972.

Morris, Aldon. *The Origins of the Civil Rights Movement: Black Communities Organizing for Change.* New York: Free Press, 1984.

Morse, Joseph Laffan, and William H. Hendelson, eds. "Indochina." *Funk & Wagnalls New Encyclopedia* 13 (1972a): 262–268.

———. "Vietnam." *Funk & Wagnalls New Encyclopedia* 24 (1972b): 317–326.

Morse, Samuel F. B. "Riot and Ignorance in Human Priest-Controlled Machines." In Moses Rischin, ed., *Immigration and the American Tradition.* Indianapolis, Ind.: Bobbs-Merrill [1835] 1976.

Moskos, Charles C., Jr. *Greek Americans.* Englewood Cliffs, N.J.: Prentice-Hall, 1980.

Moskos, Charles C., Jr., and John Sibley Butler. *All That We Can Be: Black Leadership and Racial Integration the Army Way.* New York: Basic Books, 1996.

Moynihan, Daniel Patrick. *The Negro Family.* Washington, D.C.: U.S. Department of Labor, 1965.

Mulroy, Kevin. *Freedom on the Border: The Seminole Maroons in Florida, the Indian Territory, Coahuila, and Texas.* Lubbock, Tex.: Texas Tech University Press, 1993.

Muller, Thomas, and Thomas J. Espenshade. *The Fourth Wave: California's Newest Immigrants.* Washington, D.C.: The Urban Institute Press, 1985.

Mura, David. "Japanese Americans: Strangers at Home." *New York Times* (April 29, 1992): A15.

Murguía, Edward. *Chicano Intermarriage.* San Antonio, Tex.: Trinity University Press, 1982.

———. *Assimilation, Colonialism, and the Mexican American People.* Lanham, Md.: University Press of America, 1989.

———. "On Latino/Hispanic Ethnic Identity." *Latino Studies Journal* 2 (September 1991): 8–18.

Murguía, Edward, and W. Parker Frisbie. "Trends in Mexican American Intermarriage: Recent Findings in Perspective." *Social Science Quarterly* 58 (December 1977): 374–389.

Mydans, Seth. "Japanese-Americans Face New Fears." *New York Times* (March 4, 1992): A8.

Myrdal, Gunnar. *An American Dilemma,* 2 vols. New York: McGraw-Hill, 1964.

Nagel, Joane. *American Indian Ethnic Renewal: Red Power and the Resurgence of Identity and Culture.* New York: Oxford University Press, 1996.

Nagel, Joane, and C. Matthew Snipp. "Ethnic Reorganization: American Indian Social, Economic, Political, and Cultural Strategies for Survival." *Ethnic and Racial Studies* (April 1993): 203–235.

NARF Legal Review. "Indian Religious Freedom Bills Near Passage," (Summer/Fall 1994): 1–7.

———. "A Move Toward Sovereignty: Interior Department Publishes Alaska Tribal List." (Winter/Spring 1994): 1–6.

———. "Congress Overturns Supreme Court's Peyote Ruling." Boulder, Colo.: Native American Rights Fund (Winter/Spring 1995): 1–6.

Nash, Gary B. *Red, White, and Black.* Englewood Cliffs, N.J.: Prentice-Hall, 1974.

National Advisory Commission. *Report of the National Advisory Commission on Civil Disorders.* New York: The New York Times Co., 1968.

National Center for Education Statistics. *Dropout Rates in the United States: 1993.* Washington, D.C.: U.S. Department of Education, 1994.

National Research Council. "Immigrant Children and their Families: Issues for Research and Policy." In *The Future of Children: Critical Issues for Children and Youths.* Washington, D.C.: National Research Council, Summer/Fall 1995: 79.

Neidert, Lisa, and Reynolds Farley. "Assimilation in the United States: An Analysis of Ethnic and Generation Differences in Status and Achievement." *American Sociological Review* 50 (December 1985): 840–850.

New York Times. "The AIDS 'Plot' Against Blacks." (May 12, 1992): A14.

———. "F.B.I. Agents Raid Casinos on 5 Indian Reservations." (May 13, 1992): A8.

———. "Of 58 Riot Deaths, 50 Have Been Ruled Homicides." (May 17, 1992): A17.

———. "Tribe's Land Claim Voided in Vermont." (June 18, 1992): A12.

———. "Coroner Drops Toll in Los Angeles Riot to 51 After Review." (August 13, 1992): A11.

———. "Verdict is Reached in Simpson's Trial." (October 3, 1995): A1.

———. "7 Thais Plead Guilty in Sweatshop Slavery Case." (February 11, 1996): 12.

Newsweek. "For Indians, by Indians." In Herbert L. Marx, ed., *The American Indian,* 108–110. New York: H. W. Wilson, 1973.

Nickel, James W. "Discrimination and Morally Relevant Characteristics." In Steven M. Cahn, ed., *The Affirmative Action Debate,* 3–4. New York: Routledge, 1995.

Niebuhr, Gustav. "Zunis Mix Tribe Spirit with Icons of Church." *New York Times* (January 29, 1995): A8.

Noble, Kenneth B. "California Immigration Measure Faces Rocky Legal Path." *New York Times* (November 11, 1994): A1.

Noel, Donald L. "A Theory of the Origin of Ethnic Stratification." *Social Problems* 16 (Fall 1968): 157–172.

———. *The Origins of American Slavery and Racism.* Columbus, Ohio: Charles E. Merrill, 1972.

Nostrand, Richard L. "'Mexican American' and 'Chicano': Emerging Terms for a People Coming of Age." *Pacific Historical Review* 62 (August 1973): 389–406.

Novak, Michael. *The Rise of the Unmeltable Ethnics.* New York: Macmillan, 1971.

Novotny, Ann. *Strangers at the Door.* Toronto: Bantam Pathfinders Edition, 1974.

O'Brian, David J. and Stephen S. Fugita. *The Japanese American Experience.* Bloomington, Ind.: University Press, 1991.

O'Brien, Sharon. "Federal Indian Policies and the International Protection of Human Rights." In Vine Deloria, Jr., ed., *American Indian Policy in the Twentieth Century,* 35–61. Norman: University of Oklahoma Press, 1985.

O'Hare, William. "Reaching for the Dream." *American Demographics* (January 1992): 32–36.

O'Hare, William P., Kelvin M. Pollard, Taynia L. Mann, and Mary M. Kent. "African Americans in the 1990s." *Population Bulletin* 46 (Washington, D.C.: Population Reference Bureau, Inc., July 1991): 29–30.

O'Hare, William, and Margaret L. Usdansky. "What the 1990 Census Tells Us about Segregation in 25 Large Metros." *Population Today* 20 (September 1992): 6–7.

Officer, James E. "Termination as Federal Policy: An Overview." In Kenneth R. Philp, ed., *Indian Self-Rule,* 114–128. Salt Lake City, Utah: Howe Brothers, 1986.

Ogawa, Dennis M., and Evarts C. Fox, Jr. "Japanese Internment and Relocation: The Hawaii Experience." In Roger Daniels, Sandra C. Taylor, and Harry H. L. Kitano, eds., *Japanese Americans: From Relocation to Redress,* rev. ed., 135–138. Seattle, Wash: University of Washington Press, 1991.

Okimoto, Daniel. "The Intolerance of Success." In Amy Tachiki, Eddie Wong, Franklin Odo, and Buck Wong, eds., *Roots: An Asian American Reader,* 14–19. Los Angeles: Regents of the University of California, 1971.

Oliver, Melvin L., and Thomas M. Shapiro. *Black Wealth/White Wealth: A New Perspective on Racial Inequality.* New York: Routledge, 1995.

Olson, James M., and Mark P. Zanna. "Attitudes and Attitude Change." *Annual Review of Psychology* 44 (1993): 117–154.

Olson, James S., and Raymond Wilson. *Native Americans in the Twentieth Century.* Urbana, Ill. and Chicago: University of Illinois Press, 1984.

Olzak, Susan. "A Competition Model of Ethnic Collective Action in American Cities, 1877–1899." In Susan Olzak and Joane Nagel, eds., *Competitive Ethnic Relations,* 17–46. Orlando, Fla.: Academic Press, Inc., 1986.

———. "Labor Unrest, Immigration, and Ethnic Conflict in Urban America." *American Journal of Sociology* 94 (May 1989): 1303–1333.

Olzak, Susan, and Joane Nagel. "Introduction, Competitive Ethnic Relations: An Overview." In Susan Olzak and Joane Nagel, eds., *Competitive Ethnic Relations,* 1–14. Orlando, Fla: Academic Press, Inc., 1986.

Olzak, Susan, and Suzanne Shanahan. "Deprivation and Race Riots: An Extension of Spilerman's Analysis." *Social Forces* 74 (March 1996): 931–961.

One Feather, Gerald. "Relocation" (comment). In Kenneth R. Philp, ed., *Indian Self-Rule,* 171–172. Salt Lake City, Utah: Howe Brothers, 1986.

Orfield, Gary. *Must We Bus*. Washington, D.C.: Brookings Institution, 1978.

———. *Desegregation of Black and Hispanic Students from 1968 to 1980*. Quoted in Mary Swerdlin, ed., *Education Daily* 15 (September 10, 1982): 1–2.

Osofsky, Gilbert, ed., *The Burden of Race*. New York: Harper & Row, 1968.

Pachon, Harry P., and Joan W. Moore. "Mexican Americans." *The Annals* 454 (March 1981): 111–124.

Papademetriou, D. G. "The Immigration Reform and Control Act of 1986: America Amends Its Immigration Law." *International Migration* 25 (September 1987): 325–334.

Paredes, Américo. *With His Pistol in His Hand: A Border Ballad and its Hero*. Austin, Tex.: The University of Texas Press, 1958.

Paredes, Raymund. "The Origins of Anti-Mexican Sentiment in the United States." In Ricardo Romo and Raymund Paredes, eds., *New Directions in Chicano Scholarship*, 139–166. La Jolla, Calif.: Chicano Studies Program, University of California, San Diego, 1978.

Parenti, Michael. "Ethnic Politics and the Persistence of Ethnic Identification." *American Political Science Review* 61 (September 1967): 717–726.

Park, Robert E. "Our Racial Frontier on the Pacific." *Survey Graphic* 56 (May 1926): 192–196. In Robert E. Park, ed., *Race and Culture*, 138–151. New York: Free Press, 1964.

Park, Robert E. "The Concept of Social Distance." *Journal of Applied Sociology* 8 (July–August 1924): 339–344.

———. *Race and Culture*. New York: Free Press, 1964.

Park, Robert E., and Ernest W. Burgess. *Introduction to the Science of Sociology*. Chicago: University of Chicago Press, 1921.

Parkman, Margaret A., and Jack Sawyer. "Dimensions of Ethnic Intermarriage in Hawaii." *American Sociological Review* 32 (August 1967): 593–607.

Passel, Jeffrey S. *Immigrants and Taxes: A Reappraisal of Huddle's "The Cost of Immigrants."* Washington, D.C.: The Urban Institute, PRIP–U1–29, January 1994.

Passel, Jeffrey S., and Patricia Berman. "Quality of 1980 Census Data for American Indians." *Social Biology* 3 1986: 163–182.

Patterson, Orlando. *Freedom*. New York: Basic Books, 1991.

Patterson, Orlando. "Slavery." In Alex Inkeles, ed., *Annual Review of Sociology*, 407–449. Palo Alto, Calif.: Annual Reviews, Inc., 1977.

Pear, Robert. "Platform Committee Attacks Constitution on Citizenship." *New York Times* (August 7, 1996): A9.

Pedraza, Silvia, and Rubén G. Rumbaut, eds. *Origins and Destinies: Immigration, Race, and Ethnicity in America*, 43–59. Belmont, Calif.: Wadsworth Publishing Company, 1996.

Pelofsky, Jeremy. "Mexican Immigrants Draw Lowest Wages, Study Finds." *Austin American Statesman* (July 14, 1996): D6.

Peñalosa, Fernando. "The Changing Mexican-American in Southern California." In John H. Burma, ed., *Mexican Americans in the United States*, 41–51. Cambridge, Mass.: Schenkman, 1970.

———. *Introduction to the Sociology of Language*. Rowley, Mass.: Newbury House Publishers, 1981.

———. *Chicano Sociolinguistics: A Brief Introduction*. Rowley, Mass.: Newbury House Publishers, Inc., 1989.

Perez, Lisandro. "Cubans." In Stephan Thernstrom, Ann Orlov, and Oscar Handlin, eds., *Harvard Encyclopedia of American Ethnic Groups*, 256–261. Cambridge, Mass.: The Belknap Press, 1980.

Peroff, Nicholas G. "Termination Policy and the Menominees: Feedback of Unanticipated Impacts." In John G. Grumm and Stephen L. Wasby, eds., *The Analysis of Policy Impact*, 123–131. Lexington, Mass.: Lexington Books, 1981.

Petersen, William. *Japanese Americans.* New York: Random House, 1971.

———. "Concepts of Ethnicity." In Stephan Thernstrom, Ann Orlov, and Oscar Handlin, eds., *Harvard Encyclopedia of American Ethnic Groups,* 234–242. Cambridge, Mass.: The Belknap Press, 1980.

Pettigrew, Thomas F. *Racially Separate or Together?* New York: McGraw-Hill, 1971.

———. *Racial Discrimination in the United States.* New York: Harper & Row, 1975.

Pettigrew, Thomas F., and Joanne Martin. "Shaping the Organizational Context for Black American Inclusion." In George Levinger, ed., *Black Employment Opportunities: Macro and Micro Perspectives,* special issue. *Journal of Social Issues* 43, no. 1 (1987): 41–78.

———. "Organizational Inclusion of Minority Groups: A Social Psychological Analysis." In Jan Pieter van Oudenhoven and Tineke M. Willemsen, eds., *Ethnic Minorities,* 169–200. Amsterdam: Swets & Zeitlinger B.V., 1989.

Piore, Michael J. *Birds of Passage: Migrant Labor and Industrial Societies.* New York: Cambridge University Press, 1979.

Pollack, Denan. "Mashantucket Pequots: A Tribe That's Raking It In." *U.S. News and World Report* (January 15, 1996): 59.

Porter, Judith R., and Robert E. Washington. "Black Identity and Self-Esteem: A Review of Studies of Black Self-Concept, 1968–1978." In Alex Inkeles, James Coleman, and Ralph Turner, eds., *Annual Review of Sociology,* vol. 5, 53–74. Palo Alto, Calif.: Annual Reviews, Inc., 1979.

Portes, Alejandro. "Dilemmas of a Golden Exile: Integration of Cuban Refugee Families in Milwaukee." *American Sociological Review* 34 (August 1969): 505–518.

———. "Modes of Structural Incorporation and Present Theories of Immigration." In Mary M. Kritz, Charles B. Keely, and Sylvano M. Tomasi, eds., *Global Trends in Migration,* 279–297. Staten Island, N.Y.: CMS Press, 1981.

Portes, Alejandro, and Robert L. Bach. *Latin Journey.* Berkeley, Calif.: University of California Press, 1985.

Portes, Alejandro, and Ruben G. Rumbaut. *Immigrant America: A Portrait.* Berkeley and Los Angeles: University of California Press, 1990.

Portes, Alejandro, and Richard Schauffler. "Language Acquisition and Loss Among Children of Immigrants." In Silvia Pedraza and Rubén G. Rumbaut, eds., *Origins and Destinies: Immigration, Race, and Ethnicity in America,* 442–443. Belmont, Calif.: Wadsworth Publishing Company, 1996a.

Portes, Alejandro, and Min Zhou. "Self-Employment and the Earnings of Immigrants." *American Sociological Review* 61 (April, 1996): 219–230.

Poston, Dudley L., Jr., and David Alvírez. "On the Cost of Being a Mexican American Worker." *Social Science Quarterly* 53 (March 1973): 697–709.

Poston, Dudley L., Jr., David Alvírez, and Marta Tienda. "Earnings Differences between Anglo and Mexican American Male Workers in 1960 and 1970: Changes in the 'Cost' of Being Mexican American." *Social Science Quarterly* 57 (December 1976): 618–631.

Pottinger, J. Stanley. "The Drive Toward Equality." In Barry R. Gross, ed., *Reverse Discrimination,* 41–49. Buffalo, N.Y.: Prometheus Books, 1977.

Powers, Daniel A., and Christopher G. Ellison. "Interracial Contact and Black Racial Attitudes: The Contact Hypothesis and Selectivity Bias." *Social Forces* 74 (September 1995): 205–226.

Price, John A. "The Migration and Adaptation of American Indians to Los Angeles." In Howard M. Bahr, Bruce A. Chadwick, and Robert C. Day, eds., *Native Americans Today,* 428–439. New York: Harper & Row, 1972.

Prucha, Francis Paul. *American Indian Policy in the Formative Years.* Cambridge, Mass.: Harvard University Press, 1962.

Quint, Howard H., Milton Cantor, and Dean Albertson, eds. *Main Problems in American History*, vol. 1, 4th ed. Homewood, Ill.: Dorsey, 1978.

Rainwater, Lee, and William L. Yancey. *The Moynihan Report and the Politics of Controversy*. Cambridge, Mass.: MIT Press, 1967.

Randolph, A. Philip. "Address to the Policy Conference." In August Meier, Elliott Rudwick, and Francis L. Broderick, eds., *Black Protest Thought in the Twentieth Century*, 2nd ed., 224–233. Indianapolis, Ind. and New York: Bobbs-Merrill, 1971a.

———. "A. Philip Randolph Urges Civil Disobedience Against a Jim Crow Army." In August Meier, Elliott Rudwick, and Francis L. Broderick, eds., *Black Protest Thought in the Twentieth Century*, 2nd ed., 233–238. Indianapolis, Ind. and New York: Bobbs-Merrill, 1971b.

Rawick, George P. "From Sundown to Sunup: Slavery and the Making of the Black Community." In Silvia Pedraza and Rubén G. Rumbaut, eds., *Origins and Destinies: Immigration, Race, and Ethnicity in America*, 60–72. Belmont, Calif.: Wadsworth Publishing Company, 1996.

Reimers, David M. *Still the Golden Door*. New York: Columbia University Press, 1985.

Reinhold, Robert. "Police Are Slow to React as the Violence Spreads." *New York Times* (May 1, 1992): A1, A12.

Reisler, Mark. *By the Sweat of Their Brow: Mexican Immigrant Labor in the United States, 1900–1940*. Westport, Conn.: Greenwood, 1976.

Reiss, Tom. "Home on the Range." *New York Times* (May 26, 1995): A11.

Rhoades, Everett R., Russell D. Mason, Phyllis Eddy, Eva M. Smith, and Thomas R. Burns. "The Indian Health Service Approach to Alcoholism Among American Indians and Alaska Natives." *Public Health Reports* 103 (November–December 1988): 621–627.

Richardson, Lynda. "A Suburb Seeks Clues After a Lawless Night." *New York Times* (May 13, 1992): A13.

Riesman, David, Nathan Glazer, and Reuel Denney. *The Lonely Crowd*. New Haven, Conn.: Yale University Press, 1950.

Riis, Jacob A. *How the Other Half Lives*. New York: Hill and Wang, 1957.

Robinson, J. W., and J. D. Preston. "Equal-Status Contact and Modification of Racial Prejudice: A Re-examination of the Contact Hypothesis." *Social Forces* 54 (1976): 911–924.

Robinson, William L., and Stephen L. Spitz. "Affirmative Action: Evolving Case Law and Shifting Philosophy." *The Urban League Review* 10 (Winter 1986–87): 84–100.

Roche, John P., and Milton M. Gordon. "Can Morality Be Legislated?" In Kimball Young and Raymond W. Mack, eds., *Principles of Sociology*, 3rd ed., 332–336. New York: American Book, 1965.

Rodman, Hyman. "Technical Note on Two Rates of Mixed Marriage." *American Sociological Review* 30 (October 1965): 776–778.

Rohter, Larry. "Revisiting Immigration and the Open-Door Policy." *New York Times* (September 19, 1993): 4.

Romano, Octavio Ignacio. "The Anthropology and Sociology of the Mexican Americans." *El Grito* 2 (Fall 1968): 13–26.

Romo, Harriett D., and Toni Falbo. *Latino High School Graduation: Defying the Odds*. Austin, Tex.: University of Texas Press, 1996.

Romo, Ricardo. *East Los Angeles: History of a Barrio*. Austin, Tex.: University of Texas Press, 1983.

Romo, Ricardo, and Harriett Romo. "Introduction: The Social and Cultural Context of the Mexican American Experience in the United States." In Rodolfo O. de la Garza, Frank D. Bean, Charles M. Bonjean, Ricardo Romo, Rodolfo Alvarez, eds. *The Mexican American Experience: An Interdisciplinary Anthology*, 317–333. Austin, Tex.: University of Texas Press, 1985.

Roosevelt, Franklin D. "Executive Order 8802." In Gilbert Osofsky, ed., *The Burden of Race*, 400–401. New York: Harper Torchbooks, 1967.

Rosen, Bernard. "Race, Ethnicity, and the Achievement Syndrome." *American Sociological Review* 24 (1959): 47–70.

Rosenbaum, Robert J. *Mexican Resistance in the Southwest: "The Sacred Right of Self-Preservation."* Austin, Tex.: University of Texas Press, 1981.

Rosenberg, M. P. "Bilingual Ed: A Report." *The Texas Observer* (May 1, 1981):1, 11–16.

Rosenberg, Morris, and Roberta Simmons. *Black and White Self-Esteem: The Urban School Child.* Washington, D. C.: American Sociological Association, 1972.

Rosenberg, Morris, Carmi Schooler, Carrie Schoenbach, and Florence Rosenberg. "Global Self-Esteem and Specific Self-Esteem: Different Concepts and Different Outcomes." *American Sociological Review* 60 (February 1995): 141–156.

Ross, Sonya. "More Blacks Get College Degrees But They Still Receive Lower Pay." *Austin American-Statesman* (September 16, 1993).

Rostow, Eugene V. "Our Worst Wartime Mistake." *Harper's Magazine* (September 1945): 193–201.

Rothenberg, Paula S. *Race, Class, and Gender in the United States: An Integrated Study.* New York: St. Martin's Press, 1995.

Roy, Joseph T., Jr. "Organized Hate in America." *Civil Rights Journal* 1 (Fall, 1995): 9–13.

Roy, Prodipto. "The Measurement of Assimilation: The Spokane Indians." In Howard M. Bahr, Bruce A. Chadwick, and Robert C. Day, eds., *Native Americans Today*, 225–239. New York: Harper & Row, 1972.

Rubenstein, Richard E. *Rebels in Eden.* Boston: Little, Brown, 1970.

Rumbaut, Rubén G. "A Legacy of War: Refugees from Vietnam, Laos, and Cambodia." In Silvia Pedraza and Rubén G. Rumbaut, eds., *Origins and Destinies: Immigration, Race, and Ethnicity in America*, 315–333. Belmont, Calif.: Wadsworth Publishing Company, 1996.

Rustin, Bayard. "A Workable and Christian Technique for the Righting of Injustice." In August Meier, Elliott Rudwick, and Francis L. Broderick, eds., *Black Protest Thought in the Twentieth Century*, 2nd ed., 233–238. Indianapolis, Ind. and New York: Bobbs-Merrill, 1971.

Ryan, Alan. "Apocalypse Now." In Russell Jacoby and Naomi Glauberman, eds., *The Bell Curve Debate*, 12–29. New York: Times Books, 1995.

Ryan, William. *Blaming the Victim.* New York: Vintage Books, 1971.

Sakamoto, Arthur, and Satomi Furuichi. "Wages Among Japanese-American Male Workers: Functional Form and the Issue of Parity." *Research in Social Stratification and Mobility*, vol. 15 (forthcoming).

Salzman, Jack, ed., *Bridges and Boundaries: African Americans and American Jews.* New York: The Jewish Museum, 1992.

San Miguel, Guadalupe, Jr. *"Let All of Them Take Heed": Mexican Americans and the Campaign for Educational Equality in Texas, 1910–1981.* Austin, Tex.: University of Texas Press, 1987.

Sanchez, George I. "Pachucos in the Making." In Wayne Moquín and Charles Van Doren, eds., *A Documentary History of the Mexican Americans*, 409–415. New York: Bantam Books, 1972.

Sanchez, George J. *Becoming Mexican American: Ethnicity, Culture and Identity in Chicano Los Angeles, 1900–1945.* New York: Oxford University Press, 1993.

Sandefur, Gary D., and Trudy McKinnell. "American Indian Intermarriage." *Social Science Research* 15 (December 1986): 347–371.

Sandefur, Gary D., and Arthur Sakamoto. "American Indian Household Structure and Income." *Demography* 25 (February 1988): 71–80.

Sandefur, Gary D., and Wilbur J. Scott. "Minority Group Status and the Wages of Indian and Black Males." *Social Science Research* 12 (March 1983): 44–68.

Sanders, Jimy M., and Victor Nee. "Immigrant Self-Employment: The Family as Social Capital and the Value of Human Capital." *American Sociological Review* 61 (April, 1996): 231–249.

———. "Limits of Ethnic Solidarity in the Enclave Economy." *American Sociological Review* 52 (December 1987): 745–773.

Sawhill, Isabel V. "What About America's Underclass?" In Kurt Finsterbusch, ed., *Sociology 91/92,* 175–184. Guilford, Conn.: Dushkin Publishing Group, Inc., 1991.

Schermerhorn, Richard A. *These Our People.* Boston: D. C. Heath, 1949.

———. *Comparative Ethnic Relations.* New York: Random House, 1970.

Schlesinger, Arthur M., Jr. *The Disuniting of America.* New York: W. W. Norton & Company, 1992.

Schneider, Barbara, and Yongsook Lee. "A Model for Academic Success: The School and Home Environment of East Asian Students." *Anthropology and Education Quarterly* 21 (December 1990): 358–377.

Schneider, Barbara, Joyce A. Hieshima, Sehahn Lee, and Stephen Plank. "East-Asian Academic Success in the United States: Family, School, and Community Explanations." In Patricia M. Greenfield and Rodney R. Cocking, eds., *Cross-Cultural Roots of Minority Child Development,* 323–349. Hillsdale, N.J.: Lawrence Erlbaum Associates Publishers, 1994.

Schoen, Robert, and Lawrence E. Cohen. "Ethnic Endogamy among Mexican American Grooms: A Reanalysis of Generational and Occupational Effects." *American Journal of Sociology* 86 (September 1980): 359–366.

Schoen, Robert; Verne E. Nelson, and Marion Collins. "Intermarriage among Spanish Surnamed Californians, 1962–1974." *International Migration Review* 12 (1978): 359–369.

Schofield, Janet Ward. "Black-White Contact in Desegregated Schools." In Miles Hewstone and Rupert Brown, eds., *Contact and Conflict in Intergroup Encounters,* 79–92. Oxford: Basil Blackwell Ltd., 1986.

———. "Improving Intergroup Relations Among Students." In James A. Banks and Cherry A. McGee Banks, eds., *Handbook of Research on Multicultural Education,* 635–646. New York: Macmillan Publishing, 1995.

Schofield, Janet Ward, and H. Andrew Sagar. "The Social Context of Learning in an Interracial School." In Ray C. Rist, ed., *Desegregated Schools,* 155–199. New York: Academic Press, 1979.

Schuman, Howard, and Lawrence Bobo. "Survey-based Experiments on White Racial Attitudes toward Residential Integration." *American Journal of Sociology* 94 (September 1988): 273–299.

Schuman, Howard, and Shirley Hatchett. *Black Racial Attitudes: Trends and Complexities.* Ann Arbor, Mich.: University of Michigan Institute for Social Research, 1974.

Schuman, Howard, and Michael P. Johnson "Attitudes and Behavior." In Alex Inkeles, ed., *Annual Review of Sociology,* 161–207. Palo Alto, Calif.: Annual Reviews, Inc., 1976.

Schuman, Howard, Charlotte Steeh, and Lawrence Bobo. *Racial Attitudes in America.* Cambridge, Mass.: Harvard University Press, 1985.

Schwarz, Benjamin. "The Diversity Myth: America's Leading Export." *The Atlantic* (May 1995): 57–67.

Scott, Douglas D., and Melissa A. Connor "Post-mortem at the Little Bighorn." *Natural History* 95 (June 1986): 46–55.

Scott, Robin Fitzgerald. "Wartime Labor Problems and Mexican-Americans in the War." In Manuel P. Servín, ed., *An Awakening Minority: The Mexican Americans,* 2nd ed., 134–142. Beverly Hills, Calif.: Glencoe Press, 1974.

See, Katherine O'Sullivan. "For God and Crown: Class, Ethnicity, and Protestant Politics in Northern Ireland." In Susan Olzak and Joane Nagel, eds., *Competitive Ethnic Relations,* 221–245. Orlando, Fla.: Academic Press, Inc., 1986

See, Katherine O'Sullivan, and William J. Wilson. "Race and Ethnicity." In Neil J. Smelser, ed., *Handbook of Sociology*, 223–242. Newbury Park, Calif.: Sage Publications, 1988.

Seller, Maxine S. "Historical Perspectives on American Immigration Policy: Case Studies and Current Implications." In Richard R. Hofstetter, ed., *U.S. Immigration Policy*, 137–162. Durham, N.C.: Duke University Press, 1984.

———, ed., *Immigrant Women*, rev., 2nd ed. Albany. N.Y.: State University of New York Press, 1994.

Sheppard, Nathaniel, Jr. "Hate Groups Find a Home in Cyberspace." *Austin American-Statesman* (December 23, 1995): A1, A3.

Sherwood, Mary. "Striving Toward Assimilation." *Corpus Christi Times-Caller* (December 29, 1988): D14–16.

Siegel, Paul M. "On the Cost of Being a Negro." *Sociological Inquiry* 35 (Winter 1965): 41–57.

Sigelman, Lee, and Susan Welch. "The Contact Hypothesis Revisited: Black-White Interaction and Positive Racial Attitudes." *Social Forces* 71 (March 1993): 781–795.

Simmel, Georg. "The Stranger." In Kurt H. Wolf, translator, *The Sociology of Georg Simmel*, 402–406. Glencoe, Ill.: Free Press, 1950.

Simmons, Roberta G. "Blacks and High Self-Esteem: A Puzzle." *Social Psychology* 41 (March, 1978): 54–57.

Simon, Julian L. "Don't Close Our Borders." *Newsweek* (February 27, 1984): 11. Reprinted in Steven Anzovin, ed., *The Problem of Immigration*, 129–131. New York: H. W. Wilson, 1985.

———. *The Economic Consequences of Immigration*. New York: B. Blackwell, 1989.

———. "Why Control the Borders?" *National Review* 45 (February 1, 1993): 27–29.

Simpson, George Eaton, and J. Milton Yinger. *Racial and Cultural Minorities*, 4th ed. New York: Harper & Row, 1972.

Singer, Lester. "Ethnogenesis and Negro Americans Today." *Social Research* 29 (Winter 1962): 419–432.

Skinner, B. F. *About Behaviorism*. New York: Alfred A. Knopf, 1974.

Sklare, Marshall. "American Jewry: Social History and Group Identity." In Norman R. Yetman and C. Hoy Steele, eds., *Majority & Minority*, 2nd ed., 261–273. Boston: Allyn and Bacon, 1975.

Smith, James P., and Finis Welch. *Race Differences in Earnings: A Survey and New Evidence*. Santa Monica, Calif.: The Rand Corp., 1978.

———. *Closing the Gap: Forty Years of Economic Progress for Blacks*. Santa Monica, Calif.: The Rand Corp., 1986.

Smith, Jerry E. *Hopwood et al. v. Texas*. The United States Court of Appeals for the Fifth Circuit 94–50569, 1996.

Smith, Lillian. *Killers of the Dream*. Garden City, N.Y.: Doubleday, 1963.

Smith, Starita. "Racial Classifications More Than Just Black and White." *Austin American-Statesman* (May 26, 1996): A1, A16.

Smothers, Ronald. "Restaurant Chain Promises Revolution in Race Policies." *New York Times* (January 31, 1993): 12.

Snipp, C. Matthew. "American Indians and Natural Resource Development: Indigenous Peoples' Land, Now Sought After, Has Produced New Indian-White Problems." *American Journal of Economics and Sociology* (October 1986): 457–473.

———. *American Indians: The First of This Land*. New York: Russell Sage Foundation, 1989.

———. "American Indians Today." In *National Rural Studies Committee: A Proceedings of the Annual Meeting*, Las Vegas, Nevada, May 14–16, 1992: 16–26.

Sone, Monica. "The Stubborn Twig: 'My Double Dose of Schooling.'" In Maxine Schwartz Seller, ed., *Immigrant Women*, rev., 2nd ed., 243–248. Albany, N.Y.: State University of New York Press, 1994.

Southern Poverty Law Center. "Violent Hate Crimes Remain at Record Levels." *Intelligence Report* (March, 1994): 1–5.

———. *Klanwatch Intelligence Report* (March 1994).

———. "Before They Were Patriots." *False Patriots: The Threat of Antigovernment Extremists.* 1996a.

———. "Bias Incidents Reported During 1995." *Klanwatch Intelligence Report* (February 1996b): 7–23.

———. "For the Record." *Klanwatch Intelligence Report* (August, 1995): 13–18.

———. "National Alliance: North America's Largest Neo-Nazi Group Flourishing." *Klanwatch Intelligence Report* (May 1996c): 5–8.

Sowell, Thomas. "'Affirmative Action' Reconsidered." In Barry R. Gross, ed., *Reverse Discrimination,* 113–131. Buffalo, N.Y.: Prometheus Books, 1977.

Sparks, Sam. *Hopwood et al. v. Texas.* United States District Court, Western District of Texas, Austin Division, No. A 92 CA 563 SS, August 19, 1994.

Spearman, Charles. "General Intelligence Ojectively Determined and Measured." *American Journal of Psychology* 15 (January 1904): 201–293.

Spencer, Robert F. "Language-American Babel." In Robert F. Spencer, Jesse D. Jennings, et al., eds., *The Native Americans,* 37–55. New York: Harper & Row, 1977a.

———. "The Urban Native Americans." In Robert F. Spencer, Jesse D. Jennings, et al., eds., *The Native Americans,* 523–537. New York: Harper & Row, 1977b.

Spencer, Robert F., Jesse D. Jennings, et al., eds. *The Native Americans,* 2nd ed., New York: Harper & Row, 1977.

Spicer, Edward H. "American Indians." In Stephan Thernstrom, Ann Orlov, and Oscar Handlin, eds., *Harvard Encyclopedia of American Ethnic Groups,* 58–114. Cambridge, Mass.: The Belknap Press, 1980a.

———. "American Indians, Federal Policy Toward." In Stephan Thernstrom, Ann Orlov, and Oscar Handlin, eds., *Harvard Encyclopedia of American Ethnic Groups,* 114–122. Cambridge, Mass.: The Belknap Press, 1980b.

Spickard, Paul R. *Mixed Blood: Intermarriage and Ethnic Identity in Twentieth-Century America.* Madison, Wisc.: The University of Wisconsin Press, 1989.

St. Cartmail, Keith. *Exodus Indochina.* Auckland, New Zealand: Heinemann, 1983.

St. John, Nancy H. *School Desegregation Outcomes for Children.* New York: Wiley, 1975.

Stanfield, John H., II. "Absurd Assumptions and False Optimism Mark the Social Science of Race Relations." *Chronicle of Higher Education* (July 6, 1988): B2.

Steele, C. Hoy. "The Acculturation/Assimilation Model in Urban Indian Studies: A Critique." In Norman R. Yetman and C. Hoy Steele, eds., *Majority & Minority,* 3rd ed., 282–289. Boston: Allyn and Bacon, 1982.

Steele, Shelby. *The Content of Our Character.* New York: St. Martin's Press, 1990.

———. "Affirmative Action Must Go." *New York Times* (March 1, 1995): A15.

Steinberg, Stephen. *The Ethnic Myth.* New York: Atheneum, 1989.

Steiner, Stan. *The New Indians.* New York: Harper & Row, 1968.

———. *La Raza: The Mexican Americans.* New York: Harper & Row, 1969.

Stephan, Cookie White, and Walter G. Stephan. "After Intermarriage: Ethnic Identity among Mixed-Heritage Japanese Americans and Hispanics." *Journal of Marriage and the Family* 51 (May 1989): 507–519.

Stephan, Walter G. "Intergroup Relations." In Gardner Lindzey and Elliot Aronson, eds., *Handbook of Social Psychology,* 3rd ed. New York: Random House, 1985.

———. "The Effects of School Desegregation: An Evaluation 30 Years After Brown." In Michael J. Sax and Leonard Saxe, eds., *Advances in Applied Social Psychology,* 181–206. Hillsdale, N. J.: Lawrence Erlbaum, 1986.

———. "The Contact Hypothesis in Intergroup Relations." In Clyde Hendrick, ed., *Group Processes and Intergroup Relations,* 13–40. Beverly Hills, Calif.: Sage Publications, 1987.

———. "School Desegregation: Short-Term and Long-Term Effects." Paper presented in Tuscaloosa, Alabama, June 10, 1988 (mimeographed).

Stephan, Walter G., and Cookie White Stephan. "Cognition and Affect in Stereotyping: Parallel Interactive Networks." In Diane M. Mackie and David L. Hamilton, eds., *Affect, Cognition, and Stereotyping,* 111–136. San Diego, Calif.: Academic Press, Inc., 1993.

Stern, Gary M. "Hispanics Challenge Bilingual Education." *The Hispanic Outlook in Higher Education* (January 5, 1996): 6–8.

Stevens, Gillian. "The Social and Demographic Context of Language Use in the United States." *American Sociological Review* 57 (April 1992): 171–185.

Stevens, Gillian, and Gray Swicegood. "The Linguistic Context of Ethnic Endogamy." *American Sociological Review* 52 (February 1987): 73–82.

Stewart, Kenneth M. "American Indian Heritage: Retrospect and Prospect." In Robert F. Spencer, Jesse D. Jennings, et al., eds., *The Native Americans,* 501–522. New York: Harper & Row, 1977a.

———. "The Urban Native Americans." In Robert F. Spencer, Jesse D. Jennings, et al., eds., *The Native Americans,* 523–537. New York: Harper and Row, 1977b.

Strand, Paul J., and Woodrow Jones, Jr. *Indochinese Refugees in America.* Durham, N.C.: Duke University Press, 1985.

Stroessner, Steven J., and Diane M. Mackie. "Affect and Perceived Group Variability: Implications for Stereotyping and Prejudice." In Diane M. Mackie and David L. Hamilton, eds., *Affect, Cognition, and Stereotyping,* 63–86. San Diego, Calif.: Academic Press, Inc., 1993.

Sugimoto, Howard H. "The Vancouver Riots of 1907: A Canadian Episode." In Hilary Conroy and T. Scott Miyakawa, eds., *East Across the Pacific,* 92–126. Santa Barbara, Calif.: American Bibliographical Center-CLIO Press, 1972.

Sumner, William Graham. *Folkways.* New York: American Library, (1906) 1960.

Suzuki, David. "Correlation as Causation." In Russell Jacoby and Naomi Glauberman, eds., *The Bell Curve Debate,* 280–282. New York: Times Books, 1995.

Svensson, Frances. *The Ethnics in American Politics: American Indians.* Minneapolis, Minn.: Burgess, 1973.

Sydnor, Charles S. *American Revolutionaries in the Making.* New York: The Free Press, 1965.

Tabb, William K. "What Happened to Black Economic Development?" *The Review of Black Political Economy* 9 (Summer 1979): 392–415.

Tachiki, Amy. "Introduction." In Amy Tachiki, Eddie Wong, Franklin Odo, and Buck Wong, eds., *Roots: An Asian American Reader,* 1–5. Los Angeles: Regents of the University of California, 1971.

Taeuber, Karl E., and Alma F. Taeuber. "The Negro as an Immigrant Group: Recent Trends in Racial and Ethnic Segregation in Chicago." *American Journal of Sociology* 69 (January 1964): 374–394.

———. *Negroes in Cities.* New York: Atheneum, 1969.

Tajfel, Henry, and J.C. Turner. *An Integrative Theory of Intergroup Conflict.* Monterey, Calif.: Brooks/Cole, 1979.

Takagi, Paul. "The Myth of 'Assimilation in American Life.'" *Amerasia Journal* 3 (Fall 1973): 149–158.

Takaki, Ronald. *Strangers from a Different Shore: A History of Asian Americans.* Boston: Little, Brown and Company, 1989.

———. "At Issue: Is It Accurate to Call Asian Americans a Model Minority?" *CQ Researcher* 1 (December 13, 1991): 961.

———, ed., *From Different Shores: Perspectives of Race and Ethnicity in America,* 2nd ed. New York: Oxford University Press, 1994.

Tateishi, John. "The Japanese American Citizens League and the Stuggle for Redress." In Roger Daniels, Sandra C. Taylor, and Harry H. L. Kitano, eds., *Japanese Americans: From Relocation to Redress,* rev. ed., 191–195. Seattle, Wash.: University of Washington Press, 1991.

Taylor, D. Garth, Paul B. Sheatsley, and Andrew M. Greeley. "Attitudes Toward Racial Integration." *Scientific American* (June 1978): 42–49.

Taylor, Howard F. *The IQ Game.* New Brunswick, N.J.: Rutgers University Press, 1980.

Taylor, Patricia Ann. "Education, Ethnicity, and Cultural Assimilation in the United States." *Ethnicity* 8 (1981): 31–49.

Taylor, Paul S. *An American-Mexican Frontier.* Chapel Hill, N.C.: University of North Carolina Press, 1934.

Taylor, Sandra C. "Evacuation and Economic Loss: Questions and Perspectives." In Roger Daniels, Sandra C. Taylor, and Harry H. L. Kitano, eds., *Japanese Americans: From Relocation to Redress,* rev. ed., 163–167. Seattle, Wash.: University of Washington Press, 1991.

———. *Jewel of the Desert: Japanese American Internment at Topaz.* Berkeley, Calif.: University of California Press, 1993.

Telles, Edward E., and Edward Murguía. "Phenotypic Discrimination and Income Differences among Mexican Americans." *Social Science Quarterly* 71 (December 1990): 682–696.

———. "The Continuing Significance of Phenotype among Mexican Americans." *Social Science Quarterly* 73 (March 1992): 120–122.

tenBroek, Jacobus, Edward N. Barnhart, and Floyd W. Matson. *Prejudice, War, and the Constitution.* Berkeley, Calif. and Los Angeles: University of California Press, 1954.

Thernstrom, Abigail. "The Drive for Racially Inclusive Schools." In Harold Orlans and June O'Neill, eds., *Affirmative Action Revisited, The Annals.* (September 1992): 131–143.

Thernstrom, Stephan, Ann Orlov, and Oscar Handlin, eds. *Harvard Encyclopedia of American Ethnic Groups.* Cambridge, Mass.: The Belknap Press, 1980.

Thomas, Dorothy Swaine. *The Salvage.* Berkeley, Calif. and Los Angeles: University of California Press, 1952.

Thomas, Dorothy Swaine, and Richard S. Nishimoto. *The Spoilage.* Berkeley, Calif. and Los Angeles: University of California Press, 1946.

Thompson, Charles H. "The Conclusions of Scientists Relative to Racial Differences." *Journal of Negro Education* 19 (July 1934): 494–512.

Thornton, Russell. "North American Indians and the Demography of Contact." In Silvia Pedraza and Rubén G. Rumbaut, eds., *Origins and Destinies: Immigration, Race, and Ethnicity in America,* 43–59. Belmont, Calif.: Wadsworth Publishing Company, 1996.

Thurstone, L. L. *The Vectors of the Mind.* Chicago: University of Chicago Press, 1935.

Tierney, John. "Betting the Planet." *New York Times Magazine* (December 2, 1990).

Tindall, George Brown. *America: A Narrative Story.* New York: W. W. Norton & Co., 1984.

Tinker, John N. "Intermarriage and Ethnic Boundaries: The Japanese American Case." *Journal of Social Issues* 29, no. 2 (1973): 49–66.

Tocqueville, Alexis de. *Democracy in America,* ed. by J. P. Mayer. New York: Harper and Row, Perennial Library, (1835) 1988.

Todorovich, Miro M. "Discrimination in Higher Education." In Barry R. Gross, ed., *Reverse Discrimination,* 12–14. Buffalo, N.Y.: Prometheus Books, 1977.

Tolnay, Stewart, and E. M. Beck. "Racial Violence and Black Migration in the American South, 1910–1930." *American Sociological Review* 57 (February 1992): 103–116.

Tomás Rivera Center. *The Latino Vote at Mid-Decade.* Claremont, Calif.: Scripps College, 1996.

Ton, Mark. "America's Mixed Neighborhoods Need Support." *New York Times* (July 10,1992): A14.

Trotter, Monroe. Editorial, *Boston Guardian,* December 20, 1902. Reprinted in August Meier, Elliott Rudwick, and Francis L. Broderick, eds., *Black Protest Thought in the Twentieth Century,* 2nd ed., 32–36. Indianapolis and New York: Bobbs-Merrill, 1971.

Tsai, Shih-Shan Henry. *The Chinese Experience in America.* Bloomington, Ind.: Indiana University Press, 1986.

Tuchman, Barbara W. *The First Salute.* New York: Alfred A. Knopf, 1988.

Tucker, Belinda M., and Claudia Mitchell-Kernan. "Trends in African American Family Formation: A Theoretical and Statistical Overview." In M. Belinda Tucker and Claudia Mitchell-Kernan, eds., *The Decline in Marriage Among African Americans,* 1995, 3–26. New York: Russell Sage Foundation.

Turner, Frederick Jackson. *The Frontier in American History.* New York: Henry Holt, 1920.

Tussman, Joseph, ed., *The Supreme Court on Racial Discrimination.* New York: Oxford University Press, 1963.

Ueda, Reed. "Naturalization and Citizenship." In Stephan Thernstrom, Ann Orlov, and Oscar Handlin, eds., *Harvard Encyclopedia of American Ethnic Groups,* 734–748. Cambridge, Mass.: The Belknap Press, 1980.

U.S. Bureau of the Census. Current Population Reports, March 1994: Educational Attainment Level by Ethnicity; Population Age 25 and Over; Family Income in Previous Year by Race-Ethnicity; Occupation by Race-Ethnicity (http://www.census.gov/population/socdemo/)

———. *Historical Statistics of the United States, Colonial Times to 1970.* Washington, D.C.: U.S. Government Printing Office, 1975.

———. Current Population Reports, Series P-20, No. 438, *The Hispanic Population in the United States: March, 1988.* Washington, D.C.: U.S. Government Printing Office, 1989a.

———. *Statistical Abstract of the United States: 1989,* 109th ed. Washington, D.C.: U.S. Government Printing Office, 1989b.

———. Current Population Reports, Series P-20, No. 455 *The Hispanic Population in the United States: March 1991.* Washington, D.C.: U.S. Government Printing Office, 1991.

———. *Statistical Abstract of the United States: 1995,* 115th ed. Washington, D.C.: U.S. Government Printing Office, 1996.

U.S. Commission on Civil Rights. *The Tarnished Golden Door: Civil Rights Issues in Immigration.* Washington, D.C.: September 1980.

———. *Affirmative Action in the 1980s: Dismantling the Process of Discrimination.* Washington, D.C.: U.S. Government Printing Office, 1981a.

———. *Civil Rights: A National, Not a Special Interest.* Washington, D.C.: U.S. Government Printing Office, 1981b.

———. *Civil Rights Issues Facing Asian Americans in the 1990s.* Washington, D.C.: U.S. Government Printing Office, February 1992.

———. *Civil Rights Update* (March 1979).

———. *Civil Rights Update* (August 1979).

———. *Civil Rights Update* (September/October 1988).

———. *Civil Rights Update* (November 1988).

———. *Civil Rights Update* (March 1989).

———. *Civil Rights Update* (June 1989).

———. *Civil Rights Update* (March/April 1992).

U.S. Department of Commerce *NEWS*. "Updated Information on Nation's African American Population Released by Census Bureau, CB96–90, (June 11, 1996): Table 8 (Total Money Income in 1994 of Persons 15 Years Old and Over, by Sex, Region (Persons as of March 1995).

U.S. Department of Education. *Descriptive Study of Services to Limited English Proficient Students: Analysis and Highlights*. Washington, D.C.: Office of the Under Secretary, No Date.

U.S. Department of Labor. *A CPS Supplement for Testing Methods of Collecting Racial and Ethnic Information: May 1995*. Washington, D.C.: Bureau of Labor Statistics, October 1995.

———. Facts on U.S. Working Women, Fact Sheet No. 86–2. Washington, D.C.: U.S. Department of Labor, Women's Bureau, 1989.

U.S. Immigration and Naturalization Service. *Statistical Yearbook of the Immigration and Naturalization Service, 1994*. Washington, D.C., 1996.

Vaca, Nick C. "The Mexican-American in the Social Sciences." *El Grito* 4 (Fall 1970): 17–51.

Valdivieso, Rafael, and Cary Davis. *U.S. Hispanics: Challenging Issues for the 1990s*. Washington, D.C.: Population Reference Bureau, 1988.

Valdez, Luis. "The Tale of the Raza." In Renato Rosaldo, Robert A. Calvert, and Gustav L. Seligman, eds., *Chicano: The Evolution of a People*, 269–272. Malabar, Fla: Krieger, 1982.

Van Every, Dale. "Cherokee Removal." In Francis Paul Prucha, ed., *The Indian in American History*, 29–38. Hinsdale, Ill.: Dryden, 1971.

Van Valey, Thomas L., Wade Clark Roof, and Jerome E. Wilcox. "Trends in Residential Segregation: 1960–1970." *American Journal of Sociology* 82 (January 1977): 826–844.

van den Berghe, Pierre L. *Man in Society*, 2nd ed. New York: Elsevier, 1978.

van Oudenhoven, Jan Pieter. "Improving Interethnic Relationships: How Effective is Cooperation?" In Jan Pieter van Oudenhoven and Tineke M. Willemsen, eds., *Ethnic Minorities*, 25–42. Amsterdam: Swets & Zeitlinger B.V., 1989.

van Oudenhoven Jan Pieter, and Tineke M. Willemsen, eds. *Ethnic Minorities*. Amsterdam: Swets & Zeitlinger B.V., 1989.

Veltman, Calvin. *The Future of the Spanish Language in the United States*. Washington, D.C.: Hispanic Policy Development Project, 1988.

Veltman, Calvin. "The Status of the Spanish Language in the United States at the Beginning of the 21st Century." *International Migration Review* 24 (Spring 1990): 108–123.

Vernez, George. *Statement of George Vernez, Director, Education and Human Resources Program RAND before the Select Committee on Statewide Immigration Impact, California State Assembly*, September 22, 1993 (Santa Monica, Calif.: RAND P-7853, 1993).

Vernez, George, and Kevin F. McCarthy. *Meeting the Economy and Labour Needs Through Immigration: Rationale and Challenges*. Santa Monica, Calif.: N-3052–FF, RAND, June 1990.

———. *The Costs of Immigration to Taxpayers: Analytical and Policy Issues*. Santa Monica, Calif.: Rand, 1996.

Wagley, Charles, and Marvin Harris. *Minorities in the New World*. New York: Columbia University Press, 1958.

Waldinger, Roger. "The Occupational and Economic Integration of the New Immigrants." In Richard R. Hofstetter, ed. *U.S. Immigration Policy*, 197–222. Durham, N.C.: Duke University Press, 1984.

Walls, Thomas. *The Japanese Texans*. San Antonio, Tex.: University of Texas, Institute of Texan Cultures, 1987.

Ware, Caroline F. "Immigration." *Encyclopedia of the Social Sciences*, vol. 7, 587–594. New York: Macmillan, 1937.

Warner, Lyle G., and Melvin L. DeFleur. "Attitude as an Interactional Concept: Social Constraint and Social Distance as Intervening Variables Between Attitudes and Action." *American Sociological Review* 34 (April 1969): 153–169.

Warner, W. Lloyd, and Leo Srole. *The Social Systems of American Ethnic Groups,* 2nd ed. New Haven, Conn.: Yale University Press, 1946.

Washburn, Wilcomb E. *Red Man's Land White Man's Law,* 2nd ed. Norman, Okla.: University of Oklahoma Press, 1995.

———. "The Status Today." In Herbert L. Marx, Jr., ed., *The American Indian,* 102–104. New York: H. W. Wilson, 1973.

Washington, Booker T. *Up from Slavery.* New York: Bantam Books, 1959.

Waters, Mary C. *Ethnic Options.* Berkeley, Calif.: University of California Press, 1990.

Wax, Murray L. *Indian Americans.* Englewood Cliffs, N. J.: Prentice-Hall, 1971.

Webb, Walter Prescott. *The Texas Rangers.* Austin, Tex.: University of Texas Press, 1987.

Weggert, Karl H. *German Radicals Confront the Common People.* Mainz: Verlag Philipp Von Zabern, 1992.

Weisberger, Bernard A., "A Nation of Immigrants." In John A. Kromkowski, *Annual Editions: Race and Ethnic Relations 96/97,* 40–52. Guilford, Conn.: Dushkin Publishing Group, 1995.

West, Cornel. "Why I'm Marching in Washington." *New York Times* (October 14, 1995): E15.

White, Lynn C., and Bruce A. Chadwick. "Urban Residence, Assimilation and the Identity of the Spokane Indians." In Howard M. Bahr, Bruce A. Chadwick, and Robert C. Day, eds., *Native Americans Today,* 239–249. New York: Harper & Row, 1972.

White, Michael J., Ann E. Biddlecom, and Shenyang Guo. "Immigration, Naturalization, and Residential Assimilation Among Asian Americans in 1980." *Social Forces* 72 (September 1993): 93–117.

Wilhelm, Sidney M. *Black in a White America.* Cambridge, Mass.: Schenkman, 1983.

Wilkerson, Isabel. "Interracial Marriage Rises, Acceptance Lags." *New York Times* (December 2, 1991): A1.

Wilkinson, Doris Y. "Toward a Positive Frame of Reference from Analysis of Black Families: A Selected Bibliography." *Journal of Marriage and the Family* 40 (November 1978): 707–708.

———. "Gender and Social Inequality: The Prevailing Significance of Race." In Obie Clayton, Jr., ed., *An American Dilemma Revisited: Race Relations in a Changing World,* 288–313. New York: Russell Sage Foundation, 1996.

———. "Integration Dilemmas in a Racist Culture." *Society* 8 (March/April 1996): 27–31.

Williams, J. Allen, Jr., Peter G. Beeson, and David R. Johnson. "Some Factors Associated with Income among Mexican Americans." *Social Science Quarterly* 53 (March) 1973: 710–715.

———, Clyde Z. Nunn, and Louis St. Peter. "Origins of Tolerance: Findings from a Replication of Stouffer's Communism, Conformity, and Civil Liberties." *Social Forces* 55 (December 1976): 394–418.

Williams, John E., and J. Kenneth Morland. *Race, Color, and the Young Child.* Chapel Hill, N.C.: University of North Carolina Press, 1976.

Williams, Norma. *The Mexican American Family: Tradition and Change.* Dix Hills, N.Y.: General Hall, Inc., 1990.

Williams, Robin M., Jr. *The Reduction of Intergroup Tensions.* New York: Social Science Research Council, 1947.

———. *Strangers Next Door.* Englewood Cliffs, N.J.: Prentice-Hall, 1964.

Wilson, Kenneth L., and W. Allen Martin. "Ethnic Enclaves: A Comparison of the Cuban and Black Economies in Miami." *American Journal of Sociology* 88 (July 1982): 135–160.

Wilson, Kenneth L., and Alejandro Portes. "Immigrant Enclaves: An Analysis of the Labor Market Experiences of Cubans in Miami." *American Journal of Sociology* 86 (September 1980): 295–319.

Wilson, Pete. "Piety, but No Help, On Illegal Aliens." *New York Times* (July 11, 1996): A15.

Wilson, William J. "Race Relations Models and Explanations of Ghetto Behavior." In Peter I. Rose, ed., *Nation of Nations,* 259–275. New York: Random House, 1972.

———. *The Declining Significance of Race,* 2nd ed. Chicago: University of Chicago Press, 1980.

———. *The Truly Disadvantaged.* Chicago: The University of Chicago Press, 1987.

———. "A Response to Critics of *The Truly Disadvantaged.*" In Robert G. Newby, ed., *The Truly Disadvantaged: Challenges and Prospects,* Special Issue, *Journal of Sociology and Social Welfare* 16 (December 1989): 133–148.

———. "Studying Inner-City Social Dislocations: The Challenge of Public Agenda Research." *American Sociological Review* 56 (February 1991): 1–14.

———. *When Work Disappears: The World of the New Urban Poor.* New York: Alfred A. Knopf, 1996.

Winegarten, Ruthe. *Black Texas Women: 150 Years of Trial and Triumph.* Austin, Tex.: University of Texas Press, 1995.

Wirth, Louis. "The Problem of Minority Groups." In Ralph Linton, ed., *The Science of Man in the World Crisis,* 347–372. New York: Columbia University Press, 1945.

Wittke, Carl. *We Who Built America,* 3rd ed. Englewood Cliffs, N.J.: Prentice-Hall, 1964.

———. *The Germans in America.* New York: Teachers College Press, 1967.

Wojtkiewicz, Roger A., and Katharine M. Donato. "Hispanic Educational Attainment: The Effects of Family Background and Nativity." *Social Forces* 74 (December 1995): 559–574.

Wood, Peter B., and Michelle Chesser. "Black Stereotyping in a University Population." *Sociological Focus* 27 (February 1994): 17–34.

Woodrum, Eric. "Japanese American Social Adaptation over Three Generations." Ph.D. dissertation, University of Texas at Austin, 1978.

Woodward, C. Vann. *The Strange Career of Jim Crow.* New York: Oxford University Press, 1957.

Wright, Mary Bowen. "Indochinese." In Stephan Thernstrom, Ann Orlov, and Oscar Handlin, eds., *Harvard Encyclopedia of American Ethnic Groups,* 508–513. Cambridge, Mass.: The Belknap Press, 1980.

Wrong, Dennis H. "How Important Is Social Class?" In Dennis H. Wrong and Harry L. Gracey, eds., *Readings in Introductory Sociology,* 3rd ed., 480–488. New York: Macmillan, 1977.

Yancy, William L., Eugene P. Ericksen, and Richard N. Juliani. "Emergent Ethnicity: A Review and Reformulation." *American Sociological Review* 41 (June, 1976): 391–403.

Yerkes, Robert M., ed., *Psychological Examining in the United States Army,* vol. 15. Washington, D.C.: National Academy of Sciences, 1921.

Zambrana, Ruth E. *Understanding Latino Families: Scholarship, Policy and Practice.* Thousand Oaks, Calif.: Sage Publications, 1995.

Zhou, Min, and John R. Logan. "In and Out of Chinatown: Residential Mobility and Segregation of New York City's Chinese." *Social Forces* 70 (December 1991): 387–407.

Name Index

Subject Index

Boldfaced entries denote end-of-chapter Key Terms.